*The endpapers are bird's-eye
views of Sydney (front) and
Melbourne (back) c. 1877,
reproduced from the 1879
engravings published by William
Collins Sons and Co., London.*

A NEW HISTORY
OF AUSTRALIA

A NEW HISTORY OF AUSTRALIA

Edited by

F. K. CROWLEY

Professor of History in the
University of New South Wales

 HOLMES & MEIER PUBLISHERS, INC.
101 Fifth Avenue, New York, N.Y. 10003
IMPORT DIVISION

WILLIAM HEINEMANN MELBOURNE

William Heinemann Australia Pty Ltd Melbourne

Copyright © F. K. Crowley, 1974
First published 1974

National Library of Australia Card Service Number
and International Standard Book Number 0 85561 035 2

Designed by David Wire

Wholly set up and printed at
The Griffin Press Adelaide

Contents

The Contributors

1   A. G. L. Shaw, Professor of History,
Monash University, Clayton, Victoria.

2   J. J. Auchmuty, Vice-Chancellor,
University of Newcastle, Newcastle, N.S.W.

3   Michael Roe, Reader in History, University
of Tasmania, Hobart, Tasmania.

4   T. H. Irving, Senior Lecturer in Government,
University of Sydney, Sydney, New South Wales.

5   The late G. L. Buxton, formerly Senior Lecturer
in History, University of Adelaide, Adelaide,
South Australia.

6   B. K. de Garis, Senior Lecturer in History,
University of Western Australia, Nedlands,
Western Australia.

7   F. K. Crowley, Professor of History, University
of New South Wales, Kensington, New South Wales.

8   Ian Turner, Associate Professor of History,
Monash University, Clayton, Victoria.

9   Heather Radi, Senior Lecturer in History,
University of Sydney, Sydney, New South Wales.

10   J. R. Robertson, Senior Lecturer in History,
Faculty of Military Studies, University of
New South Wales, Duntroon, A.C.T.

11   G. C. Bolton, Professor of History,
Murdoch University, Perth, Western Australia.

12   W. J. Hudson, Associate Professor of History,
University of New South Wales, Kensington,
New South Wales.

Abbreviations

A.E.H.R.	Australian Economic History Review
A.J.P.H.	Australian Journal of Politics and History
A.Q.	Australian Quarterly
C.P.D.	Commonwealth Parliamentary Debates
C.P.P.	Commonwealth Parliamentary Papers
E.R.	Economic Record
H.R.A.	Historical Records of Australia, Series I
H.R.N.S.W.	Historical Records of New South Wales
H.S.	Historical Studies, formerly Historical Studies: Australia and New Zealand
L.H.	Labour History
R.A.H.S.J.	Royal Australian Historical Society Journal
T.H.R.A.P.	Tasmanian Historical Research Association Proceedings

Preface

During the last twenty years the study of Australian History has attracted some of the best scholars in the humanities, and some of the most dedicated teachers in the schools, colleges and universities. At the same time, an increase in the number of research students has been matched by the establishment of new specialist journals, by the growth in the number of historical societies, associations and trusts, and by a very rapid increase in the volume of publishing. This book reflects all those trends. It brings together a diverse group of historians, some well established as historians and writers, and others who will shortly become so, all of whom differ from one another in age, experience and in political stance, as well as in their view of the meaning and purpose of history. It draws attention in footnotes and bibliography to the most significant and the most recent publications, and thereby highlights the growing volume of periodical literature and the declining use of works of the pioneer scholars. It has also involved a radical re-thinking of traditional interpretations of nineteenth century Australian history, and pioneering interpretations of Australia's development in the twentieth century.

The character of the book as a whole is chronological, that of the chapters is analytical and topical. Within this structure the authors have been free to apply their own view of the nature of general history, and to emphasize those aspects of their periods which gave them character or ethos. The result is twelve views of twelve consecutive periods of Australia's history, the periods having been chosen to highlight the significant events and turning points in Australia's development, and to emphasise the continuity which exists between contemporary Australia and its recent and distant past. This book is also a general history which is as much concerned with economic and social history as with government and politics, and which is more concerned with movements, ideas and themes than with individual events and persons. Necessarily, no one historian's interpretation is likely to be fully shared by any of his colleagues, but there is occasionally a strong case in the public interest for historians to provide a new overview of a period in the light of the most recent research and publications. That has been the principal objective of this book.

The very extensive chapter bibliography has been constructed as a tool for students and teachers, and therefore includes no unpublished works.

Frank Crowley
School of History
University of New South Wales

I

_____

1788-1810

A. G. L. Shaw

*A penal colony for Botany Bay—motives of the founders—com-
mercial and strategic considerations—the question of cost—
expected benefits—the First Fleet—landfall—the law and the
governor—Sydney Cove—shortage of supplies—the Second Fleet
—Norfolk Island—the work of Governor Phillip—the New South
Wales Corps—farming—traders and merchants—the liquor traffic
—the aims of convict transportation—discipline and punishment—religion and education—emancipists—the character of the
convicts—Governor Hunter—exploration—a costly colony—
Governor King—government revenue—whaling and sealing—
shipping—wool growing—John Macarthur—Samuel Marsden—
cattle—exploration in the South—settlements in Van Diemen's
Land and on Port Phillip Bay—Hobart—the Aborigines—the
liquor problem—the Governor and the New South Wales Corps
—the work of Governor King—Governor Bligh—his style of
administration—Bligh deposed—the nature of the rebellion—the
interregnum—the state of the colony.*

Australia was conceived officially when King George III announced to
parliament, on 22 January 1787, that a plan had been made 'to remove
the inconvenience which arose from the crowded state of the gaols in
the different parts of the kingdom'. At this time transportation was an
integral part of the English penal system. Many criminals were
sentenced to it directly. Many more had their death sentences
commuted, and the number thus reprieved was steadily increasing.
Between 1750 and 1775 about 1000 criminals a year had been transported to the British colonies in America, especially to Virginia and
Maryland, but the outbreak of the revolution in the colonies had
made this impossible. During the American war these people had
been accommodated in prison hulks in the Thames, but government
spokesmen had always insisted that this was only a temporary expedient until trans-Atlantic transportation could be renewed. When
the war was lost, something else had to be done, and after prolonged
dithering, the solution adopted was to establish a penal colony at
Botany Bay in New South Wales, which Captain James Cook had
discovered in 1770.

Was this a sufficient reason for founding the colony? There are some who seem almost instinctively to look for economic motives behind important projects and would argue that commercial not penological considerations must have determined the government's decision. Some, observing a 'swing to the East' in imperial development in the late eighteenth century, feel that this settlement was a part of it, and join the group described by Professor Inglis as seeking 'something more inspiriting: an essay in supplying an empire with masts and sails for her ships', rather than in finding a site for convicts as the stimulus for a new colony in the antipodes.[1]

To prove a negative is always extremely difficult, so it is possible that some such ideas may have been, unstated, at the back of the minds of the statesmen concerned. The government certainly received plans which lauded the opportunities which a colony would provide for trade with China and in the Pacific, for the supply of flax or timber for the navy, for a base for 'refreshment' and supplies for whalers, and for a strategic outpost in the antipodes. But whether such hopes influenced cabinet ministers is uncertain.[2] In December 1784, the First Lord of the Admiralty, Admiral Lord Howe, had commented that New South Wales was so far off that 'the length of the navigation' would limit its commercial and naval advantages; otherwise all the naval records are silent on the subject.[3] In 1785 a committee of the House of Commons considering possible sites for a penal colony had suggested Das Voltas Bay, in south-west Africa, arguing that the commercial and political benefits of settlement there would offset the cost of the penal establishment, but on investigation this locality proved too arid; political and commercial benefits notwithstanding the government refused to countenance a settlement on the Caffre Coast (near modern East London) because it did not want to antagonize the Dutch at the Cape, just as it objected to a settlement at Madagascar because of the opposition of the East India Company, which it was treating with respect after the political struggles centred on its regulation in 1783–4.[4] In fact that company's monopoly

---

[1] On this question see E. O'Brien, *The Foundation of Australia*, London, 1937; 2nd ed. Sydney, 1950: K. S. Inglis, 'Australia Day', in *H.S.*, *49*, October 1967: G. Blainey, *The Tyranny of Distance*, Melbourne, 1966, ch. 2: K. M. Dallas, 'Commercial influences on the First Settlement in Australia', in *T.H.R.A.P.*, XVI, 2, September 1968: M. Roe, 'Australia's Place in "The Swing to the East"', in *H.S.*, *30*, May 1958: C. M. H. Clark, 'The Choice of Botany Bay', in *H.S.*, *35*, November 1960: G. C. Bolton, 'The Hollow Conqueror; Flax and the Foundation of Australia', in *A.E.H.R.*, VIII, 1, March 1968: A. G. L. Shaw, 'The Hollow Conqueror and the Tyranny of Distance' in *H.S.*, *50*, April 1968.

[2] See the 'plans' of James Matra and Admiral George Young, and the anonymous proposal of 1785, in *H.R.N.S.W.*, *I*, ii, pp. 1, 11–12, and *II*, p. 359.

[3] *H.R.N.S.W.*, *I*, ii, p. 10: A. G. L. Shaw, 'The Hollow Conqueror and the Tyranny of Distance', in *H.S.*, *50*, April 1968, pp. 200–201.

[4] A. G. L. Shaw, *Convicts and the Colonies*, London, 1966, pp. 45–8: L. C. F. Turner, 'Cape of Good Hope and Anglo-Dutch Rivalry', in *H.S.*, *46*, April 1966, pp. 176–7: *H.R.N.S.W.*, *II*, pp. 9–10.

virtually removed any commercial advantages that might arise from New South Wales. Though whaling in the Southern Ocean was encouraged by bounties, it was prohibited in the area monopolized by the Company, between longitudes 57°E. and 180°, i.e., in Australian waters; and when New South Wales was founded, the governor was told that 'every sort of intercourse between the intended settlement at Botany Bay, or other place which may be hereafter established on the coast of New South Wales and its dependencies, and the settlements of our East India Company, as well as the coast of China, and the islands in that part of the world, ... should be *prevented by every possible means*'.[5]

Meanwhile the Committee for Trade and Plantations had been investigating possible means of replacing or supplementing the traditional Baltic sources of the supply of flax for the Royal Navy. In 1786–87, it made inquiries in other parts of Europe. It favoured bounties on flax grown in Scotland and Ireland. It hoped to disseminate information about flax-growing in England, in which the famous agricultural propagandist Arthur Young could help. It recommended encouraging cultivation in Canada. It did not however even consider the possibility of obtaining supplies from the Pacific.[6]

If commercial considerations seem remote, was international rivalry important? Certainly both Spaniards and French, especially the latter, had shown and were showing interest in the Pacific, as the writings of de Brosses, and the voyages of de Bouvet, Bougainville, Surville, Marion du Fresne and de Kerguelen indicated. In August 1785 La Pérouse had followed them, three months after reports had reached London that he had been instructed to establish a settlement in New Zealand.[7] Though these were false, nonetheless he had been ordered to explore the west coast of New Holland and to sail to New Zealand via Tasmania, and at the same time the French made contacts with Annam and reconstituted their East India Company. Since the Dutch were established at the Cape of Good Hope and in the East Indies, these activities, together with the renewal in 1785 of the Franco-Dutch alliance which had caused such trouble during the American War of Independence, and the threat of still closer Franco-Dutch co-operation which emerged during the domestic strife in Holland in 1786–7, may have influenced British ministers. On the other hand, a British post had been established at Penang in 1786, and negotiations proceeding

---

[5] My italics. From the Instructions issued to Phillip in *H.R.A.*, *I*, p. 15. See also references cited in A. G. L. Shaw, 'The Hollow Conqueror and the Tyranny of Distance', in *H.S.*, *50*, April 1968, p. 202.

[6] See references cited in A. G. L. Shaw, 'The Hollow Conqueror and the Tyranny of Distance', in *H.S.*, *50*, April 1968, pp. 196–8.

[7] G. C. Bolton, 'Broken Reeds and Smoking Flax', in *A.E.H.R.*, *IX*, March 1969, p. 67, quoting despatches from the Duke of Dorset, British Ambassador in Paris, 5 May and 9 June 1785. For French exploration in these years see J. Dunmore, *French Explorers*, Oxford, 1965, *I*, p. 260 ff.

with the Dutch about a commercial station on the island of Rhio (near the later site of Singapore) seemed to take care of the Indian Ocean. No one heeded western or north-western Australia, and Australia does not seem to have been considered relevant to the strategic studies made on the defence of India in the 1780s; Pitt ignored New South Wales when planning operations in the Pacific against Spain at the time of the Nootka Sound crisis in 1790, and no government spokesman mentioned strategic considerations when later rebutting criticism of the 'extravagant scheme' at Botany Bay.[8]

For all that, it is possible that La Pérouse's expedition to the Pacifc seemed to call for counter-measures. Though the reports which he sent to Paris from the Easter Islands and the Sandwich Islands in April–May 1786 would have leaked through to London too late (if at all) to influence a decision made in August, they might have helped to influence the change from what appears to be the strictly military-penal operation envisaged in Phillip's first commission (12 October 1786) to the more elaborate plans outlined in his second (2 April 1787), with the addition of the specific instruction that since Norfolk Island 'may hereafter become useful', he should settle it 'and prevent it being occupied by the subjects of any other European power'.[9] This occupation was not immediately for flax. No flax-dressers were sent with the expedition. Reports on it were still untested, and the government merely recommended experiments in flax cultivation, just as it had suggested in 1776 when Captain James Cook was setting out on his second great voyage of Pacific exploration, that he might bring home seeds, following the hope expressed by Joseph Banks, who had accompanied Cook on his first voyage and had already gained fame as a botanist, that the plants might thrive in England.[10] As for timber, though that growing on Norfolk Island had been reported good, it was not mentioned in Phillip's instructions; the island was a long way away, and there was still no shortage in the Bombay shipyards of the Indian timber which seemed so satisfactory that it was even making the Thames shipbuilders anxious about Indian competition.[11]

8 A. G. L. Shaw, *Convicts and the Colonies*, London, 1966, p. 55: G. C. Bolton, 'The Hollow Conqueror; Flax and the Foundation of Australia', in *A.E.H.R.*, VIII, 1, March 1968, pp. 14–15: J. Ehrman, *The Younger Pitt*, London, 1969, pp. 408-10: H. T. Fry, 'Cathay and the way thither—the background to Botany Bay', in *H.S.*, 56, April 1971, p. 497: B. E. Kennedy, 'Anglo-French Rivalry in South-East Asia, 1763–93', in *Journal of Southeast Asian Studies*, IV, September 1973, p. 200.

9 *H.R.A.*, I, pp. 1-16.

10 *H.R.A.*, I, pp. 13, 45, 101, 104: A. G. L. Shaw, 'The Hollow Conqueror and the Tyranny of Distance', in *H.S.*, 50, April 1968, p. 199: J. C. Beaglehole, Ed., *Journals of Captain Cook on his Voyages of Discovery*, Cambridge, 1967, III, p. 1513: J. C. Beaglehole, Ed., *The Endeavour Journals of Joseph Banks*, Sydney, 1959, II, p. 10.

11 R. G. Albion, *Forests and Sea-Power*, Harvard, 1926, pp. 35, 365-8, Cf. T. Laslett, *Timber and Timber Trees*, London, 1875, pp. 112–14, and T. S. Gamble, *Manual of Indian Timbers*, Calcutta, 1881, pp. 283–92.

But the possibility of thus anticipating or counterbalancing any French designs arose from the plans which had already been made for New South Wales, which seems to have been chosen as the site for a penal settlement in July 1786 more or less by default. The government had ruled out building penitentiaries because of their expense and its reluctance to interfere with local control of prisons. It had rejected special penal establishments at home, as at Milford Haven, or in the Scottish Highlands, or on the roads, or in coal mines, because of fears of local opposition. Unguarded transportation to inhabited colonies, such as Nova Scotia, Newfoundland or Honduras, was impossible for the same reason, just as settlement on the African Caffre Coast would offend the Dutch. Proposals to exchange prisoners for Christian slaves in Tunis or Algiers, or to establish a settlement on the tropical west coast of Africa, were denounced as too cruel, and south-west Africa was too arid. Considering the need for a site where the convicts were so isolated that they could be easily guarded and yet 'might soon be likely to obtain means of subsistence', available places under British control were relatively few, and the increasing urgency of the convict problem induced ministers to rely on the 'accounts given by the late Captain Cook, as well as the representation of persons who accompanied him on his last voyage'. The advantages were based not on commerce or imperial development, but on economy. It was said that the land was so fertile that the settlement would be self-sufficient in two years; it was so isolated that 'return would be difficult', and the cost of guarding the prisoners would therefore be small. Thus while 'no man could doubt' that it was 'necessary ... to send ... incorrigible criminals out of the Kingdom', as Pitt said in defending the settlement in the House of Commons in 1791, 'no cheaper mode of disposing the convicts could be found'; he apparently disagreed with the opinion of the 1784 committee that the cost of a penal settlement was so great that it could only be justified if there were compensating 'Political and Commercial Benefits'.[12]

Whatever some optimists might hope, these were not likely to be great. According to Cook, 'the country produces hardly anything fit for man to eat ... [nor] any one thing that can become an article in trade to invite Europeans to fix a settlement upon it'. Banks thought it 'barren ... in a very high degree'.[13] All they could hope for was that hard work might produce changes in time, but as that time had not yet come, it was no wonder that many of the first arrivals were disappointed when they discovered their visions of a fertile semi-tropical paradise most ill-founded.

[12] A. G. L. Shaw, *Convicts and the Colonies*, London, 1966, ch. 2: E. O'Brien, *The Foundation of Australia*, Sydney, 1950, pp. 119–26: C. M. H. Clark, *Select Documents in Australian History, 1788–1850*, Sydney, 1950, pp. 30–33.

[13] From Cook's *Journal*, quoted in C. M. H. Clark, *Sources of Australian History*, London, 1957, pp. 49–55: J. C. Beaglehole, Ed., *The Endeavour Journals of Joseph Banks*, Sydney, 1959, *II*, pp. 112–13.

For a generation they were hemmed in to the coast, on poor soil, unable to find how to cross the range of the Blue Mountains, only some fifty miles away. 'When viewed in a commercial light, I fear its insignificance will appear very striking', wrote one officer. 'The country, My Lord, is past all dispute, a wretched one', lamented another; 'the outcast of God's works', complained another.[14] But in one respect Banks and Cook had been right – the country was 'very thinly peopled', and the natives 'a timorous and inoffensive race'.[15] There would be no massacres, at least by the blacks, and since the latter were nomadic huntsmen and fishermen they would not often try to impede any agricultural efforts of the colonists, or to resist the seizure of their land. Although George III gave instructions that 'all our subjects' should 'live in amity and kindness' with the Aborigines, and no one should 'wantonly destroy them or give them any unnecessary interruption in the exercise of their several occupations', he did not explain what was an 'unnecessary interruption'. It certainly did not preclude the occupation of the land, and while the natives saw no difference between plundering and hunting, their 'depredations' aroused hostility, to be followed often enough by butchery, or at least by expulsion from settled districts where they became trespassers, and by the destruction of their centuries-old way of life.

On 13 May 1787 the First Fleet, under the command of the governor of the new colony, Captain Arthur Phillip, R.N., set sail from Portsmouth on its twelve thousand mile journey to Botany Bay. Phillip's farm at Lyndhurst, Hampshire, was near that of Sir George Rose, an ex-naval officer at that time Secretary to the Treasury, who was probably responsible for appointing Phillip to the command. On board, in addition to 443 seamen, were just over a thousand people, 568 male and 191 female convicts (with 13 children), four companies of marines, 160 men plus 51 officers and NCO's, 27 with wives (with 19 children), as well as the governor and his staff of nine.

From the British point of view, the expedition was not a major enterprise, which perhaps explains some of its shortcomings in personnel and equipment. The lieutenant-governor, Major Ross, was an officer of the marines, like the deputy-judge-advocate, Captain David Collins; unfortunately the latter, though most conscientious and loyal to Phillip, had no legal training for his position. There were marine and naval officers who could be used in various capacities, such as Lieutenant William Dawes as engineer and artillery officer, Captain-Lieutenant Watkin Tench, Captain John Hunter, R.N., later to be the second governor, Lieutenant Ball, R.N., and others to go exploring, to help with the Aborigines and to sit on the criminal court, but the civilian officials were not outstanding. The Anglican chaplain (no

---

14 W. Tench, *A Narrative of the Expedition to Botany Bay*, London 1789, reprinted Sydney, 1961, p. 74 and generally ch. 17: *H.R.N.S.W.*, *II*, pp. 745, 761.

15 Quoted in C. M. H. Clark, *Sources of Australian History*, London, 1957, pp. 52, 61.

Roman Catholic was allowed) was the Rev. Richard Johnson, a Cambridge graduate, who owed his appointment to the influence of William Wilberforce. He was a most devout evangelical, at least once denounced as a Methodist, who cared for the sick and the orphaned children, tried to befriend the Aborigines, of necessity acted as a magistrate, and was one of the best farmers in the colony; but he was constantly depressed by what he regarded as the depravity of the convicts, and though helpful to the governor in a mild way, was not a tower of strength. The surveyor-general, the elderly Augustus Alt, soon had to ask for permission to retire owing to his 'various bodily infirmities'. The surgeon, John White, and his four assistants were as competent as could be expected in the eighteenth century; of these, White and Dennis Considen contributed to the natural history of the colony, Thomas Arndell became a successful settler as well as a doctor, and William Balmain was active in trade and agriculture. At a lower level the expedition was sadly lacking. There was no one with a knowledge of farming, no one who could superintend the convicts' labour, and no master craftsmen, save for the accidental presence of the ex-carpenter, clerk and architectural student, Henry Brewer, nominally a midshipman, who was appointed provost-marshall, but was soon active as a building superintendent, and 'blacksmith' Brodie, from H.M.S. *Sirius*. For farm superintendence, and for an honest storekeeper, Phillip had to rely on his own and another officer's servants.

While waiting to sail, Phillip by dint of much pertinacity got some improvements in his supplies; anti-scorbutics, and more food and clothing were added (though the new clothes for the women, and all needles and thread, were left behind), better provision was made for the sick, and he was even furnished with an extra ship so as to reduce the crowding. But he failed to obtain any of the special manpower he needed – overseers, free settlers or artificers; he did not have even a detailed list of his charges, with their qualifications and their past histories, to help him to separate the sheep from the goats or to learn something of his workforce. The government sent no lawyer, no flax-dresser, as might have been expected if it was interested in this plant, no botanist, not even an 'intelligent gardener', which was a little surprising considering the general interest in natural history at the time, and the special interests of Banks, now Sir Joseph and President of the Royal Society, if his influence was then as great as is widely asserted and subsequently became. Possibly at this moment he was more concerned with sending bread-fruit to the West Indies, for it was in November 1787 that Captain William Bligh, later to be governor of New South Wales, set out on his famous expedition in the *Bounty*, and Banks' correspondence with Phillip does not begin until after the colony had been founded.

On 18–20 January 1788, after a voyage of eight months, Phillip and the fleet arrived, without mishap, at Botany Bay, which, wrote Collins, 'afforded even to ourselves as much matter of surprise as of general

7

satisfaction'. However this appeared an unsatisfactory spot, and in a few days the expedition moved to Port Jackson, where Phillip had discovered 'the finest harbour in the world'. Here on 26 January, he hoisted the flag to found the settlement which he christened Sydney, in the cove with the 'best spring of water'.[16] During the next few days, the marines, male convicts and livestock landed, and clearing, building and planting began. On 3 February, Johnson preached under 'a great tree' the first sermon in Australia on the text, 'What shall I render to the Lord for all his benefits towards me?' though some of his audience may have doubted these. On 7 February Collins read the commissions appointing the governor and his principal subordinates, the act establishing a Criminal Court, and the Charter of Justice, Phillip made a 'pointed and judicious speech', a 'very well delivered and energetick piece of oratory', the battalion was reviewed, 'a *feu de joie* was fired, the band played several pieces suited to the business', loyal toasts were drunk and New South Wales was on its way.[17]

Ever since 26 January the settlement had been under English law, for as soon as the colonists had arrived their 'invisible and inescapable cargo of English law ... attached itself to the soil on which they stood'; at the ceremony on 7 February, this 'already established fact' was proclaimed.[18] Even Phillip's first commission, issued in October 1786, though military in character, imposed a rule of law, because the 'rules and discipline of war' which all were to obey were determined by law; but this was military law and penal discipline, suitable only for a military–penal establishment, and apparently the government decided this was not enough. In January 1787 it sponsored an act which recited that 'a colony and a civil Government should be established' at the penal settlement.[19] Parts of the 'civil government' could be, and were, established by royal prerogative. The civil court was to administer only the laws of England, so it could be lawfully established by Charter, as one had been in Gibraltar;[20] but since the criminal court was of a special character, 'with authority to proceed in a more summary way' than in England, without grand jury, and with a special 'petty' jury (of six naval or military officers, not of

---

16 D. Collins, *An Account of the English Colony in New South Wales*, London, 1798, *I*, pp. 1–2, 6: *H.R.A., I*, p. 16 ff.

17 W. Tench, *A Narrative of the Expedition to Botany Bay*, reprinted Sydney, 1961, p. 41: D. Collins, *An Account of the English Colony in New South Wales*, Lnodon, 1798, *I*, pp. 2–19: *H.R.N.S.W., II*, pp. 543, 691–2.

18 W. J. V. Windeyer, 'A Birthright and Inheritance', in *Tasmanian University Law Review, I*, 5, November 1962, pp. 636–8. This meant that Phillip's wish that slavery be illegal in the new colony was necessarily granted. See *H.R.N.S.W., I*, ii, p. 53.

19 *H.R.A.*, Series IV, *I*, pp. 4–6.

20 W. J. V. Windeyer, 'A Birthright and Inheritance', in *Tasmanian University Law Review, I*, 5, November 1962, p. 649.

twelve good men and true), whose verdict did not have to be unanimous, the Crown needed statutory authority to set it up.

So in April 1787 Phillip had been given his second commission, more civil in character. It superseded his earlier military commission and was similar to those long in use in the American colonies. The governor had to maintain law and order and was given power to grant land, control commerce, pardon criminals, raise armed forces, and issue regulations or orders. But in all these things his powers were subject to the law and controllable by the courts; if he were to try to over-ride these, he might expect repercussions from London. Like any other officer of government he had also to obey his instructions; what was somewhat peculiar in the case of the governor of New South Wales was that it might take two years or more for a reply to any query or protest to arrive from the British authorities. Unlike the American colonies, there was no Council or Assembly to restrict the governor's power, so that though any orders he might issue might not be 'repugnant to the laws of England' – that is they were subject to statute, such as a prohibition on the imposition of taxation, or the infliction of 'cruel and unnatural punishments' – but they were otherwise at his discretion, subject only to the eventual approval of the Secretary of State. Such powers the Crown had commonly granted to colonial governors ever since Queen Elizabeth I had extended them to Sir Walter Raleigh when he was attempting to establish a colony in Virginia, so if, as Tench said, the government had 'not been backward in arming Mr Phillip with plenitude of power', it had done nothing unusual.[21]

Phillip's first problem was to make sure that his settlement would survive. One can easily overlook the difficulties of pioneering at the ends of the earth, with no outside assistance available within months. The nearest comparison with Phillip's plight would be the early days of Virginia or Massachusetts, more than a century and a half before, and these precedents were not happy ones. In Virginia in 1611, though some food was obtainable from Indians, the governor reported that 'everie man allmost laments himself of being here'.[22] In New England, the personnel was better, fortunately, for the 'starving time' was so serious that half the settlers died during the first winter, and, as for the rest 'what could sustain them but the spirite of God

[21] Enid Campbell, 'Prerogative Rule in New South Wales', in *R.A.H.S.J.*, *50*, 3, August 1964, pp. 161–91: W. J. V. Windeyer, 'A Birthright and Inheritance', in *Tasmanian University Law Review*, I, November 1962, pp. 645–6: *H.R.A.*, Series IV, I, pp. 908–9, n. 22: W. Tench, *A Narrative of the Expedition to Botany Bay*, reprinted Sydney, 1961, p. 42. When Acts of Indemnity had to be passed to protect Governor Macquarie, this was because he had imposed taxation which could not be done by prerogative since the Bill of Rights of 1689.

[22] Quoted in S. E. Morison and H. S. Commager, *The Growth of the American Republic*, New York, 1942, I, p. 39.

and his grace?' with 'the mighty ocean ... a maine barre and golfe to separate them from all the civill parts of the world'.[23]

The first need was for better shelter than tents. But building was not easy for there were only twelve carpenters among the convicts plus ten more who were temporarily available from the ships, and the convicts were unwilling workmen. However, by mid-winter two stores were finished, which provided some security against theft, four officers were in huts, even if only of thatched 'cabbage tree' plastered over with clay. As it grew cold, the lack of barracks became a source of complaint, and even temporary buildings were not ready for a year after landing.[24] After the brick-kilns had been set up in 1790 more could be done, but in 1791 Phillip could still complain that he had 'only one master carpenter in this settlement'. Permanent barracks were begun in September 1792, before Phillip left, but they were not finished for another eighteen months, six years after the colony had been founded.[25]

Shortage of food was even more serious than lack of shelter. Though kangaroos were often shot, they were 'not even as good as mutton'. Fish were scarce. There was no livestock, either for food or breeding, for many had been lost on the way out; most of the remaining sheep died from eating the native grass, and the surviving cattle escaped and disappeared. Search for edible plants or shrubs was fruitless. There remained only a fast diminishing stock of salt meat.[26] The officers tried to raise grain and vegetables, but without much success. Plants came up quickly, but without manure they soon withered on the sandy soil. Most of the officers were very gloomy. 'What is to be hereafter is known only to God', wrote Johnson, 'but at present I think the appearances are against us'. Even Phillip admitted that 'perhaps no country in the world affords less assistance to first settlers'. By the end of the year, of the 1030 who had arrived, 56 had died since landing (as well as 4 killed by natives, 5 executed and 14 missing), over 100 were in hospital, and 57 'unfit for hard labour'.[27]

As time went on the situation grew steadily worse, despite the justified hopes of better results from the farms at the second settlement formed at Rose Hill, or Parramatta. Diet, always deficient in vitamin C, worsened as supplies ran ever shorter. After the supply-ship *Guardian* had been wrecked off the Cape in December 1789, no provisions arrived from England for more than two years.[28] Poor food

23 Quoted in S. E. Morison and H. S. Commager, *The Growth of the American Republic*, New York, 1942, *I*, p. 53.

24 J. Cobley, *Sydney Cove, 1788*, London, 1962, pp. 170, 201: *H.R.A.*, *I*, pp. 45–6.

25 *H.R.N.S.W.*, *II*, pp. 208, 716: *H.R.A.*, *I*, p. 310.

26 J. Cobley, *Sydney Cove, 1788*, London, 1962, p. 77: *H.R.N.S.W.*, *II*, pp. 680–81.

27 *H.R.N.S.W.*, *II*, p. 410: John Cobley, *Sydney Cove, 1788*, London, 1962, pp. 250–52, 264.

28 *H.R.A.*, *I*, p. 165.

meant that scurvy and dysentery were common. The hospital was short of blankets, sheets, soap and medicines, as well as ordinary articles of hospital diet, such as vinegar, thought to be an anti-scorbutic, currants, oatmeal, barley, sago and rice. In April 1790 the peas 'were all expended', which reduced the vitamin B_1, to add to the existing deficiency of vitamin A, and absence of C. By June the ration was down to 1800 calories with only 56 gms of protein. No wonder that little work was done, or that Phillip noted that 'we have not made that advance towards supporting ourselves which may have been expected'.[29]

On 3 June 1790 there cast anchor the first ship from London since the expedition had arrived – *Lady Juliana*, with 226 female convicts – and before the end of the month the Second Fleet proper followed. It had embarked 1017 prisoners, but a quarter had died en route, and two-thirds of the rest landed sick. To provide room for profitable cargo, they had been overcrowded; to save money they had been underfed; for fear of their misbehaviour, they had been too closely confined; but for all that, the fleet brought some relief. By 1792, more supplies had arrived, and despite drought from July 1790 to August 1791 farming at Parramatta had begun to be productive. James Ruse, who in November 1789 was the first emancipist to be granted land, had become self-supporting; of others who had received grants, Tench noted that while some 'were in a state of despondency, and predicted that they should starve', others were 'tranquil and determined to persevere'. Maize had been found easier to cultivate than wheat, and was better adapted to the inevitable hand-hoeing. Though Phillip might regret that 'the period at which this colony will supply its inhabitants with animal food is nearly as distant at present as when I first landed in this country', and he had had to send to Calcutta for supplies again, there was no longer danger of starvation. All round, prospects were brighter.[30]

Phillip had also established a settlement on Norfolk Island. As he had been instructed, less than three weeks after the first landing in Sydney, he sent a detachment to occupy it under Lieutenant Philip Gidley King, R.N., who was to become the third governor of the colony, possibly spurred on by the appearance of La Pérouse's expedition in Botany Bay a week after his own arrival. King found the famous flax-plant luxuriant there, but he had no one to dress it. He found the timber good, but since there was no harbour on the island, little could be done about it. What was more immediately important was that he found the island very fertile; clearing was easier than on the mainland, and vegetables and maize grew readily. Phillip was

29 L. Davey, M. Macpherson and F. W. Clements, 'The Hungry Years, 1788–1792', in *H.S.*, *11*, November 1947, pp. 188, 195, 199: *H.R.A.*, I, p. 181.

30 W. Tench, *A Complete Account of the Settlement at Port Jackson*, London, 1793, p. 148 and chs. 16, 17: D. Collins, *An Account of the English Colony in New South Wales*, London, 1798, *I*, pp. 215, 249: *H.R.A.*, I, pp. 371–7.

relieved to find that it reduced the demand for food, and the British government was delighted that in so doing it reduced the expenditure of the settlement. By 1792 it had taken more than 1100 people from Port Jackson and was even producing pork.

The governor was more often hindered than helped by his second in command, Lieutenant-Governor Major Ross of the marines, described by one of his subordinates as 'without exception the most disagreeable commanding officer I ever knew'. Ross refused to allow his force to have anything to do with the convicts except to guard them. He objected to his men being subject in any way to the night watch which Phillip instituted in an attempt to reduce the thieving so prevalent in the settlement in the days of shortages; though the marines were not innocent of nocturnal plundering, Ross would not have them interfered with by the well-behaved convicts who made up this primitive police-force. He almost frustrated the working of the criminal court by his objection to his officers sitting as jurors on it (fortunately most of them voluntarily agreed to do so), and he increasingly badgered the governor with demands for his men, which though perhaps reasonable in one sense, he must have known could not be met in the difficult conditions of the infant settlement. Eventually Phillip managed to get rid of him by putting him in charge of Norfolk Island, but he had little help in coping with other difficulties. He asked for free settlers, but they would not come. He wanted livestock, and received less than enough for one good farm in England. The clothing sent out was rotten. The settlement was always short of stores, and when they arrived they were 'as bad as ever were sent out for barter on the coast of Guinea'. However, Phillip's patience, dignity and perseverance enabled him to lead the settlement successfully in its battle for survival, and in part because of his promptings, the British government had come to recognize that in the future New South Wales would be more than a gaol – it would be a colony. At first settlers would be few, and for at least a generation its principal labour force would be convicts but, as he said, it 'must hereafter be a most valuable acquisition to Great Britain'.[31]

Such a change had begun before Phillip left in December 1792. He had already been told to place no limit on the number of convict servants to be assigned to any settler. His request to be allowed to make land-grants to officers had been approved, and the despatch telling him so was on the water. He had encouraged private enterprise in whaling, though the results were disappointing, and he had not stopped, even if he disliked, his officers from chartering the *Britannia* for a mercantile speculation. From all these were to spring further commercial activities, which indeed Lieutenant-Governor Francis Grose, who took over the administration, showed himself very ready to promote. Grose was a professional soldier, in command of the New South Wales Corps; but he was not in good health, and being on his

31 *H.R.A., I*, p. 67.

own admission, 'unaccustomed to business, and fearful of acting so much from my own discretion', he was willing enough to rely on his officers.[32] He appointed as inspector-general of public works at Parramatta John Macarthur, 'my counsellor', then a lieutenant in the Corps, but soon to become famous as a farmer and entrepreneur in the settlement. He welcomed the permission to give officers land and the services of convict labourers, and probably on Macarthur's advice, refused to heed Dundas's later order to reduce the number of private servants maintained at public expense.[33] If he did not, as was later alleged, transfer control from civilians to the military, for there was virtually no civil administration, he certainly relied heavily on his regiment, increased its rations, made only its officers magistrates, and quarrelled with both the chaplain in Sydney and Lieutenant-Governor King on Norfolk Island, two of the few senior men who were not in the Corps.

This regiment had been specially raised for service in New South Wales and its officers had been made liable to perform duties, like jury and magisterial service, to which the marines had earlier objected. By modern criteria, it might be regarded as a 'peculiar institution'. M. H. Ellis, in his life of John Macarthur, insists that its personnel were of the average quality of any normal regiment raised for overseas service, though possibly this is not saying much, considering the quality of the contemporary British soldier; however, although the Corps probably degenerated as time went on, especially after the outbreak of war with France in 1793, for Ellis himself refers to recruits in 1795–6 being 'of a class reckoned unmanageable even in the Savoy Military Prison', even before that the Secretary of War had admitted that the 'service was not the most eligible' (and therefore presumably not likely to attract the best type of men), and several military criminals received pardons on condition that they served in the Corps.[34] Be that as it may, its duties were not heavy, and both its officers and its men found time on their hands.

Trouble soon occurred at Norfolk Island, where, as on the mainland, a detachment of the Corps was on duty to maintain order. A whole series of quarrels and fights between the soldiers and settlers culminated in January 1794 in riot and mutiny by some of the former; but instead of supporting Lieutenant-Governor King's attempts to restore discipline, Grose over-rode the latter's authority by removing the Corps from control by the ordinary law. He forbade any constable, who of course would be a convict, to interfere with any soldier, even

[32] *H.R.A.*, I, pp. 447, 474.

[33] Memo of Sir William Macarthur, quoted in M. H. Ellis, *John Macarthur*, Sydney, 1955, p. 48: *H.R.A.*, I, pp. 416, 442, 470.

[34] M. H. Ellis, *John Macarthur*, Sydney, 1955, pp. 12, 85–7: H. de Watteville, *The British Soldier*, London, 1954, ch. 8: A. G. L. Shaw, 'The N.S.W. Corps', in *R.A.H.S.J.*, 47, 2, June 1961, p. 129: *H.R.N.S.W.*, II, p. 102: R. Glover, *Peninsular Preparation—the Reform of the British Army, 1795–1809*, Cambridge, 1963, ch. 7.

if 'detected in an unlawful act', or to take him before a justice of the peace; he gave orders that all settlers were to be deprived of their arms, and any settler assaulting a soldier was to be summarily punished by a military court. King was naturally concerned by the illegality of these orders, but for all that he felt he had to put them into force until he received countermanding instructions from London two years later; however this was only an anticipation of similar high-handed behaviour by both officers and men of the Corps in New South Wales during the ensuing years, as was shown in the cases of Boston, Baughan and Isaac Nichols, for example.[35]

But whatever their shortcomings in obedience to the law and in respecting the rights of others, the officers of the Corps soon showed themselves to be efficient farmers, and when Governor Hunter arrived in Sydney in September 1795 he was amazed at the transformation which had taken place since he had left the colony rather more than four years before. At that time the farmers had been 'small men', either well-behaved ex-convicts, to whom Phillip had been told to give thirty acres, in order to encourage them both to reform, and even more importantly, to stay in the colony, or men from the marines, with about 100 acres each, who it was hoped would help to defend the settlement.[36] The size and conditions prescribed for the grants were the same as those for the West Indies, and perhaps a little more aptly for Canada – and why should New South Wales be any different?[37] To suggest as some have done a conscious decision to establish a specifically peasant society would seem to imply greater care and forethought than there is any evidence of, for the British government knew nothing of the needs of the farmer at Botany Bay. But by February 1791 Phillip envisaged larger farms – 500 to 1000 acres with twenty men to work them. By the same ship as the first free settlers arrived in February 1793, Grose received permission to grant land to the military and civil officers. By 1796, these men, more enterprising than those hitherto on the land, with some capital acquired from their trading ventures or from 'loans' from regimental funds, with their salaries to help to tide them over difficult times, and assisted by ten servants each provided at government expense, were cultivating one-third of the land currently under crop. The most famous was Macarthur, the first man to use a plough in the colony, who showed at Elizabeth Farm what could be accomplished by a man of means and ambition, perhaps helped by his official position at Parramatta. He was, of course, unusual but not unique.[38]

35 *H.R.N.S.W.*, *II*, pp. 103, 125–31, 173 ff., 304: *III*, 64, 88, 580 ff.

36 See the Instructions issued to Phillip, Grose and Hunter in *H.R.A.*, *I*, pp. 14–15, 124–8, 441, 523–6.

37 B. H. Fletcher, 'The Development of Small-scale Farming in New South Wales under Governor Hunter', in *R.A.H.S.J.*, *50*, 1, June 1964: N. Macdonald, *Canada, 1763–1841, Immigration and Settlement*, London, 1939, p. 39 and ch. 3.

38 S. Macarthur Onslow, *Some Early Records of the Macarthurs of Camden*, Sydney, 1914, pp. 44–51.

Phillip had thought the Hawkesbury rather inaccessible, but Grose was not worried by the possibility of attacks by the natives, of misbehaviour by the settlers, or of floods, all of which were soon evident, and by 1795 more than four hundred people were living in this fertile area along thirty miles of the banks of the river. As time went on, difficulties appeared there. In June 1795 the first major clash with the natives of New South Wales occurred, when it seemed that the Aborigines should be stopped interfering with 'the peaceable possession' of the settlers' farms, lest there should be an end to 'every prospect of advantage which the colony might expect to derive' from the district. In September came the first of the floods, and there would be six more serious ones in the next fifteen years. Not only did distance add to the settlers' cost, but isolation was said to lead to misbehaviour; certainly Hunter represented the Hawkesbury farmers as the worst of a poor lot, and guilty of misconduct which not only upset the high-minded, but inevitably affected the success of their farms.[39]

They were not the only ones to run into trouble. The average debt of the farmers at Prospect, for example, though only half the average at the Hawkesbury, equalled the legal wage for unskilled labour for nearly a year, and much of it was hardly the settlers' fault. Even if they were sober and hard-working, the declining fertility of many of the farms and a bad drought in 1798–9 pressed heavily upon them. They complained that they were unfairly treated in the distribution of convict labour, and so had to pay high wages which had to be supplemented by costly issues of rum.[40] Many, perhaps most, of the settlers knew little about farming, and they lacked equipment. Since there were no livestock in the colony, there was neither manure nor draught animals. The hoe had to take the place of the plough. There were no fences, but many weeds. By 1800, although there were then about 350 small farmers cultivating about 7000 acres, of the fifty-four ex-convicts who had received grants before 1795, only eight remained on their farms, and of all who had received grants on the mainland two-thirds had left, though how many lost their lands through foreclosed mortgages and how many sold out to go home we do not know.[41]

To add to their other difficulties, the settlers had to pay very high prices for anything imported. Naturally such goods were scarce in a new settlement, even though the extreme privations of the famine years were over. At first, according to Collins, ships' masters 'kept up the extravagant nominal value which everything bore in the colony'; then the officers of the settlement agreed to form a 'ring' to buy goods

---

[39] *H.R.A., I*, pp. 183, 470, 479, 483, 499–500, 596.

[40] *H.R.N.S.W., III*, p. 468: A. G. L. Shaw, 'Labour', in G. Abbott and B. Nairn, Eds., *Economic Growth of Australia, 1788-1821*, Melbourne, 1969, p. 110.

[41] *H.R.A., II*, pp. 135 ff, 440 ff: B. H. Fletcher, 'The Development of Small-scale Farming in New South Wales under Governor Hunter', in *R.A.H.S.J., 50*, 1, June 1964, pp. 3–31.

for resale. Three times they chartered ships, but usually they purchased the cargoes that merchants brought or sent to Sydney as a speculation.[42] Their good fortune in being able to enter the trading business arose partly from the fact that the First Fleet had not carried money – and the belief that prisons do not need this offers another example of the hand-to-mouth arrangements made for the expedition – and partly from their access to London funds. Almost the only currency in the colony was paper, which comprised either an individual's promissory note, worthless outside New South Wales, or a government bill, which might be either a local store receipt, obtained from the sale of wheat or meat to the commissariat, or bills drawn on the British Treasury in London.[43] Naturally, ships' captains preferred these, and these the officers could obtain. They might draw on anticipations of their salaries, small though these might be; more important at a time when most public officials normally used for their own profit any public funds temporarily under their control, the officers could draw paymaster's bills in sterling on regimental funds in London. Thus they could buy the cargoes they were soon either to re-sell, often through agents, or to pay 'in kind' to their soldiers and servants.[44]

At first the principal traders were the paymaster, Macarthur, and the commanders of each company, Paterson, Johnston, Foveaux and Rowley, though Lieutenant Abbott and Surgeons Harris and Balmain also appear to have taken part; as Mrs Macarthur put it delightfully in 1798, 'this country possesses numerous advantages to persons holding appointments under government', and her husband 'had a handsome addition to his income by having the payment of a company and transacting the business of Paymaster to the Regiment'.[45]

But their 'monopoly' was short-lived, and soon others showed themselves capable of joining in the trade, often with less scruple than their predecessors. Not one of these 'dealers, pedlars and extortioners', as one settlers' petition described them, had 'brought a penny to the colony', yet within two or three years they could 'mount a saddle horse'; clearly they were *not* regimental officers (even of the New South Wales Corps), but 'a number of the less elevated inhabitants', including some ex-convicts.[46] Some were men who had abandoned or sold their farms, despite the prohibition on alienation. A few had

[42] D. Collins, *An Account of the English Colony in New South Wales*, London, 1798, I, p. 334: D. R. Hainsworth, *Builders and Adventurers*, Melbourne, 1968, p. 6.

[43] S. J. Butlin, *Foundations of the Australian Monetary System*, Melbourne, 1953, ch. 2: *H.R.A.*, II, p. 150.

[44] D. R. Hainsworth, *Builders and Adventurers*, Melbourne, 1968, pp. 9–11: *H.R.N.S.W.*, III, p. 729.

[45] S. Macarthur Onslow, *Some Early Records of the Macarthurs of Camden*, Sydney, 1914, pp. 43, 46.

[46] *H.R.A.*, II, pp. 136–40: D. R. Hainsworth, *Builders and Adventurers*, Melbourne, 1968, pp. 14–17.

profited by buying goods cheaply on the way out for resale on arrival. Others had accumulated capital by selling retail as agents for the officers or ships' masters, or by some other form of petty trafficking. The fact that in 1798 'some of the principal inhabitants and the whole of the military officers' felt compelled to make an agreement to restrict the purchase of cargoes to themselves suggests that a new class was entering business, as those who had formerly dealt only as agents or retailers accumulated funds which they could convert into treasury bills by buying grain from the settlers and re-selling it to the commissariat; unless this agreement was directed against the competition of such people, whom Hunter called 'improper persons', it is difficult to understand why he should have published a government order to support it. The spread of the traffic beyond the officers appears again in a petition to Hunter in 1800 seeking permission to purchase a cargo just arrived in the *Minerva*; among the eighteen signatories are no 'officers' but seven ex-convicts, three ex-soldiers and sailors, two former missionaries and four holding minor government posts.[47]

Before such people were able to join in these activities, pay-masters' bills, drawn largely for trading purposes, had exceeded £50,000 between 1792 and 1800. A few of the officers did very well, but that every one (or even the majority) was involved is almost certainly untrue, and some of the accusations of profiteering are clearly absurd, except possibly for spirits.[48] There was a limit to the 'fortunes' which could be made by fleecing impecunious ex-convict settlers, and perhaps the value of the sheep which Foveaux sold to Macarthur when he left the colony in 1801 – £2000 – is a fairer representation of the sort of profits made.

In 1801 George Bass, the former naval surgeon who had embarked on trading activities, found to his dismay when he brought out a cargo to make his fortune that the market had collapsed, glutted 'from the quantity of goods far exceeding the consumption, and glutted also because the new system of government is built upon a plan of the most rigid economy. It issues very little or no bills . . . Our wings are clipped with a vengeance'.[49] Governor King had cut public expenditure to half in Australia's first credit squeeze, and so reduced the demand for goods. On the supply side a government retail store, first mooted as early as 1792, later proposed by King for Norfolk Island, and by Collins and Hunter for the mainland, and accepted by the secretary of state in 1797, was by this time receiving regular shipments of goods for sale at a standard mark-up of only 20 or 30 per cent.[50]

47 *H.R.A., II*, p. 216–17, 437–9.

48 *H.R.A., II*, pp. 442–3: Governor John Hunter, *Remarks on the Causes of the Colonial Expenses of the Establishment of New South Wales*, London, 1802, p. 18.

49 *H.R.N.S.W., IV*, p. 587: G. Abbott and B. Nairn, Eds., *Economic Growth of Australia 1788–1821*, Melbourne, 1969, pp. 164–5.

50 *H.R.N.S.W., I*, ii, p. 637; *III*, p. 156; *IV*, pp. 117–18: *H.R.A., II*, pp. 19, 110, 153, 551.

A number of small-scale private adventurers were also in the market, as well as the major merchant house of Robert Campbell.

Campbell had made his first speculative voyage to New South Wales in 1798, spurred on by the earlier hopes of Calcutta merchants that trade with New South Wales might be profitable. He found prospects promising, and in 1800 with King's permission, settled in Sydney as a merchant. He dealt directly with his settler-customers, accepting their grain in payment for his goods, and granting them extensive credit. As a result, three years later he was warmly thanked, both by the officers (presumably the non-trading majority) for 'the very liberal and candid manner' in which he acted, and by more than two hundred settlers for delivering them from 'a most execrable Monopoly', and from being 'a prey to the Mercenary unsparing Hand of Avarice and Extortion'.[51]

But if ordinary retail trading was getting on a sounder footing, spirits – which Hunter had said in 1796 was 'the only article that I find fault with' – remained the cause of sore heads and local dissension. Convicts, soldiers and settlers alike took to the new world the love of drink which they had in the old. Officials whether in Sydney or London agreed that in moderation grog was a bounty well-deserved; unfortunately it was so eagerly sought that up to 1801 prices occasionally touched a ten-fold mark-up, though after that they fell fairly steadily to a more normal three-fold figure.[52] Officials and soldiers received regular issues, and from 1792 an evergrowing stream of spirit cargoes arrived in New South Wales, culminating in the six months from November 1799, when to supply about 5000 persons, 36,000 gallons were landed (plus 22,000 gallons of wine). Though Hunter sometimes sent away a particular cargo, he thought it impossible to prevent these large-scale importations; indeed he went so far as to argue that they were desirable to keep the prices down.[53] All classes were involved in the trade. Orders for the licensing of public houses were ignored. 'Cellars, from the *better sort of people* ... to the blackest characters ... are full of that fiery poison', wrote King in May 1800. Hunter's secretary, Captain George Johnston, was arrested for illicit spirit-dealing. Senior N.C.O.'s were active as owners of grog-shops-*cum*-gambling dens. Some officers would sell grog directly; others 'not quite so open, employ their washwomen or others in this way'.[54] Although, as Governor King admitted, spirits could 'occasion much idleness', they formed a normal part of a man's wages, though never,

51 Margaret Steven, *Merchant Campbell, 1796–1846*, Oxford, 1965, chs. 1, 2, and pp. 56–61.

52 *H.R.A., I*, pp. 376–7, 668: *IV*, p. 23.

53 *H.R.A., II*, pp. 426, 437, 550.

54 M. Roe, 'Colonial Society in Embryo', in *H.S., 26*, May 1956, p. 155: *H.R.A., II*, pp. 505, 671: Rev. R. Johnson quoted in D. R. Hainsworth, *Builders and Adventurers*, Melbourne, 1968, p. 9: Select Committee on Transportation, 1812, *Report*, p. 58.

as some have argued, a normal form of currency. Generally speaking, the promise of rum was a better incentive to work than the threat of the lash.[55] The Rev. Samuel Marsden, the evangelically-minded chaplain who first assisted and then succeeded Richard Johnson, found, like his predecessor, that without rum 'the disspirited indolent convict cannot be excited to exertions', however regrettable this might be, and in 1803, merchant Campbell wanted to land a special cargo of grog on the ground that without a 'proper distribution of Spirits for Labour', he could not get men to carry out his work.[56]

When added to other shortcoming in New South Wales, this traffic seemed to weaken the justification for transportation as a penal policy. It had been expected to be a cheap punishment and it was not. It was to be a deterrent, but its critics argued that in fact it was agreeable, and the only really irksome part was the voyage out – unpleasant, as all long sea voyages were at the time.[57] Some historians have painted the few scandalous voyages that occurred as typical, but they were not. Six ships had a mortality rate of more than 25 per cent between 1787 and 1802, notably those in the Second Fleet, but, overall, between 1787 and 1810 the death rate, including those six, was less than five per cent, and compared very favourably with that on emigrant ships on the much shorter journey across the Atlantic. Apart from this, it was argued that the moral contamination of the prisoners closely associated in the hulks, whence they emerged 'more expert in fraud' than before, was equally likely to take place in the ships on the voyage out, and in the government gangs in the colony. Among the females, prostitution was common. So what, it was asked, was gained by transportation? Allegedly the prospect of reformation. The men might learn farming, become good servants and eventually perhaps even 'prosperous and respectable settlers'.[58] But even this was doubtful. There were few respectable employers for the convicts to work for while under sentence. British and Irish emigrants preferred to go to the more accessible U.S.A. For twenty years, less than a hundred free men came to Australia to settle, and more than half of these were artisans.[59] Though there were respectable government officials and ex-soldiers who employed convict servants, the superintendents and overseers on the government farms were no models of decorum, and most employers were themselves ex-convicts. They would not be agents for

[55] *H.R.A.*, *V*, p. 601 and cf. *H.R.A.*, *I*, p. 593: S. J. Butlin, *Foundations of the Australian Monetary System*, Melbourne, 1953, p. 18 ff.

[56] *H.R.A.*, *I*, pp. 452–3; *IV*, p. 131: *H.R.N.S.W.*, *III*, p. 486.

[57] Select Committee on Transportation, 1812, *Report*, p. 12. For the voyages generally see C. Bateson, *The Convict Ships, 1787–1868*, Glasgow, 1959.

[58] A. G. L. Shaw, *Convicts and the Colonies*, London, 1966, pp. 62–3. Select Committee on Transportation, 1812, *Report*, pp. 9–11.

[59] R. B. Madgwick, *Immigration into Eastern Australia, 1788–1851*, 2nd ed., Sydney, 1969, ch. 1: *H.R.A.*, *I*, pp. 366–7, 464; *II*, pp. 127–8, 228, 241.

reformation; they might even be lax disciplinarians, and the whole process would work out as a reward for crime.

Economy would be achieved by assigning convicts to private employment, once Hunter had obeyed his instructions and insisted that all masters should feed and clothe their convict servants. But some of the men had to remain in government gangs for public works. This aroused criticism from London; it was expensive, it kept the prisoners associated, usually 'amidst all the inducements to vice which such a town as Sydney must afford to them'. The men worked for about nine hours, or less if employed on task work, and early in the afternoon their time was their own. This was necessary, for though they were fed and clothed by the government, they had to earn enough to pay for their accommodation and meet other odd expenses, and it also helped to spread the labour force, which was particularly desirable in the case of the rare skilled artisans.[60] But it could also be argued that this spare time provided opportunities for gambling or drinking or thieving, and so hampered reform, unless strictly supervised. Hence the need for discipline, but unfortunately the punishments imposed for misconduct whether at work or elsewhere were brutalizing rather than reformatory.

Since the colony had no adequate gaol and its rulers were army and navy officers, inevitably the most common penalty for any misbehaviour was what was then normal in the services – flogging. From the beginning the punishments ordered by the Criminal Court and by the magistrates were fantastically severe and eccentric – 500 lashes for a theft, 300 for abetting a bushranger or stabbing with intent to kill, 200 for stealing spirits, 150 for 'wanting to have connexion with a woman against her will', 100 for drunkenness, for stealing from a garden, for pretending to have discovered gold, 50 for forging a note, for stealing a hat, for swearing 'horrid oaths'. In the early days masters took the law into their own hands in punishing their assigned servants themselves, though King forbade this when he assumed office in 1800. Prisoners were not commonly punished by being sent to a colonial penal settlement, for conditions at Norfolk Island or Newcastle were not much worse than at headquarters; although the out-settlements were sometimes useful for getting rid of disturbers of the peace, the most common punishment other than flogging was for a prisoner's sentence to be lengthened, or for him to be ordered to wear irons, including the form of spiked collar which was later to cause Governor Darling so much trouble in the Sudds case in 1826.[61]

60 *H.R.A.*, *I*, p. 495: *H.R.N.S.W.*, *VI*, p. 149: A. G. L. Shaw, *Convicts and the Colonies*, London, 1966, pp. 71–2: T. A. Coghlan, *Labour and Industry in Australia*, 2nd ed., Melbourne, 1969, *I*, p. 49 ff.: Select Committee on Transportation, 1812, *Report* (substantially reprinted in C. M. H. Clark, *Sources of Australian History*, London, 1957, pp. 108–22).

61 This was apparently quite a common form of punishment. See D. Collins, *An Account of the English Colony in New South Wales*, London, 1798, pp. 53–4, 211–12: *H.R.N.S.W.*, *II*, p. 178; *III*, pp. 596–7. For other punishments, N.S.W., Supreme Court Papers, Criminal Court, Mitchell Library, 1/296–9.

In some cases the convicts had justified hopes that good conduct would be rewarded. King, like Macquarie later, insisted that the convicts should not be consigned to 'Oblivion and disgrace for ever', and was as ready to enrol well-behaved emancipists in the New South Wales Corps, in the Loyal Associations and in his bodyguard, as he was to grant them land.[62] Grose and Hunter pardoned less than two per cent a year; King, like Macquarie later, nearly twice as many. Though this saved money, the British government was critical of this alleged leniency, but it is doubtful if King strained the quality of mercy very far. He could recognize that as the colony developed, conditional emancipation was safe and would benefit both colony and convict. In this regard, even more important was the 'pass', or permission for a convict to work for himself, later known as a ticket-of-leave. This innovation of King's became one of the most important elements in penal policy, and was primarily a reward for good conduct, but since it saved money, it could be abused by being granted to a prisoner, whether well-conducted or not, who could earn his own living, and so take himself 'off the stores'.[63]

However, if in some cases better material conditions in the colony might reduce the temptation to crime, the government did not provide much religious teaching or secular education to help the convict in his non-material concerns, and it was admitted in 1812 that religious feelings in the colony were weak. There was only one chaplain in New South Wales until 1794, and only one on the mainland from 1800 to 1810 (with a political prisoner at Norfolk Island from 1800 to 1806). The governors and the government were apparently more interested in the things of this world than those of the next, and not even William Wilberforce could persuade the Secretary of State to send out more clergy or schoolmasters. Johnson could get no help to build his first church in Sydney, and when it was burned down in 1798, its replacement was not finished for ten years. Though some might hope that learning would be a foe to vice, the only official day schools established were for orphans, and there was a great want of 'spelling books, testaments and Bibles'. Considering the character of the new society of New South Wales, it is hardly surprising that it should be said that many successful emancipists rose to affluence rather than respectability; though Governor King insisted in 1804 that the inhabitants were 'not so generally depraved as may be imagined', his successor argued in 1807 that by far the greater part of the prisoners remained 'after their servitude the same characters as by their viscious [sic] habits they have maintained in their career of life.' Even those who became well-to-do left off thieving, he complained, 'their

---

[62] *H.R.A., IV*, p. 216.

[63] Regulations were issued on 10 October 1801 and 28 October 1802. See A. G. L. Shaw, *Convicts and the Colonies*, London, 1966, pp. 73, 83.

habits of cheating and knavery seem to be increased by the giving up the other Vice'.[64]

For some these seemed harsh verdicts. Some of the complaints are those perennially made by the middle-aged self-righteous. Some emancipists succeeded as small farmers – a quarter of them in 1803, a fifth in 1819 – and many had 'comfortable little dwellings'. A few were good mechanics, with plenty of work, who were living in comfort. Probably about eighty enrolled in one of the colony's Loyal Associations and perhaps as many in the New South Wales Corps. A score or so more of those who arrived before 1810 made a distinguished contribution to colonial life. Richard Fitzgerald, Superintendent of Public Agriculture, 'faithful factor' of John Macarthur and, according to Governor Macquarie, a 'most honest, upright, good man', and Andrew Thompson, shipbuilder and merchant, at Windsor, were both successful farmers. In different fields were bricklayer James Bloodsworth, who built the first government house, the pioneer business woman, Mary Reibey, printer George Howe who was the first editor of the *Sydney Gazette*, superintendent Hutchinson, artists John Eyre and Thomas Watling, and among the political prisoners, chaplain Henry Fulton, and surveyor James Meehan from Ireland. William Redfern, naval surgeon, transported for sympathizing with the mutineers at the Nore in 1798, was not only a successful medical practitioner, but in 1814 wrote the important report on health in convict ships which led to further improvements in the conditions on board. The so-called Scottish martyrs, Thomas Fyshe Palmer, Thomas Muir, William Skirving, and Maurice Margarot, transported in 1794 after a partisan trial, were perhaps more notorious than important, and others like the black-mailing 'Poet Laureate', Michael Massey Robinson, the able but unscrupulous lawyer and dishonest dealer, George Crossley, merchant Simeon Lord, the greatest of the colony's early entrepreneurs, Samuel Terry, 'the Rothschild of Botany Bay', publican, brewer, farmer, Wesleyan and freemason, and the ship-building traders, Henry Kable and James Underwood, were by no means high-principled, but were notable nonetheless.

Among all the convicts, political prisoners and those in any way respectable were few, and the idea that New South Wales was peopled by gallant radicals or starving unemployed is a myth – though like many myths it dies hard. Though no single simple description can do justice to some 160,000 prisoners transported during eighty years, most were a disreputable lot, poorly educated, young, urban ne'er-do-wells, with a virtually non-existent family life; two minority groups were 'atrocious villains', and those hardly done-by, victims of injustice, or martyrs to their political or social beliefs. Of the last, nearly all came from Ireland, possibly nearly 5000 over-all, and of the 1750 Irish who were transported up to 1804, about half may have been Defenders and United Irish, who had been involved in the disorders there after

64 *H.R.N.S.W., IV*, p. 446: *H.R.A., IV*, p. 471; *VI*, p. 148.

1796. They seem to have terrified both Governor Hunter and his successor, and an investigation into rumours of an Irish conspiracy in 1800 enabled Sam Mardsen and the dissolute, indebted, but well-connected acting deputy-judge-advocate Richard Atkins to show that the authorities could be as ruthless, brutal and careless of legal proprieties in New South Wales as in Ireland itself, as they ordered floggings of up to 1000 lashes to obtain information or for having intended 'to effect a plan of the most wicked and dangerous tendency (no act or fact being clearly established to amount to a capital conviction)', while they despatched others to Norfolk Island for safety's sake. In 1804 there really was a rising of 300-odd Irish at Castle Hill. This gave the New South Wales Corps its unique opportunity for action, and was suppressed without difficulty, but it led to the foundation of the settlement at the Coal River, re-named Newcastle, with 34 of the leading insurgents.[65]

When Governor Hunter had arrived in Sydney in September 1795, he had sympathized with the officers who were developing their farms, and he refused to carry out his instructions to remove their convict servants or to increase the public cultivation. The officer-farmers needed the convicts for labour; produce supplied by the government would destroy their market. But the governor soon found that Macarthur and the Corps wanted no interference from anyone in anything, and he had to face their constant opposition and even their misconduct while he struggled to control the settlement with the inadequate manpower at his disposal.[66] In 1797 Hunter's critics from the Corps were joined by radical-settler spokesmen in Scottish martyr T. F. Palmer and his associate John Boston, a speculative adventurer, who had come out free, allegedly with plans for curing fish and making salt, a man whom Hunter thought 'the colony will not derive any advantage from'.[67] The pair were not successful farmers, but they were active shipbuilders and traders, ready enough to reciprocate the governor's attitude to them, and to criticize Hunter for restricting trade in the interests of the East India Company and for failing to control the Corps, the spirit traffic, and the 'trading hucksters' who were allegedly injuring the settlers.[68] They had a case, and they had personal experience of the consequences of the governor's actions, but

[65] Papers relating to the Irish conspiracy—*H.R.A.*, *II*, pp. 575–83, 637–51; *IV*, pp. 563–77, 611–12.

[66] *H.R.A.*, *I*, pp. 533, 560, 587, 592; *II*, pp. 163–4: Hunter to Banks, 15 January 1800, Banks Papers, Mitchell Library, A83, f. 51.

[67] *H.R.A.*, *II*, p. 30.

[68] *H.R.A.*, *II*, p. 394 ff. The source of the complaints was probably Palmer, but it might have been Boston. See C. M. H. Clark, *A History of Australia*, *I*, Melbourne, 1962, p. 157: M. H. Ellis, *John Macarthur*, Sydney, 1955, p. 149: J. Ferguson, *Bibliography of Australia*, *I*, Sydney, 1941, nos. 228, 277: *Australian Dictionary of Biography*, *I*, pp. 126–7.

they showed a woeful lack of appreciation of his difficulties, which were increased by the departure of Judge-Advocate Collins in November 1796, since his temporary replacement, Atkins, was drunken and incompetent, and his successor, the self-important lawyer sent from England, Richard Dore, was so unreliable that his death after two years in office was by no means an unmitigated misfortune.

As a naval officer, Hunter was naturally concerned about maritime discovery, and only seven weeks after his arrival he arranged for Bass and the subsequently more famous Matthew Flinders to go on their first exploring expedition, to Botany Bay and up George's River – which incidentally led to the establishment of a settlement at Banks Town two years later. In 1796, in the tiny *Tom Thumb* they discovered Lake Illawarra, Port Kembla, and, on the way back to Sydney, Wotta Molla and Port Hacking. In August 1797 Bass investigated and confirmed reports of coal at Coal Cliff in the south, a month before Lieutenant Shortland, R.N., discovered it in the north near the modern Newcastle on the river which he named the Hunter. In December, Hunter gave Bass a boat to sail southwards to what was in due course called Bass Strait, where he discovered Wilson's Promontory and Western Port, and twelve months later, the governor sent out Bass and Flinders to verify Bass's and his own supposition that Van Diemen's Land was a separate island. They proved this by sailing around it, and in 1799 Flinders rounded off the explorations of the period by discovering Glass House Bay, near the modern Brisbane. As well as these voyages, Hunter visited the newly discovered Cow Pastures, on the Nepean River, shortly after his arrival, and in 1798 sent an expedition to the south-west, which examined the country as far as the present day site of Goulburn. Being, like so many of his contemporaries, intensely interested in natural science, he always arranged for the collection of specimens and drawings of local animals and plants, as well as coal, for despatch to Banks and others in England, and he gained a unique distinction in having promoted the expeditions which secured the first specimens of the lyre-bird and reported the discovery of three of Australia's peculiar fauna – the koala, the platypus and the wombat.

In developing the settlement Hunter was hampered by a constant shortage of labour, for the war-time demand for convicts in English dockyards reduced the number sent to New South Wales from nearly 5000 between 1788 and 1792 to less than 2000 between 1793 and 1799.[69] This cut down the public works he could carry out, but he called on local landowners to repair roads, and after the log gaol he built in Sydney had been burned down, he succeeded in persuading property owners to provide the labour needed to replace it in stone. To meet the cost he showed initiative in imposing an 'assessment' on permission to land spirits – the first attempt to raise revenue in the

69 *H.R.A., II*, pp. 563–4.

colony.[70] He recognized the legal difficulty involved in levying a 'regular duty', and thought this should be done in England, but the English government took no notice of his two recommendations on the subject, and left King to face the same difficulty of raising revenue without authority.

Meanwhile the Secretary of State had observed that nearly half the men and more than three-quarters of the women and children were being supported by the government. The expenses of the colony seemed never-ending. Hunter had failed to control the liquor traffic, had not stopped the military officers trading, and worst of all, though repeatedly told to economize, he had not done so. Extravagance was a perennial cause of complaint from London, and after being several times reprimanded for this reason, on 5 November 1799 he was re-called. Self-confessed 'a very plain man, bred to the honorable and respectable profession of a seaman', he was out of his depth as governor of New South Wales, and he sank, riddled by the volleys of his critics in Sydney and the broadsides of his superiors in London, despite his 'most upright intentions'; for, as his successor King said, he was 'most shamefully deceived by those on whom he had every reason to depend for assistance, information and advice'.[71]

Economy was the major issue for King when he took over the administration in September 1800. Botany Bay was to have been an economical means of dealing with English criminals. They cost about £23 or £24 per head in the hulks, less about £13 for the value of their labour, leaving a net sum of about £10. New South Wales was to have been self-subsistent in two years, but five years after its foundation, it seemed to be still costing over £40,000, or £13–14 per convict, and in 1798 it was twice as much. King cut expenditure drastically, at the cost of a temporary trade squeeze, and during his six years he drew bills worth less than Hunter had drawn in his last three. Owing to the high cost of transport for the larger numbers sent out between 1800 and 1804, the cost per convict to the British government did not fall, but expenses in the colony did.[72] Increased imports and a run of good seasons reduced the cost of supplies for government and settler alike. King reduced the price the commissariat paid for grain, enforced the payment of debts owing to the Crown, reduced the number of convict servants allowed to officials at public expense from 356 in 1800 to 94

---

[70] G. J. Abbott, 'Government Works and Services', in G. J. Abbott and N. B. Nairn, Eds. *Economic Growth of Australia 1788–1821*, Melbourne, 1969, p. 309: *H.R.A.*, I, p. 593; II, pp. 374–6, 451.

[71] *H.R.A.*, II, pp. 429, 608.

[72] For government expenditure see A. G. L. Shaw, *Convicts and the Colonies*, London, 1966, pp. 58–9, 60–61, 71: G. J. Abbott and N. B. Nairn, Eds., *Economic Growth of Australia 1788–1821*, Melbourne, 1969, pp. 109, 149: G. J. Abbott, 'A Note on the Volume of New South Wales Treasury Bill Expenditure, 1788–1821', in *Business Archives and History*, VI, February 1966, pp. 81–4.

in 1804, and cut the numbers being victualled by government from about 60 per cent to 40 per cent of the population.[73]

However, for all his economizing, King wanted to help and not to hinder the settler. He distributed livestock as premiums for efficiency, kept down prices through the newly established government store, and assigned more convict servants to settlers, especially after the arrival of more than 2000 male and 500 female prisoners in three years after 1800.[74] The rise of 50 per cent in the population while King was in office also improved the market for grain and induced a corresponding increase in the acreage under cultivation. At one and a half acres per head, this normally produced enough grain for the colony; unfortunately, floods periodically brought shortages, so despite the development of private farming in what was later looked back on as a 'golden age', New South Wales was not yet regularly self-sufficient in grain. However it was on the way to becoming so.

King extended Hunter's efforts to raise a local revenue, which might eventually make it self-sufficient financially at least for local affairs. In 1802 he imposed a variety of port fees and import duties, part of which were credited to the Orphan Fund to pay for the much-needed institution which he had founded two years earlier for the colony's neglected children, and part to the Gaol Fund, used not only for completing the gaol, but also for building a bridge over the Tank stream (on the site of the modern Bridge Street), repairing roads, detecting illicit stills and apprehending bushrangers.[75] In 1807 Castlereagh commended the levying of duties, and despite the warning of Jeremy Bentham in his *Plea for a Constitution* in 1803, their illegality was ignored by the Colonial Office until 1819; the idea of raising a local revenue for local works was too attractive.[76]

King's economy measures, which reduced the foreign exchange available through Treasury Bills and made it more difficult to pay for imports, caused difficulties for a number of traders. It forced them to extend credit to their customers, who took years to repay them, and caused a tremendous amount of litigation. It also emphasized the need for another source of overseas income, so the search for a 'staple' became more serious, as merchants became all the more anxious to find a means to carry away the profits they gained from importing.[77] Earlier Portland had hoped to recoup some of the government's

---

[73] *H.R.A., V,* pp. 601–2.

[74] *H.R.A., IV,* p. 466: A. G. L. Shaw, *Convicts and the Colonies,* London, 1966, p. 363.

[75] *H.R.A., II,* pp. 532–3; *III,* pp. 13, 406, 626–7; *IV,* pp. 490, 599–601.

[76] *H.R.A., VI,* p. 202; Series IV, *I,* p. 883 ff.

[77] G. J. Abbott 'Governor King's Administration', in G. J. Abbott and N. B. Nairn, Eds., *Economic Growth of Australia 1788–1821,* Melbourne, 1969, pp. 167–9: *H.R.A., V,* p. 201 ff: M. Steven, *Merchant Campbell, 1769–1846,* Melbourne, 1965, pp. 23, 45.

expenditure through the export of coal or timber, just as there had been ideas of exporting flax, cotton, tobacco and wine, all of which had proved vain. Phillip had raised the possibility of using whaling vessels to bring the convicts out, so that they could return home with their oil, and the English whaling firm, Enderby and Son, had hoped to use the existence of New South Wales as a means of opening the South Pacific to their ships; but the idea was not workable. The first whalers reported bad weather; the Enderbys objected that fishing from New South Wales would destroy the Southern Whale Fishery; and the East India Company, particularly nervous that 'camouflaged colonial whalers' might want to sneak into the China market, was alert to defend its trading monopoly despite the possibility that unless it were relaxed Americans might gain a strong foothold in the Pacific trade.[78]

Sealing seemed more promising. The animals were plentiful in Bass Strait and off New Zealand, and as the ships used to catch them were smaller than the whalers, and therefore easier to come by, they could be based on New South Wales and therefore be less disturbing to the East India Company. King thought seal oil and skins 'the most considerable among the very few natural productions of this country that can be esteemed commercial'. This seemed 'our only staple', he told Banks. Robert Campbell argued that in time it would 'lessen considerably the expense of the establishment to the Mother Country', and proceeded to try to organize the export of skins and oil, by sending shipments first to China, via India, and then, in 1805, rather daringly, but with the governor's support, to London in his ship, *Lady Barlow*. However, this not only violated the rights of the East India Company, but it also aroused 'a violent clamour' among the English whalers.[79] However much it may be argued that New South Wales was established to expand British trade, its commercial progress seemed to threaten, not to foster, vested British interests, and so could not be allowed. For twenty years no plans for New South Wales trade had been thought of; now that the matter was raised, its possible dangers were insisted on. Banks was sympathetic to the colonists. He shared the orthodox doctrine that 'the whole benefit of the colony, either in consumption or in produce, should be secured as far as possible to the mother country', and therefore firmly opposed opening the trade between Australia and China whose development some claim to be one of the reasons for founding the colony; but he wanted New South Wales to become 'a blessing instead of a burden', and

---

[78] *H.R.N.S.W.*, *V*, pp. 644–5: D. R. Hainsworth, *The Sydney Traders*, Sydney, 1972, pp. 89–90: M. Steven, *Merchant Campbell, 1769–1846*, Melbourne, 1965, p. 131: Banks memorandum, Banks Papers, Mitchell Library, A78–3, f. 268.

[79] *H.R.A.*, *III*, pp. 635–6: *H.R.N.S.W.*, *VI*, pp. 100–102: M. Steven, *Merchant Campbell, 1769–1846*, Melbourne, 1965, pp. 122, 128, and ch. 5: D. R. Hainsworth, *Builders and Adventurers*, Melbourne, 1968, p. 84 ff: D. R. Hainsworth, *The Sydney Traders*, Sydney, 1972, ch. 10.

hence he urged the encouragement of sealing and the production of fine wool, and he argued that if trade between England and Australia up to latitude 9° South were freely permitted, this would encourage 'our enterprising colonists', and lead to settlements which would anticipate the French in this area. But such ideas seemed too revolutionary, and a bill to modify the privileges of the East India Company and the restrictions on Anglo-Australian trade was abandoned. All that could be arranged was to allow Campbell to re-export his oil and his seal skins, instead of having them confiscated.[80] The tyranny of corporate privilege was more potent than the tyranny of distance.

A possible sandalwood trade appeared, but it too encountered the difficulties imposed by the East India Company's monopoly in the China market.[81] King would have liked to help, but he did not want to violate the law or disregard his instructions directly in this connection, as he had done with Campbell's oil in the *Lady Barlow*. He did not oppose strictly the building of ships in the colony, and, like his predecessors, winked at such breaches of the regulations, so a colonial shipping interest, with vessels locally built, bought, or acquired as prizes, now appeared on the commercial horizon.[82] From the pioneer builders, emancipists Henry Kable and James Underwood, building and ownership spread to Lord, Campbell, Palmer, Macarthur, and their respective partners and associates, as well as a host of smaller fry, including two other emancipists, Andrew Thompson and Thomas Reibey. Some shippers entered the whaling field again, and King not only encouraged the British government to send out merchandise in the whaling ships, but also encouraged the Enderbys and the South Sea whalers to revert to Australian waters.[83] As a naval officer his attention constantly turned to the Pacific, and in 1801–2 in conjunction with the London Missionary Society he arranged for the opening of a trade in pork with Tahiti, but it soon lapsed, despite the colonists' appreciation of the 'abundance of animal food' which it provided.[84]

What was to be of far greater importance eventually, though less significant than the fisheries until at least the 1820s, was the growing of fine wool. At first the graziers of New South Wales, including John Macarthur, had shown no particular interest in wool, or for that matter in sheep. Macarthur owned none as late as July 1794, and

[80] M. Steven, *Merchant Campbell, 1769–1846*, Melbourne, 1965, p. 121 ff: *H.R.N.S.W.*, *VI*, p. 86 ff., 108 ff., 222, 240.

[81] D. R. Hainsworth, *Builders and Adventurers*, Melbourne, 1968, p. 107 ff: D. R. Hainsworth, 'In search of a staple: the Sydney Sandalwood Trade, 1804–09', in *Business Archives and History*, *V*, February 1965.

[82] D. R. Hainsworth, *Builders and Adventurers*, Melbourne, 1968, p. 76 ff: *H.R.A.*, *V*, pp. 8–9, 203, 320–25.

[83] *H.R.A.*, *IV*, p. 304; *V*, p. 321: *H.R.N.S.W.*, *V*, p. 448.

[84] *H.R.A.*, *III*, p. 432; *IV*, p. 230: H. Maude, *Islands and Men: Studies in Pacific History*, Oxford, 1967, ch. 5.

when he discussed the proper economy for New South Wales in 1796, the possibilities of sheep-raising and wool-growing had apparently not occurred to him. Two years later his wife was still writing of his flocks only in terms of mutton, though like a number of others he had purchased a few of the Spanish breed of sheep which had been brought from the Cape of Good Hope in 1797.[85] In 1800, when he was planning to leave the colony, he offered to sell his 600 sheep to the government. King, thinking they would be 'a great acquisition', wanted to buy, and sent home samples of the fleeces hoping to persuade the British government to authorize the purchase. Before he could receive a reply, Major Foveaux, the largest flock-master in the colony, when posted to take command at Norfolk Island, offered his 1400 sheep to the government too, but on this Macarthur was too quick. He bought them for himself, and then insisted that the government buy these from him, as well as his own sheep, at a 66 per cent mark-up, and demanded that their increase over the next two years be included too; since King expected that the price of sheep would fall during that period, he called off the deal.[86] Meanwhile Macarthur changed his mind about leaving, but having quarrelled with the governor, and fought a duel with his commanding officer, he was sent home under arrest.

He reached London in November 1802, and shortly afterwards certain British manufacturers approached him (not, be it noted, the reverse), and he was able to put his case as a breeder. Fortuitously, he arrived at a propitious moment, and found the renewal of war with Napoleon jeopardizing wool supplies from Europe. Banks had been impressed by some of the samples King had sent home two years before, and though in 1803 he argued that perhaps Macarthur was 'too sanguine', in 1804 he recommended a grant of one million acres to Macarthur's proposed company for promoting fine-woolled sheep in New South Wales, which even if the scheme failed would greatly benefit the colony.[87] The Committee of the Privy Council which examined the proposal reported favourably, though more cautiously than Banks, and recommended only Macarthur's 'alternative allotment on a small scale', namely 5000 acres, with another 5000 to follow.[88] But Macarthur's case had been won. He removed Foveaux's contribution from the history of his flocks, and persuaded everyone to forget that others in New South Wales were as interested in sheep as he was; as his biographer has put it, 'it was certain in view of his

[85] *H.R.A.*, II, pp. 89 ff, 98: S. Macarthur Onslow, *Some Early Records of the Macarthurs of Camden*, Sydney, 1914, pp. 45, 48.

[86] *HR.A.*, II, p. 538 ff; *III*, pp. 215, 345–6 and n. 133.

[87] H. B. Carter, *His Majesty's Spanish Flock*, Sydney, 1964, pp. 184–5, 430–2. *H.R.N.S.W.*, V, pp. 225, 365, 370–73, 459.

[88] S. Macarthur Onslow, *Some Early Records of the Macarthurs of Camden* Sydney, 1914, p. 65: *H.R.N.S.W.*, V, pp. 399, 480–81.

nature that, in the circumstances, his own enthusiasm would soon persuade him that what had come to pass was the product of his own rare foresight and conscious effort'.[89]

Macarthur took the opportunity of buying seven rams and three ewes from the royal flock, but he faced the problem of getting them out of the country. This was illegal, but since only a fortnight after the sale Banks told Governor King that he could expect the royal sheep would 'soon spread ... over the country', one may guess that he, like Macarthur, knew how to get over the difficulty. Since King told Banks in 1805 that Macarthur, on his return to New South Wales, had expressed gratitude for what Sir Joseph had done for him, the story of Banks' hostility at this time may be doubted; it rests only on James Macarthur's report of what his father had said after the latter's opposition to Governor Bligh had understandably resulted in a mutual dislike between Banks and Macarthur.[90] For his grant Macarthur selected land on the fertile Cowpastures, now apparently the only 'unappropriated range of 5000 acres that contains 500 acres of dry pasture on which I should think it safe to feed sheep', though the year before there had been 'Tracts of Land adapted for Pasture ... so boundless' that virtually they had 'no assignable limitation'. However, since twenty years later there were in New South Wales only 250,000 sheep, and neither 13,000,000 nor 5,000,000 as he had variously forecast, some of Banks' early doubts may have been justified.[91]

In general the colonists were more interested in meat than in wool. Since the price of mutton varied between 2s. and 1s. a lb. between 1800 and 1810, while the British market for fine wool was difficult to reach, uncertain and fluctuating, this was not surprising.[92] King was 'well convinced ... of the great advantage that might be derived by the improvement of the Fleeces', but Marsden, according to the governor 'the best practical farmer in the country', took a different view. For eight years he had been interested in improving the breed of sheep, and in the view of Macarthur's biographer, M. H. Ellis, 'as a prophet of the fleece he ranked as early as, and possibly higher than' Macarthur, but he stressed the importance of mutton.[93] Each year he

[89] M. H. Ellis, *John Macarthur*, Sydney, 1955, pp. 220–25. Waterhouse wrote later that 'most who had the Spanish sheep were particular about them', *H.R.N.S.W.*, *VI*, p. 111.

[90] *H.R.N.S.W.*, *V*, pp. 459, 674–5; *VI*, pp. 691, 699: H. B. Carter, *His Majesty's Spanish Flock*, Sydney, 1964, pp. 292–8: S. Macarthur Onslow, *Some Early Records of the Macarthurs of Camden*, Sydney, 1914, p. 101.

[91] *H.R.N.S.W.*, *V*, pp. 225, 371–2, 707, 709: S. Macarthur Onslow, *Some Early Records of the Macarthurs of Camden*, Sydney, 1914, p. 72 ff: *H.R.A.*, *V*, p. 556 ff: G. J. Abbott and N. B. Nairn, Eds., *Economic Growth of Australia 1788–1821*, Melbourne, 1969, pp. 226, 240: H. B. Carter, *His Majesty's Spanish Flock*, Sydney, 1964, pp. 430–31, 497, n. 44.

[92] G. J. Abbott and N. B. Nairn, Eds., *Economic Growth of Australia 1788–1821*, Melbourne, 1969, pp. 236–7.

[93] *H.R.A.*, *V*, pp. 450, 557–8: M. H. Ellis, *Lachlan Macquarie*, 2nd ed., Sydney, 1953, p. 319.

selected for breeding those 'Male Lambs ... such as promised to be hardy in their Constitution, weighty in their Carcass', and, only lastly be it noted, 'fine in their Fleece'. He did not always choose the ram 'with the finest Fleece to Breed from', for he considered 'the pure Spanish Breed much more delicate ... and lighter in Carcass' than crosses. When in England in 1809, like Macarthur he won the praise of English manufacturers for his wool, and like him, he acquired five merinos from the royal flock. Time was to prove that these, if bred pure, would flourish and improve, but for the moment Marsden felt assured that even by crossbreeds the wool 'already so fine, will rival if not surpass the best wools in the world', for the soil and climate were so propitious.[94] That Macarthur foresaw that Australia would profit from the expanding English market for wool, and could also 'enjoy the pleasing Consolation that our labours were contributing to the Support and prosperity of that parent Country to whom our Debt of Gratitude can never be paid' places his name, in Ellis's words, 'upon the all too slender roll of the world's successful prophets'; but for a decade his 'feeble attempt' to further the industry was 'almost unheeded, and altogether unassisted', and it played no very significant part in the economic life of the community.[95]

Graziers were also concerned with cattle in a country whose stocking had been very slow. Many died at sea, and it was not until 1800 that there were 1000 head in the settlement. Next year King made a contract with Campbell which eventually brought a further 300 head to New South Wales, and so helped to put the livestock industry on its feet. He sold steadily from the government herds to private individuals, and he successfully forbade the killing of females. He did not buy for the commissariat, but as the population increased the private market expanded; the price of beef varied between 2s. 6d. and 1s 9d. per lb. between 1800 and 1810, so that cattle grazing was not only profitable for the moment but seemed at this time to hold out more certain prospects for the future than wool did. Between 1800 and 1810, cattle increased twice as fast as sheep, and for twenty years from 1806 the value of the former exceeded that of the latter. Here was scope for the capitalist farmer, for the type of people whom Lord Castlereagh when secretary of state thought desirable in New South Wales – 'Settlers ... of responsibility and Capital who may set useful Examples of Industry and Cultivation, and from their property and Education be fit persons to whose Authority the Convicts may properly be entrusted' – as he granted permission to John and Gregory Blaxland to go to the colony in 1805.[96]

94 *H.R.A.*, V, pp. 563–5: *H.R.N.S.W.*, V, p. 414: R. Bell, 'Samuel Marsden – Pioneer Pastoralist', *R.A.H.S.J.*, 56, March 1970: H. B. Carter, *His Majesty's Spanish Flock*, Sydney, 1964, p. 439.

95 M. H. Ellis, *John Macarthur*, Sydney, 1955, p. 247: S. Macarthur Onslow, *Some Early Records of the Macarthurs of Camden*, Sydney, 1914, p. 317.

96 *H.R.A.*, V, p. 490. Cattle in 1800 – 1,000, in 1810 – 11,000; sheep in 1800 – 6,000, in 1810 – 31,000.

King was anxious to extend the colony geographically as well as economically, and if his suggestion for a new settlement in the far north (Queensland) was ignored, that for the south was not. Late in 1800 Lieutenant Grant, R.N., sailing from London, had made a running survey of the present Victorian coast, and next year King sent him to make a further survey of it between Cape Otway and Wilson's Promontory. In 1802 King sent Lieutenant Murray, R.N., on a similar errand, and in February he found the entrance to Port Phillip Bay, explored Corio Bay, and took formal possession of the area. Two months later Flinders, investigating the unknown southern coast of Australia in detail, and not knowing of Murray's visit, also examined the bay. Since he and Bass had confirmed the existence of Bass's Strait in 1798-9, it had become known to be valuable for its fisheries, and to be an important means of communication, so that King became concerned about its security. He recalled that in 1788 he had been sent to occupy Norfolk Island to anticipate a possible French settlement there. He knew that in 1792 and 1793 Bruny d'Entrecasteaux had made extensive surveys in the River Derwent; now he found that another French expedition had been sent to the antipodes under Nicholas Baudin. One of his ships reached Sydney in April 1802, about three weeks before Flinders arrived in May to recount the story of his meeting the French off the south Australian coast. King did not believe that the French were merely engaged in scientific work. He told Banks that he suspected that they had in mind a settlement in the west, and thought, as he had officially recommended on 21 May, a week after Flinders' arrival, that this made it the 'more incumbent on us to make a settlement at a place so advantageously situated as Port Phillip is'. He became even more suspicious while the French ships were refitting in Sydney and their officers were reported talking about a French settlement, and on top of this, soon after they left he heard of their stopping at King Island. He determined to take no chances about asserting British claims to Van Diemen's Land, and declared he would form an English settlement there if only he had an officer suitable to take charge of it. When H.M.S. *Glatton* arrived in March 1803 he had one. He commissioned Lieutenant John Bowen, R.N., to establish himself in the River Derwent, and in September 1803 Bowen did so, at Risdon.

The British government had meanwhile acted on King's earlier recommendation and decided to form a settlement at Port Phillip. It wanted to provide accommodation for more convicts now that peace had returned, and it was worried because 'the attention of other European powers has been drawn to that part of the world'.[97] This expedition, under the command of the former deputy judge-advocate of New South Wales, David Collins, was a larger-scale affair than Bowen's enterprise at the Derwent. It consisted of 455 people, including 299 convicts, and basically was planned as a penal settlement,

97 *H.R.A.*, *IV*, pp. 8-9.

like Norfolk Island, subject to the Sydney government. Collins found Port Phillip a disappointing spot and he decided to move. He considered Port Dalrymple, in northern Tasmania, but for commercial reasons finally picked on the River Derwent, a good harbour and whaling base. He chose a site slightly lower down the river than Bowen's Risdon, and on 20 February 1804 began unloading his stores at what was to be called Hobart Town, on Sullivan Cove. Six months later the Risdon settlement was abandoned. By then King had received the instructions sent in June 1803 to send Lieutenant-Colonel Paterson to Port Dalrymple on the River Tamar to form a post in the north as well, since an establishment near the 'eastern entrance to Bass's Straits' was 'in a political point of view peculiarly necessary'. Though Paterson was delayed by bad weather, he 'Hoisted His Majesty's Colours with the usual Ceremony' on 11 November 1804, and thus made effective British claims to both the north and the south of Van Diemen's Land.[98]

One cannot say that the infant settlements immediately flourished, for as with New South Wales in the early days they were neglected. The English government 'forgot' to establish law courts, and never sent a patent for the deputy judge-advocate. The secretary of state never acknowledged a despatch from Hobart, and sent no more supplies or convicts from London. Its only constructive action was to order the removal of settlers from Norfolk Island to Van Diemen's Land, which helped to raise the population to 1000 in the south and 277 in the north by 1810, and thus to provide the basis for future agricultural development and for a potentially valuable if temporarily expensive penal settlement. In the meantime the colony's existence ensured that there would be no hostile French settlements in south-eastern Australia.

But if Van Diemen's Land showed promise of being a valuable colony to Great Britain it also quickly appeared as a scene of disaster for the Aborigines. 'You are to endeavour by every means in your power to open an intercourse with the natives and to conciliate their good will', Collins was told. He had not been on the Derwent three months when a major clash occurred and fifty natives were killed. In due course an occasional white was speared. There was conflict in the north as in the south. Officially, as in New South Wales, the government recognized the Aborigines' rights and wished to protect them; but these rights were never defined. The English settled on the Aborigines' land and took their food; in return, the natives interfered with the Englishmen's livestock. The natives were then attacked in retaliation, and so relations went from bad to worse, as had happened in New South Wales. There too, the idea of the 'noble savage' disappeared on close acquaintance. In 1802 King had strictly forbidden any act of injustice, let alone cruelty, to the natives, but by 1805 he had been converted to the belief that the Aborigines were all treacherous and

[98] *H.R.A.*, *IV*, p. 304: *H.R.A.*, Series III, *I*, p. 588.

ungrateful, and felt compelled to resort to military measures to protect the settlers, more and more of whom would have agreed with the convict artist Watling, who as early as 1794 had insisted that 'irascibility, ferocity, cunning, treachery, filth and immodesty' were their principal characteristics.[99]

As time went on King also ran into difficulty with the rum traders and with the New South Wales Corps. He succeeded in cutting down spirit imports, and during his six years' administration only about 115,000 gallons were landed, compared with one-third of that amount (plus 22,000 gallons of wine) landed in Hunter's last six months, thus reducing the annual consumption of legal supplies from about seven gallons per head to about three. Writing in 1803 from immediate observation, the hypercritical botanist Caley[100] admitted that liquor 'became very scarce'; though its high price may have increased traders' profits on each sale, and also sly-grogging, it also reduced consumption. King certainly found it impossible to stop smuggling and illicit distilling, but his offer of rewards for seizures in May 1806 had some success, and for his liquor policy generally, including his opening of a brewery at Parramatta in 1804, he deserves more credit than he usually receives.[101]

With the Corps he was less successful. He had had trouble with military pretensions on Norfolk Island and though the officers of the Corps had come to play a less important part than before in the colony's commercial life, they remained a strongly knit body anxious to assert their position, and resentful of outside criticism. As early as August 1801 Lieutenant Grant had told Banks that King was worried by the influence of the military in the criminal court; since its jury was composed entirely of naval and military officers, and the former were rarely present, the officers of the Corps always could and sometimes did deliver an unjust verdict. 'How far ought I to expect impartiality when those officers were tried by others of their own Corps?' demanded King in 1803. Certainly the behaviour of the officers as jurors amply justified the requests of both King and his successor that the courts be reformed.[102] Colonel Paterson, commanding the Corps, and anxious for peace with the civil authority, agreed. 'Most of the disquiet which has agitated this settlement . . . is chiefly to be attributed to the unfortunate mixture of civil and military duties

---

99 *H.R.A.*, *III*, pp. 592–3; *V*, pp. 306–7, 497: T. Watling, *Letters from an Exile at Botany Bay*, London, 1794, quoted in B. Smith, *European Vision and the South Pacific*, Oxford, 1960, p. 139.

100 G. Caley, *Reflections on the Colony of New South Wales*, reprinted Melbourne, 1966, pp. 78–9.

101 *H.R.A.*, *V*, pp. 264, 752: *H.R.N.S.W.*, *VI*, p. 72. Contemporary consumption in England was also equivalent to about three gallons of proof spirit per head per year, but four-fifths of this was beer.

102 *H.R.A.*, *III*, p. 245; *IV*, pp. 160, 243, 350; *VI*, p. 151: Banks Papers, Mitchell Library, Sydney, A78–3, f. 23.

which exist in this country. But for this, ... the most entire concord would be maintained between the officer in command and the officers of the New South Wales Corps', he commented in 1801, and he was himself soon to run into trouble with disobedient military subordinates when in command at Port Dalrymple, because they wanted to be a law unto themselves, which at least some of the Corps seemed to regard as their right.[103]

With friends in London, some did not hesitate to misrepresent a governor's policy in order to resist any measure they objected to. In this, their leader was John Macarthur, though whether his desire to run the colony was based on the conviction that he knew better than anyone else what was good for it, or solely on a wish to increase further the large, though often exaggerated, fortune he had acquired in New South Wales is difficult to decide. He induced Paterson to criticize King for refusing to buy unwanted grain from the settlers, an economy measure which incidentally affected the settlers' merchant creditors. Then when King showed that he doubted the fairness of the trial of a naval lientenant for assaulting Macarthur and another officer of the Corps, Macarthur organized a social boycott against the governor and attacked Paterson, his commanding officer, for refusing to join it. When this led to a duel and thus to an order for Macarthur's arrest, the latter decided to give a dinner to the men under his command at Parramatta, and illegally to serve free spirits to them – an action which might have led to a riot had not two subalterns in the Corps showed a greater sense of responsibility than their arrogant, self-righteous and quarrelsome superior.[104] For the moment, King got rid of his unruly and over-mighty subject by sending him to England under arrest, though the latter could no more be tried in London, for lack of witnesses there, than he could be in Sydney, for the lack of enough impartial officers to make up a court-martial; however, since during his absence all was not quiet in New South Wales, apparently he was not the sole promoter of strife, as King might have wished to believe.

There were disputes over rations; over the enforcement of the spirits regulations; over an alleged preferential supply of liquor to the visiting French; over King appointing ex-convicts to his bodyguard (though there were such in the New South Wales Corps); over the commandant at Newcastle, a marine, Lieutenant Menzies, giving orders to the subaltern in charge of the detachment of the Corps there; over King's asking Corps officers, Ensign Barrallier and Surgeon Harris, to carry out civil duties; and inevitably over trials in the criminal court. To add to this friction, drawings and 'inscriptions' appeared in the barrack-yard and anonymous satirical verse circulated attacking King, which some of the Corps officers seemed as ready to bandy about

---

103 *H.R.A., III*, p. 292: *H.R.N.S.W., V*, pp. 546–7.

104 *H.R.A., III*, pp. 274 ff.; 321–5. On Macarthur's fortune see M. H. Ellis, *John Macarthur*, Sydney, 1955, pp. 206–7.

as they were unwilling to assist the governor to enforce obedience to his orders. No wonder that in May 1803 King should have felt impelled to ask for leave of absence, a request the British government decided to interpret as a resignation, perhaps in the light of a threat he had made the preceding June, even though it took it two years to despatch a successor to Sydney.[105]

Despite all this, King accomplished substantial reforms in New South Wales. His success in helping the private settlers enabled him almost to give up government farming. The increased demand for convicts as servants enabled him to reduce his expenditure. He supported the fisheries, and the shipping and timber industries, and was as ready to encourage the growth of fine wool as he had been to assist the emancipist farmer. Though he was unable entirely to prevent the smuggling and illicit distillation of spirits, supplies were less than before his arrival. To make his control more effective, he suggested introducing into New South Wales the excise laws of England. Significantly, he refrained from doing so himself on the ground that though not 'repugnant to the laws of England', it would be 'a stretch of power', and sought the opinion of the English law officers on the question; typically his suggestion went unnoticed.[106]

He did not receive from London the support he deserved. Macarthur, far from being punished in England, returned with favours. The government did not heed King's criticisms of the officers of the New South Wales Corps, who continued to be an irritant whom the governor was blandly told to live in harmony with. As time went on his health began to fail. He drank too much. He suffered from gout. He often lost his temper and his sense of proportion. His worries about his finances and for his family got the better of him. He made large claims for government cattle. He took special terms at the store for merchandise he had an interest in, and when his successor Governor Bligh arrived, he persuaded the latter to give his wife an extensive land grant (which he called 'Thanks'), possibly in exchange for a grant which a few days earlier he had given to Bligh – two transactions which were not reported to London. He ended his career as a tragic figure, but certainly not the failure which some would regard him. Caley was right to describe him as a 'man of ability and keen penetration', and if Phillip had helped the colony to survive its first five years, King a decade later succeeded in making its economy for the first time not only viable, but almost flourishing, and had put it so firmly on its feet that it could withstand without too much difficulty the violent upheavals of the four years that followed.

When Bligh took over the administration in August 1806, he hoped to continue and improve the work that King had begun. In an attack on the colony's traders, he decided that soldiers should be paid by

---

[105] *H.R.A.*, *III*, p. 527; *IV*, pp. 244, 428.

[106] Memo by Atkins 30 August 1805, in King Papers, Mitchell Library, A 1980-2, p. 297 ff: *H.R.A.*, *V*, pp. 634, 655.

paymaster's bills, which were acceptable to visiting ships' masters, instead of in copper coin, or other currency, which was not.[107] Of more concern to officers was the ban Bligh decided to impose in February 1807 on the use of rum either as an incentive payment or an article of barter, on pain of losing 'all indulgencies granted them by the Crown', a penalty that meant a great deal, though he knew that any attack on the spirit traffic would arouse 'the marked opposition of those few who have so materially enriched themselves by it'.[108] These included Macarthur, who in 1807 made a profit of 154 per cent on the legal re-sale of a purchase of 378 gallons, watered down to 447 gallons, and several other officers of the Corps who operated illegally, apparently with the connivance of its officer commanding in Sydney, Major Johnston. But as Bligh was convinced of the evils arising from 'the monopoly and barter' of rum he was ready to attack its purveyors in every way and even to sell spirits from the store to the settlers.[109]

Bligh next attempted to regulate the paper currency circulating in the colony. He had encountered trouble from the 1806 floods, quadrupling the price of wheat, which had raised the legal question of the obligation of those whose debts were expressed, as they often were, in wheat rather than in money. Macarthur had bought, apparently as an investment, a promissory note issued in 1805 by the now wealthy emancipist Andrew Thompson expressed in this way. In 1806 he demanded payment in full in wheat. Thompson argued that he was liable only for the money value indicated by the old price of wheat, and the Civil Court, with chaplain Fulton and merchant Thomas Moore assisting Judge-Advocate Atkins, decided in his favour. Shortly afterwards, to prevent any repetition of this problem, Bligh issued currency regulations forbidding the issue of notes drawn in any other way than in sterling money, and in due course, on appeal, he upheld the Court's verdict in Thompson's case; though opinions differ on the correctness of this decision, that Bligh should have refused to hear Macarthur speak in support of his plea is hardly defensible and perhaps not surprisingly caused the latter to sever social relations with yet another occupant of government house.[110]

During his short term of office Bligh managed to fall out with most of Sydney's other commercial men too, apart from Thompson, his

---

107 M. Steven, *Merchant Campbell 1769–1846*, Melbourne, 1965, p. 163.

108 D. R. Hainsworth, *Builders and Adventurers*, Melbourne, 1968, pp. 25–30. The rate of profit of 154% was probably more usual than the rhetorically exaggerated figures of 500% or 1000%.

109 *H.R.A.*, VI, pp. 534, 552–5: M. Steven, *Merchant Campbell 1769–1846*, Melbourne, 1965, pp. 162, 174–5.

110 J. V. Byrnes, 'Andrew Thompson, 1773–1810', in *R.A.H.S.J.*, 48, 2, June 1962, pp. 120–23: H. V. Evatt, *Rum Rebellion*, Sydney, 1938, p. 109: *H.R.N.S.W.*, VI, p. 198, 485 ff.: S. J. Butlin, *Foundations of the Australian Monetary System*, Melbourne, 1953, pp. 68–70, and n. 97: *Sydney Gazette*, 5, 12, 26 July and 2 August 1807.

agent, and Campbell and Palmer, two of his officials. He seemed less sympathetic to the trading community than his predecessor. Generally both obeyed their instructions to protect the East India Company's rights, but neither was entirely consistent in this. In January 1805 King had permitted Campbell to send his illegal cargo of oil to London in the *Lady Barlow*, but in May 1806, refused to allow the United States owned *Criterion* to land a cargo from Canton; in September Bligh curtly refused permission for Lord and his associates to send a ship to Fiji and China, but next February allowed Campbell's colonial-built brig *Perseverance* to sail for Canton, allegedly to 'procure the necessaries of life so much wanting' – an action which aroused suspicions of favouritism.[111] However, King had appeared to wish to expand and diversify the economy; Bligh, admittedly faced on his arrival with the effects of the 1806 floods, was more concerned with subsistence. 'Our utmost exertions' must be to agriculture, he argued. To this sheep would have to take second place, for if 'a few Individuals were to have all the Servants they pretend should be allowed them' for grazing, the farmer 'would want his Labourer and the Inhabitants Grain for their common consumption'.[112] To Bligh, New South Wales was a penal colony, not a trading settlement. A contretemps over the port regulations led to Lord, Kable and Underwood finding themselves in gaol for a month for writing in a manner 'highly derogatory to His Excellency's high rank and authority'. He was hostile, to put it mildly, to Lord's associates, Francis Williams, whom he deported, and Captain Wilkinson of the *Star*, whose case led to representations being made in London; also to the Blaxlands, to Macarthur's partner Blaxcell, and to Macarthur himself, his sheep, his land grants, and his trading.[113]

Simeon Lord insisted that trade and government in New South Wales was 'nothing but Party Business'.[114] This was inevitable so long as it was so closely controlled, but it made it the more necessary for the governor to try to keep his hands clean. Bligh's favouritism to Campbell and Thompson roused the opposition of their commercial rivals; and while antagonising the trading interest, he proceeded to irritate others. On the voyage out, he had quarrelled with Captain Short, R.N., for what the secretary of state justly thought 'very trivial causes'. He complained that the rank and file of the New South Wales Corps associated too much with the convicts, and he allegedly connived at the Sydney constables under Provost-Marshall Gore insulting

111 D. R. Hainsworth, *Builders and Adventurers*, Melbourne, 1968, p. 108 ff.: M. Steven, *Merchant Campbell 1769–1846*, Melbourne, 1965, p. 149: *Sydney Gazette*, 28 December 1806: *H.R.A., VI*, p. 193.

112 *H.R.A., VI*, pp. 122–3.

113 *H.R.N.S.W., VI*, p. 278: D. R. Hainsworth, *Builders and Adventurers*, Melbourne, 1968, pp. 45–6: M. H. Ellis, *John Macarthur*, Sydney, 1955, pp. 269–70.

114 D. R. Hainsworth, *Builders and Adventurers*, Melbourne, 1968, pp. 94–5.

soldiers; perhaps the constables were only trying to keep the soldiers in order, but certainly Gore was cordially disliked by most people who knew him.[115] On the personal level Bligh shouted such abuse at its members and interfered so much with its affairs that its acting commander, Major Johnston, felt obliged to make formal complaint to the commander-in-chief about his 'oppressive conduct'.[116]

Bligh refused to grant land to newly arriving settlers, like Dr Townson and the Blaxlands, even though they bore letters from the secretary of state. He interfered with the medical department and suspended D'Arcy Wentworth from duty, for allegedly using the labour of convict patients for his own benefit, though he flatly refused to tell Wentworth what was the charge against him; at the same time on his own farm on the Hawkesbury he employed every aid he could help himself to from the public stores, which, despite his assertions to the contrary, he showed no signs of paying for. In May 1807, after six Irish state prisoners, technically free men, had been tried for conspiracy and acquitted, he high-handedly, though probably not illegally, ordered them to be deported.[117] In July, he ordered certain leaseholders and occupiers of Domain Land in Sydney, to quit their houses; unfortunately most were already Bligh's opponents, and this naturally intensified their anger and could be represented as persecution. Legally the governor was justified, and probably the resumption was desirable, but in implementing this order Bligh as usual was unnecessarily violent, and his reported reply to a probably incorrect suggestion that he was violating the laws of England – 'Damn your laws of England, don't talk to me of your laws of England' – strengthened the opposition his action had aroused, and might appear to substantiate Macarthur's report that earlier Bligh had damned the law – 'my will is the Law' – and the Privy Council, and the secretary of the state – 'he commands at home, I command here'.[118]

Whatever his language, Bligh had not breached the law, even by employing the emancipist perjurer attorney, George Crossley, as his legal adviser, for the statute forbidding such a person to practice applied only in England, and not in New South Wales, though it was unfortunate that Crossley was the only competent lawyer in the colony, and that the British government had failed to send out a qualified deputy judge-advocate.[119] Like King and Hunter before him,

115 G. Caley, *Reflections on the Colony of New South Wales*, reprinted Melbourne, 1966, p. 146, n. 16: *HR.N.S.W.*, VI, 344.

116 *H.R.N.S.W.*, VI, p. 652 ff.

117 *H.R.N.S.W.*, VI, pp. 259, 313–28, 363–4, 368–9, 522–7: *Sydney Gazette*, 7 June 1807.

118 H. V. Evatt, *Rum Rebellion*, Sydney, 1938, ch. 26: G. Mackaness, *The Life of Vice Admiral William Bligh*, Sydney, 1951, pp. 400–401, 444–6: M. H. Ellis, *John Macarthur*, Sydney, 1955, pp. 270, 299–301.

119 C. H. Currey, *The Brothers Bent*, Sydney, 1968, p. 37: K. G. Allars, 'George Crossley – An Unusual Attorney', in *R.AH..S.J.*, *44*, 5, January 1959: *H.R.A.*, III, pp. 75, 246.

Bligh strongly recommended that the judicial arrangements be changed to curtail the influence of the military, but his wish that the courts be regulated by rules similar to those in force in England does not suggest a plan for overthrowing the rule of law. He opposed the proposal that a council should control the governor, and issued regulations on currency, spirits and other matters as freely as his predecessors, all of which were perfectly proper. In September 1807 he removed Surgeon Jamison from the magistracy, apparently for sympathizing with Wentworth, and in January 1808 he also removed Captain Abbott, but he accepted without demur the court's unfavourable decision when Macarthur prosecuted Bligh's officials for trespass in seizing the copper boilers of stills which the governor had claimed were illegally imported. Furthermore, in the complicated series of events arising from the allegation that Macarthur had allowed a convict to escape in one of his ships in violation of the port regulations, he followed only due legal processes in prosecuting him for seditious conduct in resisting arrest and writing in such a way as to incite hatred of the government.[120] When proceedings began on 25 January 1808 Macarthur argued that he could not expect a fair trial in a court presided over by his debtor, Atkins. When the officers comprising the jury accepted this argument, and asked that Atkins be replaced, Bligh insisted that this could not be done – as it was later remarked at Johnston's court-martial in England, an accused might as well challenge a judge at assizes – but he might be criticised for not having suspended Atkins earlier, as he undoubtedly had power to do, especially since he had described the judge-advocate as 'a disgrace to human jurisprudence'. As it was, when the officers refused to proceed with the trial or to deliver up the papers concerning it which they had seized, Atkins accused them of 'practices which he conceives treasonable', and on 26 January Bligh ordered them to appear at Government House next day. For Bligh this was fatal, for it so compromised the officers that Macarthur was able to persuade them that their interest as well as his lay in 'overthrowing the tyrant', and to convince the rather supine military commander in Sydney, Major Johnston, that this was necessary to preserve the peace of the settlement. The Corps went into action without delay, deposed the governor and placed him under arrest. Probably Macarthur and the officers had pre-arranged the whole affair, but it seems very unlikely that anyone else knew anything about it, or would have agreed that the action was necessary.[121] However, the action of the officers of the Corps had several

120 *H.R.A., II*, p. 280; *III*, p. 246; *VI*, p. 150–52: G. Mackaness, *The Life of Vice Admiral William Bligh*, Sydney, 1951, p. 447 and notes: H. V. Evatt, *Rum Rebellion*, Sydney, 1938, p. 143, ch. 23: Banks Papers, Mitchell Library, Sydney, A85, folio 189. Macarthur was never tried for breaking the port regulations, so it is not possible to say whether or not he would have been found guilty.

121 G. Mackaness, *The Life of Vice Admiral William Bligh*, Sydney, 1951, pp. 402–4, 418: *H.R.N.S.W., VI*, p. 433.

precedents in recent British colonial history, and one could argue that since communication with London took so long, the deposition of the governor was the only practical way of controlling his activities.

On their way to New South Wales in 1809, the new governor, Colonel Lachlan Macquarie, and his wife met at Rio de Janeiro some of the rebel supporters going home. *'Even by their own account* the conduct of those persons who had acted against the Governor was not to be justified or even excused', noted Mrs Macquarie in her diary.[122] Next year, from Sydney Macquarie reported that he could discover no act of Bligh's which could justify his deposition; but for Macarthur the moment for rebellion had been opportune. He expected his brig *Harrington* any day to return from China. Had she arrived with Bligh in power, she would not have been allowed to land her cargo; so, wrote the deposed governor, 'one would almost pronounce as a certainty from this circumstance that McArthur [*sic*] had calculated the exact time when the Government would be subverted, for the additional purpose of bringing on illegal communications with the East Indies'.[123] However, there is no doubt that Bligh's normal behaviour was calculated to excite irritation. Dr Joseph Arnold, the naval surgeon who came out in the same ship as Macquarie, attended Bligh professionally in New South Wales. His opinion of his patient reinforces that of others – Bligh was 'so uncertain in his manners, so violent in his conduct ... so eloquent in his diction that he overpowers and affrights every person that has any dealings with him'. Macquarie told his brother that Bligh was a 'most disagreeable Person to have any dealings or Publick business to transact with, having no regard to his promises or engagements ... His natural temper is uncommonly harsh, and tyrannical in the extreme ... He is a very improper Person to be employed in any situation of Trust or Command, and he is certainly very generally detested ... more especially by the higher Classes of People'.[124]

To Macarthur the rebellion was due to 'the dread that was entertained of the six officers being sent to gaol, and of the resentment that would have been excited among the soldiers, and inhabitants'; to the judge-advocate at Johnston's later court-martial it seemed 'the first cause of grievance was the detention of a ship of yours; the next about a post taken away from your ground'; to most contemporaries in New South Wales it was due to Bligh's determined efforts to put down the spirit traffic, and to control trade closely.[125] Probably, though not

122 Quoted in G. Mackaness, *The Life of Vice Admiral William Bligh*, Sydney, 1951, p. 473.

123 *H.R.A., VII*, p. 331: D. R. Hainsworth, *Builders and Adventurers*, Melbourne, 1968, pp. 49–50.

124 Joseph Arnold, Letters, 18 March 1810, Mitchell Library, Sydney, A1849–2: G. Mackaness, *The Life of Vice Admiral William Bligh*, Sydney, 1951, p. 507.

125 G. Mackaness, *The Life of Vice Admiral William Bligh*, Sydney, 1951, p. 461, and ch. 44.

certainly, the governor had the support of the small settlers at the Hawkesbury, but they could not greatly influence events at Sydney.[126] Like Dr Arnold, and the staunchly loyal settler George Suttor, the botanist, Caley, admitted that Bligh's 'meaning was for the general interest of the colony', but all the same thought him 'an unfit man to be Governor'.[127] His temperament was against him, he lacked the patience and ability to oppose the intolerant, intriguing and ever-discontented if always self-righteous Macarthur, whose ambitions were aided by malcontent officers in a corps which had been too long in the colony.

On 31 December 1809, twenty-three months after the rebellion, the arrival of Governor Macquarie restored legitimate government in New South Wales. In the meantime apart from a small number of semi-political trials – like those of Gore, Crossley, Campbell, Suttor – and a complete change in the magistracy and in official personnel, the insurrection appeared to have brought no great change in the colony. In turn three military officers administered its affairs – Major Johnston, Lieutenant-Colonel Foveaux, arriving from London en route to Norfolk Island, and Lieutenant-Colonel Paterson, commanding officer of the New South Wales Corps and the official lieutenant-governor of New South Wales, who belatedly returned to Sydney from Port Dalrymple. They promised to economize, but did not. They deplored the spirits traffic, but did not seriously attempt to control it. Johnston and Foveaux were circumspect in granting land, and did little more than make up for Bligh's extreme parsimony, but Paterson was lavish; on the other hand all three administrators distributed government cattle with a very free hand. The rebel supporters soon began to quarrel among themselves, and particularly with Macarthur, but all were agreed not to restore Bligh to authority. When Paterson set him free on condition he returned to England, he found to his dismay that he only went to the Derwent, though the chief result of that was to give him the opportunity to infuriate Collins and to antagonise the inhabitants of Hobart Town almost as much as he had those of Sydney.

Some of the leaders, including Johnston and Macarthur, had already departed to justify their conduct in London. For all his apparent confidence Macarthur's letters to his wife show his anxiety of the outcome, and his forebodings were justified. In 1811 Johnston was tried by court-martial in London, found guilty and cashiered. Since his defence rested on justification, his conviction was Bligh's acquittal, but whether the court's rider to its sentence that 'novel and

---

126 B. H. Fletcher, 'The Hawkesbury Settlers and the Rum Rebellion'. *R.A.H.S.J.*, *54*, 3, September 1968, p. 217.

127 *H.R.N.S.W.*, *VII*, p. 23: G. Caley, *Reflections on the Colony of New South Wales*, reprinted Melbourne, 1966, pp. 154-5.

extraordinary circumstances' offered a partial extenuation for Johnston's conduct refers to its thinking that there was provocation by Bligh or that he was merely the tool of Macarthur is uncertain. The latter could only be tried in Sydney, but as Macquarie had been ordered to arrest him if he returned, he decided he could not go back. Fearing the worst, he suffered a sentence of banishment untried, until in 1817 the secretary of state promised him that he would not be prosecuted, and therefore he could safely return to his home, his wife and his sheep.

Society in Sydney embraced many of the frustrations and short-comings of society in Britain. Here was no utopia, no easy way to salvation, no place to offer any solution to man's personal dilemmas or tragedies. Materially its progress had been slow, for a shortage of labour and the desire to economise had continually held up public works, and Hunter, King and Bligh were all better able to send home lists of works needed than lists of works completed. In 1804 settler George Suttor thought Sydney was still less like a town than a camp 'mixed with stumps and dead trees', with only 2100 inhabitants and 675 houses cobbled up by amateurs, all but one of wood, and rarely fully glazed.[128] The colony still had no staple product, was barely self-sufficient in food, and economically remained dependent on the uncertain foundation of treasury bills and convicts, which meant on British government expenditure. Except as a penal settlement, it was contributing nothing to imperial prosperity, save having anticipated any possible French occupation, and during the war it had not been greatly used for convicts. The total population was only about 10,500, or about 12,000 including Van Diemen's Land, and as these included about 1000 military, there was a large 'dead weight' on the settlement's economy. Macquarie was right to describe the colony he found as 'barely emerging from infantile imbecility', the population depressed by poverty, agriculture languishing, and public buildings delapidated. Its greatest interest to Englishmen seemed still to be its flora and fauna, including its Aborigines.

All the same there were signs of change. Dr Arnold noted that 'thirty years ago this place was entirely a forest', but in 1810, 'a person coming into Sydney Cove would think himself in the midst of a large city; if he dines on shore he finds all the luxury and elegance of the finest English tables'. For a farewell ball to Bligh, Government House was 'neatly decorated and brilliantly lighted, the ball room hung round with festoons of flowers', just as it might have been in England. Comparing 'the powers, the ingenuity, and the resources of civilised man, with the weakness, the ignorance, and the wants of the savage' who had been depossessed, Lieutenant James Tuckey, R.N., could behold 'a second Rome, rising from a coalition of banditti, ... giving

128 G. Suttor, Memoirs, Mitchell Library, Sydney, A3072, f. 60: J. M. Freeland, *Architecture in Australia*, Melbourne, 1968, pp. 25–6.

laws to the world, and superlative in arms and in arts'. More soberly the committee inquiring into its affairs in 1812 reported that New South Wales was then 'in a train entirely to answer the ends proposed by its establishment'.[129]

129 James Tuckey, *Account of a Voyage to establish a Colony at Port Phillip in Bass's Strait*, 1805, p. 189: Select Committee on Transportation, 1812, *Report*, p. 16.

2

1810-30

J. J. Auchmuty

*The crossing of the Blue Mountains—the limits of settlement—
the Hunter Valley district—the outstations—Norfolk Island—
Van Diemen's Land—the felonry—the Aborigines in the two
colonies—the clergy and the churches—the Church of England—
Roman Catholics—lunacy—education—the press and literature—
teaching—editors—commerce—manufacturing—architecture—the
Bigge inquiry—economic recessions—the currency—wages and
barter—Macquarie's holey dollars—the Bank of New South Wales
founded—a Savings Bank established—banks in Van Diemen's
Land—insolvencies—government income—the legal system—the
Charter of Justice—the legal officers—the New South Wales Act
—separation of Van Diemen's Land—the first Legislative Council
—personalities and eccentrics—the cost of living—sport and
leisure—Brisbane's administration—the Sudds and Thompson
case—a changing community.*

When Lachlan Macquarie took up office as governor on 1 January
1810, he had a tremendous advantage over his predecessors in that he
was accompanied by his own regiment and, at least until the 73rds
became contaminated by environment, he could rest assured of strong
personal support against the feuding leaders of the colonial economy.[1]
As the first military governor in succession to a series of naval men, a
new direction was given to the expansion of the colony.[2] The settled
area was still hemmed in on all sides and despite efforts by Ensign
Barrallier in 1802 and 1803 and the surveyor D. D. Mann in 1807 to
break through the barrier of the Blue Mountains, it was 1813 before
this formidable obstacle, asserted to be impassable for man, was
crossed by Gregory Blaxland, William Lawson and William Charles

---

[1] The most recent study of Macquarie's administration is by C. M. H. Clark,
A History of Australia, I, iv, Melbourne, 1962. See also A. Hewison, Ed., *The
Macquarie Decade: Documents illustrating the History of New South Wales, 1810–
1821*, Melbourne, 1972.

[2] The best recent account of early New South Wales expansion is to be found in
T. M. Perry, *Australia's First Frontier: The Spread of Settlement in New South
Wales 1788–1829*, Melbourne, 1963.

Wentworth. It was crossed not purely out of scientific curiosity nor because of a shortage of agricultural land. Blaxland had been searching for new pastures for his expanding herds of cattle since the summer of 1810–11, but since so much of the County of Cumberland, the settled area between the mountains and the sea, was still ungranted, Governor Macquarie did all in his power to prevent any settlement in the newly discovered Bathurst plains, although he did appoint Surveyor George William Evans to delineate a possible route to the interior along which William Cox succeeded in establishing a permanent road in 1814 and 1815.

With the completion of the road, great pressure was exerted on Macquarie to allow immediate transmontane settlement, largely because the capacity of the Cumberland plain pastures had been reduced by over-stocking, periodic droughts and floods, and occasional plagues of caterpillars. Yet from the governor's point of view the Cumberland area was not fully occupied and any dissipation of settlement would ensure less effective control by government. In fact, between 1812 and 1821 no less than 228,000 acres in Cumberland were granted to settlers in the area bounded by Windsor in the north and Appin in the south and centring on Liverpool and Parramatta out to Penrith. 1813, 1814 and 1815 were all drought years and in 1815 the government transferred some of its own stock to Bathurst and others sent cattle down to the Illawarra plain. But it was 1820 before Macquarie granted permission for settlers in general to graze on the inland plains and then only as a temporary relief; no title to land was granted and the sole qualification for grazing across the mountains was the possession of stock. He had made a preliminary effort to estimate the value of the new lands by settling ten farmers across the mountains in 1817, in which year, writing from Sydney, he also warned Lord Bathurst, the Secretary of State, that 'Disposable Lands are now getting Very Scarce in this part of the Colony'.[3]

Between 1788 and 1830 the non-aboriginal population of New South Wales increased from approximately 1,000 to 35,000. All governors attempted to prevent the spread of people outside currently settled areas in order to control the convict population. But the most significant steps were not taken until 1826 and 1829 when the government set limits beyond which it did not allow land to be occupied even on a grazing basis and at the same time the permitted area was divided into nineteen counties; even so, the overstretched survey department led by Oxley, Evans and Meehan was normally heavily in arrears with its work. The governors knew as well as anybody else that arbitrary limits on settlement had no long-term validity. The 1826 regulations were promulgated by Governor Darling 'until His Majesty's pleasure shall be known';[4] those of 1829 were issued 'for the present'.[5]

3 *H.R.A., IX*, p. 713.

4 *H.R.A., XII*, p. 378.

5 *Sydney Gazette*, 17 October 1829.

A different form of control on settlement was removed in September 1825, when the practice of victualling settlers on taking up their property ceased. Until 1817, settlers, their families and assigned servants received government rations for eighteen months after they had occupied their farms; this period was reduced to six months from 1817 to 1825, and whilst grants to ex-convicts were not normally greater than 100 acres, free settlers could get as much as 3,000 and of course some of them obtained over the years many such grants. By the late twenties John Macarthur's Camden estate by grant and purchase exceeded 60,000 acres, while the surgeon D'Arcy Wentworth had been awarded at least 17,000 acres and his sons had 3,450.

Development on the Bathurst plain was slow. Macquarie visited the site of the present city in May 1815; settlers were firmly established by 1818 and in the following year William Lawson was appointed as Magistrate for Westmoreland and as Commander of the Bathurst post. But the cost of transport along Cox's road over the Blue Mountains was very expensive and the real development outside the Cumberland area during the governorships of Macquarie, Brisbane and Darling was in the Hunter Valley district. When Macquarie arrived in 1810, the population of Newcastle as a convict settlement for hardened criminals annually averaged one hundred, as it had since the establishment of this settlement in 1804. So long as Newcastle remained a receptacle for the most dangerous criminals, there was little possibility of rural development along the Hunter River Valley, though by 1813 it was clear that that valley was considerably more promising for successful farming than was any other area so far discovered. It had a rich alluvial soil suitable for all types of agriculture whilst the Bathurst plains were suitable only for sheep; transport by sea was of course much cheaper than by land waggon and, by good luck or design, the survey of the Hunter Valley proceeded much more rapidly than that of the Bathurst plains; a new settler could get his certificate of land grant, his assigned servants and his six months' rations much more quickly. If a rural population were to develop, then somewhere else had to be found for the convicts. By 1822 Newcastle, a town of some 1,000 people, with a handsome church which could hold 500, had ceased to be a penal settlement and the convicts were moved further north to Port Macquarie and in 1824 to Brisbane. Although the Hunter Valley was the last district to be occupied and available to settlers before 1810, by the 1820s it was the most populous and extensively used area with a population of the order of 4,000 or perhaps 14 per cent of the total white population of the mainland colony.

By 1830 the settled areas of New South Wales – the nineteen counties as defined in Governor Darling's order of 14 October 1829 – extended from the River Manning in the north to the Shoalhaven in the south and inland to the modern Australian Capital Territory, Yass, Cowra and Wellington. The most remote stations were some 200 miles from Sydney, and some 3,500,000 acres had been appropriated in one way or another, of which less than 15 per cent was in the original area of the County of Cumberland. Outside the clearly delineated area of the nineteen counties were the penal establishments at Port Macquarie and Brisbane; the temporary settlement set up by David Collins at Port Phillip Bay in what we now call Victoria had been closed, though the overland route from Lake George had been discovered by Hume and Hovell in 1824 and from the same year there had been protective forts in what is now the Northern Territory, first at Fort Dundas on Melville Island, then at Fort Wellington on Raffles Bay north of present-day Darwin, from which the troops were finally withdrawn late in 1829. In the same year, after a series of false starts at Western Port and Albany, on the advice of Captain James Stirling a lasting settlement was established at Perth and what is now the state of Western Australia had its infant beginnings. Stirling was its first governor from 1829 to 1839.

Governor Phillip, on his original landing in 1788, had been directed to annex something over one-third of the land area of the Australian continent and of course also the adjacent islands, a phrase which Governor Macquarie interpreted as including not merely New Zealand but also Tahiti, and the early colony had quite a considerable trade, especially in pork, with the tropical paradise thought to be the islands of love. The limits of the first annexation were from Cape York in the north in latitude 10°37′ south to South Cape in 43°39′ south and inland so far as the 135th degree of east longitude. When the trading port was built at Melville Island in 1824 annexation was pushed back from the 135th meridian to the 129th and this was stretched over the whole inland area in Sir Ralph Darling's commission as governor in 1825; finally the whole of the continent was declared British when Perth was settled in 1829.

This was a gigantic expansion of the British Empire without population or forces to back it. Once the penal settlement and subsequent colonial development of New South Wales appeared assured, all kinds of strategic and commercial considerations supervened. The French, the hereditary enemy, must be kept out; the rights and privileges of the East India Company must be protected or evaded according to need, and the commercial fleets of all other nations must be controlled to the advantage of the few British occupants of the Australian mainland. Hence temporary military bases on the south and west were to keep out the French, who as late as 1826 were still considering the colonization of New Zealand; those on the north were expected to attract Malayan and Chinese and other South Asian commerce.

But if the British government was eager to extend its authority over the whole of Australia, it was also willing, on grounds of expense, to relinquish control if not ultimate possession of Norfolk Island, whose occupation had been a first direction to Governor Phillip on his arrival in 1788. In fact, there were at that date some members of the British cabinet who pressed for the establishment of the original settlement on Norfolk Island in preference to Sydney Cove. When it was discovered that the spars from the Norfolk Island pine were not suitable for naval use, that flax was not a major product, and that the island had no safe harbour facilities, opinions changed, and as early as June 1803 the British government was directing Governor King to reduce the Norfolk Island establishment by transfer of inhabitants to Van Diemen's Land. Originally it was proposed to settle those transferred from Norfolk Island at Port Dalrymple in the north of Van Diemen's Land; ultimately a greater number were established at what came to be known as New Norfolk on the Derwent, some 21 miles north of Hobart. It was a slow process. The Norfolk Islanders were unwilling to move; the naval governors of New South Wales procrastinated on strategic grounds. Governor King wished to preserve the settlement as a supply depot for whalers or for ships on the route to China and also acclaimed its value in the production of pork. Total evacuation was ordered in Governor Bligh's instructions in 1805, but there were still several hundred inhabitants when Macquarie arrived.

Macquarie had no seaman's notion of the value of island territories. Immediately he entered fully into the plans for total evacuation and his early despatches record his complete support for the project, but he was prevented from this simple military activity by a continuous shortage of shipping, and it was 18 February 1814 before the evacuation was finally completed with the destruction by burning of the greater part of the buildings and the salting down of all the cattle, pigs and sheep which could be caught – only a few wild pigs and goats and a number of dogs were left behind. Norfolk Island did not remain for long uninhabited. Commissioner Bigge in his report recommended the establishment at Moreton Bay, Port Curtis and Port Bowen, all along the eastern coast of Australia, of prisons for the worst description of convicts. But the old concern for naval strategy was still felt in London, and Bathurst firmly turned down the recommendation, directing instead that Norfolk Island should be re-occupied on grounds primarily of the difficulty of escape from an isolated island some hundreds of miles out in the ocean. It had taken more than ten years to evacuate the island but less than one year to re-occupy it. Bathurst signed his despatch on 22 July 1824; it received enthusiastic approval from Governor Brisbane and a military detachment was disembarked on 6 June 1825, to find that the progeny of the wild pigs and goats were very numerous and that it was possible to use the stone walls of the destroyed buildings as a basis for the new occupation.

Brisbane's successor, Ralph Darling, held strong military views on convict discipline. None but the most desperate criminals were to be sent to Norfolk Island and to ensure the harshest discipline he refused to send any women whether convict or free. By 1827, 64 soldiers and 150 convicts were in occupation, firmly held down despite mutinies both on the voyage and on the island. But his attitude in sexual segregation was not upheld and when Darling was directed from

London to replace the bachelor commandant, Captain Donaldson, with the married Colonel Morisset, who had previously been in charge at Newcastle, he was compelled to give way and from 1828 discrimination ceased. The early years 1825–1828 were the most terrible in the island's chequered story: soon there was an easing of convict discipline, and new proposals, which took years to bring to an issue, whereby the island should be a happy home for free farming settlers rather than a convict hell.

Governor Macquarie's authority on arrival also extended over Van Diemen's Land. Indeed, he felt fortunate that his legitimate predecessor Bligh was still on board ship in the Derwent Estuary when he sailed into Port Jackson at the end of 1809 with instructions to replace the deposed governor in power for one day, prior to taking over himself. With such a distance between the two representatives of the British Crown such satisfaction to traditional honour was impossible, and Macquarie in due course had to face Bligh's criticisms of the lieutenant governor, David Collins, who had refused to participate in a colonial civil war on his behalf. When Macquarie arrived, Van Diemen's Land was still administered as two separate settlements from Hobart and Port Dalrymple, which were entirely penal settlements of the sister colony.[6] But when Collins died in 1810 and was succeeded as lieutenant governor by Colonel Thomas Davey (1812–17) the latter was directed to consolidate the two administrations. Macquarie was no respecter of lieutenant governors; critical of Collins, he was harshly unfair to Davey. Both lieutenant governors were friendly outgoing people with inadequate training for the type of treasury mind expected in the expenditure of public funds. It was typical of Macquarie that though he condemned their public activities he was full of sympathy for their dependent wives and children.

Any consideration of Macquarie must take into account the fact that the rectitude of his public character was continuously affected by his emotional sympathy for those in any kind of misfortune. With Davey's successor, William Sorell, Macquarie established much better relations, as indeed did the people of Van Diemen's Land, where he was so popular that he was presented in 1821 with plate worth 500 guineas, a circumstance so unusual in early Australian history as to be noteworthy. Under Sorell the reputation of Van Diemen's Land for progress and prosperity led after 1817 to a steady flow of free immigrants, to intensive building development and, as in New South Wales, to the development of a bank. Unhappily, Sorrell's private life was by no means as publicly approved of, since His Majesty's representative lived openly with another man's wife though he had a wife and family at home in the British Isles whom he had great difficulty in supporting.

---

6 For this period generally see R. M. Hartwell, *The Economic Development of Van Diemen's Land 1820–1850*, Melbourne, 1954: W. G. Rimmer, 'The Economic Growth of Van Diemen's Land: 1803–1821' in G. J. Abbott and N. B. Nairn, Eds., *Economic Growth of Australia 1788–1821*, Melbourne, 1969.

In London private faults were measured against approved public achievement and Bathurst felt compelled to recall Sorell in 1824 since he was indefensible against the criticism from isolated individuals which poured into the mail from Hobart to London.

Some of the harshness in Macquarie's fundamentally sympathetic character was caused by the material with which he had to work. Anyone who considers the early history of Australia must recollect that all the basic work in the community was done by convicts; they were the servants to the owners of estates, available to free settlers till after Macquarie's era; they built every church and public building and were the beasts of burden in all expeditions of exploration; when they had earned tickets of leave these same convicts were transformed into constables and supervisors of road gangs. In other places reference has been made to the character and the reputed offences of the transported classes but whatever may be our view of the state of law and punishment in the British islands at the turn of the century, it is obvious that at the end of the earth the unfree population had to be treated with firmness, even severity, if the settlement were to survive. In fact, as so often in other parts of the world, it was not the government in Britain, nor yet its representative the governor in Sydney Cove, who proved the harshest taskmasters.[7] It has ever been the failure of imperial powers from the days of the Romans or of Renaissance Spain to control their officers at the perimeter of empire. Much legislation favourable to the indigenous populations is drafted in the imperial capital only to be quietly ignored in the overseas provinces.

Every early governor of New South Wales wished to show favour to Aborigines; every home government expected it; yet the difference in civilizations proved too great to be bridged.[8] Governor Macquarie in 1814 could write to the Secretary of State: 'it seems only to require the fostering Hand of Time, gentle Means and Conciliatory Manners to bring these poor Unenlightened People into an important Degree of Civilization and to Instill into their Minds, as they Gradually open to Reason and Reflection, A sense of the Duties they owe their fellow Kindred and Society',[9] yet his own Supreme Court judge, Barron Field, was equally firm in the other views, proclaiming in an address to the Philosophical Society of Australasia his belief that Aborigines were

[7] On the convict system generally see L. L. Robson, *The Convict Settlers of Australia*, Melbourne, 1965: A. G. L. Shaw, *Convicts and the Colonies*, London, 1966. An important contemporary enquiry was the Select Committee on the Gaols, whose report was published in the *Papers* of the House of Commons, 1819, *VII*, 579.

[8] For a survey of colonial opinion on the Aborigines see D. J. Mulvaney, 'The Australian Aborigines: 1606–1929: Opinion and Fieldwork, Part I: 1606–1859' in *H.S.*, *30*, May 1958. See also C. D. Rowley, *Aboriginal Policy and Practice*; *I*, *The Destruction of Aboriginal Society*, Canberra, 1970: and B. Bridges, 'The Aborigines and the Law: New South Wales 1788–1855', in *Teaching History*, *4*, *3*, December 1970.

[9] *H.R.A.*, *VIII*, p. 368.

without faculties of 'reflexion, judgment or foresight' and were incapable of civilization. At least it was a sign of advancing colonial civilization that the Aboriginal problem could be discussed at a supposedly intellectual level in a Society which was to be the ancestor of the various State Royal Societies in Australia. But nevertheless it was a matter of contemporary complaint that the colonial chaplain, Samuel Marsden, seemed considerably more interested in the eternal salvation of Pacific Islanders than he was in the conversion of Aborigines. Whatever view we may take of this attitude, and presumably it was based on results and achievement, it is a sign of increasing social consciousness that in December 1813 a Public Meeting was called in Sydney which resulted in the foundation early in the following year of the New South Wales Philanthropic Society for the Protection and Civilization of such of the natives of the South Sea Islands who may arrive in Port Jackson. The driving force was Samuel Marsden but as in all matters humane or philanthropic, D'Arcy Wentworth, J. T. Campbell and others were involved under the patronage of Governor Macquarie and Lieutenant Governor O'Connell, whilst the greater part of the work was done by the Rev. William Cowper. When in 1814 the governor appointed a committee to run a school of Aborigines, five of the seven members were also associated with South Sea Islanders, but this group did not include Marsden though it did include Rowland Hassall, who as a former missionary in Tahiti was an obvious choice for the first committee of the Philanthropic Society.

Governor Phillip had firmly laid down that there could be no slavery in a free land and consequently no slaves, whether African or Aboriginal. Yet save as guides on journeys of exploration Aborigines proved of little economic value to the European settler and were often the cause of considerable economic loss. Great hopes were held in the early days of converting and civilizing them, but by 1810 the attitude of goodwill to aborigines had turned to one of critical disgust at their unwillingness to adopt European clothes except for amusement, or to settle down at farming or any other regular occupation. Governor Macquarie, in the tradition of gubernatorial protection, decided to approach the civilizing process by establishing a native institution at Parramatta where both sexes would be educated from an early age and at the same time he established a farm at the north side of Port Jackson where some sixteen natives were to be taught to be farmers. The choice of Parramatta for the institution, which was opened under the care of William Shelley in January 1815, was conditioned by the fact that Parramatta was the meeting place of the Aborigines for regular corroborees, which under Macquarie became official ceremonies at which chieftaincies were confirmed and honours conferred; there was banqueting and a distinguished attendance of official and other personages of the governing class. The institution opened with six girls and six boys, and the *Sydney Gazette* for some years annually reported the prizegiving, but Shelley died early, to be succeeded by his wife, and students were always hard to come by and harder still to retain, so that by 1826 despite all the fine statements proclaimed annually the institution languished away.

At least on the mainland of Australia it was possible, though not necessarily probable, for the two races to remain apart, but there was no such possibility in Van Diemen's Land, where the clash of civilizations was much more disastrous than in New South Wales. When Lieutenant Governor Arthur arrived in Hobart in 1824 he found relations so bad that within a month he issued a proclamation warning the settlers and others that if they fired at, injured or destroyed defenceless Aborigines, then they would be prosecuted in the supreme court. It is claimed, though on inadequate evidence, that an estimated aboriginal population of 5,000 in 1803 had diminished to 500 when Arthur took up the reins of office. Against these 500 Aborigines the settlers in 1824 numbered 12,643, of whom almost 6,000 were convicts, less than 10 per cent of whom were female. Such a sexually one-sided society was bound to be a sickly place, and Aboriginal attacks on settlers met with savage reprisals. Arthur found any policy of friendship quite out of the question for his people and thought up a plan of placing all Aborigines in island sanctuaries or otherwise cut off from the farming and grazing white population. As guardian of the Aborigines on Bruny Island he appointed G. A. Robinson, who became his principal adviser on methods (which ultimately failed) to prevent the extermination of a whole native race. In 1830 an attempt was made to round up all the remaining Aborigines and to settle them on native reserves or enclosures: the attempt was a ghastly or humorous failure, according to the point of view. Some 3,000 of the white population, fully armed with a heterogeneous collection of weapons, took the field for a period of weeks as if on a hunting drive and finally struggled home in the latter part of November 1830 with the tally of two natives killed and two others captured.

Saxe Bannister, the very incompetent attorney-general of New South Wales under Brisbane and Darling, was the only high government official to continue an interest in the protection of the Aborigines after leaving the colony. In 1830 he published in London a work entitled *Humane Policy: or Justice to the Aborigines of New Settlements.* Bannister, despite his failures in court, was a distinguished legal scholar who was opposed to transportation as a policy and who wrote many pamphlets on behalf of native populations everywhere. There were many who had no more compunction in killing an Aborigine than in shooting at a bird in flight. Such people have existed and continue to exist in many parts of the world but it was the claim of the British occupiers of the land that they were the bearers of a superior civilization and more particularly of a higher religion. By the 1820s there was much ecclesiastical competition for black souls. The clergy of the established church had been joined, much against their will, by Roman Catholic priests, who could claim at least a quarter of the population as their own, and by missionaries, generally Congregationalist or with

Methodist enthusiasm, sent out by the London Missionary Society, first to the Pacific islands from which many drifted to Sydney Cove: and then from 1823 there was the great Scottish Presbyterian figure of John Dunmore Lang to preach and to organize, to become an orator and great political figure, to formulate and express views on every-thing Australian whether immigration or form of government, educa-tion or journalism. Archibald Macarthur in Hobart was the first minister to conduct Presbyterian services in Australia but his ordina-tion was suspect in the eyes of some, including John Dunmore Lang, and it was left to the latter to be the foundation stone of his form of church order.

The first Methodist minister, the Rev. Samuel Leigh, arrived in 1815 in answer to local appeal. Quietly devout, he accomplished much on circuit, co-operating closely with his theologically like-minded Anglican colleagues. He built the first Australian Methodist church at Castlereagh in 1817. By 1820 Leigh had some twenty preaching places on his circuit, including one at Windsor on land given by Samuel Marsden, with whom he established a close friendship and who sent him to minister briefly in New Zealand, hoping the voyage would be good for Leigh's health. Leigh preached frequently in Anglican churches and was essentially a pastoral rather than a political cleric such as his Presbyterian bonfrere. Leigh visited England for the sake of his health in 1820 and 1821 and returned accompanied by the Rev. William Horton, whom he established as the first resident Methodist missionary in Hobart.

There is considerable argument about the influence of the churches in the early life of New South Wales and Van Diemen's Land. David Mann, writing of the early 1800s, declared the churches to be well attended and morals to be no worse than elsewhere,[10] but he is a lone voice defending a situation of affairs few others found so rosy. Obviously convicts and guards were compelled, in accordance with British tradition, to be church goers, and so also responsible govern-ment officials, but for the rest there are few commentators to agree with Mann. In discounting his views however, it must be remembered that all the early clergy in New South Wales, no matter what their denomination, were of the evangelical persuasion and took a very gloomy view of all human effort, so their condemnation is frequently grossly exaggerated.

The early chaplains in New South Wales and Van Diemen's Land were appointed as government officials obedient to authority in accordance with the Rules and Discipline of war: the clergy of the established church in early days also had a monopoly of religious responsibility in the settlement. Samuel Marsden, who came out as assistant chaplain to the Rev. Richard Johnson in 1793, had the longest spell of authority though several times superseded or passed over in the search for ecclesiastical discipline. The original chaplains

10 D. D. Mann. *The Present Picture of New South Wales*, London, 1811.

were appointed by government but were ecclesiastically subject to the Bishop of London, a state of affairs which continued until the appointment of the first archdeacon, Thomas Hobbes Scott, in 1824, who was made responsible to the Bishop of Calcutta; so did the commercial and trading influence of the East India Company's organization of the southern seas pass over into Australian affairs.

The early Anglican chaplains were all sprung from the evangelical mould, Old Testament Christians who judged their fellow free citizens hardly and so were even harsher towards the convict population. Their religion was one of rules and regulations rather than of sympathy and kindness; they believed in an ordered society and were very conscious of their own privileged position in such a society. Marsden had been slow to over-develop this consciousness and it is ironical that the cause of its over-development was probably an action of Governor Hunter, the first of the early governors with a naturally religious temperament. He made Marsden a magistrate in 1795 and as time went on the chaplain, usually resident at Parramatta, spent more of his time on farming, the duties of the magistracy, the organization, financial and managerial, of the London Missionary Society, the Church Missionary Society, and the British and Foreign Bible Society and in the establishment of missions to the Maoris in New Zealand than on the pastoral care of those near at hand.

It may have been a sheer accident that it was the Rev. William Cowper who preached the first sermon in New South Wales before Governor Lachlan Macquarie but it was no accident, but rather a very deep concern over the immediately rebellious past, that led the minister at St Philip's mother church to choose as his text a passage from the first Book of Samuel: 'Arise, anoint him: for this is he'. The sermon as it developed was hopefully confident that a veritable David had been sent to rule, though the preacher was hardly prepared to make at so early a stage in the governor's career too much out of another verse in the same sixteenth chapter: 'Look not on his countenance or on the height of his stature . . . for the Lord seeth not as man seeth; for man looketh on the outward appearance, but the Lord looketh on the heart'. Many in the colony looked harshly on Marsden, but for the clerical ex-convict Fulton or the long-lived and hard-working Cowper, or the friend of Aborigines, Cartwright, there was always sympathy if not support; it was difficult to find clergy willing to work in convict settlements so far from home, and the 70,000 settlers in the new Australian world of 1830 had only some 15 or so Anglican priests to minister to them in New South Wales and Van Diemen's Land.[11]

[11] The early Anglican clergy in New South Wales, in approximate order of their arrival were: Richard Johnson; Samuel Marsden; Henry Fulton; William Cowper; Robert Cartwright; John Youl; Richard Hill; John Cross; G. A. Middleton; Thomas Riddall; Thomas Hobbes Scott; Thomas Hassall; F. M. Wilkinson; Mathew Devenish-Meares; J. E. Keane; John Vincent; Elijah Smith, and C. P. N. Wilton. There were also, of course, a number of Army chaplains who gave assistance such

Archdeacon Scott, who took up his duties in 1825, was in salary and status almost on a par with the governor and proved an exact but unpopular administrator. A graduate of St Alban's Hall, Oxford, he originally came out as secretary to Commissioner Bigge, to whom he was connected through his sister's marriage. Subsequently ordained, he was a quiet country parson in the north of England when he was invited to come out to New South Wales with membership of the Legislative Council and rank and precedence next to the lieutenant-governor. He was a master of infinite detail and profoundly interested in educational as in ecclesiastical affairs, continuously on the go over his vast territories and increasingly independent of his bishop in Calcutta, with whom contact was slow and unsure. Scott, with the support of Lord Bathurst, was largely responsible for the creation in 1826 of the Church and School Corporation which set aside some one-seventh of the land of the colony for the support of the Anglican church and an educational system under its control. The Corporation for a brief few years gave the United Church of England and Ireland a positive advantage in the community, but despite all Scott's best efforts was never a success, and was suspended in 1829 and dissolved in 1833. So the real crisis in church and educational affairs was postponed until the governorship of Sir Richard Bourke. Emphatically, however, Scott was not a careerist as has been imagined by many because of the background to his appointment. After five years in New South Wales he was happy to return at one-tenth the salary to his quietly humble position as a country rector in the Diocese of Durham, where he lived out his days in devoutly peaceful service; he was succeeded in Sydney by William Grant Broughton, ultimately to be the first Bishop of Australia.

New South Wales and Van Diemen's Land were British not English colonies, and it was early clear that the United Church of England and Ireland could not be exported with all the protective privileges of the establishment. John Dunmore Lang came to claim equal rights for the Scottish establishment and at all times some 20 per cent of the convict population was of Roman Catholic background; some of the military and in due course of the emancipists also belonged to the same faith. Governors in New South Wales and Van Diemen's Land were sympathetic to the religious needs of these compulsory exiles though Macquarie deported the first priest, Father Jeremiah O'Flynn,

---

as James Bain, Chaplain to the N.S.W. Corps 1792–94, or Benjamin Vale, who came out as Assistant Chaplain to the 46th Regiment in 1814 and caused a lot of trouble to Governor Macquarie. John Youl later joined the first Anglican chaplain, Robert Knopwood, in Van Diemen's Land. Knopwood served in Van Diemen's Land from 1804 to 1839; Youl from 1818 to 1827 and William Bedford, who replaced Knopwood as Senior Chaplain, from 1823 and ministered till his death in 1852.

For information on the early history of the Anglican clergy see K. Cable, 'Some Anglican Clergy of the 1840s', in *Descent*, 1969, *4*, 2, pp. 41–55.

who arrived illegally in 1817.[12] Fathers Conolly and Therry arrived with the authority of the Colonial Office in 1820 and worked devotedly in both colonies, at least in the early years, to the happiness of their co-religionists and also with the full approval of Sorell and Arthur in Van Diemen's Land and Macquarie and Brisbane in New South Wales.[13] Governor Macquarie, a freemason of long standing, personally set the foundation stone of St Mary's Cathedral in Sydney on 29 October 1821, while Sorell provided on behalf of the government the land for a similar building in Hobart; throughout the colonies Protestants of all classes contributed to building funds and offered hospitality to the travelling priests as they sought out the Roman Catholic flock. Clerically their church was much in a minority but the number of the faithful, however degraded in life some might be, remained fairly constant, and it was 1826 before an additional priest, Father Daniel Power, arrived in the colony to conduct the scattered services in the guardrooms, police barracks, hospital rooms, stores or private homes, which provided the only opportunities for the public performance of Roman Catholic rites.

If Protestant public opinion was in general sympathetic to the plight of its Roman Catholic fellow countrymen, the British government in London was not equally sympathetic. Although the Roman Catholic population was always considerable it was over thirty years before the first priest was allowed legal residence. The privileged position granted in 1826 to the Church and School Corporation; the continued practice of educating Roman Catholic orphans under the care of Anglican institutions; and the controls exercised in government establishments on Roman Catholic religious services, all combined to create and foster religious antagonism in the nineteenth-century air when such antagonisms were increasingly obvious in Europe and the United Kingdom. The sympathies of Governors Macquarie and Brisbane were not reflected by Darling, who found Father Therry difficult to handle, and by 1830 it was obvious in both the Anglican and Roman Catholic organizations in New South Wales and Van Diemen's Land that the time had come for the establishment of ecclesiastical discipline along traditional lines; no longer could bishops in Calcutta or Mauritius exercise either influence or control in the days of slow communication. It was this absence from traditional organization which led to the development in the Australian colonies of a self-sufficient and independent laity, of considerable lack of harmony at times between laymen

[12] Three Irish Roman Catholic priests, Fathers James Dixon, James Harold and Peter O'Neil, had reached N.S.W. as convicts in 1800 sentenced for alleged conspiracy in the Irish rebellion of 1798, but except for a brief period in 1803 and 1804 were not allowed to minister publicly to their co-religionists.

[13] See E. M. O'Brien, *The Foundation of Catholicism in Australia: Life and Letters of Archpriest John Joseph Therry*, Sydney, 2 vols., 1922: P. J. O'Farrell, *The Catholic Church in Australia: A Short History*, Melbourne, 1968: P. J. O'Farrell, *Documents in Australian Catholic History: 1, 1788–1884*, Sect. 1, London, 1969.

and their clerical leaders, considerable erratic behaviour on the part of some of these clerics, culminating later in disobedience to their new episcopal superiors, and it also made it possible for representatives of several British dissenting communities, especially the Congregationalists, to gather a following and exert active spiritual leadership.

In the establishment of a Society for Promoting Christian Knowledge among the Aborigines; in the continued support of the Benevolent Society, founded in 1818 at a meeting of the Bible Society; in the formation of the Sydney Institution in whose reading room periodicals and newspapers were available for the general public; and even in the appointment of the colonial Poet Laureate, Michael Robinson, by Governor Macquarie, we can see the development of the colony into something more than 'a rascally community' and a 'distant colony of convicts', although this was the way it was still regarded by Lord Bathurst as late as 1821 when Brisbane was being appointed to succeed Macquarie. And the important point about all these societies and also the growing Masonic Order was that they formed a meeting place for freemen and emancipists, for government officials, merchants and other settlers.

Prior to the establishment of these various societies it could be claimed that the clergy and the medical officers provided the only sympathetic or uplifting force in the colony, but when we read the harsh condemnation of Aboriginal customs and morals uttered by Marsden and his fellow churchmen, it must ever be remembered that if the Christian missionaries denigrated Aboriginal lives and customs, these evangelical Christians spoke equally harshly of their white fellow men. Hospital accommodation was provided in the colony long before the first church; the erection of the Sydney Hospital by D'Arcy Wentworth, Alexander Riley and Garnham Blaxcell in the early days of Macquarie's rule not only created much local controversy on financial grounds but also in subsequent years attracted many envious eyes on the part of other government servants not so adequately, as they thought, provided for in the way of accommodation.

The first mental asylum was established at Castle Hill in 1811 under the superintendency of the Rev. Samuel Marsden. He was succeeded in 1814 by the free settler George Suttor, who although without any background training, quarrelled with the visiting surgeon and was accordingly removed. Even less was known about mental illness than about other forms of human disorder in the early nineteenth century before the discovery of anaesthetics and subsequently the whole gamut of drugs.[14] When Castle Hill was closed in 1825 the inmates were transferred to the Liverpool Courthouse, which served as an asylum until 1835.

Even with the limited number of free citizens in early New South Wales society there was much social competition. But the educated

14 For an account of the treatment of mental illness in N.S.W. during the period 1788–1850 see J. Bostock, *The Dawn of Australian Psychiatry*, Sydney, 1968.

class was very small indeed. Contemporaries asserted that fewer than half the convict population could read and write, and though convict success stories are generally based on a good educational background, the proportion belonging by birth and origin to the middle and upper classes was minute. When convicts arrived governors always felt that those of the educated classes, who had usually been transported for forgery, ought to form a special class, and it was a peculiarity of the convict system as it developed in New South Wales that to be transported for forgery was almost a qualification for minor clerical appointment in government service. Others were immediately accepted as schoolmasters in the homes of the wealthier settlers, and some few were allocated to emancipist merchants whose natural abilities were frequently greater than their educational qualifications. A number became associated with the legal system, which had been their apparent ruin. All the early governors show in their despatches a distinguished literary style and the tradition was continued by Macquarie, Brisbane and even Darling. But in so far as there was any development of literary taste or of culture in either of the colonies it was both slow and accidental.

Macquarie, by his patronage of Michael Robinson and Francis Greenway, as well as by his support of explorers and engineers, and by his encouragement of the architectural interests of his aide-de-camp Lieutenant John Watts, showed considerable interest in the more practical aspects of cultural development. Brisbane before his appointment was already well known as a distinguished astronomer: in fact as governor of New South Wales it was suggested that he was far more interested in the southern heavens than in the people beneath them. By the time Darling arrived there was a heatedly critical and competitive public press, which neither he nor Arthur in Van Diemen's Land appreciated. It is difficult to discover in any detail what literature was available to private citizens in the colonies but it is clear from the style adopted by all the early writers that they possessed a knowledge of English, European and classical literature which they expected their readers to appreciate. The *Sydney Gazette and New South Wales Advertiser*, originally commenced in 1803, had resumed publication after the Bligh rebellion when Macquarie took up office in 1810, and its editor, George Howe, who played a great part in the development of a local colonial literature, especially poetry, supplemented his official salary not only by commercial activities but also by acting as a private tutor. His press produced the first Australian art book and the first volume of Australian poetry; his son, Robert, who succeeded him in 1821, published the first Australian periodical and the first volume of poems by a native-born Australian poet.

The art book *Birds of New South Wales and their Natural History* was by J. W. Lewin, a naturalist of some ability who had a disappointing life in New South Wales but who nevertheless, through the Linnean Society, was associated with many European natural scientists. Just as today world interest is focused on Australian mineral resources, so in the first half century of colonial existence there was a comparable interest in Australian flora and fauna inspired by Sir Joseph Banks and Dr Solander but continued for many subsequent years. The best known lines in *The First Fruits of Australian Poetry* by Judge Barron Field, are concerned with the kangaroo, and though Michael Robinson and many others had published much verse in Sydney before him, his was the first book. Field, who was a very good scholar, had commenced author prior to coming to Australia, publishing his *Analysis of Blackstone's Commentaries* in 1811; he had lived in very literary surroundings in London so that he could claim friendship with Charles Lamb, about whom he later wrote a book, Wordsworth, Coleridge, Blake, Hazlitt and Leigh Hunt.[15] In contrast the first native-born Australian to publish a volume of verse, Charles Tompson, whose *Wild Notes from the Lyre of a Native Minstrel* was published by Robert Howe in 1826, could only look to the Rev. Henry Fulton as his tutor for introduction to a wider world of inspiration. Yet so competent was the joint achievement that the pupil had the nerve to publish in the *Sydney Gazette* of 17 December 1829 a translation of an English schoolboy's Latin prize poem on Australia.

Eccentric achievements of this order make it very difficult to estimate real educational standards in the Australian colonies though it is known that prior to 1830 not more than one-quarter of the population of school-going age were regular attenders at school. Moreover, by the standards of today the school curriculum, especially in post-elementary schools, must seem very peculiar indeed. In 1827 Robert Wilkins Giblin, who had for some twenty years conducted a boarding school at Kingston-upon-Thames, arrived in Van Diemen's Land, driven to emigrate because of the severe economic depression in England and the needs of a large and growing family. On 27 January 1827 he advertised in the *Hobart Town Gazette* that he proposed in the immediate future to open an Academy at Kangaroo Harbour near the ferry to Hobart Town, and the advertisement continued: 'Terms – in Greek, Latin, French, English, Grammar, Reading and Orthography on an improved plan, Writing, Arithmetic Vulgar and Decimal, with the course of Foreign Exchanges, Mathematics, Geography, History, Merchants Accompts, according to age, about £60 per annum. Accomplishments and other Branches requiring Occasional Masters extra charges. Frequent lectures on Astronomy, the Mechanical Powers, Hydraulics, Pneumatics, Electricity, Chemistry &c. &c., will be given'. Unhappily the Academy, which he called Clarence House, was as financially unsuccessful as his English boarding school despite the fact that for both he claimed the patronage of H.R.H. the Duke of Clarence – subsequently William IV – and later in 1827 Lieutenant-Governor Arthur appointed Giblin as Master of the King's Orphan School. Similar and frequent advertisements appeared both in Sydney

15 See the Introduction by N. D. McLachlan in *The Memoirs of James Hardy Vaux*, London, 1819, reprinted London, 1964.

and in Hobart Town but rarely with such an ambitious wealth of detail.

The Howes were an erratic family. George came out as a convict and re-established himself in society as a typical eighteenth-century man of reason: his son Robert, after early dissipation, turned methodistical and accordingly there was a marked change in the general tone of the *Sydney Gazette*, evidenced also in Australia's first periodical *The Australian Magazine: A Compendium of Religious, Literary and Miscellaneous Intelligence* which had a short life in 1821 and 1822. To Robert Howe goes the credit for making the *Gazette*, for a short time, the first daily newspaper in the colony, after 1827 to be followed by many others, while his brother George Terry Howe established the first newspaper in Launceston in 1825 and enjoyed a short career as a Tasmanian printer in that town and in Hobart. The Howe dynasty are the real founders of Australian literature. The *Gazette*, and their printing presses, gave the earliest opportunities for colonial expression. Very different opportunities were available to W. C. Wentworth in 1819 when he published in London his *A Statistical, Historical and Political Description of the Colony of New South Wales and its Dependent Settlements in Van Diemen's Land* or at Peterhouse, Cambridge, when he achieved second place for his poem 'Australia' in the contest for the Chancellor's Gold Medal. Wentworth was Australian through and through, though his education was English, and his opportunities through his father's wealth and family connections, imperial. But he had a great influence on the Australian reading public when on 14 October 1824 his newspaper, the first to compete with the semi-official *Gazette*, appeared. In May 1826 the *Australian* was followed by the *Monitor*; competing newspapers also appeared in Van Diemen's Land, and since government was still paternalistic without any elective element, the press became the opposition, where every critical mind could get full play for self-expression.

Some of the editors were men of considerable intellectual ability. Robert Wardell, who was associated with Wentworth in the *Australian*, a Cambridge Doctor of Laws, was easily the ablest barrister to practise in the early New South Wales courts; James Ross, also a Doctor of Laws, of the University of Aberdeen, edited not only the official *Van Diemen's Land Gazette* but also the independent *Hobart Town Chronicle*; E. S. Hall, the first editor of the *Monitor* had also been the first cashier of the Bank of New South Wales and from his arrival in 1811 with a recommendation from William Wilberforce had been in the forefront of every philanthropic movement in New South Wales. Amongst the eccentric contributors to the press of the 1820s was another Aberdeen Doctor, but of Divinity, Laurence Halloran, who kept himself in hot water all his time in the colony by the libellous nature of much of his writing. But Halloran serves as an example of the majority of the early ephemeral writers in Australia. It was impossible for anyone, except perhaps the government printer, to make a living from the printed word, so many were also acting as teachers or schoolmasters, sometimes in private families, sometimes in organized private schools, or working under the Church and School Corporation. Halloran, who was a prolific publisher of pamphlets of indifferent quality, was a first class teacher and, coming out as a convict who was immediately granted a ticket of leave, had considerable emancipist support when he established the first Sydney Grammar School, and later was briefly head of an institution called the Sydney Free Public Grammar School. However well he could teach his pupils, Halloran, who was obviously a very eccentric, if intellectually able, clergyman, could never get on with their parents, so his educational contributions to individual students were very spasmodic. An examination of the advertising pages of the *Sydney Gazette* draws attention to the frequent establishment of private schools in early colonial days by widows and others not necessarily qualified for much more than child-minding: but equally it is clear that the clergy and other individual private tutors could greatly influence their pupils as Henry Fulton did Charles Tompson.

It was primarily in the philanthropic societies and in the commercial life of the colonies that the various classes made contact.[16] Officialdom and the military officers ran the government and controlled the convict population but the dominant private activity at Sydney Cove was commercial with maritime interests, and in the hinterland of New South Wales and Van Diemen's Land of course, agricultural or pastoral. By Macquarie's time the older inhabitants had come to regard the colonies as their home and those free men coming out from the British islands came out primarily to trade, while the convicts awaited their transformation into emancipists in the hopes of joining them. Under Macquarie New South Wales at any rate ceased to be predominantly a penal institution and showed every sign of developing into a dynamic society.

There were of course many setbacks. By 1810 Calcutta greatly influenced the development of Australian commercial life; a number of Indian trading firms had their New South Wales partners or agents, of whom 'Merchant' Campbell (Robert) was one of the earliest,[17] but in 1811–12 there were too many shipments from India to be absorbed by the colonial market and consistently between 1810 and 1830 the imports from India far exceeded the exports to that country so that, as W. C. Wentworth pointed out, there was a constant outward flow of 'treasure' from New South Wales.[18] There were continuous

16 For the commercial history of this period see M. J. E. Steven, 'The Changing Pattern of Commerce in New South Wales, 1810–1821', in *Business Archives and History*, III, 2, August 1963, and Part IV of G. J. Abbott and N. B. Nairn, Eds., *Economic Growth of Australia 1788–1821*, Melbourne 1969.

17 See C. E. T. Newman, *The Spirit of Wharf House*, Sydney, 1961, and M. Steven, *Merchant Campbell, 1769–1846*, Melbourne, 1965.

18 W. C. Wentworth, *A Statistical, Historical and Political Description of the Colony of New South Wales, and its Dependent Settlements in Van Diemen's Land*, London, 1819.

commercial depressions between 1812 and 1815, another in 1825 which resumed in 1827; in other years like 1817, 1819 and 1820, excessive flooding had to be contended with. In addition, in 1814 when the 73rd Regiment was replaced by the 46th of only half its strength, there were so many fewer mouths to feed as to cause serious loss to stockholders. However, in general there was a shortage of meat and an over-supply of wheat, at least in the good years: most of the food supply was produced by emancipists, who by 1821 owned some 71 per cent of the land under cultivation. Wheat and meat were largely for internal consumption; wool was the principal source of export funds and export was steady and continuous, at least from 1812 when prices were high in Europe because of the Napoleonic wars and consequent continental blockade. They remained high till 1818, after which they began to decline and by that year the export of wool from Van Diemen's Land more than equalled that from New South Wales. In 1822 John Macarthur was awarded two gold medals by the Society of Arts in London for the quality and quantity of his exports to the English market; this was at a time when there was much enthusiasm for wool as Australia's basic staple, engendered by the Bigge report. Exports of wool increased from a small quantity in 1812 to no less than 2 million lbs in 1830.[19] The first medal for wine produced in New South Wales was granted in London in 1823 to Gregory Blaxland.

From the very beginning, the colonies of New South Wales and Van Diemen's Land were continuously short of clothing; the convict ships never brought enough for their passengers, and accordingly the government itself had to move into manufacturing with a factory at Parramatta, which lasted through the twenties. Flax was grown haphazardly and was processed both by the government and privately, while the emancipist Simeon Lord commenced hat-making in 1813. Sydney was dotted with windmills and there were also water mills and even a steam engine at Sydney's Cockle Creek from 1815, all for flour-milling. The government encouraged brewing but until 1823 severely discouraged distilling, which prior to that year was carried out extensively and illegally chiefly by those of Irish descent. Other evidence of manufacturing industry was to be found in iron works, boat building, tanneries or in the supply of building materials.[20]

Macquarie is the great builder of Australia's national history.[21] He was the founder of New South Wales as a civil colony, and he studded it with churches, hospitals, law courts and other official buildings to

19 See J. Ker, 'The Wool Industry in New South Wales 1803–1830', in 2 parts in *Business Archives and History*, *1*, 9, 1961, and 2, 1, 1962: E. A. Beever, 'The Origin of the Wool Industry in New South Wales', in *Business Archives and History*, *5*, 2, 1965. See also *8*, 2, 1968.

20 G. P. Walsh, 'The Geography of Manufacturing in Sydney, 1788–1851', in *Business Archives and History*, *3*, 1, 1963.

21 See G. J. Abbott, 'Government Works and Services', in G. J. Abbott and N. B. Nairn, Eds., *Economic Growth of Australia 1788–1821*, Melbourne, 1969.

a degree which brought severe criticism from Commissioner Bigge, and at an expense which greatly irritated the Colonial Office. In this activity he was fortunate to have as his architect, the convict Francis Greenway.[22] Convicted of forgery, he arrived as a convict in 1812 and by 1816 had been appointed Civil Architect and Assistant Engineer. For the next few years there was a regular flow of buildings bearing his imprint: the lighthouse at South Head, Sydney Harbour, now represented on the coat of arms of Macquarie University; the courts still existing in Queen's Square; churches at Windsor and Liverpool; and his masterpiece St James in the centre of Sydney. All these were completed before criticisms by Commissioner Bigge of wasteful public expenditure and of the cost of some of Greenway's designs. These led to a series of triangular disagreements between governor, commissioner and architect. As an architect Greenway had to work in close association with the government engineer, Major Druitt, who also made a considerable contribution to the road system of New South Wales, and the engineer found it difficult to provide the architect with workmen of the quality required for his designs. Greenway was continued as Government Architect by Governor Brisbane but he was no longer in the position of power he had briefly enjoyed under Macquarie. Without official support his work was less successful prior to his final dismissal from his public appointment in November 1822.

No discussion of the rule of Macquarie or of his immediate successors can be complete without frequent references to the Bigge Report, or, more correctly, the three Bigge Reports, on the State of the Colony of New South Wales, on the Judicial Establishments in New South Wales and Van Diemen's Land, and on the State of Agriculture and Trade in the Colony of New South Wales.[23] These were published as command papers of the House of Commons and later of the House of Lords in 1822 and 1823 but had been a long time in gestation. As Secretary of State, Lord Bathurst had become increasingly concerned about the effectiveness of the whole transportation policy and in consequence began to doubt the purpose and validity of British government policy in the Australian colonies. The expansion of New South Wales expenditure under Macquarie brought severe criticism by government, and by 1817 the secretary of state was seeking an examination of the foundations of British policy in the South Pacific. But it was January 1819 before John Thomas Bigge was appointed as

---

[22] See M. H. Ellis, *Francis Greenway*, Sydney, 1949; 2nd edition, 1953: M. Herman, *The Early Australian Architects and Their Works*, Sydney, 1954.

[23] All three were published in the *Papers* of the House of Commons (1822, XX, 448; 1823, X, 33; 1823, X, 136). Much has been published on the Bigge reports, including recently J. Ritchie, *Punishment and Profit*, Melbourne, 1970: J. Ritchie, *The Evidence to the Bigge Reports*, Melbourne, 1971: J. M. Bennett, 'The Day of Retribution – Commissioner Bigge's Inquiries in colonial New South Wales', in *American Journal of Legal History*, XV, 2, April 1971, pp. 85–105: and T. G. Parsons, 'Does the Bigge Report follow from the evidence?' in *H.S.*, *58*, April, 1972.

commissioner to investigate 'all the laws, regulations and usages of the settlements'. Bigge had already established a reforming reputation in Trinidad as chief justice, but was no very welcome visitor to Macquarie, who was increasingly enjoying his opportunity for personal rule. Bigge, accompanied by Thomas Hobbes Scott as secretary, arrived in Sydney in September 1819 and spent some two years in the colony. His reports provide a mine of information but must always be used with care as his sources of information were often suspect and his method of obtaining it most unjudicial. Macquarie may increasingly have developed into an autocrat but his philosophy of government was far more favourable to the residents of New South Wales than any views of Commissioner Bigge. The commissioner's honesty is not in question, but by background and training and through the group he associated with in the colony, he inevitably produced a report unfavourable to Macquarie but also critical of any development towards responsible government.

Bigge was severely critical of Macquarie's ambitions and at times egocentric designs, yet New South Wales is studded with memorials to the governor's energy and far-sightedness. He had only to see a new area, when he could imagine it populated with a central market town which he hastened to name, lay out and dot with public buildings in streets named after significant political and military leaders of the day. His enthusiasm knew no bounds and he displayed more confidence in the future of Australia, a word he deliberately introduced to replace New Holland, than any of his contemporaries, such as John Macarthur or the young W. C. Wentworth. It used to be the fashion to be cynical at the extent of Governor Macquarie's enthusiasm for commemorating himself, his friends and relatives, as well as the great and near great who might be influential in political circles at home, but it is now realized that there was more than mere flamboyance in the governor's unceasing activity. There was a severe commercial depression in the early days of Macquarie's rule. The 1810 Civil War in Tahiti reduced contact with the islands to which Macquarie appointed William Henry as a justice of the peace in September 1811; despite the shortage of pork from Tahiti by 1812 the colony was glutted with imports which nobody could pay for and in December of that year Campbell and Co., whose English agent, William Wilson, had gone bankrupt the previous year, was itself brought down. This was a mighty crash, for Robert Campbell was the earliest, largest and most reputable merchant the colony had supported. The Campbell and Co.'s connexion with Sydney Cove was originally established in 1796 and the firm was an offshoot of a major commercial organization in Calcutta. The depression obviously created a serious unemployment problem and it was Macquarie's policy to meet the ensuing economic crisis by an extensive policy of road-making and public building. Such obvious activities gave ample opportunity for criticism from the days of Commissioner Bigge to our own, yet the policy had contemporary merits quite apart from our pride in it today.

Compounding the effects of the economic depression was the continuing currency problem.[24] It will be recalled that Governor Phillip was sent out from England in 1788 without any store of coin. It seemed obvious that money was unnecessary in a convict economy and soldiers and government officials had their pay credited to accounts in the United Kingdom. However sensible this policy may have been to the simple-minded, it made no allowances for the fact that Governor Phillip by his second commission of April 1787 could grant pardons in the colony; that by 1790 there was already one free settler, to be followed by a continuing stream; and finally that occasional foreign ships and their crews visiting Sydney Cove and later Van Diemen's Land might wish to have some ready cash for exchange purposes.

Legally, trade with the Pacific islands, such as the trade with Tahiti, was domestic trade, but from the earliest days ships came which had commenced their voyages not necessarily in England but in India or the United States, and by the time Macquarie took over in 1810 the colonies were flooded with coins of all kinds and places of issue, guineas side by side with guilders, ducats with rupees. On his way to New South Wales Macquarie had called at Cape Town, where the governor, the Earl of Caledon, recommended to him a young banker, a fellow Ulsterman, John Thomas Campbell, and he was taken into the Macquarie party and appointed by Macquarie as his secretary. For the next eleven years Campbell's influence on the development of New South Wales was very considerable; he was loyal, honest and devoted to his master and his interests but his greatest contribution to the changing economy of New South Wales may have been in the currency and banking areas. Campbell had early served in the Bank of Ireland before going to the Cape, where he is supposed to have had further banking experience; after he ceased to be government secretary at the end of 1820 he remained in the colony as a supporter of the claims of the emancipists for civil liberties and of the establishment of a Legislative Council. Briefly in demand for administrative assistance by Governor Darling, he was also for a short time Collector of Customs and in 1829 to the satisfaction of the majority became a member of the Legislative Council when that body was enlarged. Accordingly, when reference is made to Macquarie's opinions and decisions on currency and banking problems, it must be recalled that though the decisions were his own they were based on sound and competent advice, something very few early governors received from the advisers they were provided with.

Wages in 1810 continued to be paid in cash and kind with standard equivalents established where barter was involved. Barter could result in much litigation. In a transaction involving wheat, was payment to be made at the price of wheat prevailing when the original agreement was entered into or when the due date arrived? There was accordingly

---

[24] For this problem see S. J. Butlin, *Foundations of the Australian Monetary System*, Melbourne, 1953; reprinted Sydney, 1968.

a shortage both of cash and of credit and the obvious solutions appeared to be an influx of coin and the establishment of a bank. Neither solution was immediately acceptable to the authorities in London. Shortly after his arrival Macquarie sought approval to establish a bank 'as nearly as possible on the same system and principle as the Government Loan Bank at the Cape of Good Hope', but his request was firmly refused in 1812. Rum continued to be part of wages, so also did tobacco, but, despite barter, reckoning was calculated in money terms and promissory notes were in circulation, for as little as 1/- in New South Wales, for 3d. in Van Diemen's Land. Forgery was inevitable, adding another time-consuming activity for legal authorities who, like the officers, were not above profiting from the peculiar exchange arrangements of the colonies. Thus Ellis Bent, the Deputy Judge-Advocate, arrived with 57 gallons of brandy for which he had paid £17 2s. 0d. and which he sold for £142 10s. 0d. Bent, who also trafficked in currency notes, records that a pipe of Cape wine costing £20 could be sold in New South Wales for six times the purchase price.

Trafficking in currency notes was standard commercial practice. All notes were not equally reliable; employers of labour were accused of retaining the good and paying their employees with those notes considered doubtful. The term 'currency' was employed to describe something purely local, not valid for exchange in London, so that currency lads and lasses were native Australians for whom the southern continent and not the United Kingdom was home. Currency, therefore, was primarily promissory notes, but also included coin of whatever origin, which could only be exchanged for sterling, normally treasury bills on London, at a discount. The normal difference in value between currency and sterling could be 20 per cent to 25 per cent, i.e., it took £1 5s. 0d. currency to purchase £1 sterling. In the general state of the colony, it would appear that some individuals carried huge sums in promissory notes around with them in their pockets. In the *Sydney Gazette* of 26 September 1812, Michael Hayes claimed that the contents of his pocket book stolen at the races in Sydney on the previous 22 August included notes to the value of £293 6s. 4d., ranging from one of £140 7s. 0d. in the name of Michael Robinson, to one of £1 in that of Charles Cross, and also included in the eleven entries a conditional balance on behalf of Mohammed Cassam, apparently one of the occasional lascars to land from visiting ships. Since the promissory notes were only payable to Michael Hayes' order they were of somewhat dangerous value to the thief and Hayes offered a £5 reward for their return.

Although the proposal for a bank was rejected in 1812, in the same year Macquarie received a considerable supply of coin in the form of 40,000 silver dollars. Accounts continued to be kept in pounds, shillings and pence, but the dollar was not only the normal medium of exchange but from 1822 to 1826 it appeared as if a dollar-based currency was to be established almost 150 years before it was finally

adopted. Macquarie's dollars were adjusted rather oddly before circulation. The intrinsic value of a coin in the eighteenth and nineteenth
centuries had to be very close to its nominal face value, otherwise it
became worth while to clip bits off it so as ultimately to make a
profit from the accumulated silver clippings. Today coins are purely
tokens and a mint makes a profit for government out of its coinage
activities. Macquarie directed that the dollars he had received and
whose intrinsic value over the years varied from 4s. 2d. to 5s. should
have their centres cut out and be circulated in two parts; the major
part, the ring or 'Holey' dollar, was valued at 5s. and the centre piece,
the 'Dump', at 1s. 3d. These new coins were put into circulation in
September 1813 and every effort was taken to ensure that they would
not be exported in the many trading ships which had taken away the
silver but not the copper of past years. It was a long time before the
coin in circulation was sufficient to eliminate promissory notes or
payment in kind or even barter, but credit which is so essential to
commercial development was more easily obtainable after the establishment of the Bank of New South Wales in 1817, although from the
very early days of the colony at Sydney Cove there had been individuals willing, like D'Arcy Wentworth, to make advances at interest.
The wealth of the officers of the New South Wales Corps and of other
government and military officials, where such wealth was accumulated,
was created by monopoly importing rights and the consequent opportunity to profit from making advances.

The existence side by side of currency and sterling financial transactions led to confusion; as well, the currency notes were often worn and
torn as they passed through many hands, and occasionally they were
forgeries or worthless. The absence of an expanding coinage to meet
the needs of an expanding economy also helped to persuade Macquarie
that a bank was essential if New South Wales were to prosper; against
his own judgement and Secretary Campbell's consistent advice, there
was however the firm decision of Lord Liverpool in his despatch of
26 July 1811, definitely refusing to authorize such a proposal. But
Macquarie was never hide-bound by authority; in fact, like Nelson,
he had a faculty for turning a blind eye to apparently clear and
definite orders and directions, and indeed he sometimes departed
grievously from what would normally be accepted as the truth in his
despatches home. In fact, where his own interests, or the apparent
interests of his colonial dependency were concerned, he had a remarkable faculty for self-deception. In 1816 he received as his legal adviser
Deputy Judge-Advocate John Wylde, who happily told him that since
he was not prevented by his instructions from giving a charter of
incorporation to a bank then the implication was that he could grant
one. After all, a charter was not 'contrary to the letter or spirit of any
existing Act of Parliament or in conflict with any of those principles
upon which such charters in the mother country at least have been
granted'; furthermore, the governor was specifically authorized to
create cities and towns which included the power of incorporation.

The necessity for a charter lay in the need to establish joint but limited liability and without such limitation it is doubtful if subscribers to the bank's funds could have been found. But it is to be presumed that Macquarie kept from his legal adviser any information on the despatch which firmly refused to authorize the establishment of a bank and it shows the governor's carefulness that he hesitated for four months before reporting its establishment to London.

The despatch to Lord Bathurst of 29 March 1817 did at least acknowledge that the latter's predecessor Lord Liverpool, now the prime minister, had not approved his banking proposals, but otherwise the despatch was somewhat economical of the truth and very critical of the Judge-Advocate Ellis Bent, to the contrasting advantage of Judge-Advocate Wylde, who obviously played, as did his father Thomas Wylde who had come to New South Wales with his son, a large part in the bank's establishment. The original meeting to establish public support for the bank was held in the judge-advocate's rooms on 20 November 1817; to this meeting 14 persons were invited. A further meeting took place on 22 November and on the following day Macquarie issued a proclamation supplemented by another two days later finally abolishing both currency and barter and laying down that all payments and reckonings should be made in sterling. It was subsequently agreed that all 'currency' contracts should be scaled down by one third since the premium on sterling was calculated somewhat extravagantly.

Further meetings decided that the bank's capital should be £20,000 and prior to the issuance of the charter on 22 March 1817 some £6,000 of this capital had been promised. The bank opened for business on 8 April, 1817 with J. T. Campbell as president and D'Arcy Wentworth, John Harris, Robert Jenkins, Thomas Wylde, Alexander Riley and William Redfern as directors. None of these gentlemen was an emancipist save Redfern, though emancipists had taken an important part in the preliminary meetings and were the wealthiest section of the community; Redfern is something of an anomaly since there was a resolution on the books declaring that emancipists could not be directors but the resolution seems to have had only temporary and personal reference. Wentworth, Harris and Redfern were all from the medical establishment; Wylde, a man of means, had been a London attorney; Jenkins and Riley had been agents and merchants since their arrival in the colony. D'Arcy Wentworth was the wealthiest of the directors in the colony with much practical experience of a different character from the more theoretical experience of his president and fellow County Armagh man, J. T. Campbell. Wentworth somewhat irritated his fellow directors by continuing to make advances on his own account on better terms than those offered by the bank but he denied that anyone had suggested on his election that he should be prevented from using his own money in any way he thought proper.

The Bank of New South Wales, one of the oldest and most successful of Australian institutions, had a chequered existence in its early years. By 1819 Macquarie knew that the Home Government had denied his authority to grant a charter but he made no public announcement and postponed as long as possible any acknowledgement of the despatch. As drafted by Judge-Advocate Wylde, the charter was valid for seven years and Commissioner Bigge, who acknowledged the value of the bank in his report, recommended that the easiest way out of the situation was to let the invalid charter drop at the end of its supposed validity in 1824. Instructions to this effect were sent to Governor Brisbane but these instructions were anticipated by a re-issue of the charter with minor amendments in 1823. It was September 1827 before Governor Darling finally informed the bank of a verdict originally transmitted in 1818, but by that time the bank had surmounted many crises including a defaulting cashier and was but one competitive bank among many, well able to maintain itself as a mere partnership, capable of suing and being sued in the name of the president.

On its establishment the Bank of New South Wales was authorized to issue notes ranging from 2s. 6d. to £5 but it met with competition both from the deputy commissary general and later from other organizations which occasionally developed into permanent banking establishments. It was authorized to charge 10 per cent interest on its advances to clients, an increase of 2 per cent on the immediately prevailing rate of interest, and by obtaining a considerable share of government business including a permanent deposit from the Orphan Fund did have advantages denied to the private mercantile houses: on the other hand, as is shown in the case of D'Arcy Wentworth, one could continue to act on one's own account and still be a significant bank stockholder.

Since the bank was not prepared to enter into the small savings field and since at various times government regulations denied to convicts the right to retain money in cash at least during the early part of their sentence, a savings bank for small depositors was established in 1819 at the instigation of Judge Barron Field and under the superintendence of Robert Campbell Sr. But it made limited progress in the first ten years despite a guarantee of $7\frac{1}{2}$ per cent annual interest on deposits of over £1 left in the bank for over a year. There was no compulsion on the part of convicts to bank with the savings bank; the Superintendent of Convicts, William Hutchinson, and others were active in soliciting deposits, but many convicts preferred to hide their money rather than reveal their resources, so much so that Governor Darling in 1829 directed that any such money found should be confiscated and handed over to the Benevolent Society. Nevertheless, Campbell's Bank, as it came to be called, is the precursor of the State Savings Bank of New South Wales and of the whole system throughout Australia which ultimately developed on a considerable scale.

The 1820s saw the increasing development of the two Australian colonies, but especially New South Wales, away from a convict and towards a free economy. Such a development required more money in circulation and more capital for the loan market. In every year there were considerable imports of funds from England for the support of the administrative system and equally an excess of imports over exports to maintain the growing population. The Bank of Van Diemen's Land came into being on 15 March 1824; the Bank of Australia in Sydney in July 1826; the Tasmanian Bank in Hobart had a brief existence from 1826 to 1829. But Van Diemen's Land was prolific in banking establishments, the Derwent being opened on 1 January 1828, the Cornwall Bank at Launceston on 1 May in the same year, and finally the Commercial Bank commenced business on 29 June 1829.

Increased banking opportunities were not a sign of prosperity despite the great influx of British capital in the late 1820s with the formation of the Australian Agricultural Company, which established itself north of the Hunter in New South Wales in 1826, and of the Van Diemen's Land Company which also commenced operations in 1826. Imports were vastly in excess of exports and many merchants found themselves in considerable financial difficulties only being able to trade at a loss; the years 1827–30, which were years of considerable population increase, were also years of increasing court litigation connected with inability to meet due payments. The number of writs connected with debt increased by 400 per cent between 1825 and 1829.

The greater part of the expense of the colony was met from London but there were two local systems of government income – the Police Fund and the Orphan Fund. Every three months three-quarters (after 1818 seven-eighths) of the colonial revenue, received chiefly from import duties and port dues, were paid into the Police Fund, the balance going to the Orphan Fund; many of the local salaries were paid from the Police Fund. Revenue was also obtained from road tolls, but many roads, cemeteries and school houses were established by public subscription, establishing the modern Australian practice of matching local subscriptions by central government grants. Fees were charged in most government offices and these again went towards the payment of locally appointed officials. By modern standards, road tolls were heavy, rising on the Sydney-Parramatta turnpike to as much as 3s. for a four-wheeled carriage drawn by four horses; whilst each head of horned cattle cost 2d., the lowest charge. Even higher tolls were charged on the ferries such as that from Pitt Town to Wilberforce.

With Lachlan Macquarie came a new and more effective attitude to law enforcement and withal his own regiment to ensure it. For twenty-two years the colonies had survived without a properly qualified legal officer either to advise the governors or to ensure that convicts, much less free men and emancipists, were guaranteed natural justice. The office of deputy judge-advocate-general sounded the very echo of professionalism but successive judge-advocates, as they were abbreviated, were almost inevitably military officers with little learning other than their native wit; in New South Wales only one was a trained, though very incompetent, lawyer. The possible extent of their power was quite foreign to the principles of English civil law as they had evolved over the centuries, for the single officer played many parts; he was at once committing magistrate, public prosecutor and judge. True, as a judge he was only *primus inter pares*, for he sat with two lay colleagues and might be compelled to pronounce a judgment of which he disapproved but, obviously, his power, in the hands of an able man, like Captain David Collins the first judge-advocate, could be very extensive. His successors in New South Wales were a disgrace to the office. Major Edward Abbott in Van Diemen's Land though he knew no law was both just and honest.

With Ellis Bent, the first fully qualified competent legal adviser to be appointed, Governor Macquarie established a firm friendship on the seven months' voyage out and for the first few years of Macquarie's rule the judge-advocate lent himself to the support of every procedure which would establish the rule of law on a firm footing after the revolutionary disorder of the Bligh period. John Macarthur was safely out of the country, so he could not be tried for high treason, while the officers of the New South Wales Corps, subject to military law, were being court-martialled in Britain.

Nevertheless it was obvious to the authorities in the Colonial Office and to any others at home who followed the courts martial or who studied the problems faced by successive officers administering the government of New South Wales, that a legal system more in keeping with the rights of free citizens must be established or else the colony could be nothing more than a convict prison.[25] Hardly had Bent taken up office than he also turned to the same point, advocating the appointment of a judge, the abolition of the position of deputy judge-advocate and its replacement by the appointment of an attorney-general and, more significantly, he also supported the introduction of trial by jury; for this last Macquarie was also an enthusiast. The British government was only partially convinced. The Letters Patent known as the Second Charter of Justice for the Colony of New South Wales were proclaimed in Sydney on 12 August 1814, but the office of judge-advocate remained and the authority of that officer, based on military law, over and above the authority of the new civil judge was stressed. The Supreme Court of Civil Judicature had for its first judge, Jeffery Hart Bent, a brother to the advocate-general, and he sat in conjunction with two justices of the peace. But the right of trial by jury was firmly and resolutely denied and it might have been well for Macquarie and his future peace of mind as governor if he had accepted all the implications of this refusal instead of creating trouble for himself later by appointing emancipists as justices of the peace, to the great vexation and annoyance of the 'exclusives' or 'pure merinos', the would-be native aristocracy led by John Macarthur. Under the 1814 charter there was an appeal from the Supreme Court to the governor

25 On the relations between the Home and Colonial governments see J. J. Eddy, *Britain and the Australian Colonies: 1818–1831*, Oxford, 1969.

– advised in legal matters by the judge-advocate; there was also for minor matters in each of New South Wales and Van Diemen's Land a Governor's Court or Lieutenant-Governor's Court under the presidency of the judge-advocate or deputy judge-advocate.

The nine years of judicial practice under the authority of the charter of 1814 were unhappy years for legality and justice.[26] Ellis Bent sank sadly to his grave after a distinct breach had occurred in his relations with the governor; his brother, the judge of the Supreme Court of Civil Judicature, Jeffery Hart Bent, proved quite intractable and for over two years in New South Wales drew full salary as judge without sitting on the bench for more than a brief few days, though during his ample leisure he created as much trouble for the governor as any single human being could; after all, since he was neither convict nor emancipist but held a commission from the Prince Regent which gave him considerable independence from his governor, he could not be dealt with summarily. Much of the opposition which developed towards Macquarie during the later years of his rule was concerned with the basic problem of the future of the emancipists.[27] Was a convict to be tarred with the convict brush all through life? Even after he had served his sentence, returned to civil society and perhaps entirely recovered his social position! The outstanding early governors of New South Wales – Phillip, Hunter and Macquarie – held firmly that the future of the new colony lay with the reformation, consequent acceptance and reward of those citizens transported for their country's good. Judge Jeffery Hart Bent refused, however, to open his court without a minimum of two free lawyers in the colony to appear before it. His brother Ellis had made a virtue of necessity and had allowed three convict attorneys – George Crossley, George Chartres and Edward Eagar – but not Michael Robinson, Macquarie's poet laureate – to appear before him as agents though they were warned not to consider themselves attorneys of the court and told that if 'respectable' solicitors arrived to practise in the colony then the permission to appear as agents would be withdrawn. Jeffery Bent refused point blank to accept this compromise and when he finally sat on 1 May 1815, having arrived the previous July and been sworn in on 12 August 1814, immediately found himself in a minority against his colleagues on the bench – the two magistrates William Broughton and Alexander Riley. It was a sore blow to his pride that he, a barrister of near ten years' standing, could and should be outvoted by two mere laymen, legally untrained. Broughton and Riley

---

[26] For an account of the early legal and constitutional system see C. M. H. Clark, *Select Documents in Australian History: 1788–1850*, Sydney, 1950, Section 7: C. H. Currey, *The Brothers Bent*, Sydney, 1968: C. H. Currey, *Sir Francis Forbes*, Sydney, 1968: A. C. V. Melbourne, *Early Constitutional Development in Australia*, 2nd ed., Brisbane, 1963.

[27] See P. E. Le Roy, 'The Emancipists, Edward Eagar and the Struggle for Civil Liberties' in *R.A.H.S.J.*, *48*, 4, August 1962.

were as firmly in favour of ensuring justice by permitting the appearance of 'agents' as representatives of litigants as the judge was opposed to the debasement of the court by the acceptance of ex-convicts as would-be officers of the court.

A judge who was at perpetual loggerheads with a governor; who was prepared to organize opposition to the governor's administration; who felt himself to be above the law and who consistently communicated criticism of the government of New South Wales to the authorities in London, had either to be recalled or afforded a victory by the recall of the governor. Bent was recalled, though in another despatch Macquarie was criticized for losing his temper and acting illegally himself.

As permanent successors to the brothers Bent, the home government appointed as judge-advocate, John Wylde, who arrived in October 1816, and as Justice of the Civil Court, Barron Field, who arrived some four months later in February 1817. The Bents had been brothers, the two new legal officers were close friends and in fact Wylde, the brother of a future lord chancellor of England, Lord Truro, had nominated Field, a descendant of Oliver Cromwell, to be his colleague. Strangely enough, the successive advocates-general, Ellis Bent and John Wylde, proved much more liberal in outlook than the two judges, Jeffery Hart Bent and Barron Field. While the greater part of the New South Wales Act 4 George IV c 96 of 1823 was drafted by Francis Forbes, formerly chief justice of the Supreme Court of Newfoundland, who was to become the first chief justice of the newly-constituted Supreme Court of New South Wales, his drafts were largely based on the Report of the Commission of Inquiry on the Judicial Establishments of New South Wales and Van Diemen's Land signed by John Thomas Bigge and this Report not only surveys the past judicial history of the colony but also contains much of the evidence on which its conclusions were based. Bigge's views, of course, were not necessarily triumphant. The Colonial Office, in the person of James Stephen, had its say and considerable influence was exercised by some members of parliament on the passage of the bill through the Commons. The citizens of New South Wales lobbied extensively in London: Edward Eagar, who was also supported by former governor, Macquarie, on behalf of the emancipists; Marsden, John Macarthur and others violently against trial by jury or a Legislative Council; William Charles Wentworth favourable to a Legislative Council though not specifically a representative of the emancipists.

The act of 1823 authorized the issuance by the King of a new Charter of Justice for New South Wales which would allow for the severance of the judicial systems in New South Wales and Van Diemen's Land. Each was to have its own chief justice. No longer were appeals to be made from the Van Diemen's Land courts to the governor of New South Wales taking advice in legal matters from his judge-advocate, and courts of Quarter Sessions were to be created which in the case of New South Wales under the chairmanship of

John Stephen met at Parramatta, Windsor and Liverpool as well as Sydney. Justices of the peace continued to adjudicate as previously, but with more limited powers of punishment, whilst courts of Petty Sessions were established where two or more magistrates could impose heavier penalties. Soon the growth of population outside the Sydney area became so great that a full-time stipendiary magistrate, Donald McLeod M.D., was appointed at Parramatta, to be followed in due course by others at other centres; similar circumstances in Van Diemen's Land were met by the creation of six districts with full-time police magistrates at £400 p.a. in 1827. The modern system of justice in Australia properly derives from the Act of 1823. The current chief justice of New South Wales is the lineal successor of Sir Francis Forbes, that of Tasmania of Sir John Pedder. Both were men of probity, honour and ability and the public reputation of the legal system was slowly but surely transformed.

By an order in Council of 1825 the government of Van Diemen's Land ceased to be subordinated to that of New South Wales, though Colonel George Arthur continued to be entitled lieutenant-governor. As a result of separation, distinctive legal interpretations of the 1823 Act arose in the two colonies, as Forbes was by nature more liberal in his outlook than Pedder. A hotly discussed section of the Act empowering trial by jury was interpreted by Forbes to require that free men should be tried by juries of their fellows, but limited this right to the courts of Quarter Sessions; in contrast, Pedder ruled that the Act only introduced trial by jury in cases before the Supreme Court. It was one of the duties of the respective chief justices to certify that local Acts of the Legislative Council were not repugnant to the laws of England and here again, from the point of view of the emancipist population in New South Wales, Pedder was more reactionary than Forbes, for in 1827 he certified an Act for the licensing of proprietors of newspapers as not repugnant to English law, whereas the comparable Act in New South Wales was rejected by Forbes despite the fact that the bill had been introduced on instructions from Secretary of State Earl Bathurst.

The chief justices in the two Australian colonies were not solely judicial officers; they were also the first members of the respective governor's Legislative Councils created by the Act of 1823. The other members of the first Legislative Council in New South Wales were the lieutenant-governor, Colonel William Stewart, Frederick Goulburn, the colonial secretary, James Bowman, the principal surgeon, and John Oxley, the surveyor-general, and since Governor Brisbane did not attend personally it became the practice for Chief Justice Forbes to preside. The Council was re-constituted in 1824 when Archdeacon Thomas Hobbes Scott replaced John Oxley and again in 1825 when three representatives of the colonial merchants and landowners were named members by Bathurst – Robert Campbell, the colony's leading merchant who had first arrived in 1798; John Macarthur, the colony's leading landowner who had come out with the New South Wales

Corps in 1790, and Charles Throsby, who came out as a naval surgeon in 1802 but whose position in the colony as a landowner and explorer was established after his retirement from the public service in 1809. The non-official members had been chosen by Bathurst from a list of ten submitted by Brisbane and their appointments were proclaimed by Governor Darling on 20 December 1825. The choice brought immediate protest except in the case of 'Merchant' Campbell, so called to distinguish him from John Thomas Campbell, originally Macquarie's official secretary, whose name had also been included in Brisbane's list. Protest meetings demanded the right of public election but for the time being without success, and when the Council was again re-constituted in 1829 it was still a nominated though much larger body, with seven official and seven non-official members compulsorily presided over by the governor. So Chief Justice Forbes after four and a half years of presidency was excused from a duty many, including the chief justice, thought incompatible with his high judicial office. It was 1842 before election was permitted for a proportion of the members of the Council and the same Act 5 & 6 Victoria c 76 ensured there would be no distinction between emancipists and other free citizens in eligibility for jury service or for membership of the Legislative Council.

W. C. Wentworth in his book published in 1819 had urged the concession of representative government to New South Wales similar to that accorded to Canada in 1791, but his firm opponent John Macarthur not only brought strong pressure to bear against any such democratic ideas at Whitehall but by his own personal domination of the Legislative Council ensured that his restrictive views should have full opportunity for expression. With the establishment of the Legislative Council it received authority to impose such levies and duties as might be necessary for local purposes though the pre-existing power of the governor to impose such demands of his own volition was not removed. Individual members of Council were not themselves entitled to propose laws or ordinances, all of which must still originate from the governor, and of course before any law was promulgated the chief justice was required to certify that it was not repugnant to the laws of England.

A fundamental problem to face government of any kind in New South Wales, and to a somewhat lesser extent in Van Diemen's Land, was the almost pathological hatreds which existed between leading citizens in the community. The psychological stresses and strains suffered by human beings living in confined conditions at the other ends of the earth are today still subject for scientific inquiry, but for government officials and army personnel the Australian colonies were just as much prisons as they were for the convicts. There was no escape for any from the routine of day-by-day monotony and there was the added sense of responsibility, often a hopeless sense, as communications with the homeland were postponed, which was not felt by the convicts subject to continuous if often brutal direction and control.

It would be pointless to record all the futile and insignificant details of these personal disagreements and their effect on life in the colony but if Mrs Macarthur was always admired and respected, her husband John, often bordering on lunacy, was an irascible and impossible colleague;[28] emancipists and exclusives refused to mix even at the governor's table; the officers of the 46th Regiment made a vow before arrival not to mingle socially with ex-convicts even at the governor's command. The Rev. Samuel Marsden was an old-testament Christian whose views on law and its enforcement had not been affected by the new dispensation; his punishments, ordered in his capacity as a justice of the peace, were savage; his organized persecution of individuals with whom he fell out, like Dr Henry Grattan Douglass, was a poisonous element in the community. It is normal to attribute convict law-breaking pre-eminently to alcohol and of course it is true that rum was the customary, almost the only, recreation. The convicts' betters were no doubt also addicted to the bottle, but rum and bad wine cannot be blamed for all or even a major part of the dissension and ill-feeling permanently endemic, more particularly in the colony of New South Wales. Van Diemen's Land had its eccentrics, like the Rev. Robert Knopwood, or its incompetents, like Dr Bromley, but until later it did not have the same permanent cleavage between sections of the population, partly because that population was very small, but more particularly because when the first emancipists gained their freedom there were few, if any, free settlers to attempt to keep them in their place. The movement of free settlers into Van Diemen's Land was a later phenomenon than in New South Wales.

Nevertheless, Van Diemen's Land never had anything so outrageous as the refusal of Judge Jeffery Hart Bent to pay the turnpike fees on the Sydney-Parramatta toll road and his further refusal to pay the £2 fine imposed by the police magistrate, D'Arcy Wentworth, on the grounds that 'as Judge of the Supreme Court he was by no means amenable to any criminal jurisdiction in the Territory'; compared with him the naval surgeon Edward Foord Bromley, who misappropriated £7000 or £8000 of Van Diemen's Land funds prior to his suspension in 1824 by Lieutenant-Governor Arthur, who inherited him with approving recommendations from Sorell, was a much more typical type of careless administrator. Bromley had already come under criticism in the Bigge report for bringing into Sydney on his arrival as surgeon of the general convict ship *Wellington* no less than 150 gallons of spirits, one hogshead and six bottles of wine with 10 baskets of tobacco as well as other articles purchased at Rio de Janeiro for sale in New South Wales. Small wonder that the right of such free entry was thereafter denied.

Any form of luxury was very expensive either in Sydney or in

28 See M. H. Ellis, *John Macarthur*, Sydney, 1955, 2nd ed., 1967.

Hobart – as much as four times as dear as in London, it was sometimes claimed. Meat, whether beef, mutton or pork, and bread were the staple diet. Frequently the meat was salted; in poor seasons the bread very expensive – as much as 13½d. for a two-pound loaf. In 1812 eggs were 2s. a dozen and fowls 6s. the pair. Like the publicans, bakers were licensed and since their product was essential, it was price controlled. For vegetables there were potatoes and anything else was uncertain but all was washed down by enormous quantities of spirits, as much as 4 gallons per head of population being consumed in 1818 despite a tax of 18s. a gallon. Port was available in 1811 at 72s. a dozen but white wine imported from Europe or South Africa was more expensive. Serious efforts were made by Macquarie to reduce the number of licensed houses, but the reduction from 110 in 1814 to 46 in 1820 was accompanied, according to contemporaries, by a vast increase in private distilling, unauthorized sale and consequent dissipation and this is stated also to have been the experience in Hobart in Arthur's time. The alternative or supplementary drink was tea and quite early in their history Australian colonists had also acquired a reputation in this form of consumption.

If prices were high by contemporary British standards, so also were wages; as high as 7s. 6d. to 10s. a day in 1820 in Hobart. The week-end habit grew early in Australia since convicts were given time off on Saturday afternoons to attend to their own household gardens: the first sign of the long week-end appears in the *Sydney Gazette* of 24 April 1813, when the regular Saturday market, a typical borrowing from English practice, was transferred to Friday. In the same year on 11 March the first fair in New South Wales was held at Parramatta, where cows fetched £27 to £30 a head and horses, sheep and pigs were also on sale.

From the earliest days there had been occasional horse racing and by 1804 the practice of celebrating the date of the first landing – 26 January 1788 – had begun. Australia Day celebrations were the prerogative of the emancipists. The *Sydney Gazette* of 27 January 1813, describes the elegant and sumptuous ball and supper given by Isaac Nichols for some fifty guests which lasted from 7 p.m. to 4 a.m.: in contrast, the governor's great receptions were connected with royal birthdays and Christian festivals and though there was a special allowance of spirits for soldiers and convicts, it was some time before there were any emancipist guests. The Sydney Turf Club was founded in 1825 with Sir John Jamison, son of one of the colony's first surgeons, as its president, but D'Arcy Wentworth had already been financing and organizing races for years. Sir John also became president of the Australian Racing and Jockey Club when it was founded in 1828 and, like Wentworth, also conducted races under his own private sponsorship. Thus all the main ingredients of contemporary Australian life were catered for by 1830: the long week-end; heavy drinking; the opportunity for gambling, and of course commentators were agreed that the climate produced a race of young Australians physically if not mentally superior to their parents.[29]

The departure of Macquarie and the publication of the Bigge report mark the end of an epoch.[30] The rule of Brisbane (1821–5) was an interregnum, the calm before the storm. Colonial political life comes to bitter fruition under Darling (1825–31) but the issues are not resolved for many years after his time. Macquarie, by the establishment of firm foundations, made political developments possible, but if he is one of the greatest of Australian governors, he would have been a failure had he been faced with Darling's difficulties. Before the establishment of responsible government the character of the governor made an imprint on the whole of colonial society: there was no pretence at democracy in a convict prison: the beginnings of it can be noted under Brisbane. It was no longer possible for a governor to control every detail of administration himself, so in the absence of elected representatives of the people, permanent officials, not always competent, achieved greater power. Brisbane accused his colonial secretary, Frederick Goulburn of studied disobedience, while John Macarthur, an unreliable witness, accused the secretary of being as despotic as Bligh; his attorney-general, Saxe Bannister, though a distinguished scholar and author, proved inadequate for his post, far inferior as a barrister to Dr Wardell, the associate of W. C. Wentworth in editing the *Australian*. It was the failure of his subordinates which resulted in Brisbane's recall: for himself he loyally carried out London policy and was generally sympathetic to all colonial development. Already a Fellow of the Royal Society when he came out, a peninsular hero and the friend of Wellington, Brisbane was as anxious of scientific as of political fame. So he is now chiefly remembered for his contributions to astronomical science and its development in the southern hemisphere. His astronomical books and apparatus he left for future Australian generations; his Parramatta catalogue of the Southern Stars earned him the Gold Medal of the Royal Astronomical Society, of which he became vice-president; the Royal Society of Edinburgh, of which he was President from 1833 to his death, gave him its Keith Medal for his magnetic observations made in his private observatory in Scotland. For Brisbane to be governor of New South Wales was a strange interlude in an otherwise busy and very distinguished military and scientific career. For every other governor, service in New South Wales was the main achievement of his career; Brisbane was far more

29 All aspects of social conditions in the pioneering years have been illustrated in R. Ward and J. Robertson, Eds., *Such was Life: Select Documents in Australian Social History: 1788–1850*, Sydney, 1969. See also R. Ward and K. Macnab, 'The Nature and Nurture of the First Generation of Native-born Australians', in *H.S.*, 39, November 1962.

30 Selections from Macquarie's defence of his administration (*Papers* of the House of Commons, 1828, *XXI*, 477) have been published in C. M. H. Clark, *Sources of Australian History*, London, 1957, pp. 123–35. Macquarie had written a pamphlet in 1821 entitled *A Letter to the Right Honorable Viscount Sidmouth.*

famous as a soldier and as an astronomer than as a governor, but he would have made a superlatively good constitutional ruler of the later kind. He possessed very great gifts but was very ill-served and was glad to return to his northern stars.

When Darling arrived an opposition press was fully developed and W. C. Wentworth had taken the lead in the agitation for representative institutions, trial by jury and equality for the emancipists.[31] Darling came to Sydney via Hobart where Lieutenant Governor Arthur was granted local independence from the governor of New South Wales. From the personality point of view this independence was hardly necessary, however much it was appreciated by the people of Van Diemen's Land, since Darling and Arthur were from the same military conservative world, each with previous experience in government in more backward or racially more variegated colonies – Arthur in Honduras and Darling in Mauritius. Each governor was directed to consider the advice of an Executive Council which was bound to secrecy and by bringing out his brother-in-law Henry Dumaresq, Darling ensured greater loyalty from his senior officers than had been obtained by Brisbane. But in the new climate of public affairs efficient administration was no longer enough and the inflexible opposition of Wentworth and the latter's capacity to stir up public indignation together with his continuing influence in London ensured that Darling faced similar problems to those of his predecessors in Australia. Much was made of the Sudds and Thompson affair. These were two Army privates who deliberately committed offences, the punishment for which was transportation, in order to obtain their discharge from the forces. So sentenced by the court, Darling commuted the sentences to seven years hard labour in the chain gangs. The two men were then publicly drummed out of the 57th Regiment in chains and irons to deter any of their fellows from similar action. The commutation was found to be illegal but before Sudds could be released he was dead and all of Darling's critics were in full cry, with Wentworth loudly threatening impeachment. There was a valid reason for Darling's action, however wrong it may have been, and observers then and since have exonerated him from direct responsibility for Sudds' death. Nevertheless it provided a rallying point for opposition, and in subsequent years relations between Darling and Forbes, the chief justice, gradually improved as the governor found it was wiser to listen to advice than to be pilloried later for error.

Nevertheless Darling suffered from the same fate as all early governors of New South Wales and Van Diemen's Land. He was unable to control the private information critical of government actions which was made available to both sides in parliament in England. Despite public disavowals, British cabinet ministers like Bathurst, parliamentarians like Wilmot Horton, and civil servants like James

---

[31] See the published lecture by A. G. L. Shaw, *Heroes and Villains in History: Governors Darling and Bourke in New South Wales*, Sydney, 1966.

Stephen all conducted private correspondence with Australian residents during the period 1810–30 and at all times there was the correspondence with scientists and philanthropists like Sir Joseph Banks or William Wilberforce which could be brought to bear in influencing government. A governor could have no idea of the contents of these communications; he would have been far better off with a parliamentary opposition and a free press, had he only known it. John Macarthur through the patronage of Lord Camden was able to re-establish his credit with government despite the Bligh rebellion and after his return in 1817 each governor in turn felt the power of his influence at home, much magnified by the wide circle of friends he made during his eight years exile from New South Wales, and from the fact that he obtained the ear of Commissioner Bigge during his inquiry into the affairs of the Australian colonies.

In 1830 40 per cent of the population of both colonies were of convict origin and at least 90 per cent were convict connected. The modern disparity between the populations of New South Wales and Tasmania did not then exist; under 40,000 people were resident on the mainland and nearly half that number in Van Diemen's Land, where since 1817 convicts had been sent out direct from the United Kingdom instead of being transferred for additional punishment from New South Wales. In the late 1820s there had been a steady increase not merely in the annual intake of convicts but also in the size of the military establishments, creating new economic problems for the respective administrations and additional criticism from the vociferous free population anxious for self-government, which was obviously becoming inevitable with the growth of a free native-born population.

3

1830-50

Michael Roe

Liberalism and Governor Bourke—Wakefield and South Australia—Governor Arthur and Van Diemen's Land—Western Australia—the sale of Crown lands—free immigrants—convictism—the Constitution Act of 1842—the New South Wales Legislative Council—Gipps, Fitzroy and Grey—resumption of convict transportation—separation movements—the governors of Van Diemen's Land—South Australian politics—Western Australia—local government in the colonies—the judiciary—the public service—woolgrowing and the squatters—maritime industries—government spending—mining—agriculture—commerce—urban industries—population—the depression of the 1840s—ideas and beliefs—religion and the churches—moral enlightenment and temperance—education—literature, the arts and science—colonial culture—the squattocracy—urban elites—the aborigines—convicts and emancipists—women—the free immigrants—the common people.

Down to 1842 the dominant motif in colonial politics was the operation of that liberalism which made the 1830s remarkable in Britain's political and intellectual history. Central to constitutional debate throughout the years 1830–50 was the relationship between colonies and imperial centre. This involved political organization, land policy and migration. Ideas and expediency, each springing from both Britain and Australia, interplayed; the mixture varied according to time and colony. Australian colonists cared little for the doctrinal niceties of British liberalism, but blew with the winds of change so as to secure power for themselves.

In New South Wales the champion of liberalism was Richard Bourke, governor from December 1831 to December 1837.[1] Born into the Irish Ascendancy in 1777, Bourke served well during the French wars. From 1814 to 1825 he lived in Ireland, a squire-magistrate of model responsibility. Although Bourke was a Whig, the Tory government appointed him to Cape Colony, of which he was governor 1827–8. He strove to conciliate natives outside the colony's borders and

---

1 See H. King, *Richard Bourke*, Melbourne, 1971.

to give civil rights to those within. On moving to New South Wales Bourke transferred his sympathy for Irish peasants and African natives to that community's underdogs. His support of the emancipist-liberal faction against the exclusives became the lodestone of politics.

This first became evident in Bourke's remodelling of the judicial system under the 1828 Judicature Act. Even before Bourke arrived, a local act of 1830 gave most expirees and pardoned convicts right of jury service in those civil cases where either party opted for jury trial.[2] Exclusives grudged even this, but simultaneously Bourke and the Colonial Office were agreeing that he should extend jury trial. In 1833 Bourke moved for allowing option for jury trial in criminal cases. The measure provoked a characteristic response: exclusives in the legislature were hostile, mass petitions supported Bourke, and he showed his toughness by passing the bill on his own casting vote. Australian law thereafter assimilated to the British model, especially after an imperial Act of 1839 gave the colony sovereignty in this field.

Bourke otherwise displayed his sympathies. He suspected the colony's big men of persecuting their poorer fellows, both convict and free, and therefore sought to reduce their power as justices. In 1836 he appointed crown commissioners to arbitrate in land disputes, where otherwise the grandee might have ousted any weaker rival. Bourke gathered his friends about him, and so replaced Alexander Macleay as colonial secretary with his own son-in-law, Edward Deas Thomson. He tried (vainly) to have Sir John Jamison nominated to the legislature and voluntarily presented annual financial statements to that body. He encouraged religious minorities, especially the Roman Catholic interest. Bourke was a strong, principled man, with an arrogant streak. The exclusives fought back. In the councils Bourke met opposition both from the gentry-nominees and from civil servants like Macleay and C. D. Riddell, colonial treasurer. Settlers alleged that the government encouraged convict insubordination and general lawlessness. The Sydney *Herald* voiced these and other complaints against the 'court and convict' alliance. As the 1828 Act approached the end of its original seven-year term, exclusives strove to persuade the imperial government to deliver the colony unto themselves. They argued that justices should decide who was worthy to serve on juries and to vote for a proposed Legislative Council. The outstanding exclusive propagandist was James Macarthur, whose excellent book, *New South Wales: Its present state and future prospects*, was the centrepiece of his lobbying campaign in London, 1836–7.

The emancipist-liberals, still led by Jamison and W. C. Wentworth, capitalized on Bourke's goodwill. The Sydney *Gazette* and *Monitor* answered the *Herald* in ample measure. Roman Catholics rallied to the governor, sometimes supported by Protestants who backed his aspersion of any exclusive claims by the Church of England. 'Little

2 A. C. V. Melbourne, *Early Constitutional Development in Australia*, 2nd ed., Brisbane, 1963, p. 193 ff.

men', ex-convict and always-free, who had interest in politics, joined these other groups in the Australian Patriotic Association, 1835. This too aimed at filling the power vacuum which the expiry of the 1828 Act seemed likely to create. The Association argued that a strong executive was preferable to a Macarthur-style oligarchy, but favoured representative institutions, broadly based. The colonists' agitation led not to replacing but to prolonging the 1828 statute, pending the Constitution Act of 1842. The interim was rather a limbo in political history. The exclusives and emancipists still had their grudges, but these became less vital. From 1840 the exclusives forsook opposition to ex-convicts receiving civic rights, recognizing that the home government had accepted Bourke's view and that the end of transportation made the matter less significant. Colonial politicians tended to form a united front against the new governor, George Gipps, against imperial land policy, and in support of representative institutions.

Interesting though the impact of 1830s liberalism was in New South Wales, a more dramatic chapter was the foundation of South Australia. Ideology inspired this colony as directly as any in the history of European expansion. The ideologue was Edward Gibbon Wakefield, an Englishman who edited the works of Adam Smith and applied Smith's principles, even some of his genius, to 'the Art of Colonization'. Admitted to Gray's Inn in 1813, he worked in the diplomatic service. Widowed in 1820, he aroused scandal by abducting a minor in 1826. He pursued his schemes with tremendous, sometimes neurotic vigour, and wrote prodigiously. His influence was greatest in New Zealand where he himself lived from 1853. Wakefield wanted to create societies wherein the pursuit of self-interest led to ineffable social harmony. Colonies did not spontaneously so develop, he argued, because colonial land was available too easily and this destroyed the economy's balance. Government must ensure that land sell at a 'sufficient' price: sufficient to compel the worker to remain a worker, until such indefinite time as thrift and industry could win him decent independence. Concentration of both settlement and workforce, thus achieved by the sufficient price, would foster wealth through division of labour, and a social structure hierarchical yet mobile. Within this frame, all operations of economy and man should be free – free migration, free institutions, free worship. Wakefieldianism attracted utilitarians and dissenters, philanthropists and philosophers, radicals and reformers, all characteristic of the time in Britain. 'Although the promoters had their worldly purposes, and although their ranks constantly changed as the South Australian project passed through its various stages, there was to be found, behind all the plans, the idealistic hope that the new colony would be a land free from political patronage and the evils of a privileged church'.[3]

The pre-history of South Australia indeed was complex. In January

[3] D. H. Pike, *Paradise of Dissent: South Australia 1829–1857*, Melbourne, 1957, p. 52.

1829 Wakefield, in prison for a statutory misdemeanour, received a visit from Robert Gouger. Dissenter in religion, radical in politics, Gouger had determined to use his administrative ability in colonial enterprise. From this meeting came the first proposals for a new colony, and Wakefield's fundamental treatise, *A Letter from Sydney* (London, 1829). Purporting to argue from experience that the Australian colonies were suffering from excessively generous granting of land, this booklet persuaded many that the sufficient-price concept might introduce a new era of colonial history. The National Colonization Society was founded in London in consequence. Soon afterwards came news of Charles Sturt's navigation of the Murray, which concentrated attention on the St Vincent Gulf area. Gouger submitted three plans to the Colonial Office in 1831, and became secretary of the South Australian Land Company which wove grandiose dreams. The Colonial Office feared lest settlement under such auspices mean profit for the promoters and loss for the rest, and so the company dissolved late in 1833. That December, a new South Australian Association, dominated by Gouger and the classicist-parliamentarian George Grote, resumed the initiative.

The association's schemes, revised by Colonial Office and parliament, hatched the South Australian Act, 1834. It provided for the proposed colony to be administered jointly by the Colonial Office and a Colonisation Commission of South Australia, in effect nominated by the association. The Colonial Office was to appoint a lieutenant-governor, who would share local hegemony with a resident commissioner. John Hindmarsh, a naval veteran, and J. H. Fisher, respectively filled those posts. The Crown was to sell its land at no less than twelve shillings per acre; proceeds would meet emigration and other costs. There would be no convicts, and the colony was virtually promised self-government when its population should reach 50,000. Meanwhile a nominee council would assist the governor.

The pioneers of South Australia prepared for that destiny. Their dominant spirits were 'ambitious middle-class townsmen'[4] often radical in both politics and religion. Optimism, enthusiasm, greed, all played their parts. Finance was raised through the South Australian Company, dominated by a Baptist businessman, G. F. Angas: just as Wakefield's doctrine could appear (as it did to Karl Marx)[5] a rationalization of capitalist exploitation, so South Australia was a massive real-estate gamble as well as an ideologues' Utopia. The company attended to labour as well as land, assisting the commission to select working-class migrants. The screening of applicants was fairly careful, but its efficacy ambiguous. The first ships left for South Australia in the northern spring of 1836, and began to arrive late in the year.

[4] D. H. Pike, *Paradise of Dissent: South Australia 1829–1857*, Melbourne, 1957, p. 145.

[5] H. O. Pappe, 'Wakefield and Marx', in *Economic History Review*, IV, 1951, pp. 88 97.

Over the next few years South Australia largely assimilated to the Australian norm. The division of authority between Hindmarsh and Fisher caused friction from the outset, and in October 1838 George Gawler arrived to take their combined offices. In 1840 the Colonisation Commission gave way in Britain to the Land and Emigration Commission, which attended to South Australia only a little more directly than to the other Australian colonies. The process of settlement in South Australia was as haphazard and strife-strewn as elsewhere. The sufficient price provoked intensity of speculation, not of settlement. Immigrants flowed in, but also instructions that administrative costs were to be minimal. To cope with the immigrants, Gawler flouted the instructions; his promotion of public works and rural development (himself directing the Survey) caused his replacement by George Grey in May 1841.

Yet the cutting of South Australia down to size was not the whole story. Assimilation went both ways, with the new ideas (apropos land and migration particularly) so important in South Australia's foundation coming to influence eastern Australia too. Religious life in early South Australia had a distinctively radical and non-conformist temper. The political liberalism of the colony's founders also left its mark, notably in the establishment of Adelaide city corporation – on 31 October 1840 Australia's first formal poll elected its members. From 1839 some colonists agitated for broader constitutional change.

Neither the 1828 Act nor the liberalism of the 1830s much influenced Van Diemen's Land while George Arthur remained there (1824–36). 'The Government of the Colony is nominally vested in the Lieutenant Governor and an Executive Council', wrote Auditor-General G. T. Boyes in his diary for 1835; 'I say nominally, because the Executive Council as a body is powerless. The real government is composed of Colonel Arthur, his two nephews and [R. L.] Murray, the Editor of the Tasmanian Newspaper'.[6] The two 'nephews' were John Montagu, promoted to colonial secretary in August 1835, and Matthew Forster, chief police magistrate. Arthur ruled through such men, tied to himself by financial and family bonds. They had competence worthy of their master and the early 1830s saw the apogee of Arthur's ideal – a social economy in which men of substance employed convicts and developed the island, in return for the government's bounty of assigned labour and granted land.

Dissent always existed. Its chief medium was a vigorous, vitriolic newspaper press. Henry Melville and Gilbert Robertson were the journalists most active against Arthur, and R. L. Murray's influence in the government was the counter-measure of their weight. They constantly charged government with corruption and profiteering: Arthur and his nephews did make fortunes in Van Diemen's Land, their style being that of Indian nabobs rather than of latter-day

---

6 Quoted in W. A. Townsley, *The Struggle for Self-Government in Tasmania 1842–1856*, Hobart, 1951, p. 26.

colonial servants. Opposition to government developed also within the mercantile and even the landed community. Public meetings in 1831 and 1832, a political association in 1835, argued for constitutional rights. The community was riven as deeply as was New South Wales, but with less clarity of faction and principle. 'Every man might claim, or forfeit benefits the government could bestow, and thus multitudes had personal grievances, or unsatisfied expectations', wrote John West, the near-contemporary, brilliant historian; 'the hostilities of the day were almost invariably associated with some sense of individual wrong'.[7] The feeling against Arthur showed personality and spite rather than doctrine. The lieutenant-governor showed a corresponding imbalance in regarding his recall (January 1836) as an affront, albeit he had then spent twelve years straight in the island and recently had been told by James Stephen that 'Of all the Governors which this department has employed in my time, you have enjoyed the most uninterrupted reputation ... and the strongest hold upon the favourable opinion of your official superiors'.[8] Arthur later served in Canada and India, where in 1844 he was nominated provisional governor-general. Ill-health thwarted the fulfilment of probably the most remarkable career of any imperial servant who worked in Australia.

The new wave of the 1830s came to Van Diemen's Land with John Franklin, lieutenant-governor 1837–43. Famed as an arctic explorer, Franklin was generous and innocent. His brilliant, forceful wife, Jane, encouraged his hopes to establish freer institutions, culture, and amity. Economic vagaries and imperial policy (especially in flooding the island with convicts) defeated them. Moreover Franklin quarrelled with Montagu, Forster, and the Arthur clique generally; newspaper criticism became almost as extreme as under his precursor. Montagu caught the ear of the Colonial Office, and demonstrated how potent was that faculty in determining Australian politics. Franklin was recalled in disgrace and humiliation. He sought redemption in further arctic exploration, on which he died in 1847.

The constitution of Western Australia became similar to that of the other colonies in the 1830s, and then stood still. The Legislative and Executive Councils foreshadowed by the Act of 1829 first met in February 1832. Immediately colonists called for some representation, even for elections. After long negotiation, four non-officials joined the Legislative Council in 1838. Successive governors were James Stirling (to 1838) and John Hutt (1839–46).

New attitudes thus affected constitutional issues up to 1842. Their wider impact by then had affected policies concerning convicts, free migrants, and land. The details were complex, but everywhere worked liberal themes: development of free market forces, abolition of privilege, philanthropy (real, if shallow), belief that men of the past

[7] J. West, *The History of Tasmania*, Launceston, 1852, I, p. 176.

[8] Quoted by A. G. L. Shaw in 'Sir George Arthur', in *Australian Dictionary of Biography*, Melbourne, 1966, I, p. 36.

were usually wrong or corrupt whereas present ideals were pure.

Substitution of grant by sale was the vital fact concerning Crown land. Informed British opinion moved in favour of sales from the mid-1820s: thereby colonies would defray their costs and so qualify for political independence. Wakefieldians pushed for sales throughout Australia not only as propagandists for their ideology, but also to ensure equality between any Wakefieldian colony and the rest. The imperial government showed Wakefieldian influence in proclaiming the Ripon Regulations, 1831–2. Henceforth Crown land was alienable only by auction, at a five shilling per acre minimum. The regulations applied generally, although in Van Diemen's Land, Arthur (aware that free market forces must imperil his system) thwarted them by issuing many promises of grant, while in Western Australia virtually no one wanted any land not already alienated. Wakefieldian principles and administrative convenience combined to limit sales in New South Wales to the nineteen counties.

Over the decade the new system altered in accord with a rather desperate effort to meet local exigencies. A uniform price of £1 per acre prevailed from the outset in South Australia, and this created pressures which in 1839 increased the minimum price for the eastern colonies to twelve shillings. The next year lands' administration became the business of the Land and Emigration Commission.[9] Colonial Secretary of State Lord John Russell, in Wakefieldian vein instructed the commission to prepare a comprehensive policy. It proposed that New South Wales be divided into three parts: south of the Murrumbidgee land would sell at a fixed one pound per acre; the middle district would not change; later a northern district would follow the southern plan. In the southern district, moreover, purchasers could buy for £4000 any 4000 acres from an eight-square mile 'special survey', a scheme already operating in South Australia. Overall, the hope was to encourage British investors to buy first the best land in the fixed-price regions and so to instigate ramifying activity. Great disfavour met the plan in New South Wales: colonists foresaw the central district languishing under its proposed 'dismemberment' while Gipps not only agreed with this but maintained that the fixed price provisions, above all the special survey, were too generous. Similar misgiving arose in Britain and during 1841 the plan was dismantled. The next year the Australian Land Sales Act provided for sale by auction at a minimum of £1 per acre throughout Australia, with the right of buying 20,000-acre blocks at that fixed price.

Meanwhile the New South Wales governors had contended with 'squatting' – the occupation of Crown land, often far beyond the counties, for grazing. Squatting was the dominant economic growth of the period, and depended on extensive use of vast areas: imperial Wakefieldian theory, urging concentrated settlement and land sales at high prices, stood contrary to colonial reality. Bourke and Gipps

9 See P. Burroughs, *Britain and Australia 1831–1855*, Oxford, 1967, ch. 7.

both saw the contradiction, and that they had to recognize squatting, if only to police it. A local Act of 1836 extended beyond the counties permission to graze for a £10 licence; in 1839 a stock tax was added. Both provided for supervision, through Crown lands' commissioners.[10]

Land was an important issue in the debate over self-government. Wakefieldian reformers upheld extended local power yet insisted that colonial land was an imperial concern, to be administered for the benefit of all Britons, then and thereafter. This insistence caused colonists, who saw the land as theirs alone, to become ever more hostile to the Wakefieldians, theoretically their allies in the cause of liberty. In New South Wales especially, settlers felt that they were being sacrificed to the doctrines and jealousy of South Australia's backers. Bourke and Gipps endorsed this contention.

Free migration was a happier aspect of the new reformism. It meshed with the self-government cause (since Wakefieldians and administrators affirmed that a penal colony could never achieve that boon), and with land sales (as thence might come the money to subsidize migration and so counter the distance and penal image which blemished Australia as a migrant haven). Virtually coincident with the Ripon Regulations, commissioners for emigration were appointed.[11] Although they survived only a year, permanent government activity in this field had begun, a significant departure in British administrative-constitutional history and in Australian development. Secretary to the commissioners was T. F. Elliott, who in 1837 became agent-general for emigration and from 1840 the dynamic member of the Land and Emigration Commission.

Big problems beset this question. How much of the land fund should go to migration; how to spend most effectively what money there was; how to attract and identify migrants of good quality: these controversies tossed back and forth before answers crystalized. In 1842 the Colonial Office prescribed that half of the land fund should thus be spent, half on other colonial works. Control of finance came to rest in London after the 'bounty' scheme, whereby colonists received subsidies for organizing the despatch of migrants to themselves, fell into chaos early in the 1840s. Scandals and complaints as to the quality of migrants never ceased, but probably became less justified in later years. Anyway, the migrants came in significant numbers.[12]

---

[10] See P. Burroughs, *Britain and Australia 1831–1855*, Oxford, 1967, pp. 150–56.

[11] See P. Burroughs, *Britain and Australia: 1831–1855*, Oxford, 1967, p. 69 ff: R. B. Madgwick, *Immigration into Eastern Australia 1788–1851*, London, 1937, p. 93 ff.

[12]

	To Australia	To N.S.W.
1831–35	14,047	8,140
1836–40	53,835	29,663
1841–45	40,306	38,395
1846–50	74,455	38,518

From P. Burroughs, *Britain and Australia 1831–1855*, Oxford, 1967, Appendices 2 and 3.

As British reformers upheld free migration, so did they attack the convict system.[13] The anti-slavery tradition, strong among both Wake-fieldians and British élites generally, found convictism abhorrent. Further, the right to convict labour was a form of privilege, so detestable to all liberals and especially to South Australian investors, anxious lest their colony suffer any handicap as against the others. Various official enquiries culminated with the 'Molesworth' House of Commons Committee, 1837–8. Dominated and manipulated by Wake-fieldians, its report scarified transportation and especially assignment. The Colonial Office already had such sympathies and in mid-1838 it instructed that assignment was to end; from 1840 all transportation direct to New South Wales ceased for some years.

Convicts still existed: in resolving that problem the reformers were at their weakest. Both the Molesworth committee and the Colonial Office approved more gaols in Britain, intensified use of Norfolk Island, and gang labour especially in Van Diemen's Land. Helping the committeee to such conclusions was the pamphleteering of Alexander Maconochie, who had gone to Van Diemen's Land as Franklin's private secretary and there developed a very ambitious scheme of convict treatment. It proposed that all punishment aim at regeneration; prisoners should work co-operatively, and every stimulus be given to good conduct. As commandant at Norfolk Island, 1840–44, Maconochie had his chance at practice – but a modest chance, as Lord John Russell lost faith in him before he began. The chief burden of the changes fell on Van Diemen's Land, whither convicts poured, to be organized into gangs as well as the administration could manage. The imperial authorities issued high-minded directives – most notably apropos the probation system (1842), whereby convicts were to pursue a *cursus honorum* from gang to wage-earning. But the island became more deeply mired in convictism, while New South Wales abandoned that character.

Residents of both colonies suspected these changes. Many denied the reformers' postulate that penalism and self-government were incompatible; they wanted both. In 1836–8 James Macarthur, fearing emancipists' political weight, had endorsed abolition, but even he changed sides and most gentry thought assignment too valuable to forsake. The emancipists agreed, having as well a sentimental-political attachment to convictism. In Van Diemen's Land the new order appeared wholly for the worse, denying assigned labour yet maintaining convict costs and vice.

The Constitution Act of 1842 divided political history, especially in New South Wales. There the Act created a Legislative Council of thirty-six members, twenty-four elective and twelve (half Crown officials, half private persons) nominee. A £20 franchise restricted the vote to stable and solvent men, but did not discriminate against ex-convicts; candidates for election had to own substantial wealth. The

---

[13] A. G. L. Shaw, *Convicts and the Colonies*, London, 1966, especially ch. 12.

constitution gave 'representative' government: legislation dealing with local issues had to pass Council, and might originate there. The governor could withhold his approval from legislation, and the imperial government disallow it. Crown lands and their revenue were reserved from the legislature's orbit; 'schedules' to the Act specified the paying of £81,600 for executive and judicial salaries (so guaranteeing the Crown's servants independence from the legislature), and for aid to religion.

Within these new forms the colonists pressed for greater power as against the imperial centre. The movement had a long history, stretching back at least to the rebellion of 1808. In the 1820s and 1830s emancipists and exclusives battled so fiercely because each aspired to succeed to imperial power. Colonists in the old legislature protested every imperial exaction, especially the requirement that local revenue meet police and gaol expenses. Had there been no 1842 Act the movement would have swelled anyway: the points at issue were important, yen for power was strong, and rancour (especially in depression years) deep.

Nevertheless the new Act made politics more interesting and fluent, as was evident in the first elections. The campaign itself spread from December 1842 to June 1843. 'The keynote . . . was dissatisfaction with the Imperial Act under which the election was being held and a desire for a greater degree of self-government.'[14] Foremost in such opinion remained W. C. Wentworth, a successful candidate for Sydney. The electorate returned other brilliant men – Richard Windeyer (whose name will recur), Charles Cowper (future premier), T. A. Murray (squire of Yarralumla), William Bland (war-horse of the emancipist liberals). The Sydney electorate was hardest fought; election day there saw mob ferocity. Once in session, Council prepared itself against executive. The 'schedule' moneys were insufficient for government needs; Gipps had to ask the Council for more, and in recompense admitted its right to debate the spending of both this and the schedule sums. The right was used, especially to reduce judicial and police costs. Loathing taxation, the legislators also forced postponement of a plan for 'District Councils', local government bodies with power to raise revenue. They refused to present a 'humble' address to Gipps, and altogether bordered on contumely.

The governor sharpened the situation. 'Inflexible both in principle and character, Gipps had an admirable if not a sympathetic nature', according to one historian, while another sees him as 'governed by high principles, a strong sense of justice, and unostentatious generosity'.[15] He came to New South Wales after an honourable career in military engineering and administration. His ideas on colonial government had

---

[14] R. Knight, *Illiberal Liberal*, Melbourne, 1966, p. 42.

[15] R. Knight, *Illiberal Liberal*, Melbourne, 1966, p. 28: S. C. McCulloch, *George Gipps*, Melbourne, 1966, p. 6.

developed in 1836–7 as he served on a commission investigating the troubles of Lower Canada; it advised against granting extended powers over local finance. Under pressure of events, Gipps came to see the Council as his antagonist – a justifiable attitude, but one which ensured its own truth – and manoeuvred against it. He, like the Council, was especially sensitive on finance: whereas it grudged tax, he grudged expenditure. In logic these attitudes could ally, but in fact they grated. Gipps appeared as a governor who ground the colonists and spent a minimum for their betterment.[16]

Anger against governor, constitution, and depression, boiled over in April-May 1844, when Gipps announced plans for dealing with land occupation and ownership.[17] Theoretically his was a sensible, even brilliant, design to meet those two difficult and contrary problems: how to adhere to the imperial principle that land sell at no less than £1 per acre, how to control (and tax!) squatting. Gipps proposed two sets of regulations. The first allowed leasehold for £10 a year per station (normally twenty square miles); the second provided for gradual purchase of the station, in instalments of 320 acres for £320, each instalment guaranteeing secure tenure for eight years. Most politically active colonists joined in the antagonistic response, working through public meetings and petition, the classic 'out-of-doors' media, and through the legislature. Squatters bemoaned their insecurity of tenure, and claimed pre-emptive rights (i.e. the first offer to purchase should the Crown put their runs to sale). A Legislative Council committee endorsed these arguments, as part of a broadside attack on the 1842 Land Act. That should be repealed, went the committee's refrain, and local authorities determine its successor. Feeling rose high enough to prompt talk of revolution, and Gipps asked that imperial troops stay at full strength.

The Council fought on other fronts during 1844. The most important of many other committees reported on 'all grievances not connected with the lands'.[18] It sought responsible government, virtually in the modern sense – that the legislature should determine membership and judge actions of the executive. This committee attacked the district councils scheme and the exaction of police costs, stressing that no longer did transportation benefit the colony. Fretting over revenue continued during the session. The legislature sought further to undercut the executive by appointing Francis Scott as its agent in the House of Commons. The intellectual force of the attack matched its stridency.

16 K. Grose, 'Sir George Gipps: Prince of all Skinflints?', in *R.A.H.S.J.*, *50*, 6, December 1964.

17 B. Dyster, 'Support for the Squatters, 1844' in *R.A.H.S.J.*, *51*, 1, March 1965: K. Buckley, 'Gipps and the Graziers of New South Wales, 1841–6, in *H.S.*, *24*, May 1955, and *26*, May 1956.

18 Discussed in A. C. V. Melbourne, *Early Constitutional Development in Australia*, 2nd ed., Brisbane, 1963, p. 308 ff.

Arguments flowed in fine language, backed with weighty documentation. Wentworth and Windeyer, the early standard bearers, had charisma and erudition. The land-regulation fight had won to their side Robert Lowe, then a nominee councillor. A lawyer, and distinguished Oxford scholar, Lowe had migrated in 1842, hoping to improve his sight. He soon displayed that ability which was to make him Chancellor of the Exchequer under Gladstone. Lowe's biting of Gipps's hand, which appointed him councillor, owed something to the twist of his character, but accorded too with his veneration for the constitutional rights of Englishmen. In Council and out (especially through the *Atlas* newspaper), Lowe thrashed the governor with verve, wit, and learning. He resigned his nominee seat in August 1844, but won election in the April following.

The next few years saw some easing of the colonial-imperial conflict. The squatters quickly came to hope after the storm of mid-1844 that the British government would meet their demands; after delay and confusion the Australian Land Sales Act 1846 and a consequent Order-in-Council March 1847, did grant them pre-emptive rights and fourteen-year leases. The squatting interest therefore slackened its drive against the government. In 1846 commentators distinguished three Council parties – government, squatters, and opposition.[19] Even within the last, feeling fluctuated between moderates and Lowe-Windeyer extremists. The extremists suffered set-backs when the respectability spurned the call of the *Atlas* for a boycott of the Queen's Birthday levee, 1845; and when Britain's repeal of the Corn Laws aborted their campaign against the imperial duty on Australian grain – a campaign which espoused the wheatgrower just as that of 1844 did the pastoralist, and which identified with the radical spirit of the British Anti-Corn Law League.

Moderation strengthened with the departure of Gipps, one more Australian governor to be beaten and broken at the task. Sir Charles FitzRoy succeeded him in August, 1846. Of aristocratic background, FitzRoy disparaged constitutional nicety; he conceded to the legislature, even connived with local against imperial interests. Had he been a free agent, he might have led a complacent New South Wales into responsible government. Imperial policies destroyed that chance. Their evil genius was Henry George Grey, Earl Grey, Colonial Secretary of State from June 1846 to February 1852. Long a colonial reformer, Grey accepted Wakefield's view as to the importance of colonies but interpreted that importance differently. He was a man of intellect, principle and determination – characteristics destined to arouse rather than impress Australian opinion. The land policy of 1846–7 was one result of Grey's accession; the squatters welcomed it, but public opinion became increasingly prone to see the imperial government and the squatters as coalescing to deny other colonial

19 R. Knight, *Illiberal Liberal*, Melbourne, 1966, p. 133.

interests any right in the land. Robert Lowe, once the squatters' champion, became their scourge – and many others underwent the same conversion, if less dramatically. Grey attracted still further antagonism with his plans for constitutional change and renewed transportation.

In mid-1847 Grey submitted for Australian comment a new constitution. 'There was to be a pyramid of institutions, rising from municipal bodies at the bottom to bicameral colonial legislatures and a federal assembly at the top'.[20] In New South Wales, politicians criticized every aspect, but especially the revival of district councils, which would elect members of the lower house. Grey next had the scheme considered by the Privy Council Committee on Trade and Plantations. A re-draft, making bicameralism and district councils optional, went before parliament in 1849. Australian criticism continued, and Grey also withdrew his federation idea before the bill passed. Thus the Australian Colonies Government Act, 1850, was scarcely a victory for Grey; giving New South Wales only a lower £10 franchise, and vague promise of further change, it won little esteem there either.

Grey's concurrent pushing of his convict schemes did more to foment anger. Time had proved the changes of 1838–40 premature: the alternatives to assignment had failed. In 1844 Britain began sending to Port Phillip as well as to Van Diemen's Land 'exiles', men holding tickets of leave. The scheme had but moderate success, and so there revived plans for a new penal colony. Gladstone, on the north-east coast, was selected, but difficulties smothered the scheme in mid-1846. Coincidentally the New South Wales Legislative Council was asked whether it would accept resumed transportation. After much equivocation the Council agreed in April 1848; Grey undertook to transport only men with tickets-of-leave or conditional pardons, and to finance the concurrent migration of equal numbers of free people.

This harmony soon ended. Public opinion was more critical of transportation, on moral and social grounds, than was the Council; Grey broke his promises about free migration. As the *Hashemy* and *Randolph*, the first transports under the new scheme, approached Sydney, colonial feeling became remarkably militant. On 1 June 1849, the Council repudiated its agreement with Grey, while two tremendous public meetings on 9 and 18 June sounded a note of rebellion. The transports sailed on to Moreton Bay, where employers were found. Four more shiploads followed, and Grey hoped that Moreton Bay might be his loophole: both there and in New England squatters contemplated separation from New South Wales in order to facilitate reception of exiles.[21] But in Sydney politicians and people stood

20 J. M. Ward, 'Henry George Grey', in *Australian Dictionary of Biography*, Melbourne, 1966, *I*, p. 482.

21 A. C. V. Melbourne, *Early Constitutional Development in Australia*, 2nd ed., Brisbane, 1963, pp. 408–9.

hostile. The New South Wales Association for Preventing the Revival of Transportation was a vigorous and interesting body, comprehending all liberal and radical opinion.[22]

Meanwhile the second general election, mid-1848, had further sharpened the anti-imperial cause. The squatting representation declined, which both reflected and boosted feeling that squatters and imperial government had united in their will to monopolize the colony's lands. Lowe, supreme exponent of this view, won election for Sydney after a campaign organized by men of comparatively humble rank (Henry Parkes their leader) and directed towards working-class sentiment. The new legislature showed yet keener appetite for the spoils of self-government: one group of aspirants, descended from the old emancipist party, gathered around Wentworth. Other factions probably had similar, if less patent hopes.[23] The honeymoon with FitzRoy therefore ended. The bitterness of 1844 never quite returned, but the Annual Estimates of Revenue and Expenditure (especially in 1849) were contested, and public meetings were militant. At mid-century most politically conscious residents of New South Wales were straining for greater constitutional change than the Australian Colonies Government Act granted.

Quest for local power motivated Australian politics outside New South Wales throughout the 1840s, albeit with less brilliance and force. Even within the mother colony proceeded the separation movements – in Moreton Bay, New England, and, more importantly, Port Phillip. British associates of the pastoral pioneers there had suggested a separate colony as early as 1836. Reality was much more modest: William Lonsdale was police magistrate in charge from September 1836 to October 1839, when C. J. La Trobe became superintendent. The colonists soon began to plead for independence; Russell's 'dismemberment' proposals of 1841 would have virtually clinched the matter and their abandonment heightened frustration. The representation of Melbourne and the Port Phillip district in the New South Wales legislature under the 1842 constitution irked more than it satisfied. Gipps and Grey both endorsed separation in consequence of their stress on local government, but as Grey's constitutional proposals vacillated, Port Phillipians became more militant. In 1848 they elected Grey himself as a Council representative, in protest against their situation. The Australian Colonies Government Act created modern Victoria and gave it the same constitution as New South Wales.

Various elements tensed Van Diemen's Land politics. Upholding the incompatibility of penalism and free institutions, the Colonial Office exempted the island from the 1842 Constitution Act. Failure of the gang system strengthened discontent. The depression of the early

[22] See J. M. Ward, *Earl Grey and the Australian Colonies: 1846–1857*, Melbourne, 1958, p. 203 ff.

[23] See J. Forrest, 'Political Divisions in the N.S.W. Legislative Council, 1847–1853' in *R.A.H.S.J.*, 50, 6, December 1964.

1840s was as ruinous as in New South Wales. The island's counterpart to the storm of April 1844 came in 1845 when settler nominees in the Legislative Council, led by Richard Dry and T. G. Gregson, fought the financial stringency threatened by the Estimates. On 31 October six nominees paralysed the government with a 'walk-out'; public opinion lauded them as 'the patriotic six'. Sir John Eardley-Wilmot, lieutenant-governor 1843–6, sympathized with the colonists' problems yet described this opposition as 'radical, in fact Jacobinical'. A year later Wilmot received his recall, prompted in part by his failure to manage the convict system: doubly then was he a victim of the colonial-imperial dialectic, and his death in Hobart, February 1847, made him, even more than Franklin or Gipps, its martyr.

The next lieutenant-governor, Sir William Denison, was not the martyr type. Of renowned high-bourgeois family, his own chief skill was as a military engineeer. Denison was a Tory, his tactics often crude. He endorsed most of Earl Grey's policies, especially continued transportation, and this became the flashpoint. Local opponents of transportation were articulate in expression, sophisticated in organization. At Launceston in January 1849 they founded the Australasian League for the Abolition of Transportation, which soon attained inter-colonial vigour. Denison complained of public meetings which aspired to 'take upon themselves the whole of the legislative and executive functions of this government' and saw the anti-transportationists as a gang of bankrupt rebels.[24] In the Legislative Council, opposition to Denison was strong but not crippling. Meliorating influences were economic improvement and the Australian Colonies Government Act, which established the same representative government as elsewhere.

South Australian claims for more liberal government received some answer in an 1842 imperial Act which created a nominee Legislative Council (three official members, four private) and repeated the promise of representative institutions. The new Council little affected Sir George Grey, who rather used it to over-ride both Colonial Office and local opinion. F. H. Robe, lieutenant-governor from October 1845 to August 1848, showed less talent and toughness: a Tory and a High Anglican, he had all the wrong qualifications. One policy which especially aroused his subjects was the attempt to restrict sales of potentially metal-bearing land and to collect royalties from the mineral wealth of land already alienated. In October 1846 the private legislators had their 'walk-out' on this issue. Robe prepared to concede, but Earl Grey was more insistent; when the colonists did win – in August 1848 the Supreme Court ruled against royalty-collection – their enthusiasm was the more strident. Robe meanwhile had pressed for state aid to religion. Anglican legislators and the Colonial Office supported him, but the South Australian League for the Maintenance of

24 Quoted in M. Roe, *Quest for Authority in Eastern Australia 1835–1851*, Melbourne, 1965, p. 77.

Religious Freedom mounted a campaign comparable in technique and intensity with that of the anti-transportationists elsewhere. Nevertheless aid did operate from 1846 to 1851.

Robe's successor, Sir Henry Fox Young, had troubles, but palliatives too. His public works programme met opposition for its cost and alleged enhancement of Young's own properties. The ending of the royalties issue had softened colonial feeling, however, and discussion of Grey's constitution lessened concern for local grievance. This discussion had a strong radical tincture – colonists criticized the federation scheme, imperial retention of the land fund, the idea of an upper house (which might spawn a local ascendancy), and the non-responsibility of executive to legislature. The Australian Colonies Government Act, when it came, was little more popular in Adelaide than in Sydney.[25]

During the 1840s Western Australia's scanty population wrestled not with constitutional debate, but with basic issues of land and labour. An odd passage in this story was the settlement of a Wakefieldian model colony at Australind near Bunbury; from 1840 to 1844 it battled the environment, and lost. Arguments over land echoed those in New South Wales. The minimum price was increased to £1 per acre in 1840, government hoping thereby to halt speculative acquisition; colonists replied that the price should be five shillings, to attract capitalists and build an emigrant fund. When instead the imperial government prescribed the same long lease for Western Australia as for New South Wales under the Act and Order of 1846–7, prospects for growth dimmed accordingly. Therefore settlers asked that Britain send convicts, the first of whom arrived in mid-1850. This difference in growth between Western Australia and the other colonies left it untouched by the Australian Colonies Government Act. New governors in the decade were Andrew Clarke (1846–7), and Charles FitzGerald (1848–55).

Antipathy to local government bodies as agents of taxation not only aborted the district councils schemes but dominated the history of all such institutions. Legislation in New South Wales, commencing with a Parish Road Act 1833, managed to produce only four puny Road Trusts by mid-century. When Governor Bourke first suggested the incorporation of Sydney in 1835, a public meeting so forcefully attacked the scheme, for its threat of taxation, that Bourke abandoned his plan. Gipps revived it in 1840, but exclusives sought to deny the municipal franchise to ex-convicts and so delayed progress. Two years later, with a non-discriminatory £25 franchise prevailing, the first polls took place. The electors disparaged candidates of traditional respectability, choosing those of humbler background and recent wealth. Corporation politics proved petty but strenuous; efforts to provide

25 D. H. Pike, *Paradise of Dissent: South Australia 1829–1857*, Melbourne, 1957, p. 411 ff: J. M. Ward, *Earl Grey and the Australian Colonies: 1846–1857*, Melbourne, 1958, p. 152 ff.

basic services had only moderate success. Councillors quarrelled among themselves and with the Legislative Council, a rival for power and prestige. In 1849 the legislature appointed a committee to enquire into the corporation. It discovered, and exaggerated, favouritism, extravagance, self-interest – in short, corruption. A few market commissions had developed meanwhile: that at Parramatta prompted the first, and keen, public election in New South Wales in February 1841.

Earlier still was the first election for Adelaide's corporation. Here the respectability did dominate at first – but only for a year, after which new men took over, only to become so factious that the government replaced them with a commission in 1843–51. Lieutenant-Governor Young established elective district boards in 1849, hoping to prompt road improvements. Big proprietors won election, and struck minimal rates. Even so hostility to this impost and to a current wagon tax provoked a 'great confederated Anti-Dray and Land Tax League'. The dray tax ended, and many small farmers didn't pay rates, 'though perhaps as much from poverty as principle'.[26]

The Act which created the Sydney corporation did so for Melbourne too. The first election on 1 December 1842, was 'a great day in Melbourne, the precursor of many an election Saturnalia'.[27] Factionalism was always vigorous, abetted by sectarian division and extravagant journalism. As elsewhere, money was short yet the power-urge strong. Both factors created antipathy towards the executive, which grew when the Council espoused Port Phillip separation. The corporation's history bespoke the ardour of contemporary politics, but it did only a little to make Melbourne handsome, or even decent.

Road boards operated in Tasmania from the early 1840s, contributing a modicum to development. Both Franklin and Wilmot believed that Hobartians should take some administrative and financial responsibility for their city. Threat of further taxation killed their first bills, but in 1846 a Court of Commissioners was elected, after some excitement. The court was happy to make decisions and wield patronage, less happy to levy rates. Its legal powers, especially concerning taxation, were disputed. Denison and the commissioners blamed each other for the confusion, and in September 1847 the court adjourned forever.[28]

The judiciary had its part in colonial politics both in the struggles against imperial control and in domestic factionalism. In New South Wales, Francis Forbes (chief justice, 1824–37) backed Bourke's liberalism; he saw the colony as amenable to the norms of British justice. W. W. Burton (judge, 1832–44), contrarily, insisted New South Wales

26 D. H. Pike, *Paradise of Dissent: South Australia 1829–1857*, Melbourne, 1957, pp. 409–10.

27 E. Finn ('Garryowen'), *Chronicles of Early Melbourne*, Melbourne, 1888, *I*, p. 260.

28 M. Roe, 'The Establishment of Local Self-Government in Hobart and Launceston', *T.H.R.A.P.*, XIV, 1, December 1966.

was far removed from those norms, by reason of its moral and criminal depravity. The exclusives used his authority in their anti-emancipist campaign, and James Macarthur lobbied the Colonial Office in hope of gaining Burton's succession to Forbes. Instead the prize went (till 1844) to James Dowling, who reflected the changing times by supporting emancipist civil rights without becoming a partisan. J. W. Willis had a sadder experience. Arriving in the colony in 1838, he soon showed himself a man of many quarrels; among his antagonists were Dowling and the Roman Catholic interest. To ease matters Gipps appointed Willis to Melbourne in January 1841, but soon political society there divided for and against him. The paraphernalia of petition, counter-petition, editorial, counter-editorial, inflamed the schism, till Gipps removed Willis in June 1843. Long discussions in Britain ended in ambiguous judgement on the step's validity. A more dramatic amoval was that of Algernon Montagu by Denison in Van Diemen's Land in December 1847. It followed Montagu's ruling that a dog tax was invalid: this threatened the legality of all local revenue-raising and so boosted the opposition to Denison. Montagu was vulnerable because of the confusion of his own finances and the Privy Council supported Denison. The disallowance by Charles Cooper (sole judge in South Australia, 1838–52) of the royalties on mineral-producing land further demonstrated how the Bench's verdicts could link with politics.

Judges were important in colonial society. Montagu and Willis occasioned scandal, but most were respectable and solid: Dowling, Alfred Stephen (N.S.W. judge, 1839–44; thereafter chief justice), and John Pedder (V.D.L. chief justice from 1824) were prototypes. Some possessed intellect – Forbes, William a'Beckett (N.S.W. judge from 1844, future chief justice of Victoria), and Roger Therry (N.S.W. judge from 1845). Similar judgements apply to the high executive officers of government. They often tangled with politics and factionalism, especially in the earlier years – witness the pro- and anti-governor factions within the executives of Arthur, Bourke, and Franklin. It was Lady Franklin's accumulation of influence, supplanting his own, which caused John Montagu to persuade the Colonial Office that Franklin was incompetent. In New South Wales the 1842 constitution tended to consolidate the executive against the legislature's opposition; in Van Diemen's Land Wilmot avoided great antagonism of his officials, while Denison did antagonise but had the strength to override. Never were executive officers absolute in their support of governors, even in the legislature.

The public service, like the Bench, contributed men of social worth. Edward Deas Thomson characterized that large number which settled in New South Wales; after twenty years as colonial secretary he entered the post-1856 Legislative Council and intensified his good works for the University, the Infirmary, and the Benevolent Society. His family intermarried with that of his erstwhile precursor and antagonist, Alexander Macleay, whose sons contributed still more than did Thomson to Australian culture. J. G. N. Gibbes, collector of customs 1834–59, also founded an Australian family, having married the sister of Murray of Yarralumla. Among Van Diemen's Land officials G. T. Boyes merits the historian's respect for his depiction, in diary and watercolour, of the life around him, while J. E. Bicheno (colonial secretary 1842–51) pursued in Hobart the interests that had made him a Fellow of the Royal Society and secretary of the Linnean Society. R. D. Hanson, an associate of Wakefield's and long-time attorney-general, played an extraordinarily large and varied part in the history of South Australia.

Most officials were busy men. The high-rankers not only supervised their departments but served on the executive councils. The importance of this institution was primarily symbolic, but still sizeable – 'its very existence at least suggested that government was conducted not by an autocrat, but by a cabinet, which, if not responsible, was bound together by a common purpose and shared responsibilities.'[29] Departments were small by modern standards, yet accomplished much: the wealth of extant archival material makes the point, shaming later nineteenth century decades. Especially important were the Survey departments, leaders of which included George Frankland (Van Diemen's Land, 1828–38) whose mapping was superb, and William Light (South Australia, 1836–9) who planned Adelaide on the best contemporary principles. However hard they worked, officials never extinguished colonists' criticism, yet those twin engines of nineteenth-century reform, efficiency and rectitude, had deeply affected Australian administration by 1850.

The most important fact in the economic history of the period was the expansion of wool-growing. Sample export figures were:

1830	1,967,309 lbs.
1835	4,210,301
1841	12,959,671
1845	21,865,270
1850	41,426,655 [30]

In the British market prices fluctuated around fourteen pence per lb., reaching as high as twice that sum in 1836 and 1837, and falling a few pence below it in the mid-1840s and again late in the decade. Superior wool always fetched three or four times as much. The total export value for 1850 was almost two million pounds. Further income derived from tallow in which form a fat sheep could realize five or six shillings.

---

29 W. A. Townsley, *The Struggle for Self-Government in Tasmania, 1842–1856*, Hobart, 1951, p. 39.

30 In 1850:—

N.S.W.	14,270,622 lbs.
V.D.L.	5,855,100
P.P.	18,091,207
S.A.	2,841,131
W.A.	368,595

From T. A. Coghlan, *Labour and Industry in Australia*, London, 1918, *I*, pp. 276, 503–4.

For most of settled Australia, wool by 1850 had become the 'staple' – an export-income earning commodity, sustaining and inspiring other economic activity.

The geographical dimension of the industry was enormous. Sheep continued to grow in Van Diemen's Land and older New South Wales, but increasingly men swung their eyes and ambitions to more distant regions. By 1850 sheep grazed on a vast swathe of land, 200 miles and deeper, from Brisbane to Adelaide and beyond. The most rapid expansion came early in the period, as did its most remarkable chapter, the occupation of Port Phillip. From Van Diemen's Land in the south, Melbourne and Geelong so being created, from New South Wales in the north, men and sheep thronged to this elysium. Sometimes a professional explorer set the tracks. For example T. L. Mitchell charted the Murray-Darling system and reported the fertility of Australia Felix, the western district of Port Phillip; and P. E. de Strzelecki travelled through the Alps into Gippsland. Often the flockmaster was his own scout.

If he were to be successful, this new squatter had to possess further qualities of the superman, or at least of the entrepreneur. He had to amass capital, buy dependable sheep and equipment, organize men and materials, select land, hold it against competitors (European and Aboriginal), survive disease and hazard, and learn new skills. Pioneer squatting life was tedious, lonely, even brutal, set in a strange environment; it had little attraction save anarchic freedom and the promise of wealth. The squatters came from all ranks of society, including ex-convicts, small farmers, grantees of earlier years and the sons and agents of all these; a significant newer element were recent immigrants, often of some social standing, conscious of 'being a superior caste'.[31] From all these circumstances developed the squatter's vehemence in demanding that government grant him security over the land he occupied.

Various factors encouraged the industry. The New South Wales market for meat, especially at the commissariat, had shrunk and so discouraged that alternative enterprise. Sheep-breeders among the gentry, John Macarthur their prototype, had developed a merino suitable for Australian conditions, while from Van Diemen's Land came a Saxon strain. The pastures and climate of the interior promoted a fine wool, such as the British market increasingly demanded and as Europe relatively failed to supply. Sheer quantity of land offset poorness of soil and lack of rivers. Inland transport was possible, by virtue of the bullock and his driver, and overseas freight was cheap in terms of weight-value; moreover the commodity withstood time and travel. The pioneer could manage with minimal equipment and so saved costs. Capital came in remarkable fecundity from Britain, and to a lesser extent from within the colonies. As Macarthur had

---

31 M. Roe, *Quest for Authority in Eastern Australia, 1835–1851*, Melbourne, 1965, p. 57.

persuaded Bigge, somewhat prematurely, convict assignment dovetailed with pastoral growth, providing cheap shepherds. The most recent historian of the pastoral age in New South Wales, G. J. Abbott, has argued that not so much the export earnings of wool, but rather physical expansion of the industry produced the richest pickings. The fore-runners sold disposable stock to newcomers, and thus won bigger profits than on other parts of their business. Spread was the dynamic of success rather than vice versa.[32]

Entrepreneurial skill comparable to that of the squatter himself appeared in the bankers and middlemen who serviced him. 'The banking system was transformed' in the pastoral hey-day, says its historian. 'In place of a few localized unit banks relying on capital for loanable funds, content with a restricted business and averse to serious competition, there were a number of large banks ... engaged in aggressive competition'.[33] The banks developed a foreign exchange market and channelled capital inflow. British-based institutions tended to dominate, but a remarkable local achievement was that of the Derwent Bank, which engineered the opening of Port Phillip from Van Diemen's Land. Similarly, firms which learned to specialize in wool-dealing met and even encouraged larger output. They cleared two outlets of sale: either in the colonial towns, by auction, to merchants, speculators, and firms which processed wool further before re-selling it; or in England on consignment, with the grower still owner, but the administration conducted on his behalf. In 1850 these alternatives had about equal favour, with perhaps one-tenth of the clip being shipped direct to England by growers.[34]

While squatters found wealth and adventure in continental vastness, the ocean continued to offer its same prizes. Retrospect makes it easy to see why the land proved so superior a resource: whereas the maritime industries were predatory and exploitative, annihilating sources of future supply, sheep grew wool and bred each season; convicts could escape by sea, but received salutary discipline on land; the market for maritime produce fluctuated, and even – in the vital case of whale oil – tended to decline. Yet retrospect also suggests that maritime activity had certain superior qualities, not only economic, but moral-cum-social. The obverse of pastoralism's suitability for convicts was that the sea encouraged a free and affluent workforce, while consequent skilled industries were ship-building, cooperage, and lumbering. The seaman's exploration of coast and ocean was as remarkable as the squatter's by land, his courage and tenacity no less.

To describe the dimensions of maritime industry is hard. For whaling and sealing, its most important constituents, there was boom

[32] G. J. Abbott, *The Pastoral Age*, Melbourne, 1971.

[33] S. J. Butlin, *Foundations of the Australian Monetary System: 1788–1851*, Melbourne, 1953, p. 10.

[34] A. Barnard, *The Australian Wool Market 1840–1900*, Melbourne, 1958, pp. 47–57.

in the 1830s, then recession for a few years, followed by strong revival of whaling in Van Diemen's Land but less in New South Wales, at least for local interests. Up to 1835 seal-whale products earned more than wool, and T. A. Coghlan estimated that by 1850 the industry had earned £3,000,000 in exports from Sydney and £1,200,000 from Van Diemen's Land.[35] It attracted interest in the newer colonies too – everywhere men initially looked to the sea as provider, if not friend. One important result of Australian whalers' searching through southern seas was their impetus to the colonization of New Zealand. Various entrepreneurs had stations there; the arrival of a rich oil-catch in Hobart, October 1833, caused many locals to become 'crazy to leave' for a settlement in the South Island, meant to exploit the field.[36] New Zealand offered flax and pork as well as whales and seals, and maritime enterprise embraced this and other Pacific produce. The sandalwood trade of the south-west Pacific, conducted from Sydney and Hobart, has received closest scholarly attention, probably as of right.[37] Pearls, coconut oil, trepang, even preserved heads, were among lesser items.

Government spending remained an important element in the economy, albeit no historian has precisely measured it. Convicts not only provided labour but drew British capital to feed and administer them. Colonists raged against off-setting costs – especially police and gaol expenses – but the balance went far the other way. Similarly, although local funds paid administrators' salaries, the empire bore such concealed items as their training. The Wakefieldian-liberal re-formers attempted to diminish spending on the colonies, a purpose which accorded with permanent realities of public finance and also the burgeoning fashion of laissez-faire. Even so, money gathered from land sales was re-invested in emigrants and other works, while South Australia itself had to receive direct aid in her bankruptcy of the early 1840s. In seeking convicts Western Australia asked for subsidy, and their reception duly helped make the colony viable.

Government spending, maritime industry, and wool were the three successive staples of early Australia; the fourth was mineral wealth, which sounded its first trumpets in South Australia of the 1840s. Not golden trumpets: silver-lead came first, near Adelaide in 1841, then copper at Kapunda in 1842, Burra in 1845. The results were such as mineral discoveries were to produce time and again in Australia's history: 'new towns, new wealth, and new jobs attracted more immigrants to South Australia than to any other colony. Farmers benefited from the wider market, ships came for copper ore and brought other

[35] T. A. Coghlan, *Labour and Industry in Australia*, London, 1918, *I*, p. 510. See also R. M. Hartwell, *The Economic Development of Van Diemen's Land 1820–1850*, Melbourne, 1954, pp. 139–43.

[36] J. M. R. Young, *Australia's Pacific Frontier*, Melbourne, 1967, p. 8. See also E. J. Tapp, *Early New Zealand*, Melbourne, 1958.

[37] D. Shineberg, *They Came for Sandalwood*, Melbourne, 1967.

trade. Land sales boomed, and Adelaide enjoyed a brief heyday as the most prosperous of all the Australian capitals.'[38] Both in Britain and Australia capitalists hastened to exploit the resource, with varying honesty and varying success. Local capitalists resented overseas capitalists; workers were militant in expressing demands. Other mining ventures ranged across the colonies. Gold had its part – in the geological researches of Rev. W. B. Clarke, in the observations of artisans and shepherds, even in the hopes of some forty men who 'rushed' to an alleged discovery near Melbourne.[39]

Agriculture, especially wheat-growing, differed markedly in importance from colony to colony. The dominance of wool in New South Wales had the side effect of restricting expansion in this sector, especially after 1840. Nevertheless 'dungaree' market-farmers made a fair living by continuing the exploitation of river lands near Sydney – 'whose carts may be met twice a week on their way hither, laden with grain, hay, vegetables, fruit, and the varieties of fowls; they occupy the stalls in the market, and their places could hardly be supplied by any other class of persons'.[40] Every town sustained their counterparts. Tenant farmers developed holdings on some of the big estates – even on squattages, despite the insecurity of tenure; while at a further extreme were shifting, often shifty fellows (the first people in Australia to be called 'squatters'), who camped wherever they could and frenzied their wealthier neighbours by allegedly stealing stock, harbouring runaways, and misbehaving generally. Some of the old landowners concentrated on agriculture, especially cereals but venturing into tobacco, vines, cotton, fruits: the prototype was Alexander Berry of Shoalhaven, significantly active in moves which led in 1843 to the Legislative Council putting a duty (of one shilling, reduced to sixpence by imperial decree) on imported grain. Squatters themselves often cultivated for domestic needs. In Van Diemen's Land mixed farming was general among all types of landholders; wheat was exported in sizeable quantities, largely to New South Wales, but also to England. The industry stagnated in the 1840s, just as that in South Australia began to achieve export significance.

Approximate figures for wheat acreage were:

	N.S.W.	P.P.	V.D.L.	S.A.	W.A.
1835	47,111	—	33,931	—	1,156
1840	72,993	1,940	60,813	1,059	1,670
1845	76,428	11,466	65,079	19,000	3,313
1850	70,720	28,510	64,650	41,807	4,416 [41]

[38] D. H. Pike, *Australia: The Quiet Continent*, Cambridge, 1962, p. 93.

[39] G. Blainey, *The Rush That Never Ended: A History of Australian Mining*, Melbourne, 1963, chs. 1 and 2.

[40] Quoted in E. Dunsdorfs, *The Australian Wheat-Growing Industry 1788–1948*, Melbourne, 1956, p. 87.

[41] E. Dunsdorfs, *The Australian Wheat-Growing Industry 1788–1948*, Melbourne, 1956, p. 532.

The average yield fluctuated around fifteen bushels. Total figures for area under cultivation (e.g. 1850 – N.S.W., 153,000; P.P., 52,340; V.D.L., 168,820; S.A., 65,000) leave many acres still to be explained: allowing for all possible uses, a large part must have been fallow. The figures confirm that Van Diemen's Land was more agricultural, in relation to population and area, than were the mainland colonies, but that South Australia was accelerating in this direction. That colony produced the most notable contribution to agricultural technique: John Ridley's reaper. The general standard of farming was mediocre but so it was in most places. Agricultural societies, with shows and competitions, strove to improve matters. Individuals among the bigger, older land-owners contributed to the theory and practice of scientific agriculture – more theory in New South Wales and more practice in Van Diemen's Land.

The cattle industry has an unduly small place in the historical literature. Coghlan estimated that there were 800,000 head in Australia in 1840 and 1,900,000 ten years later. Squatters often grazed sizeable numbers especially in their first years; for some, cattle remained very significant in terms of income-earning and land-use.[42] Meat, hides, bone and tallow were minor but appreciable exports. Dairying had developed close to self sufficiency by 1850.

Earlier reference to services which smoothed the wool-growers' way indicated the presence of a merchant-financier group, protean in its activities and profound in its contribution to economic growth. 'A Sydney merchant', wrote one of them, S. A. Donaldson, in 1838, 'must be a very acute financier – a complete man of figures – a constant observer and watcher of our fickle and changeable markets – a judge of goods – a proficient in foreign exchanges – a close calculator of discount and interest; moreover must be a good salesman; as we have no brokers in whom we can trust, and no clerks who take a lead in our affairs'.[43] Export and import, financing and debt-collecting, selling and buying, auctioneering and bidding – most magnates did most of these tasks. Often they were themselves investors in primary industry, and normally were mediaries between banks and squatters. They underpinned the local banks, insurance houses, and company flotations. Better communications by land and sea especially attracted their interest – in the late 1840s both South Australia and New South Wales underwent 'railway mania'.

Commerce linked Australia with the outside world. The point need hardly be developed apropos Britain whither went wool and whence came capital and manufactures. Less obvious in retrospect is the trade with Asia, much of it being re-sale of British goods, but including

---

[42] G. L. Buxton, *The Riverina: 1861–1891*, Melbourne, 1967, ch. 1.

[43] Quoted in B. Dyster, 'Prosperity, Prostration, Prudence', in A. Birch and D. Macmillan, Eds., *Wealth and Progress*, Sydney, 1967, p. 51.

two-way deals in primary produce.[44] Britain's attempt (1838–49) to establish at Port Essington, near Darwin, a base for trade with the archipelagos of south-east Asia interested politicians and businessmen in Sydney. Mercantile enterprise in the Pacific led to the establishment and supply of many trade posts, and to British intervention in New Zealand. James Busby was appointed Resident there in 1832, largely because of pressure from Sydney, and Australian revenues met his costs; in 1840 William Hobson succeeded, with the status of Consul, and for that year was subordinate to Gipps. Missionaries based on Sydney were active throughout the Pacific, while deserting sailors (often ex-convicts) spread political and technical expertise. Thus Australia was already an agent of Pacific imperialism. Recent historians have stressed that this did not mean simply an imposition of European norms upon the simple savage: rather, many islanders were sophisticated enough to use the newcomers for their own economic and political purposes.

In 1850 Sydney had about 54,000 residents, Hobart and Melbourne each 23,000, Adelaide 14,500. Port-function and administrative centralization explain less than completely why urbanization was so high, and uniformly high despite variations in the several colonies' economic structures. The ultimate reason was probably social and psychological – that people wanted to live in cities – rather than economic. Nevertheless urbanization had important economic consequences: residential building was always vigorous and urban services developed. The Australian Gas Light Company (Sydney, 1836) was one consequent enterprise of unusual competence and longevity.

Such industry and manufacturing as did exist centred in the towns. This was not exclusively the case – of an estimated 479 industrial enterprises throughout Australia in 1848, 223 were flour mills which developed wherever need and power (especially water-power) coincided.[45] The mining of coal – in which Newcastle dominated, but many other localities participated – was dispersed also, while the heaviest enterprise, an iron smeltery, worked (from 1848) a hundred miles west of Sydney. But the tanneries, breweries, foundries, soap and candle works, which comprised most manufactories, clustered in the capitals. Perhaps the most interesting business was the parent of the Colonial Sugar Refining Company, which began operations near Sydney in 1841.

The industry of most sophistication and skill was ship-building, with its ancillaries of cooperage, sail-making, rope-works. All the big ports had their shipyards, Hobart most remarkably. Peter Degraves, whose interests in brewing, building and finance perhaps qualified him as Australia's first industrial tycoon, sent a vessel of 560 tons into

44 See A. C. Staples, 'Maritime Trade in the Indian Ocean, 1830–1845', in *University Studies in History*, 1966: G. Blainey, *The Tyranny of Distance*, Melbourne, 1966, especially p. 317.

45 T. A. Coghlan, *Labour and Industry in Australia*, London, 1918, *I*, p. 515.

the Derwent in 1847. Many other colonial ships reached at least half that size. Steam, increasingly used in all industry, had its impact here – Sydney shipwrights built a steamship as early as 1831. The ship-yards serviced those many vessels – steam and sail, intercolonial and international – which maintained communications vital in every aspect of Australian life.

The story here outlined was essentially one of 'wealth and pro-gress'. These were the outstanding attributes of the Australian economy – the level of wealth in any community is more important than the source from which that wealth derives. Population figures give some measurement of growth:

	N.S.W.	P.P.	V.D.L.	S.A.	W.A.
1836	76,845	224	43,895	546	1,549
1845	149,261	31,280	64,000	22,460	—
1851	187,243	97,489	70,130	66,538	5,886

This table indicates that economic conditions varied according to period and place. A crude listing of the prosperity of the colonies would place Port Phillip first, then old New South Wales, a sizeable gap to South Australia, then Van Diemen's Land, another gradation to Western Australia, which indeed was outside 'wealth and progress'. The most eccentric graph was South Australia's, running from the stagnation of the early 1840s to prosperity and population boom of a few years' later. Port Phillip always enjoyed affluence, which gold intensified. The heyday of Van Diemen's Land came early in the period; thereafter prosperity fluctuated, but the population figures bespeak exhaustion of currently usable resources.

Running across all such generalizations was the depression of the early 1840s. Both in New South Wales and Van Diemen's Land local houses began to withdraw credit from about mid-1840. The process somersaulted along for the next few years, resulting in thousands of bankruptcies in all colonies. South Australia suffered least – the crisis there was one of public rather than of private finance, locals having but restricted investments to lose; Van Diemen's Land suffered hardest, or at least longest, well into 1845. The phenomenon had many interest-ing aspects, some of which appear inexplicable.[46]

The point at issue concerning the cause of the depression is why credit contracted. The truest answer might be that it had to, some time – that the extraordinary circumstance was earlier bounteousness. Colonists paid ten per cent for as much as they could get, and British capitalists gave them a great deal – thus Gipps saw his colony's troubles as resulting from gross over-capitalization, itself (he said) the product on one hand of local indulgences in luxuries, on the other of British greed in seeking profit on capital loans. This boom created inflation in wages, prices and costs, which both undercut spending

46 See S. J. Butlin, *Foundations of the Australian Monetary System, 1788–1851,* Melbourne, 1953, chs. 9 and 10: B. Dyster, 'Prosperity, Prostration, Prudence', in A. Birch and D. Macmillan, Eds., *Wealth and Progress,* Sydney, 1967.

power and intimidated entrepreneurs once they had a moment's disquiet. In New South Wales the disquiet might have resulted from the drought of 1838–9: wheat prices rose high, then fell, leaving millers with debts which their flour could no longer redress, while the payment for wheat imports with specie created a currency crisis. In Van Diemen's Land, conversely, the New South Wales drought intensified the boom, by expanding the market for grain, but the aftermath was all the harsher. Disquiet everywhere might also have followed from the sheer physical expansion of wool-growing, which raised the squatters' costs, made speculation riskier, and security more hypothetical. The wavering of colonial confidence soon had its effect in Britain, especially as it followed the discouragement imparted by South Australia's troubles. So the capital inflow diminished, accelerating the debacle and linking Australia with a world-wide shrinkage of trade and investment. Sales of Crown land fell with particular sharpness, imperilling government finances, which coincidentally had to meet the costs of immigration, arranged in boom-time. In 1842 Gipps withdrew government deposits from the banks, further stultifying them. The end of transportation further cut government spending in New South Wales. Bankruptcies and unemployment deepened the gloom.

The relation of the depression to wool-growing is particularly complex. Many pastoralists crashed. Falling markets denied their earlier profit from stock sales; tallow-boiling was some, but often insufficient compensation. The drop in wool prices 1843–4 impeded recovery. Yet in terms of total sheep number, of output in weight and value, in population of squatting districts, the industry continued to grow.

The depression produced much debate and some innovatory legislation. The New South Wales Bankruptcy Act of 1842 enabled an insolvent to maintain control of his own resources if this promised to enhance his capacity to repay. Imprisonment for debt was abrogated. Other statutes allowed stock and prospective wool-clips to be legal security for advances. The legislature also initiated moves for government credit to be issued on land mortgage and for enforced reduction of interest rates, but imperial authority squashed them. Gipps did issue £50,000 of debentures to pay migration costs. Employers everywhere tended to blame high labour costs for the depression and so urged yet further immigration; meanwhile urban unemployment created problems met by philanthropy, parliamentary enquiries, and (at least in Sydney) a rudimentary dole. The Van Diemen's Land legislature so firmly backed the high-cost-of-labour argument that it voted £60,000 for migration in 1841. The result was to worsen unemployment, and Lieutenant-Governor Wilmot did more to aid recovery. He drew on the convict and military fund, pared government expenses, and enabled some ex-probation convicts to sail to the mainland.

Further elements helped restore solvency. Banking and finance houses voluntarily reduced interest. Imports never returned before 1850 to the luxury-level of the 1830s. Land sales began to recover, except in Van Diemen's Land. Financiers and businessmen learned caution; self-help and savings provided more solid foundations for economic growth. British investors perhaps lost more heavily than Australian borrowers. Under all, the wealth of wool continued strong. The depression was dramatic, but not decisive.

Ideas shaped political and even economic development. The foundation of South Australia provided the most obvious instance, but there were others. The constitutional debates invoked basic statecraft and principle. Wentworth was a fine spokesman of eighteenth-century Whiggery, Lowe of nineteenth-century Liberalism. The British anti-Corn Law movement reverberated in the campaign for free entry of Australian corn into imperial markets, the Evangelical tradition in the anti-transportation leagues. Lowe's campaign for Sydney in 1848 was one of several indicators that old-world radicalism had its Australian counterpart. Henry Parkes hailed Lowe's election as 'the birthday of Australian democracy'; a few months later another radical sounded less jubilant and more extreme:

While Europe is striking off the fetters which despotism has forged for the people, and the voice of truth is scattering to the winds the *divine rights* of Princes, and such obsolete humbugs, we, who dwell under a Government more despotic, and more oppressive than any in the world, do not make the least manifestation of sympathy with the general movement of progress.[47]

By late 1850 two Sydney organizations sought to remedy that want. The Constitutional Association had its greatest triumph in helping organize the anti-transportation outburst of 1849, using propaganda redolent of Paris in revolution; the Australian League, founded by the Presbyterian cleric-politician J. D. Lang, was Utopian, republican, and nationalist. The nationalist theme, earlier hinted in the title of the Australian Patriotic Association of 1835, also operated within the Australasian League which not only achieved federal organization but even adopted a national flag. In Van Diemen's Land opponents of Wilmot's municipal legislation invoked 'the principle of passive resistance', and South Australia too had leagues devoted to political and social rights.

Thinking apropos economic problems was more rudimentary, but interesting nevertheless. Wakefield's emphasis on labour supply was the one point at which most colonists agreed with him: the long, tangled debates over migration – bond and free – witnessed this. Likewise land policy raised such issues as whether a new community should invest capital in land purchase and whether any restraint should prevail against the land-use immediately most profitable. The merits of diversification were much argued, especially by critics of the squatters and by advocates of protective duties. Both debates had

47 Quoted in R. Knight, *Illiberal Liberal*, Melbourne, 1966, p. 206.

some subtlety, as did discussion of the depression's cause and remedies. The plans for mortgage-based credit and for accelerated migration indicated that some colonists grasped the notion of recovery through expenditure, while the validation of wool-clips and stock as securities was a classic frontier response, breaking old-world norms.

The history of the churches offers a convenient guide-line into more specific areas of colonial thought. In a material sense, these were buoyant years for religion. Whereas the foundation of the early colonies displayed minimal regard for spiritual matters, now the state gave generous subsidies to all Christian groups ready to accept them: from 1836 in New South Wales, 1837 in Van Diemen's Land, 1840 in Western Australia, 1846 in South Australia. That this aid was multi-denominational supported the proposition, never clinched with utter precision, that the Church of England had no unique status of establishment. Encouraged by state money but also by enthusiasm from metropolis and colonies, the creeds built churches and provided clergy, the latter at a ratio of more than one per thousand population. Activity concentrated on towns, but spread to the frontier; satellite organizations were busy and varied. By mid-century the colonies conformed to the religious fashion of the modern western world. About a quarter of the population attended church each week, almost everyone acknowledged nominal belief. Yet indifference and 'practical paganism' especially among the common people, were evident and deplored. 'Public feeling is all on the side of the form of religion, how much of the power exists among us, the searcher of hearts alone can tell.'[48] Historians cannot surpass this contemporary judgement, but a review of the several denominations will give it texture.

The Church of England claimed about half the colonies' population. Its leader, W. G. Broughton (archdeacon from 1829, bishop from 1835) had intellect, determination, and strength. He and other colonial Anglicans – notably F. R. Nixon, bishop of Tasmania from 1842, and Augustus Short, bishop of Adelaide from 1848 – responded to the Tractarian movement, currently active in England. They were therefore more conscious of their historic role, and more critical of the liberal-democratic tang of Australian society. Conversely, liberals of the day suspected the Church of England more than the Church of Rome as threatening civil and religious liberty. Low-church Anglicans also distrusted Tractarians, and disputes resulted.

These decades were especially remarkable for the Roman Catholic church. Under the patronage of Governor Bourke it emerged from almost squalid retreat to vigour, if not aggression. Largely Irish and ex-convict, the laity was active and devout – no other denomination had comparable strength within the proletariat. Catholics asserted their political opinions and civil rights: not only did the Australian

---

[48] Quoted in J. Barrett, *That Better Country*, Melbourne, 1966, p. 204, and generally. See also M. Roe, *Quest for Authority in Eastern Australia: 1835–1851*, Melbourne, 1965, chs. 1, 5 and 6.

church receive state aid, but from 1842 its bishops took territorial titles, the first to do so in British dominions since the Reformation. Mission work proceeded among both Europeans and Aborigines, the mission-monastery at New Norcia, north of Perth, remaining one of Australia's most exotic institutions.

Five individuals represent Catholic activity: J. B. Polding, W. B. Ullathorne, J. J. Therry, W. A. Duncan, and Caroline Chisholm. Polding, an Englishman and a Benedictine, came to Australia in 1835 as first bishop. Over forty-two years he showed many qualities of the saint. His strength was work among convicts; inevitably his role diminished with the years, but remained great. Ullathorne preceded Polding in New South Wales by two years, as vicar-general. He was a genius in organization and publicity. Ullathorne could have become a colonial bishop, but returned to Britain in 1841, soon to become a dominant figure in the English church. Therry was an Irish priest, whose arrival was still earlier, 1820. Through to his death in 1864 he served in New South Wales and Van Diemen's Land, everywhere winning the fierce loyalty of Irish Catholics. In Hobart Therry wrangled from 1844 with his bishop there, R. W. Willson – one expression of pervasive hostility between Irish rank-and-file and English leaders. Different tension – that felt by laymen reluctant to forsake all authority to priests – became associated with W. A. Duncan. After migrating to New South Wales as a Catholic schoolmaster, Duncan became editor of the church's excellent newspaper, the *Chronicle*, in 1839. Following an intra-church quarrel he conducted his own *Weekly Register* in 1843–5. Duncan was an intellectual of many gifts, and argued for wide distribution of wealth in the tradition of Catholic social justice. This linked him with Mrs Chisholm, who came to New South Wales in 1838 and soon embarked on philanthropic labours – managing an immigrants' home, arranging employment for women, settling families on the land. In 1846 she returned to England and launched a one-woman campaign on behalf of family migration to Australia.

Whereas the Catholic church flourished in Australia, transplantation wilted Presbyterianism. Its following suffered from manifold divisions – partly the counterpart of events at home (where the 1843 'Disruption' led to the Free Church secession, repudiating all connexion with the state), partly the consequence of local circumstances. J. D. Lang, dominant Presbyterian in New South Wales, was gifted as writer, teacher, and politician, but not as a leader. He quarrelled voraciously as he pushed his own interests and causes, which included free immigration (of Scotsmen), Port Phillip independence, democracy, and the scourging of priests. Lang's counterpart in Van Diemen's Land was John Lillie, much more restrained yet very able, and the church's guide through years of steady if slow growth. In Melbourne several Presbyterians of note were active before 1850, anticipating the later Scots ascendancy there. South Australia's most interesting contribution came early: the colony's founding statute provided that ministers of either the Church of England or the Church of Scotland might be appointed chaplains: an admission of equality between the two British churches which Presbyterians stressed in their denial that the Church of England had unique colonial status.

The smaller sects had greater influence and interest than their mere numbers might suggest. Methodism repeated its British success in moving a comparatively limited following with fervour. In the early 1840s a Methodist revival swept the agricultural districts around Sydney, and local primitive groups styling themselves Australian Methodists developed both there and in South Australia. The latter colony was notable for its sympathy with Congregationalism. That creed gave Adelaide its dominant churchman, T. Q. Stow – preacher, philanthropist, and publicist. John West, also a Congregationalist minister, exercised similar influence in Launceston. Congregationalists everywhere led movements for Protestant union and, conversely, against Catholicism: the latter was the more vigorous cause. The Baptists also were stronger in South Australia than elsewhere, although the most interesting minister, John Saunders, worked at Sydney (1834–47), achieving eminence comparable to that of Stow and West. Lutherans, Quakers, Unitarians, miscellaneous 'free' congregations, Christian Israelites, Mormons and Jews, all played some part in religious life.

The chief secular creed of the day was a variant of liberalism. It developed from the eighteenth-century Enlightenment, and so stressed individualism, rationality, the importance of the temporal world, and man's power to solve its problems. The creed tended to be egalitarian, and hostile to privilege and pretension, especially of the clergy. Utilitarian emphasis on the greatest good for the greatest number fused with Romantic belief in everyman's perfectibility. This perfection would develop through self-respect, self-discipline, and self-improvement. The moralistic emphasis was strong, and the creed could be termed 'moral enlightenment'.

The temperance movement, which then swept Australia, as the English-speaking world generally, well expressed moral enlightenment. To temperance spokesmen, alcohol was society's terrible curse, from which man must free himself through that act of will embodied in taking the pledge. 'Rest at nothing short of this consummation', urged one of the many temperance journals, – 'one so benevolent, so honourable, so desirable, and so glorious – the absolute sovereignty of temperance'.[49] Another medium for moral enlightenment was phrenology – that theory that an individual's pysche might be analysed by a study of his cranium, and that remedial action could then correct any aberration. Simplistic, often exploited by charlatans, phrenology nevertheless encouraged reformers in education, anthropology, criminology, and medicine.

[49] Quoted in M. Roe, *Quest for Authority in Eastern Australia: 1835–1851*, Melbourne, 1965, p. 171.

Yet more important was the concept that cultural activity could transform society and men as moral enlightenment required. This was the burden of thousands of essays and speeches, the apologia for every cultural venture. With all their hyperbole and repetition the spokesmen of culture truly believed that they could redeem the basic ills of colonial life – materialism, heterogeneity, alienation. Culture would unify, elevate, and inspire.[50] The history of colonial culture thus belongs to the propagation of moral enlightenment, and these comments fittingly introduce that history. Nevertheless its composition is determined by criteria of intrinsic worth.

Culture can thrive only among the educated, and the provision of schooling was a fundamental concern of thinkers and politicians. Each colony had a large number of purely private schools, while the churches continued in Australia their traditional interest in this activity. Increasingly important was the role of the state. From the mid-1830s in the two older colonies, from the mid-1840s in the two younger, governments accepted responsibility for subsidizing education. Thus arose the great, endless controversy as to what forms of religious instruction should government allow (or enforce) in schools receiving such bounty. Anglicans and Roman Catholics generally argued that denominational schools were necessary to maintain true religion and that the state should support such schools; most other groups, liberals especially, argued that money should go only to schools teaching very generalized religion. Most governors themselves inclined to the generalist school, but hesitated to offend churchmen. By 1851 the governments of the eastern colonies subsidized both kinds of school, South Australia had a generalized system, while in Western Australia only Roman Catholics received denominational subsidy.[51]

At mid-century probably about one-half of children aged between eight and twelve attended school at any particular time. Considerably more would have gained basic literacy, somehow, sometime. Mobility of pupils was great, and standards of teachers varied still more. The first union of pedagogues was the Professional Literary Association (Sydney, 1850) which sponsored a fine periodical, *Australian Era*. Among educational administrators were future historian, G. W. Rusden, who established many New South Wales 'National' schools, and Thomas Arnold, son of the great Rugbeian and inspector of Van Diemen's Land schools from 1850 to 1856.

Superior schools developed steadily. In 1830–31 Sydney acquired two: Sydney College, financed largely by emancipists, and J. D. Lang's Australian College. The Church of England followed with King's School, Parramatta. In Van Diemen's Land the Franklins aspired to establish Christ College virtually as a university; instead it emerged as an Anglican seminary. Anglicans also founded Hutchins

---

50 See G. H. Nadel, *Australia's Colonial Culture*, Melbourne, 1957.

51 See A. G. Austin, *Australian Education, 1788–1900*, Melbourne, 1961, chs. 2 and 3.

School, Hobart, and Launceston Church Grammar School. Noncon-
formists responded with the Hobart Town High School (1849), notable
for its experimental curriculum. Simultaneously and similarly Adelaide
gained St Peter's from the Anglicans and a High School from anti-
Anglicans. Mid-century also saw the constitution of the University of
Sydney.

Various media offered more generalized education. Mechanics Institutes failed in their nominal aim to introduce the working-class mass
to learning, but did provide a forum for the literary-minded. Libraries
and reading rooms operated both for profit and self-help, while governments subsidised museums and galleries. Retailers offered culture's raw
materials – books, music, paintings, artists' ware, musical instruments.
Newspapers were remarkable not only in gross number everywhere,
but in sometimes achieving world-standard quality. Lowe's *Atlas* and
W. A. Duncan's *Weekly Register* were as much reviews as newspapers,
including social and literary criticism and original work. The thirty-
odd little (and brief-living) magazines more deliberately cultivated
such fields.

Creative writing offered one man of outstanding talent – the poet
Charles Harpur. Born of convict parents at Windsor in 1813, Harpur's
life was dismal enough, yet he gave himself to thought and literature.
'Moral enlightenment' was his phrase and he lauded temperance,
culture, liberty, and nationalism. Judith Wright sees in his work the
two continuing preoccupations of Australian writers – 'the twin themes
of exile ... and of hope'.[52] His most appealing poems were nature
lyrics but he made respectable attempts at more involved and experimental work. Other creative writing had more historical than literary
interest. Local penmen were able and busy enough to meet the strong
demand for verse and for hack drama. The first novel in time (1830–31)
was *Quintus Servinton*, a partly-autobiographical account of a Van
Diemen's Land convict, Henry Savery. Similar in theme, but more
vigorous and thoughtful, was *Ralph Rashleigh*, probably by James
Tucker and written in New South Wales around 1840, although not
published until 1929. Charles Rowcroft, a settler in Van Diemen's
Land 1821–5, subsequently wrote several novels about that experience,
the best being *Tales of the Colonies* (1843). Mary Theresa Vidal
similarly used her sojourn in New South Wales 1840–45, and her first
book *Tales for the Bush* (1845) was written and published in Australia.

More impressive were documentary works. Journalism reached its
apotheosis in historical writing. J. D. Lang (*New South Wales*; *Cooks-
land*; etc.), Henry Melville (*Van Diemen's Land*; *Australasia*), John
West (*Tasmania*) all wrote for the press as well as composing excellent
histories. West's work (published in 1852) approached genius in style,
judgements, and range. Australian travel and reminiscence prompted
several good books, outstandingly Alexander Harris's *Settlers and
Convicts* (1846) which described Sydney and up-country life in splendid

---

52 J. Wright, *Charles Harpur*, Melbourne, 1963, p. 29.

prose and detail; the son of a nonconformist clergyman, Harris underwent a spell of riotous living and army service before migrating to New South Wales where he lived until 1841. Thereafter he travelled and published widely, maintaining an active interest in social reform. Having elements of fantasy and romance, *Settlers* might merit ranking as Australia's first major novel; Harris did explicitly attempt this form in *The Emigrant Family* (1849) but with less success. *Settlers* also belonged to the extensive 'advice to migrant' literature; especially was it akin to the writings of Caroline Chisholm and John and Samuel Sidney – Harris and they encouraged the migrant to seek social justice in Australia, and all documented the life of ordinary people. The most famous, and very perceptive, writer of a traveller's account was Charles Darwin. *Belles Lettres* included James Martin's *The Australian Sketch-Book* (Sydney, 1838), which explored the consciousness of being an Australian, and Thomas McCombie's *Australian Sketches* (1847), one of Melbourne's first contributions to literature.

Much pictorial art had a documentary, migrant-attracting purpose, and reached the same high level as its literary equivalent. Supreme was the work of John Glover, already sixty-three when he migrated to Van Diemen's Land in 1831, but destined there to paint superb vistas of man in nature. Conrad Martens and J. S. Prout were other good landscapists while portraiture had its master in T. G. Wainewright who may have poisoned three relatives for gain, and certainly committed massive forgeries, for which he was transported in 1837. Behind these leaders stood ranks of both professionals and amateurs whose extant work is always interesting and often impressive. The same judgement applies to architecture: John Verge, E. T. Blacket, James Blackburn and J. L. Archer were the most able designers of buildings, duly to become posterity's part-envy, part-pride. Drama and music met varied tastes, with much élan and some talent. The great names included Isaac Nathan, already famed as a composer before migrating in 1841; J. P. Deane, a violinist who led his family's chamber orchestra in both Hobart and Sydney; Eliza Winstanley, a Sydney girl who became an actress of old-world reputation; and Marie Carandini, 'the Tasmanian nightingale'.

Many colonists dabbled with experiments, especially in medicine, but Australia's chief scientific relevance remained its fauna, flora, and geology. The most notable local presentation of research appeared in the *Tasmanian Journal of Natural Science* (1842–9), while John Gould's *The Birds of Australia* (1840–48) was the pre-eminent fruit of a visitor's work. Exploration was another facet of research: F. W. L. Leichhardt (northern Australia, 1842–8), E. J. Eyre (especially in seeking an overland route from Adelaide to Perth, 1840–41), Charles Sturt (central Australia, 1844–6), were the mightiest heroes, extending the boundaries of both knowledge and courage. Comparable was the odyssey of G. A. Robinson, as he gathered the remnants of Aboriginal Tasmanians, 1829–34. The various expeditions of maritime discovery which called at colonial ports enlivened local salons and linked

Australia with such men as Darwin, T. H. Huxley, O. W. Brierly, and Owen Stanley.

Earlier references to phrenology and education have indicated that the social sciences received attention. Convicts and Aborigines were the particular groups of interest whom Australia offered the sociologist. Alexander Maconochie was the most interesting prison reformer, but various clergymen and transport surgeons made contributions. Maconochie also was interested in the Aborigines, concerning whom colonial discussion offered the gamut of possible judgements and forecasts. The Aborigines' most sympathetic observers were Eyre, Sir George Grey, and the South Australian artist, G. F. Angas.[53] Social statistics was the field of normal sociology most deeply cultivated, notably by William Westgarth of Melbourne and Ralph Mansfield of Sydney.

Historians will differ in their general estimate of the quality of colonial culture. Some might consider its sheer 'colonial' character – that is, having standards and practitioners drawn from Britain rather than from native growth – as a detraction. They could argue further that much of the cultural output was mediocre, and that its history proved less about Australia than that man will make some effort at cultural expressions, however discouraging his environment. Notwithstanding these arguments, the story here outlined was one of achievement and vitality, the more remarkable in view of Australia's origin; moral enlightenment generally had a strong hold in Australia by mid-century. Most colonists at least paid lip-service to the ideals of self-perfection and moral rectitude, and gave higher priority to this world's concerns than to those of eternity. Much of the European, and certainly the English-speaking world, currently embraced such ideas; they gained ground still faster in the colonies because of the relative freedom there from class division and traditional belief, because of the rapid material progress all around, and because of the many opportunities open to individualist ambition. The vigour of the anti-transportation movement, which incorporated many themes of moral enlightenment, was the clearest symbol of the creed's dominance.

To judge the quality of society is one task of social history: others are to distinguish the types of person within society and assess both their attitudes, and attitudes to them. The integration of 'social' with other branches of history complicates the task. Outstanding for both his economic importance and his origin in this period was the squatter. His attributes as superman and entrepreneur, his consciousness of 'being a superior caste', caused the squatter to assert himself against the government; he saw himself as being forced to undertake an inherently repellent way of life so that his own investments and Australia at large might flourish. Yet increasingly he became an object of general execration: squatting was accused of preventing intensive land-use, of

53 See D. J. Mulvaney, 'The Australian Aborigines: 1606–1929: Opinion and Fieldwork, Part I: 1606–1859', in *H.S.*, *30*, May 1958.

creating class distinction, of allying with imperial despotism, and of fostering barbarism in the interior. 'The pursuit which, beyond all others, is at present most essential to the material interests of the colony, has morally and socially a debasing tendency', wrote a contemporary.[54] The argument had some validity, especially when passion for land encouraged hostility towards law, rivals, and aborigines. Yet the squattocracy established its power. In doing so, it overshadowed the gentry landowners who had received grants in the 1820s. Men who had invested heavily in their freehold estates were at a disadvantage against the squatter, with his economic and physical mobility. Some gentry crumpled and disappeared. Others benefited sufficiently from the wool boom to survive. This was most obviously true in Van Diemen's Land, where the gentry generally retained their land, albeit having to recognize that in Australian terms they were smallish fry.

Atop the urban hierarchy were bankers, merchants, administrators, and professions. Lawyers were important both in public affairs, and as guardians of rights which the uncertainties of a new-world situation often made vulnerable. Medicos were relatively abundant, because many came to Australia in the convict service; they contributed to learning, to politics, and also to mutual back-biting. Officers of the imperial regiments continued to give Sydney and Hobart a regimental air and social variety. Commander of troops in New South Wales in 1838–47, was Sir M. C. P. O'Connell, who had first gone there with Governor Macquarie in 1809, and soon afterwards married Bligh's daughter; his son and secretary, Maurice, was a leading candidate in the first Legislative Council election for Sydney.

The existence of urban élites, sustained by the remarkable disposition of all colonists to throng to the capitals, had a significant impact on Australian life. They were, by and large, the patrons of culture and enabled it to attain fair standards. The point had a wider application: the existence of big towns, including élite groups, meant that Australia embraced a great range of social experience. The towns offered gaiety and sophistication, while up country other colonists wrestled with primitive necessities.

Transplantation put particular strains on upper class Britons. Some consoled themselves by reflecting that in a new land they had opportunity to mould destiny, but others suffered alienation. Hence arose that bitter, cantankerous, aspect of colonial life, best analysed by John West apropos Arthur's domain:

The spirit of contention was promoted by the peculiar fabric of society. The great majority of the colonists were below the period of human life, when the temper becomes cautious and the passions calm. Its narrow sphere magnified their temporary importance. Every man might claim, or forfeit benefits which the

[54] Quoted in M. Roe, *Quest for Authority in Eastern Australia, 1835–1851*, Melbourne, 1965, p. 75.

government could bestow, and thus multitudes had personal grievances, or unsatisfied expectations.[55]

Not only did the old colonies' élites show this darker side of Australian life. South Australia was at the other pole to Arthur's Van Diemen's Land, yet 'fractious individualism' characterized its politics.[56] Every colonial institution – the churches most obviously, but not uniquely – suffered rifts and schisms. Landowners and squatters (and labourers too) felt jealousy not only for each other but towards newcomers of their own kind, who might break established control over that commodity the group possessed. Vituperation and scandal saturated the press and no doubt much conversation too.

As the historian seeks to investigate humbler segments of society, his difficulties increase. A mark of social submersion is incapacity to contribute to the historical record; hence it is difficult to see through the eyes of any outgroup. Their existence nevertheless demands that the effort be made. Furthest out of any Australian group were the Aborigines. Between 1830 and 1850 they felt the full blast of Europe. Extinction of the Tasmanians hastened on, while pastoralists drove and killed Australians off tribal land. The imperial authority, vulnerable to humanitarian and Evangelical pressure, strove to cushion the impact, but with little effect; instead, this became yet another source of discord between metropolis and periphery. Abuse broke over Governor Gipps when he brought to justice and the gallows seven men for a massacre of aborigines at Myall Creek, New South Wales, in 1838; the New South Wales legislature consistently refused to validate Aborigines giving evidence in criminal cases; and settlers and legislators throttled the Port Phillip Protectorate scheme (1838–50), through which missionaries were to settle aborigines on stations where they might learn European ways. Local missions met with less hostility, but scarcely more success.

The white man found only a little use for the Aborigine. In Port Phillip a native police force worked sufficiently well to prompt emulation in old New South Wales from 1848. Some pastoralists tried aborigines as station hands, but the experiments rarely succeeded. Others had some recognition as domestic servants, or domestic pets: at one country house in the 1843 election a candidate was cheered by an 'admiring crowd of natives profusely decorated with pink calico' (pink being the candidate's colour).[57] The story had a few brighter aspects. Some missionaries, explorers, philanthropists, and social scientists looked upon the Aborigines with sympathy approaching understanding. There were even hints of political recognition. 'Thomas Tomru, Ab. Nat. Chf.' signed his mark to the New South

[55] J. West, *The History of Tasmania*, Launceston, 1852, *I*, p. 176.

[56] D. H. Pike, *Paradise of Dissent: South Australia 1829–1857*, Melbourne, 1957, p. 392.

[57] M. Herman, Ed., *Annabella Boswell's Journal*, Sydney, 1965, p. 64.

Wales Loyal Address on Victoria's succession. When in 1845 the legislature appointed a committee on the Aborigine question, one witness it heard was Mahroot, a Sydney boatman and erstwhile member of the Botany Bay tribe. He told of his fellows' way of life, their collapse under European impact, and their suspicion of European philanthropy. So one Aboriginal voice reached the historical record. For the rest, the natives' response to the European was either submission or retaliation. At its most extreme, in the western district of Port Phillip, retaliation seemed to contemporaries to run close to 'civil war', and interfered with pastoral expansion – but not for long.[58]

The second Australian out-group were convicts. Numbers entering Australia were:

	N.S.W.		V.D.L.	
	M	F	M	F
1830–5	17,287	2,574	10,647	1,492
1836–40	12,014	2,722	7,541	1,193
1841–5	1,605	nil	15,546	3,383
1846–50	3,690	nil	4,949	3,522 [59]

To generalize about the convicts is difficult. Often a convict's differentiation from an 'ordinary' man was notably slight rather than otherwise. Two particles of evidence show the complexity of determining whether this differentiation grew or shrank in the last decades of transportation: improved administration of Britain's criminal law meant that an ever higher proportion of convicts were criminal, yet they committed fewer gross crimes in the colonies.[60] Certainly the concurrent free migration and economic development of the period reduced the convicts' significance in politics and society. This was especially true in New South Wales, but even in Van Diemen's Land the convict remained subordinate. Australian colonists willed transportation to mean remarkably little in their lives; one consequence was that despite their various histories vis-à-vis penalism, the temper of the colonies varied relatively little.

Still, transportation did mean something, especially to those who endured it. Up until 1840 the majority spent much of their sentence under assignment. The Molesworth committee exaggerated in presenting this as often a life of ease. Probably most masters were harsh, and their hands held the whip; government supervised them, but for government too the general tenor was 'increasing severity', at least until the later 1830s.[61] That severity found harshest expression in the various colonial stations of further punishment – at Moreton Bay (till 1837), Norfolk Island, Port Arthur and its juvenile satellite Point

58 P. Corris, *Aborigines and Europeans in Western Victoria*, Canberra, 1968, especially p. 86.

59 A. G. L. Shaw, *Convicts and the Colonies*, London, 1966, pp. 366–8.

60 A. G. L. Shaw, *Convicts and the Colonies*, London, 1966, pp. 164, 227.

61 A. G. L. Shaw, *Convicts and the Colonies*, London, 1966, ch. 9.

Puer. Moreton Bay under Patrick Logan around 1830 and Norfolk Island under John Price twenty years later went nearest to that terrestrial hellishness traditionally associated with all these stations. Generally life there, as in the penal gangs which were always an alternative to assignment and succeeded it altogether after 1840, was ugly, brutal, sex-perverted, if in all this different only in degree from any closed, all-male, institutional life.

Most convicts accepted their life, with resentment. James Tucker, Alexander Harris, and a convict balladist Francis McNamara, all witnessed grousing against the system's tyranny. Some convicts escaped, some disobeyed, most worked to minimum. The females at their 'factory' in south Hobart expressed themselves when exhorted by lieutenant-governor and chaplain one day: 'they all with one impulse turned round, raised their clothes, and smacked their posteriors with loud report'.[62] At Norfolk Island in 1834 and again in 1846 convicts rose in rebellion. There were other moments of active disobedience, but the total was small. Even more than Afro-American slaves and much more than European serfs, the convicts stayed passive.

This was the more striking in that many of the more interesting convicts were political rebels: agricultural rioters (464 in 1830–31), would-be agricultural unionists (six in 1834), North Americans involved in the Canada rising (148 in 1840), Chartists (72 in 1839–42; eight in 1848), and Irish nationalists (seven in 1848, while many other Irish convicts continued to be products of social disturbance, rather than of criminality). These numbers were only a fraction of all convicts, but political radicals will always be a minority. Colonial politics attracted a very few: notably the Irish nationalist Patrick O'Donohoe, whose *Irish Exile* newspaper (Hobart, 1850–51) argued for social justice with great verve; and William Cuffey, a negro tailor of Chartist sympathies who had planned to raze London in August 1848, and who later advocated various popular causes in Hobart.

Transportation brought other interesting men to Australia, especially to Van Diemen's Land. Savery, Tucker, McNamara, Wainewright, were writers and artists already mentioned; the latter category also included W. B. Gould, Frederick Strange, and Alfred Bock. Frederick Thomas contributed to the literature of penalism in *The Horrors of Transportation* (Newcastle-on-Tyne, 1849), while J. F. Mortlock and Mark Jeffrey were later to compose two outstanding convict narratives. Free colonists might have minimized convictism, but these men left records which will ever recall that strange, sometimes terrible, heritage. Nor was this heritage utterly negligible in contemporary society and politics. The emancipist political activity of the 1830s clinched that point, and historians have tended to overlook that even later ex-convicts and their sons continued to adhere in faction. They dominated the Sydney corporation throughout the 1840s and from

---

[62] Quoted in K. E. Fitzpatrick, *Sir John Franklin in Tasmania*, Melbourne, 1949, p. 81.

1848 the Wentworth group in the legislature was 'rooted in early associations, family connections and local prejudices' of convict origin.[63] Here, then, was still operating Australia's peculiar brand of nativism. Its feastday was 26 January, its hero Wentworth, its literary expression his history and poem, and more recently, James Martin's *Australian Sketch-Book*. It merged with ideological nationalism – most notably in the Australian Patriotic Association – but its drive was the emancipists' belief, noticed by James Macarthur, that the colony was 'theirs by right'. In 1849–50 the Tasmanian Union, an embryonic political party, sought backing from ex-convicts by invoking similar emotion; it had little immediate success, although in 1852 a similar faction swept the first polls for the Hobart corporation.

Such active assertion belonged only to a minority. Many ex-convicts spent everyday lives, virtually untouched by their past. Others constituted a lumpenproletariat, free of any social commitment, even marriage – masculinity dominance was overwhelming among convicts and ex-convicts. These people lived and died as historical neuters. Overall the importance of the ex-convict, like that of the convict, diminished. Just as free colonists willed transportation to affect society remarkably little, so they generally kept the ex-convict submerged. In Van Diemen's Land especially, where the sheer number of convicts was great, conventions developed in counter-response. Freecomers ruled affairs, and in return public discussion avoided reference to convict origins. Such rules did not prevail absolutely, but were nevertheless significant.

The mass of women, whatever their background, served as mates, mothers, and domestics; but a few had some more public function. The arse-slappers of south Hobart were at one pole among this minority and Lady Franklin (a witness of that display: oh, glorious confrontation!) was at the other. Caroline Chisholm represented, albeit she transcended, many workers for good causes; Mary Theresa Vidal, a handful of contributors to culture. Moralist movements everywhere called on female support, and in Australia both temperance and anti-transportation exemplified the rule. The care of female convicts allowed a few women to show administrative skill. Mary Reibey remained still a living proof that her sex was compatible with commercial entrepreneurship; Ann Drysdale and Caroline Newcomb were Port Phillip squatters, as able as any.

As already suggested from point to point, the humbler free migrant grew steadily in significance. This was a truism apropos the new colonies, but applied also to New South Wales and even in some measure to Van Diemen's Land. John West generalized from the island's experience to argue that the migration of free workmen 'revolutionised the state of the colonies . . . If his industry raised him, he yet retained the sympathies of his early life: he remained

[63] Quoted in M. Roe, *Quest for Authority in Eastern Australia 1835–1851*, Melbourne, 1965, p. 85.

distrustful of the rich, jealous of rank, and fond of the equality of human rights'.[64] West had recognised what might be called 'the immigrant claim' – to social and political decency in the new home. That the state had assisted most migrants only increased this assertiveness, seeming to predicate a guarantee of such decency. Horace's dictum that those who cross the sea do not change their minds was not wholly true: the circumstances under which the migrant left Britain combined with new-world opportunities to maximize his awareness of self.

Most migrants came from England, but there was some variety, duly reflected in Australia. Ireland contributed many, especially after the 1846 famine: hence developed Orange-versus-Green antipathy, strong especially in the 1840s, and also Australian support for Irish nationalist movements. From Scotland came enough Gaelic-speakers to cause some Presbyterian services to be given in that language, while South Australia's Germans comprised the first bloc of continental Europeans. Coloured minorities were the Chinese, Indians, New Hebrideans, and other Pacific islanders whom labour-hungry squatters had contracted into Australia. Their experience is beyond the historian's recall. Yet the best-authenticated fact about such labour – that the men flouted their commitments – suggests an affinity with other assertive migrants.

These, the common people of Australia, earned their living in ways appropriate to that status. The small farmer might be petty squatter, tenant, or freeholder. Generally, some provision operated for sale of Crown land in blocks of eighty acres or so;[65] there still continued complaints that government neglected closer settlement, the 1846–7 legislation being especially attacked on this point. Market-suppliers around the towns were probably more successful than other small farmers, although many a South Australian, producing wheat and fruit, approached the yeoman ideal. Others lived in isolation and at subsistence level – yet even then enjoying independence and displaying those stoic virtues which the small settler has contributed to the Australian tradition. Such is the picture in Harris's *Settlers and Convicts* and in the yet more authentic, although later written, *Bush Life in Tasmania* (1891) by James Fenton.

The pastoral worker was as essential to Australia's prosperity as were squatters and sheep. Very often was he a convict – or later an ex-convict or Australian native. Few immigrants had either wish or ability to do the task, shepherding especially. The very appearance of the bushworkers set them apart – 'strange, wild-looking, sunburnt race, . . . they appear as though they had never lived in crowds, and had lost the desire and even the power to converse'.[66] Months of isolation – a drunken spree – brutal treatment by employers – brutal

[64] J. West, *The History of Tasmania*, Launceston, 1852, *I*, p. 57.

[65] See especially D. N. Jeans, 'Crown Land Sales and the Accommodation of the Small Settler in N.S.W., 1825–1842', in *H.S.*, *46*, April 1966.

[66] Quoted in R. Ward, *The Australian Legend*, Melbourne, 1958, p. 93 and generally.

treatment of Aborigines – such was the bushman's life. Yet it offered freedom, and in relations with his fellows the bushworker developed that 'mateship' later Australian nationalists were to venerate. Alexander Harris chronicled mateship and with it the bushman's hardihood, class-consciousness, and scepticism – other constituents of 'The Australian Legend'. R. B. Ward, historian of the 'Legend' sees the convict period as decisive in settling such traits within the Australian self-image.

The urban worker lacked any depictor like Harris or Fenton, yet did much to set the tone of Australian life. The apostles of moral enlightenment addressed him primarily, and won a fair response, evident in savings banks, temperance societies, and self-owned suburban homes. The urban worker further expressed himself in politics, providing both target and support for the radical movements mentioned previously. Another interesting passage came in Sydney in 1843–4, when the depression inspired a 'Mutual Protection Association'. This sounded 'the immigrant claim' very loud, and helped persuade the executive that 'as the people had been brought here ... it was the duty of the government to rescue them from destitution'.[67] The long-term issue which roused most feeling was competition in the labour market. The worker was wary of any immigration, and that of convicts above all. The anti-transportation movement received his support, and its strength enhanced his standing.

The towns had their bawdy side. Pubs and brothels abounded. Several Sydney newspapers catered for sport and liquor interests, telling of pugilist Tom Sparks and pedestrian Billy King, the flyman pieman of Parramatta. An earlier hero was bushranger Bold Jack Donohoe, the original Wild Colonial Boy, sung in ballad and sculpted on pipe bowls; born in Dublin and transported in 1825, his bushranging career began in 1827 and ended in death from a policeman's bullet. Mobs appeared at elections, on Boyne Day, at executions – and Sydney's Cabbage-Tree Hat mob was permanent. In sum, colonial life was varied, colourful, ebullient. Different people put different gloss on those basic qualities. The *Sydney Morning Herald*'s editorial for New Year 1850 stressed the rapid material progress of New South Wales. This had accrued moreover 'without any of those extraordinary accidents to which some other countries are indebted for a mushroom precocity of growth. We owe nothing to gold-dust or precious stones'.

---

[67] Quoted in M. Roe, *Quest for Authority in Eastern Australia, 1835–1851*, Melbourne, 1965, p. 91.

4

1850-70

T. H. Irving

*The ruling class—the working classes—the nature of responsible
government—the debate on the New South Wales constitution—
the constitutions of Victoria, South Australia and Tasmania—the
anti-transportation movement—the role of government—railways
—assisted immigration—the land question—the gold rushes—
the New South Wales goldfields—the Victorian goldfields—the
Eureka rebellion—effects of gold rushes—the conservatives—the
liberals—the radicals—trades unionism—the introduction of responsible government—early ministries and parliaments—democ-
ratization in Victoria and New South Wales—the Chinese—
Aborigines and Pacific Islanders—Tasmanian politics—the
pastoral industry—agriculture—rural finance—land reform—the
lands laws of New South Wales—Victoria—social tension—
constitutional conflicts in Victoria—separation of church and
state—population—loyalty.*

The twenty years after 1850 decisively shaped Australia's class structure
and its political system. In this period three processes interacted: the
rise of the urban bourgeoisie, the establishment of parliamentary
government in five colonies, and the growth of a sense of identity
among the colonists, as their efforts to form a branch of British
civilization, an empire within an empire, began to succeed. The outcome was not a classless, democratic nation, but six colonies with one
ruling class, divided six ways, and on its main fronts in Victoria and
New South Wales, restructured by the rise of the bourgeoisie.

The men who ruled the Australian colonies in 1850 derived their
authority in various ways. The officials and judges were appointed
by the British government. The leading capitalists represented the
British banking, trading and land companies. The professional
notability had British educational and professional qualifications. The
members of this ruling class had much in common with other colonists
who were making, or improving, their fortunes in the colonies. However, they were a distinct group because their families formed part of
the British upper class, they dominated and almost monopolized
colonial politics, and they controlled the key sectors of the colonial
economies, the pastoral, agricultural and mining industries.

In eastern Australia, most members of the ruling class were squatters (there were less than a thousand in 1850) or connected in some way with the pastoral industry. Since the early 1840s, however, the squatters had caused strains inside the ruling class by developing their own programme, which can best be described as pastoralism. Its basic proposition was that the pastoral industry was the country's productive interest. Additionally, it asserted that squatting was the pioneering stage of civilization, that land in Australia had no intrinsic value before the squatter pastured his sheep on it, and that the squatters suffered the privations of outback life for the good of the colony. For all these reasons the squatters demanded security of tenure, an abundant supply of cheap labour including convicts or coolies, and self-government. Naturally, as a conservative oligarchy, they did not intend to share power by widening political privileges. They defended their high rate of profit because it attracted capital to the colony, and argued that any encouragement of non-productive and hence dependent sections of the economy, such as trading and manufacturing, would harm the pastoral industry.

In the early 1850s, there was little class consciousness outside the ruling class, except the resentment that a ruling class existed at all in a new country where everybody aspired to wealth and respectability. Moreover, the English Whig notion that society was composed of interests, not socio-economic classes, was general among both conservatives and radicals. Thus, when the leading urban businessmen challenged their dependent status within the ruling class, they readily assumed that society was split by the conflict of economic interests. However, as they moved towards class consciousness, they often called these interests 'classes', attributing combativeness, collective awareness and moral and political positions to them. So, 'Publicola', writing in Henry Parkes's *Empire* in 1851, said, 'The whole population of Australia is politically and socially divided into three classes, viz. – 1st, The Squattocracy or vested interest; 2nd, the Bureaucracy or Mercantile interest; and 3rd, the Democracy or Labouring interest'.[1]

As memories of the depression of the 1840s faded, Sydney and Melbourne merchants began to diversify their activities. Typical was Thomas Barker, one of the founders of the Commercial Banking Company of Sydney in the 1830s. Now he was promoting railway development, helping to found the Royal Exchange in Sydney, and expanding his interests in steam mills, cloth factories, trading warehouses, and properties in Sydney and the countryside. Barker, and his counterparts in Adelaide and Melbourne (e.g. Henry 'Money' Miller) were sure that the supremacy of the pastoral industry in the economy was injurious to their interests. They were joined in this belief by some agriculturalists and wealthy professional men, and the clerks and shop assistants of the cities. They called themselves liberals because they thought that other interests should be equal in opportunity to

1 *Empire*, Sydney, 21 April 1851.

squatting, and because they did not accept that the civilized competition of interests in society and politics should be swamped by the ascendancy of the common people. Let there be self-government, they said, to free us from the selfish alliance of Downing Street and the squatters, and let democracy and responsible government be reached by steady and tested steps. Above all else there had to be economic development, which implied freedom to discover and exploit new resources, a steady influx of capital and skilled labour, and the cessation of transportation and of all the other practices that made the colonies 'plantation economies'.

According to the census of 1851 Sydney had over 7000 merchants, bankers, shopkeepers and manufacturers, but most of these, especially the shopkeepers and the manufacturers, were properly a part of 'Publicola's' third interest, which was an agglomeration of small and would-be capitalists. They were labouring men only in the sense that they regarded their labour power as their way to acquire capital. About 1000 worked in Sydney's 200 factories, mainly making flour, cloth, soap and sugar, and there were perhaps another 2000 skilled artisans, many of them self-employed. These men, together with several hundred publicans, were the 'democracy' – not the bush-workers, most of whom were ex-convicts, nor the unskilled labourers in the city, nor the domestic servants. Although they were a small part of the work-force they could attract considerable attention. Their skills were usually in short supply, and they cherished the 'independence' which came with either good wages or working on one's own account. A day's labour (worth 4/6) paid the weekly rent on a four-room house in 1851, and as bread and meat sold at a few pence a lb, many men extended the Sabbath in honour of 'Saint Monday'. Moreover, their self-esteem was reinforced by a family life in which their wives sought to realize their own version of independence, in the home. Very few Australian-born women entered domestic service or the clothing factories.

By 1851 the radicalism of the workingmen and their allies, which was modelled on the British political unions of the 1830s, had acquired a colonial flavour. In their view it was not sufficient that other interests besides the pastoral should be recognized; rather government must be responsible for the balance of interests in society. This clearly implied action by a strong government to provide work for the unemployed, to regulate immigration, to place small men on the land, to encourage manufacturing, and so on. They thought of themselves as upholding middle class virtues like thrift, sobriety and industriousness; they were the vanguard of a movement to unify all sections of the community, except monopolistic squatters, or, in their words, to create 'the people'. Knowing that the wealthy and 'respectable' portion of the community looked down on them as 'the working classes', they were forced to issue frequent appeals to those above them for the unity of the 'middle and lower classes'. However some of the radicals were already trade unionists who felt more sceptical about the possibility of unity with capitalists. In 1851 Melbourne and Sydney each had about a dozen 'trades societies', whose members preferred the principle of 'association' to liberal individualism, which they thought was infecting true radicalism. They hinted vaguely at the need for a redistribution of wealth and for democracy, in the interests of the working class, whom they saw as the real 'people'.

When the Australian colonies entered the decisive stage of their transition to responsible government, Britain was committed to a new form of imperial relationship with her colonies of settlement. Two developments had brought this about: the policy of free trade, and the belief, which had been growing since the American War of Independence, that the colonies of settlement should be viewed as 'developing nations', who would enhance Britain's prestige and power more effectively as her junior imperial partners than as dependencies. The constitutional basis for this new imperial design, which wonderfully identified the sentimental ties of a spreading British civilization with the material interests of all its parts, was responsible government. In the 1830s and 1840s, the development of cabinet government in Britain and of a convention in Canada by which heads of departments resigned when they lost the support of either the governor or a majority of the elected legislature, created a rough sketch of responsible government. A firmer outline appeared in 1846 when the Secretary of State for the Colonies, Earl Grey, permitted the British North American colonies to set up ministries wholly responsible to their legislatures. This occurred after a series of political crises. In contrast there was no anti-imperial 'struggle for responsible government' in the Australian colonies.[2] Rather, constitution-making was concerned with who should rule after the introduction of responsible government.

In 1850 Britain was not prepared to grant responsible government to the Australian colonies, for, according to Grey, they were lacking in population and political experience and they were not aware of their imperial responsibilities. So the enlarged powers of self-government conceded by the Australian Colonies Government Act of 1850 did not cover Crown lands and the revenue derived from them, nor did it include responsible government. However, Victoria was separated from New South Wales, and was provided with a two-thirds elected and one-third nominated Legislative Council, as were South Australia and Tasmania. The councils of these colonies could now make laws on some matters hitherto decided by the British parliament: the electoral system, local government, the judiciary and customs duties (as long as the duties were not differential). At the time, the most important concession of all was scarcely noticed: the colonies could, with British permission, rewrite their constitutions to provide for two chambers.

It is easy to misunderstand the colonists' attitudes to responsible

2 See T. H. Irving, 'The Idea of Responsible Government in New South Wales before 1856', in *H.S.*, *42*, April 1964.

government. That it was not extensively discussed did not mean that no one knew what it entailed; indeed during the 1840s the colonists of New South Wales had shown just the opposite. Most colonists wanted responsible government in some form. Although some conservatives in the early 1850s rejected it because, as William Charles Wentworth explained, they thought 'oligarchy was better than socialism',[3] the benefits that responsible government would bestow on those in power gradually overcame conservative fears. In New South Wales by December 1851 the legislature, led by Wentworth, was demanding a constitution similar in outline to Canada's: two legislative chambers, full control of local matters, and responsible government. From that time the issue of constitutional reform was debated in the belief that New South Wales would follow the Canadian pattern, and that responsible government was an integral part of self-government.

The government and the squatters dominated the select committees of 1852 and 1853 which framed the constitution in New South Wales. It was a conservative document which relied on the upper house both to check the democratic excesses of the lower house and as a means of controlling responsible government for the ruling class. After Wentworth's scheme for a hereditary aristocracy drawn from 'the Shepherd Kings' was killed by vulgar ridicule about Bunyip Aristocrats with rum kegs on their coats of arms, the committee settled for an upper house, or council, nominated by the Governor. Pensions were to be provided for those officials who might have to retire 'on political grounds', but Wentworth hoped that the council would contain some of the present officials, who would continue as members of the government. The franchise for the lower house, or assembly, was extended, but the existing distribution of seats, which greatly favoured the squatters, was retained. A further conservative bulwark was the requirement that majorities of two-thirds in both houses were necessary to alter the constitution and the electoral system. The constitution also distinguished between what were thought to be imperial and colonial subjects; land policy, of course, was a colonial subject, i.e., determined by the New South Wales parliament. Finally, compensation was offered to the squatters, if and when their lands were put up for sale. In the words of supporters of this constitution, the 'monied democrats' would control the lower house, the 'productive interest' the upper house, and the government, ruling 'by antagonism', would contain some ministers chosen from and responsible to the lower house, and others chosen from the upper house and responsible to the governor who appointed them.[4]

From 1850 there was an intermittent and loose alliance of liberals

---

[3] *Sydney Morning Herald*, 9 April 1851.

[4] The speeches of W. C. Wentworth, James Martin, M. H. Marsh and W. M. Manning in the Legislative Council were published in the *Sydney Morning Herald* in December 1852, May 1853 and August 1853.

and radicals in New South Wales in the movement against transporta·
tion, as well as in the election of the Rev. John Dunmore Lang to the
council, and in the opposition to the gold-mining regulations. At the
end of 1850 Henry Parkes established his newspaper the *Empire* as a
sign that pragmatic radicals were separating themselves from the
'socialistic' doctrinaires, who controlled the *People's Advocate* (1848–
54), the Political Association (1851) and the Democratic League (1852–
3). *The Empire* became a bridge betweeen the pragmatic radicals and
the liberals. Meanwhile, the liberals controlled the anti-transportation
movement and the New South Wales Constitution Committee of 1853.[5]
Despite their organizational differences, radicals and liberals agreed
in seeing the constitution in socio-economic terms. The radicals said
that Wentworth's constitution was 'an undisguised attempt to separate
the colony into classes ... and to check the progress of democracy'.
The proposed constitution was a check to the colony's overall economic
development, said the liberals.[6] But in their opposition to the squatters' constitution the radicals and liberals also began to merge their
analyses of the social structure. The radicals joined in the demand for
greater recognition for urban interests, and the liberals agreed that a
proper government could harmoniously compose all interests within
a single entity, 'the people'. Once 'the people' was a living feature of
society, no one need fear complete democracy and full responsible
government, both groups said.

Most of the debate on the constitution occurred before the colony
received clarification of Britain's attitude to the composition of the
upper house and the form of responsible government. It was May 1853
before despatches arrived from Grey's successors at the Colonial Office,
Sir John Pakington and the Duke of Newcastle, replying to the
council's demands of 1851. The colonists discovered that the British
government had reversed Grey's refusal to make concessions, because
of 'those extraordinary discoveries of Gold which have lately taken
place in some of the Australian Colonies, and which may be said to
have imparted new and unforeseen features to their political and
social condition'.[7] After constructing a constitution similar in outline
to that of Canada, the colony was permitted to exercise the full powers
of self-government, including the disposal of Crown lands. The colony
could decide for itself whether to elect or nominate its upper house,
but there was no mention in these despatches of responsible government. It was November 1853 before another despatch from Newcastle

5 P. Loveday, ' "Democracy" in New South Wales: The Constitution Committee
of 1853', in *R.A.H.S.J.*, *42*, 4, October 1956.

6 Letter in the *Empire*, Sydney, 9 November 1853: J. B. Darvell, 23 August 1853,
in E. K. Silvester, Ed., *The Speeches in the Legislative Council . . .* , Sydney, 1853.

7 Despatch from Pakington to FitzRoy, 15 December 1853, in C.O. 201/450. See
also Newcastle to FitzRoy, 18 January 1853, in C.O. 201/453, and the discussion in
J. M. Ward, *Earl Grey and the Australian Colonies, 1846–1857*, Melbourne, 1958,
ch. 11.

arrived advising Governor FitzRoy that the constitution should prepare for the introduction of responsible government by providing adequate pensions for the existing officials. He stressed also the importance of a bicameral legislature. The British government, of course, was not aware that the constitutions of both 1852 and 1853 already fulfilled Newcastle's vague instructions. Misled by FitzRoy's claim that 'the thinking portion of the community' did not desire responsible government, Britain thought it was prudently anticipating a future colonial demand.[8]

The truth was, rather, that both the squatters and their opponents wanted responsible government, but in a form suited to their own advantage. Until the end of 1853 the conservatives who framed the constitution believed that ministers would be individually responsible for their portfolios to either the new assembly or the Crown, that some of the present officials would remain in the government, and that those ministers in the nominated upper house would happily escape the worst aspect of democracy, the rough and tumble of 'party' politics in the assembly. James Macarthur put this point of view succinctly:

the way in which responsible government will be introduced will be this – while the entire government will not be broken up, unless on some extraordinary occasion, no government will be able to stand which does not call into its ranks the active business talent of both houses ... [To] imagine that the colonial parliament could suddenly, and at once jump into two great contending parties is absurd.[9]

By the end of 1853 it was clear why the conservative pastoralists, country gentlemen and officials were not going to get the constitution they wanted. First, despite James Macarthur's ridicule, the objective of the radicals and liberals was precisely the construction of a party to dominate the assembly and form the government. In the council, Charles Cowper could usually muster ten liberal supporters, while outside, Henry Parkes, drawing on his contacts in radical and liberal organizations since 1848, threw a wide net of correspondence over like-minded people. Second, in the last stages of the debate on the constitution in the council, the belief that ministers would be individually responsible to either the governor or the assembly collapsed when it was realized that no constitutional provision could ensure that the incumbent officials would continue as part of the government against the wishes of the majority of elected members. The pivotal question was what would happen to the present officials if they were elected to the assembly. If they were among the five leading officials for whom the constitution provided pensions then they would be expected to retire 'on political grounds'. If they were among those not

[8] For a different view of the effects of this despatch see J. M. Ward, *Empire in the Antipodes: The British in Australasia: 1840–1860*, London, 1966, pp. 84–5.

[9] E. K. Silvester, Ed., *The Speeches in the Legislative Council . . .* , Sydney, 1853.

provided with pensions, then they would become 'placemen' of the Crown, forced to vote with the government of the day, or face dismissal. In the existing 'democratic' climate of opinion, the conservatives knew that to vote with the majority would be to vote against one's conscience. So in its final form the constitution prevented the election to the assembly of those officials not provided with 'political' pensions. The implication was that in the new parliament the ministers, whether in the upper or lower house, would be collectively responsible to the majority in the assembly alone.

In Victoria, the constitution was never a very salient political issue. The novelty of having a Legislative Council at first diverted its members from thinking of reforming it. Then the gold discoveries affected the radical movement in significant ways. The Reform Association in Melbourne and the People's Association in Geelong disappeared during the first rushes, and when the radicals regrouped late in 1852 they were preoccupied with land reform. So central was this issue that the squatters, unlike their counterparts in New South Wales, felt too intimidated to take the initiative in constitutional reform. Finally, by September 1853, when the council appointed a select committee to draw up a new constitution, a common antagonism to the turbulent gold immigrants made the government and the representatives of the squatters and urban businessmen sink their differences.[10]

By this time, the 1853 select committee had reported in New South Wales. Thus Victoria's select committee, dominated by the colonial secretary J. F. L. Foster, and the attorney-general, W. F. Stawell, never doubted that in the new parliament the ministry would be wholly responsible to the assembly and the excesses of democracy would have to be avoided by a conservative upper house. Newly appointed as colonial secretary, Foster was a squatter with more insight than most of his official colleagues into colonial radicalism's quest for order and property. Victoria's constitution, he said, aimed to direct the democratic stream 'into a proper channel; to develop that conservative element in it which is too often overlooked'.[11] Both houses would be elected, but the members of the new Legislative Council would be required to own land worth £5000, and they would be elected by the wealthiest landowners, squatters, and professional men. By contrast, in New South Wales there were no property qualifications for the nominated members of the new Legislative Council. The assemblies of both colonies would be elected on a fairly similar and extended franchise, and the distribution of seats was skewed in both cases to favour the conservative rural areas, but whereas any voter for the assembly in New South Wales could be elected a member, in Victoria there was a £2000 property qualification for membership.

[10] G. Serle, *The Golden Age: A History of the Colony of Victoria, 1851–1861*, Melbourne, 1963, pp. 130–146.

[11] Quoted in G. Serle, *The Golden Age: A History of the Colony of Victoria, 1851–1861*, Melbourne, 1963, p. 147.

Constitution-making in South Australia was a serious political issue throughout the early 1850s.[12] As in New South Wales in 1844 a critical factor was the widespread feeling that the government and the elected members as a body had separate interests. This situation was the product of the commitment to civil and religious liberty among the colonists (e.g., the formation of the South Australian Ballot Association and the abolition of state aid to religion in 1851) and of the lack of a conciliatory response by the governments of Sir Henry Young (before 1854) and Sir Richard Graves MacDonnell. The initial act of the first elected council was to reply to Governor Young's opening address by demanding 'independence in all matters not affecting Imperial interests'. Unity among the elected members also occurred in attacks on provisions of the existing constitution, such as the Civil List and the presence of nominees in the council. However, it was not carried over to the details of an alternative constitution. As in New South Wales, radicals and liberals advocated adult male suffrage, secret ballot and low property qualifications for members. South Australia also saw a strong demand for a single elected chamber.

Because a select committee on constitutional reform had been unable to produce a unanimous report at the end of 1852, Governor Young felt secure enough to take the initiative when he received despatches permitting the colony the same concession of self-government as New South Wales. The government drafted a conservative constitution, with an upper house nominated for life, and then extracted a pledge from the nominees in the council that they would support it whatever the elected members proposed. As an extra precaution, Young placed Pakington's despatch stipulating a nominated upper house before the council, but did not make public Newcastle's subsequent concession that the colony could make up its own mind whether to nominate or elect its new upper house. Young matched this deception of the colonists with a series of disingenuous despatches to the Colonial Office in which he neglected to report the existence of popular opposition to his constitution but stressed the division of opinion among the elected members over the form of the upper house. In fact the constitution of 1853 was passed only after the government, relying on colonial eagerness to administer the Crown lands, persuaded six elected members (three pastoralists and three radicals) to support it in return for the half-promise that after nine years the upper house might be made elective.

During 1853, Young's deceptions and his constitution were censured so strongly that the Secretary for the Colonies, Lord John Russell, returned the draft constitution to the colony with instructions that a new council should be elected to reconsider the question. The 1855 elections showed that the colonists wanted two elected chambers and full responsible government, but MacDonnell, the new governor, was

12 D. H. Pike, *Paradise of Dissent: South Australia: 1829–1857*, Melbourne, 1957, ch. 19.

determined to enjoy his full responsibilities for as long as possible. Like Young, he presented the colonists with his own constitutional proposals, which included an elected upper house to represent landed property. Further, he continued the practice of organizing a 'court party' to support the government in the legislature. However, the opposition, led by George Kingston, was strong enough to ensure adult male suffrage for the assembly, an elected upper house responsive to the wealth as well as the landed property of the community, three-year parliaments and secret ballot. Even some conservatives, including the colonial secretary, B. T. Finniss, deserted the governor when they realised that his constitution and his influence in the legislature would have left him supreme in the government. As in Victoria, these conservatives were confident of their power to manage democracy; according to Finniss 'they preferred the possibility of a despotism within, which they could subvert, to a despotism without which was irresistible'.[13] The constitution was then amended to remove the last barriers to full responsible government.

MacDonnell had taken his main proposals from Tasmania's constitution of 1854. From its first meeting in December 1851 the new Legislative Council of Tasmania was preoccupied with the transportation question, as the elected members united in a body to embarrass the local government and persuade Britain to stop sending convicts. Eventually in 1852, the governor, Sir William Denison, had to dismiss his colonial secretary, H. S. Chapman, and another official for succumbing to this pressure and failing to support the government in a critical vote. In such a climate, the council naturally stressed the demarcation of imperial from local interests when it turned its attention to constitution-making in 1853. The elected members were so overwhelmingly conservative that there was virtually no discussion of the constitution's provisions for responsible government. The constitution was not completed until late 1853, but it was the first to receive the Royal assent, because at the last moment the Council removed the list of powers reserved to the Crown, in order to speed up its introduction. The British parliament also struck out the list of imperial powers from the other constitutions and the two-thirds clause from that of New South Wales.

The nearest Australia came to an organized inter-colonial struggle for self-government was the anti-transportation movement of the early 1850s.[14] In New South Wales the opposition to convicts in the late 1840s was half-hearted because the urban bourgeoisie were torn between their moral repudiation of transportation and their vestigial support for pastoralism. In 1850, however, they were provoked by Earl Grey's contention that the Legislative Council had never decisively

13 B. T. Finniss, *The Constitutional History of South Australia . . .* , Adelaide, 1886, p. 353.

14 J. M. Ward, *Earl Grey and the Australian Colonies, 1846–1857*, Melbourne, 1958, ch. 8.

rejected transportation because the pastoral industry could not survive without convicts. Their spokesman, John Lamb, replied to Grey in August 1850 by moving in the council for an Address to the Queen praying that 'no more convicts ought under any conditions to be sent to any part of the colony'. The squatters continued to search for a compromise. After their proposals that the colony should take 'exiles', that is, convicts thought to be partly reformed after a period in a British prison, and for a new northern penal colony whose ticket-of-leave men could be expected to drift south, were defeated, they walked out of the chamber and Lamb's motion was then carried unanimously.

A change had come over the anti-transportation movement between 1849 and 1850. Formerly the radical workingmen were the organizers of the movement, but in the Anti-Transportation Association, formed in 1850, business and professional men were dominant. Moreover, not only did they succeed organizationally, collecting 36,000 signatures to their petitions, but also they were now more vehement than the radicals in their rejection of pastoralism. As one liberal lawyer warned at an anti-convict meeting in 1850, 'It is the worship of the golden fleece among ourselves that we have chiefly to fear'.[15] Six large employers of labour in Sydney jointly argued that the resumption of transportation would increase the cost of protecting property, divert capital from the colony and discourage the sort of immigrant who could both produce and consume manufactured goods. Even in the country areas at this time, anti-convict speakers saw the colony's future in urban bourgeois terms. In Bathurst, for example, one speaker asked:

Are we to consider this country as having no other resources than those of sheep and cattle? No! No! These must soon reach their limit, other vents for industry must be found; mines and manufactures brought into play; a pastoral country is ever a scattered and a poor one.[16]

John Lamb concluded that as a result of the transportation question,

a feeling of hostility was springing up between the gentry and the middle class, while the passions of the lower orders were becoming inflamed.[17]

Earl Grey became alarmed when FitzRoy warned him that the 'lower orders' were becoming discontented with the British government. So, in June 1851 he revoked the 1848 Order in Council, which had made possible the resumption of transportation. However, in his view, the colony was a sheep-run on which there would be always a shortage of labour, and he said repeatedly that he expected the colonists to ask for transportation to be resumed in some form.

15 Speech of G. K. Holden in *Sydney Morning Herald*, 18 September 1850.

16 *Sydney Morning Herald*, 20 September 1850, p. 3.

17 Report of Legislative Council debate in *Sydney Morning Herald*, 7 October 1850.

Grey's insensitivity to colonial feelings was resented everywhere except Western Australia. Moreover Port Phillip and South Australia, neither of which had ever officially received convicts, had long regarded the 'expirees' coming from Tasmania's underdeveloped economy as a source of contagion. Thus there were good reasons to form an inter-colonial confederation to end transportation to eastern Australia. From January 1851 the Australasian League for the Abolition of Transportation co-ordinated the activities of existing anti-convict committees in Hobart, Launceston, Melbourne, Geelong and Sydney. Under its auspices, a similar committee was established in Adelaide. On four occasions, delegates from some or all of the four eastern colonies met in conference. The league took no concerted action, but as a warning that united colonial resistance was possible, it had some impact in England where its representatives helped to persuade the Colonial Office to take the final 'no-convict' decision in December 1852. Changes in British penal practice and in attitudes to secondary punishment were also influential in ending transportation to eastern Australia.[18]

The most combative phase of the anti-convict agitation began when the news arrived in March 1852 of Grey's stubborn insistence that Tasmania must continue to take convicts. The occasional militancy of the colonial radicals paled before that of an outraged bourgeoisie. The latter now stressed the 'constitutional aspect' of the convict question; if the colonies had self-government and if the liberals were in power, they would not have to take convicts. Now it was Cowper's turn to talk of fighting and sacrifice and it was Lamb who spoke of separation from Britain. The Roman Catholic Archdeacon McEncroe said that, 'if pushed, he felt that there was a point at which loyalty itself became a crime'.[19] In this period the league became a symbol of emerging national consciousness.[20] On letterheads and pamphlets, at league meetings and on colonial vessels, the league flag appeared: five silver stars, in the form of a cross, on a blue ground, with the Union Jack in the top left-hand corner. It was the league that began that awkward tradition of offering a money prize for the composition of an Australian anthem. Later, Gilbert Wright, the league's secretary, when arguing for a National Day to celebrate its achievements, said, 'We should ... aim at nationality – at individuality – at a character. We should not blend our associations with the histories of the Old World! Why not have an era – a chronology of our own?'[21]

[18] See A. G. L. Shaw, *Convicts and the Colonies*, London, 1966, pp. 347–50: J. M. Ward, *Earl Grey and the Australian Colonies, 1846–1857*, Melbourne, 1958, pp. 213–14. Transportation of convicts to Western Australia ended in January 1868.

[19] *Empire*, Sydney, 8 April 1852.

[20] C. S. Blackton, 'The Dawn of Australian National Feeling, 1850–1856', in *Pacific Historical Review, XXIV*, May 1955.

[21] Letter to the editor of the *Sydney Morning Herald*, 16 June 1853.

In the course of the anti-transportation movement, the urban businessmen moved towards class consciousness by widening their economic and political horizons. They discovered that they could not reject the convict system without breaking with pastoralism, without leading a popular movement, and, in the Australasian league, without dedicating themselves to building a balanced, self-sufficient and inter-colonial economy. Whether in Sydney, where the *Empire* said 'Our trading intercourse is a common inheritance – we are necessary to each other',[22] or in Launceston, whose delegate in Sydney said 'The Australias were one',[23] the league linked anti-convictism to national economic development. More narrowly, the pay-off for the bourgeois conscience, which abhorred transportation on moral grounds, was, as Wright declared, that in obeying their moral instincts they were also acting 'on the nicest calculation of their material interests'.[24]

Economic development to the bourgeoisie meant a more diversified economy, and a bigger skilled labour force and home market through immigration. A few even dreamt of exporting Australian goods to Asia and the Pacific. However, just as important was a new economic and social order: the businessmen wanted class relationships and the values on which they were based to be different from those they associated with pastoralism. While coping with such issues as railway development, immigration and land policy, they began to sketch the outlines of this order.

The colonial capitalists spoke of 'free trade' and 'laissez-faire' but they relied heavily on the government, not only to remove existing restrictions on the economy but also to encourage 'the germs of industry'. They organized chambers of commerce as political pressure groups in Sydney, Melbourne and Hobart, and by 1852 the chambers succeeded in reforming the tariffs of the three colonies along similar, simplified lines – 'one of the best things done by us', as Cowper wrote to Parkes.[25] They were anxious to encourage the government to survey the resources of the country and to promote the marriage of science and industry, so they formed scientific societies. The results were often pathetic or tragic. A case of cabbage-tree hats represented colonial manufactures at the Great Exhibition in London in 1851. The ill-fated Burke and Wills expedition of 1860–61 was sponsored by the Royal Society of Victoria out of scientific curiosity, inter-colonial rivalry and dreams of commercial advantage.

Most of all the capitalists required the government to undertake essential utilities which were unattractive to local and overseas investors. This particularly applied to railways, which in this period

22 Editorial in the *Empire*, Sydney, 9 February 1853.

23 As reported in the *Empire*, Sydney, 28 April 1851.

24 *Empire*, Sydney, 28 April 1851.

25 See J. A. La Nauze, 'Merchants in Action: The Australian Tariffs of 1852', in *Economic Record, XXXI*, May 1955.

were begun by joint stock companies but usually completed, and almost invariably operated, by governments. This considerable advance of state enterprise was the result of a two-pronged attack in which the capitalists, adopting the radical viewpoint, came to see that it was important for the government to discourage the growth of monopolies. Attacking the squatters, the *Empire* wrote sarcastically: 'Iron ways through the Australian bush! Let loose a flood of poor striving competitors over the land to rob me of my lordly supremacy over sheep and bunyips! Perish the thought! I take my stand upon the ancient ways; the bullock team is the national vehicle of Australia; no levelling ways for me.'[26] As well, the liberal capitalists attacked the 'adventurers and stock-jobbers' who thought more of the benefits of monopoly than of the railway's advantages to civilization in a new country, and demanded that the government buy them out. By 1870 more than a thousand miles of railway track was in use in Australia.

Assisted immigration continued through the 1850s, even to Victoria, and as always there were complaints about its quality.[27] But now, while the strongest demands were for skilled workers for the building and manufacturing sectors, and for Cornishmen to replace the copper miners in South Australia who had gone to the diggings, there were also appeals for respectable families and single females to raise the tone of urban life. The merchants applauded, and sometimes donated money to Caroline Chisholm's Family Colonization Loan Society, which began sending 'superior' immigrants in 1850, and there was talk of a return to the bounty system, in the hope that a 'free trade' in immigrants might find prospective colonists who did not lack energy and self-respect. Naturally, when some squatters resumed importing Chinese and Indian coolies during the gold rushes, and proposed that assisted British immigrants should be indentured, the outcry was loud and principled. There were racialist assumptions about the immorality of the coloured labourers, but these were translated into the fear that unskilled, uneducated labourers in a plantation economy might become a separate, inferior caste. Again the capitalists adopted the viewpoint of the radicals, this time arguing that the independence of all workers would be jeopardized, class divisions would be widened, and political rights restricted.

In both New South Wales and Victoria in the first half of the 1850s the land policy of the liberal politicians was that agricultural reserves in the unsettled districts should be opened for sale as a step towards the 'free trade in land'. They said very little about the real barriers to

---

[26] Editorial in the *Empire*, Sydney, 29 April 1853.

[27] In the years 1850-59 Victoria received 88,475, New South Wales 72,638 and South Australia 50,354 government-assisted immigrants from Britain. In the years 1860-69 the respective figures were 43,989, 21,285 and 14,702. Newly separated Queensland paid for 48,726 assisted British migrants in the 1860s. See F. K. Crowley, 'The British Contribution to the Australian Population: 1860-1919', in *University Studies in History and Economics*, 1954.

establishing a yeomanry: the high price of Crown land, the system of sale by auction, and a host of acts, regulations and administrative practices which favoured the pastoral industry at the expense of agriculture.[28] In New South Wales, while the radicals pressed for economic independence on the land, their middle-class allies agreed with the squatters and landowners that the working-class immigrants had no right to expect easy purchase of land, and that a scattered farming population was undesirable. By the end of 1852 in Victoria disappointed diggers were adding their voices to the clamour for land reform, but it was successful diggers, businessmen speculating in land, and a growing bourgeoisie resenting the aristocratic pretensions of the squatters who dominated the debate.

The radicals watched with interest as the bourgeoisie continued their public defection from 'the plantation economy'. There was already a conviction among the radicals that their values of industriousness, self-improvement as the basis for an improved society, and social harmony conflicted with the values of pastoralism. Now the radicals joined the liberals in fearing that 'squattish attitudes' (as the *Empire* called them) might be transferred from the pastoral industry to other areas of society; cotton, wine, olive and silk production were specified as objects of 'squattish' aggrandisement. All forms of monopoly, and speculative activity on a large scale, were denounced as 'squattish', while demands for indentured labour in New South Wales were seen as an indication that the squatters desired an extension of the 'plantation economy'. The result was that economic development became associated with 'the defence of civilization' and the urban workingmen and small capitalists strengthened their attachment to the liberal bourgeoisie.

The discovery of gold in commercial quantities in the three eastern mainland colonies from 1851 onwards paved the way for a long economic boom between 1860 and 1890. When alluvial mining declined in the late 1850s, unemployment increased in Melbourne and Sydney, but much of the slackness in the economy was soon taken up by the lively building industry and by the construction of railways and other public works. By 1860 the gold discoveries had invigorated the pastoral industry by creating lower freight rates to Europe for wool, good prices on the diggings for mutton and beef, and labour for fencing and dam building. The squatters also took their share of the vast inflow of British capital. Yet, each year until 1871 gold supplanted wool as Australia's main export, and this was a tremendous, symbolic blow to the squatters. More significantly, even when the export picture changed, wool never regained its key role as the staple of the economy.

Initially, the gold rushes produced economic and financial dislocation, and an unexpected increase in the supply of labour and capital. In the ten years after 1851 the non-aboriginal population of

[28] D. W. A. Baker, 'The Origins of Robertson's Land Acts', in *H.S.*, *30*, May 1958.

Australia almost trebled to 1,200,000. The gold immigrants rapidly produced a work-force with a high level of skill and literacy, and a market with a good spread of purchasing power. The majority went to Victoria, which became the most populous colony in 1854; ninety per cent of them tried their luck on the goldfields. The New South Wales fields in the 1850s probably never had more than 10,000 men at one time, but in 1855 the number of adult males passed the 100,000 mark on the Victorian diggings.

Social origin and past position counted for little among the diggers. 'This was that rare thing in the history of mankind, a social democracy; and a social democracy in which gentility and education carried with them neither respect nor reward.'[29] Moreover, at this time gold mining did not create a class structure or consciousness. Most diggers had mates and formed cooperative parties of three to six. These parties gradually became small companies, with 'sleeping partners' and employees, and in this way capitalist enterprise came to the diggings before heavily mechanized and capitalized companies appeared on some fields in the middle and late 1850s. In these conditions it was impossible for the consciousness of the diggers to be wholly anti-capitalist, or wholly acquisitive and selfish. Their search for independence was balanced by their experience of cooperative economic and social activity.

In New South Wales, the 1852 Gold Fields Management Act gave legislative force to the thirty shillings monthly licence, which it doubled for aliens, and provided harsh penalties for breaking its provisions. Further, all persons on the fields had to have licences, whereas previously traders, publicans, and perhaps a third of the diggers (those employed by other miners) had not taken out licences. While taxing small-scale capitalism on the fields, the government made concessions to the large urban capitalists who had petitioned in the name of 'labour organized by capital and science', and who asserted wrongly that the fields were monopolized by 'insulated, desultory diggers'.[30] The want of 'capital and science' already excluded the typical, small co-partnerships from mining the quartz seams, which required crushing machinery, but now they were brought into direct competition with the large mining companies to whom the Act granted leases of extensive tracts of alluvial ground. By 1853 when the colony's leading entrepreneur, Thomas Sutcliffe Mort, gave the main toast at the Gold Anniversary Dinner, the bourgeoisie were appropriating the benefits of the gold discoveries for mercantile liberalism: 'Gold is the mainspring of commerce; commerce is the forerunner of civilization; and civilization is the handmaiden of Christianity'.[31]

---

29 G. Serle, *The Golden Age: A History of the Colony of Victoria, 1851–1861*, Melbourne, 1963, p. 92.

30 *Empire*, Sydney, 15 July 1852.

31 *Sydney Morning Herald*, 14 February 1853.

Meanwhile, the radicals were attempting unsuccessfully to co-ordinate the resentment against the recent act. In late 1852 the remnants of the Political Association formed the Democratic League for the Defence of the Rights of Industry and of Free Government, but they could not interest the miners in democratic political reforms, nor the urban workingmen in the notion, popularized by James McEachern among the miners, that labour, like capital, was best defended by the rights of property. The miners had formed their own associations; as small-scale or expectant capitalists they welcomed equality of opportunity as much as the urban capitalists, and an informal alliance existed between them at this time, symbolized by their common cry of 'unlock the lands'. By February 1853 the league was collapsing, just as the government was despatching troops to the Turon River where some miners threatened to resist by force the introduction of the Act. At Sofala, men drilled and burned effigies of W. C. Wentworth. However, when the gold commissioner made only token attempts to collect the licence fees, the crowd of 15,000 dispersed. The diggers heeded a local clergyman more than the radical orators, once it was plain that the government would not absolutely prevent them getting a stake in the country. In 1853, the government justified the miners' trust by reducing the licence fee to 10s. but in the meantime most of the diggers had set out for the richer Victorian fields.

In Victoria, La Trobe's government was demoralised by the gold rushes. It was incapable of organizing the colony's finances and spent very little on amenities in the gold districts where the majority of the population resided. The licence fee of thirty shillings a month, payable in advance, was both a device to raise much-needed revenue and an instrument of social and economic control. The government feared and despised the diggers. Their deputations were received with coolness, their complaints about the state of the roads, the corruption and high-handedness of the police, and the injustice of a licence fee which fell equally on successful and unsuccessful miners alike, were largely rejected. The Legislative Council was no more sympathetic. Indeed, in 1853, when the government attempted to conciliate the diggers by giving them the vote and replacing the licence by an export duty on gold, the council blocked the government's plan. Earlier, in 1852, the Chamber of Commerce had persuaded the politicians to veto the idea of replacing gold licences with an export duty, which would force down the price of gold; Melbourne merchants never tried to form an alliance with the miners, as their counterparts in New South Wales did, to defend the principle of equality of opportunity.

Organized protests were common on the Victorian fields from October 1851, only two months after the first gold regulations were issued. The incompetence of the government and the intransigence of the Legislative Council meant that from the first the miners directed their protests against the misdeeds and failures of 'authority'. Accordingly they demanded the rights of representation and voting, in marked contrast to their counterparts in New South Wales. Further, although land reform was often raised, it was more a symbol of their hostility to the squatters than a serious demand. The miners at this stage nonchalantly believed they could realize their dream of living independently and yet fraternally and they did not see the present conflict in terms of a revolutionary situation. Like the Chartists, they believed in the efficacy of political change. Among the miners' leaders were several ex-Chartists who advocated the use of 'moral force' in the colony. Meetings, deputations, petitions and most dramatically, the passive resistance of the 'red ribbon' movement of 1853, when there was an organized refusal to take out a new licence, all showed that the mass of the diggers had turned to politics.

Sir Charles Hotham, the new governor (1854–5), arrived in June 1854, in the midst of a business recession when urban unemployment was forcing many ex-diggers back to the fields. Hotham was quite insensitive to the state of feeling in the colony. He mistook the bonhomie of his welcome from the diggers as evidence of contentment, and he refused to take the advice of his officials. In September he ordered twice-weekly licence inspections, which the miners called 'digger hunts', and encouraged the police and troops on the fields to crush resistance. On many fields, reform leagues were revived. The situation was tense at Ballarat, where there was a strong concentration of Irish diggers, and where the difficulties of making a living from mining were increasing as the seams lay deeper underground. Here, also, Hotham had to dismiss a magistrate and a police sergeant for corruption in connection with the release of a publican, Bentley, who had murdered a miner. But Hotham would not release three miners who had been singled out for arrest after a large crowd had set fire to Bentley's hotel. Their release was one of the demands of a deputation from the Ballarat Reform League, who also asked Hotham for the disbanding of the Gold Commission (which administered the licence system), the abolition of the licence, manhood suffrage, payment of members of parliament, no property qualification for members, and land reform.

For the previous three years a mass democratic movement had been flickering into life. Contacts had been established between the fields, and with Melbourne and the major towns. It was led by capable, respectable men, with backgrounds in English and Welsh Chartism, like Henry Holyoake and J. B. Humffray. Although the movement was captured briefly at Ballarat in November 1854 by supporters of 'physical force', this was the result of a momentary failure of the usual leadership, rather than a shift to a revolutionary perspective. When Hotham's only response to the deputation was to fob them off with a reference to a royal commission, which he had already appointed, and to send more troops to the field, the mood of the miners could no longer be satisfied by organized passive resistance. They burned their licences as a sign of their determination to resist with physical force the next time an injustice or harassment was committed by the authorities. Among the new leaders to emerge was Peter Lalor, an Irish engineer, whose hatred of injustice derived from a family tradition of leading the Irish lower classes against the English.[32] He led the miners in swearing an oath 'to stand truly by each other and to fight to defend our rights and liberties'. About fifteen per cent of the diggers at Ballarat took up arms, drilling and constructing a primitive stockade on the Eureka rise. But arms were scarce, leadership poor, and of the thousand diggers who followed Lalor, only 150 were left in the stockade on the Sunday morning, 3 December, when 400 troopers attacked, killing thirty of the defenders. Flushed with their easy victory, the troopers went on to terrorize the miners who lay asleep in their tents, killing three and wounding many others. Five troopers were killed.[33]

Now in Melbourne, and throughout the colony, the democratic movement burst into life, fanned by the Victorian Reform League. No jury could be found to convict any of the thirteen men, including Lalor, who were placed on trial for high treason. The Chamber of Commerce was persuaded to accept an export duty, as the most expedient way of taxing the miners, and the royal commission, strongly influenced by its chairman, the liberal William Westgarth, abolished the licence system and substituted an annual miner's right, costing £1, which carried with it the right to vote. In all this, Hotham acquiesced; at least the commission had condemned the diggers' resort to arms. The miners and their allies in the towns were more discriminating. They defended what the men at Eureka had done, but reaffirmed their preference for peaceful persuasion.

Contemporary hyperbole was misleading. Australia was not precipitated into nationhood by the gold discoveries, because their impact on the colonies was differential and because Victoria, although for a generation the most important colony in size and wealth, was not Australia. Gold created a new society with a distinctive politics in Victoria. The Victorian democratic movement was constantly preoccupied with the importance of political liberties. This was the sense in which democracy was born at Eureka: as a movement which stressed questions of political freedom, a movement unparalleled anywhere else in Australia. In New South Wales gold speeded up processes already under way and confirmed the emergence of a bourgeois hegemony resting on a wide agreement about economic development and social harmony. Tasmania lost ten thousand men to Victoria, crippling the economy, strengthening the dominance of the landed gentry, and

32 See C. Kiernan, 'Peter Lalor, the Enigma of Eureka', in *Labour and the Goldfields*, Australian Society for the Study of Labour History, Canberra, 1968, pp. 15–16.

33 The most comprehensive study of Eureka is the *Eureka Centenary Supplement* of *Historical Studies*, Melbourne, December 1954, enlarged and revised in 1965. An interesting contemporary account is by Carboni Raffaello, *The Eureka Stockade*, Melbourne, 1855, reprinted Melbourne, 1942, 1963, 1969. See also G. Serle, *The Golden Age: A History of the Colony of Victoria, 1851–1861*, Melbourne, 1963, ch. 6.

prolonging the era of master-servant relationships.[34] South Australia also lost ten thousand men, but those that remained or came back showed initiative and enterprise, and soon prospered. Her business-men pressured the government into passing a Bullion Act in 1852 which attracted gold by offering a higher price than Melbourne's; her traders opened up the Murray and her farmers provided the goods for them by doubling the acreage under cultivation in four years.

'The real Conservatives here are the aborigines, and all who, like them, would have the country remain as it is.'[35] Thus the *Empire* castigated the squatters, but there existed a more traditional con-servatism, in which responsibility from above balanced deference from below in a stable, stratified society, and in which government mediated the demands of interests and of imperfect individuals. Some land-owners, especially in New South Wales and Tasmania,[36] had become large landlords, with tenant farmers whose livelihood they controlled, whose transgressions they punished in the magistrates' courts, and whose votes they could rely on in the polling booths. In this sense the gentry conserved a way of life as well as the economic privilege of owning land. Further, by the 1850s, the largest landowners in New South Wales were also the largest squatters, while in Victoria, the style of life of the large squatters in the western district was already more suited to that of a gentry.[37] However, because these men were pioneers or speculators before they became landlords, their conserva-tism was not anti-capitalistic. In politics they despised the liberals: 'the active democrats, the traders in politics – ready and hungry for place, the men of desperate fortunes, and the young members seeking noto-riety', as James Macarthur said.[38] Their disputes with the liberals were seldom over principles, such as manhood suffrage or equality of opportunity, because the liberals rarely defended these wholeheartedly, but over the speed or extent of reform, or if they were squatters, over the rights of that particular form of capitalist enterprise. When forced to, the conservatives, especially in New South Wales, made strategic concessions to their opponents, but they were never decisively defeated, and although Macarthur and others tried, and failed, to overcome by organization their stubborn sense of political independence, they remained a political force.

Organization preoccupied the liberals. Their theory of representation

[34] H. Reynolds, '"That Hated Stain": The Aftermath of Transportation in Tasmania', in *H.S.*, *53*, October 1969.

[35] Editorial in the *Empire*, Sydney, 24 April 1851.

[36] H. Reynolds, '"Men of Substance and Deservedly Good Repute": The Tas-manian Gentry, 1856–1875', in *A.J.P.H.*, *XV*, 3, December 1969.

[37] M. Kiddle, *Men of Yesterday: A Social History of the Western District of Victoria, 1834–1890*, Melbourne, 1961.

[38] Quoted in B. Dickey, *Politics in New South Wales 1856–1900*, Melbourne, 1969, p. 8.

assumed that there was a contract between the politician and his constituents. They also believed that 'the collective power of the multitude, which is found in popular associations, if of itself a thing unwieldy and self-deranging, [requiring] a skilful hand to set it in motion [and direct it] to the accomplishment of a particular task'.[39] As well as leadership, the liberals saw the necessity of institutions to contain the political process. Again and again in the two decades after 1850 the liberals secured their ends because the conservative men of property recognized the importance of institutions 'to establish order and good government and to create a healthy conservative feeling'.[40] The liberals' prime aim was to change the political scene peacefully; their ultimate achievement was to obtain the consent of the governed in the name of democracy. As the most astute liberals said, parliamentary democracy was a conservative force in the colonies.

By the middle 1850s the liberals had developed a successful political strategy. First, harness popular support by using radical slogans, by assuming the leadership or the management of popular movements, and by building up a network of agents in the electorates. Second, construct factions in the legislature based on personal loyalty to a leader. Third, reassure the traditional conservatives by compromise and by pragmatic justifications of policy. Last, reform the electoral system and land laws to placate the masses, and to strike a symbolic blow for liberalism. Of course, the liberals were genuinely offended by aristocratic pretensions, and had a self-interested hatred of privileges unfairly acquired. These were the roots of their antagonism to the squatters. But they were not, in principle, opposed to conservatism.

The liberals were the first to realise that the cities would play a key role in the production of an Australian version of English civilization, and from this flowed much of their power over the radicals. The liberals were the entrepreneurs of civility as well as of economic growth; they sought a social existence of polite commerce and public-spirited activity. From both they expected personal fulfilment as well as profit and influence. Consequently, their organizing impulse was felt at every intersection of city life. The inactivity of local government, which the small tradesmen had dominated in Melbourne and Sydney since the 1840s, aroused the liberal zeal for civic progress. In his literary circle, the lawyer Nicol Drysdale Stenhouse encouraged the Australian-born poets Henry Kendall and Charles Harpur. In Melbourne, Sir Redmond Barry, Justice of the Supreme Court, was a great patron of the arts and the founder of the Public Library. The Mechanics' Institutes, already dedicated to social uplift, received improving attention from George Kenyon Holden, another lawyer, who, while flattering the institutes by calling them 'a people's university', lectured them on the benefits of joint-stock companies.

---

[39] Editorial in the *Empire*, Sydney, 25 March 1851.

[40] Quoted in G. Serle, *The Golden Age: A History of the Colony of Victoria, 1851–1861*, Melbourne, 1963, p. 193.

The radicals had almost no popular cultural defences to withstand the liberal challenge in this area. Politically, too, the radicals were on weak ground; in fact nothing in their analyses of society prepared them for the metamorphosis of the businessmen, from an economic interest to a ruling class. Radicals believed that all except the squatters had an equal interest in building the new society; because social relationships were democratic, classes in the colonies had to be vestiges of those in the old world. So if privilege existed, if unemployment, land monopoly and other grievances persisted, there were two solutions. Firstly, popular democracy, to sever the usurping connection between selfish interests and legislation. Secondly, the strategy of the panacea, a bold legislative act which would smash the monopolists, restore economic and social freedom to the people, and banish all other grievances. Free selection of land and protection of colonial industries were the most popular cure-alls.

There were different political situations in New South Wales and Victoria from the late 1850s, clearly evident in the position of the radical movements in the two colonies. In New South Wales the liberals had a long-standing liaison with the radicals, and they were able both to manipulate them and to soothe the fears of the conservatives. In Sydney, the wealthy Scottish Whig, John Black, led the Land League between 1857 and 1859,[41] and the Electoral Reform League flourished only while the Cowper liberals took charge of it. In Victoria, where both the liberals and the conservatives feared the preoccupation of the radicals with political liberties and where the merchants opposed tariff protection, the cleavage between democrats and conservatives could not be bridged by the liberals. Between 1857 and 1860 the Land Convention in Melbourne was the bearer of the democratic tradition which had emerged on the gold fields. As an alternative 'people's parliament' in 1857, and as the focus of a popular movement incorporating several score of local reform societies, the convention reflected the greater proportion of Chartists, Irish rebels, American supporters of 'equal rights' and European revolutionaries in Victoria's population. In addition to free selection of land before survey, the convention's demands included the six points of the charter (annual parliaments, universal male suffrage, equal electoral districts, no property qualification for membership of parliament, secret ballot, payment of members), the removal of the Chinese from the colony, and opposition to assisted immigration. The slogan, 'a vote, a rifle and a farm' was raised by the most militant of the conventionists, but the majority believed that the vote would be sufficient to get them the farm. In 1859 conventionists contested about half the seats in the general election. Moses Wilson Gray, an Irishman who was the first president, and ten others were elected, and formed a not very cohesive part of the 'Corner', which was led by another

41 See D. W. A. Baker, 'The Origins of Robertson's Land Acts', in *H.S.*, *30*, May 1958.

Irish patriot, Charles Gavan Duffy. By then, however, the convention was splitting, as protection challenged land reform as the chief radical demand and as many wage earners in the movement began to suspect all panaceas.

Some of the men who revived trade unionism in Melbourne and Sydney in 1855 were merely pursuing by new means the status and material comforts they had intended to acquire through economic independence. Others, like the British immigrants who formed a branch of the Amalgamated Society of Engineers on the ship out to Australia, were equally committed to self-improvement, but were also the bearers of a strongly developed, and exclusive, tradition of craft-conscious unionism.[42] Although wages were still high (a tradesman received between 15s. and 20s. a day in 1855) they were falling, and there was unemployment in Melbourne and Sydney.

In the late 1850s, although the trade unionists were still a minority of the urban work force, the days when 'trades societies' mainly dispensed benefits to sick and unemployed members, and when 'delegates of the trades' met irregularly, were over. Melbourne's Trades Hall was opened in 1859 after four years of formal cooperation between unions, including a short-lived attempt to set up an arbitration body. There were co-ordinated campaigns for the eight-hour day in each of the mainland colonies except Western Australia; most building workers in Melbourne and the larger Victorian towns had achieved it by 1857, in Sydney by 1861.[43] When economic conditions worsened at the end of the decade, the confrontations between workers and employers became more militant. After 1861 the unions won very few strikes, partly because some employers had also begun to combine. A seven-month lock-out by mine owners in the northern coalfields of New South Wales in 1862 put the miners' union out of action until the 1870s.[44]

The failure of industrial action in the 1860s strengthened the earlier interest of workingmen in politics. They sought to extend the principle of the eight-hour day by making it a condition of government contracts for public works; Victorian workers won this concession in 1870. To ease unemployment they wanted more public works, a halt to assisted immigration, and protection for native industry. In Victoria, the unions had formed political leagues in 1857 and 1859 and were an important, but separate, component of the democratic movement. They intervened in elections, but it was difficult to find suitable candidates before parliamentarians were paid. However, several workingmen were elected in Victoria, Charles Jardine Don being the

42 K. D. Buckley, *The Amalgamated Engineers in Australia, 1852–1900*, Canberra, 1970, ch. 1.

43 H. Hughes, 'The Eight Hour Day and the Development of the Labour Movement in Victoria in the Eighteen-Fifties', in *H.S.*, *36*, May 1961: J. Niland, 'The Birth of the Movement for an Eight Hour Working Day in New South Wales', in *A.J.P.H.*, *XIV*, 1, April 1968.

44 E. Ross, *A History of the Miners' Federation of Australia*, 1970, ch. 3.

first in 1859. There were also a few in New South Wales; for two years the miners in Newcastle financed the chairman of their union after he was elected to the Legislative Assembly in 1860.

By building a labour movement, the wage-earners separated themselves in practice from the radicals, even though they retained traces of the radical rhetoric while they searched for security as a class within the existing system. There was an artisanal form of working class consciousness among trade unionists at this time, characterized by the joining of the values of the 'independent' workingman to an assertion of the need for class action. For example, although trade unionists saw that the eight hour day would benefit them as individuals, they considered the increased control over their social environment which self-improved workingmen could exercise as a class as an even greater advantage. In much the same way, the social and cultural activities of the unions in Victoria and the political campaigns of unions both there and in New South Wales linked the search for craft exclusiveness with the broader ambition of realizing the egalitarian potential of a new country.[45]

Whereas Australia's infrequent 'national' days – like the Queen's birthday, or, in Sydney, the anniversary of the first settlement – were commonly celebrated on the harbour or at the race track, the opening of each of the four new parliaments was an occasion for decorous display and formal ceremony. Similarly, there was nothing casual about the setting up of parliamentary governments, between late 1855 and early 1857. The participants – governors, heads of departments, popular representatives and conservative upper-housemen – relished devising methods of consultation, forms of address, standing orders, and so on. At last they foresaw traditions in public life to complement and strengthen their middle-class codes of private behaviour. The main preoccupation was office – how to define it and how to get it. Power was desired for its own sake, and for the status attached to it, and any member of the assembly with a following of two or three could dream of achieving ministerial rank. The atmosphere was business-like, not crusading; politicians were unconcerned about placating constituents, satisfying interests and advocating reform. After all, there were no parties, and interest groups and popular movements, while articulate, were inexperienced in legislative politics. On the other hand the most successful politicians were those who made use of popular movements.

The handing-over of power to responsible ministries went fairly smoothly, except in Victoria and South Australia where the politicians had to overcome resistance from Governors Hotham and MacDonnell. There were no breakdowns in administration, partly because the former officials became the first responsible ministers, or, as in New

---

[45] See **R. A. Gollan**, *Radical and Working Class Politics: A Study of Eastern Australia, 1850–1910*, Melbourne, 1960, ch. 4: G. Serle, *The Golden Age: A History of the Colony of Victoria, 1851–1861*, Melbourne, 1963, pp. 241–8, 271–3.

South Wales, advised the government from behind the scenes. Nor were there any political crises, because the largest grouping in the legislatures, even after the elections of 1856 and 1857, was conservative and accustomed to working closely with the old officials. These men were not a majority, but they held the initial advantage of experience in public affairs. So there was more continuity of policy in this period than anybody expected. In Victoria, the former officials under W. C. ('Honest') Haines remained in office, except for a few weeks, until March 1858, and John O'Shanassy's ministry, which followed, was constructed of such disparate elements that no major policy change was possible. In Tasmania, a former official, F. Smith, was premier for nearly three and a half years from 1857. Much the same occurred in South Australia: three ephemeral ministries, followed by a lengthy term for a ministry including all the faction leaders, led by R. D. Hanson, who was a former official. Only in New South Wales was there something like a contest between left and right, but by the end of 1857 the Cowper-Robertson faction had established a liberal ascendancy.[46] In all four colonies, by the 1860s, the success of responsible government rested on governors who kept to their advisory role, permanent under-secretaries and other civil servants who reinforced the continuity of policy which a stable and conservative core of politicians developed, and on factions around which majorities could form in the legislatures.

There were other signs of continuity and conservatism in the political system. For a generation the ministries in South Australia, Tasmania and New South Wales were dominated by men who arrived or were born in Australia before 1850.[47] As well, the composition of the legislatures was stable. In South Australia, the assembly was dominated by 'independents' with agricultural interests. The rural gentry remained the most numerous group in the Tasmanian lower house. In Victoria and New South Wales, the urban mercantile, trading and professional men comprised 50–60 per cent of the membership of their assemblies.[48] Furthermore, all the Legislative Councils were fortresses of conservatism, their members being wealthy landowners, capitalists, or, as in New South Wales and Victoria, squatters.[49] Again, factions were not signs of a budding party system.

46 The two major works dealing with New South Wales are P. Loveday and A. W. Martin, *Parliament, Factions and Parties: The First Thirty Years of Responsible Government in New South Wales, 1856–1889*, Melbourne, 1966: and G. N. Hawker, *The Parliament of New South Wales: 1856–1965*, Sydney, 1971.

47 J. A. La Nauze, 'The Gold Rushes and Australian Politics', in *A.J.P.H., XIII*, 1, April 1967.

48 J. E. Mills, 'The Composition of the Victorian Parliament, 1856–1881', in *H.S., 5*, April 1942: A. W. Martin, 'The Legislative Assembly of New South Wales, 1856–1900', in *A.J.P.H., II*, 1, November 1956.

49 P. Loveday, 'The Legislative Council in New South Wales 1856–1870', in *H.S., 44*, April 1965: G. Serle, 'The Victorian Legislative Council, 1856–1950', in *H.S., 22*, May 1954.

In New South Wales, after the settlement of the electoral and land questions in the period 1858–61, the distinction between liberal and conservative weakened, both inside and outside the parliament, and the four factions which operated in the 1860s (led by C. Cowper and J. Robertson, H. Parkes, W. Forster and J. Martin) were heterogeneous in occupational composition.[50] In Victoria, although movements of various kinds flourished, and even the legislators readily identified liberal, radical and conservative parliamentary groupings, in fact these tendencies were cut across by the flux of factions, and by ministries, like those of J. McCulloch, that tried to embrace several interests and both conservative and democratic persuasions. Although the electoral, land, and state aid to religion and education issues produced a high degree of principled commitment among liberals, the main interest of politicians in all colonies was in issues of the 'roads and bridges' kind.[51] Finally, it was a rare electoral contest in which more than half of those on the rolls voted. In fact, there would have been more change in the political system if the colonists had not believed that their fortunate society posed no intractable problems. Although the colonists were not politically apathetic they saw no need to sustain a high level of political involvement after they had made their point.

The first timid bite at democracy in the Australian colonies left a rather uneven impression. South Australia was the most adventurous, its Constitution Act providing for triennial parliaments, manhood suffrage and no property qualifications for members of the assembly. In April 1856, South Australia also introduced secret ballot. On the other hand Tasmania legislated for secret ballot in February 1858, but for nothing else. In Victoria and New South Wales these questions produced serious conflict between conservatives and their opponents, and, in the crucial areas of manhood suffrage and equal electoral districts, a democratic advance that was more apparent than real. The Haines government in Victoria unsuccessfully resisted the introduction of the ballot in 1856 and the abolition of property qualifications for members of the assembly in 1857. Then the conservatives began to realize how gravely their predominance was threatened by the convention, and their tactics changed. Late in 1857 the Haines government introduced a bill to give manhood suffrage, but it was qualified by plural voting for property owners, a residence of three months in the electorate for those claiming the adult male suffrage, and voluntary registration on the electoral rolls. This became law and was followed by the triennial parliament act in January 1858. When the clamour from the radical democrats did not abate Haines tried to repeat the successful ploy of the suffrage act in the new context of

50 P. Loveday and A. W. Martin, *Parliament, Factions and Parties: The First Thirty Years of Responsible Government in New South Wales, 1856–1889,* Melbourne, 1966, p. 52.

51 G. R. Quaife, 'Make Us Roads No Matter How: A Note on Colonial Politics', in *A.J.P.H.,* XV, 1, April 1969.

electorate redistribution. He proposed to increase the number of seats to ninety and distribute them according to population, but to protect minorities by multi-member electorates. However, the bill lapsed when the government was defeated and resigned.

It was now the turn of the liberals to tackle electoral reform in the shadow of the convention. Already Edward Wilson, the liberal proprietor of the *Argus*, had argued strongly for the representation of interests to place a check on democracy. The O'Shanassy ministry included no democrats but it was more optimistic than Wilson, believing that political democracy in the colony would enhance the power of property. Their new bill did recognise the population principle, but it was defeated in the upper house. The government stalled while elections for a third of the council were held. The convention again mounted a sustained and militant agitation, but its effects were counter-productive. The government was persuaded to compromise, by introducing an amended bill with fifteen seats removed from the urban and mining areas, although the assembly was enlarged from 60 to 78. Suppressing reports of the outcry from the diggings, where the miners already felt penalized by the absence of convenient polling places and the registration and residence requirements in the manhood suffrage act, George Higinbotham, editor of the *Argus*, wrote 'we have established perfect political equality'.[52]

In New South Wales, the electoral reform act of 1858 ostensibly provided for secret ballot, manhood suffrage, abolition of property qualifications for membership of the assembly and equal electoral districts. The act was introduced by Cowper's liberal government, and was passed because the conservatives in the council, advised by the *Herald*, retreated. In fact, not all adult males were guaranteed the vote (there was a six-months residence qualification which twelve per cent could not meet in 1861) and plural voting was possible. Moreover, even the liberals discussed the distribution of seats according to interests; in those terms the effect of the 1858 reform was to curtail the representation of the pastoral districts and to continue the under-representation of the city of Sydney. The country towns and boroughs, where liberals stood a good chance of election, had the best ratio of seats to the adult male population. As for the ballot, liberals and conservatives alike reckoned that it would protect the working classes 'from the tyranny of the demagogues of the workshop'.[53] But there was a more important reason why conservatives were prepared to compromise in 1858. Unlike Victoria, New South Wales had a feeble radical movement which the liberals showed they could transform into a powerful electoral force, when, in the elections of 1858, the Electoral Reform League became an appendage of the government. Although

---

[52] Quoted in G. Serle, *The Golden Age: A History of the Colony of Victoria, 1851–1861*, Melbourne, 1963, p. 281.

[53] *Sydney Morning Herald*, 13 August 1859

the *Herald* railed against this 'confederacy of dupes and cheats',[54] and although angry conservatives detested and abhorred 'the conduct of men who join or pretend to join an association having for its professed objects the attainment of opposite principles to those which they endeavour to carry out',[55] the lesson for conservatives, as the liberals increased their vote, was that they should not provoke, by unwise resistance, an alliance of the liberals and the populace.[56]

The campaign against the Chinese immigrants presented another challenge to the 'mock liberals', as the *Sydney Morning Herald* now called them. There were about 40,000 Chinese in Victoria in 1859 and perhaps 10,000 in New South Wales in 1861. Mostly males, they dug for gold in low yield areas or on abandoned claims, but whenever unemployment rose or mining returns dropped the tension between the Chinese and European diggers increased. The Chinese were accused of wasting water. Their religion was despised as pagan, their customs and language were mocked, and their camps, on flimsy evidence, were decried as centres of sodomy and disease. After 1854, dozens of riots occurred, the worst on Lambing Flat, New South Wales, in 1860 and 1861. Here the Europeans repeatedly expelled the Chinese from the field, and when at last a few of the European diggers were arrested, their comrades fought a gun battle with the police. Cowper's government subsequently legislated to exclude Chinese from certain fields and to regulate their entry into the colony by imposing a heavy tax of £10 per head. Earlier, between 1855 and 1858, Victoria and South Australia had placed restrictions on the entry of Chinese, and Victoria had also imposed a residence tax. Before the Chinese started to return to China in the early 1860s, the anti-Chinese cause was popular in all classes.

The Chinese were well organized in societies with protective and social functions, and when confronted with these discriminatory measures they retaliated, as the European diggers had done in the early 1850s. They adopted petitions at mass meetings, arguing that 'We obey law, we make no noise, we have feelings like other men, we want to be brothers with Englishmen – why not let be so?'[57] In Victoria they boycotted European stores, picketed police stations, and engaged in passive resistance by refusing to pay the residence tax. Thousands were fined or arrested. But with a few exceptions, the liberal conscience was unmoved. The liberals pretended that the anti-Chinese riots were the work of foreigners, and that only ruffians participated, but their own haste to jump on the racialist bandwagon belied this. They deplored the violence and asked how Australian society could realize

54 *Sydney Morning Herald*, 2 February 1858.

55 *Sydney Morning Herald*, 5 April 1858.

56 *Sydney Morning Herald*, 3 April 1858.

57 Quoted in G. Serle, *The Golden Age: A History of the Colony of Victoria, 1851–1861*, Melbourne, 1963, p. 330.

its potential for harmony and freedom if it contained an inferior labour caste. They stressed that the Chinese were bonded servants, no better than slaves, because they were contracted to serve Chinese capitalists. But these idealistic arguments were disingenuous; the liberals supported the anti-Chinese programme for political reasons, and they were as racialist as the rest of the community. The diggers, who had the most to lose through economic competition with the Chinese, were also the most overtly racialist, but the view that the Chinese were an inferior race was virtually universal. There were other arguments, less directly based on racialist fears. Governor Hotham worried about Victoria's security and Henry Parkes warned of the danger to British civilization in Australia. Both were early versions of the 'yellow peril' thesis, that the Chinese would just keep on coming until they overran the continent.[58]

In fact by 1860 racialism in Australia was institutionalized, and violence against racial minorities had become a cultural fact. The Chinese posed a more direct threat than the Aborigines to covert notions of British racial supremacy but relationships with the Aborigines also were approached in racialist terms. None of the colonial governments had seriously attempted to treat them as British citizens, nor to police the frontier regions effectively. When the Aborigines resisted white occupation of their tribal lands, and when some engaged in sporadic guerrilla warfare, they were easily dispersed or exterminated. The obvious failure of the policy of assimilation before the middle of the nineteenth century led to a policy of protection, which meant that the Aborigines became second-class citizens. Whether in special settlements, as cheap pastoral labour, or as fringe-dwellers, the Aborigines had become an inferior caste. Yet there was no sign of general concern about this and no liberal warnings that the future ideal society was endangered.

In Queensland, where the economy was dominated still by the large landowners and squatters, there was even less liberal concern about race relations. The new colony's frontier conditions led to many clashes between European settlers and Aborigines, the worst being the massacre in 1861 of nineteen whites and subsequently of 170 Aborigines in the Midway Ranges.[59] At the same time, there were demands for cheap, coloured labour that would submit to being indentured. The squatters and large landowners at first relied on government efforts to introduce coolies from India, but in 1863 Captain Robert Towns began a brisk trade in South Sea Islanders for the sugar plantations. In the next five years two thousand Islanders were indentured. They were regarded as racially inferior, and treated with callousness and

58 See G. Serle, *The Golden Age: A History of the Colony of Victoria, 1851–1861*, Melbourne, 1963, ch. 11: R. B. Walker, 'Another look at the Lambing Flat Riots, 1860–1861', in *R.A.H.S.J.*, 56, 3, September 1970.

59 See H. Reynolds, Ed., *Aborigines and Settlers: The Australian Experience 1788–1939*, Melbourne, 1972, pp. 9–11.

often brutality. After protests from workingmen and churchmen an act was passed in 1868 to regulate conditions on the ships and to ensure that the 'Kanakas' were paid at least £6 a year and repatriated at the end of their contracts.

Tasmania in the 1850s and 1860s took fewer and smaller steps than the other colonies along the road to urban, liberal-democratic politics. Tasmania's atypical development was the result of the remnants of the convict system and of the long economic depression beginning in 1856. Convicts and emancipists still formed between 30 per cent and 40 per cent of the adult community in the late 1860s. In depressed conditions, this meant that there was more crime than in other colonies, and greater need for prisons, hospitals and charitable institutions. The depression made it difficult for urban occupations to absorb the ex-convicts, and, as there was little unoccupied farming or grazing land, they remained in a state of near-feudal dependence on their rural masters. Tasmania was the only colony in which the urban population declined proportionately, from 44 per cent in 1857 to 39 per cent in 1870, and the only colony in which the line between the free and the freed hardened.

Politics was uniformly conservative throughout the island. The faint voice of democracy in Hobart and Launceston provoked only token reform of the electoral process. Although some politicians had their customary associates, there were too many independent country gentlemen and too few urban liberals in parliament to produce more than the outlines of a faction system. Finance was the constant preoccupation and the main cause of the changes of government: there were eight governments before the fall of Sir Richard Dry's ministry in 1869. Expenditure regularly exceeded revenue because of the depressed economy and the need to spend more on welfare than other colonies. From time to time the parliament demanded, unsuccessfully, that Britain share the cost of these welfare charges, for the population contained so many of the mother country's former criminals. At other times political controversy broke out over the advantages and drawbacks of direct taxation, retrenchment, protection and free trade. Retrenchment and a moderate tariff were usually adopted.

The conservative, rural predominance was reflected in legislation. The 1856 Master and Servant Act continued the arbitrary power which magistrates had exercised in the convict period. An act in 1858 allowed rural areas to petition for the establishment of a local government, with a restricted franchise and multiple voting. Eleven local governments were set up, and so effective were the electoral restrictions that 15 to 25 per cent of the wealthiest electors held a majority of votes. Through local government the gentry gained a more direct control of expenditure on public works, especially roads, and retained their control over the police while New South Wales and Victoria were centralizing their police forces.

The colonies emerged from the gold decade preoccupied with the land question.[60] Pastoralists, farmers, capitalists, workingmen and governments had an interest in land policy, and none of them thought the present land system was perfect. Thus, the profusion of land laws – Queensland passed ten important acts in the 1860s – tried to satisfy diverse interests. An added complication in Victoria and New South Wales arose from movements for land reform, whose activities meant that the land question became an issue in the relationship between the liberal politicians and the radical popular movements.

In 1860 the pastoral industry occupied a vast arc stretching from the Darling Downs in Queensland to the western district in Victoria and up into northern South Australia. About four thousand squatters monopolized over 160 million acres, and paid less than a farthing an acre in annual rent. Except in Queensland, wool was no longer the staple of colonial economies, but the pastoral industry was prospering. The introduction of fences and dams increased its efficiency. There were twenty million sheep, compared to seventeen million in 1851. In the 1860s the number of sheep more than doubled, but in Queensland, the new pastoral frontier, both the area occupied, and the number of sheep, trebled. High hopes were also held for cattle-grazing in the Northern Territory, which was transferred to South Australian administration in 1863, but a severe drought began in 1864, and those hopes were blown away in the hot winds which over the next few years returned South Australia's northern pastoral districts to their customary arid conditions. By the end of the period bad seasons and falling wool prices brought financial problems for many squatters in other parts of the continent, and in Victoria and New South Wales, the proportion of land occupied by the pastoral industry declined slightly.

The squatters in 1860 were more confident about their prospects than their public rhetoric suggested. The squatters' runs were mostly unsurveyed, barring them from the leases promised by the 1847 Order in Council, and their tenure, based on yearly licences, was only as secure as their economic and political power. However, they were prosperous; some had exercised their preemptive rights to buy the land on which their homesteads stood, and everywhere pastoral improvements made the purchase by outsiders of their runs (by auction at an upset price of £1 per acre, with compensation for the squatter's improvements) less likely. 'Security of tenure' was their traditional cry, a witness to their corporate identity, but it was beside the point by 1860. In the early 1850s, when the governments of Victoria and New South Wales set aside land for small-scale settlement, the runs of very few squatters were affected, and by the end of the 1850s it was

60 For a general discussion of the economic history of the post-gold era see N. G. Butlin, 'The Shape of the Australian Economy, 1861–1900' in *Economic Record*, *XXXIV*, 67, April 1958, reprinted in N. T. Drohan and J. H. Day, Eds., *Readings in Australian Economics: Studies in Economic Growth*, Melbourne, 1965, 1969: N. G. Butlin, *Investment in Australian Economic Development, 1861–1900*, Cambridge, 1964.

difficult to find a parliamentarian who advocated expropriation of the squatters. In Queensland, the squatters were invulnerable; the Macalister land act of 1868, Queensland's gesture to the land reformers, provided easy terms for the purchase of pastoral as well as agricultural land. However, in South Australia, land policy in the 1860s completely overrode the interests of the squatters. Here Strangway's Act of 1868 expanded the agricultural sector of the economy by providing for certain pastoral leaseholds to be open for purchase at auction and by instalment, in blocks of up to 640 acres.

The state of agriculture produced no real problems for the squatters. There was concern for farmers as a class only in South Australia where wheat was the staple and where the number of farmers increased by a third in the late 1850s. In other parts of Australia, especially Victoria, many pastoralists themselves had diversified into agriculture. Moreover, there was no longer a threat of food shortage to arouse urban concern about pastoralism impeding agriculture. Indeed by 1860 there were about a million and a quarter acres under cultivation and South Australia was able to export wheat to Mauritius, South Africa and England, as well as to other mainland colonies. Naturally landowners who had paid a high price for land resisted any suggestion that mere occupancy should entitle the squatters to freehold tenure, but most squatters no longer made such an extreme claim. Moreover, experienced landowners knew that most of the squatters' land was unsuitable for agriculture and not worth £1 per acre as grazing land. There was, in short, no reason for landowners as a body to want to overturn the pastoral industry, especially as some landowners had themselves taken up squatting runs.

By 1860 there was a new pattern of economic activity, stressing building, transport and manufacturing, in New South Wales and Victoria. As this became the main force of economic development it helped to convince the urban businessmen that, at last, they were responsible for the country's future. Where squatters occupied land suitable for other activities, as in large areas of Victoria, businessmen saw them as restricting the growth of the home market, and discouraging economic diversification. Moreover speculators, hoping for quick profits, wanted government action to force more land onto the market. However, they did not want to destroy the pastoral industry; indeed they wanted the land laws to strengthen it as a component of a capitalist economy. The squatters were the pure milk of rural capitalism, and they needed capital now to improve their runs, expand their flocks and herds, and purchase their homestead areas. Capitalists in Melbourne, already the financial centre of Australia, and in Sydney and Adelaide, soon learnt to disparage pastoralism while assisting individual pastoralists. In Queensland by 1863, two-thirds of the sheep and horses and about half the cattle of the colony were under mortgage to Sydney capitalists. By the end of the decade, the structure of ownership of the pastoral industry had changed significantly, as bankrupt properties passed into the hands of the banks and pastoral finance companies, a result in which bad seasons were as important as the land laws.

Reform, as distinct from instrumental adjustment, of the land system was the aim of the popular movements. It was seen, primarily, as the catalyst of the wide social change which the radicals now thought necessary to achieve economic independence. But the popular movements were also responding to the effects of the growth of large-scale capitalism in a metropolitan environment. About 28 per cent of the population of Victoria and New South Wales lived in the capitals by 1870; Sydney's proportion had been steady for almost twenty years, but Melbourne's had risen, as her population was augmented at the end of the 1850s by about 100,000 ex-miners. When mass unemployment and rudimentary living conditions appeared in the cities, land reform was also demanded as an answer to these specific, and real, grievances. Finally as these grievances made class differences highly visible for the first time, land reform was urged in protest against large-scale capitalism itself and the passing of a form of society associated with the small-scale economy of the 1840s and the goldfields in the early 1850s. Significantly, the appearance of Melbourne's Land Convention in 1857 coincided with rising unemployment, and in Sydney, the Land League entered its main phase of agitation in 1859, when the unemployed demonstrated almost daily for six months. In Brisbane, too, demands from urban workingmen for land reform were barely audible until Queensland's economic crisis of 1866.

Everywhere land reform was discussed the vision of an agrarian way of life was invoked: a people united, industrious and contented with a purely domestic existence. In the 1840s agrarianism was common in the north-eastern cities of the United States and amongst the followers of Feargus O'Connor in the Chartist movement. Their arguments were echoed by Australian land reformers, who also saw life on the land as symbolizing civilization and its continuity, especially in a country without tradition, where the cities had grown up before the countryside was settled. Nevertheless, the uses of the agrarian myth in Australia were not more particular than that, and nor was myth substituted entirely for reality. While the Sydney unemployed called for land reform they were refusing at the same time to accept money raised by public subscription to send them into the interior. The workingman who apostrophized the joys of a neat cottage and the arts of cultivation in fact expected no more than a slab hut, a vegetable garden and a cow, on a suburban or edge-of-town block. He expected to earn an intermittent income by fencing or clearing, prospecting or shearing. His land-hunger had been taking this form since the 1840s, and it was not evidence that he was either a frustrated farmer, or an atavistic enemy of capitalism. Just as land was a resource for the capitalist, it was another form of a home and independence for the workingman.

In New South Wales, Cowper chaired a select committee of the council on Crown land in 1854, and decided that the government was acting fairly: the farmers were served by the policy of gazetting agricultural reserves, and the squatters by a guarantee of preemptive rights, even when their lands fell within one of those reserves. Gradually, however, the difference between adjustment and reform of the land system, and the political advantages of reform, were recognized by the liberals. Responding to cries of 'unlock the lands' from disappointed diggers, Henry Parkes chaired a select committee on agriculture in 1855. He knew nothing about the subject, but his generous use of agrarian clichés made a good impression on the workingmen. It was his newspaper, the *Empire*, which encouraged the formation of the Land League in 1857, and his select committee on working-class conditions in 1859 before which John Robertson stated, 'All I want to see is this branch of business [i.e. agriculture] in common with all others have fair play, leaving the people to take up whatever business they please'.[61]

Although the Land League was never strong, it showed the liberals that radicalism was susceptible to an appeal to equality of opportunity in the form of free selection. Thus, the liberals, while leading the clamour against the squatters' monopoly, actually took up land reform as a way of managing and satisfying a restless and discontented urban populace. As Cowper wrote in a letter to the conservative James Macarthur in 1861: 'It will be a great thing to get the Land Bills passed. This alone will put down a vast amount of agitation.'[62] When Cowper's first land bill, which made no pretence of opening up the lands, was defeated in 1858, he hastily switched his reforming zeal to the electoral question. After this was settled John Robertson, a liberal landowner, introduced two land reform bills, one of which provided for free selection. When the free selection bill was defeated in the assembly he obtained a dissolution in 1860, and after an election in which land reform was the main issue, he was able to reintroduce it and secure its passage. Because the council now refused to accept free selection, the government appointed twenty-one additional members to swamp it, but the government's opponents walked out, depriving the council of a quorum. The legislation was passed eventually in 1861 after the appointments of the council members expired and the council was reconstituted. Robertson's Alienation Act provided that up to 320 acres of Crown lands could be selected, even if unsurveyed, at a price of £1 per acre, with an initial payment of 25 per cent and the remainder within three years. The land had to be occupied and improved before the freehold title was issued. The only land excluded from selection, apart from town lots, goldfields, etc., was land containing improvements made by pastoral lessees or licence holders. Thus were the squatters compensated for their loss of preemptive

[61] Quoted in D. W. A. Baker, 'The Origins of Robertson's Land Acts', in *H.S.*, *30*, May 1958, p. 181.

[62] Quoted in B. Dickey, *Politics in New South Wales, 1856–1900*, Melbourne, 1969, p. 14.

rights in Robertson's Occupation Act which superseded the squatting system of 1847. This act provided for leases of one year to five years' duration.

In Victoria there was a decade of agitation and four major land bills before free selection before survey became law. One reason for this was the financial pressure on governments to raise revenue from the lands. It was one of the aims of the land bill which was defeated in 1857, and of the Lands Department's policies which throughout the 1860s encouraged the purchase of land by the squatters, who, with liberal credit from the banks, could pay more, and in less time, than the small settlers. Other reasons were the political strength of the squatters, and the liberal suspicion of the popular movement and of its demand for free selection before survey. After the elections of 1859, land reformers made up a quarter of the new assembly. At the same time, half the Legislative Council were squatters.

William Nicholson introduced the next land bill in 1859 but the council made over 250 amendments to it; the result was an unsatisfactory compromise between squatters, reformers and other interested parties. Two classes of land were put up for sale. 'Country' lands could be selected in small blocks, for an initial payment of half the price, which would be uniformly £1 per acre, unless the price was forced up by competition for the block. There were penalties for non-cultivation, but the government did not enforce them. 'Special' lands, including land within a mile of property purchased before the act, could not be selected, and had to be sold at auction. Using 'dummies', and secure from the penal clauses of the act, the squatters bought more than eighty per cent of the lands opened up for selection and almost all the special lands.

A new land act was soon necessary. Because the Orders in Council expired in 1862, the squatters' tenure had to be settled. Further, Brookes, the Minister for Lands in a liberal-radical ministry, led by Heales, began to issue licences for agricultural settlement. This seemed dangerously like a precedent for free selection before survey. Hence early in 1862, after a change of government, Charles Gavan Duffy's bill was passed by both houses in only a few weeks. It gave the squatters security, on yearly licences, with rents based on the grazing capacity of their runs, until the end of 1870. The ten million acres previously opened under the system of agricultural licences were proclaimed 'reserves' for agriculture, in which surveyed land could be bought at £1 per acre, with an immediate down-payment of half the price, and the rest over the next eight years. Nothing in Duffy's act interfered with the trend of purchase by the squatters; one estimate was that only one hundred bona fide selectors benefited by Duffy's act. But by 1865 a radical Reform League was again making land reform a contentious issue, and the reformers had some influence over the ministry of James McCulloch, although it also rested on conservative support. In his Land Act of 1865 the Minister for Lands, J. M. Grant, sought to placate the reformers by a scheme to lease agricultural land in small lots at 2s. per acre for five years, and the conservatives by refusing to interfere with the rental and tenure of the squatters' runs. Some expansion of small-scale settlement occurred because Grant manipulated the release of land to favour agriculturalists. Finally, in 1869 Grant presented a new land bill to parliament, drawing on his own experiences as minister and on the suggestions of selectors' organizations. The second Grant act provided for free selection, both before and after survey, in all remaining Crown lands. Lots would be leased at 2s. 6d. per acre, and the rent would form part of the purchase price. The squatters were given a new tenure of ten years, with an additional preemptive right to 640 acres since their runs were now all open to selection.

The results of the land acts were as diverse as their objectives. The squatters secured their tenure, albeit mainly through purchase. In Victoria the pastoralists bought about half the land offered for sale by the Crown in the 1860s. The city financiers happily lent them the necessary money at 8 or 10 per cent interest. Over nine million acres were alienated in the 1860s in Victoria and New South Wales, and about 17,000 selectors were living on their blocks in each colony in 1870. An unknown number of selectors failed because they lacked farming skills, or the capital (estimated at £160 a year for forty acres) to see them through the bad seasons that were common after 1864. However the acts, and the way they were administered, discriminated against small settlers, and thus deterred settlement. In the long run, the most important consequence of land policy in this period was unintended: the increase of social tension in the towns as well as the countryside. The sympathy for bushrangers was an index of this in the 1860s.[63] The small selectors were harassed by the squatters and often exploited by rapacious storekeepers. In the cities, the workingmen became increasingly disillusioned with the inability of land reform to solve what they were beginning to call 'the class question'.

In Victoria chronic unemployment and the protracted agitation for land reform contributed to the climate of social tension which was the background to the political crises between 1865 and 1868. The critical elements in the situation were the conservative role of the Legislative Council, the political requirements of the McCulloch ministries and Victoria's provincialism in asserting its right to non-interference from Britain. The Legislative Council in Victoria was constructed avowedly to act as a conservative force. The constitution-makers ruled out a nominated council so that it could not be swamped by a hostile government. Nor did they provide for a way to settle a deadlock between the houses. The council's thirty members, who were elected for ten years, represented six constituencies, only one of which was urban. The value of freehold property which a colonist had to own to

---

[63] See R. B. Walker, 'Bushranging in Fact and Legend', in *H.S.*, 42, April 1964. See also R. Ward, *The Australian Legend*, Melbourne, 1958, ch. 6.

qualify for membership was £5000; for voting it was £1000. Professional men, and after 1858, occupants of property worth £100 per annum were also entitled to vote, but in 1866 only 12,000 persons were on the rolls, about one-tenth of the assembly's electorate. By 1865 the council had shown its political colours by amending the land bills and rejecting bills to abolish state aid to religion and to pay parliamentarians. It was also plain that the council opposed tariff protection for native industries. In fact the council set itself to defend the interests of the squatters, the mercantile free traders, and all laissez-faire conservatives who deplored the use of the state for social purposes.

James McCulloch's political supremacy extended from the middle of 1863 to September 1869. In this time he decisively won three general elections in 1864, 1865 and 1868. The popular movement was controlled for him through the Liberal Reform Association and its successor, the Loyal Liberal Reform Association, which at its peak of influence in 1868 had 130 branches. Before elections, and when McCulloch was thwarted by the governor or the council, this vast organization would be reactivated by his lieutenants to threaten the obstructors of the popular will with direct action. McCulloch, however, was no tribune of the people. He was a free trader who advocated protection, a squatter who favoured land reform, and a conservative who provoked a confrontation with the upper house. Above all, he cherished power, and knew how to keep it through patronage, compromise and espousal of popular causes. Shrewdly, he included radicals such as Grant and George Higinbotham in his cabinets. Within the assembly his majority, which was always unstable, was a shifting coalition of personal coteries, groups interested mainly in single issues (the tariff, mining, land, abolition of state aid) and supporters of principled reform (such as Graham Berry). The common denominator of most of his supporters, however, was antagonism to what they saw as the council's determination to block the policies of the people's representatives in the assembly.

At the beginning of the 1860s Victoria had half as many factory workers as New South Wales. Its citizens depended on imported manufactured goods. There were always shortages, and yet men were unemployed and capitalists were looking for good investments. As wages fell in the first half of the new decade (from 9s. to 6s. a day for mechanics) many Victorian trade unionists became protectionists. In 1864, protection was firmly embraced by the radicals when Graham Berry formed the Australian Reform League. However, the working-men in the popular movement, who made protection a leading issue in the elections of 1864, and who formed the Central Protection League in 1865, were really indicating their support for the McCulloch ministry, which they saw as engaged in a legislative war on several fronts with the squatters and their allies. McCulloch's tariff of 1865 rewarded them by reducing the duties on tea, sugar and opium, and favoured the manufacturers by imposing an *ad valorem* duty of 10 per cent on other imports. However, the tariff's merit in the government's eyes was its promise of increased revenue.

The government began collecting duties at the new rates before the tariff bill was sent to the council. This was customary, but highly impolitic if there were marked changes in the tariff. Moreover, the government insisted on 'tacking' the tariff bill, a supply measure, onto an appropriation bill, which the constitution only allowed the council to accept or reject. Consequently the council rejected the composite bill. The government persisted in collecting the new duties until prevented by the courts and it obtained money in the absence of an appropriation act by repeatedly borrowing from a bank of which McCulloch was the sole local director. The government would not repay the duties collected illegally, nor would it back down from its new, and unconstitutional, position that the assembly had the exclusive right to grant supplies, and so twice more the council rejected the tariff. After a general election and the ministry's temporary resignation, the deadlock was finally solved in April 1866 when McCulloch retreated on the constitutional issue because the Colonial Office intervened to censure the governor, Sir Charles Darling, for sanctioning the government's illegal practices. The council accepted the tariff, and a further increase in duties in 1867. By 1871 factory workers in Victoria had increased threefold in ten years compared to about 10 per cent in New South Wales.

In the popular movement the sixteen-month contest was seen as a democratic struggle against wealth, privilege, monopoly and imperial interference. George Higinbotham and other radical politicians in the assembly encouraged this analysis. The opportunity to resume the struggle and to exercise parliamentary leadership again over the movement came in July 1867. When Darling was recalled in disgrace by the Colonial Office, the assembly voted £20,000 to his wife, and added onto an appropriation bill the supplementary estimate for this money. This 'tack' was not only a vindication of the assembly's earlier position but a dramatic way of emphasising the determination of a democratic colony not to bow to interference from an aristocratic Colonial Office. Victorians already felt that Britain discriminated against them by sending convicts to Western Australia and by neglecting their defence. During the next twelve months the council twice rejected 'the tack', McCulloch's government resigned twice (on the second occasion leaving the colony without a government for two months before Sladen formed a minority government) and there was another general election. Again the deadlock was ended by imperial action when Lady Darling refused her £20,000 because the Colonial Office agreed to reinstate her husband. The Sladen government resigned, and the Loyal Liberal Reform Association, which had spoken of revolution, collapsed when McCulloch returned to office. The rights of the assembly were precious to Victorians, a fact underlined by Higinbotham's assembly resolutions of 1869 on relations with the mother country, which provided both a climax and an end to anti-imperial resentment in the colony.[64]

The Victorian council finally agreed to a bill to abolish state aid to religion in 1870. A sustained public campaign from 1855 to the early 1860s by the Society for the Abolition of the Fifty-Third Clause of the Victorian Constitution had failed to convert the council, but when McCulloch formed a new government in 1870 he mollified the supporters of state aid by promising concessions in the abolition measure and a cabinet post for the leading state-aid supporter in the council. In New South Wales, the Cowper government had abolished state aid to religion in 1862, and in 1866 the government of Parkes and James Martin took an important step in the direction of secular education by providing that state aid would go to denominational schools only if they followed an official syllabus (which included 'general religious teaching'), if they barred no pupil on religious grounds and if they were a sufficient distance from a public school. The Public Schools Act of 1866 also replaced the former Boards of National and Denominational Education with a single Council of Education.

These developments indicated a growing separation of church and state which had little to do with secular sentiments. South Australia, a 'paradise of dissent' based on voluntary support of religion until 1846, ended its brief state aid experiment in 1851 with abolitionists posing as the colony's Pilgrim Fathers. In eastern Australia Governor Bourke's Church Act of 1836 allowed four denominations, Anglican, Roman Catholic, Presbyterian and Wesleyan, to share the bounty of the state. Most of the other denominations did not want state aid, but they resented, as did many lay members of the state-supported churches, the edge which state aid gave to sectarian animosities, and the power which the disbursement of state monies gave to the hierarchies in the Anglican and Catholic churches. There was also the fear that state aid was a springboard for Anglican plans to become the established church again. The typical abolitionist was nonconformist in religion. He was more likely to be middle class in occupation, young, native-born and a representative of an urban electorate than the typical State Aider. His impulse to abolish state aid was liberal; his object was to ensure religious equality, which meant that the state must stand impartially aloof from all churches. Liberalism in religion, as in colonial politics, rested on low participation; there was widespread indifference to religion in the colonies. Also, as in politics, it was conservative, in the sense that the coming of voluntaryism fixed

64 See C. S. Blackton, 'The Cannon Street Episode: An Aspect of Anglo-Australian Relations', in *H.S.*, *52*, April 1969: G. Serle, 'New Light on the Colonial Office, Sir George Bowen and the Victorian Constitutional Crises', in *H.S.*, *52*, April 1969: D. P. Clarke, 'The Colonial Office and the Constitutional Crises in Victoria, 1865–68', in *H.S.*, *18*, May 1952.

the area of influence of religion in society and, for the time being, the relative standing and influence of the various churches.[65]

In the 1860s Australia's population grew more slowly than in the 1850s; Victoria's proportion of the total population declined, and Queensland's increased, by about three per cent in both cases. In 1870 there were over 720,000 colonists in Victoria, almost 500,000 in New South Wales, 185,000 in South Australia, 115,000 in Queensland, 100,000 in Tasmania and 25,000 in Western Australia. Although the worst of the recession of the mid-1860s was over, and good seasons were returning, the colonists were no more prosperous in 1870 than they were in 1860. However, they had not forgotten the golden fifties; they were still restless and confident of both the country's resources and their own resourcefulness. Indeed 'the rush that never ended' was about to reach Queensland where gold was discovered at Gympie (in 1867), Townsville (1868) and Gilbert (1869).[66]

The consolidation of a belief in the country's future as an important area of British civilization was the distinctive development of the 1860s, and it made the colonists feel that they had a common identity. The movement of population between the colonies, the growth of inter-colonial trade, and the networks of railways (albeit with different gauges) and telegraph lines which eased travel, commerce and communication had all contributed. Political union was not really on the agenda although there was some talk of federation; at a series of conferences (1863, 1865, 1867) between the colonial governments the representatives of the ruling class could not reach a satisfactory agreement on tariff policy.

Prince Alfred, the Duke of Edinburgh, toured the colonies in 1867–8.[67] His reception showed that the emerging, common identity of the colonists was British, but that it also involved loyalty to the new country; in Victoria the crowds cheered the Duke but jeered when the Colonial Office was mentioned. To the dismay of editorial writers, the pushy *nouveau riche* disrupted the dignity of public ceremonies and celebrations, demonstrating that wealth and power were now as privileged in the colonies as a family background in the British upper class was formerly. At last, the state of 'delirious loyalty' became too much for one Irish immigrant, Henry James O'Farrell, who shot and slightly wounded the Duke at Clontarf in March 1868. As popular hysteria increased there were dark rumours of a Fenian conspiracy, and editorial surprise that European feuds could still break out in

65 N. Turner, *Sinews of Sectarian Warfare? State Aid in New South Wales, 1836–1862*, Canberra, 1972, Pt. III: R. Border, *Church and State in Australia, 1788–1872*, London, 1962.

66 G. Blainey, *The Rush that Never Ended: A History of Australian Mining*, Melbourne, 1963.

67 See B. McKinlay, *The First Royal Tour, 1867–1868*, Adelaide, 1970: P. M. Cowburn, 'Attempted Assassination of the Duke of Edinburgh, 1868', in *R.A.H.S.J.*, 55, 1, March 1969.

Australia's benign society. Yet after O'Farrell was hanged and a select committee had found no evidence of a plot, Parkes continued to talk of a conspiracy, in a bid for the loyal, protestant vote, and his government passed a savage Treason Felony Act which the Crown had to disallow. This was Australia's first 'royal tour', an occasion for the colonists, led by the liberal bourgeoisie, to show off their variant of British civilisation.

5

1870-90

G. L. Buxton[1]

*Immigration—the search for security—gold mining—copper—tin
—silver-lead—Broken Hill—'unlock the lands'—the land problem in Victoria—the Mallee—irrigation—Mildura—Gippsland—
the Robertson Acts in N.S.W.—Strangways' Act—Goyder's Line—
the Darling Downs—the farming arc—the pastoral industry—
cattlemen—indebtedness of squatters—station improvement—
rabbits—rural communities—education—country towns—town
life—rural society—trades unionism—urbanization—Marvellous
Melbourne—public health—land and building speculation—Victorian politicians—business morality—manufacturing—women in
employment—the standard of living—city life—the search for
identity—art and literature—the influence of the bush—defence
—New Guinea—the Kanaka trade—the New Hebrides—republicanism—the A.N.A.—the Chinese—racism—the Irish—'free, compulsory and secular' religion—wowsers—the Salvation Army—
colonial particularism.*

In the one hundred years after 1850, fifty-two million people left
Europe for new lands across the seas. Thirty-five per cent of these
migrants came from the British Isles. Australian history in the
nineteenth century is part of this great European emigration, and
the period 1870–90 a section of this story. There were those who sought
the greater political or religious freedom which the new territories
like America and Australia offered, including Chartists from Britain,
unsuccessful European revolutionaries from 1848, Schleschwig-Hol-
steiners seeking to escape Prussian military conscription, and Irish-
Catholics antagonistic to English rule. They frequently held strong
opinions, and this cultural baggage later produced conflicting loyalties
in the host countries. But the motives for emigration were predominantly economic. Most migrants left Europe to better themselves
materially, and despite population pressure in Europe, only extraordinarily strong pull factors in Australia, such as the lure of gold or

---

[1] G. L. Buxton died whilst this book was in preparation, and it has not been
possible to find the sources of all of the quotations and information which he
included in the draft of his chapter. *Ed.*

the offer of free or assisted passages, could attract migrants over thirteen thousand miles. For every migrant who came to Australia, ten went to America.

The first massive migration came with the gold rushes of the 1850s, when half a million unassisted free migrants flocked to Victoria. In one decade the populations of New South Wales, South Australia and Queensland doubled, whilst that of Victoria increased sevenfold. Not only was the migration of massive proportions, but the migrants themselves were predominantly young men and women. As a result of the great increase in the number of marriages and children, there was by the 1870s a rising demand for employment and a growing pressure on resources, including land. 'What shall we do with our boys?' became an increasingly common cry in Australia in the 1870s and 1880s. In Victoria, the initial surplus of males had been balanced to some extent by schemes of assisted immigration for females. Even so, the search for wives as well as jobs had led to a net outflow of males from Victoria to other parts of Australia and to New Zealand. Not until the 1880s was parity between the sexes reached in Victoria. Meanwhile, the restricted amount of land available in that small colony, and limited job opportunities – despite Victoria's policy of tariff protection – ensured the continuance of the Victorian invasion of the rest of Australia. Events in the period 1870–90, therefore, represent the long-term effects of the demographic dislocation of the 1850s.

At the same time the belief that population was wealth had inspired some colonies, especially New South Wales, Queensland and South Australia, to embark on assisted immigration schemes, while Victoria, during the building of 'Marvellous Melbourne', attracted thousands more without offering any assistance. Although this new migration reinforced some of the old world mores, many migrants had shrugged off the inequalities and traditional values of their homelands, and a new generation had grown up which owed more allegiance to Australia. The continuing rejection of traditions of privilege and rank, and the search for new solutions, led to a questioning best summed up as, 'What kind of country or society is this to be?' The rapidly growing cities, even more than rural areas, were characterized not only by a search for economic opportunity and security, but also by a search for identity, reflected in differing attitudes towards formal and informal allegiances as well as race, politics, religion and education.

Because migrants had left Europe to seek their fortunes, they were prepared to travel widely in Australia to find security for themselves and their families, and there was considerable geographical and social mobility. The 1870s began with boom conditions, particularly in the rural areas, but although the period 1870–90 was one of rapid growth, for many Australians it was increasingly marked by declining economic opportunity. Greater pressure on resources and job opportunities encouraged trade union activity in the 1880s, leading to direct confrontations between labour and capital in the depressed 1890s. The belief in British-type political processes led to an agitation for government action, in the expectation that passing laws would create opportunities or guard gains. In response to these pressures different colonies chose different solutions, and produced quite different results – as different as free trade and protection.

The search for security involved Australians in three main areas. In the great mining camps or declining gold towns, in the agricultural or pastoral districts and in the ever-swelling cities and suburbs, colonists developed new attitudes and sought to forge new values. As the amount of easily won alluvial gold declined in the late 1850s most mining camps began to disperse. Some miners joined quartz crushing syndicates or worked for wages in mining companies in the surviving gold towns like Bendigo; others continued to pursue the gold illusion wherever it led. By the 1870s they had followed it north from Victoria to the Queensland fields. Thereafter prospectors traversed the Northern Territory to reach the Kimberleys in the north of Western Australia by 1886. The end of this migration came in 1893 with the discovery of gold at Kalgoorlie in Western Australia.[2]

Gold-mining methods changed considerably during this period. Despite earlier theories that quartz crushing would not pay, particularly as the ore was poorer at depth, mines sank deeper and deeper; some had reached 2000 feet by 1890. Rock containing as little as $1\frac{1}{2}$ penny-weights of gold in each ton of ore could sometimes yield a profit. In part this was due to improved techniques. Shafts were enlarged and steam engines on the surface hauled ore from below and lowered miners in fast cages with safety catches. The miners' muscle power was gradually supplemented by pneumatic rock drills, black blasting powder by dynamite, and hand-drilled exploratory shafts by the diamond drill installed on the surface and piercing down hundreds of feet. Though many of these innovations spread slowly, Victorians gradually converted other miners to their skills or prejudices. In metallurgy Australia ultimately emerged as a world leader.

The increased capital needed to carry out these changes made it harder for individuals to amass fortunes, though the former grocer and merchant George Lansell, 'Australia's Quartz King', optimistically financed vast mining projects, won over a ton of gold from one reef alone, and retired, not to London, but to Bendigo. Other bonanzas brought more modest fortunes to speculators, rogues and honest men alike. They built their mansions, bred merinos, had their hair curled daily by a personal servant or won the Melbourne Cup; their optimism and success encouraged thousands still hoping to get rich quick. Many of these, preferring the more active and independent outdoor life of

[2] The sections on mining rely mainly on the following works by G. Blainey – *The Peaks of Lyell*, Melbourne, 1954: *Mines in the Spinifex: The Story of Mt Isa Mines*, Sydney, 1960: *The Rush That Never Ended: A History of Australian Mining*, Melbourne, 1963; *The Tyranny of Distance*, Melbourne, 1966: *Across a Red World*, Melbourne, 1968: *The Rise of Broken Hill*, Melbourne, 1968: *The Steel Master: A Life of Essington Lewis*, Melbourne, 1971.

the digger, crossed first into New South Wales, then by land and sea to the Queensland fields: Ravenswood in 1868, Charters Towers in 1872 and up the slushy tracks of tropical Cape York Peninsula to the Palmer River in 1873. Queensland could not match the Victorian fields, but from 1874 did produce more gold annually than New South Wales. Frequently its gold and metal exports exceeded those of wool, enriching and enlarging its coastal towns. Here the fears of the 1850s became a reality, as the Chinese dominated Queensland fields in the 1870s. From Cantonese districts that traditionally sent men to mine Malayan tin and later Californian gold, a continual stream arrived in Australia. By 1877 there were 17,000 on the Palmer field alone. Gradually the Australian colonies moved towards a common policy, but exclusive legislation may have been less effective than the Australian miners' insistence that companies employ Europeans. Only on the Northern Territory fields did the Chinese have one last open go.

Construction workers on the Overland Telegraph from Adelaide to Darwin had found payable gold, and despite the expensive transport, much South Australian capital was poured into the north. A few mines paid well, but heat, fever, scurvy, 'the blacks' and the distance by sea from other settled parts of Australia deterred most Europeans. Finally the South Australian government, separated from the fields by the central deserts, agreed to allow coolie labour. On two-year indentures, a diet of rice and preserved fish, and one-twelfth the wages paid to Europeans, Chinese made the mines pay. Then, refusing their return passage to Singapore, many became alluvial miners, vegetable growers or storekeepers. Others drifted across from Queensland to swell 'the yellow horde', until by 1879 the 3400 Chinese in the Territory outnumbered Europeans by seven to one. In 1881 the alarmed South Australian government imposed a £10 tax on all Chinese who crossed an imaginary line one thousand miles south of Darwin. From 1886 Chinese were not permitted to work on any new goldfields for the first two years. Partly as a result of this preclusion, by 1888 three thousand Chinese navvies were working on the Darwin-to-Pine Creek railway, and Darwin boasted 'one Chinese joss house, two Chinese shoemakers, three Chinese laundries, four Chinese cafes, five Chinese tailor shops, six Chinese gambling houses, seven Chinese brothels and so on to thirty-nine Chinese stores'.[3] The Adelaide investors lost nearly all their money but the Chinese continued to dominate Territory mining, and on the fields by the end of the century outnumbered Europeans by more than twenty to one.

Sharedealing in Victoria was lucrative for many, particularly the larger sharebrokers. Bendigo and Ballarat had busier stock exchanges than Melbourne's during mining booms, and gambling in shares attracted thousands who had first come to dig. Even the strong

[3] G. Blainey, *The Rush That Never Ended*, Melbourne, 1963, p. 95.

Methodist sanctions against gambling seem to have weakened in the case of the mining shares on which much of the life of these towns depended. After the Victorian No Liability Act of 1871 a speculator could lose only the money he had originally invested. Initially this encouraged capital investment, though it may also have increased the risk of failure in some companies. Gambling fever and an infectious optimism permeated the whole structure of the Victorian economy and society, from mining speculators to bankers, importers, politicians who built state railways so lavishly, and the land boomers and city builders of the 1880s.

Until the late 1880s, the enormous cost of financing tens of thousands of mines in Australia had been met by Australian investors and mine profits, but now overseas capital was tapped. Following the arrival of the telegraph in 1872 and cheaper rates in the 1880s, Australian mining trends and share fluctuations could be telegraphed to European investors. At the 1886 Colonial and Indian Exhibition in London, the Queensland government crushed over one hundred tons of golden stone from Charters Towers. Five million people saw the London Exhibition, and the deafening noise of the stamping mills in the crowded hall and the £6000 cake of retorted gold attracted thousands daily. English investors chasing quick profits eagerly bought shares, especially after the first 20 per cent dividend, but many paid so dear that half a million ounces of gold hardly repaid them and the boom collapsed in 1887. Even so, by 1891 Charters Towers was the second biggest city in Queensland and the most productive goldfield in Australia for the following five years.

One further flurry disturbed the long slow decline of gold mining to 1886. The Kimberleys were in one of the most remote areas mined, reached by walking, or riding a horse, or pushing a handcart or wheelbarrow three hundred miles east from the isolated port of Derby; or by paying hundreds of pounds to be landed at Wyndham only to face a solid mountain wall. A few crossed the entire continent following the telegraph from Adelaide or overlanding from Queensland. But the cost in money and lives was great and men turned willingly from these grim hardships to the Pilbara rush further south, then to the Murchison, and finally to Yilgarn east of Perth. By now the diggers had travelled the full circle around Australia and stood poised before the great gold discoveries of the 1890s – Coolgardie and Kalgoorlie.

While gold mining excited the imagination and offered the richest rewards, other minerals were also attractive. South Australia had earlier proved rich in copper. In some years when Victoria led the world in gold, South Australia had mined one-tenth of the world's copper. The earlier mines at Kapunda and Burra were supplanted in the 1860s by Moonta and Kadina, which were thought to be 'the most religious towns in Australia', strongholds of Methodism and Cornish custom, where miners 'returning home from work late at night walked to the doors of the chapels to learn how many were saved that night'. During the 1870s, South Australia replaced Cornwall as the busiest copper region in the British Empire.[4] While prices averaged over £100 per ton – a level not reached again until munitions demands in the War of 1914–18 – all was well. Captain Hancock's mine employed over 1400 men and boys in 1873, more than any other Australian mine until B.H.P.s silver-lead finds. The Wallaroo smelters had never been busier, and the three main copper towns held some 20,000 people – about two per cent of Australia's total population. Preaching miners, the tribute system, even Captain Hancock himself, were all to survive until the late 1890s. But the mines, despite careful husbanding of reserves, slowly declined. Moonta's miners departed to the hundreds of copper and tin mines in the eastern colonies; many were skilled men who had survived as their own bosses under the tribute system for thirty years and had never worked for wages.

Tin commanded a higher price than copper but was more scattered and harder to detect than the blue-green copper outcrops. It could however be mined alluvially by men without much money or experience. In 1871 on the New England tablelands of northern New South Wales near Inverell a rush began for rich tin finds; so rich was Vegetable Creek that thousands of Chinese and Australians churned a mere 150 acres of river flat for fifteen thousand tons; then deep shafts were sunk underground for a further six thousand tons. The tinlands, it was found, stretched north across the Queensland border and in 1873 this border region alone produced more tin than any other country in the world. Australia continued the world's largest tin producer for the whole decade 1873–82.

There was one further boom to excite the Australian speculator before the 1890s – the silver-lead discoveries in the Barrier ranges seven hundred miles west of Sydney. The far west had a well-earned reputation for heat, drought and dust, but depressed conditions frequently spurred mining exploration. Silver at Thackaringa was such a response, but the £8 per ton freight for the long trip down the Darling, then overseas to smelters in Wales or Germany, discouraged development. Near Tibooburra where the daily temperature for six months was over 100°F, there was barely enough water for man and beast to drink. Only dry-blowing the dusty soil was possible, and advance and retreat fluctuated with the seasons. In 1882–3 amazingly rich silver deposits were found near permanent water at Silverton. When the drought broke thousands of miners arrived and local smelters were built. The South Australian government extended its railway two hundred miles northeast from Peterborough in 1885, but refused to cross the New South Wales border, so local promoters built the Silverton Tramway Company line to bridge the short gap. Yet even as the first train arrived, Silverton was dying.

Further east, a long low hill with a jagged broken crest attracted Charles Rasp, boundary rider. A first assay reported lead and silver,

4 For an account of South Australia's Cornish Miners see O. Pryor, *Australia's Little Cornwall*, Adelaide, 1962.

and a syndicate of seven members was formed, including George McCulloch the station manager. This willingness for boss and men – capital and labour – to unite laid the basis for the vast Broken Hill Proprietary Company. During the first year doubts and inconclusive geological reports forced some members, who were contributing half their monthly wages, to sell out. Even McCulloch sold half his shares – soon to be worth over a million – for £120. Shares, half-shares and quarters were sold and resold as further money was sunk in shafts. Then at last the real wealth was discovered, rich silver chloride in soft white clay. Easily mined and smelted, it paid for the new smelters which opened in 1886.

B.H.P. shares had a nominal value of £19. The last sales for 1887 closed at £174 10s, and by February 1888 they had jumped to £409, giving the mine a market value of £6.5 million.[5] Adjacent mines shared the boom; the share markets responded and silver mining was stimulated all over Australia. Eighty brokers are estimated to have made over a quarter of a million in brokerage from silver shares alone. The gold boom seemed weak by comparison, and speculation was proportionately high and hazardous. Despite primitive living conditions, water shortages, flies and typhoid, by 1891 Broken Hill was the third largest city in New South Wales with a population of 20,000 and still growing. Its impact was spread over the economies of three colonies: Melbourne directed the company, New South Wales handled an annual £3.6 million silver-lead export, and Adelaide supplied food and stores. South Australia's wharves, railways, farms, factories, warehouses and silver smelters all benefited and its economy revived. Yet all was not success, even for so rich a mine as Broken Hill. The price of lead had fallen slowly since 1886 as had the price of silver ever since the field was first found. International monetary policies had reduced the value of a £1000 bar of silver of 1884 to only £572 in 1894 and the deeper sulphide ores were poorer and harder to smelt.

Throughout these twenty years as mining fortunes rose and fell, the boom and bust conditions directly affected the lives of thousands of Australians. Following the rushes in the hope of instant wealth and the lucky strike was uncertain and hazardous, and more suited to independent, mobile, unmarried men. Those with wives and families frequently settled for the less precarious company employment and the more stable society of the large mining towns. Even this often proved illusory and led men to seek further independence on the land. Generally, miners and mining suffered little interference from governments; indeed the nature of the industry encouraged a laissez-faire attitude. The hope of a rich discovery made miners less interested in government handouts. By contrast, those who sought independence on the land were faced with different problems. First, the Crown, in the person of colonial lands departments, laid claim to all unsold lands, and second, the pastoralists or squatters grazed enormous

---

[5] G. Blainey, *The Rush That Never Ended*, Melbourne, 1963, pp. 149–50.

numbers of sheep and cattle on these lands under leasehold arrangements. Hence government action was needed to 'Unlock the Lands'.

In their attempts to open land for settlement, the aims of the colonies were similar but their methods differed. Some sold land only after it had been surveyed, others allowed men to select land before survey. The radical aims of those who sought to overthrow the squatters contrasted sharply with the earlier Wakefieldian vision of concentrated settlement and of a transplanted English rural society. Those arguing for land reform appealed to a wide range of historical experience, from Cain and Abel to the yeomen of Old England, from Virgil to the Physiocrats and Jefferson. Utopian idealists and political anti-squatter factions alike saw the squatters as monster monopolists, obstacles to the settlement of the country, locusts eating up the bowels of the land, a race of shepherd-kings who had usurped occupancy of the land. Reform would remedy this. Every man by nature, they said, longed to possess a piece of land for his own, though not necessarily for agricultural purposes. Population would be attracted into the interior where, as men settled down and made homes, dissipation and the wandering habits which were said to be so striking a feature of colonial life would be checked. Then would every man sit on his verandah or under his fig tree smoking his pipe in contentment while the vine brought forth her fruit and the wilderness blossomed as the rose.

Pro-squatter newspaper editors and politicians, however, argued that the squatters had brought civilization to an unoccupied waste and produced a staple commanding a world market. They paid rent into government revenue, ensured rural economic and social stability, and provided political leadership. Such a view saw the selection acts as class legislation, aimed at ruining the squatter. In Victoria, greater population pressure reduced squatter domination. In the well-watered western district, tenacious Scottish pastoralists fought and consolidated; elsewhere, as the number of Victorian runs was halved, squatters were forced into the Riverina district of New South Wales or to Queensland.[6] Under Grant's 1869 Amending Act, eleven million acres in Victoria were selected before survey in nine years, and little land suitable for agriculture remained. As wheat growers moved inland in the 1870s the population of the Wimmera and northern Victoria rose by over 70,000 and new towns like Horsham and Shepparton developed rapidly. By 1877, Victoria was at last self-sufficient in wheat and had become an exporter. The protective tariff of 1866 had helped, but more important were railway extensions which brought access to metropolitan and world markets.

By the 1880s the only large areas left for aspiring farmers in Victoria were the Mallee in the north-west and Gippsland in the south-

[6] For the Victorian experience, especially in the Wimmera and Gippsland, see G. Serle, *The Rush To Be Rich*, Melbourne, 1971, and J. M. Powell, *The Public Lands of Australia Felix*, Melbourne, 1970.

east. The 1870s had seen the settlement of much of the Wimmera, on the northern fringes of which heavy grey and brown clay soils gave way to undulating mallee country, as the rainfall steadily diminished from fifteen to ten inches and even lower. In the Mallee, long parallel lines of sandhills alternated with clay flats. The whole area, covered uniformly with the multiple-trunked *Eucalyptus Dumosa*, ten to fifteen feet high, was devoid of permanent water and overrun with rabbits. Unattractive to explorers and pastoralists, the mallee finally yielded to clearing techniques developed for similar country in South Australia: scrub-rolling with heavy logs or chains or old boilers pulled by two teams of horses, followed by a good burn, then ploughing with the stump-jump plough (invented in 1876 by a South Australian farmer), sowing and reaping the first wheat crop, then sucker-bashing and stump-picking for several years. By the mid-1880s, despite the hardships, many farmers had been attracted by the virgin soil and large areas available. As in the settlement of the Wimmera, scores of wagons had crossed the border from South Australia bringing Lutheran settlers, while some Victorian farmers made a second migration north from Warracknabeal or west from Swan Hill. By 1890 five hundred farmers were growing wheat successfully in the southern Mallee, protected not only by the rising Victorian tariff, but also by the government fence, which in 1885 was run along the 36th parallel to keep rabbits away from the southern farming areas.

As farmers moved into these drier areas comparisons were made with the great deserts of Africa, Asia and America, leading inevitably to discussion of irrigation. Spurred on by enthusiasts like Hugh McColl, 'the man with water on the brain', the Victorian parliament began seriously to consider government involvement in irrigation. In 1883 Melbourne newspaper reporters were sent to California to study irrigation; Alfred Deakin espoused the cause, piloted Victoria's Irrigation Act through in 1886, and by 1888, despite problems caused by seepage, evaporation and yabbies, water flowed along 400 miles of channels from the Coulburn Weir. Meanwhile the Chaffey brothers had come from California to found a Mesopotamia of the South at the extreme northern end of the Mallee, on the Mildura pastoral run, 'a Sahara of hissing hot winds' swarming with rabbits. Outspoken criticism of 'Yankee Landgrabbers' and subsequent delays diverted them temporarily to South Australia where they founded Renmark. But when no further tenders from Mildura were received, the Victorian government renegotiated its original contract. By 1890 there were three thousand people in this teetotal settlement and Mildura's struggle for existence had begun.[7]

While some Victorians grappled with the arid northwest, others faced different problems in the thick forests of Gippsland, led by Danish settlers in the Poowong area in 1874. Aeons of 40–50 inch rainfall had produced a thick layer of decomposing vegetable matter

[7] See Ernestine Hill, *Water into Gold*, Melbourne, 1937.

and towering timber one hundred and fifty feet high. One hollow tree with an internal diameter of twenty-six feet was used for years as a church, meeting hall and school. The axe work in clearing such land was prodigious, and the undergrowth was so thick that men were easily lost. Few ventured far, even for a morning's work, without a compass, and the tall forest timber produced a different kind of loneliness from that of the arid inland. As in the Wimmera and the Mallee, women and children followed their men and shared the hardships. Indeed, without families and their labour many holdings would not have been economically viable. Richer soil and heavier rainfall in Gippsland made dairying the main occupation and the cleared land was sown with English grasses and clovers. Cream separators, co-operative factories and the railway to Melbourne completed the cash nexus.[8]

Stimulated by government bonuses, Victoria had half as many dairy cattle again as New South Wales throughout the 1880s, but further dairy expansion had to wait until refrigeration made export possible. Wheat production, still less than South Australia's, had trebled. Partly this was a result of tariff protection which had risen steadily in response to rural pressure, thus compensating for a downward trend in world prices. By the mid-1880s over 100,000 selections had been made under the 1869 amendment, and by 1890 Victorian farm produce was worth twice as much as pastoral production and three times that of mining. Even the Irish, traditionally regarded for their lack of Anglo-Saxon virtues as the most slovenly of farmers, recreated the potato-growing economy of their homeland in the Koroit-Warrnambool area and the western district. In the shire of Bungaree, in the early 1890s, 90 per cent of the 537 cultivators were of Irish descent. A few held 40-60 acres, most had eighty acres, and some 160 acres. When over-crowding had occurred earlier, some Irish had moved out into the drier wheatbelt areas where, by the late 1880s one Tipperary man had 1400 acres, seven hundred of which were in crop.

In New South Wales the 1860s had seen moderate land sales on the coast and tablelands but few inland, where the great pastoral runs remained locked-up until their fourteen-year leases expired at the beginning of 1866. The severe drought of 1864–6 had further discouraged settlers. But by the 1870s wool prices had boomed, seasons were extraordinarily good and population pressure on land was pushing men inland from South Australia and New South Wales as well as Victoria. The major difficulty was that the whole area was legitimately occupied under pastoral lease. Robertson's Acts simply (or complicatedly) offered the same land to two different lots of people under different clauses of the same legislation.[9] Historians generally have followed the views of S. H. Roberts based on the 1883 Morris and

8 G. Serle, *The Rush To Be Rich*, Melbourne, 1971, pp. 58–60.

9 For a discussion of the New South Wales experience see G. L. Buxton, *The Riverina 1861–1891: An Australian Regional Study*, Melbourne, 1967.

Ranken pro-squatter report on the land laws.[10] There is no denying much of what that report had to say about fraud, blackmail, intimidation, perjury and wholesale alienation of land to pastoral lessees; nor that the Acts were most elastic in interpretation. But Morris and Ranken's main aim was to discredit Robertson. They destroyed their minutes of evidence, suppressed the names of all witnesses, and by carefully juggling statistics concluded predictably that free selection had failed. More recent research has cast doubt on this long-established interpretation.

For the intending selector the first problem was to discover what land was actually available. Because Robertson's Acts were passed largely in response to political pressure, no steps were taken to prepare the New South Wales Survey or Lands departments, which in any case were more backward than those of any other British colony. Not even a single base line existed for the beginnings of triangulation. By the time free selection had been operating for ten years, confusion in the centralized system was immense, and delays of up to two years were common. Further, six million acres of reserves had been declared, but not surveyed, their whereabouts known only to the squatters who had recommended them on their runs. Persons paying deposits could not know whether the land they sought was available, nor could the local Crown lands agent tell them; many turned back disappointed. Abuses also occurred in the local land offices – open for selection business only on Thursdays – where the Crown lands agent was also clerk of petty sessions, and as such, on other days of the week, subservient to squatter J.P.s in the local court. It was useless for John Robertson to protest that his Acts were 'framed for honest men, not rogues'. Some squatters moved back, but most were prepared to fight. Auction purchases turned whole stations from leasehold to freehold. Improvement purchases were based on useless tanks, mobile stockyards and flying huts; and some curiously shaped blocks resulted from utilizing every room and building in the homestead. Volunteer land orders, mineral selections and several varieties of dummying completed the sorry list of subterfuges and evasions. Squatters could and did also legitimately select in their own names.

Meanwhile family selection (including some on behalf of squatters) had raised New South Wales land revenue spectacularly. In many inland districts, more than 40 per cent of the selections for these two decades were taken up in the years 1873–6. The loophole was finally closed by an amendment of late 1875, which also remedied survey deficiencies, reorganized the Lands Department and generally brought order into chaos. Much of the pressure for these changes had been directed politically through local selectors' associations, first formed in

10 'Report of Inquiry into the State of Public Lands, and the operation of the Land Laws', May 1883, in *Journal of the Legislative Council of New South Wales*, 1883, *34*, i, pp. 271–311, part-published in C. M. H. Clark, *Select Documents in Australian History: 1851–1900*, Sydney, 1955, pp. 126–34.

1873. Combined annual conferences were held in Sydney from 1876, which later led to the formation of the Amalgamated Farmers' Union (and ultimately the Country Party). In 1877 selectors' representatives were successful in rural electorates and thereafter increasingly replaced squatters in the N.S.W. Legislative Assembly.

With only slight amendments Robertson's Acts continued in force until 1883 when the Parkes-Robertson coalition was defeated, and Augustus Morris and George Ranken were appointed to investigate land matters. The 1884 Act which followed had little effect on the established pattern of growth. Despite their extended period of examination they discovered little that was new, but they showed considerable ingenuity in emphasizing faults and failures while avoiding altogether mentioning the successes. Where, for example, an area was closely settled they complained of reckless alienation without thought for posterity. And where the nature of the environment forced selectors to be graziers rather than farmers, or the railway had not been extended, they deplored the lack of cultivation. The vast numbers attracted from Victoria were without exception 'speculators' and 'blackmailers'. The squatters' misdeeds were all whitewashed, and the successful German farmers from South Australia were not mentioned. Nevertheless, Robertson's Acts, despite all their shortcomings, enabled men to attain independence on the land. The extension of railways enabled selectors to turn from grazing to wheat-growing. From 1882–8 the wheat acreage in the Murrumbidgee area increased nine-fold. In the Riverina, which Morris and Ranken argued the greatest failure, crop acreages grew from 8000 in 1861 to 200,000 in 1891, population from 10,000 to 63,000 and sheep numbers from one million to thirteen million: all this occurred in an area some 350 miles long and 150 miles wide.

South Australia, which saw the most spectacular advance on the land and the most disastrous retreat, differed markedly from the eastern colonies, where the most suitable areas for wheat-growing lay across the Great Dividing Range. A Mediterranean climate, suitable soils for wheat-growing close to the sea, and easy gradients to the heavily indented coastline, giving horse tramways and railways ready access to overseas shipping, all help to account for South Australia's early dominance in agriculture. By contrast with New South Wales' somewhat indifferent early attitude to the small man, the systematic colonizers, free settlers all, had from the beginning followed Wakefield's plan of survey before sale of 80-acre sections for small men and 4000-acre Special Surveys for capitalists. Even these latter it was assumed (correctly in many cases) would pass from government to squatter-capitalist to tenant farmer, thereby establishing a yeomanry. In the 1860s South Australia grew half of Australia's wheat and exported to all the eastern colonies as well as to Mauritius, South Africa and Britain. This heavy dependence of the economy on wheat was both cause and effect of legislative concern with agriculture. Politics was dominated by urban middle classes and farmers' representatives.

By the 1860s only one squatter remained in the lower house, though squatters could still obstruct in the council; in contrast New South Wales' squatters held one-third of Legislative Assembly seats in 1860 and still held one-fifth as late as 1880.

The exodus of farmers to the Wimmera and the Riverina (where eventually nearly 7 per cent of the population were South Australian Lutherans) prompted South Australia to accept H. B. T. Strangways' compromise Act in 1868.[11] In 1869 Surveyor-General G. W. Goyder named six Agricultural Areas, describing the soil, rainfall, ports and roads, and selection began. Lack of rain in 1869 led to the first amendment, establishing the pattern for the next two decades of an annual review of land matters. Good rains made the 1870–71 harvest a South Australian record, nearly 7,000,000 bushels at an average of over eleven bushels per acre. Agitation began for an increase in the area for sale, at least up to Goyder's Line, drawn in 1865 to mark the limits of pastoral runs affected adversely by drought.[12] Based largely on the surveyor-general's observations of vegetation changes, particularly saltbush, it corresponds roughly to the modern twelve-inch rainfall isohyet. Under the 1872 Act selection was permitted anywhere south of Goyder's line.

The period of expansion from 1872 to 1880 was spurred by extraordinarily good seasons. Each year marked a new record harvest, and prices were steady at a high 5s. 5d. per bushel. Chafing against restrictions, the *Northern Argus* suggested that 'Mr Goyder's rainfall line should be shifted out of the colony', and despite all Goyder's warnings pressure prevailed. In 1874 the whole of the colony was thrown open for selection. The basis of settlement legislation was thus no longer paternal but empirical; the farmers were to judge where wheat would grow, and while the seasons remained good they did not hesitate to advance well beyond Goyder's line. Record rainfall continued and the doctrine 'rain follows the plough' was in the ascendant. Twenty-four survey parties worked continuously to cope with selectors' demands and northern squatters were hard hit as notice of resumption was reduced from six months to as little as five days. In County Victoria, inland from Port Pirie, the population rose from 800 in 1871 to over 6000 in 1876, and more than a thousand substantial new houses were built. Railways expanded at their most rapid rate for the half-century. In 1879, despite lower prices, a record harvest yielded 14,000,000 bushels. Ports were crowded with ships, railways were overtaxed and the revenue was unbelievably buoyant. The *Northern Argus* commented that 'Some of our young men may yet be speeding the plough

11 For the South Australian experience see D. W. Meinig, *On the Margins of the Good Earth: The South Australian Wheat Frontier 1869–1884*, Chicago, 1962: J. B. Hirst, *Adelaide and the Country 1870–1917: Their Social and Political Relationship*, Melbourne, 1973.

12 'Surveyor-General's Report on Demarcation of Northern Rainfall', in *South Australia: Proceedings of Parliament and Papers*, 1865 6, 2, Paper No. 78.

on the banks of the River Finke or on the plateaus of the McDonnell Ranges in Central Australia', but already on the marginal lands there were doubts.

The years 1881–4 saw a rapid retreat back to Goyder's line, as rainfall diminished to half the average and crops failed along the frontiers. Distressed farmers petitioned for drinking water and seed wheat, and trees were planted in the forlorn hope of bringing rain. In 1882 the colony's average yield dropped to 4.2 bushels, the lowest on record. More than half a million acres were forfeited and farmers simply walked off their land, one writing sadly, 'Goyder's ghost seems to hover about' (Goyder was still alive at the time). New legislation relieved farmers but wrecked revenue anticipation. A brief break in the drought in 1883–4 sent production soaring to 14,000,000 bushels again but optimism had gone. Further drought and depression in the 1890s savagely vindicated Goyder's judgement, and there was no more talk of expansion in the north, though the annual land bill continued a feature of South Australian legislation, and many farmers reselected further south.

What had been achieved? Twenty land acts or amendments had been passed in twenty years. Effective agricultural limits had been extended 150 miles northwards, nearly two million more acres had been brought under crop and the settled area more than doubled. In the mid-north 50,000 new settlers remained. In 1884, as in 1869, South Australia still reaped harvests greater than Victoria and New South Wales combined. In the south-east and other areas closer settlement had continued to expand. In the north an empirical testing of the new country had been made and the limits of marginal lands established, though at considerable human and environmental cost. Goyder's line had gained an acceptance, not entirely forgotten amongst farmers a century later, as a reliable basis for delimiting the area suitable for agriculture. Despite all their evasive tactics, many of the squatters had been pushed back. The resistance of the pastoral lessees and the inexperience of legislators in dealing with the new environment had hindered the quest for an ideal solution, but the South Australian parliament did succeed in planting agriculturalists over a wide area of the colony and establishing a prosperous middle-class farming community. Generally this was the most successful of the attempts of the period to put 'the small man on the land'.

At the further end of Australia's fertile crescent, the Darling Downs in southern Queensland marked the northern limits of attempts to settle a yeomanry of commercial grain growers. Nowhere else in Queensland, according to D. B. Waterson, were 'the squatters stronger, the storekeepers more hostile and the selectors more significant'.[13] Like other squatters, the 'Pure Merinos of the Downs' were well established when the first Queensland selection acts were passed and they used

13 For the Queensland experience see D. B. Waterson, *Squatter, Selector and Storekeeper*, Sydney, 1968.

the same methods to hold the land, becoming equally indebted in the process. Despite their efforts, large and small selectors, including many Germans and Irish were established as graziers or farmers. By the early 1890s the Downs population had risen to 40,000.

Country land in Queensland was cheaper than in the other colonies, where the £1 per acre minimum upset price was the rule. For 15s. or, from 1876–84, for a mere 5s. per acre, Darling Downs settlers could select on rich, easily worked blacksoil plains, capable of being cropped for decades without fertilizer, as well as on patches of somewhat less fertile red soils. The main obstacle to cultivation, apart from eucalypts and cypress pine in the timbered areas, was the variable summer rainfall, particularly as suitable wheats had not yet been developed. Many therefore tried mixed farming and grew crops other than wheat, especially maize, but for these the market was more local and less predictable. When wheat did grow – at times only once in three years – the average yield was at least double that of South Australia and sometimes as high as forty-two bushels per acre. Such a crop could yield a farmer £1000 in one season and £500 – £800 was common in parts of the Downs, enabling farmers to withstand several bad years. However, technologically Downs wheat farming was as much as twenty years behind South Australia.

Although success varied with capitalization, technical skills, soil and the run of seasons, a man and his family could acquire a measure of independence. But pride of ownership was sometimes marred by virtual slave labour, as whole families struggled to increase the area under crop to 70,000 acres by 1890. Waterson sees the worst psychological effects in a sense of frustration, 'Schools emptied at harvest time and children were forced into heavy farm duties at an early age without any choice. Adolescents worked without wages. Racking tensions between patriarch and his sons were not uncommon and remorseless routine often made drudges of the women . . . ' Beyond the environment stood the storekeeper, like the one in Steele Rudd's *On Our Selection* who, when the long-awaited first year's crop of maize brought £12, took all, leaving a debt of £3 still standing. No wonder 'Dad was speechless and looked sick'.[14] Not all the crops of maize, lucerne, potatoes (and even tobacco and grapes) could counteract undercapitalization, lack of marketing facilities, and the 'pitiless accumulation of compound interest'. In such cases agriculture seemed 'more a way of life than a method of making profits'. But so long as banks regarded farms as second-rate security, needy selectors were at the mercy of storekeepers. Taking a further rake-off were monopolistic millers and middlemen. The exploitation of farmers by storekeepers was more excessive on the Darling Downs than elsewhere.

In other ways Darling Downs society was unique. There was marked fragmentation and an astonishing lack of co-operation compared with other colonies, where selectors' associations and farmers' unions were

14 Steel Rudd, *On Our Selection*, Sydney, 1889, p. 13.

commonplace, leading to effective political representation by the mid-1870s. By contrast Queensland farmers' candidates regularly failed. As late as the 1890s, Downs selectors were still returning storekeepers, millers and publicans to parliament. Perhaps the relative ease of acquiring land had reduced the common sense of grievance, perhaps isolation contributed, or perhaps it was the absence amongst these settlers of the social and intellectual quality of the Victorian gold-rush migrants and their earlier South Australian middle-class counterparts.

Even Tasmania and Western Australia attempted yeoman settlement in this period, though with little success, partly because of lack of transport and markets. In thirty years, Tasmanian cultivation increased only from 163,000 to 168,000 acres, while Western Australia's rose from 25,000 to 64,000 acres.[15] It was on the southern and eastern mainland of the continent that agricultural settlement had its greatest success, and thriving populations numbering tens of thousands settled in a wide arc from the north of South Australia to southern Queensland, fulfilling to a greater or lesser degree the yeoman ideal. By tradition the backbone of the country, uncorrupted by society, more patriotic and virtuous than the allegedly decadent city dweller, his struggle with the land made the Australian farmer hard and proud, noted for his toughness and independence. 'In his respectability and pride in property' Geoffrey Serle concludes, 'he was the antithesis of the classical Australian bush worker'.[16]

Most of the expansion of agriculture in the selection period was at the expense of pastoral land holdings in the better watered areas of Australia, and the cost of this struggle for control of the land hurt the pastoralists.[17] Paradoxically, their economic decline took place in a period of rapid growth in sheep numbers to a level not to be reached again until well into the twentieth century. The boom years of the early 1870s attracted not only farmers but many would-be graziers, and the competition from hundreds of mobile families posed serious problems for established pastoral lessees, leading them, as well as smaller graziers, to seek 'better country further out' – or at least freedom from interference. During the 1870s and 1880s the pastoral area increased continually, especially in New South Wales and Queensland. In Queensland until railways were built, sheep were less economical and the climate of central Queensland favoured cattle.[18] Markets, however, were a problem. Not until the late 1880s did beef export reach

15 See F. K. Crowley, *Australia's Western Third*, London, 1960, pp. 59–63.

16 G. Serle, *The Rush To Be Rich*, Melbourne, 1971, pp. 62–3.

17 For a discussion of changes in the pastoral industry see G. L. Buxton, *The Riverina: 1861–1891*, Melbourne, 1967, ch. 8: N. G. Butlin, *Investment in Australian Economic Development, 1861–1900*, Cambridge, 1964, ch. 2.

18 See J. Griffin, Ed., *Essays in Economic History of Australia*, Brisbane, 1967, ch. 5.

substantial levels, much of it due to the success in shipping frozen meat to the initially reluctant English market.

In the meantime, cattlemen had penetrated the further reaches of Queensland and spilled over into the Northern Territory. The great stimulus came with the expansion of Queensland mining and the arrival of hordes of hungry miners, though the overlanding of thousands of cattle southwards to Sydney and Melbourne markets still continued. In one epic feat of overlanding, Long Michael walked two thousand cattle from the Barcoo River in Queensland to the Kimberleys in Western Australia where the Duracks had settled on the Ord River. Further south, the Emanuels ran cattle on the Fitzroy River. But Queensland was the real cattle country, and between 1870 and 1890 numbers rose from 1.1 million to 5.5 million, the latter being more than half the cattle in Australia. In this respect Queensland was exceptional. For most of Australia, the pastoral industry meant sheep, and even in Queensland, between 1866 and 1891, sheep numbers rose from 7.3 million to 20.9 million. In the same period the New South Wales' total rose from 11.6 million to 55.5 million. Although some of the increase was in favoured regions like the Riverina much of the expansion was into areas which in drier (and more normal) seasons could not hope to carry such numbers of stock and which certainly could not repay the vast sums invested. In this regard the pastoral industry was as speculative and hazardous as mining.

A second response to squatter-selector competition and one with equally disastrous results in the 1890s was the conversion of thousands of acres from leasehold to freehold. The ultimate protection for the squatter was to purchase his previously leased land at a price of at least £1 per acre – an inflated price even decades later – borrowing from banks, individuals or the growing pastoral finance houses in order to do so. In the boom years the price of pastoral leasehold property had soared. Now, many who had paid dear were forced by selector competition to 'buy the station twice'. Even in 1870 71, interest on some of the largest pastoral debts was approaching one-half of the proceeds of wool sales. But this was while wool prices were high and before the extensive land purchases virtually forced on the squatters by selectors. N. G. Butlin has shown that by 1889–91, despite very much higher total debts, wool proceeds, in a time of continually falling wool prices, had not nearly kept pace, and the annual cash surplus was swallowed up without decreasing the debt. Whereas at one stage it was said, as a result of Victorian absentee investment, 'Queensland was keeping half Toorak' by the late 1880s 'Toorak was keeping half Queensland'.

There was therefore great need for both old-established squatters and the new class of grazier-selectors to maximize productivity mainly by fencing, water conservation and primitive pasture improvement. In 1871, there were some twenty thousand miles of fencing in New South Wales, most of it in the Riverina, the leading pastoral district, but within a decade three-quarters of a million miles had been erected on New South Wales runs alone.[19] Keeping pace with the boundary and sub-division fencing for intricate systems of large and small paddocks were the watering facilities: tanks, wells, dams, whims, windmills, steam engines and finally bores. Much of the cost of these pastoral improvements was paid to gangs of itinerant rural workers, the fencing and damsinking teams, who travelled endlessly across the pastoral lands. The commonest attempt at pasture improvement was ringbarking, by which every tree on millions of acres of Australia was killed while still standing. Few Australians objected to the widespread use of Chinese for this work, nor for the even more arduous years of scrub-cutting and sucker-bashing which followed. Erosion, the spread of pine scrub, the disappearance of native vegetation and general deterioration of the original environment followed; but up to double the number of stock could be carried.

Hindering all efforts to increase productivity was the rabbit invasion. In 1880 rabbits crossed the Murray from Victoria and by 1886 were thick in southern Queensland. So severe was the infestation in some areas that runs were simply deserted. Thousands of rabbits overran outback towns driving some residents to leave. Dogs gave up in disgust their attempts to kill the invaders. Under acts like the 1883 N.S.W. Rabbit Nuisance Act thousands of pounds were paid for destruction, but the rodents were unmoved, even after an 1891 Royal Commission on Rabbits. Arsenic, strychnine and acetic acid were used to poison water, bran, chaff, sticks of sandalwood and even jam; phosphorized grain was laid; traps were set, yarding machines invented and hundreds of miles of rabbit-proof netting fence erected. But where almost a million rabbits could be killed on one station in a year, and four men could yard 9827 in one day, pastures were devastated, stock-carrying capacity greatly reduced and farmers' crops ruined. Nor could major technological changes compensate. River steamers, railways, and freezing and chilling works helped, as did differential rates inspired by intercolonial rivalries. But heavy borrowing, overexpansion into marginal areas and falling world wool prices all combined to lower profitability. By 1891, for the sheepmen, large and small, economic opportunities were declining. At the same time, closer settlement and the growth of country towns provided alternative value and status systems which undermined the social and political power of the squatter.

By 1890 most of the best agricultural land in south-eastern Australia had been occupied. Around this fertile crescent, thousands of families lived in comfortable and relatively prosperous conditions. Home and family, church and school were the typical bulwarks of the farming

---

[19] N. G. Butlin, *Investment in Australian Economic Development, 1861–1900,* Cambridge, 1964, p. 75.

communities.[20] Country newspaper editors particularly praised Lutheran farmers, whose industry, thrift and frugality provide an interesting Australian counterpart to the European version of the Weber thesis. Lutheran churches and day schools formed a strong social cement, while retention of the German language perpetuated traditional culture. Pockets of Roman Catholicism were similarly maintained in small bush churches amongst families of Irish descent. Indeed, clergy of all major denominations, especially Methodists, travelled long distances in all weathers on horseback or in horsedrawn vehicles to conduct services. Besides its religious significance, the weekly gathering served an important social purpose as a time when men and women could meet to talk about farm and family and the prospects for the season.

As farming communities proliferated, rural population structure changed. Men continued to outnumber women in predominantly pastoral districts, but in farming areas and country towns the numbers of males and females were more nearly equal. Irish female immigrants, sent in large numbers as domestics, aided the balance. Greater marriage possibilities and the large families which resulted increased the youthfulness of the population. Three Darling Downs families mustered forty-nine children between them, and in 1890, in a graphic demonstration of rural fertility near Wagga Wagga, Mrs Henry Angel numbered among her living descendants thirteen children, ninety grandchildren and forty-nine great grandchildren. As the selector population spread inland colonial governments faced the problem of providing schools and teachers for this increasing horde. The Riverina, for example, in 1861 boasted some six schools of primary standard. By 1882 nearly 13,000 children attended 233 schools in the Wagga Wagga district alone. Although some difficulty was experienced with attendance during harvest-time, education was generally valued, and the annual school picnic, prize-giving, Arbor day and sports day were important social occasions in the rural calendar. Speeches on such occasions were still along Smilesian lines, emphasising self-help, perseverance and hard work.

In their opposition to secular education, Anglicans and Roman Catholics established church schools in country towns, as Lutherans did in farming areas. In South Australia a teaching order, the Sisters of Saint Joseph, expanded remarkably, particularly in view of the smaller percentage of Roman Catholics in that colony. By 1870 27 schools taught 1700 children, and by 1876, as the unsalaried teaching sisters advanced into the newly-settled agricultural areas, these had increased to over 90 schools teaching nearly 3000 children.

[20] For discussion of rural communities and country towns see G. L. Buxton, *The Riverina, 1861–1891*, Melbourne, 1967: D. B. Waterson, *Squatter, Selector and Storekeeper*, Sydney, 1968: L. T. Daley, *Men and a River*, Melbourne, 1966: D. W. Meinig, *On the Margins of the Good Earth*, Chicago, 1962: S. Priestley, *Echuca: A Centenary History*, Brisbane, 1965.

In rural communities everywhere literacy rose as colonies promoted their 'free, compulsory, secular' programmes and a much greater appreciation of secondary and tertiary education resulted. Not only did boys matriculate successfully from country high schools but town feuds could develop when one school received a graduate teacher and another did not. State schools also contributed to incipient nationalism, not only by what was taught in the classroom, but by the military cadet training scheme in which students with wooden rifles practised 'drill' in preparation for the defence of their country.

Between 1871 and 1891 hundreds of small country towns, with populations ranging from fifty to five hundred, developed in the farming areas particularly along the railway lines. Unlike their earlier pastoral counterparts, few boasted hotels at first. The school, church, hall, saleyard, store, post office and blacksmith's were more typical, with perhaps a police station later. Initially, one weatherboard or galvanized iron building served different purposes on different days. Activities and organizations included horse-racing and sports meetings, concerts and dances, progress committees, brass bands, cricket and football teams, a School of Arts, Literary Institute and Library, a Railway League and a Farmers' Union.

Marked growth also occurred in larger centres especially in New South Wales. By contrast, former mining towns in Victoria frequently declined unless they found new industries. Most depended for survival on the development of surrounding farmlands. Golden Ballarat, fourth city in Australia in 1870, with 50,000 inhabitants, had only 40,000 by 1880. Others like Castlemaine became old men's towns, as their youth departed in search of economic opportunity. In South Australia and New South Wales as well as in Victoria, towns which had served older pastoral or agricultural communities or had grown rapidly with the first rush of selectors in the 1870s often declined as the selector frontier moved on: families grew up, women passed child-bearing age, and selectors sold out to each other or to the squatter. A similar rise and fall followed the outward wave of casual workers engaged in railway construction, fencing, damsinking and ringbarking, mostly on pastoral properties, while teamsters and those employed in coaching and the river steamer traffic continually retreated before the advancing railways.

While the growth patterns of some country towns reflect the influence of these major migratory movements, others mirror the rise and fall of local or world prices and the development of new markets. Coastal ports following the fluctuating fortunes of their hinterlands are obvious examples. At Port Augusta in northern South Australia wheat exports for 1878–80 rose from almost nothing to half a million bushels. With the retreat behind Goyder's line they fell by 80 per cent in two years. When Mackay (Qld.) shared in the sugar boom between 1876 and 1886, its population trebled. In the Richmond River valley on the New South Wales coast, sugar-growing, ship-building and the booming timber trade with Sydney led to similar developments, while a more modest growth occurred in Western Australia as that colony's first significant railways thrust into the forests of the south-west.

In the more stable wheat-sheep belt, towns developed industries to process local products: flour-mills, wool-scours, tanneries, dairy factories and meat-freezing works. Bakeries, breweries and cordial manufactories supplied local requirements of food and drink, though metropolitan breweries undermined local enterprise when railways extended. Town growth itself stimulated the building trade with growing numbers of lime-kilns, brickworks and sawmills, the latter cutting redgum, native pine or cedar depending on the district. More skilled tradesmen were employed in joinery, furniture and coach factories. Heavier industry was limited, although blacksmith's shops often expanded to small agricultural machinery works. Toowoomba's iron foundry and engineering works employed 50 men in 1889. James Martin and Co., Engineers, of Gawler, twenty miles north of Adelaide, produced agricultural and mining machinery for use all over Australia. By 1883 Martins' employed 300 men and in 1888 undertook contracts for 52 locomotives for the South Australian railways.

Towns also served administrative purposes through land offices, customs houses and local court-houses. The assumption of municipal status increased local government duties; greater revenue and expenditure were involved in the creation of primitive sewage disposal systems (buckets and night carts), water supply and gas works. Civic pride grew correspondingly. In many inland towns, considerable numbers of Chinese settled. A typical Chinese camp had its own stores, joss-house, cookshop, lottery houses, fan-tan rooms and brothels, its streets and lanes lined with brick, weatherboard, iron and canvas dwellings. Usually built on cheaper low-lying ground, it was frequently a cause of complaint because of poor hygiene. The Chinese themselves were peaceable and law abiding, but the women of the camps, some married, but more of them prostitutes and almost entirely European, were frequently in court on charges of sly-grog selling, prostitution, gambling and robbery. At shearing time the camps were thronged with shearers and other nomadic workers, adding to the disquieting element.

In larger towns, hospitals as well as churches and schools sought to counteract such influences. Alcoholism, venereal diseases and scurvy, were, to judge from hospital admissions over the period, less common by 1890 in farming areas than they had been in the 1850s and 1860s when these were pastoral areas, and drink, sickness and violence had contributed to the misery of the lower orders. Some of the credit for this change must go to the evangelical sects as well as to the Baptists and Congregationalists, who had penetrated as least the larger towns, while thousands of children were encouraged to abstinence in Methodist Sunday schools by joining the Band of Hope.

The greater diversity of social activity which larger populations made possible is seen clearly in sport, entertainment and town organizations. To cricket and football were added rowing, swimming, roller

skating and cycling clubs. Polo was more of a status symbol, and carefully stratified racing clubs and gun clubs allowed social distinctions
to be maintained, as did membership of select Quadrille Assemblies
and attendance at Nomination and Subscription Balls (Admission by
Ticket Only). Lodges, including the Loyal Orange, Oddfellows and
Freemasons continued to attract membership in an age of few social
services; agricultural and horticultural, pigeon and poultry societies
held festivals and shows; and semi-political groups like Railway
Leagues met irregularly. Mechanics' Institutes, Schools of Arts, and
Literary and Debating societies arranged dramatic and musical performances, provided reading rooms and debated The Single Tax v.
Socialism (Henry George v. Karl Marx), or heard lectures on Irish
eviction and Home Rule. Little excuse was needed for a procession;
St Patrick's Day or the annual hospital fête saw the fire brigade, brass
band, tradesmen's carts, lodges, Sons and Daughters of Temperance,
Volunteer Corps and the inevitable Darktown Minstrels all willing
to join in.

Travelling circuses and Wirth's Wild West Show, variety companies – in which the proprietress herself would perform Lola Montez's
spider dance – balloon artists and Edison phonograph demonstrators
provided seasonal entertainment, often coinciding with the annual
show. Gilbert and Sullivan performances, philharmonic concerts and
visiting baritones from the Paris Opera singing excerpts from Gounod
and Meyerbeer catered for more classical tastes, while Melbourne and
Sydney actors played Ibsen's 'Doll's House' from one end of the
country to the other. Edith O'Gorman, 'The Escaped Nun', aroused
great interest with her lectures, but so violent were the antagonisms
aroused between Orangemen and Roman Catholics in the Richmond
River Valley, that at Lismore over 50 rioters were arrested by special
constables.

Local newspapers lent unity to diversity by fostering local pride
and a sense of identity.[21] They expounded the civilizing mission of the
town and its organizations and the notion of a self-sufficient regional
capital. The claims of three South Australian towns – Port Augusta,
'The Future Metropolis of Australia'; Moonta, 'If you haven't been
to Moonta you haven't travelled'; and Gawler, 'The Athens of the
South' – help to explain the extraordinary number of applications
from impossibly unlikely towns to be considered as sites for the federal
capital in the 1890s. By 1890 the centralizing influence of the capital
cities and their railway fans had not dimmed the hopes of country-
town dwellers and the industrious yeomanry. The limits imposed by
a horsedrawn technology still postponed rural depopulation.

Australian rural society, like pastoral and agricultural communities
elsewhere, was generally conservative. Country towns and their organizations for the most part reflected the values of the surrounding

21 See R. B. Walker, 'Aspects of the Country Press in New South Wales from
1850–1900', in *R.A.H.S.J.*, 50, 3, August 1964.

countryside. Until the 1860s the squatter or large landowner stood at the head of the rural social pyramid and represented country districts in parliament. But first the gold rushes and then the selector movement topped the squattocracy. By the 1870s, selectors' representatives, considered radical at the time, were successfully contesting rural seats in the colonial legislative assemblies and demonstrating that selection acts were effective in filling the gaps in rural society implicit in such antiquated legislation as the Masters and Servants Act. By the late 1880s all taint of radicalism had left the Farmers' Unions, whose members, having obtained land and many of the concessions they sought, turned conservative. But declining economic opportunity for the rest of rural society and the spread of ideas like Henry George's on nationalization of land and Karl Marx's on inequalities in the distribution of the products of labour, led to a rejection of Samuel Smiles' gospel of *Self Help,* and to the rise of more radical organizations in some country towns, providing direct opposition to traditional values.

In Creswick (Vic.) W. G. Spence became secretary of the almost defunct Amalgamated Miners' Association in 1882.[22] By 1886 the A.M.A. had 23,500 members in Australia and New Zealand. Later, in 1886, Spence was president of a second leading radical union, the Amalgamated Shearers' Union, formed by amalgamating newly-formed shearers' unions in Ballarat, Bourke and Wagga. The strongest branch was in Wagga Wagga where Arthur Rae, A.S.U. secretary and organizer, was elected to the New South Wales Legislative Assembly in 1891 on a Labor platform.

On the pastoral stations themselves, relationships between permanent station hands and squatters, or managers installed by banks or finance companies, had changed little, if only because the Masters and Servants Act was still in force and at times invoked. But as the 1880s drew to a close the need to economize made stations much less liberal with their handouts to the increasing numbers of wandering men, and antagonism directed at capital led to minor confrontations and damage to property. But until 1890 these activities were much milder than the extreme form of rural anti-capitalism practised earlier by the bushrangers, culminating with the Kelly gang's activities of 1878–80. This stemmed from the older convict – Irish – landless v. landowner tradition, and widespread sympathy with such social grievances and attitudes to authority was reflected in country newspaper columns headed 'Bushranging for the Week'. By 1890 social protest had become more coherent and articulate, and more politically oriented. Until the late 1870s the end of shearing had often been marked by general celebrations on the station, original songs and a concert, plenty of food and drink supplied, and cheers for the manager, the proprietor and the ladies present. By the late 1880s such

[22] See W. G. Spence, *Australia's Awakening: Thirty Years in the Life of an Australian Agitator,* Sydney, 1909.

performances were rare and likely to occur only where stations used non-union ('scab') labour. The first major break in relations between pastoralists and pastoral workers occurred in the shearing strike of 1890.[23] But such militancy was a far cry from the earlier unionism which had heartily endorsed Graham Berry's 'harmony of interests' advice to the 1884 Intercolonial Trade Union Congress, – 'Be cautious, be moderate, be determined'.

In the wheat-sheep belt of the fertile crescent, the gap between capital and labour, Master and Servant, had been largely filled in, and a simple picture in black and white is inadequate. Selectors who belonged to the Farmers' Union went shearing each year, and shearers who belonged to the Shearers' Union owned farms on which their wives and families lived. There had also been a profound change in the technology of shearing. The shearing machine, invented by F. Y. Wolseley of Cobran station in the Riverina, was at first ridiculed as a new-fangled implement by crack shearers remembering their two-year apprenticeship with blade shears, but at the end of one season even novices were shearing 80 or 90 sheep a day, and experienced men reached a tally of 140. Within a few days, amateurs could learn to use the new machines, and they could become effective strike breakers.

While some Australians sought their fortunes with varying success in mining or on the land, an ever increasing proportion lived and looked for economic opportunity and security in urban areas, especially in the rapidly growing capital cities. Discussing urbanization in nineteenth century Australia, N. G. Butlin pointed out that almost two-thirds of the Australian population of 1891 lived in cities and towns, a fraction matched by the United States only by 1920 and Canada not until 1950.[24] As early as the end of the nineteenth century an American had noted, 'The most remarkable concentration or rather centralization of population occurs in the newest product of civilization, Australia, where nearly one-third of the entire population is settled in and about capital cities'.[25] In the United States in 1790 (it was noted) of a population of four million, the proportion living in towns of one thousand or more was only 3.14 per cent. In Australia in 1891, of an equal population of four million, the proportion was 32.2 per cent.

In Australia's urban hierarchy there were comparatively few urban centres between the large metropolitan capital and the small bush township. In Europe the long-term pattern of urban hierarchy was fairly standard. A predominantly rural population was gradually

23 See R. Gollan, *Radical and Working Class Politics: A Study of Eastern Australia, 1850–1910*, Melbourne, 1960.

24 N. G. Butlin, *Investment in Australian Economic Development, 1861–1900*, Cambridge, 1964, p. 6.

25 Adna F. Weber, *The Growth of Cities in the Nineteenth Century*, New York, 1899, quoted in S. Glynn, *Urbanisation in Australian History 1788–1900*, Melbourne, 1970.

drawn into urban centres as a result of rapid population growth, increasing industrialization and changes in agriculture. In Australia the process was reversed; urbanization developed in advance of manufacturing industry and rural settlement, and indeed tended to promote them. From the earliest settlement a relatively large proportion had always lived in urban areas on the coast, and the continent was largely settled from these urban areas. Before the gold rushes the cities were little more than large frontier towns of 20 – 50,000. Thereafter their share of the total population grew rapidly. Between 1871 and 1891 the urban proportion of the population in Queensland rose from 39 per cent to 53 per cent, in Victoria from 55 per cent to 65 per cent, and in New South Wales from 50 per cent to 66 per cent. The timing and composition of this change varied in the different colonies.[26] In the 1880s, Melbourne gained four times as many people as the rest of Victoria. Sydney did not overwhelm New South Wales in quite the same way.

There were many reasons for the unusually high rate and degree of urbanization in Australia and its centralized metropolitan nature. Australia's capital cities did not develop naturally but were deliberately sited to fulfil some specific administrative or economic function, whether gaol services or as a base for experiments in systematic colonization, laying already the preconditions for a centralized government and economy. The transport and communication systems strengthened this beginning. Overseas communications were by sea. Cities were therefore ports, connected to world shipping lanes which carried official orders, food and staple exports. The new technological age of the second half of the nineteenth century accelerated this trend, externally with steamships linking world trade routes, internally with railway fans radiating from the existing cities. Telegraphs were a further centralizing influence.

Australia's rural labour requirements, at least for its permanent workforce, were relatively small, and much of the casual migratory labour operated from a country town base. There was rarely a lack of rural labour and the workforce did increase in this period, but city-based industry and commerce had larger labour requirements. Further, the source of much of Australia's immigration was urban. Migrants often simply moved from urban centres in the old world to urban centres in the new; having landed in urban areas they were inclined to stay there. Apart from migration, population growth was greatest where approximate sexual parity existed, and in cities and large country towns the number of males and females was nearly equal. Finally, the inflow of capital from overseas was also channelled through the cities, leading to the growth of finance institutions and further centralization. The demand for enlarged services and public utilities stimulated more expansion and a further inflow of funds.

26 N. G. Butlin, *Investment in Australian Economic Development: 1861–1900*, Cambridge, 1964, pp. 185–93.

It has been shown that the urbanization process in Australia had marked effects on the structure of the economy. The major structural change was the movement of residential and city building to the forefront in expenditure patterns, ahead of the other main areas of spending – pastoral equipment, railways and local authority works – all influenced by long-term considerations rather than short-term profitability, and requiring, in terms of employment opportunities, a high proportion of unskilled labour. Except for the period 1874–81 when the building of pastoral equipment led, residential building accounted for most investment, about one-third of all resources which went into capital formation. The long-term basis of this investment imparted a certain stability to the economy, but eventually its nature led to excess capacity, particularly in the pastoral industry and housing. Pastoral properties were frequently over-capitalized; house building eventually moved well ahead of population demand.

Melbourne's was the most spectacular boom and crash. Until the mid-1880s Melbourne's and Sydney's building rates and land prices ran parallel, stimulated by increasing immigration and marriage rates. Then, in three years from 1886 to 1888, immigration increased Victoria's population by 10 per cent; there was a net gain of 40,000 immigrants in 1888 alone, most of whom stayed in Melbourne. Between 1881 and 1891 Melbourne's population grew from just over a quarter of a million to nearly half a million; most of this was natural growth boosted by migration. Melbourne was a wonder for its times, 'a spacious city with stately public buildings and broad streets crammed with traffic, a city which was unquestionably a metropolis'.[27] About the thirtieth city in the world in numbers (though higher in wealth) and seventh city in the Empire, it was larger than most European capitals. Cable trams glided efficiently through the dense horse-drawn and pedestrian traffic; 300 trains a day left for the southern and eastern suburbs. No British city outside London could boast as many or as fine public buildings; towers, domes, turrets and spires abounded; Government House, cathedrals, the G.P.O., banks, hotels and coffee palaces contributed style or a sense of opulence; 'Corinthian, Ionic, Doric, early English, late English, Queen Anne, Elizabethan, Australian' mingled indiscriminately – 'a Renaissance gone wrong' – with gilded interiors to match; and in the suburbs, town halls and gentleman's mansions perpetuated the trend. At the end of the decade almost half of Melbourne's houses were less than ten years old, some jerry-built by urban speculators, but many, like the city buildings themselves, solid and still standing ninety years later. Two-roomed and three-roomed single fronted bungalows were still built, but more common were the suburban double-fronted, (sometimes with semi-octagonal bulge) or triple-fronted, on their one-sixth of an acre with front and back gardens. Middle and working class suburbs alike showed evidence of prosperity; cast-iron balconies and

27 G. Serle, *The Rush To Be Rich*, Melbourne, 1971, p. 272.

verandah lacework proliferated, while the newly-rich bought 10-acre to 30-acre suburban estates and built their two-storied mansions, complete with tower, flagpole, ballroom, picture gallery, shrubbery, rose garden and lawn tennis court to demonstrate their affluence, social standing and respectability.

Yet for all their pride of achievement in bricks and mortar, public health was increasingly menaced. Melbourne's Yarra was a common sewer, inky black with foul gases emanating from it, and the smells of the city were intolerable. 'Liquid refuse from kitchens, baths and laundries, factories, stables and public urinals drained into open street channels and thence into almost every watercourse or lagoon in the metropolitan area.' At night hundreds of stinking nightcarts made their noisy way to dispose of the city's sewage, some 'cutting their journeys short by depositing their loads in the streets'. Not surprising then, that the Sydney *Bulletin* repeated with glee the taunts at 'Marvellous Smelbourne'. Not until 1889, eleven years after Adelaide and nine years after Sydney, was effective public health legislation introduced for Melbourne, by which time Melbourne's death rate from typhoid was worse than London's – 558 in the city in 1889 – and diphtheria was almost as bad. This astonishing time lag in sewering 'Marvellous Melbourne' continued until well into the twentieth century.

The cost of building a city the size of Melbourne so quickly was enormous and much of the capital, particularly for the last stages of the boom, came from unwise overseas borrowing. Until the late 1880s the rate of building and rise in land prices in Melbourne was fairly well justified, but within a few years the import of capital rose to fantastic levels as Melbourne became a favourite field for British investors. Over £50,000,000 – more than for all the rest of Australia – was borrowed by Victorian governments, municipalities, banks, pastoral and mining companies, building societies and land finance companies, at unusually high rates of interest. In the second half of the decade most of this went into rebuilding the city and extending its suburbs, into land speculation, railways, water supplies and local government public works; very little went into productive industries. Local savings were also channelled, with conventional wisdom, into land purchases, which were seen as the ultimate security.[28]

Co-operative building societies, which financed most housebuilding, lent £2 million annually from 1885–7 and £4 million in 1888. Although these were generally non-speculative they also became deposit banks. Much more speculative and hazardous were the land investment companies and mortgage banks, channels for most of the imported capital for urban land speculation. They were misleading in the use of the word 'bank' in their titles, prodigal in their lending, and, like the English 'land banks' of the eighteenth century, ultimately failed

[28] G. Serle, *The Rush To Be Rich*, Melbourne, 1971, pp. 272–83. See also M. Cannon, *The Land Boomers*, Melbourne, 1966.

because of the non-negotiability of their chief asset, land, especially in a falling market. Meanwhile, the men who 'bought by the acre and sold by the foot' waxed fat in the suburban springtime with their misleading maps and advertisements, small deposits and generous terms, free rail passes, free lunches, free whiskey, free champagne, dummy bidders and blaring brass bands. The value of outer suburban lands rose five, ten and in some cases twenty times in five years, while city values rose threefold, partly in response to the introduction of the Otis hydraulic lift so that buildings rose six, nine and twelve storeys high.

Speculation in land banks and land finance companies reached a peak in 1888. In one month the public agreed to pay £2.7 million to new companies and more in future calls. One promoter had little difficulty in making £100,000 in an afternoon. When share prices steadied, speculation in land reached new heights: city land climbed to over £2000 per foot and £300,000 was unsuccessfully offered for the site of the half-built St Paul's Cathedral. In the suburbs one block of less than an acre brought over £30,000. When £50,000 was paid for 500 acres of poor soil twenty-six miles from Melbourne, *The Times* of London remarked that such a sum in England would buy an estate of 1550 acres 'with a really grand old mansion built by an eminent historical personage, a deer park, walled gardens, lawns, terraces, cedars and six park lodges, one mile and a half from a railway station and within thirty miles of London'.

In Michael Cannon's words, 'the big speculators were selling to the medium speculators, the medium speculators were selling to the small speculators, and madness was in the air'.[29] In the first nine months of 1888 land sales totalled more than £13 million. Yet by late 1889 the boom had collapsed, millions had been lost, and bankruptcies were commonplace. Many who survived did so only through secret compositions with creditors and the payment of token amounts. Benjamin Fink listed £1.5 million in debts, and paid ½d. in the £1 before departing to London for ever. The question of responsibility for this state of madness has produced some disagreement amongst historians. Geoffrey Serle has pointed out that despite Victoria's unusual government activity in public works, and its care of farmers and manufacturers by protective tariffs, there was still a strong residue of laissez-faire assumptions and a marked resistance to the idea of government being responsible for the general health of the economy.[30] He is willing to 'predicate insanity as characterizing politicians, businessmen and the whole populace'; concedes that 'nearly all the general managers and directors of the other banks participated in the rush to be rich'; lists the cautious and far-sighted who foresaw the crash; agrees that government 'took no action to check the shady activities of the boomers'

29 M. Cannon, *The Land Boomers*, Melbourne, 1966, p. 34.

30 G. Serle, *The Rush To Be Rich*, Melbourne, 1971, pp. 258–71.

and was not even policing the Companies Act of 1864 until 1888. But he questions Cannon's generalization about bribery and the degree of corruption and criminality amongst politicians. He points out that even Benjamin Fink, James Munro and Thomas Bent were popular and acceptable to the society of the day. Tommy Bent, for example, the member for Brighton and eventually premier of Victoria, was a man of tremendous force, a master of the craft of binding men and manipulating them, a master of intrigue and log-rolling. He was coarse, vulgar, unscrupulous, cunning, a liar and a larrikin; he was also a cheery good fellow with some comic gifts, generous, loyal, and widely popular among his fellow-politicians. He believed that what was good for Tommy Bent was good for Brighton and Victoria, and in 1888 formed the Thomas Bent Land Company, attracting many investors. A typical story is Bent's reported rebuff to a journalist, 'I know what you're going to say against me ... You are going to say that I have a wife and family in every suburb and that I neglect them ... I *don't* neglect them.'

In Cannon's view the activities of such men meant that 'Parliament became a sort of land speculators' club' where 'a rich state was plundered by the very men who had been elected to advance its interests'.[31] Serle postulates greater purity and the inevitability and acceptance of some use of inside knowledge by politicians. Yet in Queensland at the same time McIlwraith, the premier, was toppled by Griffith's allegations that he had used his position and foreknowledge to arrange the steel rails purchase for Queensland railways and their transport by his brother's shipping firm. Just how far the public accepted such behaviour is therefore difficult to assess. Certainly the churches provided little opposition and indeed at times so reassured those who believed that material success and prosperity were a sign of God's favour that the *Bulletin* predicted the future Australian religion would be 'Presbyterianism tempered by the rate of exchange'.

Colonial experience encouraged both overt materialism and super optimism. Most men had migrated to the land of opportunity in order to achieve that economic success which the old world had denied them. 'The local experience of mass participation in the gold lottery, the widespread abandonment of respect for law and morality in the struggle for land, even the common practice of presenting fake invoices to customs officers which a protective system cultivated, encouraged a permissive commercial ethic.'[32] With the temptations of the 1880s business morals in Victoria deteriorated even further. How far this applies to the other colonies is uncertain, but it is significant that in Queensland, a few years after the steel rails investigation, Griffith and McIlwraith formed a coalition government, suggesting that the subject was more a matter for making political capital than for any real

31 M. Cannon, *The Land Boomers*, Melbourne, 1966, pp. 29-30.

32 G. Serle, *The Rush To Be Rich*, Melbourne, 1971, p. 271.

righteous indignation. Most Australians were whiggishly bemused with the notion of the inevitability of progress, the passion to get rich quick, and 'by the last long delayed chance to make the golden pile for which they had migrated'.

While large numbers of Australians engaged in mining and land speculation in the hope of gaining quick fortunes, an increasing section of the workforce was involved in manufacturing. The major manufacturing industries were textiles and clothing, metals and machinery, building materials and food, drink and tobacco; these were by no means confined to the cities but were distributed over rural areas as well. Obstacles to the growth of manufacture, like smallness of scale, high costs, especially of Australian labour, and import competition, were more than outweighed by favourable conditions: a prosperous and increasingly concentrated consumer market, inflow of labour and capital, the existence of exploitable female and child labour, protective tariffs and government contracts, and the natural protection of distance from sources of competing bulky or perishable goods. By 1891 manufacturing employed 17 per cent of the total Australian workforce and a higher proportion of the urban population. In a further reversal of European trends, urban growth preceded manufacturing and seems rather to have stimulated it. New South Wales and Victoria easily dominated manufacturing but the question of whether Victorian protection or New South Wales free trade was more advantageous, apart from fostering infant industries, is not easily decided. By 1890, of a total manufacturing output of £60 million, New South Wales and Victoria each accounted for £22 million.

In Victoria in 1882 there were only fifteen factories employing more than two hundred workers and of these, two clothing factories, one foundry, and Swallow and Ariell's biscuit factory – said to be the fifth largest in the world – employed more than three hundred.[33] By 1888 the number employing over two hundred had doubled. New factories were established as craftsmen, brewers, tailors, clothing workers and boot and shoe makers sought independence in enterprises of their own. In 1880 the nineteen-year old Macpherson Robertson began making sweets in the bath at home with 'a sixpenny nail can, a threepenny pannikin and a bag of sugar', tramping the suburbs to sell his products to shops. By 1887 he employed thirty workers and had laid the foundations for the long-lived MacRobertson confectionery empire.

The metals and machinery industries also expanded from local manufacture of agricultural machinery and the replacement of imports, to larger enterprises like the Danks Foundry which monopolized watertap and plumbing manufacturing in Melbourne, produced steam and safety valves and pumping machinery, and in 1886 established an English branch factory. Another Wesleyan, Peter Johns,

[33] For the Victorian manufacturing industry see G. Serle, *The Rush To Be Rich*, Melbourne, 1971, pp. 69–77.

moved into lift manufacturing and installation to catch the city building boom. Ballarat's Phoenix Foundry built locomotives for the Victorian Railways, the Bendigo Rolling Stock Works built carriages and trucks, while local coach-builders catered for areas not serviced by railways. Hugh Lennon, blacksmith turned agricultural machinery manufacturer, produced six hundred ploughs a year and received gratuitous publicity when the Kelly gang used his mouldboard steel for their armour.

For women, social mobility and the chances of employment were much more limited; domestic service, making clothes and teaching marked the limits of respectable employment. In Melbourne in the early 1880s there were some 20,000 maids and cooks, half of whom were under twenty-one, and 3000 waitresses; 18,000 women and girls worked as dressmakers, milliners, tailoresses and shoemakers, about a quarter of them in factories. There were 5000 female teachers, about a third of them private governesses or music teachers. There were 2000 shop assistants, and smaller numbers of washerwomen, nurses and saleswomen. Clerking and copying in offices was still a male preserve, though in 1887 one of the banks daringly engaged its first lady typist. The formation by anxious ladies in 1885 of the Domestic Servants' Immigration Society emphasised the continual shortage of domestic servants and the preference of Australian-born girls for the 'independence' of factory employment, despite low wages.

It was the low wages, long hours and poor conditions – both for factory women and outworkers – which sparked off the tailoresses' strike of 1883, leading to higher pay and the growth of militant union membership to 300 in two years. Public opinion was stirred further by the findings of a commission on labour conditions which revealed sweating, long hours, dangerous machinery, ill-ventilated and unsanitary factory conditions, and child labour (breeding ground for larrikins and prostitutes). While conditions were rarely as bad as those in England had been, amended Factory Acts paralleled the most advanced British legislation. Yet despite Victoria's avowed protectionist policy, governments often hesitated, as in England, to extend state intervention, maintaining that it interfered with the rights of the individual. Many also protested against government interference with the age of employment, on the grounds that keeping boys at school until they were thirteen trained them in idleness.[34]

Despite these black spots there was agreement amongst observers, confirmed later by Coghlan's statistical evidence, that the standard of living for the working classes in Australia was amongst the highest in the world.[35] The most optimistic wrote of a workingman's paradise,

[34] For an important aspect of industrial conditions in this period see E. C. Fry, 'Outwork in the Eighties: An Examination of Outwork in the Infant Industries of the Eastern Australian Colonies, c. 1880–90', in *University Studies in History and Economics*, 1966.

[35] T. A. Coghlan, *Labour and Industry in Australia*, London, 4 vols., 1918.

of workers concerned not with bread but with cake and the number of plums in it, and of workingmen who, if they did not become capitalists, had only themselves to blame. Business failures and droughts had sometimes brought hardship to particular areas and industries, but conditions generally in the 1880s supported the optimists' view that for most workers all was well.

Australian workingmen had more to spend than workers elsewhere and food was cheaper in relation to income than anywhere except perhaps parts of North America. Meat consumption was easily the highest in the world, two or three times Britain's, four times Germany's, ten times Italy's. Housing standards were equally high. Labourers lived in separate houses and took pride in their gardens, artisans aspired to own their own homes, brick in Sydney and Adelaide, weatherboard in Melbourne. Yet while wages were higher and costs lower, unemployment and accidents were still possible; and friendly societies, lodges and unions were the only insurance in cases of sickness, unemployment, accident or death. There was more security in the civil service or in the banks, at least until the crashes, though this too carried its price; some banks forbade their employees to marry without an income of £200 – £250, usually reached by about age thirty. As yet there was no income tax.

Here too the role of government was questioned. Such poverty as existed could not be compared with that existing in English cities, and public and private charities alleviated much of this without poor laws and poor rates. Governments were senstive to unemployment rates, and their expenditure on public works (even if at lower wage rates) helped maintain near-full employment; free rail passes were issued to allow the seasonally unemployed to seek work in the country. But from time to time, especially in hard winters like those of 1885 and 1886, unemployment did reach crisis point in Sydney, Melbourne and Adelaide. Yet even after admitting the existence of cases of terrible poverty and hardship, government argued that there would always be suffering in large cities, especially on the fringes of poverty, and that dependence on the state should not be encouraged. In Marvellous Melbourne possibly a quarter to a third of the working class remained only marginally above the bread line. Yet the general level of prosperity remained high. Not until conditions worsened and the general decline in economic opportunity became more obvious could militant champions like William Lane stir men to action.

Within the cities, sport, entertainment and organizations paralleled those in country towns, though greater population and greater wealth extended the range and diversity.[36] On Eight Hours Day, St Patrick's Day, or any public holiday, and whenever a jubilee or exhibition called for a celebration, sporting events, processions and dances were

36 See R. E. N. Twopeny, *Town Life in Australia*, London, 1883, reprinted Melbourne, 1973.

organized. In music, art, the theatre, and literature, the cities catered for popular tastes and pretensions to culture. The achievement of the eight-hours principle had made the Saturday a half-holiday for many and gave great stimulus to organized sport. Cricket and football established themselves as national games, while horse-racing attracted vast crowds in which all classes mingled, the range extending from the wealthy, and those self-respecting artisans and unionists indistinguishable from them in dress, to that manifestation of Australia's criminal sub-culture, the larrikin. But within the cities, as in rural areas, there was, in addition to such social activity, much serious questioning of the future of the Australian colonies.

Australian historians have been criticized for their preoccupation with the search for Australian national characteristics in the second half of the nineteenth century, but this reflects the preoccupation of the more literate colonists with aspects of what has been broadly termed Australian nationalism. It is impossible to ignore the increasing self-awareness of Australian art, literature and political debate in this period. For the colonists themselves, the questions could be stated in fairly simple terms: 'What kind of country is this, and is it to become? What kind of people? What kind of society?' Just as the search for economic security took colonists to different parts of the continent and created different interest groups, so in Australian society as a whole the search for identity led to a diversity of opinions and a fragmentation which was of greater reality than the surface unity which culminated in the moves towards political federation. Australian nationalism in the period 1870–90 was a peculiarly hybrid growth and was variously expressed in attitudes to defence, allegiances and loyalties, race, religion, education and politics.

Historians have noted the rise of 'nationalist' schools of literature and art. The works of Lawson, Paterson and Furphy, and the *Bulletin*, whatever their shortcomings, are vigorous in language and content, unmistakably and unashamedly Australian. Similarly in art, impressionists of the Heidelberg school like Roberts, Streeton and McCubbin struggled with problems of light, heat, haze and distance in the new environment, to capture the unique Australian landscape on canvas. Significantly, both art and literature were preoccupied with rural and especially outback Australia, provoking the question as to where the greatest strength of Australian nationalism lay. The European nature of the Australian population, and its Britishness in particular, was reinforced by the flood of migrants who arrived in the 1880s, most to remain in the cities. Against this influence, the Australian-born percentage of the population continued to rise and accelerated the fading of Old World memories. From the 1870s onwards, the successful spread of selectors out onto the fertile crescent raised a whole new generation of country 'kids'. Many of these were later to move to the cities, but their youthful impressions were an important ingredient in Australian nationalism. 'John O'Brien's' poems specifically reject the libel that 'the flowers have no scent, and the birds have no song', or that

> The landscape is sombre and dreary and grey
> No colour its mantle adorning,

and appeal to a common experience and genuine appreciation of the Australian bush.[37]

For most Australians colonial boundaries were of little significance, except for the pinprick annoyance of the border customs house. Rural workers, miners, shearers, pastoralists, drovers and selectors all moved freely in the inland, which formed a more effective melting pot for ideas, and matrix for the Australian legend, than the fiercely jealous capital cities, so like their counterparts elsewhere that locals as well as visitors likened them to British, European and American cities. This lack of specifically Australian identity in the cities helps us in part to explain why an increasingly urban nation accepted the bush as the basis for its legends and self-image, as if this alone were uniquely Australian.[38] That the majority of Australians had long lived in cities merely intensified the appeal of 'The Great Australian Outback', and has its parallels in Englishmen's views – coloured by Goldsmith and Cobbett – of that golden age of rural bliss which preceded enclosures and industrial urbanization. But beyond sentimentalism in Australia lay a pragmatic concern for economic realities. It is significant in terms of nationalism that two of the earliest major Australia-wide unions, miners and pastoral workers, were rural in origin. The third, the Seamen's Union, is classified as an urban union because Australian metropolitan capitals were also the chief ports.

Some aspects of nationalism, and attempts to formulate answers to the question, 'what kind of country is this to be?', were discussed with greater intensity in the country, but the centre of gravity of the population lay in the capital cities, and it was here, through public debate and the daily newspapers, that most colonists became familiar with the major issues. Colonial particularism was also focused most strongly in the cities. When Melbourne politicians spoke of 'the nation' they were usually referring to Victoria. Not surprisingly, New South Wales, proclaiming its own position as the Mother colony, sought to change its name to 'Australia'. Apart from such sibling rivalry, some issues were relevant to all colonies, though in differing degrees. That the answers to common questions were formulated differently in different colonies, merely emphasises that diversity and fragmentation which reached its extreme manifestation in the varieties of legislation passed by separate colonial governments, each isolated in its own separate colonial city. Here policies were decided and laws passed, with a traditional belief in British constitutional processes,

37 'The Libel', in John O'Brien (pseud. Father Hartigan), *Around the Boree Log and Other Verses*, Sydney, 1921, pp. 36–7.

38 See R. Ward, *The Australian Legend*, Melbourne, 1958.

that by such conscious manipulations, Australian society could be moulded into the desired image. But 'farmers are not made by Act of Parliament', nor are men 'made moral by Act of Parliament', as some contemporaries at least were aware. The Kelly gang epitomized those whose vision of justice and equality, and the best methods of achieving their goals, differed from that of the respectable law-makers.

Beyond internal divergences and confrontations, though often inseparable from them, were a number of interrelated external issues. The most important of these were imperial relations, and especially defence. Colonists from time to time were alarmed by real or imagined threats. The most regular of these were Russian scares. In South Australia in 1882, residents of the seaside town of Glenelg, only six miles from Adelaide, awoke to find a Russian fleet anchored on their doorsteps. After initial panic it was decided to fraternize, and the Russians were entertained ashore at a Grand Ball attended by the governor, with music provided by Russian sailors (including one named Rimsky-Korsakov). The incident promoted defence measures: a railway and 'Military Road' were begun and two large guns were brought from England. The guns were hauled to the sandhills, to rust until the war of 1914–18.

In 1879 a British Royal Commission had emphasised the weakness of empire defences, causing considerable colonial concern. By 1883 Victoria had a ministry of defence and was voting over £500,000 for a five-year defence plan, including permanent artillery, engineers, paid militia, land batteries, mines, torpedoes for two shoal-boats and a fast gunboat outside the Heads. In 1885 a clash on the Afghanistan frontier – 'Australia's furthest line of defence' – created further alarm, while a report from Singapore brought out the fleet and the naval reserve.

The Australian Naval Force Bill of 1887, following the London Colonial Conference, concluded the quest for autonomy and the question of what was being protected, British investments or Australia. Local flotillas were replaced by an Australasian squadron to be used, under the British Pacific Fleet commander, entirely for local defence. The next year saw the publication of the anonymous *Battle of Mordialloc* describing an imaginary war between England and Russia. As summarized by Geoffrey Serle –

The Russians cut the cables, and at the close of the Melbourne Cup meeting news was heard of a huge fleet bearing down and of a secret treaty between Russia and China to partition Australia. The invaders landed at Western Port and advanced on Melbourne, and the Victorian army was slaughtered after magnificent resistance. After larrikins had plundered the city, it was burnt by the Chinese. Britain sent an expedition to reconquer the country.[39]

Though Australians were very concerned with protection of their shores, problems of coaling rendered attack by European powers

[39] G. Serle, *The Rush To Be Rich*, Melbourne, 1971, pp. 330–31.

unlikely. Threats from imaginary Chinese or more real Japanese fleets were equally improbable.

The death of General Gordon in Khartoum in 1885 roused emotion in the colonies. The New South Wales offer of a contingent for the Sudan surprised the imperial government, but subsequent offers by Victoria and Canada were refused. James Service, the Victorian premier, believed the New South Wales coup had 'precipitated Australia, in one short week, from a geographical expression to a nation'.[40] Not only was inter-colonial rivalry stirred, however, but within the Victorian legislature division was fairly even between those who blindly supported Mother England and those who mistrusted the new imperialism, disliked colonial military support for Britain, or feared foreign reprisals. James Munro saw support as rampant 'Jingoism', militarism run mad, and 'a disgrace to the country to become involved in this mean, miserable, contemptible fight in the Sudan'. Gyles Turner, supporting him, said that 'to claim patriotic virtue for the men who are ready to shoot Arabs, negroes, Abyssinians or Egyptians indifferently at 5s. a day is a miserable prostitution of terms', though of course if England were really threatened there was no question about Victoria springing to her aid.[41] The real point of agreement was that Australia should not be defenceless.

In military defences Victoria was well ahead of the other colonies. By 1889 the local defence scheme enabled Victoria to 'defy insult or attack'. A modern Zalinski dynamite gun had been ordered, and on the death of the German Emperor the Victorians, anxious to try out their new big guns, eagerly asked whether a salute should be fired. Major Tom Price, later notorious for his part against the strikers of the 1890s, commanded the Victorian Mounted Rifles; and notable citizens maintained their own troops of horse-artillery. Nearly 5000 twelve-to-fourteen year old Victorian school children trained in the school cadet corps and a further 10,000 state school children were instructed in compulsory military drill. Similar schemes operated in other colonies. In New South Wales, where cadets drilled with wooden rifles and fought mock battles, local troops like the Wagga Wagga Rifles and the Eurongilly Cavalry Detachment carried out military manoeuvres and attended the great Easter encampment of volunteer forces.[42] Yet even here there was ambivalence, and unionists especially opposed the idea of a standing army, an opposition which events of the 1890s later seemed to justify.

Two further crises, involving New Guinea and the New Hebrides, illustrate the problems of imperial relations. In 1883, the Queensland premier, Sir Thomas McIlwraith, announced that Queensland had annexed New Guinea. Victoria hastened to support the annexation,

40 G. Serle, *The Rush To Be Rich*, Melbourne, 1971, p. 199.

41 G. Serle, *The Rush To Be Rich*, Melbourne, 1971, pp. 199–200.

42 G. L. Buxton, *The Riverina: 1861–1891*, Melbourne, 1967, p. 241.

though its trade and interest in the Pacific had been far less than that of New South Wales. The major agitation had been in response to the expansion of German trading interests from Samoa to New Britain and New Ireland and pressure on Bismarck to colonize New Guinea. Each of the eastern colonies had at times proclaimed Australia's manifest destiny in the Pacific. The Queensland claims were bound up with the problems of Kanaka labour, but neither the earlier demands nor the annexation of New Guinea was primarily intended to allow or increase exploitation of the islanders; rather, the reverse was the case. Humanitarian concern and the need to control recruiting had inspired Queensland legislative attempts since the first plantation society had been set up in the 1860s and led to the prospect of a black state north of Capricorn, with many of the features of the slave areas of North America.

When Queensland cotton growing collapsed at the end of the American Civil War planters turned to sugar. The islanders had survived well in Queensland and were considered cheap, docile and relatively efficient, so that more and more were imported as sugar plantings increased. By 1868 hundreds were arriving each month, but by 1870, despite the 1868 Polynesian Labourers' Act, rumours of abuses and maltreatment were alarming many colonists and had roused strong opposition from missionaries, the navy, and the British government. Abolition was not a real possibility while political power rested with merchants, squatters and planters, but even control of the traffic was impossible so long as Queensland jurisdiction was limited to her own waters. Some atrocious crimes on black-birding vessels went unpunished for this reason, and even where neither force nor fraud was used, illiterate islanders signed contracts in almost complete ignorance of their meaning. A series of acts from 1872 closed many loopholes, but until the islands were annexed island societies continued to be broken up and depopulated, and 'guns, liquor and vice' were spread widely.

In the 'Black Labour' elections of 1883, the abolition movement, centred on the south-eastern Liberal towns and temperate farming districts stretching from Brisbane to the Darling Downs, defeated McIlwraith's Conservative northern interests – grazing, sugar and related trade and finance. From abolitionist pressure in opposition Sir Samuel Griffith's party in power now moved to legislation. In 1884 recruiting regulations were tightened and Kanakas limited to field work. The opportunity for total suppression came in 1885 when the crew of the *Hopeful* were convicted of kidnapping and murder in the Supreme Court. A royal commission reported 'one long record of deceit, cruel treachery, deliberate kidnapping and cold blooded murder', and the act which followed prohibited indenturing of Kanakas from 1890. The collapse of the sugar industry which followed in 1891–2 led to reintroduction for a further decade under a Griffith-McIlwraith coalition, despite Griffith's attempt to utilize imported Piedmontese as cheap white labour – an attempt frustrated by union agitators urging the Piedmontese to claim equal pay, which led directly to the reintroduction of Kanakas.[43] Most Australians, whether unionists or not, opposed the Kanaka trade, favouring abolition rather than control, generally on the grounds of national unity and fears of social and economic inequality in the new land of opportunity. Certainly it was widely believed that the home government disallowed the annexation of New Guinea because of its coloured labour policy.

While the colonies waited for Britain's decision on New Guinea in 1883, the Victorian government adopted the long-advocated programme of the Presbyterian mission to the New Hebrides – British annexation of all south sea islands not under foreign control. The main concern was French annexation of the New Hebrides for a penal settlement, a use to which they had already put New Caledonia, from which several hundred convicts had escaped to Australia. The Italian government, meanwhile, was warned by Britain not to implement its plans to use New Guinea for a penal settlement. Talk of the Pacific becoming a cesspool where European nations dumped their refuse gained ground when France introduced legislation to increase transportation with 20,000 of her worst criminals, officially described as 'dangerous, steeped in vice, debauchery and crime', and including some communists. Following public outcry in Victoria, the imperial government gained agreement from the French that neither would annex the New Hebrides, but soon afterwards New South Wales dissociated itself from the movement.

In 1884 the New Guinea stalemate was resolved. Earlier, with Bismarck forcing their hand, the British government had reluctantly proclaimed a mandate over all eastern New Guinea, though Australian attempts to lay down a Monroe doctrine for the Pacific were not acceptable. Now Germany occupied north-eastern New Guinea. Queensland's action was thus partly ratified, but colonial interests were clearly subservient to European claims, and Germany hoisted her flag not only on New Guinea but on New Ireland and New Britain as well. Worse was to follow. In 1886 news reached the Federal Council, meeting for the first time in Hobart, that Germany and France had reached agreement over the New Hebrides, France offering to abandon transportation if allowed to annex. With the Presbyterians in agonies in Melbourne and the Australian Natives Association organizing meetings all over Victoria, the clamour was considerable, but again New South Wales remained silent, except for jibes like the *Bulletin*'s ridicule of 'holy howlers' and the 'cocoa-nut-oil party'. However, when New Zealand joined with the Australian colonies the British government finally announced it would oppose French occupation. But early in June 1886 four hundred French marines from New Caledonia occupied the New Hebrides. Threats to send the Victorian gunboats were less effective than the impassioned speeches of Deakin

---

[43] See G. C. Bolton, *A Thousand Miles Away: A History of North Queensland to 1920*, Brisbane, 1963.

and other colonial leaders to Prime Minister Lord Salisbury at the first conference of British colonies in London in 1887. Finally an agreement for an Anglo-French joint naval commission and French evacuation was reached, but the ultimate solution of the New Hebrides problem was to remain for the young Commonwealth of Australia.[44]

Both crises had demonstrated the marked divergences between colonies, New South Wales appearing more loyal to Britain, if only because more subservient. Victoria, like Queensland, was more inclined to 'go it alone', but all attempts at foreign policy were complicated if not undone by the situation in the 'armed camp of Europe'. The demonstration that the Australian colonies, even when acting together, constituted a non-power in world affairs appealed little to Australian nascent nationalism and strengthened the case of those who favoured separation if not republicanism. Opposed to them were those who invoked the basic Britishness of Australian origins and institutions. In general however, the isolation and ineffectiveness of the colonies in international relations favoured inward rather than outward looking attempts to discover a national identity. 'Australian nationalism', Robin Gollan has written,

was more than a sentiment about a country. It was a complex of ideas and emotions, partly apprehension of present reality, partly aspiration toward an ideal future in Australia. At its heart was an equalitarian social doctrine, a belief in equality of opportunity and a conviction that in Australia men had a right to a good life.[45]

There was therefore relatively little sympathy with the aims of the Imperial Federation League which sought not only a more integrated political control of the empire with a central imperial parliament, but a closer formal union of the colonies with Britain in her imperial mission, especially in defence and economic matters. Despite Victorian enthusiasm the league lasted only a decade from its foundation in 1884.

At the opposite extreme was republicanism. The Sydney Republican Union of 1887 became the Republican League in 1888 with branches in Adelaide and Melbourne; its aim was a federation of the Australian colonies under republican rule. Essentially, republicans rejected royalty, criticized inequality and hereditary privilege, titles and a stratified society. In 1886 A. S. Bailes, an 'almost native' publican and Bendigo member in the Victorian Legislative Assembly, said in debate that while he had nothing against the Queen he hoped the

[44] For a discussion of Pacific problems see G. Greenwood, Ed., *Australia: A Social and Political History*, Sydney, 1955, pp. 125–31: A. T. Yarwood, *Asian Migration to Australia: The Background to Exclusion*, Melbourne, 1964: A. T. Yarwood, *Attitudes to Non-European Immigration*, Melbourne, 1968.

[45] In G. Greenwood, Ed., *Australia: A Social and Political History*, Sydney, 1955, p. 146.

monarchy would be extinguished when she died. 'Moreover the character of the Prince of Wales was not obviously high. He had always been mixed up with scandal wherever he had gone'. Bailes apologized in the house but Bendigo was divided between 'God Save the Queen' and 'The Bonny Flag of Australia'. Public meetings broke up in disorder, letters to the press supported both sides passionately and Bailes himself was threatened with horsewhipping. A year later a horsewhipping was carried out on a newspaper proprietor who had referred to the Queen as an 'obese old woman fond of whiskey'.[46]

When Arthur Rae, radical activist and secretary of the Shearers' Union, was elected to the New South Wales Legislative Assembly in 1891 as a Labour Electoral League candidate, his known republican sympathies were far from universally acceptable. On his refusal to sign the vote of condolence to Queen Victoria on the death of the Duke of Clarence, he was recalled to Wagga Wagga and subjected to a vote of no-confidence from a meeting of the more conservative of his constituents. The meeting concluded with the singing of the National Anthem.[47] However great the appeal of anti-British ideas to Australians at times, republicanism was a minority movement. Most colonists remained persistently loyal to Britain and demonstrated enthusiastically at the Queen's Jubilee and on other similar occasions.

As the numbers of Australian-born increased, older migrants watched anxiously. In Victoria in the 1880s, three-quarters of those over thirty were still migrants. In that climate of Social Darwinism, the question often phrased in response to the larger one, 'What kind of country and society is this to be?' was *'Would the race degenerate?'* Would the British heritage and the superior stock, free of the convict stain, breed a superior generation? Marcus Clarke saw *The Future Australian Race* fundamentally modified by climate and becoming something like the Greeks. Robert Lowe wondered what would happen when the younger generation took control, when 'the larrikin comes on the state'. Others had little doubt regarding the inferiority of the new breed, whose three chief characteristics were 'inordinate love of sport, disinclination to accept the authority of parents and superiors and dislike of mental effort; there was not nearly enough flogging in the schools'.[48]

In 1872 the Friendly Society of Victorian Natives had become the Australian Natives Association. Initially a mutual insurance society, it became a political training ground for the Australian-born, to whom alone membership was possible. By 1886 membership had risen to over 4000 in nearly sixty branches. Gold-rush towns were especially strong, but other groups like a substantial Irish-Catholic element and the Geelong Australian-rules football team were distinctive. Radical

---

46 G. Serle, *The Rush To Be Rich*, Melbourne, 1971, pp. 236, 284.

47 G. L. Buxton, *The Riverina, 1861–1891*, Melbourne, 1967, p. 282.

48 G. Serle, *The Rush To Be Rich*, Melbourne, 1971, pp. 229–30.

in tone, the A.N.A. took a nationalist stance in the campaigns for federation, annexation of New Guinea and the New Hebrides, asked why Australian history and geography were not taught in the schools and supported Bailes in his anti-monarchical stand. The English were foreigners, and the slogan 'Australia for the Australians' was coined by an A.N.A. member. By the late eighties the A.N.A. was established as a political force rejecting intercolonial prejudice and sectarianism and representing particularly 'the new breed'.

While an older generation of youth watchers kept their eyes on such activities of the colonial-born, Australians as a whole were more concerned with the presence in their midst of those of different race, particularly the Chinese, and the alleged threat they represented. Objections to the Chinese were on three grounds: economic, hygienic and moral. Since the 1850s, European miners, whenever their own returns were low, had looked unfavourably on Chinese fossickers who worked usually where other miners had left off. At times anti-Chinese feelings had reached riot proportions. But by the 1870s mining riots were rare. In the Northern Territory, Chinese were encouraged, at least by the government. Nor did Australians themselves protest when gangs of Chinese were employed for ringbarking and suckering, or as cooks, gardeners or merchants. There were strong protests, however, by the late 1880s, when some pastoralists employed Chinese as cheap shearers just when unionists were realizing that economic opportunities were declining.

Similar opposition had been aroused in the maritime dispute of 1878, when a shipping company had attempted to have 'aliens of inferior mental and physical capacity ... supersede ... the indomitable valour of British Seamen', and in Sydney the old Lambing Flat cry, 'Roll up, no Chinese', attracted larrikins who attacked Chinese and set fire to workshops. By the mid-1880s, several hundred Chinese had captured the cheap furniture trade and this led to union demands for the branding of all Chinese-made furniture. Objections on hygienic grounds had some basis. Conditions in rural Chinese camps were frequently unhealthy, as were many city areas. Hospital records show that of twelve cases of leprosy in New South Wales in 1891, nine were Chinese, one Javanese and two were Australian-born youths who had been living with Chinese. Further, traditions of filial piety required that the remains of dead Chinese be returned to their homeland for burial, and, to avoid a repetition of an unpleasant incident in Sydney, 'bones only' were to be sent after careful cleaning. Uproar followed the discovery at Albury in 1890–91 that Chinese were scraping the bones of dead countrymen, some exhumed from the cemetery, in the Bungambrawatha Creek which supplied some residents with drinking water.[49]

Moral protests similarly had some factual basis. The predominance of Chinese males over females had encouraged de facto European

[49] G. L. Buxton, *The Riverina, 1861–1891*, Melbourne, 1967, pp. 228–33.

wives, prostitution and mixed marriages. Although the Chinese themselves were quiet, law-abiding citizens, the presence of these women and other hangers-on frequently led to police action. Gambling, though common amongst Chinese, was probably no more prevalent than amongst young Australians, and the consumption of alcohol infinitely lower, though opium-smoking was perhaps a Chinese equivalent, and more immoral in European eyes. Nor were fears on account of numbers entirely groundless. In the cities, despite their concentration on some areas, Chinese were a tiny fraction of the growing urban population. A thousand or so lived in Melbourne in the eighties, while in Sydney, in the 1891 census, there were 1691 in the city itself and 1704 in the suburbs, representing, of the total male population, a mere 1.26 per cent. On the gold fields and in country towns proportions were rather different. In the wheat-sheep towns of Narrandera (N.S.W.) in the 1880s, of a total population of 1400 over 300 were Chinese, making every second man in town Chinese.[50] Given their distinctive appearance and habits, such a group could hardly be ignored. In the Northern Territory, they outnumbered Europeans by twenty to one. But the fears were not based on actual numbers. As the *Argus* observed,

The Chinese question never fails. At every meeting somebody in the hall has a word to say in regard to it, and visions of countless millions of the barbarians swooping upon the colony in a solid body rise on the mental horizons of every man present.

From time to time reports of anti-Chinese activity and repressive legislation filtered back to China and in 1887 Commissioners of the Imperial Chinese government, on their tour of the Pacific and Indian Oceans to investigate the treatment of overseas Chinese, were met by Melbourne Chinese leaders with a petition objecting to the polltax, the taxation of Chinese moving from one colony to another, and unprovoked and cowardly assaults on tea and vegetable sellers by 'the young and the simple'. Although the commissioners were treated with respect and hospitality and complained only regarding the polltax – warning that retaliation might be necessary – a sustained burst of anti-Chinese activity ensued. Part of the problem lay in the relationship between Britain and China and the fact that some Chinese migrants were British subjects from Hong Kong. Only the year before, in 1886, the Victorian government had discovered that the number of naturalization papers issued in one year were matched by the number of migrants the next, as papers were sold or sent to Hong Kong. By making secret marks on the papers customs officers were finally able to detect imposters.

The crisis marking the effective end of Chinese immigration occurred in 1888, when the *Afghan* arrived in Melbourne with 250–300 Chinese on board, mostly new migrants, as their dress, long pigtails and shaven

50 G. L. Buxton, *The Riverina, 1861–1891*, Melbourne, 1967, p. 224.

heads showed. The Trades Hall Council called an emergency meeting, orators recalled the tradition of resistance to convict landings and police guarded the ship as crowds gathered on the wharf. Inspections revealed a majority of false naturalization papers. In the face of mounting opposition, and rather than pay fines, the *Afghan* sailed for Sydney to the echoes of anti-Chinese demonstrations around Australia. A second ship was halted by the hoisting of the yellow quarantine flag and a hasty Order-in-Council declaring Hong Kong, Singapore and other eastern ports 'infected'. Meanwhile the *Afghan* and other vessels had met further opposition in Sydney. Ultimately restrictive legislation was agreed to by the imperial government, though in the meantime one genuine migrant on the *Afghan*, Ah Toy, had successfully sued the Victorian government for damages.[51]

The question, 'What kind of country is this to be?' was thus partly answered in racial terms. Cheap coloured labour, whether Chinese, Kanaka or Indian coolie, meant inequality and Australians were determined on economic and humanitarian grounds to avoid inequality. Australian Aborigines, however, were encouraged to join unions from which other non-Europeans were excluded, and no objection was raised when they were employed as shearers, some being highly skilled. Some recent commentators have made much of nineteenth century racism, but it is difficult to disentangle pure racism from economic or merely xenophobic arguments. Even the *Bulletin*'s ranting against the cheap Chinaman, the cheap Kanaka and the cheap nigger was expressing an essentially economic fear, while the rural press could champion the Chinese and acknowledge that they were 'no more immoral than our men in similar circumstances'.[52] But in the cities, anti-Chinese feeling was almost as high at times as anti-'foreign devil' feeling in some Chinese cities.

It was not difficult for most nineteenth century Europeans to believe genuinely in their racial superiority, a belief evidenced by their technologically superior industrial civilization, reinforced by scientific Social Darwinism and condoned in practice by the churches. Some views arose quite naturally from the eighteenth century concept of 'Improvement', when it was clearly shown by Bakewell and others that by selective breeding it was possible to obtain larger and stronger sheep, horses and cattle. Australian wool growers of the early nineteenth century commonly spoke of 'pure merinos of the French or Saxon *race*'. C. H. Pearson saw Australians as a naturally selected higher race 'guarding the last part of the world in which the higher races can live and increase freely, for the higher civilization'. Others wrote of the 'soft and pulpy Kanaka', and fear of intermarriage between races raised the greatest wrath. William Lane, Utopian

[51] On the question generally see M. Willard, *History of the White Australia Policy to 1920*, Melbourne, 1923: A. T. Yarwood, *Attitudes to Non-European Immigration*, Melbourne, 1968.

[52] G. L. Buxton, *The Riverina, 1861–1891*, Melbourne, 1967, p. 230.

Socialist and founder of the New Australia colony in Paraguay, could write in the Wagga Wagga *Hummer* of April 1892 that, while he would not do a black man harm, he would rather see his daughter

dead in her coffin than kissing one of them on the mouth or nursing a coffee coloured brat that she was mother to. If this is a wicked thing to say, then I am one of the wicked ones, and don't want to be good either; and I'd pray daily to be kept wicked if I thought there was any chance of my ever getting to think that the colour didn't matter.

Racialist views also formed one strand of what was popularly known as the Irish Question. By race Celtic and by religion Catholic, the substantial Irish minority frequently raised doubts in the minds of those who looked forward to Australian homogeneity, while for the Irish themselves tradition and history produced a conflict of loyalties not easily resolved.[53] In 1881 a Melbourne observer, A. M. Topp, commenting on the Irish in Australia, saw a basic incompatibility between Celtic and Anglo-Saxon. Since Roman times the Celtic Irish had been 'recognised as inferior' – morally, socially and intellectually – unable to discern truth from falsehood, given to petty bickering and lacking moral courage, characteristics which explained the perpetual anarchy in Ireland. Irish Catholics were often despised, mocked, and feared; their frequent casting in the role of scapegoat, otherwise reserved for the Chinese, may well reflect guilt feelings on the part of the Anglo-Saxon majority, unable to avoid knowledge of three centuries of English oppression in Ireland.

Experience in Ireland and America suggested that politically, Irish migrants understood best the exercise of raw power, whether of the church, the landlord or Anglo-Saxon government authorities. Respect for power and distrust of the law led the Irish to think of politics as a struggle by one group for the right to oppress and exploit another, rather than seeing change and ferment as essential features of a healthy community. In a classic demonstration of their talent for manipulative politics in Victoria, O'Shanassy and the Catholic bishops had traditionally led Catholics as a pressure group, to vote for whichever politicians offered the greatest concessions, particularly in the matter of education. A small élite, sons of Irish or Anglo-Irish gentry, including (Sir) John O'Shanassy and (Sir) Charles Gavan Duffy, lawyer and former member of the British House of Commons, held some professional qualifications and gave leadership, but migrants from Munster predominated, mainly farm workers and labourers. The conditions of rural servitude from which they came were sometimes offered in explanation of their admittedly intemperate and aggressive natures.

Half of Australia's Irish-born lived in rural districts where, given equal opportunities, they acquired land and became moderately prosperous. Father Hartigan ('John O'Brien') has depicted in *Around*

[53] G. Serle, *The Rush To Be Rich*, Melbourne, 1971, p. 302.

the Boree Log the life style of such a group of Celtic yeomanry, his poems revealing the nostalgia and sentiment of the exile; Irish melancholy and Irish laughter – the little Irish mother, the pessimistic Hanrahan, the presbytery dog, and McEvoy, the altar-boy, aged 'sixty come November' – all part of the cultural luggage of the emigrant.[54] The other half of the Irish clustered in the inner suburbs close to their place of work as manual labourers or near transport. A small but prosperous group were the wine and spirit merchants or produce suppliers, while the ubiquitous Irish publican catered for the Celtic thirst throughout the colonies.

The loyalties of those of Irish-Catholic birth or descent were somewhat confused. Traditional antagonism to the English had been slowly modified in the new country and by the 1880s British attitudes to law and politics were more acceptable. Many Irish-Australians genuinely deplored the extremities of Orange versus Green. In Irish homes pictures of the Queen, Parnell, and after 1884 even Gladstone, mingled indiscriminately, and at Catholic gatherings the Anglo-Saxon protestant Queen was toasted – even if after the Pope. During the early 1880s, Home Rule became the critical issue, as the Irish independence movement rose to a pitch not reached again until 1916. In Victoria the arrival of the young, fiery, Redmond brothers, sent by Parnell to raise funds and support, provoked Roman Catholic Archbishop Goold to write home angrily, 'Keep your red hot politicans in Ireland where they are much needed'. Both clergy and Catholic politicians feared the loss of substantial gains already made if Irish extremists gained support in Australia, while the Loyal Orange Lodge thundered 'Home Rule is Rome Rule'. But whereas in Victoria Catholic clergy generally discouraged extremist calls to action amongst their flocks, in New South Wales support for Home Rule was more open and widespread. The safest and most common course for those of Irish descent was loyalty to Australia first. Until new waves of Irish migrants disturbed the process of assimilation, most avoided extreme positions on both Irish nationalism and Australian republicanism, accounting for the strong tradition of Irish-Australian nationalism. Only in the matter of state-aid for Catholic schools was the recurrent battle fought. Because of their economic position, Irish Catholics could contribute little to building cathedrals, parish churches or convent schools, whether amongst urban labourers or in rural districts. Yet despite financial difficulties, building went ahead. The decisions of colonial governments against state-aid for church or private schools was therefore a serious blow to Catholic education in particular.

But the notion of an Australia free of inequality and privilege, where every child had a right to the same level of education, was currently acceptable to politicians, the community at large, and working men in particular, leading to the passing of the 'Free, Compulsory

---

[54] 'John O'Brien' (pseud. Father Hartigan), *Around the Boree Log and Other Verses*, Sydney, 1921.

and Secular' acts in the 1870s.[55] The debate has continued for a century, but in the 1870s and 1880s Ministers for Public Instruction led their newly formed bureaucracies in the fight against ignorance and sectarianism. Throughout the system, indoctrination was aimed at British-Australian loyalty. History, geography and literature were British, jingoistic, and openly racist; loyalty to Queen and Empire was axiomatic and further encouraged by the cadet system and the drill manual. What little moralistic, non-sectarian, 'religious' teaching was offered offended both secular rationalists and religious leaders. The Catholic view saw such a system as 'instruction, not education'.

The evangelicals failed in their attempt to restore the Bible to state schools; indeed, in response to protests from the Jewish community in Victoria to references to Christ in the *Irish National Readers*, these had been replaced with *Nelson 'Royal' Readers*, from which all references to Christianity were then removed. Small wonder that the Catholic *Advocate* in 1883 in an editorial 'The State School Leprosy' referred to 'hotbeds of vice and irreligion' in which 'gross immorality' flourished. Yet, at the time, half the Catholic children of Victoria were attending state schools, a quarter of the teachers were Catholic. In 1884, Bishop Moore threatened to withdraw Catholic children if the Bible were introduced.[56] The education debate itself was part of the wider issue – the place of religion in the new Australian society.

One major debate took place at the theoretical or doctrinal level, the second concerned more practical social problems. In the 1881 censuses the overwhelming majority of colonists professed allegiance to one or other of the Christian churches. In Victoria on any one Sunday, half the total population actually attended church;[57] possibly more attended in South Australia. But by the early 1880s the challenge to the churches was mounting and the battle had been joined – as usual, five or ten years later than in England. A whole generation was compelled to face a spirit of enquiry based on the new scientific knowledge.[58] Evolution and the cult of rationalist science as a cure for the world's ills reached a culmination in Herbert Spencer's philosophical system, widely discussed in the universities, and for a time secularists gained strength.

It was not that these ideas arrived suddenly in the 1880s; many of them had been evident in the debate on secular education in the

---

[55] See A. G. Austin, *Australian Education: 1788–1900*, Melbourne, 1961: A. G. Austin, *Select Documents in Australian Education 1788–1900*, Melbourne, 1963: C. M. H. Clark, *Select Documents in Australian History: 1851–1900*, Sydney, 1955, Sect. 4, Pt. III: P. J. O'Farrell, *The Catholic Church in Australia: A Short History: 1788–1967*, Melbourne, 1968, ch. 3.

[56] G. Serle, *The Rush To Be Rich*, Melbourne, 1971, pp. 154–6.

[57] J. Roe, 'Challenge and Response: Religious Life in Melbourne, 1876–86', in *The Journal of Religious History*, 5, 2, December 1968.

[58] See T. Suttor, 'The Criticism of Religious Certitude in Australia, 1875–1900' in *The Journal of Religious History*, I, 1, June 1960.

1870s. For many, their appeal lay in the confrontation with evangelical Christianity, its emphasis on the literal inspiration of the Bible, and the concomitant doctrines of personal salvation, Satan, sin, hell, eternal life and eternal damnation. In 1883, Mr Justice Higinbotham's 'grave, anguished, lucid, utterly honest and reverent' lecture on 'Science and Religion' split the powerful Victorian Presbyterian church asunder. In the conflict which followed Presbyterianism suffered great damage.[59] The Wesleyans remained little affected by the debate, their fundamentalist beliefs unshaken: whereas Presbyterians required a B.A. degree before theological training, Methodists did not even demand matriculation. The Roman Catholic church, with its traditional hold over the flock, could disregard 'monkeyism' on the authority of the *Syllabus of Errors* and other encyclicals. As with political beliefs, it is easy to illustrate that these questioning ideas were current, but more difficult to know how widely they were held. The assumption by Victorians of intellectual superiority may well mean that the religion *versus* science debate raged more strongly there than in other colonies, but in any case the process of change in religious belief and observance was a slow one.

While this theoretical debate continued, church leaders and their followers were engaged on another front with more practical social issues. In its negative aspect there were the moral efforts of those derisively termed 'wowsers', one clergyman noting on his arrival that 'religious people here have a good deal more influence on politics than in England'. In Victoria, Presbyterians, aided by the evangelical wing of the Church of England, and occasionally by the Catholic church, led the van. In South Australia Methodists were stronger. In the absence of mass political parties or organized pressure groups, the churches for many decades had considerable political influence on some social questions.[60] Sabbath desecration was one of the major issues, the wowser position being defined by their enemies as 'Remember to keep gloomy the Sabbath Day'. Presbyterians were the strongest sabbatarians; hence Melbourne saw the greatest repression. Only sufficient trains ran to get people to church. There was great public outcry in 1874 when 1500 railway workers held their annual outing at Mount Macedon, with dancing and liquor. Many, lost in the bush, missed the train home. Clearly excursion trains were a work of the devil.

The greatest wowser victory came over the Sunday opening of the Public Library and National Gallery. Following a change of trustees, openers dominated the Board and in 1883, while parliament was in recess, they declared Library and Gallery open on Sunday – though only during non-church hours from 1.30 p.m. to 5 p.m. Nearly 6000 attended on the first day. The innovation may have succeeded if

59 G. Serle, *The Rush To Be Rich*, Melbourne, 1971, pp. 130–31.

60 See K. Dunstan, *Wowsers*, Melbourne, 1968.

exhibits at the time had not included a rather innocuous nude painting entitled 'Chloe'. Furious newspaper correspondence followed this exhibition of depraved nudity with its pernicious influence on youth. The more moderate suggested that since 'Chloe' had been awarded gold medals, and was, in one view, a work of art, she could be shown separately to males and females, or suitably draped. Meanwhile the Sunday opening debate continued. Despite 38,000 signatories to the petition for opening and only 11,000 against, when parliament reassembled the assembly castigated the trustees and, following a vote of 35 to 12, ordered them not to re-open on Sundays. Yet both the Melbourne Zoo and Botanical Gardens were open on Sundays, as were the galleries and libraries in most other Australasian cities.

A second target was intemperance. Australians drank more heavily than Americans, though somewhat less than Britons, and the ill-effects of alcoholism were widespread, especially amongst workingmen. Both religious and rationalist groups supported abstinence, as did lodges like the Rechabites, and the 1880s and 1890s were possibly the heyday of the temperance movements. Alliances of all anti-drink organizations were formed in most colonies by the early 1880s. Dr John Singleton, a man of great compassion and one of the few, apart from the Salvation Army, who tried to help actively, led the campaign against the prescription of alcohol as medicine; and after 1880 most non-conformist churches insisted on the use of unfermented wine for communion services. But the hundreds of hotels, far more numerous than churches, remained open from 6 a.m. until midnight six days a week, and some held a further licence from midnight to 6 a.m.

The rapid growth of coffee palaces in the 1880s was a positive attempt to offer alternative beverages and unlicensed accommodation. These temperance hotels were large by any standards. The Federal was the greatest hotel Australia had ever seen. Built for the opening of the International Exhibition of 1888 at a cost of £154,000, it had seven floors, six accident-proof lifts, accommodation for 400, an ice-plant, gas light on all floors, and electric bells. Supported by politicians and the respectable of the day coffee palaces and temperance hotels paid 10 per cent dividends at first, but many went under in the crash of the 1890s. Some, like The Victoria, have survived until the present, though are now acquiring licences. Prohibition for the community as a whole was never seriously considered, despite references to the prohibitionist American state of Maine, and only isolated pockets like teetotal Mildura were ever restricted in this way. Smoking came similarly under attack, the best known illustration being the diagram of twin brothers in the rationalist E. W. Cole's *Funny Picture Book*, in which an evil-looking, debilitated, weedy youth is captioned as 'The Brother who Smoked, thereby destroying his Vital Organs, his Good Looks and Stunting his Body'.[61]

Sexual morality was one of the main battle grounds for the

61 K. Dunstan, *Wowsers*, Melbourne, 1968, p. 130.

wowsers. Apart from attacking theatres and dancing as immoral and lustful, and public bathing as likely to lead to sin, their main target was prostitution or 'The Social Evil' as it was called, and as it appears in parliamentary records. The 'Disorderly House' or 'House of Ill Fame' was extraordinarily common and openly in evidence, forming the particular target of the Social Purity leagues. Prostitution, it was suggested, was one result of the lack of employment opportunities for girls, and a direct result of employing them as barmaids. Hotels and theatres were common recruiting places, and the Theatre Royal in Adelaide, like its counterparts in the other cities, had its special bar known as 'the Saddling Paddock' where arrangements were made. Politicians and public men were regular customers at the brothels. The colonial year book regularly and unashamedly published figures purporting to list the number of prostitutes per 10,000 of population, leading to some quite misguided self-congratulation. Whole streets and even city blocks were given over to the trade, and notorious Madames like Mother Fraser and Madame Brussells appeared in court from time to time, flaunting silks, feathers and jewellery, with little il-effect on their business, chiefly owing to the difficulty of obtaining convictions. Only very slowly did wowser influence change Australian attitudes to prostitution. Their attempts at censorship were equally unsuccessful. In 1888 a conviction was gained against W. W. Collins for selling Annie Besant's *Law of Population*, which opposed large families and explained how to avoid them. Birth control measures were described in precise clinical terms, as was the sex act itself. But the idea of sexual activity for pleasure rather than procreation was considered sacriligious. The book, said the prosecution, was immoral because it told people how to indulge their passions but avoid the normal consequences, and how to sin without fear of detection. Mr Justice Windeyer's judgement in the Supreme Court reversing the decision, remarkably humane and enlightened for its time, seems to have been lost sight of by later advocates of censorship. At the same time, French novels of the Naturalist Schools were seen as 'soaked and poisoned by beastly sensuality' and, on the grounds that 'French literary vice' was as bad as escaped French convicts from New Caledonia, the Customs department raided Cole's Book Arcade in Melbourne in 1889 and confiscated works by Zola, Daudet and de Maupassant.

The final target was gambling, which appeared to affect the whole Australian community. All denominations except Roman Catholics railed against gambling, even in the form of church lotteries, whist drives and raffles. Australians, it was considered, would bet on anything and two-up was particularly prevalent. In 1880, when Melbourne's population was 282,000 an estimated 100,000 attended the Melbourne Cup meeting, and in 1890, Carbine's year, John Wren gained the stake which led him to found his Collingwood Tote. Melbourne was one of the few cities in the world which gave a public holiday for a horse race, a disgraceful state of affairs according to the moralists. Subsequently, both the land crashes and bank crashes were blamed on the gambling mania. In an attempt to avert further such disasters the Council of Churches later declared a National Day of Humiliation.

Throughout these moral struggles, colonists reasserted their faith in the power of legislation to control social conditions, yet some of the most effective amelioration came not from government action but from voluntary organizations, of which the Salvation Army was one of the most effective. Following General Booth's charge, 'Go for souls and go for the worst', the Army's uniforms and bands appeared in 1880 in Adelaide and 1882 in Melbourne. Their rowdy marches and meetings appalled many respectable churchgoers, who saw them as irreligious burlesques or mere sensationalism. Yet criminals, drunkards and larrikins were persuaded to 'Come to Jesus', despite early brushes with larrikin gangs in the streets, pelting with stones, rotten eggs, dead cats, red ochre and flour, and even the gaoling of officers who refused to pay fines for disturbing the peace.[62] Within a few years the Army's mass rallies attracted tens of thousands. Yet it was probably true that much of the Army's membership represented transfers of the dissatisfied from other denominations. Nevertheless, the Salvation Army's social work brought it increasing respect. Reclaimed working men and women, alcoholics, criminals and prostitutes sought out and spoke to the poor and outcast in terms they could understand; prisoners were met on release from gaol, and fed and cared for; custody of first offenders was given to the Army in 1884 and a government grant allowed in 1886. A Fallen Sisters' Home was established, four hundred women passing through in the first year, and a Rescue House begun for venereal disease sufferers, against much opposition from Catholics and Methodists, who declared that such an institution pandered to vice. Except for such positive measures, the social achievements of the churches, and the wowser element in particular, were not impressive in the period, even in regard to education, sabbatarianism, temperance and prostitution.

Australian colonial society thus manifested many of the conflict symptoms endemic to the development of a pluralist society. Both the search for economic opportunity and the search for identity led to the formation of a diversity of interest groups, fragmentary but interconnected in a variety of ways. The *Bulletin* could thunder 'Australia for the Australians', but the question might well be asked, 'Which Australians?' The empire loyalists with their traditional ties to Britain, or the republicans who rejected old world privilege in their search for new Utopias? The native born, as epitomized by the aggressiveness of the A.N.A., or that 30 per cent who had been born overseas and had often grown up there, absorbing all the otherness of that different cultural environment? And what of Catholic and Irish Home Rulers, still resentful of Anglo-Saxon domination and the

62 G. Serle, *The Rush To Be Rich*, Melbourne, 1971, p. 148.

Protestant ascendency, or those much praised German settlers, 'our Anglo-Saxon cousins', so soon to become 'the filthy Hun'? What of wowser *versus* secularist, science *versus* religion, unionist and protectionist *versus* free trader, conservative or liberal *versus* radical, nationalist *versus* internationalist, capital *versus* labour, skilled *versus* unskilled, rural *versus* urban? Few would have suggested in that climate of Social Darwinism that the coloured races were Australians, but what of those who would employ them in the Deep North's plantation economy?

In short, rather than a united Australia it is easier in the 1870s and 1880s to see a disjointed collection of loosely linked economies and societies fluctuating independently, riven by internal factionalism, split by inter-colonial rivalries, and groping only tentatively towards what was in many ways a federation of fear – beginning with fear of Russian, German or French imperialist expansion in the antipodes, and the inability of an undefended Australia to resist encroachment from these or the coloured races. These, and all the other hopes and fears of Australians, help to account for the real fragmentation of the period, and the transient factionalism so evident in politics. Only at the top were the dreams of a unified Australia fully formulated and given substance.

6

1890-1900

B. K. de Garis

Characteristics of the 1890s—the economic depression—the build-ing boom in Victoria—land companies collapse—difficulties of the pastoral industry—the railway building spree ends—the bank crash of April-May 1893—government policies—the financial crisis and the depression—unemployment—land settlement schemes—the long drought—farming—meat—mining—the Mari-time Strike of 1890—capital versus labour?—strikes by shearers and coal miners—established political practices—the Labor party and politics in New South Wales—Victoria—Queensland—South Australia—Tasmania and Western Australia—political groupings —parliamentary reform—industrial legislation—taxation—old-age pensions—immigration restriction—the Aborigines—the concept of the State—legislative achievements—the federal movement— the 1891 Convention—the Corowa Conference—the 1895 Premiers' Conference—the 1897-8 Convention—the federal constitution— the first referendums—the Premiers' Conference of 1899—the second referendums—interpreting the results—the British con-nexion—local loyalties—being 'Australian'—federation and nationalism—the legend of the nineties—end of an age.

In the centenary year of 1888 Australia enthusiastically celebrated its first hundred years of European settlement; colonial leaders vied with each other in a scramble for superlatives to express their pride in past achievements and unbounded confidence in the future. After faltering earlier in the 1880s, the long boom which had begun in the 1860s had gathered momentum again and seemed to be set fair to carry the colonies into the twentieth century on a continuing wave of prosperity. But such was not to be. By the end of 1889 the boom had begun to break in the very colony, Victoria, in which it had been most exuber-ant: by 1892 most of Australia was in the grip of the worst depression it had yet experienced. Falling export income, bank failures, un-employment, drought, and industrial strife made the 1890s a dismal period for many people. Yet, despite the depression, perhaps even because of it, the decade has come to be acclaimed as one of the most creative in Australian history.Many colonists became more conscious of the real inequalities which existed within their egalitarian society and this was reflected in a flurry of social and political reform. In most colonies labor parties were established to give the workingman a political voice. At the same time, the federation of the colonies was attained, and loosely associated with this was the growth of a sense of national identity reflected particularly in literature and art.

It is appropriate to begin with an account of the economic depression, because every colony save Western Australia was hit, although the timing, nature and severity of the depression varied a good deal. The roots of the depression may be traced back into the long boom which had preceded it. With overseas capital available in seemingly unlimited quantities, more and more money had been poured into the pastoral industry, urban and residential building, and railway construction. Within each of these areas the criteria governing investment were progressively relaxed. The result was over-extension in these three sectors, and a lack of balance in the economy as a whole. These structural weaknesses were for some time concealed by the continuing high level of capital inflow, but in the long run major readjustments were inevitable. It is possible, though, that the process of readjusting the structure of the economy might have been a good deal less painful had there not been an unfortunate confluence of internal and external events between 1889 and 1893. The relative weight which should be assigned to internal and external causes of the depression is a matter of controversy, as is the related issue of whether or not a major depression was inevitable at this time.[1]

The first signs of trouble arose in Victoria, where the dizzy speculative boom in city and suburban land and building had over-reached itself. By the latter part of 1888 land prices had soared to unrealistic heights and the supply of housing had outrun demand. On 22 October the Melbourne banks stepped in, raising their interest rates by 1 per cent and restricting advances for speculative purposes. These measures immediately quenched the land fever and sent values tumbling, though the volume of work in progress was sufficient to keep the building industry busy well into the following year. However, the land and building companies which had financed the boom soon found themselves in difficulties, for the large sums which they had borrowed, mostly on short terms, were tied up directly or indirectly in unsaleable real estate. The suspension of one of Victoria's biggest building societies, the Premier Permanent Building Association, in December 1889, caused a sensation; ironically, though, when a subsequent investigation showed its affairs to have been disgracefully mismanaged, public opinion was reassured. Most of the other property

---

[1] These questions are more explicitly discussed in the following works, on which the account of the depression which follows is largely based – E. A. Boehm, *Prosperity and Depression in Australia 1887-1897*, Oxford, 1971: N. G. Butlin, *Investment in Australian Economic Development 1861-1900*, Cambridge, 1964: A. R. Hall, *The Stock Exchange of Melbourne and the Victorian Economy 1852-1900*, Canberra, 1968: T. A. Coghlan, *Labour and Industry in Australia*, London, 1918, vols. 3, 4.

companies were able to stave off disaster for a time by frantically soliciting further deposits in the United Kingdom which they used to meet their existing obligations.

It was thus several years before the full impact of the break in speculation became publicly apparent. During this period heavy government spending on public works kept unemployment in check, and a run of good seasons for the farmers and graziers boosted export income. In Victoria the net result was a mild recession lasting from 1889 to 1891, before the downswing accelerated. New South Wales was at this stage relatively unaffected by the turn of events in Victoria, for its building boom had passed its peak several years earlier and without the same degree of speculation. Indeed, after a slight check in 1889 the New South Wales economy enjoyed a brief Indian summer reaching a peak mid-way through 1891. As the trend in the other colonies was closer to the New South Wales pattern than to that in Victoria, Australia as a whole entered the 1890s with an appearance of prosperity. Few realised how ill-founded this was.

In the meantime, the flow of funds from overseas had begun to dry up. For years leading British financial experts had alleged that the Australian colonies were borrowing excessively and spending rashly but their warnings had fallen on deaf ears. However the collapse of the Premier Permanent alarmed British investors. Then, in 1890, a political and financial upheaval in Argentina brought Baring's, one of London's leading financial houses, to its knees. Baring's had been involved mainly in South American securities but the debacle aroused well-founded doubts about the financial soundness of the Australian colonies. By the end of 1891 Australian banks, building societies, and mortgage companies were finding it impossible to collect further funds in Britain, and the Australian governments were encountering similar difficulties. Each of the four colonial government loans floated on the London Money Market during 1891 was initially undersubscribed; Queensland sought to raise £2.5 million and was offered only £300,000.[2] These rebuffs effectively ended public borrowing, all governments being reluctant to risk further refusals. Victoria did not approach the London market again until 1898 and the other colonies, with the exception of gold-rich Western Australia, limited their borrowings during the remainder of the 1890s to less than one-quarter of the figure for the previous decade.

For the boomers of the 1880s the day of reckoning was near at hand; the 'land banks' and mortgage companies which had been hanging on grimly since 1889 began to tumble like ninepins. Not only was there no longer any British money available, but local credit also tightened up as governments drew on the banks to make good the shortfall in their own overseas borrowing. In July and August 1891 several major 'land banks' failed, and others followed with a rush. Individual

[2] E. A. Boehm, *Prosperity and Depression in Australia 1887–1897*, Oxford, 1971, pp. 164–79.

investors and depositors hastened to withdraw their capital but for many it was too late. By mid-1892 no less than twenty-one Melbourne- and twenty Sydney-based land and building institutions had gone into suspension; several Queensland institutions were also among the casualties.[3] Some of these companies were able to reconstruct, but most of them eventually had to be wound up, often paying their creditors no more than a few shillings in the pound. The collapse of so many companies also meant that thousands of individuals were bankrupted. In Victoria, the full extent of the collapse was even then concealed from the public for the law allowed bankrupts to make secret arrangements with their creditors; in 1892 alone 78 such 'secret compositions' accounted for total debts of £5.1 million, an enormous sum at that time.[4] In the end no one knew for certain who was solvent and who was not. Rumours flew about, and public confidence reached a low ebb. To make matters worse, the liquidation of the land boom brought to light scandalous details of the way many property companies had been run. Not only had most of them been mis- managed but there were many instances of deliberate fraud and deception, particularly in the desperate period between 1889 and 1891. The overconfidence of the boomers was seen to have been exceeded only by the gullibility of the public. Once again the position was bleakest in Victoria where such prominent men as the premier, James Munro, and the Speaker of the Legislative Assembly, Sir Matthew Davies, were up to their necks in disaster. So many public men had been involved in the follies of the boom that the heart was knocked out of Victorian politics for a generation.

The spectacular company failures of late 1891 and early 1892 signalled the onset of severe depression throughout eastern Australia. Not only had urban development come to a full stop, but the other major area of private investment, the pastoral industry, was equally deep in trouble. During the boom years most runs had been mortgaged to the hilt and by the 1890s pastoralists were saddled with crippling interest commitments to be met from shrinking wool cheques; in keeping their land out of the clutches of the selectors they had delivered themselves bound hand and foot to the banks. The stag- gering expense of converting leasehold to freehold had been fol- lowed by further heavy outlay on such improvements as fencing and water conservation, which seldom brought in a matching return. Pasture deterioration and the rabbit plague held productivity down whilst rent increases on pastoral leases and the wage increases won by the 'new unions' pushed costs up. Clearly, the industry badly needed to put its house in order, and a steep fall in wool prices between 1891 and 1894, on top of a slower but steady decline in the 1880s brought

---

[3] N. G. Butlin, *Investment in Australian Economic Development 1861–1900*, Cambridge, 1964, p. 429. See also M. Cannon, *The Land Boomers*, Melbourne, 1966.

[4] E. A. Boehm, *Prosperity and Depression in Australia, 1887–1897*, Oxford, 1971, pp. 258–9.

matters to a head. Even the fall in prices, at first sight an external factor since 99 per cent of the clip was bought by overseas manufacturers, could to some extent be laid at the pastoralists' own door. For although an economic recession in Europe and America contributed to the price slump, over-production was at the root of the problem. As a result of over-investment in the 1870s and 1880s Australia's output of wool had temporarily out-stripped world demand.

Although the nature of the cost, price and productivity squeeze was imperfectly understood at the time, its effects were readily apparent. Many squatters could not meet their interest obligations and effective control of their properties passed to the banks and finance companies from whom they had borrowed. Those who in palmier days had ventured into the arid inland regions where costs were highest and productivity lowest were particularly hard hit. New investment in pastoralism stopped abruptly after 1891 and the value of land and stock was written down, with unfortunate repercussions on general income and employment levels in the colonies. A parallel slump in the prices obtained for Australia's other major exports, wheat and silver, further intensified the economic difficulties of the period.

In the third major area of boom-time investment, railway construction, the pattern was similar. Massive expenditure of overseas capital on such facilities as roads, bridges, harbours, telegraphs, and above all, railways, had been an integral and valuable feature of the thirty years between 1860 and 1890 during which, in Butlin's words, 'the foundations of an enduring western society had been established'.[5] But in the end the colonial governments had carried their railway building to excess, just as private investors had done with urban building and pastoralism. Parliamentarians had shamelessly lobbied to ensure that the railway extended to or through their constituencies and once the obvious trunk routes had been completed lines were pushed out into thinly settled districts where there was likely to be little traffic for years to come. Governments had deliberately duplicated facilities already provided by other colonies in order to draw off trade from across neighbours' borders or to hold it within their own. Moreover freight rates were kept artificially low to stimulate traffic so that although in the long run most lines were of value in encouraging economic development, in the short run few of them could pay their way.[6]

By the late 1880s some colonists had begun to feel that the costs and benefits of proposed works should be scrutinized more carefully but it was not until British capital ceased to be available that the railway spree shuddered to a halt. A pause for re-thinking was clearly desirable but the timing could hardly have been worse because the

[5] N. G. Butlin, *Investment in Australian Economic Development 1861–1900*, Cambridge, 1964, pp. 3–4.

[6] For an account of the railway boom see G. Blainey, *The Tyranny of Distance*, Melbourne, 1966, ch. 2.

sudden contraction in governmental spending accelerated the slide into depression. The slackening of economic activity was in turn reflected in falling government revenue and the colonies began to find it difficult to meet their fixed interest obligations. By the mid-1890s the annual interest bill was swallowing up between 25 per cent and 35 per cent of each colony's public revenue,[7] leaving little room for budgetary manoeuvre. Moreover, according to the conventional economic wisdom of the day, governments, like families, were expected to live within their means; indeed there was a general call for them to atone for past sins and restore their credit-worthiness by practising rigid economies. Thus at the very time when the economy was most in need of stimulation, the harassed colonial treasurers were driven into even more severe retrenchment.

All things considered, it is not surprising that 1892 was a bleak year throughout eastern Australia, but by its end the worst seemed to be over. However, 1893 brought a further body-blow – the most serious financial crisis in Australian history.[8] The crisis arose out of the prevailing economic dislocation, but it was made possible by the fragmented and rather unsophisticated character of Australia's monetary arrangements. Despite the growth of intercolonial trade and investment and the fact that more than half the banks-of-issue operated in more than one colony, there was no federal government to co-ordinate economic policy and no central bank to control banking policy. Each of the twenty-two banks in existence at the beginning of 1893 issued its own banknotes, determined its own interest rates and banking policy, and decided for itself what reserves of gold and securities were necessary. During the later stages of the boom most of them had used this freedom to slip into practices which whilst they seemed sound enough at the time, were ultimately to prove dangerous. Although few banks had taken part directly in land speculation, they had advanced a great deal of money to building and finance companies which were more intimately involved. They had also been active in financing the expansion of the pastoral industry so that one way or another a substantial proportion of their advances had been made against mortgages on land: by 1893 the land was practically unsaleable even at drastically reduced valuations.

The increasingly low ratio of reserves to liabilities held by most banks was also a source of vulnerability. Central to the whole of banking practice was the assumption that at no time would it ever be necessary to convert all notes to coin or refund every deposit, so that

---

[7] E. A. Boehm, *Prosperity and Depression in Australia 1887–1897*, Oxford, 1971, p. 174.

[8] For varying accounts of the crisis see E. A. Boehm, *Prosperity and Depression in Australia 1887–1897*, Oxford, 1971, chs. 8 and 10: R. Gollan, *The Commonwealth Bank of Australia: Origins and Early History*, Canberra, 1968, ch. 2: G. Blainey, *Gold and Paper: A History of the National Bank of Australasia Limited*, Melbourne, 1958, ch. 10: S. J. Butlin, *Australia and New Zealand Bank*, London, 1961.

most of a bank's assets could be profitably loaned or invested provided that adequate reserves of gold coin and bullion were retained. But opinions differed as to what constituted adequate reserves. Earlier in the century a ratio of reserves to liabilities of about one-third had been considered necessary, but decades of prosperity had induced a false sense of security, and by 1890 few banks had reserves exceeding twenty per cent and some fell below fifteen per cent. Another aspect of banking practice in the 1880s which was to prove a weakness was the collection of deposits in Britain as well as in Australia. By 1892 more than a quarter of the total deposits held by Australian banks was British, and this money had been loaned out to building societies and pastoralists in exactly the same way as money deposited locally. This meant that the banks were dependent on retaining the confidence of two different groups of clients, doubling the risk of a panic, without having set aside extra reserves to cover this danger.

Given these underlying weaknesses, the onset of the depression and the collapse of the land boom left some banks highly vulnerable. The funds advanced to defunct and suspended companies were either totally lost or locked up for years; many other clients could not meet their commitments, and with both city and pastoral land a drug on the market there was little to be gained from foreclosures. Moreover the failure of the land and building companies, many of which had called themselves 'banks', raised doubts about the soundness of other financial institutions. Depositors began withdrawing their money, particularly from those banks which were thought to have close links with the building boom. In March 1892 the Mercantile Bank of Australia, of which the notorious Matthew Davies was chairman, closed following a run on its coin reserves. Pressure then shifted to the Federal and Commercial, two more Melbourne-based banks. A vague assurance of fraternal support by the Associated Banks temporarily averted panic but they were steadily bled of their reserves during the remainder of the year; by January 1893 the Federal was insolvent. After two weeks of secret deliberation the Associated Banks declined to take it over, despite the earlier assurance, and the Federal Bank went into liquidation. The next to close was the Commercial, on 4 April. In its last four months of trading the Commercial experienced an excess of withdrawals over deposits of £1 million and on its final day of business lost £115,000. This time the other banks offered support but the Commercial's directors decided to suspend and reconstruct, believing that even if the local run could be stopped their English depositors would take the first opportunity of demanding their money, placing the bank in an impossible position. With the fall of the Commercial, a large bank with branches in five colonies, the crisis spread beyond Melbourne, and within the next six weeks there were twelve more suspensions. By the middle of May only nine banks had withstood the avalanche. Six of these were small and operated in one colony only; the others were Australia's oldest and biggest bank, the New South Wales, and two well-established and conservatively managed Anglo-Australian banks, the Union and the Australasia.

Throughout April and May, whilst the crisis was at its height, the commercial life of the colonies was plunged into chaos. The notes issued by suspended banks were looked at askance, and thousands of depositors found that their accounts were frozen. Employers could not pay their workmen, who in turn could not pay their shopkeepers or tradesmen; the unemployed, who could not withdraw their savings, were particularly hard hit. The morale of the community, already sapped by two years of depression, reached rock bottom.

Could the crisis have been averted, given stronger leadership? It is difficult to give an unequivocal answer to this perennial question. The unwise policies pursued by some banks during the boom had left them in a very exposed condition and it is doubtful whether they could or should have survived in the bleaker economic climate of the nineties, but most of the banks that closed were reasonably solvent. Their problem was the deterioration of public confidence, and it was here that the lack of leadership was felt. It is remarkable how much confidence in the banking system the colonial community displayed during 1891–2, and had the Associated Banks of Melbourne propped up or taken over the Federal Bank the 'run' might never have started. Their reluctance to incur heavy expense sustaining a foolish competitor is understandable, but once panic was allowed to develop it brought down the not-so-foolish and even the moderately cautious banks as well.

The Victorian government, in particular, handled the crisis poorly. Following the closure of the Federal and the Commercial, the Patterson ministry took the remarkable step of declaring a five-day bank holiday in the hope that the public might calm down if the banks were shut, apparently believing, one contemporary observed, 'that in order to put out a fire the right thing is to shower petroleum upon it'.[9] In New South Wales the Dibbs ministry boldly rushed through the Bank Issue Act, the most important provision of which empowered the government to declare bank notes legal tender for one year in order to stop worried citizens exchanging them for gold coin. This revolutionary step was resisted by the very banks it was intended to succour but when there was yet another suspension Dibbs overruled their objections and the run on the four banks which were open in New South Wales soon fizzled out. Had Patterson and his colleagues in Victoria taken similar action in January when the Federal Bank failed the extent of the crisis might have been minimized, though Boehm argues that the public might not have been prepared to accept notes as legal tender at that time, and that in any case firmer measures to protect the interests of local depositors might have provoked panic

9 *Australasian Insurance and Banking Record*, May 1893, p. 299.

on the part of the bank's British clients and hence only have post-poned the crisis.[10]

At all events the last of the suspended banks was back in business on a reconstructed basis by the end of August 1893.[11] The method of reconstruction generally adopted was the compulsory conversion of a proportion of each existing deposit into shares in the bank, the re-mainder to be available for refund after five years. This procedure greatly improved the capital structure of the banks concerned and gave them time to realize their illiquid assets in a rational way. The chief sufferers were the small depositors who could not wait for five years to retrieve their money and here again the New South Wales govern-ment showed sensible initiative, passing an act authorizing the colonial treasury to advance to such people up to half their frozen deposits. A similar scheme was adopted in Queensland.

The effects of the crisis continued to be felt long after the banks re-opened for business, indeed it might be argued that Australians have never felt quite the same about their banks again. In a more immediate way, the financial collapse was undoubtedly responsible for intensifying and prolonging the depression. In addition to the indi-viduals and businesses forced into bankruptcy by the temporary paralysis of commercial life during the crisis, there were many others who suffered from the general tightness of credit through the re-mainder of the decade as the chastened banks adopted more cautious policies and paid off their obligations. To add to the woes of the colonists, wool, wheat and silver prices all slumped still further in 1894, keeping primary industry in the doldrums. The building trade remained at a standstill as did its suppliers such as the brickyards and timbermills. Most other manufacturers were also affected by the falling demand and shortage of money; some factories closed and others laid off men, adding to the unemployment problem.

The rigours of the depression were a shock to a community which had come to take for granted a high standard of living, and all levels of society were affected though some more severely than others.[12] The respectable folk, especially the elderly and the widowed, who had invested their all in defunct companies, were left in a desperate pre-dicament, and some starved rather than accept charity. Young middle-class families who had been living beyond their means in heavily

---

[10] E. A. Boehm, *Prosperity and Depression in Australia, 1887–1897*, Oxford, 1971, pp. 309–12: cf. G. Blainey, *Gold and Paper: A History of the National Bank of Australasia Limited*, Melbourne, 1958, pp. 162–3: A. R. Hall, *The Stock Exchange of Melbourne and the Victorian Economy 1852–1900*, Canberra, 1968, pp. 157–61.

[11] For an example of a contemporary financial reconstruction see N. Cain, 'Financial Reconstruction in Australia, 1893–1900' in *Business Archives and History, VI*, 2, August 1966.

[12] M. Cannon, *The Land Boomers*, Melbourne, 1966, chs. 4 and 21: T. A. Coghlan, *Labour and Industry in Australia*, London, 1918, 3, 6, ch. 6, and 4, 7, ch. 4.

mortgaged villas in the new outer-suburban housing areas were also in trouble. Some were put out into the streets for failure to keep up their repayments; others sold their furniture to raise cash and camped in cold and empty houses. In a few Melbourne suburbs there were streets and streets of deserted houses. Those lucky members of the working class who kept their jobs were not too badly off at first for although wage cuts were universal, prices fell farther and faster, but later in the decade when the cost of living began to rise again wages did not keep in step and wage-earners, particularly the unskilled, found it hard to make ends meet. However the greatest privations were experienced by the tens of thousands of unemployed.

There are no firm unemployment statistics for the 1890s but one historian has estimated that during the trough of the depression between 25 per cent and 30 per cent of skilled tradesmen were out of work and the figure was almost certainly much higher for the unskilled.[13] It is difficult for those accustomed to the modern welfare state to appreciate how grim was the plight of the unemployed. There was no dole, no pension, no child endowment, and no health scheme to assist them. Once a man's savings, if he had any, were exhausted, he and his family were totally dependent on private charity until he could find another job; 'the forlorn and destitute workers are herding in alleys and lanes, or cowering in garret and cellar like hunted animals', reported the *Age* in 1892.[14] The Salvation Army, which had become established in Australia only a few years before, took an active part in setting up soup kitchens and distributing fuel, as did such organizations as the Ladies' Benevolent Society, the Neglected Children's Aid Society, and the Women's Christian Temperance Union. For those who were homeless, 'refuges' were opened where overnight accommodation was available. The extent of the demand for help of all kinds overstrained the resources of these voluntary organizations, especially since some of those who had previously dispensed charity were themselves in need of it.

In all colonies the governments of the day were loath to accept any responsibility for the problems of the unemployed. Obsessed with the need to balance their budgets and unable to borrow overseas, they mostly turned a deaf ear to the deputations and demonstrations which asked that public works should be started to create jobs. In 1894 the South Australian government put a few men to work on stonebreaking in return for rations, and the New South Wales government offered one day's work a week to those who wanted it 'sand-shifting' at Centennial Park. In the following year men were paid to cut down all the native shrubs and plants on church and school lands between Sydney and Randwick, a useless and disgraceful piece of vandalism. The only major project of the period was undertaken not by a

13 P. G. Macarthy, 'Wages in Australia, 1891 to 1914', in *A.E.H.R.*, X, 1, March 1970.

14 M. Cannon, *The Land Boomers*, Melbourne, 1966, p. 22.

government but the Melbourne Board of Works, which belatedly began to sewer the city. In 1892 labour bureaus were opened in the colonies most affected but these could do little for those who registered, save offer some of them rail passes to the country districts.

A turning away from the cities was indeed a characteristic of the depression era. The spectacular growth of the major colonial capitals had been a striking feature of the boom and when the crash came critics were quick to lay the blame at their door; the wasteful and vulgar ostentation of city life was unfavourably contrasted with the simple rural values of the bush. Fossicking for gold provided a living for quite a few in New South Wales and Victoria. Moreover the discovery of rich goldfields in Western Australia came at just the right time to serve as a form of large-scale outdoor relief for the eastern colonies, one South Australian politician remarking 'if it had not been for West Australia we would have had working men walking about our streets in thousands'.[15] After 1896 the Mt Lyell copper deposits in Tasmania fulfilled a similar function.

The other traditional Australian panacea of 'putting men on the land' enjoyed a revival, though the numbers involved were smaller. In Victoria for example, further tracts of the Mallee and Gippsland regions were opened up, and in Queensland the government re-purchased and sub-divided 140,000 acres on the Darling Downs. More unusual was the establishment in all five colonies affected by the depression of co-operative agricultural settlements.[16] These were in part only an extension of previous land development practice but the co-operative element was new and was adopted largely as a counter to William Lane's utopian 'New Australia' settlement in Paraguay. In New South Wales three such village settlements were founded in 1893, the biggest being that at Pitt Town with two smaller ones at Bega and Wilberforce. In Queensland in the same year twelve groups were organized and South Australia followed suit in 1894 with thirteen settlements, mostly along the River Murray between Renmark and Morgan. Tasmania's only settlement was founded at Southport also in 1894. In each case the broad intention was for a small group of men to work together on a co-operative basis under the supervision of trustees to clear and farm leasehold land, usually with some slight financial assistance from the government concerned. All these schemes got some of the unemployed out of the cities and supported them and their families through part of the depression but most of them folded up within a few years and none were really successful. The men lacked experience of agriculture and knowledge of co-operative principles, and most of the settlements were under-capitalized and poorly located.

15 J. H. Howe, in *South Australia: Parliamentary Debates* 31 July 1895, p. 753.

16 T. A. Coghlan, *Labour and Industry in Australia*, London, 1918, *4*, 7, chs. 2 and 4: R. B. Walker, 'The Ambiguous Experiment – Agricultural Co-operatives in New South Wales, 1893–1896', in *L.H., 18*, May 1970: R. E. W. Kennedy, 'The Leongatha Labour Colony: Founding an Anti-Utopia', in *L.H., 14*, May 1968.

Those which survived their teething troubles invariably switched to individual ownership of the land following internecine strife.

In Victoria a similar flirtation with agrarian utopianism took a greater variety of forms. The Village Settlement Association founded in 1892 by the Rev. Horace Tucker established seven communities several of which were reasonably successful, and following appropriate legislation in 1893 other groups including the Salvation Army took up the idea. One interesting but abortive variant was an attempted fishing village on Flinders Island to which eighteen men were briefly despatched. A slightly more successful experiment was the Labour Colony at Leongatha where the unemployed were paid subsistence wages whilst they learned to do farm work. Four thousand men passed through Leongatha in its first seven years, but like similar ventures elsewhere it was unpopular, and it is doubtful whether the average inmate stayed long enough to develop useful skills.

The exodus from the cities was most marked in the case of Melbourne which lost fifty thousand people in three years. Many must have left the colony altogether for in the course of the 1890s Victoria lost well over one hundred thousand of its citizens. This was a reflection of the utter demoralization of that colony as well as of the severity of its depression. Though New South Wales was also badly off it drew some compensation from the discomforture of its brash young neighbour, the Sydney *Bulletin* maliciously remarking on 18 November 1893 that 'The policy of the continent at large should be to declare Victoria an infected province until its moral character has been renovated and its reputation restored'. In both these colonies and also in Tasmania there was little recovery before 1895. In South Australia and Queensland the pattern was different, the depression there easing soon after the financial crisis in 1893, but each of these colonies experienced a further period of recession later in the decade when the overall trend was more favourable.

The process of recovery was complicated by the worst drought on record in Australia, which lasted from 1895 to 1903 and further crippled the already ailing pastoral industry. That a reasonable measure of prosperity had been regained by the turn of the century, despite this handicap and without the leadership of a central government, testifies to the resilience of the colonists and suggests that the weaknesses in the economy which the depression had exposed were not as deep seated as has sometimes been suggested. Within less than a decade considerable economic diversification had been achieved and the colonies had learned to make do with a great deal less imported capital and a lower level of imported goods. Investment was diverted from those sectors which had been overemphasised during the boom into neglected or entirely new industries, the development of which was further assisted by technological innovation.

Both these factors assisted wheatgrowing which began a great surge of expansion which carried through to the outbreak of the War of

1914–18.[17] New South Wales, which had hitherto imported wheat from other colonies, now began to feed itself, trebling its acreage under cultivation in the 1890s. This meant that the Victorian and South Australian surplus was available for export overseas. The mechanization of farming, fallowing, the introduction of superphosphate and other fertilizers, and the use of new varieties of seed all contributed to the improved yields per acre which were achieved. Mixed farming increased in popularity and the lavish railway building of the 1880s began to pay dividends by facilitating the extension of wheat growing into inland areas. Dairy farming made a striking rise to prominence in the 1890s, particularly in Victoria where it was encouraged by a government subsidy; with refrigerated shipping now available butter became a valuable export earner. Wine production increased in Victoria and South Australia and exports like butter, directed mainly to Britain, doubled. Fruitgrowing also expanded though attempts to export fruit were less successful at this stage. Further north, the sugar industry contrived to retain its Pacific island labour force though there was a gradual transition from large plantations to small farms clustered around central mills.

For many years prior to 1890 Australian pastoralism had been oriented principally towards wool. Meat was less highly valued because the local market was small and distance made the export of fresh meat impracticable, though some canned meat was sold overseas. The combination of fast steamships and refrigeration changed this situation, but although a trial shipment of frozen meat arrived in London in good order as early as 1879, it was not until the 1890s that a significant trade in both beef and mutton developed; Queensland benefited most. By 1895 Australia was supplying 20 per cent of Britain's meat imports. In addition to reducing Australia's dependence on a few staple exports, the sale of frozen meat softened the impact of the drought by allowing stock numbers to be drastically reduced without total loss. Little wonder that the *Pastoralists Review* considered that 'the frozen meat trade is the silver lining to the cloud that is passing over Australia . . .'[18]

The revival of mining made an even more important contribution to the recovery. In 1900 gold production earned almost as much as wool, and for a few years thereafter it actually went ahead again for the first time since the 1860s. Queensland led the way, for the Charters Towers field had begun to boom in 1886. Fossickers were busy in New South Wales and Victoria in the 1890s, and the discovery of the cyanide method of recovering gold from 'tailings' gave a new lease of life to some of the old goldfields. But it was Western Australia that really struck it rich. The Kimberley discoveries of 1885 began, in

[17] For a more detailed account than that which follows see E. Dunsdorfs, *The Australian Wheat-Growing Industry 1788–1948*, Melbourne, 1956, ch. 5.

[18] *Australasian Pastoralists' Review*, 15 March 1893. On the growth of the refrigerated export trade generally, see E. A. Boehm, *Prosperity and Depression in Australia 1887–1897*, Oxford, 1971, pp. 107–17: W. A. Sinclair, *Economic Recovery in Victoria 1894–1899*, Canberra, 1956, ch. 4.

Blaney's words, 'a lightning run of finds that in seven years stretched in a long arc one and a half thousand miles from the Timor Sea to the Great Australian Bight'.[19] The climax came in June 1893, when Hannan, Flannagan and O'Shea found gold at Kalgoorlie, centre of what was to become the 'Golden Mile', the most productive goldfield in Australia. With the eastern colonies still sunk in depression the lure of gold was irresistible and thousands flocked westward, increasing the colony's population almost fourfold in the course of the decade; by 1900 Tasmania, not Western Australia, was the least populous colony.[20]

As always, few of the diggers realized their dreams of easy wealth and by 1897 alluvial production had already begun to taper off. But the rise of deep mining boosted total gold production to even greater heights. The British capital which was no longer available to the other colonies was lavishly showered on the 'Golden West' to finance the renewed boom and there were plenty of well paid jobs in the mines for unsuccessful fossickers. The colony took advantage of its unprecedented prosperity to consolidate older industries and make good the deficiencies in its transport and communications but the spin-off from the goldfields was not confined to Western Australia. Remittances by men who had left their families in other colonies totalled £900,000 by money order alone in 1897, a much needed injection of spending money, and the gold itself was helpful in restoring Australia's balance of payments. Moreover the sevenfold increase in Western Australia's level of imports from her sister colonies during the 1890s helped to get their industries out of the doldrums. Western Australia thus entered the twentieth century on the crest of a boom which even her most optimistic citizens could hardly have foreseen in the 1880s. For the other colonies the experience of the 1890s was almost exactly the reverse, but they at least ended the decade a good deal more prosperously than could have seemed likely a few years earlier.

For the trade union movement the 1880s had been a period of growth. In the 1890s the story was very different. As unemployment rose and wages fell, thousands of unionists ceased paying their dues. The unions in turn were unable to pay their contributions to central trades and labour organizations, and were forced to disaffiliate. By the middle of the decade many unions had been dissolved and others crippled by their financial problems. In addition, between 1890 and 1894 there was a run of major strikes, each of which ended disastrously for the unions concerned. The rot set in with the Maritime Strike of

[19] G. Blainey, *The Rush That Never Ended*, Melbourne, 1963, pp. 167–8. On the Western Australian gold-rushes see F. K. Crowley, *Australia's Western Third*, London, 1960, chs. 4 and 5.

[20] On the impact of the W.A. gold rushes on the other colonies see G. Blainey, *The Rush That Never Ended*, Melbourne, 1963, pp. 194–6: E. A. Boehm, *Prosperity and Depression in Australia 1887–1897*, Oxford, 1971, pp. 117–24: W. A. Sinclair,, *Economic Recovery in Victoria 1894–1899*, Canberra, 1956, pp. 118–24.

1890, the nearest approximation to a general strike in Australian history to that time, involving some 50,000 men spread over four colonies. The origins of the strike were complex.[21] Between April and July 1890 the owners of ships engaged in the coastal trade found themselves under pressure for improved conditions and wages from one maritime union after another. Concessions were made to the wharf labourers and to some extent to the seamen, but the Marine Officers were told that a condition of any settlement with them would be the cancellation of their recent affiliation with the Melbourne Trades Hall Council. The officers rejected this ultimatum and by 16 August they were on strike.

At this stage the dispute was a relatively minor one but within a few days the wharf labourers, seamen, stewards and cooks also ceased work. For each of these unions, fraternal sympathy was reinforced by claims or grievances of their own, for the whole maritime industry was in a ferment. However, the most serious complication arose out of the pastoral industry and affected the waterfront only tangentially, though seriously. In May 1890 the Queensland Shearers' Union had forced Darling Downs pastoralists to agree to employ only union labour by persuading the Brisbane wharf labourers to refuse to handle 'non-union' wool from Jondaryan station. The president of the Amalgamated Shearers' Union, W. G. Spence, had then decided that the time was ripe for similar action in New South Wales. Already much of the shearing in the south-eastern colonies was done by unionists, and Spence determined to eliminate non-unionists altogether. During July and August the Pastoralists' Association several times offered to negotiate about the possible introduction of the 'closed shop' in the following year, once existing agreements with non-union shearers had expired, but Spence would accept nothing less than immediate capitulation. On 6 August the Wharf Labourers' Union agreed to his request that they should not handle non-union wool and on 10 August the first such bales reached Sydney. The shearing dispute was thus threatening to come to a head just as the Marine Officers precipitated the general strike of maritime unions. Spence's enthusiastic oratory about the solidarity of labour, designed to win support for the shearers, may have encouraged waterfront militancy, but in substance the two issues were not connected. Wool was carried by overseas vessels whereas the shipping dispute was confined to the coastal trade, and when the wharf labourers first came out in support of the officers they excepted overseas vessels from their ban on work. However their strike was soon

---

[21] The following account of the strike is based mainly on T. A. Coghlan, *Labour and Industry in Australia*, London, 1918, *3*, pp. 1591–1607: N. B. Nairn, 'The 1890 Maritime Strike in New South Wales' in *H.S.*, *37*, November 1961: F. S. Piggin, 'New South Wales Pastoralists and the Strikes of 1890 and 1891', in *H.S.*, *56*, April 1971: J. A. Merritt, 'W. G. Spence and the 1890 Maritime Strike', in *H.S.*, *60*, April 1973: G. R. Henning, 'Steamships and the 1890 Maritime Strike', in *H.S.*, *60*, April 1973: R. B. Walker, 'The Maritime Strikes in South Australia 1887 and 1890', in *L.H.*, *14*, May 1968.

extended to include all shipping and thereafter the two disputes became progressively more entangled.

By the end of August the battle-lines had been drawn and thereafter hostilities intensified. Although most colonies were still outwardly prosperous there was already a good deal of unemployment and the shipowners had no difficulty in recruiting non-union or 'scab' labour to load and crew their ships. Union efforts to prevent this by picketing were broken up by the police and ugly scenes occurred in both Melbourne and Sydney. When the coal miners became embroiled in the strike through their desire to deny coal to ships with non-union crews, the mines were quickly re-opened in similar fashion. The shearers themselves were not called out until 24 September. With the Broken Hill mines also closed at this time the strike had reached its climax in terms of the number of men who were out; but the end was near. The shearers returned to work after only a week, and on 17 October the Marine Officers accepted the shipowners' terms. With union coffers empty, other men trickled back to work and early in November the strike tamely petered out. Few unions had improved their position in the slightest; most were worse off than before.

The Maritime Strike has often been depicted as a deliberate trial of strength between united labour and united capital with the principle of unionism itself as the central issue.[22] Several caveats must be entered against this interpretation. To begin with, the strike was limited to the shipping, mining and pastoral industries, and though the number of men involved was large, they were mostly drawn from a few big unions of recent origins. The building and manufacturing unions which had pioneered trade unionism in Australia did not participate. Moreover even within the limits of the strike neither the employers nor the unionists were as well co-ordinated as was afterwards claimed. Such collaboration as there was between shipowners and pastoralists was a product rather than a cause of the strike. On the union side, though there were well established organizations such as the Sydney and Adelaide Trades and Labour Councils in existence, these bodies remained on the fringes of the strike, which was managed by an *ad hoc* Labour Defence Committee. In the end, individual unions accepted the terms of the appropriate group of employers. Hence it may be argued that the opposing forces were neither as comprehensive nor as monolithic as tradition has suggested.

It is also doubtful whether either side really intended to provoke a major confrontation in 1890. So far as the shearing side of the strike is concerned, the pastoralists' apparent readiness to move towards the 'closed shop' if the unions would wait a year is indicative of their desire to dampen the dispute down. Although the Pastoralists' Association was formed a month before the strike, it was not formed, as

22 See especially W. G. Spence, *Australia's Awakening*, Sydney, 1909, p. 114: B. Fitzpatrick, *A Short History of the Australian Labor Movement*, Melbourne, 1940, reprinted Melbourne, 1968: R. Gollan, *Radical and Working Class Politics: A Study of Eastern Australia, 1850–1910*, Melbourne, 1960, reprinted 1966, ch. 8.

Spence later alleged, in order to smash the Shearers' Union. Some of its members were antagonistic towards the shearers from the start, but the majority began by adopting a conciliatory policy until Spence's intransigence encouraged them to take the offensive. It is possible that the Association might in any case have taken a tougher line as it gained in strength but the evidence on this point is by no means conclusive. Spence may more plausibly be said to have courted a showdown, but it should not be inferred that his uncompromising attitude was based on the strength and militancy of his union. Rather was the reverse true; the officials of the Shearers' Union were anxious to force the issue of compulsory unionism without delay because they feared that only in this way could they hold their membership together. Furthermore, the showdown which Spence seems to have envisaged was a limited strike of the Jondaryan type, involving only the Sydney wharf labourers. He certainly did not intend that the shearers themselves should become involved, but the general stoppage of work on the waterfront sparked off by the Marine Officers upset his calculations and thereafter events rapidly moved beyond his control.

The background to the shipping side of the strike is more obscure but it is by no means certain that a major conflict was deliberately engineered there either. Given the constant barrage of union demands to which they had been subjected over the previous few years the shipowners were undoubtedly in a mood to be firm, but it is possible that they chose to dig their heels in over the claims of the Marine Officers precisely because they believed that this small and rather unusual group could be isolated from the other unions. This belief proved to be unfounded but the decision of the other maritime unions to join the strike was not simply a matter of fraternal solidarity; they each took the opportunity to press claims and grievances of their own.

On the other hand, although the strike was made up of several distinct strands which became interwoven almost fortuitously, once begun it developed into a general trial of strength. Fundamental questions about the proper limits of unionism were re-opened, notably the conflict between the belief of some employers in their right to employ whoever they chose and the belief of most unionists in their right to refuse to work with non-unionists. This was not a new issue, for it had been fought out before in the context of other industries; nor was it an enduring issue, for unionism had already become too much a part of the Australian way of life to be sloughed off. But for a few years following the Maritime Strike it was fiercely debated and in the pastoral and mining industries in particular, the battles of 1890 were fought again and again.[23]

<hr />

[23] See H. Kenway, 'The Pastoral Strikes of 1891 and 1894', in D. J. Murphy *et al*, Eds., *Prelude to Power*, Brisbane, 1970: G. Blainey, *The Rise of Broken Hill*, Melbourne, 1968, ch. 3: R. Gollan, *The Coalminers of New South Wales*, Melbourne, 1963, pp. 88–94.

In 1891 the Queensland shearers struck when the pastoralists uni-
laterally adopted a new agreement. Several hundred non-union
shearers were imported from Melbourne, with police protection, whilst
the union shearers gathered in large camps near the major shearing
sheds. After more than three months the strike ended in victory for
the pastoralists. In 1894 trouble again flared up when a new shearing
agreement was proclaimed without reference to the union. On this
occasion there was a good deal of violence and arson, culminating in
a bold attack on the *Rodney*, a river steamer hired to carry non-union
shearers up the Darling. A party of unionists captured and burnt the
steamer under cover of darkness, after first marooning the strike-
breakers on an island and setting the crew adrift in a barge. Despite
the offer of a large reward for information, the culprits were never
brought to book, but other unionists were less fortunate. In 1891,
200 of the Queensland shearers were prosecuted on such charges as
conspiracy, intimidation, and riot, often on the basis of antiquated
British statutes; 82 men were imprisoned. In 1894 another 50 Queensland unionists were imprisoned on similar charges. In the meantime,
a four-month strike at Broken Hill in 1892 over the introduction of
contract mining had also ended in the gaoling of seven union leaders
for conspiracy. Moreover 1893 and 1896 witnessed further unsuccessful strikes by the New South Wales coalminers. By the middle of the
1890s, mineowners and pastoralists had for the time being asserted
their right to choose their own employees and name their own terms.

The cumulative effect of this industrial turmoil was considerable
but complex. The majority of Australians lived in cities; mines and
shearing sheds were remote from their experience and they were easily
alarmed by exaggerated press reports that the country districts were
on the brink of civil war, and sympathetic to editorial demands for
the preservation of law and order. In some respects this was as true
of urban workers as of other city dwellers but their response was more
complicated; trade unionists, in particular, could not fail to be affected
by the spectacle of their fellows being crushed by the weight of
constituted authority. Old assumptions about the harmony of interest
between master and man were called into question and in this sense
the strikes, through their very failure, were a stimulus to change. However the changes sought were such as would improve and hence
strengthen the existing social and political framework, rather than
destroy it. The eclipse of the 'new unions' of unskilled workers and
the disillusionment of socialists and utopians such as William Lane
left the leadership of the labour movement in the hands of moderates
drawn from the old craft union tradition. Disenchantment with the
strike weapon gave rise to a new interest in alternative methods of
settling industrial disputes, and plans to secure labour representation
in parliament received a boost.

Between 1856 and 1890 each of the colonies had evolved its own
political structures and traditions but their differences were for the
most part differences of degree rather than of kind. Political life

revolved around loosely organised parliamentary factions centred on a few strong leaders. Power was gained or lost as factions formed coalitions amongst themselves or attracted temporary support from some of the many independents. In this battle of the 'ins' and the 'outs' ministries at times rose and fell with alarming frequency but overall there was sufficient order and stability for the business of government to be carried on satisfactorily. This was facilitated by the high degree of consensus about the nature of politics which existed during these years of prosperity. It was accepted that 'Good Government' was primarily a matter of equitably distributing public works and services and encouraging the rapid exploitation of resources. Only occasionally were parliaments and public opinion polarized by major issues, notably land policy, education and free trade *versus* protection. For the most part, what was good for one section of the community was believed to be good for all and the idea of class or sectional parties and legislation was anathema. These assumptions gave a paradoxical but effective monopoly of political power to the burgeoning middle class.

During the 1890s these settled political practices and beliefs came under stress and major changes occurred. Of course the transition to organized party politics had begun before 1890 but whilst the good years lasted the tempo of change was slow. With the onset of the depression however, the pressure for change intensified from both above and below. At the parliamentary level, governments found that with retrenchment and budget-balancing the order of the day they could no longer rely on their public works programmes to hold the allegiance of their followers; it became necessary to find new methods of forming stable majorities. Meanwhile, within the community, groups and individuals adversely affected by the economic downturn abandoned the notion of a 'common good' and frankly turned to political action in defence of their special interests. When the effects of the strikes are added in, it is clear that circumstances were unusually favourable for the emergence of sectional or class-based political parties, though the extent of class-consciousness let alone class-warfare, should not be exaggerated.[24] The break in prosperity was not sufficiently prolonged to slacken permanently the grip of bourgeois values on Australian society – but it did allow the forces of change to make headway in a number of directions.

In New South Wales the late 1880s had seen the formation of free trade and protectionist parties, better organized and with a more coherent body of principles than the factions of earlier years.[25] The

[24] For a brief review of the literature on class consciousness in this period see R. Lawson, 'Class or Status? – The Social Structure of Brisbane in the 1890s', in *A.J.P.H., XVIII*, 3, December 1972.

[25] For an analysis of factional politics and the rise of free trade and protection parties see P. Loveday and A. W. Martin, *Parliament Factions and Parties: The*

1890s began with the free-traders in power under Sir Henry Parkes, but after the election of June 1891 Parkes held office only by favour of an entirely new force, the Labor party, which at its first attempt had won no less than thirty-five seats. The novelty of the Labor party lay in its overt allegiance to one section of the community, the working class, from which it sought votes and to which it promised reforms. Its organization and discipline went beyond anything previously seen in the colony. From the start it had organic links with the trade union movement and a published platform to which all members were expected to adhere. Day-by-day tactics were worked out by regular caucus meetings of Labor parliamentarians. The platform of the new party was less original, being made up of proposals for the reform of working hours and conditions already formulated by the Trades and Labour Council, and some more general social and political reforms most of which were also supported by other organizations. Of socialism, Labor's policy statements contained scarcely a whiff.

Labor's spectacular arrival on the political scene took many people by surprise but it was not quite the 'bolt from the blue' that it seemed, for trade unionists had been talking about the need to enter the parliamentary arena since at least the mid-1880s. Their plans gathered momentum when in September 1889 the New South Wales parliament passed a payment of members act, to come into force after the next election. Within a few weeks P. J. Brennan initiated discussion within the Trades and Labour Council on the desirability of bringing forward Labor candidates and drawing up a platform. In January 1890 a special meeting of the Council carried Brennan's motion, and although no election was expected before 1892 plans were laid for a Labour Electoral League to be set up in every con-stituency, the first being founded in Balmain in March 1891. The importance of payment for parliamentary service is obvious, for with-out it few unionists would have been able to afford to enter parlia-ment, but it is best described as a precondition rather than a cause of the birth of the Labor party, the real origins of which lay in the character and experience of the trade union movement in New South Wales. In this connection it is worth noting that payment of members had been the rule in Victoria since 1870 without a Labor party having appeared. The idea of political action received further encouragement of a rather different kind from the Maritime Strike. The strike was initially something of a distraction in that it monopolized the time and energy of labour leaders, but ultimately its failure gave Brennan's scheme a valuable boost, particularly in the country districts. The Sydney Trades and Labour Council would almost certainly have put forward parliamentary candidates in 1891 even had there been no strike – but not on such a large scale nor with such success. As it was,

First Thirty Years of Responsible Government in New South Wales, 1856–1889, Melbourne, 1966.

when the election came on earlier than had been anticipated, Labor was relatively well prepared.[26]

Part of the scholarly controversy which surrounds labour's entry into politics relates to the question of whether the New South Wales Labor party was the first modern political party in Australia, and as such, a model for non-Labor.[27] This is the sort of dispute in which opinion counts for almost as much as fact and no answer is likely to satisfy everyone. On the negative side, it may be observed that many of Labor's organizational devices had been tried out by the free traders and protectionists before 1891. Caucus meetings, for example had been common for years though they had not been so frequent nor so binding as they were to become under Labor. Furthermore, although most of the special characteristics of the party were present from the beginning, it took several years of savage internecine strife to perfect them. However to argue that the ground had been prepared for Labor's emergence, and that it did not spring forth fully armed, is not to deny that it was a phenomenon such as Australia had not seen before.

Between 1891 and 1895 all parties tried to adjust to the changed situation.[28] In October 1891 Parkes, too steeped in the old ways to relish his dependence on Labor, retired to the back-benches, and Labor support was transferred to Dibbs and the protectionists. During its three years in office the Dibbs government was responsible for a very important revision of the colony's electoral procedures and passed some minor industrial legislation, but its popularity with Labor was dimmed by its unsympathetic treatment of the Broken Hill strikers in 1892. Dibbs himself handled the bank crisis of 1893 skilfully but had no answers to the problems posed by the depression. Meanwhile, the free-trade leadership had passed to George Reid. With his short

[26] For the details of the genesis of the Labor Party, including a lively controversy over the extent to which the Maritime Strike was responsible for diverting the trade union movement from direct action into politics, see J. Philipp, '1890 – the Turning Point in Labour History?' in *H.S.*, *14*, May 1950: J. E. O'Connor, '1890 – a Turning Point in Labour History: A Reply to Mrs Philipp', in *H.S.*, *16*, May 1951: N. B. Nairn, 'The Role of the Trades and Labour Council in N.S.W., 1871–1891', in *H.S.*, *28*, May 1957: R. Gollan, *Radical and Working Class Politics: A Study of Eastern Australia, 1850–1910*, Melbourne, 1960, ch. 8: 'Peter Joseph Brennan', in *Australian Dictionary of Biography, 3*, Melbourne, 1969.

[27] See N. B. Nairn's review of R. Gollan, *Radical and Working Class Politics: A Study in Eastern Australia, 1850–1910*, Melbourne, 1960, in *H.S.*, *35*, November 1960: P. Loveday, 'A Note on Nineteenth Century Party Organization in New South Wales', in *H.S.*, *36*, May 1961: P. Loveday and A. W. Martin, *Parliament, Factions and Parties: The First Thirty Years of Responsible Government in New South Wales, 1856–1889*, Melbourne, 1966, esp. pp. 153–4.

[28] For N.S.W. politics in the 1890s see G. N. Hawker, *The Parliament of New South Wales 1856–1965*, Sydney, 1971, especially ch. 10: A. W. Martin, 'Free Trade and Protectionist Parties in New South Wales', in *H.S.*, *23*, November 1954: N. B. Nairn, 'J. C. Watson in New South Wales Politics, 1890–1894', in *R.A.H.S.J.*, *48*, 2, June 1962. A most important work published recently is N. B. Nairn, *Civilising Capitalism: The Labor Movement in New South Wales 1870–1900*, Canberra, 1973.

legs, enormous belly, and squeaky voice, Reid was a cartoonist's delight. His laziness and vulgarity were notorious, and many other politicians, even in his own party, regarded him as an unprincipled opportunist. The Sydney public loved him. Buffoonery notwithstanding, Reid was perhaps the shrewdest politician of his generation in Australia. He won the 1894 election with a promise that he would balance the budget by directly taxing land and incomes, a policy which had the advantage of being compatible with free-trade yet appealing to the Labor party, which felt that protectionist tariffs bore too heavily on the working man. Reid then united the disparate wings of his own party and consolidated Labor support through a head-on collision with the Legislative Council, from which he emerged with as much of his programme intact as suited him. In the process the free-traders had strengthened their electoral machinery and although their disciplinary procedures were not as formalized as Labor's, by 1895 Reid could rely on a solid vote on important issues.

In the next few sessions Reid's mastery over party and parliament resulted in major social reforms being enacted together with valuable modernizing legislation such as the Public Service Act of 1895. By this time the Labor contingent had overcome their teething troubles. Their ranks had been thinned by internal disagreements on the tariff issue but those who remained were pledged to accept party discipline. In 1894 fifteen official candidates were returned plus twelve independent Labor men, four of whom later accepted an amended pledge. For the remainder of the decade Labor strength remained at about nineteen – nothing like enough to form a government but sufficient to decide which of the other parties should be in power. In J. S. T. McGowen, its official leader, and W. A. Holman, both future premiers of New South Wales, and J. C. Watson and W. M. Hughes, both future Australian prime ministers, the party had an abundance of talent. It probably owed most to Chris Watson, whose tact and patience were invaluable in solving the party's extra-parliamentary organizational problems, culminating in the formation of the Political Labor League in 1895. The bewildered protectionists came least well out of this period of adjustment. They were thoroughly outgeneralled by Reid, much to the chagrin of the liberal wing of the party which regarded itself as the natural ally of Labor. Not until 1899 were the protectionists able to regain office, by which time Dibbs had been succeeded by William Lyne.

Political developments in the other colonies must be surveyed more briefly and with an eye mainly to variations from the New South Wales pattern. Victoria in the 1880s was governed by a coalition of liberals and constitutionalists, the two parties which had been thrown up by the constitutional battles of the two previous decades.[29] At

29 On Victorian politics see G. Serle, *The Rush To Be Rich*, Melbourne, 1971: S. M. Ingham, 'Political Parties in the Victorian Legislative Assembly 1880–1900', in *H.S., 15*, November 1950.

first glance these parties were more coherent than their New South Wales equivalents but their extra-parliamentary organization was fitful and within each party there were shifting factional groups. When the land boom burst, the coalition which had presided over it was ejected from office and then slowly disintegrated. Whilst the depression was at it worst a series of unstable governments floundered with problems which were beyond their grasp. However by 1894 the old coalition and its rather heterogeneous opposition of the 1880s had regrouped into two parties, the Conservatives led by James Patterson, and the Liberals who under the leadership of George Turner held office, with one brief interruption, for the remainder of the decade.

Though sincere and hardworking, Turner was an unimpressive man of limited ability but his careful nursing of Victoria's finances proved effective, and with men like Alfred Deakin, Isaac Isaacs, A. J. Peacock and H. B. Higgins on his side of the house, his lack of imagination was more than compensated for. The Liberal hegemony in the late 1890s was underpinned by the support of a small Labor group in parliament. Founded in 1891 and re-formed as the United Labour and Liberal party in 1894, Victorian Labor held at least a dozen seats from 1892 onwards but could not improve much on that figure. It found it difficult to establish a stable extra-parliamentary machine, and was handicapped by the need to compete for working class support with a well-established Liberal party, of which it was sometimes said to be merely a faction. Certainly the Victorian Laborites were less ready than their New South Wales brethren to switch their support between the other parties, and they were sometimes upstaged by such genuinely radical Liberals as Higgins and Isaacs, but in a quieter way they exercised more influence than has sometimes been recognized. This was particularly true between 1894 and 1897 when Turner would have been hard put to it to carry on without their support.

Whereas the 1890s brought an end to coalition government in Victoria, in Queensland the trend was reversed.[30] In 1890 Sir Samuel Griffith, who throughout the 1880s had led the Liberal party, joined with his erstwhile arch-enemy Sir Thomas McIlwraith, to form what was derisorily known as the 'Griffilwraith'. There was nothing wraith-like about the coalition however, for despite five changes of leader it endured almost to the end of the decade. In giving up their separate identity the Liberals left a clear field which Labor was quick to exploit. The first official Labor representative came in through a by-election in 1891 and in 1893 the party won sixteen seats to become the largest opposition group, though not until 1898 did it accept the constitutional role of official opposition. In 1899 the Dawson ministry, though it held office for a week only, became the first Labor government

---

[30] For Queensland see D. J. Murphy *et al.*, Eds., *Prelude to Power*, Brisbane, 1970: A. A. Morrison, 'Liberal Party Organizations Before 1900', in *Historical Society of Queensland Journal*, 5, 1, 1953.

in Australia or indeed the world. Thus in terms of status Labor had achieved more in Queensland by the end of the century than elsewhere though its legislative harvest was small.

In South Australia a period of unstable factionalism drew to a close in 1893.[31] The general election of that year provided the first real test of strength of two new organizations. The United Labor party, founded in 1891 by the Adelaide Trades and Labour Council, much along the lines of New South Wales, won eight seats, and the success of two independent candidates gave Labor a total strength of ten in the new assembly. The National Defence League had been founded shortly afterwards by a group of Adelaide business and professional men and pastoralists, under the leadership of R. C. Baker, with a view to resisting both Labor and the movement in favour of a 'single tax' on land. In its membership and aims the League closely resembled a body called the National Association – better known to *Bulletin* readers as the 'National Ass' – formed by conservative property-owners in New South Wales in August 1891.[32] The National Association took an active part in New South Wales politics in the early 1890s but its adherence to the outmoded concept of supporting 'sound' men regardless of whether they were free traders or protectionists meant that the rise of party politics soon rendered it redundant. However the National Defence League gradually became the extra-parliamentary wing of the conservative group in the South Australian parliament led by Sir John Downer. In 1893 twenty-one Conservatives won assembly seats, many of them with Defence League backing. The remaining twenty-three seats were won by Liberals, and in response to the developments on their flanks this hitherto divided group united under the leadership of C. C. Kingston to form a ministry which, with Labor support, lasted until 1899. Kingston was a tough-minded man with an explosive temperament; his private life and vituperative attacks on opponents scandalized respectable society but the Adelaide working class idolized him. As Kingston's views on a number of topics were more radical than those of Labor, the alliance was a natural one, though not without its tensions, and resulted in a good deal of 'progressive' legislation.

The winds of change were less noticeable in Tasmania.[33] Although 'liberal' and 'conservative' groups alternated in office in a reasonably methodical way, these labels were not very meaningful and party organization was minimal. Trade unionism was weak until the rise of the west coast mining unions at the turn of the century, and attempts to secure labour representation in parliament met with no success

---

[31] For South Australian politics see J. B. Hirst, *Adelaide and the Country 1870–1917*, Melbourne, 1973.

[32] For an account of the formation and early activities of the Association see its journal, *Liberty*, 17 December 1894.

[33] For Tasmanian politics see M. D. McRae, 'Some Aspects of the Origins of the Tasmanian Labour Party', in *T.H.R.A.P.*, III, 2, April 1954.

until 1903. In Western Australia the situation was different again, for that colony became self-governing only in 1890 and its first premier, John Forrest, was still in power at the end of the decade.[34] It was a period of 'roads and bridges' politics in a colony hitherto starved of funds, and Forrest's ability to satisfy the demand for public works stifled opposition. However the gold which made Forrest's lavish spending possible also accelerated the rate of political development and after his departure to federal politics in 1901 the transition to party politics was rapid. The first Labor members were elected in 1901, and three years later Western Australia had its first taste of Labor government – well ahead of New South Wales or Victoria.

Overall then, it may fairly be said that by the end of the 1890s political groupings were fewer in number, more cohesive, and better organized than ever before; independents were a fast vanishing breed. In each of the major colonies the labour movement had at least one foot inside the parliamentary door and the approach of federation ensured that the stronger Labor parties would take steps to encourage their weaker brethren in order to achieve nationwide organization. On the non-Labor side the picture was more confused, for the line dividing the other parties varied from colony to colony and only in some cases did their parliamentary discipline and extra-parliamentary organization approach that of Labor. However the fiscal issue, one major obstacle to further rationalization of non-Labor politics within and between the colonies, was within sight of resolution. Another complicating factor, the divergent interests of rural and urban property-owners, had been brought into the open by depression and drought but was as yet imperfectly understood.[35] Of more immediate concern to all parties was the uncertain future course of Liberal-Labor and Liberal-Conservative relationships, and not until this was crystallised by the 'fusion' of 1909 was the transition to party politics complete.

Throughout the 1890s though, Liberal and Labor groups in most colonies worked together harmoniously and fruitfully to make possible what Manning Clark has called Australia's 'second bite' at reform.[36] After the rash of democratic measures adopted by South Australia, Victoria, and New South Wales in the 1850s these colonies had rested on their oars for thirty years and the others had made little attempt to overhaul them. However towards the close of the century Western Australia (1899) and Queensland (1890) limited the duration of parliament to three years, and Western Australia (1893) and Tasmania (1901) abolished property qualifications for members of their Legislative Assemblies and introduced manhood suffrage, to

[34] See B. K. de Garis and C. T. Stannage, 'From Responsible Government to Party Politics in Western Australia', in *A.E.H.R.*, *VIII*, 1, March 1968

[35] For a detailed study of this question see B. D. Graham, *The Formation of the Australian Country Parties*, Canberra, 1966, chs. 2 and 3.

[36] C. M. H. Clark, *Select Documents in Australian History: 1851–1900*, Melbourne, 1955, p. xii.

make these practices common to all colonies. In addition, there were three further refinements of the system of parliamentary representation. Firstly, between 1886 and 1900 all colonies followed Victoria's earlier example and commenced paying their members of parliament. Secondly, there was a general move to abolish plural voting. Hitherto in all colonies except South Australia a man who owned property in several constituencies could vote in each. For example it was alleged in 1899, not altogether jocularly, that Alexander Forrest, the premier's brother, had a vote for every one of the forty-four seats in the Western Australian Legislative Assembly.[37] Naturally plural voting was one of Labor's first targets and its abolition in New South Wales in 1893 was soon emulated elsewhere, the last colony to fall into line being Western Australia in 1907. The third important innovation was the extension of voting rights to women; South Australia (1894) and Western Australia (1899) set the lead and all parliaments had followed suit by 1909.[38]

The social legislation of the period was even more significant, for prior to 1890 very little had been done in this field. For example, whereas only Victoria had hitherto made any pretence of regulating working conditions in factories, between 1894 and 1900 all colonies except Tasmania accepted this responsibility. Adequate ventilation, sanitation, and protective screening of dangerous machinery became compulsory, conditions of apprenticeship were controlled, the employment of children prohibited, and the hours of work of women and juveniles under sixteen were restricted. Maximum working hours for shop-assistants were also specified, and provisions made for one half-day holiday in the six-day working week though this was still not the norm. The Victorian Factories and Shops Act of 1896 broke even more novel ground by establishing wages boards empowered to fix minimum wages and thus prevent 'sweated' labour and pass on the benefits of tariff protection to the employees. By 1900, twenty-two industries came under this legislation and South Australia was taking steps to copy it.[39]

The settlement of industrial disputes was yet another area in which governments began to interest themselves. At first voluntary Councils of Conciliation were tried but these achieved little. The unions were much more co-operative than before the Maritime Strike, but whilst depression conditions lasted the employers would seldom agree to refer

---

[37] *Western Australia: Parliamentary Debates (New Series)*, XV, p. 1523.

[38] C. M. H. Clark, *Select Documents in Australian History: 1851–1900*, Melbourne, 1955, pp. 374–8 lists in tabular form the dates at which eight democratic reforms were enacted in the various colonies, though with a few errors.

[39] For the details of factory legislation see W. P. Reeves, *State Experiments in Australia and New Zealand*, London, 1902, II, ch. 1. On the minimum wage see P. G. Macarthy, 'Victorian Wages Boards: Their Origins and the Doctrine of the Living Wage', in *The Journal of Industrial Relations, 10*, 2, July 1968: P. G. Macarthy, 'Employers, the Tariff, and Legal Wage Determination in Australia – 1890–1910', in *The Journal of Industrial Relations, 12*, 2, July 1970.

disputes to such bodies. Interest therefore shifted to compulsory arbitration, which Kingston had made several abortive attempts to introduce in South Australia. New Zealand showed the way with its Arbitration Act of 1894. Western Australia was the first Australian colony to follow suit, in 1900, but the New South Wales Act of 1901 was much more significant. It founded an Arbitration Court, consisting of an employers' representative, a union representative, and a judge, with the right to settle strikes and disputes and make awards binding on an industry as a whole. This device to make industrial relations 'a new province for law and order' was to become an unusual but enduring feature of Australian society.[40]

The 1890s also saw the introduction of taxation on land and incomes in most colonies. This development was applauded by Liberal and Labor sympathizers as a method of redistributing wealth; land tax, in particular, was seen as a way of exacting payment from the squatters who had locked up large tracts of land for a small outlay. It was popularized by the American writer, Henry George, who visited Australia in 1890, though his concept of a 'single tax' on land as the sole source of public revenue and a panacea for all social ills was never seriously tried. During 1894–5 Tasmania, New South Wales and Victoria all introduced land and income tax (land tax was not new in Victoria) and South Australia replaced its flat-rate taxation of 1884 with graduated taxes designed to bear more heavily on high incomes and large estates. Yet another indication of heightened social concern was the growing recognition of the need for old-age pensions. Victoria, South Australia, and New South Wales all appointed commissions to investigate the desirability and practicability of pensions schemes and in 1900 New South Wales and Victoria both passed old-age pension acts. The New South Wales scheme, the better thought-out of the two, provided for men and women over 65 years of age who had lived in the colony for 25 years and whose 'accumulated property' did not exceed £390 in value to be eligible for a pension of £26 *per annum.*[41]

Prominent amongst those excluded from the pension were Aborigines and Asians, two of the blind spots of this generation. During the 1890s the established practice of excluding the Chinese broadened into a fully-fledged 'White Australia' policy. The attention of colonial leaders was forcibly drawn to Japan by her victory over China in 1895 and the Anglo-Japanese Commercial Treaty of 1894 to which the

[40] On the origins of arbitration see W. P. Reeves, *State Experiments in Australia and New Zealand*, 2 vols., London, 1902: R. Gollan, *Radical and Working Class Politics: A Study of Eastern Australia, 1850–1910*, Melbourne, 1960, ch. 9: P. G. Macarthy, 'Wage Determination in New South Wales – 1890–1921', in *The Journal of Industrial Relations, 10, 3*, November 1968.

[41] On taxation and pensions see T. H. Kewley, *Social Security in Australia*, Sydney, 1965, chs. 2–4: W. P. Reeves, *State Experiments in Australia and New Zealand*, London, 1902, *II*, 2: C. M. H. Clark, *Select Documents in Australian History: 1851–1900*, Melbourne, 1955, pp. 642–52.

colonies were invited to adhere. At an intercolonial conference held in Sydney in 1896 they decided not merely to spurn the treaty but to take precautions against Japanese migration. Reid and others voiced fears that if a Japanese minority were allowed to build up in Australia there would be a risk of subsequent intervention by Japan. Queensland later went back on this decision and became a party to the Commercial Treaty, but the other colonies passed bills which prohibited the immigration of all Asians, Africans and Polynesians. These were disallowed by the British government, but after negotiations three colonies adopted an indirect method of exclusion used by Natal. Their acts provided for the exclusion of any intending migrant unable to pass a literacy test in a European language. This procedure, which was taken over by the federal parliament in 1901, was very flexible in that the language prescribed could be varied to suit the occasion, and had the advantage of avoiding any reference to colour or nationality, though no one was in any doubt about its purpose.[42]

Whilst the barriers to coloured migration were being perfected, there was a growing tendency in those colonies where Aborigines were still numerous for them to be confined to reserves. Under its act of 1897, Queensland provided for Aborigines and persons of mixed descent to be put under the legal charge of protectors, to be prohibited from drinking alcohol, and to live outside special reserves only if in an approved job. This legislation became a model for other parts of Australia. The intention which lay behind this change in policy was benevolent but paternalistic. It was believed that by these means the Aborigines, thought in any case to be a dying race, could be protected from further atrocities and degradation. But the price was a heavy one in that policies which had some justification at the frontier were applied indiscriminately; the Aborigines became institutionalized and lost the legal equality which had hitherto always been theirs, at least in theory.[43]

One striking fact which emerges from this review of the legislation of the period is the extent to which Australians had come to expect their governments to play an active part in the economic and social life of the country.[44] Government initiative in promoting economic development had been characteristic of the colonies from their earliest days; now they were also expected to regulate working conditions and accept the responsibility for social problems. This attitude was grounded in the utopian visions of a 'brave new world' to which the

[42] A. T. Yarwood, *Asian Migration to Australia: The Background to Exclusion 1896–1923*, Melbourne, 1964, ch. 1.

[43] C. D. Rowley, *Aboriginal Policy and Practice, I, The Destruction of Aboriginal Society*, Canberra, 1970, and *II, Outcasts in White Australia*, see especially pp. 177–86.

[44] On the general expectations of Australians about the role of the state see N. G. Butlin, 'Colonial Socialism in Australia, 1860–1900', in H. G. Aitken, Ed., *The State and Economic Growth*, New York, 1959: S. Encel, 'The Concept of the State in Australian Politics', in *A.J.P.H., VI*, 1, May 1960.

long years of prosperity had given rise, but took practical expression only when the depression revealed the gulf between vision and reality. In the work of bridging this gulf, middle-class Liberals joined hands with the Labor party, and credit for the achievements of the 1890s must be shared between these groups. In New South Wales Labor held the balance of power for most of the time but the 'concessions' made in return for its 'support' were quantitatively and qualitatively little different from the measures sponsored in Victoria and South Australia by relatively independent Liberal governments.

Both parties to the alliance tended to be pragmatic in their approach, and most Liberal and Labor parliamentarians were more interested in righting wrongs and solving problems than in following through a coherent political philosophy. This is not to say that ideas played no part in the politics of the period. The popularity of the 'prophet of San Francisco', Henry George, has already been mentioned. Following his 1890 visit single tax leagues sprang up all over Australia and their members infiltrated both the labour movement and some Liberal organizations.[45] Another American to make an impact was Edward Bellamy, a utopian socialist and the author of *Looking Backward*, a piece of political science-fiction which won a wide readership. Bellamy's leading disciple in Australia was William Lane, the editor of the Queensland *Worker*, which serialized *Looking Backward*. But Lane's departure in 1893 to found a 'New Australia' in Paraguay confirmed the waning appeal of utopianism.[46] Although less publicized than these exotic imports, British doctrines of co-operative, fabian and state socialism had their adherents. However even in New South Wales where quite a few Labor MP's were socialists of one kind or another, the Labor platform was by no means socialist in character. The need to placate middle-of-the-road opinion for electoral purposes was one reason for this, as was the anti-socialist stance of the Catholic church which was already closely associated with Labor. But the decisive factor was probably the pragmatic attitude of most trade unions which wanted improved wages and conditions rather than the reconstruction of society.[47] On the Liberal side, there were few – Bernhard Wise was one exception – whose reading had progressed from Bentham and Mill to T. H. Green, though there was a general willingness to

[45] See F. Picard, 'Henry George and the Labour Split of 1891', in *H.S.*, *21*, November 1953.

[46] On Bellamy see R. Gollan, 'The Australian Impact' in S. E. Bowman, Ed., *Edward Bellamy Abroad*, New York, 1962. The latest of a number of books on Lane and Paraguay is by G. Souter, *A Peculiar People*, Sydney, 1968. See also G. Hannan, 'William Lane – Mateship and Utopia' in D. J. Murphy *et al.*, Eds., *Prelude to Power*, Brisbane, 1970.

[47] On socialism within the N.S.W. Labor Party see P. J. O'Farrell, 'The Australian Socialist League and the Labour Movement, 1887–1891', in *H.S.*, *30*, May 1958: D. W. Rawson, *Labor in Vain?*, Melbourne, 1966, esp. chs. 1 and 4. On the Catholic influence see P. Ford, *Cardinal Moran and the A.L.P.*, Melbourne, 1966.

experiment with particular schemes borrowed from Britain, Germany or New Zealand for guaranteeing equality of opportunity.

In view of the piecemeal, ameliorative, and often derivative character of much of the 'advanced' legislation enacted it may be questioned whether the colonies altogether deserved the reputation they enjoyed around the turn of the century as a 'social laboratory'. On closer inspection a number of the reforms seem less impressive. For example, the sudden popularity of land and income tax owed at least as much to the desperate need for government revenue as to enthusiasm for the redistribution of wealth. Similarly, there are grounds for suspecting that women's suffrage was introduced in South and Western Australia not so much because Kingston and Forrest were passionately interested in women's rights as because they calculated that the majority of women in their colonies lived in those areas from which they received the strongest support. Moreover it was easy for Forrest as premier of a predominantly rural colony to please local trade unionists by passing Australia's first compulsory arbitration act. Some of the factory legislation too, was in Coghlan's words 'not called forth by the peculiar circumstances of labour in the colonies' but blindly followed British precedent with neither 'originality nor intelligence'.[48]

Nevertheless, the legislative achievements of the 1890s remain striking even when due weight has been given to these doubts and qualifications. In this period, many of the foundations of twentieth century Australia were laid. The rate and direction of political and social experimentation were surprisingly uniform across the continent and when the first national parliament met the raw materials from which broad national policies might be fashioned were ready to hand. Ironically though, the impulse towards reform and the impulse towards national union were often rather uneasy bedfellows and amidst the other excitement of the nineties, the federation movement seemed at times to be losing rather than gaining ground. However in the end the dawn of the new century brought to a close the colonial chapter in Australian history and the union of the six colonies in 'one indissoluble federal commonwealth', inaugurated on 1 January 1901, capped off an eventful decade. The significance of the decision to federate has become more and more clear with the passage of time. For if political federation did not, of itself, make Australia a nation, it certainly opened the way.

The rather halting progress of the federal cause arose in part from the fact that although federation was a political matter which required political action it cut across the political alignments of the day. Since some federalists were free-traders and some were protectionists, some Liberals and some Conservatives, the older political groups treated federation as a 'non-party' issue, and Labor's interests lay elsewhere. With the existing political machinery not available to it, the federation

[48] T. A. Coghlan, *Labour and Industry in Australia*, London, 1918, *4*, p. 2096.

movement was for many years dependent on the enthusiasm of influential individuals. First amongst these was Henry Parkes, the Grand
Old Man of New South Wales politics, who resolutely turned
his back on the Federal Council set up in the 1880s and insisted
on a fresh start.[49] In 1889 Parkes made private overtures to the
Victorian and Queensland governments and on getting a lukewarm
response, he drew public attention to the issue in a famous speech
delivered in the small country town of Tenterfield. The other colonies
believed that if New South Wales was in earnest about federation it
should join the Federal Council, but they finally assented to a conference, which met in Melbourne in February 1890. That gathering
decided that the time was ripe for a more organic union than the
Federal Council and arrangements were made for a National Australasian Convention to be held in Sydney in 1891.[50]

Each of the six Australian colonies was represented at this 'August
Assembly' and so also was New Zealand, though even at this stage
the likelihood of New Zealand federating was slight. The forty-six
delegates included many premiers and ex-premiers and there were few
who lacked cabinet experience. Parkes was appropriately voted into
the chair, where his dignified manner and long white hair and beard
made him an impressive figure, but he had not fully recovered from
a broken leg sustained a few months before and he was not the driving
force of earlier years. Once the formalities were over the real leader
of the Convention proved to be Samuel Griffith, Queensland's cool,
precise, and assured lawyer-premier and it was he who did most to
shape the draft constitution which was the main work of the Convention.[51] Though the 1891 draft was thrown back into the melting
pot at the Conventions of 1897–8 its basic framework was not fundamentally changed and hence in a very real sense Griffith was the
principal architect of Australia's twentieth century political structure.
However, there were many hurdles still to be surmounted before
federation was accomplished.

When the delegates returned to their colonies they found other
matters urgently claiming attention for the slide into depression was

49 Parkes' sincerity as a federalist and his motives for taking the initiative have
provoked a good deal of speculation over the years; no adequate study has yet been
published but for two recent comments see W. G. McMinn, 'Sir Henry Parkes as a
Federalist', in *H.S.*, 47, October 1966: J. A. La Nauze, *The Making of the Australian
Constitution*, Melbourne, 1972, pp. 6–10.

50 The reader who requires a more detailed narrative of the federal movement
must turn, in the absence of an up-to-date general history of the subject, to two
major contemporary accounts; the Introduction to J. Quick and R. R. Garran,
The Annotated Constitution of the Australian Commonwealth, Sydney, 1901:
Alfred Deakin, *The Federal Story*, Melbourne, 1944, 2nd ed. 1963, (written in
1898–1900).

51 A succinct interpretative account of the Convention and its constitution may
be found in J. A. La Nauze, *The Making of the Australian Constitution*, Melbourne, 1972, chs. 3–5.

gathering momentum. Several parliaments desultorily looked at the draft constitution, but in New South Wales, from whence a lead was sought, the arrival of the Labor party had thrown politics into confusion. Parkes resigned in October 1891 without having put the draft bill before parliament; Dibbs, the next premier, was an anti-federalist; and Labor was primarily interested in immediate reforms within the colony. By 1893 the whole movement had run out of steam and Parkes was an ailing and embittered back-bencher who no longer commanded much influence. All was not lost, however. New leaders emerged, and the economic and industrial upheavals which had temporarily drawn attention away from federation helped, in the long run, to demonstrate the dangers of disunity.

Parkes had handed on the federal 'leadership' to Edmund Barton, a Sydney barrister and protectionist politician. A tall, handsome man in his early forties, with a very erect carriage though already overweight, Barton was liked and respected but thought to be lazy. This reputation he belied by tirelessly stumping New South Wales in an effort to arouse grass-roots support for federation. It was largely at his instigation that federal leagues were formed, first in the Riverina and then throughout the colony, including Sydney. In Victoria, the Australian Natives' Association mobilized public opinion in a similar fashion and in July 1893 interested groups from the two colonies conferred at the border town of Corowa.[52] The Corowa Conference had no official standing, but it secured its place in the history of Australia by passing a resolution moved by Dr John Quick of Bendigo which suggested a *modus operandi* for the renewal of the federation movement. This was that another convention should be held but that this time the delegates should be elected by the people rather than appointed by parliaments and the constitution they drafted should be submitted directly to the electors of each colony by referendum. The merit of this scheme was that it would lift federation out of the cross-currents of parliamentary politics, but it was first of all necessary to get the parliaments of the colonies to agree to the procedure.

The first step in this direction was taken by George Reid within a few weeks of assuming office in New South Wales in 1894, when he asked the other premiers to meet him in Hobart in January 1895 to discuss federation. Federalists in and outside his own colony suspected Reid's sincerity, for he had been instrumental in preventing Parkes from proceeding with the Commonwealth Bill after the 1891 Convention, but they cautiously welcomed his initiative. The premiers duly met and agreed, though not without a great deal of debate, that another convention should be held. The decision was a crucial

---

52 On the revival of interest in federation and the Corowa Conference see J. Quick and R. R. Garran, *The Annotated Constitution of the Australian Commonwealth*, Sydney, 1901, pp. 150–55: D. I. Wright, 'The Australasian Federation League in the Federal Movement in New South Wales, 1893–1899', *R.A.H.S.J.*, 57, 1, March 1971: A. W. Martin, 'Economic Influences in the "New Federation Movement"' in *H.S.*, 21, November 1953.

one. By 1895 circumstances were very favourable in that the economy was on the mend but the lessons of the depression had not yet had time to lose their force. Moreover the unprecedented political stability of the later nineties meant that five of the six premiers present at Hobart – Reid, Turner, Kingston, Forrest and Braddon – remained in office until at least 1899 and once committed to federation were in a position to see to its accomplishment.

The new Convention met for the first time in Adelaide in March 1897. After a month's work it adjourned to allow the colonial parliaments to scrutinize its work and make suggestions; two further lengthy sittings were then held, in Sydney in September 1897 and in Melbourne in January-February 1898.[53] New Zealand was not represented this time and nor, despite renewed overtures during each of the adjournments, was Queensland. Among the other delegations there were many new faces, reflecting the shake-up of colonial politics occasioned by the depression. There were more lawyers, and the proportion of Australian-born was considerably higher, but otherwise they were not markedly different from the men of 1891. Nearly all were experienced politicians from professional or commercial backgrounds; only one delegate, William Trenwith of Victoria, could plausibly be described as a representative of the labour movement. Parkes was dead and Griffith was doubly debarred from participation by his own appointment as a judge and his colony's refusal to send a delegation; Kingston and Barton, who had been his 'adjutants', were this time elected President and Leader respectively. Barton managed the conduct of business and with Richard O'Connor and Sir John Downer did most of the detailed drafting, but he did not dominate as Griffith had done in 1891. It was a team effort. Reid and Turner jealously guarded the interests of the large colonies; Forrest, Braddon and Josiah Symon those of the small; Symon and Isaac Isaacs were the Drafting Committee's most acute critics; Isaacs, Trenwith and H. B. Higgins were amongst the ablest spokesmen for the radical point of view, William McMillan the most respected conservative. Bernhard Wise and Alfred Deakin also deserve to be listed in the front rank; Deakin, in particular, was a very effective mediator between conflicting interests and did his best work behind the scenes. His talents in this direction were much needed.

It was generally accepted that there should be a 'Commonwealth of Australia', with a bicameral federal parliament to which specified powers would be transferred, all other matters to be left with the existing parliaments of the colonies, or states, as they would become known after federation. However, thorny problems arose concerning the relationship between the two houses of the parliament, and the allocation of powers as between the federal and state governments and parliaments. Underlying these problems was the fear of the less

[53] On the conventions and their work see J. A. La Nauze, *The Making of the Australian Constitution*, Melbourne, 1972, chs. 7–14.

populous colonies that the new parliament and government would be dominated by New South Wales and Victoria, and the wish of all colonies to retain their own individuality and rights as far as possible. Compromises were necessary if federation was to become a reality and one by one these were hammered out.

The most important related to the Senate, which was to be the guardian of state-rights. To allay the fears of the small colonies it was resolved that all states should be equally represented in the Senate, and in general its powers were to be the same as those of the lower house, but though it might reject financial measures, it was not to be permitted to amend them. This last proviso was enough to ensure that federal cabinets would be made and un-made in the population-based House of Representatives – though the Senate would have to be taken seriously. Another major decision was that customs duties on intercolonial trade should end with federation and that the right to levy duties on overseas trade should pass to the federal government. This disposed of the free trade *versus* protection issue for the moment but since tariffs were the principal source of government revenue at that time the colonies were afraid of financial strangulation. The Convention's last word on this subject was a clause which became known as the 'Braddon Blot' and which provided that the federal government should return three-quarters of its customs revenue to the states. Other details of the constitution, important as they were, cannot be discussed here save to note that in addition to such obvious powers as defence, immigration, external affairs, posts and telegraphs, *et cetera*, the federal parliament was allotted a power of conciliation and arbitration in industrial disputes extending beyond a single state and the power to pay old-age and invalid pensions. Had the constitution-making process reached finality in 1891 these provisions would certainly not have been included.

When the Convention had completed its work, Victoria, New South Wales, Tasmania, and South Australia promptly arranged for their electors to vote for or against federating on the basis of the draft constitution. For some weeks before the referendum, held on 3 and 4 June 1898, public meetings were held, pamphlets were circulated, and the pros and cons were fully canvassed in the press. Very few public men openly opposed federation as such, but the particular form of it embodied in the commonwealth bill came under heavy fire from some quarters. Most Labor party leaders and some ultra-radicals complained that concessions to the small colonies had made the bill undemocratic and they advised their supporters to vote against federation for this reason. Others, usually at the opposite end of the political spectrum, claimed that the bill inadequately protected the interests of their colonies and produced elaborate statistics 'proving' that their governments would be bankrupted. Then again, in every colony there were those who feared the impact of intercolonial free trade on local industries.

Federalists naturally felt obliged to reply to these objections and so

the debate came to centre less and less on the desirability or otherwise
of federation and more on particular clauses of the commonwealth
bill and their probable effects. However the 'Billites', as they were
called, also took every opportunity to stress the benefits which
federation might bring, such as commercial unity and national defence
and immigration policies, and appealed to national sentiment with
such slogans as 'One People – One Destiny'. As federation cut across
normal party lines *ad hoc* pro- and anti-federal organizations were
hastily formed to conduct the campaign in each colony. Most of those
who had been at the conventions supported federation but H. B.
Higgins of Victoria was amongst those who felt that the bill was not
democratic enough, and in New South Wales, George Reid confirmed
the fears of sceptics by announcing that although he personally would
vote 'Yes' he felt obliged to point out to the electors that the bill did
not entirely safeguard their interests. Reid has been severely criticised
for acting in this way but it must be said in his defence that his
objections to the bill were consistent with the line he had followed
at the Conventions, and as premier he had a particular responsibility
to his colony. Until very recently assessments of Reid's contribution
to the federation movement were coloured by the dislike and distrust
with which other leading federalists such as Barton, Wise and Deakin
regarded him. The tide of opinion has begun to turn in Reid's favour
but the last word on this subject has yet to be said.[54]

When the votes were counted it was learned that there was a
majority in favour of federation in each of the four colonies; in three
of them the verdict was unequivocal, but in New South Wales the
'Yes' vote fell short of the 80,000 minimum which the parliament of
that colony had prescribed. An impasse had been reached. Federation
without New South Wales would have been like a marriage without
the bride, but the other premiers were loath to agree to Reid's
immediate invitation to discuss amendments which might make the
bill more acceptable to his voters. However after a general election
had confirmed, albeit by the narrowest of margins, that Reid was still
entitled to speak on behalf of New South Wales, the other colonies
bowed to the inevitable. The premiers met in Melbourne in January
1899 and agreed upon six amendments to the commonwealth bill, five
to meet the wishes of New South Wales and one to meet the wishes
of Queensland, which had begun to emerge from hibernation. Several
of the alterations, though controversial at the time, have proved in-
consequential, but two at least were highly significant. One of these
was the decision to restrict the application of the 'Braddon Blot' to
the first ten years after federation; thereafter the federal parliament
would determine the most suitable arrangements. The other was a
stipulation that the federal capital was to be located in New South

[54] For a discussion of some of the pros and cons see W. G. McMinn, 'G. H. Reid
and Federation: The Case for the Defence', in *R.A.H.S.J.*, *49*, 4, December 1963:
L. E. Fredman, 'Yes-No Reid: A Case for the Prosecution', in *R.A.H.S.J.*, *50*, 2,
July 1964.

Wales though at least one hundred miles from Sydney – but that until a suitable site was agreed upon the new parliament should meet in Melbourne.[55]

Following the Premiers' Conference, Reid declared unambiguously for federation and he and Barton campaigned shoulder-to-shoulder prior to the second referendum, held on 20 June 1899. This time the 'Yes' vote comfortably exceeded the necessary target, and the other colonies then re-affirmed their decision by even larger majorities than before. The federal battle had been won but a few formalities remained. On 2 September the voters of Queensland also opted for federation but Western Australia, though it had participated in the Conventions, now hung back. The fast growing population of its goldfields region favoured federating and even talked of forming a separate colony to achieve this, but the dominant agricultural, pastoral and commercial interests believed that the colony was still too undeveloped to risk union with its more advanced neighbours. Forrest himself was a federalist at heart but he was reluctant to take the lists too openly against his own staunchest supporters and sought face-saving amendments. He thought he saw his opening when prior to enacting the commonwealth bill as a statute of the imperial parliament, the British government put forward amendments of its own. However the other colonies, whilst they grudgingly compromised with Britain, refused any concessions to Western Australia, which then at the eleventh hour voted to federate on the same terms as the others.[56] All six colonies were thus original members of the Commonwealth of Australia.

Altogether, just under six hundred thousand votes were cast in the 1899 series of referendums and of these just over two-and-a-half were in favour of federating for every one against.[57] In Victoria, Tasmania and South Australia there was a pro-federation majority in every constituency; in the other three colonies significant pockets of opposition were outweighed by strong support elsewhere. Complete unanimity could hardly be expected on such an issue. It is true that nearly 40 per cent of those on the electoral rolls did not vote either way, but where voting is optional there is always substantial absenteeism and in this case there was no established party machinery and no army of hopeful candidates to get the vote out. No doubt there was some apathy, as well as some hostility, but on the whole it seems fair to conclude that the decision to federate was a popular one and the notorious reluctance of Australians since 1900 to approve constitutional

[55] J. A. La Nauze, *The Making of the Australian Constitution*, Melbourne, 1972, ch. 15.

[56] J. Bastin, 'Sir John Forrest and Australian Federation', in *The Australian Quarterly*, *XXIV*, 4, 1952.

[57] A convenient analysis of the voting figures is printed as an appendix to R. S. Parker's, 'Australian Federation: The Influence of Economic Interests and Political Pressures', in *H.S.*, *13*, November 1949.

amendments, makes the clear vote in favour of an entirely new constitution even more impressive.

As the complications involved in interpreting the referendum results indicate, the success of the federation movement is more easily described than explained. In a sense, federation was a logical and even an obvious step; no barriers of race, language or culture separated the colonies, and those responsible for running them had long been aware of the administrative advantages likely to accrue from some sort of closer association. The United States and Canada had, in their different ways, set precedents for the federation of groups of British colonists occupying new continents, and it was a commonplace of after-dinner rhetoric that Australia would some day follow suit. Despite nearly half a century of separate self-government the colonies were still recognizably members of the same family and fraternal jealousies notwithstanding, the great improvements in transport and communications which occurred in the late nineteenth century had drawn them closer together than ever before. The adoption of Eastern Standard Time in 1895 symbolizes this togetherness. Nevertheless, self-governing communities do not give up their autonomy lightly. It is true that the extent to which federation would, in the end, erode the autonomy of the states, was not foreseen at the time, but even so it is natural to assume that urgent and compelling reasons for federating must have been operative. Such reasons are, however, not easy to identify.

In the 1880s, agitation about the future of the Pacific region and irritation at Britain's reluctance to heed their wishes in the matter led directly to the establishment of the Federal Council, but interest in the Pacific had dwindled long before 1890. The need for unified defence arrangements supplied the immediate context against which Parkes re-opened the federal question in 1889, but it was a pretext rather than a cause, and the years during which the federation movement made the most headway were unusually free of war scares. The need to preserve their antipodean Eden from racial 'pollution' too, concerned the colonists less in the 1890s; the Chinese had already been effectively shut out and moves to exclude the Japanese were to some extent in advance of public opinion. Of course the fact that these problems were not urgent does not mean that they were irrelevant. Imprecisely directed feelings of insecurity were already deeply embedded in the Australian character, and memories of crises in the 1880s and earlier undoubtedly predisposed some politicians to advocate federation and some electors to vote 'Yes' on referendum day. But it is misleading to list defence, concern about the Pacific, and the White Australia policy as 'causes' of federation in the simplistic manner that this has often been done.

Economic factors certainly contributed to the success of the federation movement, but here again the issues are by no means straightforward. By 1890 the economic interests of the six colonies were becoming intertwined. Trade between neighbours was almost equal to the trade of each colony with Britain; banks, pastoral firms, importers and to a lesser extent manufacturers had established intercolonial agencies; and there had been a good deal of investment across colonial boundaries. Yet the six artificially defined segments of what was becoming a more and more integrated economy were controlled not just separately but in competition with each other. Railway freights were manipulated to divert trade from its natural channels and above all there were the irksome customs houses at the borders of each colony. Whilst the good years lasted no one worried unduly about these illogicalities but the manner in which one colony after another succumbed to the depression and the financial crisis demonstrated graphically both the extent to which the colonies were interlocked and the need for central direction of the economy. And whereas the problem of reconciling differing tariff policies had once seemed an immovable barrier to federation, some colonists now saw the need for this as an irresistible reason for federating. However the influence of these considerations is difficult to assess. Insofar as general benefits to the whole community were anticipated, support for federation was obviously generated, but the economic interests of governments, colonies, regions, industries and individuals overlapped and conflicted in a confused and confusing manner. For example, some regions and industries expected to gain from federation, particularly through the abolition of inter-colonial tariffs, but in most cases these putative gains were likely to be registered at someone else's expense and 'yes' votes cast on this basis in one part of Australia were balanced by 'no' votes elsewhere. Thus the well-established manufacturers of Melbourne supported federation in the hope that it would open up new markets in other colonies. Adelaide manufacturers opposed federation because they feared that unrestrained competition from Melbourne rivals operating on a larger scale would put them out of business. Since the only electorates in South Australia to register a 'no' majority were in the factory districts of Adelaide it seems reasonable to assume that their fears were shared by their employees and were translated into votes. But as practically everyone in Victoria voted for federation the significance in terms of votes of the hopes of the Melbourne manufacturers is much more obscure. It is likely then, that some of the opposition to federation was evoked by real or imagined economic threats; it is more difficult to prove that economic causes were responsible for the general movement in favour of federation, though clearly they played a part.[58]

---

[58] The article by Parker cited in the previous footnote has sparked off a continuing debate. See G. Blainey, 'The Role of Economic Interests in Australian Federation', in *H.S.*, *15*, November 1950: J. Bastin, 'Federation and Western Australia: A Contribution to the Parker-Blainey Discussion', in *H.S.*, *17*, November 1951: R. Norris, 'Economic Influences on the 1898 South Australian Federation Referendum', and P. Hewett, 'Aspects of Campaigns in South-Eastern New South Wales at the Federation Referenda of 1898 and 1899', both in A. W. Martin, Ed., *Essays in Australian Federation*, Melbourne, 1969.

Further difficulties arise when the relationship between the decision to federate and the growth of nationalism is examined. Though some progress had been made towards the evolution of a national identity the loyalties of late nineteenth century Australians were perplexingly tangled. Emotional links with Britain remained strong; the individual colonies commanded the affection and even the patriotism of their inhabitants; and yet most colonists also thought of themselves as Australians. Priorities varied between these three loyalties but few could altogether escape the pull of each and none of the crises of the period were serious enough to make a clear-cut choice necessary. This point is illustrated by Australia's reaction to the outbreak of the Boer War in 1899. Critics of the morality of the British cause were engulfed in a tidal wave of patriotic fervour and troops were at once despatched to aid the motherland in her hour of need. On the other hand, part of the enthusiasm for the war sprang from a desire to prove the virility of Australian manhood and the fitness of the embryonic nation to take its place in the world. However, although the outbreak of war followed hard on the heels of the decision to federate, the colonies vied amongst themselves for the right to send troops and the early contingents were despatched separately by each colony.[59]

Loyalty to Britain took many forms. At one extreme, a handful of imperial federationists sought to institutionalize the relationship by setting up a parliament at Westminster in which the whole Empire should be represented. This plan attracted little support but its failure should not be taken to mean that the British connection was no longer valued. Most Australians felt some personal allegiance to the Queen and were proud to be part of what they believed to be the greatest empire the world had known. They understood Australia's relationship to Britain by analogy with the family and assumed that like all grown children the colonies had the right to call for parental help when necessary whilst rejecting parental interference. Since the existing constitutional arrangements seemed to work in more or less this way, attempts to re-define them aroused little interest. There was, though, a vociferous minority who clamoured for all ties with Britain to be severed and ridiculed the attachment of their fellows to the royal family. This point of view was kept constantly before the public by the Sydney *Bulletin* but it would be rash to assume that the *Bulletin*'s many readers all agreed with its editorial policies. In any case, the *Bulletin* writers and other republicans and radicals were often amongst the staunchest believers in the inherent superiority of the Anglo-Saxon racial stock. Moreover, underpinning both pride in the Empire and pride of race was the rich inheritance of British

[59] See B. R. Penny, 'Australia's Reactions to the Boer War – a study in Colonial Imperialism', in *The Journal of British Studies, VII*, 1, November 1967: B. R. Penny, 'The Australian Debate on the Boer War', in *H.S.*, 56, April 1971: A. P. Haydon, 'South Australia's First War', in *H.S.*, 42, April 1964.

culture which was still an inescapable part of the birthright of every Australian.[60]

In view of the vast distances which separated the colonies in their formative years and the varying circumstances of their foundation it was natural that local loyalties and traditions should have arisen. Later the experience of separate self-government added a political dimension to colonial patriotism, which manifested itself in tariff and railway wars, disputes over borders and rivers, and everlasting inter-colonial slanging-matches between politicians and newspapers.[61] However the attachment of colonists to their colonies was also an important stage in the gradual process by which Britons-in-exile became Australians. Furthermore, local loyalties, however strong, were shallowly rooted, in that the character of society differed relatively little from one colony to another. As William Gay wrote, in 1895, 'A Man from Ballarat does not in Hobart, in Cooktown, or in Coolgardie, feel among foreigners. There is less diversity of local prejudice, of dialect, and of custom between the north and south and east and west of the whole of this Continent than there is between the north and south and east and west of England.'[62] This homogeneity, partly based on common British origins, was fundamental to the consciousness of a common Australian nationality transcending colonial boundaries and different from, though not necessarily incompatible with, loyalty to Britain, which gained in strength towards the end of the century. Most colonists were now Australian rather than British born and they began more frequently to ask themselves what it meant to be an Australian. Artists, creative writers, journalists, and politicians came in their various ways to focus less on the immense similarities which still existed between British and Australian society and more on novel aspects of the local environment and local modifications of British manners and mores. Belief in the existence and worth of distinctively Australian personal and social characteristics was reinforced through the popularization of myths and images quarried from what was now a century of experience of Australia.[63]

60 For further material on loyalty to Britain see D. Cole, 'The Problem of 'Nationalism' and 'Imperialism' in British Settlement Colonies', in *The Journal of British Studies, X*, 2, 1971: D. Cole, 'The Crimson Thread of Kinship': Ethnic Ideas in Australia, 1870–1914, in *H.S., 56*, April 1971: R. Ward, 'Two Kinds of Australian Patriotism', in *The Victorian Historical Magazine, 41*, 1, February 1970.

61 On colonial patriotism see H. Reynolds, 'Australian Nationalism: Tasmanian Patriotism', in *The New Zealand Journal of History, 5*, 1, April 1971: S. P. Shortus, ' "Colonial Nationalism": New South Welsh Identity in the mid-1880s', in *R.A.H.S.J., 59*, 1 March 1973.

62 W. Gay and M. E. Sampson, Eds., *The Commonwealth and the Empire*, Melbourne, 1895, pp. 26–7.

63 In addition to sources already cited, see C. S. Blackton, 'Australian Nationality and Nationalism, 1850–1900', in *H.S., 36*, May 1961: M. Roe, 'An Historical Survey of Australian Nationalism', in *The Victorian Historical Magazine, 42*, 4, November 1971: R. Ward, *The Australian Legend*, Melbourne, 1958, chs. 7–8.

By the 1890s then, the word 'Australia' stood for a people as well as a continent – but it still meant little politically. The consciousness of colonists that they were Australians did not necessarily imply any desire to bring about political union, for national sentiment was primarily cultural and cultural unity already existed. Citizens of the separate colonies could and did enjoy the poetry of 'Banjo' Paterson or the stories of 'Steele Rudd', they could rejoice in test match victories over England or bask in reflected glory when Nellie Melba took Europe's opera houses by storm, regardless of political boundaries. Indeed there is a sense in which political nationalism was scarcely possible until such time as a nation-state came into being, around which emotions might cohere. Hence although consciousness of belonging together certainly helped to make federation possible, one must be wary of thinking of nationalism as the propulsive force behind the federation movement. A more appropriate concept is that of nationalism as a magnet drawing the colonies towards their destiny. Most of the leading federalists drew inspiration from dreams of the glorious future open to a united Australia and as their plans took on definite shape, their vision came to be more widely shared. Australia, it was hoped and believed, was fated to become another America, a new-world power which would dominate the southern seas.

Over against this vision stood the pull of loyalty to the existing colonies, the strength of which was such as to rule out any scheme for complete unification. Colonial patriotism also manifested itself in the concern for 'state rights' so characteristic of the federal conventions and some, at least, of the 'no' votes cast at the referendums. On the other hand, there were those who looked to federation to confer benefits on their colony or to increase its sphere of influence. Loyalty to Britain was less of a problem. Though the persistence and pervasiveness of the British connection had an inhibiting effect on the development of nationalism, it was not an obstacle to the success of the federation movement. Imperial federationists saw local federation as an essential preliminary to their own goal; republicans saw it as a means of moving towards independence. Others were content that federation under the crown, along the lines proposed in the Commonwealth Bill, would not of itself alter the status quo, for the federated colonies would jointly stand in the same relationship to Britain as they formerly had done severally.

The decade of the 1890s has long been regarded as one of the most noteworthy in Australia's history, rivalled only by the 1850s. In Vance Palmer's words, '. . . there has grown up a legend of the Australian nineties as a period of intense artistic and political activity, in which the genius of this young country had a brief and brilliant first flowering'.[64] Palmer himself emphasised the literary and artistic achievements of the 1890s, which he saw as an expression of emergent nationalism; others have laid their stress on the political achievements

[64] Vance Palmer, *The Legend of the Nineties*, Melbourne, 1954, p. 9.

of the decade, particularly the birth of the Labor party, which has also been seen as an expression of nationalism. Politics and culture have thus been linked together by their common basis in national sentiment, and it is this heady mixture of ingredients which has given the legend its remarkable potency. It is of course true that the 1890s encompassed an unusually large number of major events and that some of these also make convenient pegs on which to hang discussion of important long-term forces at work in Australian society. Nevertheless, by focusing undue attention on a single decade, and oversimplifying the relationship between some of its principal features, the legend has distorted rather than enhanced the significance of the period.

Belief in the 'special' character of the 1890s can probably be traced back to the 1920s. In the aftermath of the War of 1914–18 Australia seemed to many of its older citizens to have undergone vast changes, often for the worse, since the heady days of their youth. This was particularly true of writers and journalists, many of whom as young men without dependants had been relatively untouched by the hardships of the depression. They remembered only the gay times and professional opportunities of an age when every country town boasted several newspapers and the great metropolitan dailies and weeklies were at their peak. G. A. Taylor's, *Those Were The Days*, published in 1918, inaugurated a steady stream of reminiscences by such men which included *The Romantic Nineties* by A. W. Jose (1933), *Naught to Thirty-Three* by Randolph Bedford (1944), *Lost Years* by E. H. Collis (1948), and *Bohemians of the Bulletin* by Norman Lindsay (1965). The titles alone are indicative of a legend in the making. Literary historians and critics such as Vance Palmer, H. M. Green, A. A. Phillips and T. Inglis Moore, anxious to encourage contemporary writing by showing that it was deeply rooted in Australian history, assisted in the process. Though uneasily conscious of the inferior quality of much of the literature, these men drew attention to the hitherto neglected 'Joe Wilson' stories of Henry Lawson and to Joseph Furphy's much misunderstood masterpiece, *Such Is Life*, and thus gave the legend a firmer basis.

In cultural terms, the central affirmation of the legend-makers was that in the 1890s Australian literature threw off the crippling shackles of the British connection and began for the first time to produce poems and stories written and published in Australia for an Australian audience and enshrining Australian attitudes and values. These attitudes and values were originally those of the most distinctive of Australians – the convict, the digger, the bullock-driver, the drover, the cocky-farmer – but through literary popularization, so the argument runs, they permeated the entire population. The characteristic forms of writing in this literary explosion were the bush ballad and the short story, the staple fare offered by the Sydney *Bulletin*. The leading exponent of the bush ballad was 'Banjo' Paterson, whose *The Man From Snowy River*, was the first Australian best-seller, but dozens of other rhymsters, most of them now totally forgotten, turned out similar work. *While The Billy Boils*, Henry Lawson's first major collection of short stories, enjoyed a success comparable with that of Paterson's verse, and other popular story-tellers included Edward Dyson, Ernest Favenc, Louis Becke, 'Price Warung', Albert Dorrington and Alex Montgomery. Then, towards the end of the decade, Steele Rudd's *On Our Selection* stories took the reading public by storm and outbid even Lawson for popularity. It was indeed one of the features of the period that within the space of ten years some twenty or thirty writers burst into prominence, most of them being given their start by the *Bulletin* which in 1890 had embarked on a policy of encouraging local writers to produce 'Australian' material.

The literature of the 1890s was, however, remarkable more for its quantity than its quality. Most of the stories were graceless in style, unstructured, and lacking in depth of characterization. The stereotypes and conventions of romantic literature had been replaced by another set of stereotypes and conventions with the virtue only of being more indigenous. A few of Paterson's ballads can still stir the emotions but even the best of his work cannot stand up to critical analysis; many of the other balladists wrote crudely rhymed doggerel. The only works for which enduring literary value can be claimed are *Such Is Life*, which though written in the 1890s was not published until after the turn of the century and not appreciated fully for thirty or forty years after that; some of Lawson's stories, though not necessarily those which won him popularity with his contemporaries; and the complex and symbolic poetry of Christopher Brennan, which no stretch of the imagination could incorporate into the Australian legend. Once these facts are accepted the true significance of the period becomes clearer. For the first time in Australian history literature had become an integral part of the popular culture – an unsophisticated literature for an unsophisticated audience. This phenomenon was short-lived. Certainly by the end of the War of 1914–18 it was over and C. J. Dennis was the last poet to enjoy the adulation of the man-in-the-street as Paterson and Lawson had done.

By no means all the writers of the 1890s belonged to the stockwhip and wattle-blossom school. Even in the pages of the *Bulletin* no more than one third of the poems and stories dealt with overtly Australian subjects. Much of the poetry, in particular, concerned itself with such traditional topics as life, love, and death, in the stilted manner of the worst British verse of the Victorian era. Of the better known poets, Brennan, Victor Daley, and Bernard O'Dowd all either ignored or explicitly rejected the bush. On the fiction side, there was a vogue for Kipling-esque stories about the Pacific islands, and a steady demand for romances. Had there been best-seller lists, Ethel S. Turner's *Seven Little Australians* would have given 'Clancy of the Overflow' a good run for his money. Moreover the increased readership for locally produced literature did not imply any slackening of demand for imported works by such writers as Mark Twain, Rudyard Kipling, Arthur Conan Doyle, Ouida, Marie Corelli, and the expatriate

Australian Guy Boothby. In the light of these facts, glib generalisations about the relationship between literature and the growth of nationalism should be treated with caution. On close inspection it is surprising how few even of those stories and ballads which were concerned with outback life celebrated the glories of mateship, manly independence, or the joys of life on the land, and how many were either grimly sardonic or downright bitter.

On the political side, the legend of the 1890s probably owes something to the dissatisfaction of twentieth century writers and historians with the Australian Labor party of their own day, for this had led to the romanticization of the uncorrupted labour movement of the 1890s. The infant Labor parties were from their birth dominated by moderate and pragmatic men little different from the labour leaders of subsequent decades. To suggest otherwise is to conflate the utopian idealism of the 1880s, the class-warfare rhetoric of the strikes, and the parliamentary activities of the 1890s, in an alarmingly unhistorical manner. The actual achievements of the early Labor parties have often been over-emphasised at the expense of the 'middle class' Liberals; in similar fashion the 'legendary' view appropriated nationalism to the Labor party, the unions, and the working class generally. These claims must be modified. Furthermore, insofar as the claims made for the Labor party can stand, this is true primarily for New South Wales. Indeed the legend of the 1890s is generally rather New South Wales-centric.

Another reason for the cloud of nostalgia which has come to envelop the 1890s, less often articulated but also less controversial, is that this decade genuinely embodied the last days of an old way of life and the first fruits of a new. In 1890 there was still one horse in Australia for every two people, and the horse and buggy was an indispensable form of transport even in the great cities. Yet fast steamships had already reduced the country's isolation, bringing a stream of distinguished visitors such as Henry George, Mark Twain, the Webbs, the Hallés, and the divine Sarah Bernhardt. Modern transport had also made it possible for the first of what was to become a long line of Australian sportsmen to visit Europe regularly, and modern communications conveyed immediate news of their triumphs. The 1890s also saw the arrival in the colonies of further harbingers of the technological age. Electric street lighting was introduced in Melbourne in 1890; the first X-rays in Australia were taken in 1896. The cinema and the motor car both made their debut in the colonies before federation was consumated. In 1900 many of these innovations were still curiosities, the real impact of which had yet to be felt, but the signs of the times were there for those willing and able to read them.

7

1901-14

F. K. Crowley

A new nation—Britannic Australians—federal government in-
augurated—Barton's policy—first federal elections—the China
Contingent—the Boer War—the navy and the telegraph—new
national institutions—White Australia policy—the tariff of 1902
—the federal record of 1902-03—the drought—the economy—
urbanization—arbitration—'three elevens' in federal politics—
Commonwealth Arbitration Court established—New Protection—
the basic wage—the tariff of 1908—the rise of the A.L.P.—social-
ism—the fusion of 1909—liberalism—federalism—early defence
arrangements—changing opinions about imperial defence—an
Australian navy launched—compulsory military training institu-
ted—Australia and the empire—the economy 1905-14—assisted
immigration—industrial unrest—wheat growing—urbanization—
improvements in communications—the A.L.P. in office—in the
states—the work of the Fisher government—the land tax—the
Commonwealth Bank—constitutional referendums—economic
and political achievements—the Australian character.

In 1901 Australia's political unity was superficial. The dreams of the
constitution-makers and the slogans of the federalists had not made a
nation overnight. There was no fully developed and widespread
sense of national identity. Nor was there a fervent nationalism nurtured by conflicts, revolutions or crises. The politicians and newspaper
editors who asserted that a nation had been born on 1 January 1901
were expressing a hope, not pointing to a fulfilment. A new 'state'
had come into being on New Year's Day 1901, when the Commonwealth of Australia had become a federated self-governing member of
the British Empire; and the new prime minister was justified in
boasting that it was 'the first time in history in which it is allowed to
one body of men to govern a whole continent'.[1] But Australia was not
a 'nation-state' because its citizens had had no experience of loyalty
to a single national government, and the six state (formerly colonial)
governments retained autonomy in the management of their lands,
railways, roads, schools and most industrial matters.

1 Edmund Barton, quoted in the *Maitland Daily Mercury*, 18 January 1901.

Loyalty to colony or to city transcended loyalty to the newly-established federal government. Parochialism was rampant. The combative jealousy between Sydneysiders and Melbournians, strongly determined by history and geography, was nurtured by competitive businessmen, stock exchanges, newspaper proprietors and government statisticians. The staid and self-satisfied South Australians of Adelaide's Establishment still congratulated themselves that they had never suffered from the convict 'taint', whilst Tasmanians felt a closer affinity to London than to Melbourne and Adelaide. There was also the petulant antipathy to eastern-staters among the residents of Perth in far away Western Australia, who were sure that federation would cost them money, and the feeling amongst the cane-growers in the tropical north of Queensland that they did not really belong to Australia. The uneven distribution of the population between and within the states accentuated this localism. In 1901 two-thirds of Australia's population of 3,750,000 lived in New South Wales and Victoria, and one-quarter of the total lived in Sydney and Melbourne.[2] There was also antipathy between the primary producers of the rural districts and the city workers who were said 'to live off the farmers' backs'. This was accentuated by the high and growing proportion of the population which lived in urban areas. One-third of the total population lived in the six capital cities, two-thirds lived in cities and towns. Much of the private capital sent from Britain in the last half of the previous century had been invested in building the cities and suburbs.[3]

There was no fully developed Australian self-image. Most Australians who thought about the matter referred to themselves as Anglo-Australians or Scottish Australians or Irish Australians, or, paradoxically, as 'independent Australian Britons', or 'Britons of the Empire',[4] or even as Britishers first and Australians second. Not only did recently arrived immigrants still regard England as 'Home', so did some second and third generation Australians who had never been to Britain, and for them it was an expression of a genuine emotional attachment to the birthplace and the culture of their parents or grandparents, an attachment to their books, poetry, songs and sentiments. The typical Australians—the suburbanites, the factory hands, the cockey farmers and the sundowners – were probably best described as Britannic Australians because of their dual loyalty. In one respect they were conscious of being citizen subjects of the British Empire, and sharing a sentiment of racial kinship with the people of Britain; they were also pleased to share in the reflected glory of an Empire which safeguarded their country's existence. In another respect

[2] The Census of 31 March 1901 was conducted independently by the six state governments, though to a fairly uniform plan. See *Official Year Book of the Commonwealth of Australia: 1901–1907*, I, 1908, p. 160 ff.

[3] N. G. Butlin, *Investment in Australian Economic Development 1861–1900*, Cambridge, 1964, p. 6.

[4] Edmund Barton's phrase in *C.P.D.*, 7 July 1903, *14*, p. 1797.

they were vaguely loyal to their own birthplace, or to their adopted country, and sensed that being Australian was different from being a resident of the British Isles. But they had never been forced by a national emergency involving Australia to declare which loyalty should come first, and never expected that they would have to do so. Nor did they seem to want to develop either loyalty to any great degree.[5] Most Australians had no desire to establish a closer political union with Britain in the form of an imperial federation, least of all the Australian Irish, whilst at the same time they seemed reluctant to forego their existing loyalties for a new national allegiance or patriotism. It would therefore be an exaggeration to say that in 1901 there existed in Australia 'a happy blend of imperialism and nationalism'. Many Australians did not worry about either.

There were no well-established national traditions which could be taught in the state-run primary schoolrooms where most Australians learned civics and history. On the contrary, the traditions in these schools were British and the history was British and European. The teachers used maps of the world on which were marked in red the possessions of the British Empire, and taught their children to salute the Union Jack, to sing 'God Save the King' and to be proud of the Royal Navy and of an Empire which controlled one-quarter of the world's land surface, and one-fifth of its population.[6] Only in the Catholic parish schools run by Irish teachers were the children taught to value other principles and other traditions. The Irishness of the Catholic clergy and laity owed much to the constant re-stocking of the clergy and the religious orders from Irish seminaries and other training institutions. Hence in their schools and churches they kept alive the values and the attitudes of Old Ireland. They had also brought to Australia the old-fashioned brand of Irish patriotism, and were concerned that it should not be smothered by the propaganda of the Anglophiles. But the Catholic classrooms were no more seminaries of sedition than the 'godless' state schools were seedplots of immorality and vice; Irish Australians (perhaps constituting twenty per cent of the population) might love Old Ireland, but they did not wish to overthrow the Australian government in order to demonstrate it.

The symbols of loyalty in Australia were British, not Australian.

[5] For comments on Australian nationalism in the early federal period see C. S. Blackton, 'Australian Nationality and Nationalism: The Imperial Federationist Interlude 1885–1901' in *H.S.*, *25*, November 1955: C. S. Blackton, 'Australian Nationality and Nationalism, 1850–1900', in *H.S.*, *36*, May 1961: C. Grimshaw, 'Australian Nationalism and the Imperial Connection: 1900–1914', *A.J.P.H.*, *III*, 2, May 1958: P. C. Campbell, 'Australian Nationalism', in *R.A.H.S.J.*, *14*, 6, 1928: M. Atkinson, Ed., *Australia: Economic and Political Studies*, Melbourne, 1920: R. Ward, 'Two Kinds of Australian Patriotism', in *The Victorian Historical Magazine*, *41*, 1, February 1970.

[6] See S. G. Firth 'Social Values in the New South Wales Primary School 1880–1914: an analysis of school texts', in *Melbourne Studies in Education*, 1970.

The King of England was Australia's head of state. The laws were enacted in his name and enforced by His Majesty's ministers, judges and police forces. The highest court of appeal was the Judicial Committee of the Privy Council in London, and Australia had no foreign policy of its own. The nature and standards of professional training in the law, medicine, education or engineering were determined by English or Scottish universities, whilst from the British Isles came all Australia's governors and most of its Anglican and Catholic bishops. There was no Australian national anthem, no army and no navy. There was no flag, until a public competition late in 1901 produced a winning design from 30,000 entries which, understandably, incorporated the Union Jack as well as the Southern Cross, but which the Sydney *Bulletin* thought had no artistic virtue and no national significance, a

bastard flag ... a true symbol of the bastard state of Australian opinion, still in large part biassed by British tradition, British customs, still lacking many years to the sufficiency of manhood which will determine a path of its own ... The flag represents the old generation, the old leaven.[7]

There were no Australian medals or decorations, and the highest honour to be earned in war was the Victoria Cross and in peace a knighthood conferred by the King or membership of the King's Privy Council. The loyal toast was always dutifully given at official dinners, and public gatherings dispersed only after playing the British national anthem. There were no long-established and influential groups of artists in Australian cultural life. There were few opportunities in Australia for talented musicians, performers, and painters, and most had to travel overseas to gain recognition and an income. Many, like the singer Nellie Melba, or the painters Roberts, Streeton, Lambert, Fox and Meldrum, spent more time out of Australia than in it, and those who remained at home were provincial, isolated and backward in world terms. There were no national balladists whom the reading public at large was prepared to accept as purveyors of a national ethos, and the 'Bush School' of native-born poets and creative writers which had flourished in the 1880s and 1890s was already on the decline.[8] Apart from a few bushrangers and explorers – and some horses – there were no heroes in national history, except those shared with the Old Country. In war, the heroes were Kitchener and Gordon. In literature they were Shakespeare, Dickens and Kipling. Australian explorers, politicians and 'horse poets' offered no serious competition to imported traditions or heroes. What was British was Best, except, of course,

[7] *Bulletin*, Sydney, 18 September 1901.

[8] See H. W. MacCallum, 'The Literature of New South Wales', in *British Association for the Advancement of Science: Handbook For New South Wales*, Sydney, 1914, pp. 76–82. See also G. Serle, *From Deserts the Prophets Come: The Creative Spirit in Australia 1788–1972*, Melbourne, 1973, ch. 6.

among those Irish Australians who had had personal experience of British colonization in Ireland.

The dominance of Britishism in Australia was further accentuated by the homogeneity of the Australian population. Three-quarters of the total population had been born in Australia, but most were the children of immigrants from the British Isles. The character of the Australian population had been shaped by more than a century of immigration predominantly from the United Kingdom. Furthermore, Australian governments had always offered special inducements by way of assisted passages and easy access to Crown land to British immigrants with the express intention of preserving Australia as a white and British community. In one respect this homogeneity was a disability rather than an asset, because the demographic character of the Australian community at the turn of the century was more British than it was Australian: most of the English, Welsh and Scots of the nineteenth century had not settled in separate communities, but they and their children had fused into a social amalgam which had rarely existed even in the Home Country. The national loyalties and religious observances of the Irish proved to be the more durable of the imported traditions, but time, distance from Ireland, and the lack of village discipline eventually modified the week-day habits of the Australian Irish. They, too, learnt to be pro-British Australians as well as anti-English Irishmen. The exact proportions of the national elements which had formed the Australia of 1901 were not recorded, but it seems that their numbers were in proportion to those existing in the British Isles: about sixty per cent of Australians born in the United Kingdom had come from England and Wales. However, this fusing of Britannic Australians did not constitute a nation, any more than similar cross-bred enclaves made nations of Britain's west coastal ports. The Australian people, like their ideals and outlook, were a blend of the imported and the indigenous, and did not yet constitute an identifiable nation-community or nation-state.

National feeling had not matured greatly by the day on which more than a hundred thousand people gathered in Centennial Park, Sydney, to watch the ceremony inaugurating Australia's first national government, and to see Edmund Barton, the New South Wales leader of the federation movement, sworn in as Australia's first national prime minister. But throughout Australia the press saw a special significance in this triple coincidence of events – a new year, a new century, and a newly united nation – and in a spirit of optimism and exuberance expected to see a new national pride develop and a glorious destiny emerge for the newly united Australian nation. The Australian people, it was said, had a broader measure of political privilege and a more generous share of individual freedom and public liberty than their forefathers who had founded the Australian colonies. They inherited, also, those proud traditions which had made the statesmanship and the policy of Britain the admiration of historians and the models of constitution-makers. 'We share the national life and thought of an Empire of which the peer has yet to make itself known', declared the *Sydney Morning Herald*. 'We are guarded in our isolation by the iron wall of a navy which is admittedly incomparable, and by a military prestige built up on a record which has never known complete defeat. We have within our borders, in our but partly discovered and exploited natural resources, all the material guarantees for prosperity and greatness. We enter on the new year and the new century a united Australian nation.'[9]

Edmund Barton decided to seek election to the first federal parliament as the member for Hunter (N.S.W.), and on 17 January 1901, in the West Maitland Town Hall, he announced the policy which his cabinet proposed to put to the people at the first federal elections, and which he expected the new federal parliament to endorse.[10] He pointed to the main administrative problems which faced the federal government, and he raised many of the controversial issues which were to dominate Australian politics until 1914. His speech also laid the foundations of several national policies which were to give a special character to public life for more than half a century. In it he combined practical proposals to inaugurate federal government with a moderately liberal approach to social issues, a moderately protectionist view of financial questions, a conservative view of electoral and constitutional problems, and a racist policy on demographic issues. His chief concern was with the financial problems likely to follow from the economic union of the six states, since customs revenue, which had been a main source of state income, was now exclusively federal; for the first ten years the federal government was obliged to return three-quarters of it, but after that date it could decide on the best arrangement for the future. Because most of the state governments had previously adopted protectionist trade policies, or relied on their customs houses for much of their annual income, Barton believed that a national free trade policy in relation to overseas imports was impracticable. The problem, therefore, was to decide what level of indirect taxation through import duties was needed in order to provide all seven governments with an adequate income, and also maintain employment and profits in those industries which had been established behind tariff barriers. In short, Australia's major national task as it began a new experiment in government was to solve an economic problem and one which affected most of the population because it concerned their employment and their cost of living.

Barton and his cabinet ministers were protectionist in varying degrees, and it would have been odd if the first federal government had not produced a protectionist policy. Whatever were the fiscal views of the cabinet, the national government had to compensate the six state governments for their loss of income from both import

---

9 *Sydney Morning Herald*, 1 January 1901, Leader.

10 *Maitland Daily Mercury*, 18 January 1901, part-published in F. K. Crowley, *Modern Australia in Documents, I*, 1901–1939, Melbourne, 1973, pp. 1–3.

tariffs and border duties, for, without inter-state free trade, there would have been no federation. It had also to provide the new national government with a substantial income of its own in order to pay the staff of the new federally-run customs, post and telegraph, and defence departments. Barton declared unequivocally that the federal government would not impose land or income taxation, which were the most important devices left to the state governments to increase their own incomes. He therefore proposed a moderately protective tariff, thoroughly liberal, of 'purely Australian character', 'a practical and businessman's tariff', federal in so far as it would protect the interests of the state governments and one which would therefore maintain employment and provide 'revenue without destruction'. It would not be so high as to stifle imports and thereby restrict revenue, nor so low as to provide the governments with an inadequate income and cripple existing industries. Barton reassured the states by saying the 'the Ministry will not take any action that will have the effect of destroying state industries, and the Commonwealth will not be ushered in by the pattering of the feet of people driven out of employment'. Had the state governments known where to look for an omen as to their financial future they would have found it on Flemington Racecourse on 5 November 1901, where the first Melbourne Cup of the new century was won by Revenue, the hottest favourite to go to the post up to that time.

The creation of a federal political union, together with a new trading entity and a common purse, gave the fiscal issue a new dimension in a community which was heavily reliant on trade and which looked to government to provide the basic communications and utilities from its own income or from its own overseas borrowing. Governments were expected to construct the roads, railways, harbours and other public works which were needed in pioneering communities, and which also provided large-scale employment. Most of these had been paid for in the past by raising loans in London and paying the annual interest out of local revenue, leaving to a later generation the obligation to repay the principal. Colonial socialism or colonial governmentalism had long been a conspicuous feature of the Australian colonies, encouraged by both entrepreneurs and wage-earners in their own different interests; government had indeed become 'a vast public utility, whose duty it is to provide the greatest happiness for the greatest number'.[11] The initial federal system of finance was therefore tied to meeting the needs of the states and their

11 W. K. Hancock, *Australia*, new ed., Brisbane, 1961, p. 55. For discussion of this feature see H. V. Evatt, *Liberalism in Australia*, Sydney, 1918, ch. 9: N. G. Butlin, 'Colonial Socialism in Australia', in H. G. J. Aitken, Ed., *The State and Economic Growth*, New York, 1959: W. P. Reeves, *State Experiments in Australia and New Zealand*, London, 2 vols, 1902: A. Métin, *Le Socialisme sans Doctrines*, Paris, 1901: S. Encel, 'The Concept of the State in Australian Politics', in *A.J.P.H.*, VI, 1, May 1960: B. E. Mansfield, 'The State as Employer: An Early Twentieth Century Discussion', in *A.J.P.H.*, III, 2, May 1958.

governments, who were the real developers of Australia, and whose incomes had to be guaranteed in the national interest.

In his first policy speech Barton also proposed to establish an inter-state commission which would deal with difficult inter-state economic problems (not established until 1913 and then short-lived), especially the preferential freight rates charged by the state government rail-ways, the continuance of which was inconsistent with the idea of a common market and the concept of national economic unity. Several other proposals involved large-scale federal expenditure. He suggested that a nation-wide scheme of old age pensions be established, that a transcontinental railway be constructed between Kalgoorlie and Port Augusta, and a new railway from Sydney to Broken Hill, as well as a uniform railway gauge between Melbourne, Sydney and Brisbane. Presumably, the financing of all these projects – except perhaps the railways – would come from the federal government's one-quarter share of the total income from customs and excise. Barton's optimism also extended to promising an early decision on the future site and construction of the federal capital, (in which all land would be leased and never sold) the establishment of an efficient federal civil service, the creation of the High Court ('one of the great bulwarks of popular rights and the guardian of the States and Commonwealth against encroachment one by the other'), and legislation to deal with inter-state conciliation and arbitration, but only in cases of national in-dustrial crises. On two other issues Barton was less liberal, though these were views which were not shared by all the ministers in his cabinet. He was reluctantly prepared to introduce full adult franchise at federal elections because two states had already given the vote to women, but he did not believe that women should sit in the federal parliament.[12] He also hoped that there would be no rash amendments to the federal constitution.

Barton was firmly committed to establishing a White Australia by legislating against any influx of Asiatic labour and the further importa-tion of Kanakas for the sugar industry, a policy quickly endorsed by Alfred Deakin, the new federal attorney-general, who applauded the principle of preserving civilized Australia for the white man and as a white man's country. Indeed, the theme of White Australia ran through most of Deakin's platform speeches thereafter, and always produced a sympathetic response from his audiences. As he had long been a leading spokesman of both the federal movement and pro-tectionism in Victoria, and as he was by repute the most inspiring public speaker of his day – 'the silver-tongued orator' to his admirers, 'the supreme word spinner' to others – he was influential in preserving this essential element in the settled policies of the formative years of federalism. Most of the candidates at the first federal elections, as well as all the leading state politicians also endorsed the principle of a

12 See B. D. Graham, 'The Choice of Voting Methods in Federal Politics, 1902–1918', in *A.J.P.H., VIII*, 2, November 1962.

White Australia, though the issue was vigorously contested in Queensland. In that state the sugar planters believed that their future would be in jeopardy if Barton's proposals were implemented, whilst the Labor candidates hoped that it would be, and that Australia would be saved from 'the coloured curse', and from becoming 'a mongrel nation torn with racial dissension'. Their approach to the issue was more blatantly racist than Deakin's, and they saw Australia as 'the last chance of the white race'. 'What about the coloured alien, and the Chow and the Hindoo?' asked the editor of the Brisbane *Worker*;

> 'Fellow voters', says Australia,
> 'Do not let yourself be gulled:
> From the flock of White Australia,
> Let the coloured sheep be culled'[13]

The first federal elections held on 29–30 March 1901 did not produce clear-cut results.[14] No party won a majority in the House of Representatives or the Senate, but after the election it was found that the Labor party would generally support Barton and his protectionist ministry, rather than Reid, the free-trade leader who had served as premier of New South Wales and had been nick-named 'the great Australian Yes-No' because of his ambivalent attitude to federation. However, it is not possible to say whether the results of the election meant a great deal more than this. There was no fully developed party system in state or federal politics; only Labor candidates shortly after the federal election organized themselves into a disciplined party; and there had been no single issue on which the whole election had been contested. Candidates had stood under a great variety of banners and labels – protectionist, free-trader, high tariffist, low tariffist, compromise tariffist, ministerialist (supporters of Barton), protectionist Labor, free-trade Labor, Labor, independent. Some traded on their previous reputations as state politicians, some promised to look after provincial or state or working class interests, and others merely promised to legislate for the national good. Almost all of them had expressed a view about the tariff question, and hence this was the main divisive issue in both the House of Representatives and the Senate. Most of the extreme free-traders came from New South Wales, and the more ardent of the protectionists from Victoria, though none of the protectionists believed in protection to the extent of prohibition, and all of the free-traders believed in raising revenue by tariffs. The members from the other four states held views somewhere between those dominant in the two most populous states, and in the ultimate the free-traders did better in the Senate, the protectionists in the

13 *Worker*, Brisbane, 30 March 1901, 'Editorial Mill'.

14 For election results in the years 1901–14 see C. A. Hughes and B. D. Graham, *A Handbook of Australian Government and Politics 1890–1964*, Canberra, 1968.

House of Representatives. A compromise of the kind already advocated by Barton was the only possible outcome, whereby in effect the New South Wales tariff would have to go up and the Victorian tariff come down.[15]

The first federal election did not produce a nationally minded legislature. Considering the over-representation of the small states in the Senate, and the high proportion of state-minded politicians in the House of Representatives, the first national parliament, which assembled in Melbourne in May 1901, was more a body of state delegates than of national legislators, and it retained this character until the federal system and the growth of a Labor party created a new class of professional federal politicians. The parliament was also similar in other respects to the Conventions which had created it. Occupationally the lawyers were as dominant in the legislature as they had been in the federal movement, accounting for a quarter of the total membership, and for seven of the nine federal ministers. Overall, the professions were greatly over-represented, and the wage-earners under-represented.[16] Nevertheless, some of the best of the state politicians had been attracted to the federal scene.

From the point of view of the average Australian the establishment of the national government was not especially important. The customs houses, the post offices, and the military volunteers had come under new management, but the clerks in the public offices and the men behind the telegraph counters were the same as had been there previously. The state governments still ran the railways, built the bridges, made the roads and ran most of the schools, and the unemployed expected the state governments to provide relief works from public funds when times were hard. The merchants and importers merely paid their taxes to differently-styled officials, whilst the farmers and graziers sold their products as best they could through private agents and complained about the high prices they had to pay for manufactured or imported goods. The change of government responsibilities had no influence on the standing of Australian stock in the London money market, nor in bringing the long drought in the pastoral districts to an end, nor in stopping the continent-wide plague of rabbits. Nobody expected the federal government to do anything drastic or hasty, and the local parliaments went on with business as usual.

The Australian federation had not been created after a revolutionary or violent struggle between triumphant colonies and a defeated Motherland, and nobody expected any revolutionary changes to follow in the relationship between Australia and Britain. There had been no strong opposition to Australian federation in the British parliament, and its members were much more willing to see its

15 Discussion of the polling in the *Argus*, Melbourne, 2 April 1901, Leader.

16 See F. K. Crowley, *Modern Australia in Documents, 1*, 1901–1939, Melbourne, 1973, pp. 8–10.

consummation than the Anti-Billites in New South Wales. Nor did most Australians look forward to the day when they could 'cut the painter'. Separatists and republicans, who had had some success in the 1880s, had long since lost most of their disciples. The Australians were emotionally and sentimentally loyal subjects of the British Crown. They eagerly welcomed Lord Hopetoun as the first governor-general, they paid gushing tributes to the memory of the late Queen Victoria, who had died shortly after the inauguration of the Commonwealth, and they were grateful that the Duke and Duchess of Cornwall and York had been sent out to Australia to open the first session of the federal parliament in Melbourne. Besides, at the time of federation the Mother Country was at war in South Africa and in trouble in China, and the Australia-wide displays of loyalty to the empire were accompanied by the more practical gesture of volunteering to serve in Australian contingents within the imperial armed services.

In May 1901 the Australian China Contingent returned to Sydney and its members were warmly thanked by their former commanding officer for their help during the difficult times which followed the Boxer Rebellion. Originally consisting of 451 naval volunteers from New South Wales and Victoria, the contingent was employed for nine months on police duties in Peking and Tientsin, where according to General Gaselee, commanding the British contingent, their appearance was 'an object lesson not only to foreigners, but also to our Indian fellow subjects, of the patriotism which inspires all parts of the British Empire'.[17] Meanwhile, the new federal minister for defence, the former premier of Western Australia, Sir John Forrest, and the first head of the Australian Army, General Sir Edward Hutton, who had recently been on active service, were arranging for a Commonwealth Contingent of volunteers to be raised to help Britain suppress the Boer guerillas in South Africa. The state governments had already sent several contingents of infantry and mounted bushmen, and there was no shortage of amateurs, as well as men from the Volunteer Forces who were willing to respond to the call to arms for Australia's first national expeditionary force.

The first battalion of the Australian Commonwealth Horse sailed for South Africa on 19 February 1902 with an injunction from the lieutenant-governor of New South Wales to maintain 'the same high character for dauntless courage, for subordination, for discipline, and for resourcefulness which your brothers from Australia have so deservedly won'.[18] Not as many voices were heard then, as had been heard during the previous three years, to criticize the jingoism of the politicians and journalists who had urged Australians to spend their 'last shilling and last man' in the furtherance of British policy in

17 *C.P.D.*, 6 June 1901, *I*, p. 781. The South Australian government had also lent the *Protector* for service during the Rebellion.

18 Mr Justice Owen, quoted in *Sydney Morning Herald*, 20 February 1902.

South Africa;[19] the public debate during the early stages of the Boer War had become less significant as the war had lengthened. The war was being fought 'to protect British subjects from oppression and injustice', and so that Great Britain in the interests of empire should remain as paramount in South Africa as she was in north-eastern Africa. Australians had always looked to Britain to keep open their links with British ports, more specially the Suez Canal, the Cape routes, and the network of coaling and cable stations which guaranteed access to the markets of the Home Country. Thus patriotic support for the war in South Africa had sound foundations in economic survival, which was made quite clear by Edmund Barton when he explained to federal parliament in January 1902 that

the bond of Empire is not one only of mere patriotism – on which terms I think the bond of itself ought to be maintained if there were no ulterior considerations – but also one of self interest ... in the event of Britain at any time losing the control of the passage of the Suez Canal, the route by South Africa would become most important as the trade route from Great Britain to India and Australia.[20]

More than 16,000 volunteers from Australia did their duty when the trumpet sounded, and served with the British Army in South Africa between October 1899 and June 1902. Their return home was the occasion for a rash of fulsome newspaper editorials and public speeches extolling the gallantry and patriotism of the colonial troops, and glorying in the final success of British arms. 'The lion's cubs had rallied to the dam' and the Union Jack fluttered above the veldt where civilization and British justice now reigned unchallenged. Most Australians and their churchmen felt that the empire had successfully passed through a great trial, and were proud that the ties which bound all parts of the empire together were more closely woven than ever before; as Mr Justice Owen remarked, 'although we have changed our skies we have not changed our strength. We are not degenerating, but are of that old British bull-dog breed ... worthy descendants of that noble stock'.[21] The volunteers formed their own association of returned soldiers, and municipal councils began to erect memorials on which were inscribed the names of those comrades in arms who had served their empire and country in the Great Boer War, and the reminder – 'lest we forget'. To the historians of a later generation

---

[19] For this well used phraseology see speeches by McDonald and Barton in *C.P.D., 10*, 11 June 1902 and *14*, 7 July 1903. For detailed accounts of Australia's involvement see B. R. Penny, 'Australia's Reactions to the Boer War – a study in Colonial Imperialism', in *Journal of British Studies*, 7, 1, November 1967: B. R. Penny, 'The Australian Debate on the Boer War', in *H.S., 56*, April 1971: A. P. Haydon, 'South Australia's First War', in *H.S., 42*, April 1964.

[20] *C.P.D.*, 14 January 1902, 7, p. 8743.

[21] *Sydney Morning Herald*, 20 February 1902.

they also served as memorials to the early death of republicanism and separatism.

At the close of the war several other events illustrated Australia's close identity of interest with Britain. At the Colonial Conference in London during July and August 1902, which had been arranged to coincide with the coronation of Edward VII and which took place at a time when imperial fervour and colonial interest in the organization of the empire was at its peak, arrangements were made for the continued naval protection of both Australia and New Zealand.[22] Barton agreed that Australia should pay an increased annual subsidy to help maintain a British squadron in Australian waters, which was to be enlarged and to be partly manned by Australians. This arrangement, which followed the forming of the Anglo-Japanese Alliance in January 1902 to meet the threat of Russian expansion in the Far East,[23] secured the interest of Britain, Australia and New Zealand in the Pacific, though there was some criticism in Australia of an arrangement which continued the payment of 'tribute' and which did not provide for the creation of a separate Australian navy. The latter Barton believed to be premature, because its cost would have been beyond the means of the new federal government, and furthermore the strength of the empire navy required it to be concentrated under one command, and not consist of autonomous local squadrons. He appealed to Australians not to be niggardly in relation to the subsidy, but to realise that their contribution was being made to the empire as a whole and not merely to Australia.[24] In any case, the agreement was of a limited duration, and during that time sufficient Australians would be trained to provide for the manning of an Australian navy when the occasion was opportune. Later in the same year the All-British Pacific Cable was completed between Australia and Canada. It then became possible for the first time to send a telegraph message from the antipodes to London through both eastern and western hemispheres; the western route had been opened to Australia in 1872. The significance of the occasion was illustrated by the first telegram sent to the King which read: – 'as the cables are entirely British, this first message to pass the sunrise by one route, and the sunset by the other, is appropriately addressed to the Sovereign of the British Empire, on which the sun never rises or sets'.[25] Thus by the end of 1902 Australia's lines of communication with the Home Country were secured by the all-red submarine telegraph, by the British navy, by the defeat of the Boers

[22] For a general discussion of the conferences of 1902–11 see J. E. Kendle, *The Colonial and Imperial Conferences, 1887–1911*, London, 1967.

[23] See I. H. Nish, 'Australia and the Anglo-Japanese Alliance, 1901–1911', in *A.J.P.H.*, IX, 2, November 1963.

[24] *C.P.D.*, 7 July 1903, *14*, pp. 1772–1802: *Sydney Morning Herald*, 18 October 1902.

[25] *Courier*, Brisbane, 4 November 1902.

in South Africa, and by the coaling stations along the Suez and Cape of Good Hope routes to Britain.

Meanwhile the first national parliament had been debating the programme submitted to it by Barton's government.[26] Although there were three identifiable groups in the parliament – protectionists, free-traders and members of the Labor party – no one group dominated the proceedings, and the legislation which resulted arose from a consensus amongst the members about the basic tasks of the new parliament and government. Since May 1901 it had endorsed legislation which enabled the national government to recruit and manage its civil service in the various departments which it had taken over from the state governments, or which it had established to carry out its special federal functions. Entrance to the federal service was to be solely by competitive public examination, promotion was to be by merit and ability, and federal public servants were guaranteed a minimum living wage and protected against political patronage or interference; the politicians were thereby relieved of the responsibility of looking after their servants, who were to be placed under the surveillance of the Public Service Commissioner's inspectors, who were in Deakin's words 'the business doctors of the public service', and who were 'to move about among the branches of the service, and to make suggestions whereby it may be more economically administered and made more profitable to the community'.[27] By the end of 1903 federal parliament had adopted first-past-the-post voting for its own elections, as well as universal adult franchise, thus virtually forcing those states which had not already granted the suffrage to women for their own parliamentary elections to do so – Victoria, Queensland, New South Wales and Tasmania. There had been practically no agitation for federal female franchise – or any other female franchise – and hence it appeared to be an act of true male philanthropy, except to the visiting feminist Jessie Ackermann, who thought it was only another example of male expediency to forestall the inevitable.[28] Federal parliament also established the High Court, and passed a national Patents Act which reduced the cost of registering new inventions. It had also endorsed the acceptance of administrative control over British New Guinea, and the 1902 Naval Agreement which Barton had discussed at the recent conference in London.

Parliament established two major national policies designed to

[26] The most detailed and comprehensive discussion of federal legislation for the period 1901–14 is in G. Sawer, *Australian Federal Politics and Law, 1901–1929*, Melbourne, 1956.

[27] *C.P.D.*, 19 June 1901, *1*, p. 1302.

[28] Jessie Ackermann, *Australia from a Woman's Point of View*, London, 1913, pp. 215–16. There was an unsuccessful woman candidate at the federal election of 1903. See N. MacKenzie, 'Vida Goldstein: the Australian Suffragette', in *A.J.P.H.*, *VI*, 2, November 1960. Forty years later the first female legislator arrived in Canberra.

protect the character of Australia's population and its economy. The most important, but the least controversial, was the White Australia policy, which ensured the maintenance of the British character of the Australian population and its protection from contamination by 'inferior' races and sweated labour.[29] This was the most enduring of all the settled policies to arise from the pattern of political acceptance in the years 1901–14. There had long been widespread support throughout Australia for the permanent exclusion of Asians and Africans, whether on racist, industrial or any other grounds. Some protagonists held that the coloureds of the world were lower down God's scale of creation than the whites, whilst other were convinced that there could only be a viable standard of living and adequate social reforms in Australia if wage-earners were protected from competition with cheap Asian labour; Asian labour was 'too thrifty, too hard-working and too provident'. Alfred Deakin asserted that 'this note of nationality is that which gives dignity and importance to this debate. The unity of Australia is nothing if that does not imply a united race ... At the very first instant of our national career we are as one for a White Australia ... It is the Monroe doctrine of the Commonwealth of Australia'.[30] The only real dispute was over the method to be adopted in order to implement the policy. Labor members favoured a 'snow-white policy' which would have excluded all coloured races without exception and without subterfuge. However, the majority of parliamentarians preferred to use the device of a dictation test in a European language (changed in 1905 to a prescribed language), which could be administered to undesirable immigrants who would then be deported on 'educational' grounds.

The majority of members of the federal parliament also agreed that no more Kanakas should be imported into Queensland after 1904, and that all Pacific Islanders be expatriated from Australia by 1906. The Queensland sugar planters were offered a rebate of excise duty on sugar, soon changed to a bounty on production, if they employed white workmen in place of Kanakas.[31] The growers were at first adamant that they would face ruin as the result of the policy, but it soon became apparent that whites were capable of hard work in the tropics, provided they were adequately compensated for it; in consequence, ever since then Australians have paid a much higher price for their sugar than the prevailing price on world markets. The seamen in the coastal (but not overseas) ships were also protected against competition from coloured seamen, and the importing of migrants

29 See A. T. Yarwood, *Asian Migration to Australia*, Melbourne, 1964, ch. 2: D. Cole, 'The Crimson Thread of Kinship: Ethnic Ideas in Australia, 1870–1914', in *H.S.*, *56*, April 1971: F. K. Crowley, *Modern Australia in Documents, I*, 1901–1939, Melbourne, 1973, pp. 13–18.

30 *C.P.D.*, 12 September 1901, *4*, p. 4807.

31 A. Birch, 'The Implementation of the White Australia Policy in the Queensland Sugar Industry, 1901–12', in *A.J.P.H.*, *XI*, 2, August 1965.

under contracts or employment indentures was prohibited. A special act gave the federal government control over the naturalization of citizens. Thus the first federal parliament's main contribution to the development of a distinctive national identity was to build an ethnic wall around the community so as to preserve it from economic dislocation and the social consequences of intermarriage between Europeans and Asians. Thereafter all political parties were dedicated to cultivating what the Australian Labor party later described as 'an Australian sentiment, based upon the maintenance of racial purity'.[32]

The second new policy was the adoption of a national customs tariff. This was an unavoidable obligation of the federal compact, but soon came to be an economic corollary of the policy of immigration restriction. The wearisome debates on the individual items in the tariff schedule lasted for almost a year, as one after another the manufacturing, commercial and importing interests badgered members of parliament seeking favourable treatment. Debates on the principles of political economy were noticeably infrequent; 'who is to get what' was the question at issue, not the inherent virtues of free trade or protection. A series of compromises was eventually reached which imposed duties of 5 per cent to 25 per cent on imported goods and which thereby favoured the moderate protectionists. This occurred mainly because George Reid, the leader of the opposition in the House of Representatives, and his free-trade supporters in both houses, were compelled to agree to a level of duties which guaranteed a reasonable income to the state governments from their three-quarter share of the total revenue raised by the national government from customs and excise. However, the free-traders could not have hoped to retain their membership of parliament if they had abolished industries which had become self-sufficient behind protective tariff barriers. Labor members were divided on the issue, except when they helped to prevent a duty being imposed on imported tea and kerosene (used for lighting), which were important items in the wage earner's weekly budget. Ultimately the tariff of 1902 satisfied neither group of fiscal protagonists. However, New South Wales lost when Sydney ceased to be a free port, whilst the state governments gained more than they had expected. They not only achieved complete interstate free trade for the movement of their products, but under the management of the federal treasurer, Sir George Turner, they received additional amounts from the surplus revenue which the federal government did not spend; Turner had previously been premier of Victoria during the financial crises of the 1890s and had entered federal politics with a reputation for parsimonious bookkeeping. It was later discovered that his surplus should have been spent improving the run-down federal postal department.

[32] From the Objective of the Federal Labour Party, July 1905, in Australian Labour Party, *Official Report of Commonwealth Conference*, Melbourne, 1905, pp. 25-7.

The dictation test and the tariff wall were the main achievements of the first national parliament, and both illustrated the dominant materialism of the politicians and their electors: the first important national tasks to be attended to concerned the economic health of the community and its standard of living. On several other important issues the parliament did not make a great deal of progress. The Defence Act of 1903 established little more than the principles that the forces should consist almost entirely of citizen soldiers, and that there would be no overseas compulsory military service in wartime; Parliament was reluctant to commit itself to expensive military or naval establishments, and in any case nobody wanted a large standing army commanded by 'gold-laced officers'. Amongst other unresolved matters was parliament's inability to agree to a site for the national capital, or to the establishment of the Inter-state Commission, because the cost would have been too great. It did not create a federal system of industrial arbitration, mainly because it was under pressure from Labor to extend any such system to certain categories of state government employees, and this was not supported by the majority of members. Nor would parliament approve a system of bonuses which would have given a boost to the iron and steel industry. These failures drew attention to the contrast between Barton's comprehensive programme of 1901 and the actual achievements of parliament by 1903, and one contemporary observer attributed the lack of progress to 'an amount of protracted wrangling that would have discredited an inexperienced shire council in the back-blocks'.[33]

In September 1903 Sir Samuel Griffith, formerly premier and then chief justice of Queensland, was appointed first chief justice of the High Court, and Sir Edmund Barton (prime minister) and R. E. O'Connor (government leader in the Senate) left the federal cabinet to take the other two positions on the bench of the new court. All three of the judges had been active in politics and were conservative and imperialist; all had been involved in the federation movement, and all were expected to put their knowledge of the federal constitution to good effect when interpreting its clauses. Deakin succeeded Barton as leader of the protectionists and as prime minister, a choice which was popular with all sides in politics, as Deakin had long been acknowledged as one of the few gentlemen in the rough-and-tumble of Australian politics. He had been personally popular in the Victorian parliament, where he had acquired a reputation for promoting irrigation and factory legislation. He was always courteous and never ill-natured, and shunned both good living and High Society. By the time he took office the federal system was functioning smoothly. The common market had been established between the states, and the state governments had gained financially by the transfer of certain of their previous responsibilities to the national government. Most of

33 H. G. Turner, *The First Decade of the Australian Commonwealth*, Melbourne, 1911, p. 55.

them found that the return of three-quarters of the customs revenue by the federal government provided them with an adequate income. Furthermore, the federal government had already proved to be cautious in its financial policies and moderate in its exercise of legislative powers, and had not interfered with the right of the states to borrow capital in order to finance their public works. Indeed, had it done so, by becoming a competitor for loan funds, the economic and social condition of many breadwinners would have been a great deal worse than it was, because the continued borrowing of money helped to provide employment on public works at a time when many primary producers and urban workers dependent on handling wool were suffering from the most severe drought in Australia's history.[34] The public debt of the six states rose by £24 million in the first four years of federal government, half the new loan money having been borrowed by New South Wales; the large expenditure in New South Wales, Victoria, Queensland and Western Australia was incurred in railway construction. Although an increasing proportion of the new loans was raised within Australia, eighty-three percent was still owing in London in 1904.[35]

A dry period, which had begun in the inland wool-growing areas in the mid-1890s, became progressively worse and culminated in the catastrophic season of 1902. The drought, which lasted until 1904, devastated large areas of the sunburnt country in the sweeping inland plains of Queensland and western New South Wales. It destroyed millions of livestock and reduced the sheep population of Australia to less than half what it had been in 1891. It also ruined thousands of settlers and drove many of them from the outback into the coastal cities. Those pastoralists who managed to survive had to contend with a plague of rabbits, which permanently devastated vast areas of marginal pastoral land already weakened by years of over-stocking. The surviving squatters also had to endure low wool and stock prices, and the reluctance of banks and other financial institutions to lend them money for improvements or for protection against the rabbits. As Australia was heavily dependent on selling primary products to English manufacturers and borrowing capital from British-based banks, and as Australian sheep stations supplied most of the raw material needed by English woollen mills, the economic health of the new federation was poor during the first five years of the century. There was little new investment of overseas capital in pastoral enterprises, and few immigrants were attracted from Britain to take up sheep stations or farms in the outback areas. Itinerant unskilled bush workers had great difficulty in finding employment.

However, important pockets in the near-coastal rural areas escaped the worst of the drought, and most wheat-farmers in New South Wales,

[34] See T. A. Coghlan, *Labour and Industry in Australia*, London, 1918, *4*, pp. 2138–9, 2152–4.

[35] *Official Year Book of the Commonwealth of Australia*, *3*, 1910, pp. 836–40.

Victoria and South Australia were able to keep their land under cultivation. Fruit growers in the Murray irrigation districts did well, and so did the miners at Kalgoorlie on Western Australia's eastern goldfields. Gold production reached its peak in 1902, the year in which the 350-mile water pipeline was completed linking Kalgoorlie and other desert towns with the Mundaring Weir near the western coast. Western Australia's population and wheat acreage rose rapidly; most of the new arrivals came from Victoria, very few from overseas.[36] In fact, there was only a slow growth in Australia's total population in the years 1901–5, from 3,765,000 to 3,984,000, partly because the average size of families were declining, and partly because there was a negligible gain from net migration. The feature of Australia's demographic development most noticed by contemporary visitors was the concentration of people in the coastal commercial centres, especially in the suburbs of Melbourne and Sydney, where most of the factory industries were located. At the time of the Census of 1901, 43 per cent of the working population was employed in commerce, transport and manufacturing (18 per cent in factories), whilst only 40 per cent were employed in primary production,[37] and during the next decade the former rose whilst the latter fell.

It was this concentration of industrial and urban wage-earners, and hence of voters, which had a considerable influence on Australian politics and government, and helped to focus public interest on such issues as tariffs, wages and industrial employment.[38] Nevertheless, farmers and their spokesmen considered that life on the land was inherently more virtuous, as well as more healthy, more important and more productive than life in the towns, and foremost among the exponents of the evils of city life were the country newspapers which were convinced that cities vampire-like sucked the blood from their surrounding country; and none more so than Sydney, which had over one-third of the state's population 'where they add nothing to our productiveness, our wealth or our exports'.[39] It was rare during the early years of the twentieth century for anyone to defend the cities and to justify their growth on the grounds that so long as the country sent down plenty of raw material for shipment from the pastoral, agricultural and mining industries, so long would the raw material be bought and sold and mortgaged in those places, and the more that was sent down the more effort would be required to handle it,

36 F. K. Crowley, *Australia's Western Third*, London, 1960, chs. 5, 6.

37 Professional 69,899: Domestic 50,335: Commercial 188,144: Transport and Communication 118,730: Industrial 350,596: Primary Producers 494,163. *Official Year Book of the Commonwealth of Australia, 1901–1907, 1*, 1908, p. 169.

38 See E. T. McPhee, 'The Urbanization of Australian Population', in P. D. Phillips and G. L. Wood, Eds., *The Peopling of Australia*, Melbourne, 1928: *Urbanization in Australia*, being *Australian Economic History Review*, X, 2, September 1970.

39 *Queanbeyan Observer*, 1 August 1905.

and the more would the producers need supplies and equipment manufactured in the cities, as well as railways and other conveyances to sustain their commerce. Hence, the greater the number of men who went on the land, the greater would Sydney and Melbourne become, quite apart from the employment generated within the cities by their own growth and by the policy of tariff protection.[40]

Although the parties in the federal parliament had reached a compromise in 1902 over the nature of the national tariff and had agreed to observe a fiscal truce for the time being, both Deakin and Watson, the Liberal and Labor leaders, believed that the Australian standard of living needed additional safeguards besides the barriers already erected against the import of Asian labour or of cheap manufactured goods. Trade unionists and Labor politicians were convinced that Australian workmen needed help in improving the wages and working conditions offered by Australian employers, whilst Liberal politicians believed that the community ought to be protected against the irresponsibility of either employers or wage-earners who attempted to gain their objectives by lock-outs or strikes. After the industrial disturbances of the early 1890s in eastern Australia, some parliaments had legislated to provide minimum standards of working conditions in shops, mines and factories, and it was widely acknowledged, though not enforced by general legislation, that eight hours a day, and forty-eight hours a weeek, was the maximum expected of most wage-earners: the celebration of Eight Hours Day with parades and public sports was an annual festival in every state capital. Some states had also established boards, commissions or courts to settle disputes over wages and conditions of employment. A wages board system existed in Victoria and South Australia, and by the turn of the century there were arbitration courts in Western Australia and New South Wales. These quasi-judicial committees or courts were expected to bring the influence of the state to bear on matters which were likely to disturb the 'People's Peace'. Hence, most governments, employers and employees had become convinced that neither laissez-faire nor combative collective bargaining was in the best interests of all concerned, and that legislation by democratically elected parliaments should declare strikes and lock-outs to be illegal, and those who engaged in them to be subject to legal penalties. As the Brisbane *Worker* hopefully declared, 'Arbitration will take from us, it is said, and truly, the power to cease work. But while we have the power to vote that will not matter a great deal. We can hit Capitalism harder at the ballot box than we ever did on strike.'[41]

During the 1890s the creation of an industrial tribunal to keep

40 See the article by C.W., 'The Australian City', in *Sydney Morning Herald*, 8 June 1907.

41 *Worker*, Brisbane, 26 March 1904. For a general discussion see R. Gollan, *Radical and Working Class Politics: A Study of Eastern Australia, 1850–1910*, Melbourne, 1960.

the peace on a national scale had also been proposed, and this was adopted by the constitution-makers; a clause was inserted into the federal constitution enabling parliament to deal with disputes which occurred in more than one state at the one time, the wording being 'Conciliation and arbitration for the prevention and settlement of industrial disputes extending beyond the limits of any one State'. But although many federal politicians and trade union leaders supported the idea in principle, they disagreeed strongly about the degree to which any new national authority ought to interfere with the right of the state governments to determine their own standards of industrial employment, especially for their own employees. Most Liberal politicians supported some form of federal compulsory conciliation or arbitration, though they insisted that it be reconciled with the basic notion of federalism, which was to preserve the respective rights of federal and state authorities. On the other hand, Labor politicians, who saw in compulsory arbitration a means of achieving a larger share of the community cake at a time when trade union strength was very weak, were much more centrally minded, and were convinced that a nation-wide system of arbitration should be created, whatever might be its adverse effect on the federal compact. A number of trade unions were already federally organized, but gained no benefit from it. Furthermore there was no uniformity in conditions of employment in the same occupations in different states. Labor leaders were also influenced by the unsuccessful and bitterly contested week-long railway strike in Victoria early in May 1903,[42] which persuaded them that the federal parliament might be used to discipline state governments which were not sympathetic to Labor. The strike was one of the major industrial disturbances of the first ten years of the century and was the first large-scale disruption of a government public utility. It began when militant unionists made 'excessive' demands on the Irvine government, and it ended in unconditional surrender of the men. A strike of public servants is 'a monstrosity as well as a crime', declared the Melbourne *Age*, 'since it must always be a strike against Parliament, which in other words is a revolt against the people who make Parliament'.[43] The Victorian parliament agreed with these sentiments.

One of the earliest champions of industrial conciliation and arbitration was the federal minister for Customs, C. C. Kingston from South Australia, who had introduced arbitration into his state whilst premier in the 1890s, and who had also pioneered female franchise and other reforms. He resigned from Barton's government in 1903 because he could not persuade his colleagues to extend the power of the proposed federal arbitration court to deal with seamen employed in all ships engaged in the coastal trade, whether they were Australian-registered

[42] See L. Benham and J. Rickard, 'Masters and Servants: The Victorian Railway Strike of 1903', in J. Iremonger, *et al.*, Eds, *Strikes: Studies in Twentieth Century Australian Social History*, Sydney, 1973.

[43] *Age*, Melbourne, 16 May 1903.

ships or not. Soon afterwards the Barton government shelved the bill to establish the court, because ministers did not agree with the majority in the House of Representatives who wanted to extend federal authority to cover working conditions in the state government railways, which were not only the states' main security for their public debts but employed a very large permanent and casual workforce – all potential Labor voters.

By the time of the second federal election in December 1903 it was clear that industrial arbitration had taken the place of the tariff as the most divisive issue in national politics. Deakin stated unequivocally that 'to strike a blow at the railways would be to strike a blow at that state of self-government which we are entitled to preserve', whilst Watson, the Labor leader, insisted that there should be an arbitration system applying to the whole of Australia, because existing state acts could not deal adequately with such employees as seamen and railway workers.[44] As the Labor party had become a political *tertium quid* and its support was essential if either Deakin or Reid wished to enact industrial legislation, it was possible for Watson to insist that the federal parliament should endorse Labor's proposal; as Watson remarked, 'it mattered not to the Labor party which set of men carried out their measures. They were only concerned with the measures brought out.'[45] For over a year Labor's political strength on this issue, and the inability of the others to come to an agreement amongst themselves, kept the arbitration issue unresolved.

The result of the December 1903 election did not greatly change the character of federal politics. Free-traders, protectionists and Labor candidates were returned to the House of Representatives in almost equal numbers, and this political contest with its 'three elevens' continued for another six years, bearing no resemblance whatever to English cricket or to the Westminster two-party political system. During a luncheon speech to the Australian Natives' Association early in 1904 Deakin had likened the situation to a game of cricket with three teams: 'What a game of cricket you would have if there were three elevens in the field instead of two, and one of those elevens sometimes playing on one side, sometimes on the other, and sometimes for itself.'[46] The analogy was taken up by the press, but it greatly exaggerated the extent of discipline among the 'teams', especially amongst the two loosely-knit groups of parliamentarians led respectively by Deakin (high tariffists) and Reid (low tariffists). Both were divided on most other matters, in much the same fashion as Labor members differed among themselves on the tariff question.

The arbitration issue produced as much heated debate between the

[44] Deakin's speech – *Argus*, Melbourne, 30 October 1903: Watson's – *Wagga Wagga Express*, 14 November 1903.

[45] *Wagga Wagga Express*, 14 November 1903.

[46] *Argus*, Melbourne, 2 February 1904, part-published in F. K. Crowley, *Modern Australia in Documents, I*, 1901–1939, Melbourne, 1973, pp. 56–7.

three groups as the tariff issue had done. It upset one ministry and wrecked two others. It antagonized all state governments and greatly delayed the work of the national parliament. In April 1904 the Deakin government resigned when the House of Representatives supported a Labor motion to extend the power of the federal court to state government employees. J. C. Watson then formed a Labor party ministry which, in the opinion of the Melbourne *Argus*, was,

of course, entitled to a fair and reasonable chance of showing what, as a minority, it can do. One minority, led by very able and experienced men, has confessed itself unable to govern further, having regard to the present divisions of the House. Another minority, led by men of no experience, has undertaken the task. It will now have an opportunity of feeling something of what it has, with no compunction, inflicted for years past.[47]

John Christian Watson, a New Zealander by upbringing and a compositor by trade, had been a member of the New South Wales parliament since the early 1890s, and had opposed the federal constitution because of the electoral principle of equal state representation in the Senate. He was elected to the first federal parliament and was chosen as the first party leader.[48] But Australia's first national Labor government only lasted four months. Watson resigned when the House of Representatives defeated his proposal to include a substantial measure of preference to unionists participating in the decisions of the proposed Arbitration Court. Eventually the Reid-McLean coalition government, a temporary coalition of the free-traders with some protectionists formed in August 1904, piloted an amended bill through both houses of parliament. This was the main achievement of the second federal parliament (1903–6). The act established a federal tribunal and a system of compulsory conciliation and arbitration to deal with inter-state disputes. But not long afterwards the High Court declared that the Arbitration Court had no power to deal with state government railway servants, and by implication with any other state employees, so that the political struggle in the federal parliament on that issue was seen to have been wasted effort. The High Court agreed with Deakin that to give the federal Arbitration Court jurisdiction over state employees would undermine the basic principle of the federal constitution, which safeguarded the autonomy of the state governments within their own jurisdiction; this view remained paramount until the complexion of the majority of the High Court bench changed in the 1920s.

It was not the federal Arbitration Court's constitutional powers which gave it an important role in Australian society, but the lead which the court gave to state authorities and the encouragement it

47 *Argus*, Melbourne, 25 April 1904.

48 For a brief discussion of his leadership problems see H. S. Broadhead, 'J. C. Watson and the Caucus Crisis of 1905', in *A.J.P.H.*, *VIII*, 1, May 1962.

gave to trade unionism. Mainly because arbitration courts would only deal with the representatives of organized associations, there was a rapid increase in the number of trade unions in Australia, and membership more than trebled in the years 1906–14.[49] At the same time the president of the federal Arbitration Court, Henry Bournes Higgins, a former Victorian M.L.A. and M.H.R., adopted a style of approach to industrial affairs which he described as 'a new province for law and order', and which was widely accepted.[50] Although not a member of the Labor party, Higgins had served as attorney-general in the short-lived Watson government, and his appointment to the High Court, together with that of Isaac Isaacs, brought a new and less conservative approach to the deliberations of the bench. Higgins succeeded O'Connor, the first president of the Arbitration Court, and Higgins's influence was soon felt.

To some extent the opportunity for this was provided by the Deakin government's policy of New Protection, which succeeded arbitration as the main issue in national politics in the years 1905–8. Deakin had returned to office in July 1905, with Labor support, and until November 1908 led the longest and most successful of the early federal administrations. He committed his government to a legislative programme which involved a further extension of industrial protection by legislation. This policy, which was the subject of a special white paper presented to parliament in October 1907, tried to ensure that a manufacturer who benefited from the federal protective tariffs against overseas competition should charge a reasonable price for the goods which he produced, and should provide fair and reasonable wages and conditions of work for his employees; the government declared that 'The "old" Protection contented itself with making good wages possible. The "new" Protection seeks to make them actual.' Employers were to be told that if they desired higher duties then they must give higher wages.[51]

Several acts of the federal parliament in 1905 and 1906 attempted to apply the principle of conditional protection on a national scale, in some instances offering inducements by way of a bounty or a rebate of excise duty, in others attempting by regulative or restrictive provisions to compel employers to conform. The idea of New Protection derived from the industrial legislation of the 1890s, and was the Liberal answer to industrial regulation: it fell short of statutory

---

49 1901–68,218: 1906–147,049: 1911–344,999: 1914–523,271: *Official Year Book of the Commonwealth of Australia, 1901–1919, 13*, 1920, pp. 982–6. See also M. Atkinson, Ed., *Trade Unionism in Australia*, Sydney, 1915, and J. T. Sutcliffe, *A History of Trade Unionism in Australia*, Melbourne, 1921.

50 See H. B. Higgins, *A New Province for Law and Order*, Sydney, 1922: N. Palmer, *Henry Bournes Higgins*, London, 1931.

51 *New Protection – Explanatory Memorandum in Regard to, C.P.P.* 1907–8, 2, pp. 1887–9. See also J. A. La Nauze, *Alfred Deakin*, Melbourne, 1965, 2, p. 410 ff.

compulsion, which the Labor party wanted, and yet was far too radical for the conservative free-traders. In some instances the federal Arbitration Court was given the task of declaring what ought to be 'fair and reasonable' wages (without being given any guide as to the meaning of those words), and no judicial decision roused greater interest in the first decade of federation than that given in the Harvester Case on 8 November 1907. None had such long-term significance. In his judgement in this case Mr Justice Higgins, largely by intelligent guesswork, determined a minimum living wage for an unskilled male Australian worker of 7s. per day for a six-day working week, based on the grounds of 'the normal needs of the average employee, regarded as a human being living in a civilized community', and not on the grounds of his employer's capacity to pay it.[52]

Ultimately, the High Court invalidated most of the New Protection legislation, either because it believed that the federal parliament had no power to interfere with the internal industrial affairs of the states, or because the constitution had not given the parliament the power to legislate on labour generally or to control monopolies which might not have the best interests of Australia and its wage-earners at heart. Nevertheless, the experiment with New Protection on a national scale had important long-term industrial and political consequences. From it came the judicial standard of 7s. per day for all unskilled labourers, and the concept of an Australian needs-based minimum wage – the basic wage, which dominated thinking about industrial affairs for the next sixty years. From it also came the firm Labor conviction that only by altering the federal constitution and thereby by-passing the 'small oligarchy of non-elected irremovable judges' could national industrial justice be obtained. The public spectacle of disagreement on the High Court bench had not added majesty to the court's decision, as the *Round Table* observed:–

Probably the electors would be more resigned to the burial of this legislation in the cemetery of the High Court, if all the judges had joined in making the funeral. But a most remarkable feature of the decisions has been that in almost every case the same three judges, Chief Justice Griffith, and Justices Barton and O'Connor, have signed the death certificate, while the other two, Justices Isaacs and Higgins, equally competent legal physicians, have solemnly declared that the Act has been buried alive.[53]

Whilst the debates about the nature and extent of federal arbitration were continuing, the liberal protectionists were insisting that the

[52] *Commonwealth Arbitration Reports*, II, 1906. See also P. G. Macarthy, 'Justice Higgins and the Harvester Judgement', in *A.E.H.R.*, IX, 1, March 1969: P. G. Macarthy, 'Labor and the Living Wage, 1890–1910', in *A.J.P.H.*, XIII, 1, April 1967: M. R. Hill, 'The Basic Wage, 1907–1953', in *A.Q.*, XXV, 4, December 1953.

[53] *Round Table*, London, March 1912, p. 360. For an early comment on the political complexion of the court see the *Bulletin*, Sydney, 1 October 1903, p. 9. The main Acts declared invalid were the Trade Marks Act of 1905, the Excise Tariff Act of 1906 and the Australian Industries Preservation Act of 1907.

compromise tariff of 1902, on which the New Protection policy had been based, was inadequate to ensure the full development of Australian manufacturing and other industries. This issue had been one of the most contentious at the federal election of 1906, and although the liberal protectionists did not poll well, Deakin's government continued to be supported by the Labor party, and its fiscal policy of tariff protection was supported by a large number of Labor members. The government therefore placed its protectionist proposals before parliament in August 1907, and, after marathon debates in both houses, a protective tariff was eventually enacted in June 1908, which also gave a unilateral five per cent margin of preference to British-made goods.[54]

The debates were lengthy because Reid's free-traders and the free-traders within the Labor party realized that the protectionists were too strong in numbers and that this was their final chance. This was the last general debate on the most divisive issue which had been inherited from nineteenth century politics, and the free-traders lost the battle. As in 1902, the free-traders were compelled to submit to an increase in protective duties, whilst the protectionists claimed that the new tariff was insufficiently protective. However, in its general incidence the tariff of 1908 was much more protective than the compromise of 1902, and may be regarded as the first fully protective tariff. The Deakin government also allied with it a further extension of New Protection, and at the same time the Labor party's national conference formally incorporated New Protection into its own policy. It was fitting in these circumstances that the prime minister who was responsible for the first national protective tariff should have been both a Victorian and a protegé of David Syme of the Melbourne *Age*, whose paper had led the first successful agitation for a protective tariff forty years earlier.

The establishment of a system of federal arbitration in 1904, the various experiments with New Protection legislation in 1905–7, and the adoption of a national protective tariff in 1908 had all taken place in a political situation of flux and instability. But during these years there emerged in Australian state and federal politics marked differences of objective and method between the new Labor parties and the other groups with whom the Labor parties had at first allied themselves, chiefly the liberal protectionists and the urban radicals. This was illustrated by the way in which the Labor parties organized their state and federal conferences, gradually defined their platforms, and disciplined their parliamentary representatives by the use of the pre-selection of election candidates, by the signing of the party Pledge by all endorsed candidates, and discussion of issues in a caucus consisting of all the members of the party belonging to a particular parliament at any one time. Members pledged themselves to support

[54] Australian tariff history has attracted few scholars. See V. M. Segal 'The Development of Tariff Protection in Australia', in *A.Q.*, IX, 2, June 1937: A. J. Reitsma, *Trade Protection in Australia*, Brisbane, 1960.

the party's Objective, as well as a Fighting Platform and a General Platform, the two latter owing much of their detail to Australian liberals and radicals, and something to overseas influences; they were remarkable in their combination of racist, nationalist, socialist, reformist, militarist and idealist objectives. The decisions reached by the majority of members of caucus on questions of methods and minor matters became binding on all members in the parliament, whether they approved of them or not. The latter principle was, in effect, an extension to parliament itself of the well known principle of corporate cabinet responsibility, but was heartily disliked by Labor's parliamentary opponents who eschewed tight discipline and regimentation, and insisted that they should maintain their independence as representatives of electorates, and not become delegates of classes or of groups within the electorates. Critics of Labor also felt that a written undertaking in the form of the Pledge to be honest and faithful was likely to have the opposite effect, and that a gentleman did not need such a crude form of coercion in order to make him remain true to his ideals.

Liberalism of the type espoused by Deakin and his Victorian protectionists, which lay somewhere between the extreme forms of socialism and conservatism, appeared to be on the decline electorally. Labor obtained a continuous increase in support from the voters, and frequently at the expense of those liberals who were closest to it in objective – the 'as-good-as-Labor' men. In three successive federal elections Labor candidates increased their share of the valid Representatives vote from 19 per cent to 36 per cent, and their seats from 14 to 26; in the Senate elections they did correspondingly well. Most of their success was at the expense of the liberal-protectionists, whose share of the vote fell from 46 per cent to 24 per cent in 1901–1906, though some of this was due to vote-splitting under the first-past-the-post system of voting. Labor parties formed minority short-lived governments in the federal and Western Australian parliaments in 1904, and in the years 1903–6 they entered into coalition governments in Queensland and South Australia. Their success stemmed partly from the fast-growing trade unions (523,000 members by 1914), partly from their obvious appeal to class interests in urban, industrial and working class electorates, and partly from their single-minded devotion to the objective of taking a greater share of the wealth of the community away from the employers by raising wages and reducing the hours of work. Their principles also appealed to many 'brain workers' and to small employers and storekeepers.[55]

55 The rise of political Labor parties in this period has been studied extensively. See V. S. Clark, *The Labour Movement in Australasia*, Westminster, 1906: *Round Table*, London, September 1912, pp. 657–77: G. V. Portus, 'The Labour Movement in Australia, 1788–1914', in M. Atkinson, Ed., *Australia: Economic and Political Studies*, Melbourne, 1920, ch. 4: V. G. Childe, *How Labour Governs*, London, 1923: B. Fitzpatrick, *A Short History of the Australian Labour Movement*, Melbourne, 1944: L. F. Crisp, *The Australian Federal Labour Party 1901–1951*,

By this time colonial governmentalism or state socialism had been further developed by the six state parliaments. The number of state government employees was rising, especially in the public utilities, parliaments were taking more interest in the regulation of industrial employment and in social welfare, and their financial resources were being used to promote large-scale rural settlement. Labor members had endorsed this trend, and in some instances had been decisive in accelerating it. But by doing so they had made many voters apprehensive about the long-term consequences of this policy for the nature of the capitalist economy, because Labor proposed a more extensive use of the powers of government to interfere with the economic organization of society than had been customary. The Liberal politicians were also becoming aware that they were being encouraged to adopt a greater degree of interference and regulation than their own supporters were prepared to endorse. The free-traders and the conservatives were more outspoken. Before and during the federal election campaign of 1906 George Reid declared that the real issue in Australia was the growing menace of 'the socialist tiger'; he launched an anti-socialist campaign designed to discredit the Labor party by branding it as extremist, and also in the hope of uniting the non-Labor groups into one non-Labor party, presumably led by himself. In April 1906 George Reid and W. A. Holman, representing the New South Wales Free Trade and Labor parties respectively, engaged in a lengthy public debate over two evenings on 'Socialism as defined by the Objective and Platform of the Labor Party', which was reported in full in the Sydney *Daily Telegraph* and eventually published as a pamphlet.[56]

Many of the anti-socialist candidates polled well. They were also able to exploit some of the recent statements by Catholic bishops who were extremely worried about the materialist preoccupations of Australians, and who feared that extreme forms of socialism of the 'foreign' or 'Communistic' or 'European' type would become popular and subvert existing social conditions.[57] Anti-socialists could also dwell

London, 1955: R. Gollan, *Radical and Working Class Politics: A Study of Eastern Australia, 1850–1910*, Melbourne, 1960.

[56] See the account of the historic debate in H. V. Evatt, *Australian Labour Leader: The Story of W. A. Holman and the Labour Movement*, Sydney, 1940, ch. 26. Another two contemporary controversialists were A. St. Ledger, *Australian Socialism*, London, 1909, and W. M. Hughes, *The Case for Labor*, Sydney, 1910. Two leaders of the movement gave interesting explanations of the rise of socialism – W. G. Spence, *Australia's Awakening*, Sydney, 1909, and J. C. Watson, 'The Labour Movement', in *British Association for the Advancement of Science: Handbook for New South Wales*, Sydney, 1914. See also R. N. Ebbels, *The Australian Labor Movement: 1850–1907*, Sydney, 1960, ch. 8, and I. Turner, *Industrial Labour and Politics: The Dynamics of the Labour Movement in Eastern Australia, 1900–1921*, Canberra, 1965.

[57] *Freemans Journal*, Sydney, 16 September 1905, pp. 17–19. See also A. E. Cahill, 'Catholicism and Socialism – The 1905 Controversy in Australia', in *The Journal of Religious History, I, 2*, December 1960.

on the written platform of the political Labor movement, especially that part which threatened 'the collective ownership of monopolies and the extension of the industrial and economic functions of the State and the Municipality'. Although Labor leaders eschewed ideological programmes, when they were pressed by their opponents they readily admitted that if their objectives were realized they would lead to a substantial degree of evolutionary socialism. However, none of the parties to the controversy was able or willing to agree to a definition of socialism, as a contemporary remarked:

it is something to all men and something different to each point of view. It is a philosophy and an ethical scheme, a religion, an economic interpretation of history, a legal concept, a popular and progressive movement, a revolution or evolution, the hope of mankind, or the last evil days of this world.[58]

At the time of the discussion on the national tariff of 1908, though not because of it, the federal Labor conference prohibited any further alliances with other political groups, and in November 1908 Labor withdrew its support from Deakin's national government. Andrew Fisher, who had replaced J. C. Watson as Labor party leader, then formed a short-lived Labor administration; Fisher was a Scottish immigrant of the 1880s who had become an active unionist whilst mining in Queensland, and had also served in the Queensland parliament. But the introduction of the protective tariff and the Labor conference decision prohibiting alliances had persuaded many members of the national parliament that the only hope for stable government, and thereby control of the Labor minority, lay in the formation of a single non-Labor party. One of the difficulties which prevented the achievement of this was the personal mistrust of Reid by Deakin; another was that the protectionists disliked the conservatives amongst the free-traders. But towards the end of 1908 Reid resigned as leader of the free-traders and was succeeded by Joseph Cook, a former protectionist and also a former Labor leader. Fisher's speech at Gympie in March 1909 was a forthright and very thorough statement of Labor's aims and did much to frighten the conservatives into a non-Labor alliance, especially by proposing to establish a federal land tax in order to break up the big estates.[59] Fisher's speech also took place during a five-months' struggle over wages between the trade unions and the mining companies at Broken Hill, which had led to unemployment, poverty, distress and occasional acts of violence.[60]

Against this background a fusion was negotiated between Deakin's protectionist group (ten in number), Cook's free trade group and the

---

58 H. V. Evatt, *Liberalism in Australia*, Sydney, 1918, p. 63.

59 *Courier*, Brisbane, 31 March 1909.

60 See G. Osborne, 'Town and Company: The Broken Hill Industrial Dispute of 1908-9' in J. Iremonger, *et al.*, Eds., *Strikes: Studies in Twentieth Century Australian Social History*, Sydney, 1973.

Corner group, of which the unofficial leader was Sir John Forrest; Forrest had left Deakin's government in 1907 because of its reliance on Labor. Fisher was forced to resign when parliament resumed in May 1909 and Deakin then formed the first composite Liberal government supported by most of the non-Labor members of the federal parliament. This inaugurated the two-party political system in Australian national politics and provided a powerful example to the non-Labor groups in the state parliaments. The conservatives thought the new situation was a wholesome state of affairs. Labor leaders, especially the vitriolic W. M. Hughes, described the fusion as an act of gross opportunism. Liberals who were left out or who stayed out of the fusion said Deakin had betrayed liberalism. Deakin was obviously pleased to have become – though reluctantly at first—the leader of such a large party, but nevertheless was uneasy that he had presided over the death of Australian liberalism: it had been 'crushed between the upper and nether millstones'.[61]

The fusion, later Liberal government, of 1909–10[62] was one of the most successful in federal politics, but its life was cut short by the sweeping victory of Labor at the federal elections of April 1910. This was the first time in the history of federal politics that a single party had won a clear majority in both houses of parliament, and also the first occasion on which the Labor party was able to form a majority government in federal politics; it had won a majority in South Australia ten days earlier, and shortly afterwards also captured the lower house in the New South Wales parliament, and thus held power both in the federal parliament and in the parliament of the largest state. The Liberals blamed the federal debacle on the apathy of the electorate: only sixty-three per cent voted. However, many electors obviously objected to the blatant opportunism of the liberal and conservative politicians who had organized the fusion. The Adelaide *Advertiser* rightly commented that 'the Fusion further strengthened Labor, because Labor could point to it as the embodiment of the Conservative idea. The middle party, absorbed in the Fusion could no longer be distinguished from the Tory extremists with whom its leaders had made friends'.[63] It was some time before the newly-christened Federal Liberal Union and Liberal party clarified their objectives.[64]

[61] This was the accurate forecast of the editor of the Brisbane *Courier* on 14 December 1906.

[62] See *Round Table*, London, August 1911, p. 502 – 'To avoid misunderstanding, it should be pointed out that the term "Liberal" is frequently used in Australia to denote the whole body of those opposed to the Labour, or Socialist policy; and includes not only persons to whom the name would be given in England, but also many who in that country would be called Conservatives, or even Tories. Compare the names "Republican" and "Democrat", as applied to the great political parties of the United States.'

[63] *Advertiser*, Adelaide, 15 April 1910.

[64] See the *Argus*, Melbourne, 26 May 1909, and the *Age*, Melbourne, 29 May 1909 for the original compact.

The decade which ended in 1910 with the electoral victories of the Labor parties had been the age of liberal experiment. The liberals, and especially the Deakinite liberal-protectionists, were committed to an all-round policy of protection – of the population, its industries, its manufactures, and its standard of living. They were successful in achieving it because they rightly judged the sentiment of the electorate and because they were voluntarily given the support of the Labor party who agreed with many of their objectives. Labor gave this support because it had less in common with the loosely-knit group of free-traders, which contained a higher proportion of social conservatives than the Deakinite protectionist party. However, the Labor party had not made or unmade the governments of the first decade of federalism, nor did it hold the balance of power and wring concessions from Deakin's liberals. Indeed, by supporting Deakin's government of 1906–8 the party lost its independence, which it realized when it later withdrew that support and found that it could not govern alone.

The liberals were not prepared to go as far as Labor demanded in the regulation of economic conditions. Nor were they prepared to interfere seriously with the financial rights of the state governments. Their statemindedness was neither an irrational parochialism nor a rigid conservatism. It was a legitimate view of the nature of the original federal compact based on the presumption that the electorate as a whole did not want a greater degree of centralism. Especially was this so in the 'smaller' states. As early as 1906 their leaders had been grumbling about the disadvantages of the federal union, feeling that they were no longer their own masters. The Western Australian parliament agreed to a resolution in September 1906 suggesting that the state should withdraw from the federation, and there was strong anti-federal feeling in South Australia at the same time. In the years that followed localism, provincialism and parochialism all still existed just as strongly as in 1901, and quickly came to the surface when arbitration or state finances were being discussed. By 1908 the Hobart *Mercury* was thundering that the situation was rapidly degenerating into 'Bastard Unification',[65] whilst the Melbourne *Argus* claimed that state rights had been ignored in the federal Arbitration Act, Transferred Properties Bill, Surplus Reserve Bill, and in the New Protection policy, and that the states' Senate was dominated by the socialists and state rights were never considered.[66] Deakin well expressed the liberals' viewpoint when he remarked that

it is the preservation of that poise and balance between the centrifugal and the centripetal tendencies which makes the true federalist at one time the antagonist of State aggression, and at another time the antagonist of the undue aggrandisement of the central Government. In the poise and balance of the two lies the very essence of the life of a Federal Constitution, as in

[65] *Mercury*, Hobart, 9 May 1908.

[66] *Argus*, Melbourne, 10 October 1908

the solar system the planets move in their orbits, neither falling into the sun to be consumed, nor passing into outer space.[67]

Nor was the liberals' desire to impose limits on government authority a conservative view of politics. Rather, it was based on the conviction that there was a point beyond which the government should not interfere with the rights of the individual, whether he was an employer, an employee or self-employed. In the first decade of the century the liberals did much to make the formative period of Australian national government a successful venture in industrial experiment and federalism, and it was the irony of history that they should lose power after being convicted of political opportunism, and yet be replaced by a party whose rhetorical dedication to 'support in return for concessions' had been an equally obvious example of political opportunism.[68]

The arrangements which were made in this decade for the military and naval defence of Australia reflected the growing Australian-ness of politicians. However, as the politicians, newspaper editors, journalists, pamphleteers and publicists all took part in bringing about a marriage of nationalist and imperialist objectives, it is impossible to apportion credit for the special type of defence policy which had been established by 1914. There were two phases in this development. The first was conditioned by Australia's long experience of colonial dependence on Britain and its lack of sovereign national status. The second was influenced by major changes in the structure of world politics. In the early years of the twentieth century Barton, Deakin and most of their liberal and conservative supporters were unwilling to commit Australia to an independent naval defence programme, partly because it would have been too costly for the federal government to bear, and partly because it was unnecessary in view of Australia's junior role in the empire. In any case the Home Government did not favour separate local seagoing fleets, preferring that the colonies and dominions should contribute financially to the maintenance of naval squadrons based in various regions of the world, but operating strategically on behalf of the empire as a whole. Naval power was the basis of all imperial foreign and trade policies – 'the Empire floats upon its fleet', and the British admiralty considered that local navies tied to geographical areas would weaken central control in times of emergency. This was the Blue Water policy which Barton and the

---

[67] *C.P.D.*, 22 March 1904, *18*, pp. 777–8.

[68] The apportioning of credit for the Liberal successes in the years 1901–1910 remains a matter of debate amongst historians and political activists. The most useful articles are by P. Loveday, 'Support in return for Concessions', in *H.S.*, *55*, October 1970: H. Mayer, 'Some Conceptions of the Australian Party System, 1910–1950', in *H.S.*, *27*, November 1956: D. W. Rawson, 'Another Look at Initiative and Resistance', in *Politics*, *III*, 1, May 1968, and replies to this article in later issues of that journal: P. B. Westerway, 'Cliches on Australian Politics, 1900–1950', in *Melbourne Historical Journal*, *3*, 1963/64.

federal parliament endorsed, after some hesitation and much public criticism, in 1903; it was also agreed at that time that Australia would supply the crews, but not the officers, for four of the ships in the Royal Navy's Australian Squadron.

With regard to military defence, there was no great problem. The imperial government was happy to see the nucleus of dominion forces established and to assist by seconding senior officers to command them. A military force was created in 1901–03 by the general officer commanding, Major-General Sir Edward Hutton, which was somewhat smaller than the sum of the colonial forces which had existed at the time of federation.[69] In addition, the early defence acts established the principle that all men between eighteen and sixty should be compelled to give military service on the home front in time of war. As it was not thought possible that Australia would be involved in the wars of the Old World, no provision was made for compulsory military service in overseas countries, though it was presumed that Australians would loyally volunteer to serve the Flag if the Mother Country were ever in danger. This, too, was thought to be highly unlikely, since the Royal Navy policed the world's shipping lanes and was the most powerful force which the world had ever known; the white ensign guaranteed a white Australia. Advocates of military conscription in peace-time had few adherents, mainly because despite the imperialist fervour which had been generated by the Boer War, there was still a widespread antipathy to any proposal which smacked of militarism. Besides, Australian trade unionists had already experienced confrontation with the military forces during the labour troubles of the early 1890s and did not wish to see the national government develop a powerful military arm.

At the suggestion of the premier of New South Wales, J. H. Carruthers, the Premiers' Conference of February 1905 agreed that in future 24 May, the late Queen Victoria's birthday, should become a public holiday known as Empire Day, and that special lessons should be taught in the state schools 'to imbue children with the Imperial Sentiment'; they should be taught that

Countries separated by the bulge of a hemisphere, peopled by races divergent in colour, creed, language, and laws, look up to the one flag as they do to the one sun, and see there the symbol of that mutually guaranteed peace in which they live and prosper – the peace of the strong man armed who keepeth his court.[70]

About that time both imperial and colonial opinion about empire defence began to change.[71] The attitude of the British government

---

[69] W. Perry, 'Military reforms of General Sir Edward Hutton in the Commonwealth of Australia: 1902–04', in *The Victorian Historical Magazine*, 29, 1, February 1959.

[70] Editorial in the *Daily Telegraph*, Sydney, 24 May 1905.

[71] See *Round Table*, London, August 1911, p. 498 ff.

was powerfully affected by the changing balance of power amongst the main European nations, and especially by the aggressive naval armament programme adopted by Germany, which concentrated British attention on the North Sea.

The attitude of the Australians was influenced by 'the Awakening of the East', and especially by the rapid rise of Japan as an expansionist power in the Pacific, following her sudden and unexpected defeat of the Russians at Mukden in March 1905 and her destruction of the Russian naval force in May 1905. Most Australians would have echoed the *Daily Telegraph*'s comment – 'we have been slumbering beside a volcano, the danger of which was never until now suspected'.[72] Australians had always been conscious of their remoteness on the periphery of the empire as 'a lonely outpost of European civilization in a region which is profoundly alien', and many felt that their white, British and democratic way of life was in danger of being engulfed by the 'hundreds of millions of land-hungry Asiatics',[73] a threat which they referred to as the 'Asiatic Menace' or the 'Yellow Peril'. At the same time, the nationalist spirit which had already found expression in a great variety of protective policies in trade, industry and employment was reflected in a demand for a more distinctive Australian contribution to Australia's and to the empire's defence. The old policy of 'One Flag, One Fleet, One Ocean' had worked well when there was no challenge to Britain's naval or trading interests. But Britain was now facing a major rival in Europe, and hence the only guarantees of Australian security were the possibility that the American fleet might replace the British fleet as the guardian of Anglo-Saxon Destiny, and the existence of the Anglo-Japanese Treaty (renewed in August 1905), which, however, some Australians thought might be used by Japan to modify the White Australia policy.[74]

By the time of the Imperial Conference of 1907 Deakin had decided that Australia ought to be allowed to make a more independent contribution to its own defence. On his return home he suggested to the federal parliament that an Australian coastal naval unit should be established, and a citizen militia organized on the Swiss model.[75] Neither of these proposals was novel, but much depended on the attitude of the Home Government. The events of 1908–9 in Europe, when the major powers finalised their war mobilization plans and when Britain decided to out-match Germany's naval programme, persuaded the British government and the Admiralty that there would

[72] *Daily Telegraph*, Sydney, 24 May 1905.

[73] *Round Table*, London, February 1911, p. 188.

[74] *Round Table*, London, September 1912, pp. 719–21.

[75] See his speech on Defence Policy, *C.P.D.*, 13 December 1907, *42*, p. 7509 ff. See also J. A. La Nauze, *Alfred Deakin*, Melbourne, 1965, 2, ch. 23: G. H. Gill 'The Australian Navy: Origins, Growth and Development', in *R.A.H.S.J.*, *45*, *3*, November 1959: G. L. M. Macandie, *The Genesis of the Royal Australian Navy*, Sydney, 1949.

be some benefit in allowing Australia to develop its own naval force. In 1908 federal parliament put a large sum into a trust fund for future expenditure, and early in 1909 the Fisher government ordered the building of three destroyers in Britain. In November 1909 the Deakin government approved of the new scheme of naval defence adopted at a recent Imperial Defence Conference, at which the admiralty had agreed to allow the dominions to build their own navies. An Australian unit of the Eastern Fleet was to be built, which in wartime would be placed at the disposal of the imperial authorities. This was a year after the U.S. Pacific Fleet had steamed through the heads of Sydney Harbour on a goodwill mission at the invitation of Prime Minister Deakin, an event which had an astonishing impact on Australians whose knowledge of naval matters had hitherto been derived from school history books. On the shores of Sydney Harbour, and later of Port Phillip Bay, the biggest crowds to assemble in Australia's history watched the Great White Fleet of sixteen white-painted battleships drop their anchors; they marvelled at the might of their neighbour across the Pacific.[76] The governments provided lavish banquets for the ships' officers, whilst the marines and the sailors were welcomed with immense public enthusiasm. This great American fleet at the gates of Australia's capitals – was it a proclamation of Australian national manhood acknowledged? But where was Australia's own navy, to meet its kinsmen?

The first ship of the Australian navy, the destroyer *Parramatta* was launched on the Clyde in February 1910 and, together with the *Yarra*, reached Australia in November 1910. Eventually, on 4 October 1913, the first squadron of the Royal Australian Navy steamed into Sydney Harbour. It consisted of a battle-cruiser, three light cruisers and three destroyers, and was owned, financed and, later, manned by Australians. Very large and demonstrative crowds welcomed the ships on their arrival in Farm Cove, and fervently patriotic speeches were made at the welcoming banquet. Not since the days of the Boer War had there been so much public jingoism.

The creation of the Australian navy was generally applauded as a truly patriotic and responsible decision, except by a few older-generation imperialists who thought that the Admiralty had made the wrong decision in 1909. Most Australians were proud to be 'shouldering the burden of nationhood' and could now claim a dignified and self-reliant role in their own defence. Admiral Henderson, who had been sent out to review the situation in 1911, further inflated the national ego by proposing a grandiose scheme of rapid naval expansion. The atmosphere of self-congratulation generated by the arrival of 'our own ships' was marred only by unseemly wrangling amongst politicians eager to claim personal credit for the conception of the

---

76 See, for example, the reports in the *Age*, Melbourne, 31 August 1908 and 1 September 1908. See also R. Megaw, 'Australia and the Great White Fleet, 1908', in *R.A.H.S.J.*, *56*, 2, June 1970.

R.A.N. (Royal in 1911), and by unsportsmanlike critics who pointed out that Australia was as totally dependent on the Royal Navy as it had ever been; that Australia could not even supply the officers to steer its own ships; and that the cost of a local naval unit was enormous compared with the previous annual 'tribute' paid to the British government.[77]

Events in the Pacific had also persuaded many Australians that the existing system of military defence was inadequate to meet future dangers. Fisher outlined a full-scale defence scheme in March 1909 which involved military conscription for youths from ten to twenty years of age. Compulsory military training of youths was established by the Deakin government later in the same year, the system being enlarged and the period of training extended by the Fisher government in 1910, after it had received a report from the distinguished British field-marshal, Lord Kitchener, who had visited Australia at the invitation of the Deakin government.[78] From 1911 all males between twelve and twenty-five were liable to some form of compulsory military training.[79] A military college was established at Duntroon in the Australian Capital Territory in June 1911 under the command of Brigadier-General W. T. Bridges, primarily to train the officers needed for the newly-established system of compulsory military training.

The introduction of compulsory military training did not receive community-wide support, and had only come about because most political leaders had changed their minds rather suddenly, and wanted to regard military defence as being above party politics. Deakin himself had moved slowly and reluctantly towards the idea of compulsion, but several Labor leaders were amongst the first to support the principle. The first federal party leader, J. C. Watson favoured the Swiss system,[80] and the federal Labor Conference of 1903 advocated the creation of a citizen military force; five years later it accepted the principle of compulsory military training, which was a distinct departure from the policy of radical political parties in other western countries, who did not agree that the working classes had anything worth defending. By 1911 W. M. Hughes and other federal Labor leaders were claiming the total credit for its adoption, a situation which the pacifists and socialists who had memories of the 1890s thought was quite extraordinary. However, it was not long before the Labor parliamentarians found that they were out of company with many of their supporters, and as time passed the gap between the political and industrial leadership of the Labor movement widened.

[77] *Round Table*, London, February 1911, p. 192.

[78] His Report is printed in *C.P.P.*, 1910, 2.

[79] See the three articles on the new army scheme in *Daily Telegraph*, Sydney, 25, 26, 27 February 1908. See also *Round Table*, London, August 1911, pp. 511–12 and December 1912, pp. 170–72.

[80] In an interview reported in the *Advertiser*, Adelaide, 1 September 1902.

The prosecution of youths who had not registered for military service or had not attended their periods of drill or camp training provoked an outcry from a dissident minority of trade unionists, who circulated a large quantity of anti-conscription leaflets.[81]

By 1914 Australia had established an autonomous system of military training which was intended to create an army of citizen-soldiers, and a system of naval defence which could be integrated with the British navy in time of war. The former consisted largely of compulsory soldiers, the latter entirely of volunteer seamen. These two principles reflected the consensus of national and imperial sentiment in Australia. The word Imperialist was no longer a term of reproach in the same category as Jingoist, and the desire for local defence was not thought to be separatist but in the best interests of both nation and empire. The new slogan was 'self-defence of the parts, with co-operative defence of the whole'. Defence policy assumed that the only danger would come in the form of a seaborne invasion, probably from the north, although there was the possibility that Germany might follow an aggressive policy in the Pacific Islands: Australia had reluctantly taken over responsibility for administering Papua (formerly British New Guinea) in 1906, and had thereby become a neighbour of the German colonists in New Guinea. Only in the unlikely event of the British navy and the Australian squadron being unable to prevent such an invasion would there be a need for a large Australian army. But it was still necessary to be prepared for this remote possibility. Australians did not therefore want autonomy in defence, only to share in imperial defence and to be heard when important matters affecting the Pacific were being discussed in London. Australians also wanted to be warned if there were sudden changes in policy or in the international situation. This was the tenor of the pleas of all Australian politicians who attended the succession of imperial and defence conferences at Whitehall in the years 1907–12,[82] and their views were received with growing sympathy and increasingly informative discussions; but there was no real participation in decision-making. British foreign policy and imperial defence continued to be the sole prerogative of the British government and parliament, and this was made quite clear in the discussions which concerned the New Hebrides in 1906,[83] the Declaration of London in 1911, and the renewal of the Anglo-Japanese Alliance in the same year; the decision to extend that alliance had already been taken before the Australian and other

[81] See L. C. Jauncey, *The Story of Conscription in Australia*, London, 1935, and the speech by the Labor Minister of Defence, Senator G. F. Pearce, in *C.P.D.*, 5 October 1911, *60*, pp. 1086–7.

[82] See I. R. Hancock, 'The 1911 Imperial Conference', in *H.S.*, *47*, October 1966: C. Grimshaw, 'Australian Nationalism and the Imperial Connection 1900–1914', in *A.J.P.H.*, *III*, 2, May 1958.

[83] See R. C. Thompson, 'The Labor Party and Australian Imperialism in the Pacific, 1901–1919', in *L.H.*, *23*, November 1972.

dominion representatives were asked for their opinions.[84] Australia could not have diplomatic relations with foreign powers in her own right, nor an independent foreign policy.

Fortunately for the Australians, the climate and the market greatly improved after the turn of the century. After years of depression followed by years of drought the Australian economy made a remarkable recovery, and the gross national product nearly doubled between 1904 and 1913 because of the increased production of minerals, wool, wheat, dairy products and manufactured goods.[85] After about 1905 there was a mood of optimistic expansion amongst financiers, businessmen and state governments, many of whom looked to overseas investors to provide the necessary loans for speculation and development. They were increasingly able to finance much of their own capital development, though more than half the total debt in 1914 had been subscribed by the London money market. Most state governments were convinced that Australia's prime need was to settle the inland farming areas, and hence launched programmes to open up new areas of Crown land, or to re-purchase land compulsorily from private owners who had not developed it. New government railway lines were laid to implement programmes of closer settlement[86] which also provided for a rapid expansion of inland irrigation works and many new coastal harbour improvements; Australia then had the greatest per capita railway mileage in the world. The main objective was to increase the export of wheat, meat, dairy products and fruit in a period when wool was recovering slowly and gold production, though still very high, was declining. However, it was popularly believed that this was not feasible unless a new generation of ready-made pioneers was available, and hence state governments made a determined and costly effort to attract British immigrants to fill up the 'Empty Spaces' of the outback.

Large-scale assisted immigration schemes, which had been in abeyance since the 1870s and 1880s, were revived with great enthusiasm by all state governments, and in the years 1906 to 1914, 393,048 British immigrants reached Australia, nearly half of whom had received some form of government assistance to make the voyage from the British Isles, either in the form of a free or part-paid passage, or an offer of cheap land.[87] In 1908 the annual intake was over 20,000

84 See P. Lowe, 'The British Empire and the Anglo-Japanese Alliance, 1911–1915', in *History, LIV*, 181, June 1969.

85 There is a useful survey of the economy in this period in G. Wood, *Borrowing and Business in Australia*, London, 1930, ch. 9. See also V. G. Childe, *How Labour Governs*, London, 1923, Introduction, and L. F. Fitzhardinge, *William Morris Hughes*, Sydney, 1964, *I*, p. 248.

86 For example see S. Glynn, 'The Transport Factor in Developmental Policy', in *A.J.P.H., XV*, 2, August 1969.

87 Government-assisted 184,605: other 208,443. See F. K. Crowley, 'The British Contribution to the Australian Population: 1860–1919', in *University Studies in History and Economics*, 1954.

immigrants. By 1910 it was over 38,000 and by 1912 over 88,500, and in that year nearly 47,000 were assisted immigrants. At this time the birth rate was stable, but the death rate was falling, and the combination of net national increase and net migration led to a very substantial increase in population of one million between 1903 and 1914, to reach 4,940,000. This was a rapid rate of growth for such a small community and it had very sudden economic and social consequences, which trade unionists were quick to discover. For more than a century the wage-earning classes and their representatives had been opposed to government-sponsored immigration, believing that immigration ought to be allowed to vary in accordance with wages and employment conditions in Australia. They had good grounds for their opinion. Too often immigration schemes had resulted in the indiscriminate introduction of penniless immigrants, who merely increased the already swollen ranks of urban labourers. Now, in the years 1910–14, history was repeating itself, and at a time when the general level of unemployment never fell below six per cent of the workforce, and reached a very high level in the industrial suburbs of Melbourne and Sydney, and especially amongst the unskilled day labourers. Wages did not rise significantly in towns or country districts until after 1910 and even then there was a rapid increase in prices. In this situation there was a good deal of industrial unrest, which was reflected in stop-work meetings and strikes, several of which were on a large scale, especially amongst miners. There were very serious strikes by New South Wales coal miners in November 1907, and from November 1909 until March 1910.[88] The conservative governments blamed 'the glib tongues of the loud-voiced agitators';[89] the unionists blamed money-grubbing monopolists and their political dupes in state parliaments. There was a lengthy dispute at Broken Hill during the first five months of 1909,[90] and a five-week long general strike in Brisbane early in 1912.[91] The ostensible cause of that trouble was a claim by some men in the tramways to wear, on duty, a badge indicating union membership. But the situation quickly worsened and all forty-three trade unions associated with the Trades Hall went on strike. The streets were thronged with idle men intent on stopping everyone else from working. Violence and hooliganism were frequent occurrences during the following weeks, until the police and special

[88] See B. Fitzpatrick, *A Short History of the Australian Labor Movement*, Melbourne, 1940, ch. 9: I. Turner, *Industrial Labour and Politics: The Dynamics of the Labor Movement in Eastern Australia, 1900–1921*, Canberra, 1965, ch. 2.

[89] Premier Wade in *N.S.W. Parliamentary Debates*, 16 December 1909, XXXVI, p. 4570.

[90] See G. Osborne, 'Town and Company: The Broken Hill Industrial Dispute of 1908–09', in J. Iremonger, *et al.*, Eds., *Strikes: Studies in Twentieth Century Australian Social History*, Sydney, 1973.

[91] See A. A. Morrison, 'The Brisbane General Strike of 1912', in *H.S.*, *14*, May 1950: *Round Table*, London, June 1912, pp. 472–95.

constables restored order, and the men returned to work on the employers' terms, defeated and disillusioned. This militancy not only reflected long delayed improvements in wages and working conditions, but was symptomatic of a growing strength in the ranks of organized labour which was itself to some degree influenced by overseas trends brought in by migrants.

The land settlement schemes, based on family unit cultivation, did not provide many jobs for agricultural labourers.[92] Nevertheless, the protagonists of the immigration programme took a long view of its benefits in creating more jobs, bigger markets and in strengthening the Anglo-Saxon character of the Australian community. They also claimed that if white British Australians did not fill up 'the wide brown land' some other races would soon do so, evidently echoing the sentiment of President Theodore Roosevelt of the U.S.A. that 'an unmanned nation invites disaster'. Partly due to government activity, and partly to technological and market conditions, there was a very rapid growth of the area under crop, and especially in the dry-farming wheat-growing districts of New South Wales and Western Australia.[93] Many 'new chums' were attracted by the offer of cheap land, easy access to credit, new railway lines, and the opportunity to make a new home for themselves in the more hospitable climate of Australia; some were also attracted by the vision of having a home and a farm of their own, and by the prospect of being their own masters. The area under wheat almost doubled between 1901 and 1914 and the yield improved markedly following the breeding of new strains of wheat developed by William Farrer and the widespread use of superphosphate and other chemical fertilizers. By then the wool-growing industry in the sparsely settled outback districts, which had always been an important source of national prosperity, had recovered from the long drought of the 1890s. The years 1904–6 were especially good, and the season 1905–6 produced a record wool clip of over one million bales, of which more than eighty-two per cent was sold by auction in Australia. There after there was a steady rise in wool prices, and an increase in the yield, and the wider adoption of wheat-sheep farming in the closer settled areas. The increase in the volume of overseas trade and hence in the annual income from the export of wool, wheat, meat and butter seemed to justify the vigorous public works and immigration policies of the state governments, and it appeared as though Australia had been launched upon a new era of pioneering. At the same time, the increase in population spread the burden of annual loan interest payments in such a way that increasing public indebtedness was hardly noticed.

[92] See P. G. Macarthy, 'Labor and the Living Wage, 1890–1910', in *A.J.P.H.*, XIII, 1, April 1967: C. Forster, 'Australian Unemployment 1900–1940', in *E.R.*, 41, 95, September 1965.

[93] E. Dunsdorfs, *The Australian Wheat-Growing Industry 1788–1948*, Melbourne, 1956, ch. 5: F. K. Crowley, *Australia's Western Third*, London, 1960, ch. 6.

One other result of the development and migration programme was not so heartily welcomed by state authorities: the population of the urban areas continued to grow out of proportion to rural population. In 1908 Sydney and Melbourne each had more than 500,000 people in the city and suburbs, Adelaide 180,000 and Brisbane 137,000. Many of the newly-arrived migrants preferred to live in the crowded slums of the inner residential districts of the big cities, or in their fast expanding outer suburbs, rather than in weatherboard huts on new farm sites; they also seemed to prefer the known uncertainties of commercial and industrial employment to the unknown but obviously arduous life of pioneering virgin farms in the back-blocks. However, it was not only the perversity of migrants or Australians which accelerated urbanization, but the growth of factory employment in response to the growth of the population, and the demand for new houses and offices. Factory employment, as a proportion of the workforce, grew slowly, but the number of employees grew quickly, especially in the two big eastern cities; factory hands were engaged in processing primary products and producing food, drink, clothing and building supplies. By 1914 industrial production made a significant contribution to the national income, but in a community whose general economic health was heavily dependent on the state of the seasons and the fluctuating prices on world markets. Britain was the largest single supplier of imported manufactured goods, and although Germany and France had begun to buy more of Australia's wool and minerals, Britain was still the country's major market.[94]

At this time Australia experienced the first of the great technological advances of the twentieth century in communications.[95] There were notable developments in shipping. Australia's overseas trade was greatly enlarged and accelerated when the windjammers were replaced by the coal-burning steam ships for the carriage of goods, although in the Australasian trade this was a slow change compared with that of the North Atlantic, partly because of the comparative lack of traffic, and partly because of the long distances on the Australia run which made coaling difficult and expensive. However, the new steamers were equipped to carry refrigerated cargoes of meat, butter and fruit, which gave a great boost to closer Australian settlement, and subsequently the ships were also fitted with facilities for wireless telegraphy. The first long-distance experiments in Australia with 'wireless' were conducted between Queenscliff in Victoria and Devonport in Tasmania in

---

94 *Official Year Book of the Commonwealth of Australia*, 7, 1914, pp. 520, 529.

95 There is a dearth of writing on Australia's technological history. For examples of the topics that follow in the text see F. K. Crowley, *Modern Australia in Documents*, I, 1901–1939, Melbourne, 1973, – wireless, p. 91; telegraphs, p. 39; telephones, pp. 106, 189; electricity, pp. 65, 89; motor cars, pp. 73, 122, 142; aeroplanes pp. 144, 188, 213. There is an excellent book on farming technology – F. Wheelhouse, *Digging Stick to Rotary Hoe: Men and machines in Rural Australia*, Melbourne, 1966, reprinted Adelaide, 1972.

July 1906, and in August 1912 the federal government opened a Wireless Telegraphy Station at Pennant Hills in Sydney. The multiplication of the world's overland and submarine telegraph and telephone systems also greatly improved Australia's commerce and overseas trade. The Pacific telegraph cable had been opened in November 1902, to supplement the route via Darwin and the Cocos Islands, and in 1907 Sydney and Melbourne were connected by telephone. Five years later the first automatic telephone exchange in Australia was installed at Geelong in Victoria.

Meanwhile electric light was gradually being used to supplement and then replace coal gas in the lighting of houses, factories and streets. Sydney's Pyrmont power-house opened in July 1904 and soon councils and municipalities were thinking of using the new energy source as a substitute for horse trams and cable trams. Motor cars had also come into use as a substitute for horse-riding, cycling or walking. Early models were seen around the turn of the century, but not until 1905–6 was there a sufficient number to meet the needs of those who had the considerable amount of money needed to buy them; those who could not travelled by steam train or by electric tram. Most of the vehicles were fully imported, and were very noisy and smelly, and disrupted horse-traffic, especially in built-up areas. They also created hazards for pedestrians, miniature dust-storms for housewives, and two new social menaces – the road hog and the drunk driver. State parliaments soon legislated to register the vehicles, license the drivers, and impose speed limits on them so as to prevent 'furious driving in public places'. The young men were quickly attracted to the new 'motor bikes'. It was not long before the mails were being delivered to the post offices by motor vehicles.

The ships that annually took away Australia's wheat, wool and other primary products also brought back a great variety of goods from British and American factories. Amongst them were the new wind-up gramophones with their Edison records, which brought people in the antipodes so much closer to other continents overseas. They could actually hear the great singers of the day – their own Madame Melba too – as well as the great orchestras of England and the voices of the statesmen of Europe; they could even dance to Viennese waltzes in their own drawing rooms. Promoters of the travelling variety shows which visited Australia as a part of their world tour also brought with them cinematograph projectors that actually showed 'moving pictures', as well as stills of the great wonders of the world. And some very fortunate Australians even saw an aeroplane or two, which had arrived by sea and been used to demonstrate man's new mastery over the tyranny of distance. A Wilbur Wright powered biplane actually took off in Sydney in December 1909 and covered 100 yards in five seconds. In June 1912, the first air race in Australia's history resulted in a win for an Australian: William Hart, the Parramatta aeronaut, successfully completed a flight from Botany to Parramatta and return: 'Wizard' Stone of the U.S.A. declined to take off because of turbulent conditions. Hart had travelled at over a mile a minute.[96] In July 1914 the first aerial mail was taken from Melbourne to Sydney.

During the years 1910–14 Labor had spectacular electoral successes as a mass political party. It also made some of its most significant contributions to Australian public life. Labor held office in the federal parliament from April 1910 until June 1913, in New South Wales from October 1910 until November 1916, in Victoria for a short time in December 1913, in South Australia from June 1910 until February 1912, in Western Australia from October 1911 until July 1916, and in Tasmania from April 1914 until April 1916. In all seven parliaments it was the official opposition where it was not the government. One immediate consequence of these victories was that the two-party political system became firmly established in Australia, as most of the non-Labor groups united in political parties for self-protection. Another effect of Labor's sudden rise to office was the realization amongst Labor leaders that parliamentary systems which were tied to written constitutions were imperfect instruments for instituting radical social reforms. Before the Labor party's advent to power, its leaders hoped, and its critics feared, that if it captured the Australian parliaments it would try to change the whole social order. The least the critics expected was a very rapid extension of municipal and state socialism, and an attempt to nationalize monopolies concerned with the production of coal, sugar and tobacco. However, the exercise of power and responsibility, and a growing sensitivity to the uncommitted middle class voters, made Labor politicians work out a compromise between their platforms when in opposition and their activities when in office. They had also to learn that federal and state Labor politicians did not always see eye-to-eye on major economic and social issues.

State Labor ministers quickly found that the Legislative Councils, whose rights to reject legislation were safeguarded by written constitutions which could only be altered with their consent, did not favour socialism in any form. They also discovered that the best method of gaining and keeping political power in the states was to promote the roads-and-bridges policies which had been traditional in the Australian colonies since the middle of the previous century. Hence, when in office they adopted the role of developers, and their policies were therefore indistinguishable from those of their Liberal predecessors. Some state Labor leaders even acquired a keen states-rights approach to national affairs. A few state Labor governments by-passed the upper houses by establishing state trading or retailing undertakings by executive action, in the hope that the working people would benefit if capitalist businesses were compelled to compete with collectively-owned or state enterprises, thereby reducing consumer prices. But not many of these undertakings achieved their original objectives, and none of them justified the alarmist apprehensions of the conservatives that they were the first instalments of 'creeping

[96] There is an account of the affair in the *Sydney Morning Herald*, 1 July 1912.

socialism'.[97] Labor's other contributions to states affairs came in the form of extensions of the arbitration system and of the government secondary education system, together with schemes for cheap workers' homes, and improved welfare services for the sick and the aged. Two of the state Labor leaders achieved reputations for forthright administration which have stood the test of time, John Scaddan in Western Australia and W. A. Holman in New South Wales.[98] It was Holman's Labor government which enabled Broken Hill Pty Ltd to begin its steel works at Newcastle in October 1912.

When the Fisher federal government took office in 1910, after receiving one of the most decisive mandates ever given to an Australian political party, most Labor supporters thought that the Labor leaders would be able to establish a wage-earners' paradise by legislation. On the other hand the conservative wing of the Fusion-Liberal party was appalled at the prospect of being governed by a gang of political amateurs and paupers, who were clearly bent on 'milking the rich' and turning parliament into a mere recording apparatus for caucus and conference decrees – 'Proposals are framed elsewhere; theirs but to help in carrying them out'.[99] However, men like Andrew Fisher, George Pearce and King O'Malley were not revolutionaries, or even very radically-minded, and they did not theorize about their own platforms, let alone about socialism. Fisher was a keen clear debater, who was dedicated to preventing a recurrence in Australia of the financial and employment problems of the early 1890s, and was convinced that the parliamentary system could effect this. W. M. Hughes, the leader of the Waterside Workers Union, published a widely-read pamphlet entitled the *Case for Labor*, which was, however, weak in theory, and was not concerned with the ultimate structure of society but with the short-term methods of putting more money into the pockets of Labor party supporters. Hughes was always proud that his waterside workers did better by not going on strike. Most Labor leaders eschewed the left-wing militants of the Victorian Socialist party[100] or the Industrial Workers of the World, a revolutionary industrial and political organization which had originated in the United States, and

[97] See R. S. Parker, 'Public Enterprise in New South Wales', in *A.J.P.H.*, IV, 2, November 1958: H. V. Evatt, *Australian Labour Leader*, Sydney, 1940, ch. 68: J. B. Brigden 'State Enterprises in Australia', in *International Labour Review, 16*, 1, July 1927: F. W. Eggleston, *State Socialism in Victoria*, London, 1932: J. R. Robertson, 'The Foundations of State Socialism in Western Australia, 1911–16', in *H.S., 39*, November 1962: D. J. Murphy, 'The Establishment of State Enterprises in Queensland 1915–1918', in *L.H., 14*, May 1968.

[98] J. R. Robertson, 'The Internal Politics of State Labor in Western Australia, 1911–1916', in *L.H., 2*, May 1962: H. V. Evatt, *Australian Labour Leader: The Story of W. A. Holman and the Labour Movement*, Sydney, 1940.

[99] H. G. Turner, *The First Decade of the Australian Commonwealth*, Melbourne, 1911, p. viii. For a summary of the arguments against the party pledge see H. V. Evatt, *Liberalism in Australia*, Sydney, 1918, pp. 59–60.

[100] See I. Turner, 'Socialist Political Tactics, 1900–1920', in *L.H., 2*, May 1962.

which had recently arrived in Australia; nor would they be associated with the advocates of direct action. Labor leaders could not afford to appear before the electors as extremists if they wished to be returned to parliament. Labor members were keen to make parliament and the arbitration system work, and even when they had found that neither the High Court nor the electorate would allow any increase in the legislative powers of the federal parliament so that they could implement their objectives on a national scale, they did not abandon their commitment to constitutional government and the gradual education of the electorate to vote in their favour. They were also keen defenders of the prevailing standards of moral decency, as was made clear when the federal conference resolved –

That this Conference repudiates with indignation the charges levelled against the Australian Labour movement of endeavouring to weaken the sanctity of the marriage tie and to sap the foundations of religious belief; and we furthermore declare our firm conviction that the success of our efforts to improve the material condition of the community would result in the elevation and not the degradation of marriage, and would enable the sublime teachings of the Founder of Christianity to be brought home as a living reality to those members to whom, owing to the misery and privation in which society, as now constituted, has engulfed them, they remain but a mere abstraction.[101]

Most of Labor's numerous and impressive legislative achievements in the years 1910–13 were extensions of Deakin's liberal programme of 1905–8, and combined a special interest in nation-building with modest proposals for industrial and social welfare.[102] For example, the nation-wide old-age pensions scheme initiated by the Deakin government in July 1909 and financed from surplus federal revenue was extended to naturalized citizens, to women at the age of sixty and to pensioners owning their own homes; the pension was subject to a means test on income and property.[103] Invalid pensions were instituted and a maternity allowance – the £5 'baby bonus' – was paid to all mothers after 1912 without any test of means. Federal government employees were allowed to appeal to the federal arbitration court and were given compensation if injured at work. The government also introduced compulsory preference to trade unionists in federal employment, and extended the authority of the federal arbitration court to domestic servants and agricultural employees.

An Australian paper currency replaced the bank notes of the private trading banks in 1910, by the simple device of compelling the banks

101 Australian Labor Party, *Official Report of the Commonwealth Conference, 1905*, p. 27.

102 See G. Sawer, *Australian Federal Politics and Law: 1901–1929*, Melbourne, 1956, ch. 6.

103 See T. H. Kewley, 'Social Services in Australia (1900–10)', in *R.A.H.S.J.*, *33*, 4, 1947: T. H. Kewley, *Australia's Welfare State*, Melbourne, 1969.

to pay such a high tax on their own notes – ten per cent – that they would no longer find it profitable to issue them. For the first time there was issued a note of a lower denomination than one pound – 10s., thereby giving the working classes access to a more convenient form of currency than heavy coins. At the same time the system of recouping the state governments at the rate of 25s. per capita per annum for their loss of customs and excise revenue was adopted for a ten-year period. Both these financial innovations had previously been supported by the Liberals, and the Fusion government had proposed to make the latter scheme inviolate by incorporating it into the federal constitution. However, the electors rejected this proposal by a narrow majority at a referendum held in conjunction with the election of 1910, though they accepted the principle that the federal government should take over management of the debts of the state governments when this was convenient. This type of ad hoc federal-state financial relationship, which was to last for the next seventeen years, illustrated the very imperfect adaptation of the governments to federalism; finance was the most vital element in that relationship and yet no real progress had been made in determining the respective financial rights of all seven governments.

Many of the achievements of the Fisher government had been adopted from its predecessor, or were a necessary obligation of any federal government which was still involved in laying the foundations of the federal system. Work was begun in 1912 on constructing the east-west transcontinental railway to link Port Augusta with Kalgoorlie (completed in October 1917), and on surveying a new north-south line from South Australia; the federal government, at the request of the South Australian government, had taken over the responsibility for administering the Northern Territory in January 1911. Australia House in London was constructed to serve as a headquarters for the high commissioner, the first being Sir George Reid. A uniform postal charge of one penny on a letter from anywhere to anywhere was introduced in 1911, thereby replacing the six different postal scales which had been operative since before federation. Arrangements were made to administer the Australian Capital Territory, and Canberra was named. The selection of the site of the capital territory had taken the federal parliament – meeting in Melbourne, but with frequent trips for members to sites all over New South Wales – eight years of discussion, arguments and voting, mainly because of interstate jealousy between New South Wales and Victoria. In terms of the constitution, the capital had to be within New South Wales but not closer than 100 miles to Sydney, presumably for fear of corruption or contamination. When the decision was made it was dubbed 'The Surrender to Sydney Influences Act', because members chose Yass-Canberra instead of Dalgety, which was as far as it was possible to get from Sydney on the way to Victoria. Another four years elapsed before the governor-general's wife, Lady Denman, announced on 12 March 1913, 'I name this Capital of Australia Canberra'. The residents of the territory were delighted that the original name of the place had been retained and that the capital had not been given some unpopular or ridiculous name: the Minister of Home Affairs, Mr King O'Malley, wanted it called Shakespeare, and one of many hundreds of other suggestions was Sydmeladlperbriho. The occasion called for numerous patriotic speeches. The prime minister, Mr Andrew Fisher, hoped to see Canberra become the seat of learning and the arts, as well as of politics. The governor-general pointed out that the choice of the site had been a necessary compromise, but that compromise was the essence of British self-government, and, furthermore, that the people should not cavil at the expense of creating another city because Sydney and Melbourne were already overcrowded. Mr King O'Malley took the opportunity to declare his belief that God had commanded the English-speaking peoples to secure the control of and constitutionally govern the earth in the interests of civilization, whilst Mr W. M. Hughes, the Attorney-General, pointed out that Canberra was the visible sign of a continent – 'The people are incapable of nourishing abstract ideals. They must have a symbol.' He also noticed that there was no trace at the ceremony 'of that race we have banished from the face of the earth'.[104]

The Fisher government extended the nation-wide scheme of compulsory military training and established an administration for Australia's new navy. Apart from the abolition of postal voting at federal elections (which favoured Labor's opponents), only two of the Fisher government's other legislative achievements were totally foreign to the liberalism of the Deakin era. The first was the imposition in 1910 of a land tax to be levied on unimproved properties over £5000 in value, with no such exemption for absentee owners, which was ostensibly designed to 'bust up the big estates', by taxing the monopolists out of existence, and thereby make more and cheaper land available for the needy.[105] Because this was not only a federal tax but a direct tax, it infuriated the conservatives, who claimed that they were being plundered by a class-biased government; the state governments were also apprehensive about the federal government competing with them for income. The land tax failed to achieve the rural millenium, and did not attract many farming votes for Labor, but it prevented a degree of monopoly in the urban areas. Because it raised a substantial income, later governments found ways of justifying its continuance.

The second distinctively Labor contribution to Australia's new national institutions was the establishment of the Commonwealth

104 For the speeches see *Sydney Morning Herald*, 13 March 1913. For accounts of the origin of the Capital Territory see G. E. Sherington, 'The Selection of Canberra as Australia's National Capital', in *R.A.H.S.J.*, *56*, *2*, June 1970: D. I. Wright, *Shadow of Dispute: Aspects of Commonwealth-State Relations, 1901–1910*, Canberra, 1970, ch. 2.

105 See H. Heaton, 'Land Settlement and Legislation', in M. Atkinson, Ed., *Australia: Economic and Political Studies*, Melbourne, 1920, esp. pp. 373–5.

Bank by legislation in 1911 as a competitive trading and savings bank capitalised by the federal government.[106] It was to be managed by a governor, appointed by the government, who would be responsible to parliament as his board of directors. This annoyed the private trading banks as well as those state governments who owned savings banks. The Commonwealth Bank opened for business as a savings bank in July 1912 and as a trading bank in January 1913, with Denison Miller as its governor. It was an immediate and lasting success, though it did not fulfil the hopes of those Labor parliamentarians who had bitter memories of the bank crash of 1893, and who would have preferred an institution with central banking functions and one which could have been used by the federal government and the treasury to drive the private trading banks out of business. But the Fisher government was not committed to bank nationalization, or to land nationalization, or to using its new role as banker and issuer of currency to take over the whole financial and economic system. It preferred merely to make the capitalist system work a little more favourably in the interests of the wage-earners, the small investors, the small farmers, and the street-corner grocers and shopkeepers. Federal Labor was not anti-capitalism, or anti-business; it objected to big landowners, big financiers and big businesses, especially monopolies (but not trade union monopolies) and trusts and combines which were not subject to trade union pressures or the ballot box.

For this reason it found the restraints of the federal system particularly irksome; by protecting the rights of the states, the constitution prevented the federal parliament from controlling interstate corporations and Australia-wide industrial conditions. Baulked by the decisions of the High Court, which had prevented the introduction of New Protection, and also nurturing a simple faith in the supposed commonsense of the predominantly working class electorate, the Fisher government appealed to the people. It asked that the federal constitution should be amended to give parliament greater powers so as to by-pass both the High Court and the state parliaments. The government was especially keen to have the power to nationalize monopolies, which would have made it Australia's largest single employer of labour, a policy which was well expressed by the party's first federal leader:

As against the endeavour of the Liberals to regulate monopolies into good behaviour, following generally the lines of the Sherman law of the United States, the Labour party urges that monopolies should be nationalised, on the ground that only the owners can successfully regulate a business.[107]

106 See K. E. Beazley, 'The Labor Party and the Origin of the Commonwealth Bank', in *A.J.P.H.*, IX, 1, May 1963: R. Gollan, *The Commonwealth Bank of Australia: Origins and Early History*, Canberra, 1968.

107 J. C. Watson, 'The Labour Movement', in *British Association for the Advancement of Science: Handbook For New South Wales*, Sydney, 1914, pp. 129–30.

In 1911 and in 1913 the Labor government put a variety of proposals to the electors to give federal parliament power over much of the nation's economic and industrial activity – over all trade and commerce, monopolies, corporations, employment and wages.[108] At both referendums neither the electorate as a whole nor a majority of the states agreed to the proposals, though the dissenting majority was much less on the second than on the first occasion; in 1913 the 'Yes' vote was 49.4 per cent and Queensland, South Australia and Western Australia agreed. The referendum proposals were opposed by the Liberals, by the states'-righters, by those who feared the consequences of industrial unification or the monopoly of trade unionism, and by some of Labor's own supporters in the states, who were opposed to centralizing political power in the one government. Especially was this the case in New South Wales, where Premier Holman had publicly disagreed with the policies of Fisher and Hughes, and was strongly supported by the local rank and file. However, the federal leaders did not abandon their hope that if the proposals were not so far-reaching or so numerous they would ultimately be acceptable to the people, thereby ignoring the message which had already become clear, namely, that when voters were in doubt, or suspicious of the real intentions of politicians, they tended to vote 'No'. The Australian constitutional referendum was obviously a conservative instrument of federalism.

By 1913 federal politics had settled into a straight-out contest between the Labor and Liberal parties, the former advocating a rapid centralizing of power in the federal parliament and an increase in the activities of government in the community, the latter insisting that the federal system needed decentralized authority, and that governments should govern, not socialize. At the election of May 1913 the Fisher government was narrowly defeated at the elections for the House of Representatives, and for more than a year the Cook Liberal government faced a Labor-controlled Senate and tried to govern with a majority of only one in the House of Representatives. Eventually, by attempting to abolish preference to unionists in government employment, Cook was able to create a situation of an unresolvable deadlock between the two chambers, which was the constitutional pre-requisite for a double dissolution of parliament.[109] At the ensuing elections in September 1914 Labor returned to office with a substantial majority in both the Senate and the House of Representatives, and in the following year the Labor party controlled six of Australia's seven governments. But by then the war in Europe had begun and the formative years of Australian federalism had been brought to an abrupt close.

What had been achieved during those years? Economically, Australia was much more unified in 1914 than in 1901 through the operation

[108] See C. Joyner, 'Attempts to Extend Commonwealth Powers 1908–1919', in *H.S.*, 35, November 1960: C. Joyner, *The Commonwealth and Monopolies*, Melbourne, 1963.

[109] See *Round Table*, London, September 1914, p. 733 ff.

of the common market between the states and several new tariff and industrial policies, although Australian industries were still heavily reliant on British industry, commerce and capital. In political terms Australia was also much better qualified as a nation in 1914 than it had been at the inauguration of federation. There was a national navy and a nation-wide system of military defence. There was a national bank, a national currency, nation-wide postal rates, cheaper telegraphic rates, a national old-age and invalid pension scheme, a maternity bonus, and a site had been chosen for a national capital. The distinctly new national achievements of the early years of federation had become the settled policies of parliament and people, more particularly the White Australia Policy, the White Ocean Policy,[110] Old Protection, New Protection, the commonwealth arbitration system, and the concept of the living wage. All of these were the achievements of the federal system of government, and hence by 1914 the people had become accustomed to look to the national, rather than to the state governments for the attainment of some of their community goals. Federalism had therefore brought into being a national awareness which was characterisically Australian in its combination of interests and objectives, and which had not been present amongst the six federating colonies in 1901. Nevertheless, the historical experience had been brief. There had been no acute crises to generate national fervour, and state parochialism was still highly significant. A visitor to Australia had commented that after almost a decade of federation, Australia presented a paradox. There was a breezy, buoyant imperial spirit. But a national spirit was practically non-existent.

You drop from Imperialism to something like parochialism in Australia, with little of the real national spirit intervening – though it exists and must increase.[111]

He complained that he had heard too much talk about state advancement and too little about Australia's advancement, and far too much disparagement of one state by another.

After fourteen years' experience of federal government the five million Australians were still inclined to speak of themselves as Victorians, South Australians and New South Welshmen, though there were signs, other than economic and political, which suggested that significant changes had been occurring in the national make-up. The Census of 1911 had shown that in the preceding thirty years the Australian-born proportion of the population had risen from 63 per cent to 83 per cent and although 98 per cent were probably of British descent, some indigenous traits had emerged. Visitors had little

110 This was the policy that the federal government should not subsidize a mail service if the ship concerned employed even one coloured cook. See Reid's speech in *Sydney Morning Herald*, 19 April 1905.

111 J. F. Fraser, *Australia: The Making of a Nation*, London, 1910, pp. 11–13. See also *Round Table*, London, August, 1911, p. 507.

difficulty in distinguishing Australians by their accent from Americans, Canadians and other English-speaking people, and within Australia there were no political frontiers or military borders which prevented the free movement of people between the six states and thereby the sharing of common attitudes. The Australian wage-earners were particularly mobile. The working men of the farming districts and the pastoral outback moved freely, and constantly, in search of jobs, whilst the seasonal character of many rural occupations such as shearing, harvesting, and fruit-picking freed the bushworkers from the restraints of village life. A building boom in a capital city, the opening of a new goldfield in a remote region, or the construction of a new country railway quickly attracted workmen, merchants, bankers, agents and professional men from less prosperous districts. Despite the long distances which separated the cities and towns, and the homesteads from one another in the sparsely settled outback, Australians behaved in a remarkably similar manner.[112] One of the reasons for this was that, in the main, the Australian wage-earners were also literate, and there was scarcely a country town or goldfield centre which did not have a weekly or even tri-weekly newspaper: a newspaper plebiscite in 1910 on the wisdom of selecting Yass-Canberra for the nation's capital involved sending a questionnaire to 802 newspapers – 287 of them in Victoria, 283 in New South Wales, 113 in Queensland. News and views arrived quickly from the capital cities and from overseas by the electric telegraph, and thereby helped to overcome 'the tyranny of distance' which had once been the chief drawback of living in the back-blocks of the antipodes.

Visitors to Australia did not discern a lively cultural development, but they did notice a greater independence of mind amongst working men than in Britain, as well as a dislike of foreigners, especially Asians, and of Englishmen who referred to Australians as 'colonials'. Most Australians were opposed to the ideas of an aristocracy of birth, a state-established church, and a military caste. They liked to think that they had a reputation for being progressive in the matter of the franchise, and in legislating to protect the wage-earners against harsh employers. They were keen to provide elementary education for all children, whether in government or church schools, and their governments were now making secondary education available to the children of the working classes, some of whom might even be able to go on to one of the six universities. Visitors were always impressed with the Australians' interest in all forms of sport. Australian Rules football was well-established as the 'national' winter game in Victoria, Tasmania, South Australia and Western Australia. Rugby was the popular game in New South Wales and Queensland. In Victoria the Victorian

112 For some contemporary comments on Australian attitudes see M. Atkinson, 'The Australian Outlook', in M. Atkinson, Ed., *Australia: Economic and Political Studies*, Melbourne, 1920, ch. 1: C. H. Northcott, *Australian Social Development*, New York, 1918.

Football League games attracted very large crowds, and the weekly postmortems on the performance of the club teams were already an established feature of Melbourne's social life. In summer, cricket was popular in all states. So also were tennis (Australians won the Davis Cup in 1907), cycling and the new sport of surfing. Australians also had a weakness for drinking and gambling, two of the best-known habits of Australians since 1788: Tattersalls sweeps, then located in Hobart, were very popular, as were two-up, and on- and off-course betting on horse-racing.

The wowsers and the sabbatarians – in particular the half million Methodists – still had much influence on governments, and were able to restrict hotel trading hours and the playing of sport on Sundays, as well as to keep a firm control over the tone of vaudeville acts open to the public, and the circulating of filthy books and indecent post-cards. But there were signs that the changes in social customs and attitudes which had been taking place in Britain since the death of Queen Victoria had been echoed in the antipodes. More especially was this so concerning the behaviour of women. By 1914 mixed bathing was permitted on the beaches, divorcees were not automatically socially ostracized, public dances were not considered to be large-scale temptations to immorality, and a growing number of women were seeking employment other than in domestic service. There was a decline in church-going amongst the Anglicans and the non-conformists and, especially amongst trade unionists and Irish Catholics, there was a simmering discontent with the governing consensus, which looked upon Australia as a replica of England – its economy, its society and its values. Nevertheless, the Australian community was materially well-off compared with those in other capitalist countries, and its chief interest was a self-concerned devotion to improving the material conditions for the greatest number of its white inhabitants. In 1914 Australians celebrated 126 years of material progress. So far, only the Aborigines had suffered.

8

1914-19

Ian Turner

*Outbreak of war in Europe—the Australian response—Germans
in the Pacific—the A.I.F. formed—the end of the* Emden*—the
economy—internal security—the A.I.F. in Egypt—the attack on
the Gallipoli Peninsula—Lone Pine—the evacuation—the Anzacs
—recruiting—the home front—manufacturing—the primary industries—finance—inflation—strikes—the War Census of 1915—
Hughes visits Britain—Australians on the Western Front in 1916
—in the Middle East—conscription for overseas military service—
the referendum campaign of 1916—the Labor party splits—the
Nationalist party formed—Australians on the Western Front in
1917—in the Middle East—the New South Wales Strike—the
referendum campaign of 1917—Australians on the Western Front
in 1918—the Armistice—the Australian soldier—Hughes in
Britain—at the Peace Conference—economic and political effects
of the war—the federal election of 1919—repatriation—industry
and employment—social attitudes—affairs of the intellect.*

At 12.45 p.m. on 5 August 1914, the prime minister, Joseph Cook,
called together in his Melbourne office the representatives of the
Australian press. He told them: 'I have received the following
despatch from the Imperial government – war has broken out with
Germany.' The news was not unexpected. For a week, cables had been
passing between London and Melbourne concerning precautions
against the possibility of a European war. A federal election was in
progress, following the double dissolution of both houses of parliament which Cook had secured after the Labor-controlled Senate had
twice rejected a vital government measure. Government and opposition leaders had warned the people of the danger of war and had
pledged Australia's support for the Mother Country. The governor-
general had already informed London of the 'indescribable enthusiasm
and entire unanimity throughout Australia' for the Imperial cause.[1]

---

[1] The standard work on Australia's part in the War of 1914–18 is C. E. W. Bean,
Ed., *The Official History of Australia in the War of 1914–1918*, Sydney, 12 Volumes,
1921–42; a condensed version is C. E. W. Bean, *Anzac to Amiens*, Canberra, 1946.
The standard work on the home front is E. Scott, *Australia During the War*,

Sir Ronald Munro-Ferguson hardly overstated the case. Yet in the last century the colonizers of Australia had come to think of themselves not as exiled Britons but as native Australians. Many articulate voices had come to distinguish themselves from their country of origin – politically, socially and culturally. And the proud moment of the proclamation of the Commonwealth of Australia was still fresh in the minds of all but the youngest generation of Australians. How then to account for the overwhelming atavistic response? From early years the very isolation of the Australian colonies seemed to promise security. Safe within the encircling oceans, the colonists dreamed of creating a new, homogeneous society and culture which would, for some, reproduce the British model, for others grow out of and beyond it. So long as Britannia ruled the waves it seemed that the dream could become reality. Instead, the decades before the war saw the emergence of Russia as an Asian power, a powerful German Asiatic squadron with bases at Tsingtao and Rabaul and also in the Carolines, and clear evidence of Japanese naval power. The dream turned into nightmare, and the 'teeming hordes' of Asia came to haunt the Australian imagination.

The British naval squadron no longer seemed adequate protection: it could at any time be withdrawn from the Pacific to meet the growing German threat in the North Sea, and in any case Japan was Britain's ally. Australia hedged its defence bets by investing heavily in a naval squadron to keep the 'Yellow Peril' from Australian shores and by training its young citizens to repel the Asian hordes should they breach the naval defences and invade. Australia's destiny was, however, still bound up with Europe; its foreign relations were, like those of the entire Empire, still conducted by Great Britain. The British declaration of war on Germany on 4 August 1914 automatically involved Australia.

German perfidy in invading Belgium en route to France, the heroic resistance of 'gallant little Belgium', the noble acceptance by Britain and France of their treaty obligations, and the beastliness of the Hun, were the central themes of early pro-war rhetoric. More cynical theories of the origin of the war – the struggle for the redivision of the world, imperial rivalry in the Balkans and the Middle East, national pride leading to a fall – received short shrift. The issue was civilization against barbarism. The official Australian response to the crisis was immediate and eager. A few days before the outbreak of war the retiring Liberal prime minister, Cook, declared on the hustings that 'all our resources in Australia are ... for the preservation and the security of the Empire'.[2] The same night, the leader of the

---

Sydney, 1936, which is Vol. XI of *The Official History*: the quotation in the text is from p. 13 in the Scott volume. There are two books of documents which cover the period: L. L. Robson, *Australia and the Great War: 1914–1918*, Melbourne, 1969: F. K. Crowley, *Modern Australia in Documents, I*, 1901–1939, Melbourne, 1973, pp. 214–314.

2 *Argus*, Melbourne, 1 August 1914.

Labor opposition, Andrew Fisher, capped this by pledging that 'Australians will stand beside our own to help and defend her to our last man and our last shilling'.[3] The Liberal government agreed to place the Australian naval squadron at the disposal of the British high command and to despatch an expeditionary force of 20,000 men 'of any suggested composition to any destination required by the Home Government'.[4] A month later the Labor party scored an easy win in the elections, capturing 42 of the 75 seats in the House of Representatives and 31 of the 36 seats in the Senate. The first steps had already been taken to implement the Australian commitment, and Fisher's new government honoured its predecessor's pledge.

The public response was equally enthusiastic. In the last few days of the crisis, masses of people who until then had shown little interest in foreign affairs were alerted to the imminence of war. Crowds gathered outside newspaper offices awaiting the arrival of the London cables. When news came of the outbreak, 'some were enthusiastic, some evidently gratified; some seemed over-weighted by the import of the news, some were openly pessimistic. But the general feeling was one of relief that the terrible waiting and uncertainty of the last few days was over'.[5] Whatever there was of national identity was submerged in the surge of emotion for the home country: some 98 per cent of the population were of United Kingdom descent (including over 20 per cent of Irish, a distinction which was to become significant later), and of these some 400,000 had arrived from the United Kingdom in the ten years before the war. The overwhelming sentiment was expressed by a *Bulletin* poet:

> For Britain! Good old Britain!
>   Where our fathers first drew breath,
> We'll fight like true Australians,
>   Facing danger, wounds or death.[6]

There was in this something of a child's solicitude for his parent, something of a young adult's claim for parental recognition that he had reached maturity. There was no shadow of feeling that the interests of child and parent might not be one.

Patriotic citizens sported allied colours. Aero Club, Rifle Club and Motor Cycle Club members offered their services; a wealthy Sydney retailer offered 'himself and his cars'. Shopkeepers disavowed any connection with German automobiles or pianos. Melbourne wharf-labourers, Newcastle coalminers and West Australian goldminers

[3] *Argus*, Melbourne, 1 August 1914.

[4] Announcement by the Prime Minister published in the *Argus*, Melbourne, 4 August 1914.

[5] *Argus*, Melbourne, 6 August 1914.

[6] Frank Johnstone, 'Sons of Australia', quoted in I. Turner, *Sydney's Burning*, Sydney, 2nd ed., 1969, p. 3.

worked off some job rivalries in the name of anti-Germanism. Victorian football clubs imposed a 6d. surcharge on admission prices for patriotic funds (however, attendances fell sharply) and one club changed its colours from the red, white and black of Germany to the red, yellow and black of Belgium. Irish-Australians declared their intention of burying the Home Rule hatchet for the duration. The only warning notes were sounded on the left. Within the labour movement there was, as well as radical nationalism and the chauvinism of White Australia, a tinge of anti-militarism and internationalism. The several socialist sects were at first disoriented by the adherence of so many leading European socialists to their countries, right or wrong, but they quickly moved into opposition. The revolutionary syndicalists of the Industrial Workers of the World (the 'Wobblies', as they were universally known) denounced the war from the outset: 'If they [the politicians of Australia] want blood, let them cut their own throats.'[7] But these were tiny minorities. The dominant note in the labour movement was perhaps one of sorrow. The *Australian Worker* wrote:

We must protect our country. We must keep sacred from the mailed fist this splendid heritage. But we hope no wave of jingo madness will sweep over the land, unbalancing the judgement of its leaders, and inciting its population to wild measures, spurred on by the vile press, to which war is only an increase in circulation, and every corpse a copper. God help Australia! God help England! God help Germany! God help us![8]

This was apprehension rather than dissent. The movement generally supported the patriotic expression of its leaders. The changeover to a Labor government on 17 September 1914 confirmed Australia's support for the Empire's war.

The presence of German nationals and shipping in and around Australia was an early preoccupation. Reservists of the German army and Germans of military age were ordered to register and were later interned. Some eminent German scientists, visiting Australia for a meeting of the British Association for the Advancement of Science, were permitted to attend the conference and were later repatriated, except for two of their number who were potential soldiers. German merchant ships in Australian ports were placed under arrest. One, the *Pfalz*, was sailing through the Port Phillip heads at the moment of Cook's announcement of the war; she was stopped by a shot fired from a shore battery across her bow – the first shot fired by Australian forces in the war. More serious was the presence in the Pacific of a strong German naval squadron, headed by the cruisers *Scharnhorst* and *Gneisenau*, and the existence of German garrisons in New Guinea and other Pacific islands. The Australian naval squadron, led by the

7 *Direct Action*, quoted in I. Turner, *Sydney's Burning*, Sydney, 2nd edition, 1969, p. 5.

8 *Australian Worker*, Sydney, 6 August 1914.

battle-cruiser *Australia,* abandoned its defensive role and set out in search of the German ships. A British request, however, diverted it to silencing the German garrisons. An expeditionary force of three battalions was raised hastily and sent to German New Guinea; Australian forces saw their first action and suffered their first casualties in subduing the German post at Rabaul. In the meantime the German naval squadron was playing hide and seek in the Pacific, eventually destroying a British squadron at Coronel on the west coast of South America and being in its turn annihilated near the Falkland Islands.

These were major naval engagements but the decisive battles, it was evident, would be fought in Europe. There, the Germans had passed through Belgium and had penetrated deeply into France. The strategic dogma of the time was that victory could be won quickly by the rapid advance of giant armies, spearheaded by cavalry, and the occupation of the enemy's seat of government. But this dogma was founded on an outmoded military technology. The German race to the sea was checked. By the time the first battle of Ypres in November 1914 the war of rapid movement froze to a halt on a line stretching from Switzerland across northern France and Flanders to the English Channel. The Germans dug in and used machine-guns – a late nineteenth century invention – to defend their positions. The French and the British did the same. New techniques – trenches, sandbags, barbed wire, quick-firing weapons – transformed mobile expectations into a static war. It was for this war that Australia's expeditionary force was destined.

The initial objective was the supply of three brigades of infantry and one Light Horse Brigade, under the command of Brigadier-General W. T. Bridges, for whatever purpose the Imperial government might require. The 20,000 men of this Australian Imperial Force were expected to come largely from those who had served in the militia or in the Australian contingent to the Boer War. These might be supplemented by such volunteers as could measure up to the high physical standards which had been set. Such was popular enthusiasm – and the conviction that the war would soon be over – that the government had no need to appeal for volunteers. No sooner were recruiting offices opened than men flocked to the colours, at first from the cities and then, as the news gradually spread through the outback, the men of the bush.[9] By the end of August the first contingent was already filled. Its soldiers were in training on sporting grounds in the capital cities, dressed in a distinctive local uniform whose 'crowning mark' was the digger hat, 'the cachet of [the Australian's] nationality wherever he fought', sporting the 'Rising Sun' emblem (in fact a cluster of rifles with bayonets attached) on its up-turned brim.[10] By the end of the year, over 50,000 men had enlisted – enough to add a second division to the contingent initially promised,

9 See 'Harney's War', in *Overland, 13,* Spring 1958.

10 E. Scott, *Australia During the War,* Sydney, 1936, p. 254.

as well as the 3000 reinforcements who would be needed each month once the troops went into action. Later, unfavourable comparisons were drawn between these early recruits who were held to have joined up out of dare-devilry and a desire to see the world, without due concern for the seriousness of the occasion, and those who enlisted when the reality of the war became clear. But there was no lack of warmth among the tens of thousands who lined the streets of Melbourne and Sydney to cheer the men of the First Division, marching to their points of embarkation and singing the song of the day:

> Should Auld acquaintance be forgot?
> No! No!   No! No! No! Australia will be there,
> Australia will be there![11]

The thirty-eight transports packed with Australian and New Zealand volunteers made rendezvous at King George's Sound in the far south-west of the continent. On 1 November 1914, escorted by one British, one Japanese and two Australian cruisers (the *Melbourne* and the *Sydney*), they sailed into the Indian Ocean. There the German cruiser *Emden* had been doing considerable damage to allied shipping and shore installations. On the morning of 9 November, contact was made with the *Emden* off the Cocos Islands. The *Sydney* closed in, engaged her in battle and finally drove her ashore, a shattered and helpless wreck. It was Australia's first significant victory, and it was greeted with great jubilation.

The Fisher government meanwhile applied itself to the problems of the home front. Despite a steady growth in manufacturing industry, the basis of the Australian economy remained unchanged – the export of primary products and the import of manufactured goods. In particular, the metal industry was not yet sufficiently developed to provide secondary industry with essential machinery and machine tools. Germany had been a major buyer of Australian exports. The direct trade was now stopped, and beyond that it was necessary to ensure that Australian primary produce did not reach Germany through neutral nations. The war placed new strains on British manufacturing industry, making it an uncertain supplier of imports. Shipping was commandeered for war purposes and freight and insurance charges rose sharply. Throughout the country there was uncertainty about the future. The stock exchanges closed for several weeks and there was a short-lived run on the banks. Local manufacturers, unsure of the domestic market, began to lay off workers. And, to add to all this, primary producers were suffering a drought.

At the outbreak of the war, the *Australian Worker* had warned: 'Thousands of unemployed will be created; unscrupulous greed will seize the opportunity to raise the necessaries of life to famine prices.'[12]

---

[11] 'Australia Will Be There', by W. W. Francis, quoted in E. Scott, *Australia During the War*, Sydney, 1936, p. 218.

[12] *Australian Worker*, Sydney, 6 August 1914.

A dramatic fall in living standards was indeed the war's first major impact on most Australians. Unemployment doubled in those unions which reported the number of their members out of work. Prices and rents rose noticeably during the last months of 1914 and began to rocket from the beginning of 1915. The half-hearted attempts of state governments to control prices came to nothing, while the various wage-fixing tribunals stopped operations and declared a wage-freeze. For the labour movement, this contrast made mockery of the government's promise that, while Australia's entry into the war would entail sacrifices for the Australian people, these would be shared evenly. Many believed, rightly or wrongly, that 'boodlers' were cornering scarce commodities in order to enhance their profits, and that governments were doing little if anything to end this exploitation. This sense of grievance against the unloading of the burdens of war onto the working class laid the basis for the conflict between trade unions and Labor governments which was to erupt in 1916.

The government was also concerned with questions of security – defence against the 'enemy within' and the prevention of information about war preparations and troop movements reaching the other side. Although there were only some 36,000 men and women of 'enemy' birth in Australia at the outbreak of war, there were many thousands more – particularly in the Barossa Valley in South Australia, the Victorian wheatlands and Southern Queensland – of German descent. Patriotic prejudice was directed against these people. Towns, rivers, mountains lost their German-sounding names, and even the humble 'German sausage' became 'baloney'. Mysterious lights were interpreted as attempts to communicate with enemy shipping lurking offshore; flights of birds were seen as aeroplanes, and whales as submarines. Anonymous correspondents sent copious reports to the authorities on the 'suspicious' behaviour of their neighbours. People suspected of having German connections suffered economic discrimination and social ostracism.

There were, however, serious matters at stake. In the early days of the war, London instructed that enemy reservists should be rounded up, and in October 1914 came the further instruction that all enemy subjects whose conduct was suspicious should be detained. Internment camps were set up for the confinement of such people. The fear of enemy aliens was confirmed by an extraordinary incident at Broken Hill on New Year's Day, 1915, when two Turks declared their own war on Australia and opened fire on a train-load of picnickers, killing four and wounding several more. The attorney-general W. M. Hughes, remarked that this reinforced the need to keep the enemy behind barbed wire. In October 1914 parliament gave the federal government wide powers under a War Precautions Act to require the registration and control the movement of aliens, as well as to prevent money, goods and information falling into enemy hands, and to 'make regulations for securing the public defence of the Commonwealth' – a dragnet provision on which the High Court later placed an extremely liberal interpretation. Censorship was quickly introduced – none too early for the safety of Australian troops en route for the war, as the interest of the press in conveying news of the sailing of the first contingent seemed to outweigh its concern for the men's safety.

Turkey had entered the war on Germany's side in October 1914, a few days before the first contingent sailed. The Turks threatened the allied powers at two points – on their common frontier with the Russian Empire and through their control of the east bank of the vital Suez Canal. The British High Command was concerned to meet this threat, and Lord Kitchener, the secretary of state for war, decided to divert the 'colonial' contingent to Egypt. Meanwhile, in London, the Australian high commissioner, Sir George Reid, had reached the same conclusion but for a different reason – Reid was concerned that the available accommodation would not provide adequately for the troops through an English winter. The Australian and New Zealand governments agreed, and, before Christmas, the first contingent was under canvas at Mena, five miles out of Cairo and almost in the shadow of the Pyramids – a 'ragged island of men and horses dropped in a sea of sand'.[13] The second contingent, which included a brigade of infantry under Colonel John Monash, joined them there in February 1915. The 'colonials' were grouped into an army corps, the A.N.Z.A.C., under the command of General William Birdwood, an outstanding British cavalry officer who had served in South Africa and India. The corps included the First Australian Division, led by General Bridges, and a New Zealand and Australian Division, under the British general A. J. Godley.

Their training was tough. They criss-crossed the desert, humping rifle and bayonet and pack and waterbottle, their horses dragging supply carts and cannon. They fought mock battles in the sand, bivouacked on sand, and dragged 'home' wearily through still more sand. The dreary routine was broken only by the hurried departure of two battalions for the Suez Canal to counter a Turkish foray which petered out before it could establish a bridgehead on the west bank. Camp life was tedious and little was done to counter boredom. The men spent their spare time gambling (two-up was the great game), writing home, organizing impromptu horse-races and other sports, cursing the sand and the flies, and everlastingly whingeing. But Cairo was close at hand. The Anzacs were a volunteer army, selected for their physical excellence, and, at six shillings a day for the privates, comparatively well paid. In Cairo, they met the 'Tommies'. They scandalized British officers by their irreverence towards the discipline and class distinctions of the British army and they lorded it with good-natured disdain over the subservient, underpaid and undersized 'other ranks' of the British 'Territorials'.

For the Egyptians – 'wogs' was the usual name – the Anzacs felt both resentment and contempt. 'Should White Australia defend Black

13 'S. De Loghe', (F. S. Loch), *The Straits Impregnable*, Melbourne, 1916, p. 37.

319

Egypt?'[14] – particularly a Black Egypt that did its best to rob White Australia of its money in every sale of food or booze or sex? There was respectable entertainment to be had in Cairo, but the city had its dark side – 'the loathsomeness of the native quarter, where humanity is to be seen in its grossest debasement'.[15] Often the 'six-bob-a-day tourists', as the men of the A.I.F. were dubbed, preferred the city's flesh-pots to its intellectual delights. Many went absent without leave to taste the forbidden fruits of the Wadir, Cairo's brothel quarter. Two such, staggering into camp in the early morning, were asked their names; they answered 'Burke and Wills'. On the night before their departure from Egypt, a brothel brawl over money became the 'battle of the Wadir', and the Anzacs burned the place down. For his censorious reports of Australian behaviour, the official correspondent, C. E. W. Bean, earned an unpopularity among the soldiers which took him a long time to live down. Despite the free issue of contraceptives for prophylactic purposes, many men were hospitalized with venereal disease, which was regarded as a 'self-inflicted wound' and then much more difficult to cure than now. Many did time in the military 'boobs'. Some suffered the ultimate punishment, to be dishonourably discharged and sent home. But most survived to fight on Gallipoli.

Between the Mediterranean and the Black Sea, on the shores of which lay Russia's only all-weather ports, was the Sea of Marmara. To the south of this sea lay Turkey; to the north lay the remains of the once-mighty Ottoman Empire in Europe – including the ancient city of Constantinople which the Turks had made their capital. At the Mediterranean end of the sea were the narrow straits called the Dardanelles, overlooked from the north by the sudden cliffs and barren hills of the Gallipoli Peninsula. The Turks were exerting military pressure on the Russians. The British High Command, urged on by the inventive first lord of the admiralty, Winston Churchill, determined to relieve this pressure on their ally. The first move was an attempt to force the Straits by naval action, which ended in disaster. The next was to open the Dardanelles to the passage of allied shipping by capturing the north shore. This was to be effected by a landing on Gallipoli. On 1 April, all leave was stopped for the Anzacs. They broke camp and embarked on a stream of shipping flowing through Alexandria. Their destination was secret, but latrine rumour guessed rightly that it was Lemnos, an offshore island, and then Gallipoli. The plan was for British and French forces to land at Cape Helles, the foot of the peninsula, and take the range called Achi Baba, and for the Anzacs to land near Gaba Tepe, ten miles north of Helles, and take Hill 971 on Sari Bair. From these two heights, to be captured

[14] H. Matthews, *Saints and Soldiers*, Sydney, 1918, p. 81.

[15] E. Gorman, *With the Twenty-Second: A History of the Twenty-Second Battalion, A.I.F.*, Melbourne, 1919, p. 15.

on the first day, the artillery would be able to subdue the Turkish forts and dominate the straits.

The Australians 'had come at last to the ancient test; and in the mind of each man was the question – how would they react to it?'[16] Soon after dawn on 25 April 1915, the men of the 3rd Brigade of the First Division of the A.I.F. stormed ashore at Anzac Cove, a rugged and difficult part of the coast a mile north of their intended landing point. They were met by solid rifle and artillery fire which cost them their first heavy toll of dead and wounded. But they established their beach-head and held off a formidable Turkish counter-attack mounted by Mustapha Kemel later in the day. By then they had penetrated only half a mile inland and were still far short of their first objective. Sixteen thousand men and stores had already been landed, but over 2000 were already casualties – among them Captain J. P. Lalor, a grandson of the miners' leader. Both General Birdwood and General Bridges contemplated an immediate evacuation so that A.N.Z.A.C. might reinforce the British at Cape Helles, but General Hamilton, cruising offshore on the *Queen Elizabeth*, decided that evacuation was impossible: 'There is nothing for it but to dig yourselves right in and stick it out.'[17]

The Anzacs did just that. They clung precariously to the foothills of Sari Bair in a complex of trenches and dugouts, overlooked by the Turks who were often no more than a hundred feet away. During the next three months, the lines did not change substantially, despite British attacks in the Cape Helles sector, which involved the 2nd Australian Brigade, and a massive and unsuccessful attack by the Turks on the Anzac beachhead on 19 May. 'It's the monotony we revile, not hard work or hard fare,' one soldier wrote.[18] The same outlook, the same dreary bully beef and army biscuits; the scarcity of tobacco, the irregularity of mail from home, the shortage of water; the fleas and the flies; as the summer wore on, the endemic dysentery. Turkish snipers harassed the men in the Anzac trenches until they provided themselves with periscopes in order to take sight for the return of fire. They were plagued by showers of hand bombs from the Turkish trenches which, when the fuses were long enough, they caught and threw back; later, they retaliated with improvised jam-tin bombs. 'Beachy Bill', the Turkish gun whose shrapnel rained down behind the lines, was an everyday menace to the man 'drawing water for his unit, directing a mule convoy [or] merely returning from a bathe or washing a shirt'.[19] There was ever-present danger, and little comfort and little rest.

For the British High Command, Gallipoli was a sideshow. The real

16 C. E. W. Bean, *Anzac to Amiens*, Canberra, 1946, p. 79.

17 Quoted in C. E. W. Bean, *Anzac to Amiens*, Canberra, 1946, p. 112.

18 H. Dinning, 'Glimpses of Anzac', in *The Anzac Book*, London, 1916, p. 17.

19 H. Dinning, 'Glimpses of Anzac', in *The Anzac Book*, London, 1916, p. 18.

war was being fought on the Western Front. Nevertheless General Hamilton explained patiently that no progress could be made unless he was given more men, and the British government sent reinforcements. The new plan was for the Australians to capture the southernmost Turkish strongpoint, Lone Pine, and to drive up Sari Bair, while a British landing would attack Sari Bair from the other side, at Suvla Bay. 'Furphies' (so called because the Furphy water-tank was a convenient place to exchange gossip) spread among the men of a new offensive, and the atmosphere grew tense. 'On many there dawned for the first time the fact that for them the prospect of return was vanishing,' wrote Bean. 'The vision was now one of battle after battle after battle. Men felt themselves to be between two long walls from which there seemed to be no turning except death, or disabling wounds.... The fond dream of the return home was silently surrendered ... men's keenness now was ... for the credit of Australia.'[20] At 4.30 in the afternoon of 6 August 1915, the artillery began a heavy bombardment of the Turkish line at Lone Pine. The Australians began to mass in their trenches. 'Can you find room for me beside Jim here?' asked one. 'Him and me are mates an' we're going over together.'[21] At 5.30 they went over, attacking out of the setting sun. Heavy Turkish rifle and machine-gun fire killed many of the first wave. Those who survived found the Turkish trenches so strongly roofed that they could not force entry. So they swept over the Turkish front-line and into the communications trenches behind, and took the Turks with rifle and bayonet from the rear. Within half-an-hour Lone Pine had fallen, but the battle continued for the next four days. The trenches were clogged with dead – 2000 Australians and 5000 Turks. The corpses began to rot in the sun, but there was neither time nor space to bury them until 10 August, when the worst of the fighting was done. Lone Pine was one of the high points of Australian military achievement on Gallipoli. It was here that seven Victoria Crosses were won.

The Anzac attack, delivered by the 4th Australian Brigade, and the New Zealand Brigade, supported by some Indian troops, failed when the troops lost their way in the maze of gullies on the slope of Sari Bair. But it was the colossal failure of the attack by the British Corps at Suvla Bay which was the main reason for the failure of the whole operation. Hamilton asked for still more men to renew the attack, but by now there were willing ears in London to listen to criticism of Hamilton's command – including that made by the Australian correspondent, Keith Murdoch. The British government replaced Hamilton by Sir Charles Munro. Munro recommended evacuation. Kitchener sought the opinion of the local commanders and found only Birdwood in favour of staying put; he visited Gallipoli himself and recognized the inevitable. On 22 November he recommended

20 C. E. W. Bean, *Anzac to Amiens*, Canberra, 1946, pp. 141–2.
21 C. E. W. Bean, *Anzac to Amiens*, Canberra, 1946, p. 145.

partial evacuation. Unwilling to divert further forces from the Western Front, the British government ordered that the evacuation be complete. By way of finale, a few days later a violent thunderstorm, followed by a torrent of rain and an icy hurricane, reduced water rations to two pints a day and left the Australians – many of whom had not seen snow before – shivering and miserable in their inadequate gear.

The plan for evacuation was brilliant. It provided for withdrawal in three stages, in a context of deception. The A.N.Z.A.C. command ordered a three-day cease fire (the 'Silent Stunt') to accustom the Turks to a new situation. Thereafter, periods of vigorous activity were alternated with periods of silence. The first two stages went without a hitch, though the troops were still unaware that this was more than a winter regrouping. The final stage provided for the embarkation of 20,000 men on the nights of 18 and 19 December, covered by a rearguard of 1500 who would move from position to position maintaining an intermittent fire. These in their turn would move out of the trenches and onto the waiting small craft, leaving a handful of rifles rigged to fire spasmodically for a further half-hour, and two landmines to block any last minute Turkish interference. The whole operation cost only two Anzac casualties. The last of the staff pushed off the deserted beach at 4 a.m. Three hours later, the Turks attacked – to find only booby-traps and ironic messages of welcome.

The Anzacs showed a strange reluctance to leave Gallipoli. Many demanded the application of established trade union principle – first on, last off. 'I hope *they* won't hear us marching down the *deres*,' one man said to Birdwood on the final day.[22] They had suffered a military defeat which would materially affect the further course of the war, but they had experienced a personal and national triumph. For one British observer, the poet John Masefield, they had taken on a legendary quality: 'For physical beauty and nobility of bearing they surpassed any men I had ever seen; they walked and looked like the kings in old poems'.[23] For themselves, they had confronted deprivation and death with stoic endurance and sardonic humour – 'next thing you'll be wanting flowers on your grave'. They had reinforced the established values of the Australian bush. A man was judged by his performance, not by his birth, and by how he stood with his mates. They lived closely with their officers and gave them respect – if they proved worthy – but not servility. They revered 'Birdie' (Birdwood) but were contemptuous of the upper-class officers of the British staff. They whinged continually as they improvised shelter and equipment from whatever was at hand. They had come to know their own manhood and that of their fellows.

Success or failure, right or wrong, victims of imperial rivalry or

[22] C. E. W. Bean, *Anzac to Amiens*, Canberra, 1946, p. 178.

[23] J. Masefield, *Gallipoli*, New York, 1916, pp. 25–6.

defenders of freedom from the German-Turkish yoke, they did what they had to do as well as they knew how, and because they had done if they came to symbolize, for themselves as well as for others, the demand and the guarantee that the maturity of their nation be recognized. They went from Gallipoli, leaving behind them 7594 Australians killed, 2431 New Zealanders killed, and 19,500 Australians and 5140 New Zealanders wounded: fewer than 100 were taken prisoner.

> Bury the dead
> By whose dying, splendidly,
> In that harsh dawn, volley-litten,
> Was our new war-saga written –
> We who 'had no history'.[24]

Australians first read of Gallipoli in their newspapers of 29 April. Eight days later came the detailed and stirring account of the distinguished British war correspondent, Ellis Ashmead-Bartlett:

Here [the assault on 'an almost perpendicular cliff'] was a tough proposition to tackle in the darkness, but those colonials, practical above all else, went about it in a practical way... this race of athletes proceeded to scale the cliffs without responding to the enemy's fire.... I have never seen anything like these wounded Australians in war before. Though many were shot to bits, without the hope of recovery, their cheers resounded throughout the night.... They were happy because they knew that they had been tried for the first time and had not been found wanting.[25]

The first casualty lists from Gallipoli, and the news of the sinking of the passenger liner *Lusitania*, aroused Australians to the grim severity of the times. At last people understood that this would be a long and bitter struggle. The immediate response was a wave of patriotic determination which swept thousands of men into the A.I.F.: 12,500 volunteered in June 1915, twice the April tally. But even this was not enough. In mid-June, the Australian government asked the British government whether it would accept all the recruits that Australia could provide. The British replied that they wanted every available man.

For the first time the government set out to persuade young men to enlist. Recruiting committees were formed and recruiting meetings held. Appeals were made at exhibitions of moving pictures, now beginning to replace live theatre as the major popular entertainment. A debate developed over the propriety of continuing sporting activities at a time of national crisis. Golfers regretted that they could not enlist in great numbers but offered to donate the cost of trophies to patriotic

---

24 J. A. Allen, 'Dardanelles – 1915', quoted in K. S. Inglis, 'The Australians at Gallipoli – I', in *H.S.*, *54*, April 1970, p. 224.

25 *Argus*, Melbourne, 8 May 1915.

funds. Race-goers insisted on the morale-building value of their sport. Prime Minister Fisher opined that the healthy outdoor sports, such as football, were preparation for the 'more serious business ahead'.[26] Soon after Gallipoli, however, the *Australasian* deplored 'the unhappy fact that the professional footballer ... and not the patriotic and gallant Australian soldier lavishing his life on Turkish ridges is still [the] idol' of Victorian youth.[27] In August the enlistment was announced of the notorious sports promoter, John Wren, who had offered £500 to the first Australian to win the Victoria Cross and paid the money over to the family of Private Albert Jacka. Wren was discharged from the army nine weeks later, having taken part in several recruiting meetings and risen to the rank of corporal. Recruiting peaked in July (36,000) and August (25,700) but was never again to reach such heights. In September 1915 the Universal Service League was formed, under the patronage of leading politicians of both parties, leaders of all religious denominations, and prominent professional men, to agitate for the abandonment of voluntary recruiting in favour of conscription.

Australian women, too, were swept along by the patriotic tide. Wives, mothers and daughters were urged to encourage their men to enlist; many did, convinced that it was a noble cause for which they offered up their sacrifice. The more enthusiastic took pleasure in presenting young men in civilian clothes with white feathers as symbols of their cowardice. Many enlisted as army nurses. But, for most, 'war work' meant assisting in providing comforts for 'our boys'. Red Cross branches were set up to provide aid to the sick and wounded and to prisoners of war. Organizations such as the Cheer-Up Society in Adelaide offered a cheery farewell to the boys as they left for the front, and a cheery welcome to the wounded when they arrived home. One legless soldier was reported as saying in the Cheer-up rooms: 'It's great to be without 'em, girls. You see, I suffered terribly with corns, and I don't feel 'em now.'[28] Other women offered, through the Comforts Fund, material well-being for the boys on active service. The enthusiasm with which the ladies knitted socks and mufflers and packed food parcels was not, however, always matched by the efficiency with which these were delivered to the front, nor the warmth with which they were received. One soldier sardonically recalled receiving on Gallipoli a parcel containing hair oil, pyjamas, cigars, and a booklet advising that Henry Clay pipes would be sent post-free to any part of the front.[29]

Yet others offered comfort of a more intimate kind. The suffragette and socialist, Adele Pankhurst, warned of a growth in the 'white slave'

26 *Truth*, Melbourne, 27 March 1915.

27 *Australasian*, Melbourne, 22 May 1915.

28 F. J. Mills, *Cheer Up: A Story of War Work*, Adelaide, 1920, p. 71.

29 A. J. Boyd, 'What Frank Thought', in *The Anzac Book*, London, 1916, p. 109.

traffic. *Truth* agreed that prostitution had increased but questioned whether the prostitutes had been forced into the game or had entered it of their own accord.[30] There was general alarm at the presumed increase in venereal disease – 'presumed' because V.D. was not yet legally notifiable – not only among the men abroad but also at home. A debate developed over whether legalized prostitution would be an effective safeguard against the scourge. A New South Wales parliamentarian, Dr Richard Arthur of the White Cross League, warned reinforcements on their way to Gallipoli against the 'flighty girl' who permitted 'liberties', and against drink which inflamed sexual desires and weakened self-control.[31] Emboldened by their victory in an early closing referendum in South Australia, the ladies of the Women's Christian Temperance Union and those whom *Truth* called 'wowsers' successfully extended their campaign for six o'clock closing of hotel bars to other states.

On the economic front, Australia was moving closer to self-sufficiency, as well as supplying Britain with important raw materials, and was financing the growing war effort from internal sources. A start had been made on the establishment of government-owned factories to manufacture munitions and other military supplies before the war. The Broken Hill Proprietary, having been offered inducements by the N.S.W. Labor government, opened its steelworks at Newcastle in June 1915, amid trenchant criticism from some sections of the labour movement that Labor policy was for a state-owned steelworks. B.H.P. provided steel for the manufacture of shells, the production of which was undertaken by government workshops in Victoria and Queensland and by private firms elsewhere, but Australian knowhow lagged behind the rapid changes in military technology. Australian troops nevertheless continued to be equipped with rifles and bayonets from the government small arms factory, until 1915 when the supply of weapons fell short of the recruits and British arms were used to supplement Australian. Australian factories provided the A.I.F. with an adequate supply of uniforms and – most important of all the infantryman's needs – boots, on which the Australians obstinately continued to insist, despite the claim of British manufacturers to produce a superior product.

After the early uncertainty, primary producers found their interests secured by the contingencies of war. Faced with the possibility that American meat packers might artificially inflate prices, the British government contracted to buy the whole of Australia's beef and mutton exports for the duration of the war. Australia gave Britain, at her request, first option on the purchase of the wool clip. In the first years of the war, British demand was almost entirely for crossbred wool, which represented only a third of the total. Wheat farmers had

30 *Truth*, Melbourne, 20 March 1915.

31 R. Arthur, *Keep Yourself Fit: An Address Given at the Camps in Queensland and New South Wales*, Sydney, n.d.

suffered a disastrous drought in 1914–15, leaving no export surplus, but 1915–16 promised a bumper crop and, European sources having dried up, Australian sales prospects were good provided that adequate shipping at reasonable freight rates could be found. The military demand for shipping, and the losses from German naval action, prevented an immediate solution to this problem, and the crop was acquired and stock-piled by the federal government's newly formed Wheat Pool. Metals presented a special problem. The base metals were of major significance to the munitions industry, but the marketing of these had been virtually controlled by German firms and Germany had been the major buyer. The Australian government, on the insistence of Attorney-General Hughes, sought Australian and Imperial legislation to enable the cancellation of contracts with German firms. Hughes introduced local legislation against 'enemy contracts' and this loophole was blocked.

The war imposed severe strains on Australia's finances. Pre-war, the federal government had been able to finance its operations, including major public works, without recourse to public borrowing, although the states were heavily indebted to overseas lenders. The Labor government hoped to finance the war effort in this way, but it soon became apparent that normal revenue would not suffice. The British treasury would not permit continued Australian borrowing on the London money market, and Australia was thrown onto its own resources. Three major measures were taken. An embargo on the export of gold enabled an accumulation of gold reserves and a consequent rapid increase in the note issue, which contributed largely to wartime price inflation. New taxes – a more steeply graduated land tax, death duties, and, in the 1915-16 budget, the first federal income tax – provided considerable new revenue. And in July 1915, Prime Minister Fisher announced the first Australian War Loan (£5,000,000 at 4½ per cent) and appealed to the patriotism of Australians to support the loan. It was over-subscribed by £8,400,000.

This was, it seemed, a community which had adjusted well to a war commitment escalating rapidly beyond the early sanguine expectations, and which was wholehearted in its support of that commitment. But there was a simmer of discontent below the surface, which was soon to boil. The prime cause was the price-inflation/wage-freeze scissors in which the workers found themselves. In 1915, this produced not so much industrial action, because the condition of the labour market was not favourable to strikes, as demands from the unions that the political wing of the movement take action. The unions were in a strong position; as well as the Fisher government, Labor governments were in power in five of the six states. Of these, the newest and most innovatory was that led by T. J. Ryan in Queensland, which came to power in May 1915. As well as promising sugar-growers support against the near-monopoly Colonial Sugar Refinery, and meatworkers, building workers and miners state action to provide employment, Ryan introduced a brand of 'consumer socialism' in food production and distribution and in banking and insurance. He also legislated for the eight-hour day. Beyond that, he promised to introduce price control.

This was the most emotive issue for the labour movement. It may have been, as Ernest Scott has suggested, that the causes of rising prices were the drought-created scarcity of foodstuffs, the virtual cessation of the inflow of British manufactures, and monetary inflation.[32] But the labour movement observed sourly the apparent efforts of producers and middlemen to 'corner' the supply of scarce commodities, and accordingly blamed inflation on 'the hogs of society, the exploiting rascals of the people's everyday food, [who] are trading on misfortune and making the poor pay the bill'.[33] At the Commonwealth Labor Conference in May 1915, the unions demanded that a new referendum be held to give the commonwealth the power to control prices. Despite some state-rights objections from state politicians, the proposal was carried. The following month Attorney-General Hughes secured the passage of a bill for a referendum, to be held in December. Four months later Andrew Fisher, growing weary of the continual divisions within the Labor caucus, resigned his office to succeed Sir George Reid as high commissioner in London. Hughes, the cabinet strong man, was elected by caucus to succeed him as prime minister. Hughes was already having second thoughts about the referendum, which the Liberal opposition had condemned as a threat to wartime unity. He convened a meeting of state premiers who undertook instead to introduce legislation to transfer the required powers to the federal government for the duration of the war. Hughes accepted the offer – which was not in the event honoured – and the labour movement was immediately in uproar. It was this more than anything else which shook the faith of the unions in the Labor politicians, whom they regarded as their parliamentary delegates.

Trade union discontent provided fertile ground for socialists and and syndicalists who were not impressed by appeals for industrial peace in time of war. Despite a favourable award on hours and conditions of work in December 1915, and the pleas of their federal president, W. M. Hughes, waterside workers in eastern ports mounted a series of strikes in 1916 against the 'famine' price of bread and for wage increases. At Broken Hill, militant metal miners moved past their union leadership, itself reckoned militant, to implement an I.W.W. slogan: 'If you want the 44-hour week, take it!' The union swung behind the men, the prime minister promised an immediate hearing in the arbitration court, and the demand was won. In New South Wales, coal miners struck for a reduction in working hours; the shortage of coal supplies threatened war production and the prime minister arranged a resumption of work on the miners' terms. In

[32] E. Scott, *Australia During the War*, Sydney, 1936, pp. 656–7.

[33] W. Wallis in *Labor Call*, Melbourne, 15 July 1915.

Queensland and New South Wales, militant shearers also used 'direct action' tactics – 'Give the warm weather and the blowflies a chance!' – to force wage increases, despite the efforts of the A.W.U. leaders to prevent a strike. It was a remarkable series of strikes. In all, during 1916, 170,000 workers were involved in over 500 industrial disputes for a total loss of 1.7 million working days – and this in a year when Australian soldiers were confronting their first major engagements on the Western Front. Industrial unrest was a symptom of the beginning of a loss of faith in the war. Working-class discontent exploded in a bitter fight over military conscription, a split in the Labor party, and the fall of Labor governments.

The war on the Western Front had been at virtual stalemate throughout 1915, but strategic opinion continued to insist that victory could only be won by making a decisive break in the enemy's defences. The British command set itself to raising, from the homeland and the Empire, the additional men needed to mount a summer 1916 offensive. In furtherance of this, the Australian government in September 1915 conducted a War Census, designed to assess the available resources of manpower and wealth, Attorney-General Hughes indicating that the government believed that these resources should not be used haphazardly but in a planned way. In November, the Commonwealth Statistician reported that there were 600,000 'fit' men of military age in Australia. ('Men were deemed fit if they described themselves as being in good health, not having lost a limb, and being neither blind nor deaf.'[34]) The government asked them all three questions: 'If willing to enlist now? ... If not willing to enlist now, are you willing to enlist at a later date? ... If not willing to enlist, state the reason why, as explicitly as possible.'[35] A wide section of the labour movement condemned these measures as dangerously close to conscription. One vocal opponent was tarred and feathered by returned soldiers. On 15 December, Hughes, by now prime minister, called for 50,000 volunteers to form new units of the A.I.F. and another 16,000 per month for 'reinforcements at the front'. They were needed, he said, to achieve a 'speedy and glorious victory'.[36] A few days later, British Prime Minister Asquith called for a million more men for the Imperial armies, and in January 1916 he introduced conscription.

Late in 1915, the British government invited the dominion prime ministers to meet with the Cabinet to discuss the progress of the war. Hughes accepted eagerly, arriving in London in March 1916. He believed that his hosts were 'a little at a loss to know what to do with me'.[37] He threw himself into a round of public engagements which

---

[34] E. Scott, *Australia During the War*, Sydney, 1936, p. 310, n. 42.

[35] The form is reproduced in F. K. Crowley, *Modern Australia in Documents, I, 1901–1939*, Melbourne, 1973, pp. 249–50.

[36] His 'Call to Arms' is reproduced in F. K. Crowley, *Modern Australia in Documents, I, 1901–1939*, Melbourne, 1973, pp. 248–9.

[37] W. M. Hughes, *The Splendid Adventure*, London, 1929, p. 39.

led an Australian classicist to compare him to Demosthenes, and he was made a freeman of various cities and collected an impressive array of honorary degrees. His attendance at Cabinet left Hughes with a poor opinion of Asquith – 'he looked upon action as a kind of disease . . . life terrified him'.[38] Hughes' opinion was apparently widely shared, since late in 1916 Asquith was replaced as prime minister by Lloyd George; but Lloyd George, although a stronger and more capable leader than Asquith, was never entirely successful in imposing his will on the British 'brass'. Hughes was not able to persuade the British command to group the Australian divisions in France into a single army under Birdwood, but he secured an agreement that the Australian troops would be used together whenever possible. He opened discussions, which were successfully concluded after his return to Australia, for the purchase by Great Britain of Australia's export surpluses of wool and wheat, and, when he ran into difficulty with the allocation of shipping and with exorbitant freights, he bought for the Commonwealth a fleet of fifteen somewhat sea-worn ships for £2,000,000. The French government convened an Economic Conference in Paris in June. Asquith, a free-trader, declared that Britain would be a 'looker-on', and was not keen for Hughes, an advocate of ruthless economic war, to attend. But pressure from within Britain and from France ensured Hughes a seat in the British delegation, and the conference decided on an aggressive post-war economic policy. Hughes arrived back in Australia on 31 July 1916, to an enthusiastic welcome – and a growing undercurrent of dissent.

While the prime minister was in London, the A.I.F. was involved in its first fighting in France. Two Anzac corps arrived in France in 1916. II Anzac Corps under General A. J. Godley took over the Armentières sector, while I Anzac Corps under General W. R. Birdwood fought in the Battle of the Somme. This was the Australians' first experience of trench warfare in settled country. The pleasures of towns like Armentières were available only a few miles from the front line, while London was accessible to the wounded and to men on leave. The trenches were more carefully built and more strongly fortified than those on Gallipoli, and behind the front line were support trenches and long lines of communication trenches up which came supplies and reinforcements and down which went the wounded. The dead were buried where they fell.

The new British commander was Sir Douglas Haig, who believed that victory could be won by a successful allied breakthrough on the River Somme. The French armies, however, had suffered appalling losses during their successful defence of Verdun, and the Somme attack had to be largely carried by the British. In the weeks leading up to the attack, raids and counter-raids, the heaviest artillery fire they had yet experienced and their first taste of poison gas introduced the Australians to a new kind of war. The British attack opened on 1 July,

[38] W. M. Hughes, *The Splendid Adventure*, London, 1929, p. 42.

after five days of artillery bombardment the main effect of which was so to chew up the land between the two front lines as to make orderly advance by the infantry impossible. The attack failed, as did a further one on 14 July, at enormous cost. The first major Australian engagement was an assault on 19 July by the Fifth Australian Division, with British support, on Fromelles in the Armentières sector, to the north of the main battle – a move designed to pin down the German troops in that area. It was preceded by a bombardment which gave advance warning to the Germans, who had also observed the preparatory movements of the inexperienced Australian infantry. The allied artillery did not succeed in silencing the German machine-guns and the attack was costly. Units of the Fifth Division broke through the German lines but were cut off by a counter-attack. The survivors were finally forced back to their original positions. The operation achieved nothing. It cost 5500 Australian casualties and put the Fifth Division out of operation for many months.

Four days later, the First, Second and Fourth Divisions (the Third was still in training in England) were thrown into a futile attempt to break through the German defences at Pozières. The First Division went 'over the top' at 12.30 a.m. on Sunday, 23 July. After bitter close-at-hand fighting with bombs and machine-guns, they won some ground and dug in. The Germans retaliated with three days of massive artillery fire. Having lost 5300 casualties, the First Division was relieved by the Second. 'They looked like men who had been in Hell ... drawn and haggard and so dazed that they appeared to be walking in a dream.'[39] The Second Division renewed the assault across a waste land where the village of Pozières had once stood. They were under continual artillery bombardment and their advance was caught on the German barbed wire. They dug in, preparing for a new attack. An officer wrote: 'We had to drive the men by every possible means and dig ourselves. The wounded and killed had to be thrown to one side – I refused to let any sound man help a wounded man; the sound men had to dig'.[40] Many succumbed, under the intolerable strain, to the condition known as 'shell-shock'. The attack won a little more ground but the Division was exhausted. Having suffered 6800 casualties, it was relieved by the Fourth Division on 6 August. The slow advance continued, still under heavy artillery fire which had by now destroyed most landmarks and made the attackers' objectives unrecognizable. The Fourth lost 4600 men. They were relieved on 15 August by the First Division which had been reinforced to two-thirds of its original strength. In one week of fighting, the First lost another 2650 men and were relieved by the Second. Five days and 1300 men later, the Second was withdrawn and the Fourth once more thrown

[39] Sgt. E. J. Rule, quoted in C. E. W. Bean, *Anzac to Amiens*, Canberra, 1946, p. 249.

[40] Lt. J. A. Raws, quoted in C. E. W. Bean, *The Australian Imperial Force in France 1916*, Sydney, 1929, p. 659.

into the attack. It cost the Fourth Division another 2400 casualties to reach their furthest point, Mouquet Farm, about a mile from the starting point of the battle, where the Germans finally halted the advance. The division pulled out through heavy shellfire: 'Our men were walking as if they were in Pitt Street, erect, not hurrying.'[41] The A.I.F. had suffered greatly, and to no effect. Haig's next move, in which for the first time he used – or rather misused – tanks, was held by the Germans and the Somme returned to stalemate. Both sides had suffered very heavy casualties. The thirty acres around Pozières Windmill were soaked with more Australian blood than any other piece of land, before or since, in the nation's history. The survivors were transferred to Ypres, a relatively quiet sector of the front, where they proceeded to dig in for the winter.

But Haig was not yet finished. Together with the French commander, Joffre, he resolved on a final thrust. The three Australian divisions were sent back to the Somme to take part in an attack on Bapaume. There they were rejoined by the Fifth Division which had been rebuilt with reinforcements. This time, the artillery barrages not only tore up the earth but converted it into a sea of mud. The roads over which motor lorries were carting supplies gave way and infantry moving towards the front line took two hours to cover every mile. The men of the A.I.F. had come to believe that their sacrifices at Pozières had been wasted, and their morale was down. Nevertheless they went twice into the attack, but each time bogged down in mud. The first battle of the Somme was over. The Australians had won no battles but they had established a reputation as game fighters, and they withdrew once more to the comparative comfort – despite rain, frost and snow – of their winter trenches.

The Australian and New Zealand Light Horse Brigades had been left behind in Egypt, together with British troops, to counter the possibility of a Turkish attack through the Sinai desert and across the Suez Canal. They repulsed the Turks at Romani, losing several hundred casualties – but few prisoners, as they had agreed on 'a voluntary and unwritten law that no sound man should allow himself to be taken prisoner, and no wounded man should be permitted to fall into enemy hands'.[42] Led by General Henry Chauvel, and accompanied by a Camel Brigade, the Light Horse late in 1916 pushed the Turkish army back across the desert and into Palestine. They were, the British commander wrote, 'the keystone of the defence of Egypt'.[43]

Meanwhile, the prime minister had returned to Australia, and the *Sydney Morning Herald* had welcomed him with the comment: 'If Mr Hughes' picture of the present state of the war is a reflection of his knowledge, he is bound to introduce compulsory service in some form,

41 C. E. W. Bean, *Anzac to Amiens*, Canberra, 1946, p. 263.

42 H. S. Gullett, *The Australian Imperial Force in Sinai and Palestine, 1914–1918*, Sydney, 1923, p. 185.

43 C. E. W. Bean, *Anzac to Amiens*, Canberra, 1946, p. 286.

so that our supply of reinforcements shall not come to an end.'[44] Indeed, the position was acute. Recruiting had been high at the start of the year, following the prime minister's 'Call to Arms', but had then fallen off, so that by mid-May the total recruits for the previous six months were 47,000 short of the 128,000 required. Then in July came the battle of the Somme. Australian newspapers did not tell their readers the truth about the failure, but the huge number of casualties could not be hidden. Through the British command, General Birdwood told the Australian government how many reinforcements would be needed to keep the five Australian divisions at fighting strength. Suggestions were floated to break up the Third Division and distribute its men among the four divisions which had been decimated on the Somme, and to bring the Light Horsemen from the Middle East and convert them into infantry. On 30 August, the prime minister told parliament what was needed: a special draft of 32,500 men in September and 16,500 a month thereafter. Recruiting had been running at around 6000 a month. The people would be asked to vote on whether Australia should follow Britain and introduce compulsion for overseas military service.

The lines were already drawn. The Universal Service League had been campaigning for compulsion for nearly twelve months. Radicals had met this campaign by forming Anti-Conscription Leagues. The trade union movements in Victoria and New South Wales had, in September 1915, declared against conscription in any form. The N.S.W. Labor party warned its members, including Prime Minister Hughes and N.S.W. Premier W. A. Holman, against associating with the U.S.L. Between March and May 1916, the three eastern states' branches of the Labor party resolved to oppose the introduction of conscription. In June, a Trade Union Congress which claimed to speak for 280,000 unionists declared its 'uncompromising hostility' to conscription and agreed on a ballot of unions on the calling of a general strike if conscription were introduced.[45] Hughes was confronted on his return from London with a labour movement that was hopelessly divided, and already the press was speculating that 'it is hard to see how a split in the party can be avoided'.[46] He addressed great meetings in Melbourne and Sydney, urging a more vigorous war effort but not referring directly to conscription. The N.S.W. Labor party countered with its first anti-conscription rally – a meeting variously estimated at sixty and one hundred thousand in the Sydney Domain.

The parliamentary Labor party was deeply divided. The federal parliament had the constitutional power to legislate for conscription, but Hughes did not have the numbers in parliament, even with the support of the opposition, to get conscription through. Hoping that a

44 *Sydney Morning Herald*, 2 August 1916.

45 See I. Turner, *Industrial Labour and Politics*, Canberra, 1965, p. 102.

46 *Sydney Morning Herald*, 5 August 1916.

massive popular vote would force his dissident colleagues into line, the prime minister asked his cabinet to initiate a referendum on conscription. They agreed, by five votes to four. The parliamentary party agreed by 'a bare majority of one'.[47] Hughes was later criticized for his decision to hold a referendum, but in reality he had little choice. Once the legislation to hold the referendum was passed, Hughes set out to win the support of the labour movement. He was rebuffed by the Victorian and New South Wales executives, N.S.W. Premier Holman declaring that Victoria had 'succumbed to the pressure brought to bear by the workers', while the N.S.W. decision had been 'pre-determined' by a trade union grouping known as the Industrial Section.[48] The West Australian branch of the party was the only one to offer Hughes any comfort – it allowed its members freedom of action. On 15 September, the N.S.W. branch expelled Hughes and Holman from the party. Undeterred, Hughes plunged into the campaign:

Australians! This is no time for party strife. The nation is in peril, and it calls for her citizens to defend her. Our duty is clear. Let us rise like men, gird up our loins, and do that which duty and self-interests alike dictate.[49]

It was a bitter fight. The prime minister issued a list of the twenty-two Labor parliamentarians who would be available for the 'Yes' campaign. The leader of the anti-conscription faction, Frank Tudor, who had recently resigned from cabinet, issued a list of thirty-four 'No' supporters. The government called young men up for home service on 2 October. Hughes threatened wholesale prosecutions for draft-evasion, whereupon three anti-conscriptionist ministers resigned. The labour movement believed that the October call-up was in anticipation of conscription for overseas service. A special trade union conference called a national one-day stoppage in protest and resolved on further industrial action in the event of conscription being introduced. Huge crowds heard orators present emotionally loaded cases for 'Yes' and 'No' at meetings which were often tumultuous and sometimes the occasion of minor violence. Among the largest were those addressed by Daniel Mannix, the Catholic Coadjutor-Archbishop of Melbourne. Mannix was deeply distressed by the wrongs inflicted on the Irish people during the recent Easter Rising, and he condemned the 'sordid trade war' and those who would conscript Australians to fight in it. Wild accusations were tossed about. For the 'No' side it was alleged that the government was planning to abandon White Australia and to replace conscripts with coloured immigrants. The 'Yes' supporters claimed that the 'No' campaign was the work of pro-Germans, Sinn

[47] W. Webster, M.H.R., quoted in L. C. Jauncey, *The Story of Conscription in Australia*, London, 1935, p. 158.

[48] See I. Turner, *Industrial Labour and Politics*, Canberra, 1965, pp. 106–7.

[49] *Sydney Morning Herald*, 19 September 1916.

Feiners, the I.W.W. and similar disloyalists. 'Yes' advocates urged women voters not to abandon their menfolk at the front. A 'No' leaflet, 'The Blood Vote', asked:

> 'Why is your face so white, Mother?
> Why do you choke for breath?'
> 'O, I have dreamt in the night, my son,
> That I have doomed a man to death.'[50]

It was the Industrial Workers of the World who provided the most dramatic incident of the campaign. An anarcho-syndicalist offshoot of an American labour organization, the Wobblies had first organized in Australia in 1907. They had won some influence among itinerant and unskilled workers by their uncompromising advocacy of 'direct action', but it was their outspoken opposition to the war which had won them national attention – largely hostile. In 1915, one of their leaders, Tom Barker, had published what was perhaps the most famous Australian poster of the war:

To arms! Capitalists, parsons, politicians, landlords, newspaper editors, and other stay at home patriots. Your country needs you in the trenches! Workers, follow your masters![51]

Barker was charged with prejudicing recruiting and sentenced to six months' gaol. Now into the middle of the referendum campaign was thrown the arrest of twelve members of the I.W.W. on charges of conspiring to burn down a large part of Sydney in order to secure the release of Barker from prison and to prevent the introduction of conscription. A newspaper headlined: I.W.W. ASSASSINS WANT YOU TO VOTE NO.[52]

The referendum of 28 October showed a narrow majority (72,476 in a poll of 2,247,590) for 'No'.[53] New South Wales, South Australia and Queensland voted against conscription, the other states for – especially Western Australia, where the 'Yes' vote was twice as high as the national average. It seems likely that, while the overall vote of the soldiers was for conscription, the vote of those who had seen active service was against. Analysis of the results suggests that, while the

---

[50] W. R. Winspear, in Claude Marquet, *Cartoons: A Commemorative Volume*, Sydney, 1920, p. 55.

[51] Quoted in I. Turner, *Sydney's Burning*, Sydney, 1969, p. 15.

[52] Quoted in I. Turner, *Sydney's Burning*, Sydney, 1969, p. 48.

[53] *C.P.P.*, 1917–19, *IV*, p. 1469. The conscription campaigns of 1916 and 1917, and the results are discussed in F. B. Smith, *The Conscription Plebiscites in Australia 1916–17*, Melbourne, 1965: I. Turner, *Industrial Labour and Politics*, Canberra, 1965, chs. 4 and 7: L. L. Robson, *Australia and the Great War 1914–1918*, Melbourne, 1969: J. M. Main, *Conscription: The Australian Debate 1901–1970*, Melbourne, 1970: F. K. Crowley, *Modern Australia in Documents, I, 1901–1939*, Melbourne, 1973, pp. 266–72, 296–301.

labour movement's campaign had carried the majority of working-class voters for 'No', it was the votes of the usually non-Labor farmers which defeated conscription.

The referendum consummated the split in the Labor party. When the parliamentary party met on 14 November, a Queensland member moved want of confidence in Hughes' leadership. Realizing that the numbers were against him, Hughes led his twenty-four followers in a walk-out, leaving forty members behind in the party room to confirm the expulsion of the prime minister and to elect Frank Tudor as their new leader. Similar divisions occurred in the state parliamentary parties, except for Queensland. A special federal conference of the party in December resolved on the expulsion of all federal members who had supported conscription or had left the party to form another party, and thus finalized the split.

Hughes had already announced the formation of a National Labor party, and had formed a new government with Liberal support. In January 1917, the two parties fused to form the Nationalist party. Holman acted similarly in New South Wales. Both Hughes and Holman were hesitant to go to the electorate and manoeuvred to extend the lives of their parliaments, while the anti-conscriptionists had taken great heart from their victory and were demanding early polls. Public opinion was against the prolongation of parliament and Holman decided to risk an election. His Nationalist coalition won a handsome victory. A motion to prolong the life of the federal parliament was defeated in the Senate, and Hughes too led his Nationalist coalition into an election. Labor now held only two instead of five state governments, and Hughes had gained confidence from the New South Wales result. The poll was held on 5 May 1917. Voting was not yet compulsory, but more than three-quarters of the electors went to the polls. The Nationalists won an additional four seats in the House of Representatives, to give them 53 out of 75, and all eighteen of the available Senate seats. Overall, the Labor vote dropped from its 1914 Senate high-point of 52.15 per cent to 43.7 per cent. The anti-conscriptionists' victory was not carried over into the election. Opposition to conscription did not mean opposition to the war. The hard-core working class vote in the eastern cities stayed solid, but the farmers moved back to their traditional position and away from Labor.

The war was not going well for the allies in the early months of 1917. The rival front line trenches were static. The Australian divisions were entrenched in the mud before Bapaume – 'mud ... along miles and miles of country that is nothing but broken tree stumps and endless shell holes'.[54] C. E. W. Bean painted a grim picture of 'an Australian in the trenches ... standing in mud nearly to his waist, shivering in his arms and every body muscle, leaning back against the trench side,

---

[54] C. E. W. Bean, *Letters from France*, London, 1917, p. 198.

fast asleep'.[55] The Germans declared open season on allied shipping with their submarines and threatened to starve Great Britain into submission. The March Revolution in Russia, prompted by intense war weariness, had caused the Tsar to abdicate. The new government declared its intention of continuing the war, but the revolutionary movement was growing. French morale was flagging. Almost the only good news was America's declaration of war on Germany, but American manpower was untrained and American industry was not geared to the needs of the war. Yet still the allied command thought in terms of another massive infantry offensive and a knock-out blow. For this they needed men.

The Australian government had pledged support, but conscription had been defeated, so the target was re-adjusted. The aim now was 5,500 men a month – the bare minimum needed to maintain the existing strength of the A.I.F. Donald McKinnon, newly appointed director-general of recruiting, built an elaborate network of recruiting committees throughout the country. He was a man with flair and imagination and the campaign took on new dimensions. A *Speaker's Companion* contained a woman's pledge to give her favours only to a man who had served his country – 'If there are not enough soldiers to go round I will cheerfully die an old maid' – and a poem by Henry Lawson:

> A nation's born where the shells fall fast,
> Or its lease of life renewed.[56]

Large foosteps painted on the pavement led men to recruiting depots. A parade of horses with empty saddles invited the eligible to fill them. Films – both documentaries of the army at war and features such as 'A Hero of the Dardanelles' – encouraged young men to enlist. A special appeal was made for a 'Sportsmen's Thousand' to 'Play up, Play Up, & Play THE Game'.[57]

The 1917 spring offensive was to begin in April. Meanwhile, the Germans had decided on a new strategy – to pull back to the just completed, heavily fortified Hindenburg Line, there to stand fast while the submarine war brought Britain and France to their knees. Probing operations carried out by the A.I.F. near Bapaume confirmed the German withdrawal. In high spirits, the Australians pushed their cautious advance across the devastated no-man's-land towards positions from which they might support the British offensive. The Hindenburg Line was protected by barbed-wire entanglements, 'very wide, in double belts, boldly patterned with angles intended to cause attacking troops to divide and crowd into spaces murderously covered

[55] C. E. W. Bean, *Letters from France*, London, 1917, p. 202.

[56] Quoted in L. L. Robson, *The First A.I.F.: A Study of Its Recruitment 1914–1918*, Melbourne, 1970, pp. 125–6.

[57] From the plate facing p. 135 in L. L. Robson, *The First A.I.F.: A Study of Its Recruitment 1914–1918*, Melbourne, 1970.

by machine guns'.[58] The plan was to throw tanks in to flatten the wire and to follow with infantry. The offensive opened on 9 April with a British feint on the northern sector. The main attack was that of the French on the Aisne. The Germans had advance warning, and a fortnight's fierce fighting left the stalemate much where it was. On 11 April, despite Birdwood's doubt about the prospects, the A.I.F.'s Fourth Division assaulted the Hindenburg Line just east of Bullecourt. The tanks were not a success. They were delayed by a blizzard, from which the infantry also suffered, and their armour proved too thin to withstand the German shells. The use of tanks inhibited artillery bombardment and the Australians attacked virtually without support. Despite this, they took a section of the Hindenburg Line and held it until they ran short of ammunition. The Germans counter-attacked and they were forced to withdraw with the loss of 1170 prisoners. At one point in the see-saw fighting, when the artillery had at last been allowed to open fire, the Australians recaptured a position from which they had been dislodged. They suffered a barrage from their own artillery, which had not been informed. The Brigade which spearheaded the attack suffered 2339 casualties out of 3000 men. A soldiers' song lamented:

> If you want to find the privates, we know where they are,
> They're hanging on the old barbed wire.

The rash decisions and the abysmal staff work which led to this defeat shook the confidence of the Australians in tanks, and in the British command.

Further south, a strong German force attacked a section of the line held by the thinly-spread First Division. The Germans succeeeded in penetrating between the Australian strongposts and in overrunning some artillery positions, but they were driven back by skilful use of the new Lewis light machine-gun. On 3 May, as the French offensive was drawing to its unsuccessful end, the Australians – this time the Second Division – were again thrown against Bullecourt. A preliminary bombardment had reduced the village to rubble and the plan was for the infantry to advance in the wake of a creeping barrage. Once more the wire was not demolished and the attackers were pinned down by machine-gun fire along the entanglements. Once more the fighting see-sawed and sections of the German trenches repeatedly changed hands. One brigade, however, succeeded in taking 600 yards of the Hindenburg Line; the First and later the Fifth Divisions were brought in to reinforce the Second, slightly extending the Australian enclave and holding it despite fierce German artillery fire and a series of counter-attacks headed by flamethrowers. The Australian advance, and a successful British attack on the Germans' other flank, forced the Germans to withdraw to their second line of defence. Half a mile of rubble and shell-torn earth had been captured, at a cost to the

[58] C. E. W. Bean, *Anzac to Amiens*, Canberra, 1946, p. 328.

A.I.F. of 10,000 casualties. The decimated divisions were reinforced by men who had recovered from their wounds, and the Australians were withdrawn to rest.

The defeat on the Aisne had destroyed the morale of the French army and it was torn apart by mutiny. Nevertheless Haig resolved to test his belief that the Germans could be defeated by a successful British attack in the north, at Ypres. The Third Australian Division had moved into the front line under General John Monash in December 1916. It was part, together with the New Zealand and a British Division, of II Anzac Corps. The Corps' task was to take the village of Messines. The attack had been carefully prepared. For months, tunnelling companies had been working to lay nineteen huge mines deep underneath key points in the German defences. Those at Hill 60 were manned by an Australian company whose task it was to defend the workings against German counter-tunnelling. The British bombardment began seven days before the attack was due. As the infantry moved up to the front line, they came under fire from German shells containing phosgene gas. Just before dawn on 7 June the mines were exploded; it is said that Lloyd George heard the explosion in 10 Downing Street. The three divisions advanced and took Messines. In the afternoon the Fourth Division, which had been withdrawn from its rest, moved through Messines under heavy artillery fire and advanced the allied line still further. This was one of the few successful operations on the Western Front. It won some two miles of territory, eliminated an awkward German bulge into the allied lines, and secured the flank for the major attack further north, towards Passchendaele. But the price was high. II Anzac Corps, engaged in the Messines sector, lost 10,178 Australians and 4978 New Zealanders in a week's fighting.

Haig planned his major offensive for late July. In the absence of effective French support, Lloyd George was doubtful, but Haig's views prevailed. Australian gunners, tunnellers, and (for the first time) airmen from the Australian Flying Corps took part in the preparatory softening up. Haig attacked on 31 July with twenty divisions, including the Third Australian, on a fifteen-mile front. He won some ground, and then the rain came. 'The battlefield became a bog; in every depression the flooded craters lay brim to brim like the footsteps of monstrous animals in the slimy margin of some primeval waterhole.'[59] The advance was smothered in mud. The men responded characteristically. It was said that a soldier, walking along the duckboard, saw an Australian hat lying on the mud. He picked it up and discovered a man's head. He began to help the man out, to be told: 'Hang on a minute, dig, till I get me feet out of the bloody stirrups.'

Haig held to his belief that further massive attacks would break the German morale, and resolved to renew the assault. The 'diggers'

[59] C. E. W. Bean, *The Australian Imperial Force in France 1917*, Sydney, 1938, p. 721.

of I Anzac Corps (the affectionate nickname was by now in general use) were to be brought out of their resting place to spearhead the drive. At dawn on 20 September 1917, Haig's eleven divisions went 'over the top'. The First and Second Australian Divisions were side by side – a great morale booster – in the centre of the force. The Battle of the Menin Road swept over the German front line and won a mile of ground, at a cost to the Australians of 5000 casualties. The Fourth and Fifth Australian Divisions moved through their successful comrades to take Polygon Wood and carry the fight to the Germans' second line. On 4 October, Haig used the First, Second and Third Australian and the New Zealand Divisions to spearhead an attack on the strategically important Broodseinde Ridge, but at the cost of 6432 Australian casualties and about 1700 New Zealanders. The huge losses had strengthened Lloyd George's doubts about Haig's strategy, but Haig persisted and poised his army for an assault on Passchendaele. The Third and Fourth Divisions were again in the forefront of the fighting, but again the rains came and the advance bogged down in mud. Passchendaele was finally taken by the Canadians, with Australian support, on 10 November. The third battle of Ypres was over, and the Australians were withdrawn from the front line. The battle had lasted for fifteen weeks and had cost the two sides over half a million casualties – among them, 38,000 Australians. It had worn down, but not broken, the German defences. It had advanced the British line by five or six miles, and given Haig his 'victory'.

In the Middle East, British infantry and the Australian Light Horse continued the fight to drive the Turks back from the Suez Canal and Egypt – unsuccessfully until General Allenby assumed overall command, and Chauvel took command of the horsemen of the Desert Column. The winter rains were not far away and Allenby had to move quickly. He encouraged the Turks to believe that he would try to take Gaza, while preparing a bold thrust towards their inland base at Beersheba. After a rapid march across the desert, the British infantry attacked the township from the west. The men of the Anzac Mounted Division came in on foot from the east, but their advance was halted by the Turkish defence. Beersheba had to be captured before nightfall, or both men and horses would be without water. Chauvel was ordered to mount a Light Horse attack from the south. It was their first cavalry charge. The Light Horsemen galloped for Beersheba, through artillery, and then machine-gun, and finally rifle fire. They swept over the Turkish trenches and stormed them from the rear with rifle and bayonet. Beersheba was taken, and at minute cost, either in men or in the horses they loved.

The smell of water, cold and sweet, was released on the dusty air. Standing, weary and patient, out among the ridges, the horses smelled it, and a whinny ran from line to line.[60]

60 F. D. Davison, *The Wells of Beersheba*, Sydney, 1933, p. 76.

It was one of the last major cavalry campaigns of the war; thereafter machines would take over from horses. Allenby's troops moved west from Beersheba to take Gaza, then north to drive the Turkish army from Jerusalem.

Win, lose or draw, the part played by Australian troops on the Western Front and in the Middle East was presented to the Australian people in the most favourable possible light. But the long casualty lists could not be hidden, and they produced the first serious questioning of Australian participation in the war. A Peace Alliance had been formed in October 1914. It had adopted the demand of the British Union of Democratic Control for a peace without annexations and without indemnities,[61] based on the right of all nations to self-determination and the arbitration of international disputes, but it had had little influence except on the extreme left. The rejection by the allied powers on 30 December 1916 of German peace feelers and of U.S. President Wilson's proposal for a negotiated peace produced a wider response. Labour organizations began to join in the demand that the allies declare their terms for peace and enter into negotiations. The secretary of the Peace Alliance commented that 'there is a deep feeling of war weariness that if taken in hand can be developed and used to checkmate the jingoism feeling and ultimately bring about a stop-the-war feeling'.[62] In June 1917 the N.S.W. branch of the Labor party laid the blame for the war at the door of capitalism and called for a negotiated peace. The Victorian, Queensland and South Australian branches followed suit.

Then, on 2 August 1917, there began a 'general strike' of workers in New South Wales, 'the biggest industrial upheaval ever experienced in Australia'.[63] It began with the attempt of the N.S.W. Railways and Tramways Commissioners to introduce into their workshops a method of work accounting which the unions condemned as 'speed up' – an attempt to force the workers to increase the intensity of their labour. It was a seemingly small issue to give rise to such a big dispute, but such was the frustration and discontent among workers, not only with their immediate condition but with the war itself, that, as the unions' secretary said, 'the difficulty was not in getting men to come out, but to keep them in'.[64] Within a few days, as well as railway and tramway workers, road transport workers, miners and maritime workers were out on strike. The unions saw themselves as threatened

[61] See I. Turner, *Industrial Labour and Politics*, Canberra, 1965, p. 169.

[62] F. J. Riley, quoted in I. Turner, *Industrial Labour and Politics*, Canberra, 1965, p. 172.

[63] Quoted in I. Turner, *Industrial Labour and Politics*, Canberra 1965, p. 141. See also D. Coward, 'Crime and Punishment: The Great Strike in New South Wales', in J. Iremonger, *et al.*, Eds., *Strikes: Studies in Twentieth Century Australian Social History*, Sydney, 1973.

[64] Quoted in I. Turner, *Industrial Labour and Politics*, Canberra, 1965, p. 147.

with 'a general reduction of work, longer hours, and more degrading conditions of labour'.[65] The N.S.W. government declared:

The Enemies of Britain and her Allies have succeeded in plunging Australia into a General Strike. For the time being they have crippled our Country's efforts to assist in the Great War. AT THE BACK OF THIS STRIKE LURK THE I.W.W. AND THE EXPONENTS OF DIRECT ACTION. . . . Who is for Australia and the Allies?[66]

The N.S.W. and federal governments set out to defeat the strike. 'Free' labour was recruited, coal stocks and transport were commandeered, gas and electricity were rationed, the leaders of the Union Defence Committee were arrested on charges of conspiracy. After three weeks out, the railwaymen began to drift back to work. The government stood firm for unconditional surrender and the unions had no option but to concede. The railwaymen returned to work on 10 September, the last of the strikers (the seamen) on 8 October. It was a total defeat. 'Loyalist' strike-breakers and newly formed 'loyalist' unions were given preference in employment over the defeated unionists. Many hundreds of railwaymen, miners and waterside workers were refused re-employment. The Defence Committee secretary, E. J. Kavanagh, said:

It took just twenty-seven years of hard work to bring [trade unionism] to that state of perfection. It was built up by arbitration and knocked down in twenty-seven days by direct action.[67]

The government had established its ability to govern without, or against, the unions – but at the cost of growing working-class disaffection. The gulf between Sydney and Ypres was wide.

The huge casualties on the Western Front – over 50,000 Australians, nearly one in six of the total force, had been killed or injured – lent point to Lord Carson's comment in England that the necessary supply of heroes must be maintained at all costs. But recruiting was falling off – from around 4,500 a month early in 1917 to around 2,500 a month later in the year. 'The general welfare became subservient to class and individual animosity', reported the director-general of recruiting, 'and the trouble grew as the effects of war weariness began to make themselves felt'.[68] Every effort was made to keep up the numbers. Women were encouraged to tell their men: 'You must go!' Allowances were increased for the dependants of married men. Labour organizations accused employers of imposing 'economic conscription' by sacking eligible men. Pressure was put on theatre managers to allow recruiting

[65] *The Striker*, being a special issue of the *Australian Worker*, Sydney, 13 August 1917.

[66] Quoted in I. Turner, *Industrial Labour and Politics*, Canberra, 1965, p. 146.

[67] Quoted in F. K. Crowley, *Modern Australia in Documents, I*, 1901–1939, Melbourne, 1973, pp. 290–91.

[68] Quoted in E. Scott, *Australia During the War*, Sydney, 1936, p. 398.

speeches at intervals, but the managers objected that this would reduce box-office takings. Horse-racing, boxing and drinking hours were curtailed. But to little effect.

There were several potential scapegoats. The I.W.W. were obvious – but since November 1916 their efforts had been concentrated on winning the release from gaol of their twelve imprisoned fellow-workers, and their organization was finally declared illegal and destroyed in July 1917. People of German origin or descent were accused of crimes ranging from disloyalty to sabotage and espionage; the police systematically investigated the complaints but found little or nothing to support them. The sectarian bitterness created by the suppression of Irish nationalism and the conscription campaign continued to flower, and 'Loyal Orange' partisans took the opportunity of tarring the whole of Catholicism with the 'disloyal' brush. But the simple truth was that, in Australia as in every other belligerent country except the newcomer, America, more and more people were losing their enthusiasm for a war which seemed to have no end. On 7 November, Prime Minister Hughes announced that the government would hold another referendum on conscription for overseas military service. The question to be put to the people was: 'Are you in favour of the proposal of the Commonwealth Government for reinforcing the Australian Imperial Forces oversea?'[69] The precise proposal was that voluntary recruiting should continue, but that any leeway between this and the required 7000 men a month should be made up by conscripting fit, single men between the ages of 20 and 44, the order of their induction to be determined by lot. The *Worker* promptly labelled this a 'Lottery of Death'.[70]

The government decreed that electors of enemy origin and their children were disqualified from voting and closed the rolls two days after the referendum was announced. The anti-conscriptionists felt that there were 'fearful odds against us this time ... with thousands disenfranchised and the trade unions weakened by a nine-weeks strike'.[71] The campaign was even more bitter, and the rival propaganda more extreme, than that of 1916. For the 'No' side, A. W. Foster wrote in a special no-conscription issue of *Ross's Monthly*: 'Husbands for our future brides under Conscription – Chinese, Japs., and Hindoos.'[72] The 'Yes' campaigners issued *The Anti's Creed*:

I believe the men at the Front should be sacrificed.... I believe that treachery is a virtue ... that disloyalty is true citizenship ... that desertion is ennobling.... I believe I'm worm enough to vote No.[73]

[69] Quoted in E. Scott, *Australia During the War*, Sydney, 1936, p. 414.

[70] *Australian Worker*, Sydney, 15 November 1917.

[71] M.E.L. (M. E. Lloyd), *Sidelights on Two Referendums*, Sydney, n.d., p. 80.

[72] *Ross's Monthly*, 8 December 1917, quoted in I. Turner, *Industrial Labour and Politics*, Canberra, 1965, p. 163.

[73] Quoted in J. M. Main, *Conscription: The Australian Debate, 1901–1970*, Melbourne, 1970, pp. 91–2.

The prime minister made the Queensland premier, T. J. Ryan, a national figure when he instructed that an issue of the Queensland *Hansard* containing an anti-conscription speech by Ryan be refused transmission through the post. This was fresh in Ryan's mind when, a week later, Hughes was hit by an egg while addressing a 'Yes' meeting at Warwick. Ryan refused to treat the matter seriously, whereupon the prime minister directed the formation of a commonwealth police force.

The 'Yes' supporters were confident of victory, but they were disappointed. The majority against conscription had grown to 166,588 in a slightly smaller total vote (2,196,906).[74] Victoria joined New South Wales, Queensland and South Australia in voting 'No'. Analysis of the figures suggests that some Labor voters who had supported 'Yes' in 1916 now voted 'No', that many 1916 'Yes' voters abstained from voting, and that the farmers once more voted 'No'. Hughes declared:

... it is not we who have failed, but the people of Australia. ... I cannot forgive those [tens of thousands] of men who, grown fat on this war, pretended that they desired Australia to do her duty, and went to the ballot box and voted against her doing it.[75]

Before the poll, Hughes had declared that his government could not continue to govern unless it were given power to conscript; now he tendered his resignation to the governor-general. After some negotiation, he was invited to form a new administration. Hughes' own position was for the time secure, and the labour movement had not regained sufficient strength to mount an effective challenge to his government. But the referendum had enhanced the questioning of Australia's continued participation in the war.

The victory of the Bolsheviks in November 1917 freed the German army from its commitment to the Eastern Front. The German command resolved on a final, decisive offensive on the Western Front in the following spring. On 21 March 1918, the German army launched a mass attack astride the River Somme in the direction of the important rail junction, Amiens. They broke through the British lines and advanced rapidly, recapturing the territory across which the Australians had fought twelve months earlier. The Australian divisions had been resting in the northern sector, near Messines. There, their depleted ranks had been replenished by a dwindling flow of recruits and by men who had recovered from their wounds. The five divisions (the proposed Sixth had been broken up to provide reinforcements) had been re-grouped, to their great satisfaction, in an Australian Corps which, at the end of May 1918, came under the command of General Monash with Brigadier Thomas Blamey as chief of staff. At Messines, they heard of the German breakthrough. 'We all had the feeling,'

[74] *C.P.P.*, 1917–19, *IV*, p. 1469. See n. 53 in this chapter.

[75] *C.P.D.*, 1 January 1918, *83*, p. 2938.

wrote one infantry officer, 'that if we could only get down there it would be all right!'[76] Four days later, the Third and Fourth Divisions were sent south to plug the gap in the British lines. In a week's hard fighting, they played a major part in stopping the German advance at Villers-Bretonneux and Dernancourt. They lost 1800 men.

This was the turning point of the final German offensive, but the German command proceeded with its plans. An attack on the northern sector broke through the British lines south of Ypres; the First Australian Division was hastily diverted from Amiens to help repulse the German advance. Held in the north, the Germans resumed their attack on Amiens. The Australian Corps held a substantial part of the British line. The German attack was preceded by a mustard gas bombardment of the reserve line which incapacitated many of the Australian reserves. Australian units spearheaded a copy-book operation which retook Villers-Bretonneux after the Germans had captured it from inexperienced British troops. It was during this engagement that the German air ace, the 'Red Baron', von Richtofen, was shot down. The British R.A.F. claimed that one of its pilots was responsible, but C. E. W. Bean gave the honour to an Australian machine-gunner, firing from the ground.[77] The action had been successful, but it had cost the A.I.F. dearly. Three battalions which had been in the field since 1916 now had to be disbanded to provide reinforcements for other units. Between 21 March and 7 May 1918 the Australian Corps suffered 15,083 casualties.

At home, enlistments were running at about 2000 a month – except in May, when nearly 5000 volunteered in the wake of the alarming German spring offensive, and a lowering of the age limit for recruits. This was well below the number needed to keep the Australian divisions at full fighting strength. The director-general of recruiting reported that irreconcilable political differences were 'a disturbing and discouraging factor'.[78] In April, the governor-general had called a recruiting conference of political, business, trade union and community leaders. The Labor leader, Frank Tudor, told the conference that he and his colleagues were present as individuals, and that they could not bind their organizations. It was a frank admission of the growing anti-war sentiment within the labour movement. The N.S.W. Labor Council called for an immediate armistice and declared its refusal to take part in any further recruiting campaigns. The Commonwealth Labor Conference in June 1918 declared in favour of a negotiated peace, and resolved on a rank-and-file ballot to determine the party's attitude to recruiting. The consensus on the war had broken, very much along class lines. Middle-class Australia was still

[76] C. E. W. Bean, *Anzac to Amiens*, Canberra, 1946, p. 409.

[77] C. E. W. Bean, *The Australian Imperial Force in France During the Main German Offensive 1918*, Sydney, 1937, appendix 4, pp. 693–701.

[78] Quoted in E. Scott, *Australia During the War*, Sydney, 1936, p. 438

fervently behind the war effort, but working-class Australia had come to believe that the allied demand for unconditional surrender was a cloak for national aggrandisement. The news of Australia's part in the final battle of the Somme, and an impassioned campaign, produced a somewhat larger inflow of recruits in the last four months of the war, but it was apparent that the nation was growing weary of sacrifice.

Although the allied leaders did not expect it yet, the end was at hand. The allied commander, the French Marshal Foch, correctly believed that the main German threat was still in the northern sector. He thought that the German offensive had been interrupted by the losses they had already suffered, and he planned to use the Australian Corps for a disruptive surprise attack at Amiens. But before Foch could move the Germans struck at a weakly defended part of the line on the Aisne front. Their intention was to divert allied troops from the north, but they succeeded in breaking through and advancing thirty-two miles in three days – the most rapid advance of any army since August 1914. On 3 June, the Germans reached the River Marne, only fifty-six miles from Paris. They renewed their attack on 15 July and made some further advances. But the French armoured counter-attack on 18 July precipitated a general German withdrawal from the Marne, and, in the opinion of French historians, this was the decisive battle of 1918. Meanwhile, Foch had planned what was to become the final allied offensive – by the British in the north, the French in the centre and the newly-arrived Americans in the south.

In the relative quiet which followed the German spring offensive in Flanders and on the Somme, the Australians improvised a new style of fighting which they called 'Peaceful Penetration'. Small patrols, acting in true bushman's style on local initiative, infiltrated the German lines without the warning of prior bombardment and captured enemy strongpoints. These operations were interspersed with small-scale local offensives. One of these – a successful attack on Hamel, south of the Somme – was Monash's first operation as Corps Commander. In it, he set the pattern for the subsequent use of tanks by British forces.

The final allied offensive began on 8 August; it was designed to recapture the ground won by the Germans in their spring offensive and to crack the Hindenburg Line. Spearheaded by 450 British tanks, which broke the German front, with two Australian squadrons operating in the air, the British, Canadian, French and Australian divisions swept through the German lines and overran the German artillery south of the Somme. Five more days of fighting won more ground, until the front line was advanced by some six miles. It was this battle which first revealed that German morale was weakening. The Australians had established their superiority, and a German commander reported that his troops would no longer confront them. 'August 8th was the black day of the German Army in this war', Ludendorff later wrote. '[It] put the decline of that (German) fighting power beyond all doubt.'[79] The engagement had cost the Australians 6000 casualties, but this was the turning point of the war on the Western Front. The German command had given up hope of total victory.

Monash resolved to pursue 'an aggressive policy' directed towards the elimination of the German forces south-west of the Somme Bend and the capture of the German strong-points of Mont St Quentin and Péronne, to the river's north.[80] The Second and Fifth Divisions took the south-west bank of the Somme on 29 August, and Monash moved his men to the north. On 31 August, he threw two depleted battalions against Mont St Quentin. Relying on shock tactics, the men advanced 'yelling like a lot of bushrangers'.[81] The Germans were taken unawares and surrendered. In the next two days the Australians pressed home their advantage and captured Péronne. They had suffered a further 3000 casualties, but they had played a major part in forcing Ludendorff to withdraw to his last line of defence.

The first attack on the outposts of the Hindenburg Line was made on 18 September, in rain and fog, and was entirely successful. Two Australian divisions, reduced to some 7000 men, again played a leading part; they captured 4300 prisoners at a cost to themselves of 1260 casualties. It was now time for a concerted attack on the Line – a three-pronged drive by British, French and American forces. The Australians were given the task of carrying the main attack of the British sector, an assault on a strongly defended portion of the German line where the St Quentin Canal ran for three miles through an underground tunnel. The Australian battalions had been seriously depleted by casualties. Now they were further reduced by the belated granting of home leave in Australia to the original Anzacs, those Gallipoli veterans who had survived the fighting in France. The British commander ordered that some battalions be broken up in order to bring those remaining up to operation strength. 'What right had any bastard of a general to give an order like that? It was their battalion.' The men refused to accept the order, they appointed their own 'officers' and continued to prepare the offensive. They won their point: 'the wiser of the Australian commanders ... knew that in the A.I.F. there was a force of intelligent public opinion which could never be disregarded as this order had disregarded it'.[82] What was at stake was mateship, tradition, and the prestige of the Australian fighting men who, said Monash, were sportsmen who 'would refuse to play unless [their] score was displayed on the board'.[83]

[79] Quoted in C. E. W. Bean, *Anzac to Amiens*, Canberra, 1946, p. 473.

[80] J. Monash, *The Australian Victories in France in 1918*, London, 1920, p. 167.

[81] Capt. E. T. Manefield, quoted in C. E. W. Bean, *Anzac to Amiens*, Canberra, 1946, p. 481.

[82] L. Mann, *Flesh in Armour*, Melbourne, 1932, pp. 319, 322.

[83] C. E. W. Bean, *The Australian Imperial Force in France During the Allied Offensive, 1918*, Sydney, 1942, pp. 876–7.

Monash was given two American divisions to augment his force and began his main attack on 29 September. In one week's fighting, the Australians achieved their objective, breaking through the Hindenburg Line to Beaurevoir and – the farthest point of their advance – Montbrehain. They were relieved by the Americans, and they withdrew:

Troops more fatigued had rarely been seen and yet, by sheer determination, they overcame the weakness of the body and marched back in excellent order to their new positions. But their strained, pallid faces revealed what they had passed through, and numerous transport units along the roads respectfully and in silence pulled their vehicles to one side that the war-worn men might not have an extra step to march. It was the mute and eloquent testimony of brave men to heroes.[84]

This was the last time that Australian infantrymen were in action. They, the survivors, were sent to rest on the banks of the Somme near Amiens, thirty miles to the east, from where two months earlier they had begun their advance. On 5 November they were ordered back into the line. But by then Bulgaria had suffered a major defeat in the Balkans, the Turks had suffered a major defeat in Palestine in September 1918 – in which the Australian Mounted Division had played an important role – while the Austrians had been defeated at the Battle of Vittorio Veneto in October 1918. Germany was also confronting the prospect of revolution, and on 10 November the Kaiser fled to Holland. The German command signed an Armistice on 11 November 1918, and the killing was at last over. In Sydney, the news was greeted with huge enthusiasm:

Suddenly, from cottage and mansion, flat and lodging, everyone who could walk turned an eager face towards the city.... Every thoroughfare held a hurrying procession, the heads of which were thrusting into Martin Place, while the tails were miles out in the residential areas. Every man, woman, and child came into the city to 'celebrate'.[85]

It was as much a sigh of relief as a hymn to victory.

This had been the bloodiest of all wars, and a lot of the spilt blood was Australian: of 417,000 men and women who had voluntarily enlisted in the Australian forces, 330,000 had served overseas, while of these two-thirds had become casualties and nearly 60,000 had died – the highest casualty rate of any Empire army. Not only had they served as soldiers with distinction in the Middle East and on the Western Front, but many had also served in the Australian Flying Corps, and on Australian ships attached to the Grand Fleet or posted to anti-submarine activities in the Mediterranean. They had earned for themselves the reputation of being first-rate fighters – indeed, it

[84] A. D. Ellis, *The Story of the Fifth Australian Division*, London, n.d., p. 380.

[85] *Sydney Morning Herald*, 12 November 1918.

seemed as if they had been repeatedly used as the 'shock-troops' of the war – and they believed themselves to be a fighting force of a special mould.

General John Monash, himself urbane, Jewish, highly educated and sophisticated, an engineer whose clear, cool thinking led to his emergence as one of the supreme staff officers of the war, assessed the qualities of the Australian fighting men, as did C. E. W. Bean, very much in terms of the traditions of the bush. Monash noted that they were volunteers and of 'high physical standard', that they adapted readily to unfamiliar circumstances, that they had both a 'sense of duty' and an 'instinct of comradeship' (others said 'mateship'), that they showed a 'curious blend of a capacity for independent judge-ment with a readiness to submit to self-effacement in a common cause', that they were 'easy to lead but difficult to drive'. Indeed, Monash had resisted strong pressure from the British General Staff to intro-duce the death penalty for such offences as desertion. He concluded:

The democratic institutions under which he was reared, the advanced system of education by which he was trained – teaching him to think for himself and to apply what he had taught to practical ends – the instinct of sport and adventure which is his national heritage, his pride in his young country, and the opportunity which came to him of creating a great national tradition, were all factors which made him what he was.[86]

They left France, and their dead, behind them, and they carried with them the beginnings of a legend:

At last they were moving.... [Harry] felt, now, that it was almost wrong for them to be leaving that blasted land. He felt as if he were deserting those back there.... As if, almost, they all ought to go back and die there where they belonged.... It seemed, now that he was leaving the war and the old familiar landscape of death, that his life and the life of this generation was finished. They were the dung for the new flowering and fruit of the future.[87]

It was perhaps the greatest tragedy of this tragic war that the future did not flower. Later, men would speak of the 'ashes of victory', would ask what the human sacrifice had meant, would question the motives of those who demanded that so many millions die. But, for most Australians who had lived through those years of insane destruc-tion, it remained unhappily true that, for the first and only time, they had identified with a cause bigger than themselves and had known what it meant to be a man.

The last year of the war was marked by growing dissension over Australia's participation. Labour organizations had already declared during 1917 for a negotiated peace 'without annexations or indemni-ties', and their disaffection from the government had been strengthened

---

86 J. Monash, *The Australian Victories in France in 1918*, London, 1920, p. 290.

87 L. Mann, *Flesh in Armour*, Melbourne, 1932, pp. 316–7.

by the general strike and the referendum. Sectarian bitterness was rife. The hostility between the 'win-the-war' camp and the 'shirkers' was intense. As he had pledged, Hughes offered his resignation as prime minister to the governor-general following the referendum defeat. Within his new Nationalist party, there were some, led by West Australian and Treasurer Sir John Forrest, who wanted to dump Hughes, but Hughes won a decisive vote of confidence from his colleagues. Others urged a new election, fought on the conscription issue, but the majority decided against 'any course of action that will hand the Government of the Commonwealth over to the official Labour party'.[88] After discussions with various political leaders, the governor-general renewed Hughes' mandate. Forrest became the first Australian to be recommended by his country for elevation to the British peerage and a seat in the House of Lords. He declined to resign from the government, but ill health caused him to do so several months later and in September he died at sea en route to England. The by-election which followed gave victory to the Labor party.

The Imperial government had reaffirmed its recognition of the dominions' contribution to the war effort by inviting dominion leaders to meet with the Imperial War Cabinet in June 1918. Hughes and his minister for the navy, Joseph Cook, represented Australia. It marked, Hughes said in extravagant vein, 'a landmark in the development of Empire government', the first occasion on which 'the Dominion representatives shared, on terms of perfect equality with Britain, the actual government of the Empire'.[89] There was much to concern Hughes and his colleagues about the state of that government. For four years they had poured men and money into 'the sink of France and Flanders'. They now realized, hearing Lloyd George's report on the German advance, that they 'were possibly in a worse position than before the battle of the Marne' (the culmination of the German offensive in 1914).[90] The augmented War Cabinet turned to a consideration of the major questions of the day: the quality of the British command, the threatened exhaustion of the reserves of manpower, a strategy for turning defeat into victory which their advisers then believed would not be possible until 1919 or 1920. The Australian representatives were at the centre of power. By 20 August, when the War Cabinet went into temporary recess, the tide of battle had unexpectedly turned.

Hughes found time for the interests of the Australian forces, too. He visited them in France, on the eve of their successful attack on Hamel, and delivered a 'stirring address'.[91] He argued successfully for home leave for the Anzacs, and for a winter respite for the Australian

---

[88] Quoted in E. Scott, *Australia During the War*, Sydney, 1936, p. 433.

[89] W. M. Hughes, *The Splendid Adventure*, London, 1929, pp. 56–7.

[90] W. M. Hughes, *The Splendid Adventure*, London, 1929, p. 63.

[91] J. Monash, *The Australian Victories in France in 1918*, London, 1920, p. 55.

Corps. He was again in France, early in September, in time to con-
gratulate the Australians on the capture of Péronne. With victory in
sight, the War Cabinet turned its attention to the terms of peace.
Hughes' estimate of Australia's contribution to the war led him to
break with imperial tradition and insist on independent representation for his country at the Peace Conference. He won his point,
despite the doubts expressed by his cabinet at home. His conception
of Australia's interests led him to oppose President Wilson's 'Fourteeen
Points' in some important respects – notably the fate of the German
colonies in the Pacific, reparations, and post-war population and
trading arrangements. His hard line won him the respect of the
French leader, Clemenceau.

The Peace Conference met in Paris on 18 January 1919. President
Wilson's proposals provided the basis for discussion; in essence, these
called for the creation of a League of Nations, decolonization, the
right of all peoples to self-determination, and free movement of goods
and people. Hughes expressed reservations about the occupation of
former German colonies in the North Pacific by the Japanese but
was over-ruled by the British. He fought vigorously for Australia's
right to annex the German colonies in the South-West Pacific, arguing
that control of these islands was essential to Australian security, but
he was unsuccessful. He reluctantly agreed to accept a League of
Nations mandate over the islands when it was conceded that Australian law, particularly that relating to immigration and trade, would
prevail. He argued strongly that Germany should make full financial
reparation for the costs of the war; the conference adopted a compromise resolution which met most of his demands – although, in the
event, Germany did not meet the bill. He objected to the Japanese
demand for the inclusion of a racial equality clause in the Covenant
of the League of Nations, on the ground that this might jeopardize the
White Australia policy, and his stubborn opposition led President
Wilson to declare this clause out of order. Later, Hughes expressed
regret that the conference had not accepted his tough anti-German
line, but in fact, through shrewd belligerence and a skilful use of his
hearing aid, he had had most of his own way. For Hughes, the Peace
Conference was a great symbolic landmark for Australia – 'a formal
recognition, not only by Britain, but by Foreign Powers, of the complete autonomy of the Dominions and of their equality of status with
the United Kingdom'.[92] Australia was not to act with full autonomy
for another twenty-odd years, but the point had been made. The prime
minister arrived back in Melbourne on 30 August 1919 to 'a reception
like that of a victorious general with the laurels of a campaign fresh
upon him'.[93] A fortnight later, he moved in the House of Representatives that Australia ratify the Treaty of Versailles:

[92] W. M. Hughes, *The Splendid Adventure*, London, 1929, p. 236.

[93] E. Scott, *Australia During the War*, Sydney, 1936, p. 818.

What has been won? If the fruits of victory are to be measured by national safety and liberty, and the high ideals for which these boys died, the sacrifice has not been in vain. They died for the safety of Australia. Australia is safe. They died for liberty, and liberty is now assured to us and to all men. They have made for themselves and their country a name that will not die. . . . We turn now from war to peace. We live in a new world, a world bled white by the cruel wounds of war. Victory is ours, but the price of victory is heavy. The whole earth has been shaken to its very core. Upon the foundations of victory we would build the new temple of our choice.[94]

The 'new temple' was a not uncommon theme in Australian rhetoric. But the great age of Australian optimism was over; the difficulty was that there was agreement on neither architect nor design.

Australia emerged from the war weakened by the loss of her maimed and dead and by the monstrous burden of a £350,000,000 war debt, but in other ways she had been strengthened by the war. Manufacturing had grown dramatically, particularly in the metal industry. Primary production was buoyant, and new trading patterns had been established. Transport and communications had been extended and refined, and Australia had at her disposal a fleet of shipping for coastal and overseas trade. The primacy of the federal government had been established in the affairs of the nation. The independence of Australia had been recognised in the affairs of the world. But perhaps the most immediate impact of the war on Australian society was in the divisions it fomented: capital against labour, government against the unions, ex-servicemen against civilians, the war generation against their children, the traditional modes of behaviour against the new. Hughes was right to say that the earth had been shaken to its very core. The post-war years saw the kaleidoscope reforming in new and unfamiliar patterns. To many these were frightening – everywhere they saw the hand, and the bomb, of the Bolshevik at work. 'Bolshevism' became a giant coverall which encompassed everything from revolutionary agitation and labour unrest to the 'new woman', loose morals, and jazz.

The news of the storming of the Winter Palace in Petrograd reached Australia on the day that the prime minister announced the second conscription referendum. It went almost unnoticed until radical Russian emigrés spread the news through the labour movement of the early decrees of the Soviet régime – withdrawal from the war, and the takeover of the factories by the workers. Weary of the war and frustrated by its defeats, the labour movement was looking for new ideas and quick solutions. Repeated but unsuccessful attempts were made to reorganize the trade unions into one big union, which was thought of as the basis for a new 'industrial' administration of society. A group of militant unions broke away from the N.S.W. Labor party in 1919 to form an Industrial Socialist Labor party, but they enjoyed no success and soon returned to Labor. A sustained campaign against

[94] *C.P.D.*, 10 September 1919, *89*, p. 12179.

the continued imprisonment of the 'I.W.W. Twelve', convicted of conspiracy, led to the appointment of two royal commissions of inquiry and, in 1920, to their release. Trade union militants and socialists joined in forming a Communist party, an Australian section of the Third (Communist) International, in October 1920; they tried with much infighting, and little success, to apply Bolshevik principles to Australia. Following a showdown between unions and political leaders, a special conference of the Labor party adopted a 'socialist objective' in October 1921, but this remained an objective rather than becoming part of the 'fighting platform'. The fervent discussion and eager acceptance of the various radical and revolutionary formulae involved the leaders and activists of the labour movement, but it was often remote from the rank and file. Nevertheless, it reflected a broad working class sympathy for what the Bolsheviks were attempting, and the widespread industrial and social unrest in the wake of the war.

By 1918, the Labor party was beginning to recover from the electoral consequences of the 1916 split, and it entered the federal election of 1919 with high hopes. There was continuing opposition among the Nationalists to the leadership of Hughes. Australia's most able Labor politician, T. J. Ryan, had resigned as premier of Queensland to enter federal politics (he was succeeded in Queensland by E. G. Theodore) and was in charge of the Labor campaign. Most of the 'returned soldiers' were by now back in their homes and Labor hoped to win their vote. The Farmers' Union, precursor of the Country party, was making a strong run, however, and preferential voting was to be used for the first time in a national election. In the event, the Labor vote fell slightly from 1917, although the inroads made by the Farmers' candidates on the Nationalist vote enabled Labor to capture five seats, giving it twenty-six in a house of seventy-five. Hughes, the 'little digger', had held the support of the returned soldiers, and he was commissioned to form his fourth government in four years. But his abrasive personality, his dictatorial attitude towards his colleagues, and his lack of concern for the details of administration had made him many enemies.

It had not been easy to find the shipping for the 270,000 men – about a third of them wounded or incapacitated – who had to be brought home from the United Kingdom, France and the Middle East. The ships were overcrowded, the food was bad, there was little done to entertain the men and on some ships alcohol was banned; there were complaints about the privileges – including the companionship of nurses – enjoyed by the officers.[95] But the ships were found, and virtually all the 'boys' were home by December 1919. It was, Monash said, the best piece of 'staff work' he had been associated with.[96] Back home, the governments faced the difficult task of

[95] See Leslie Parker (Angela Thirkell), *Trooper to the Southern Cross*, London, 1934, Melbourne, 1966.

[96] F. Scott, *Australia During the War*, Sydney, 1936, p. 827.

'repatriation' – returning the servicemen to civilian life. Many simply went back to their old jobs, though there were some who found these already filled by boys, or, in the case of clerks in offices and banks, by young women who were being paid less than half the male wage. Some 36,000 men signified a desire to become farmers; the government provided the money for land, stock, grain and machinery, but all too often the land was marginal and the farms were over-capitalized. Others were established in small businesses, in which many 'went broke'. Still others were given trade or professional training. Special grants were made to enable ex-servicemen to buy houses and furniture and to bring their 'war brides' out from the United Kingdom and France. Provision was made for the incapacitated and for the widows and children of the dead. All this was highly satisfactory, and very costly, but there was one running sore. The federal government had promised servicemen that after the war they would receive preference in employment, but this cut right across the labour movement's principle of preference to unionists. The Returned Sailors' and Soldiers' Imperial League of Australia, formed late in 1916, acted as a pressure group and lobby in support of the special interests of its members. All the governments except Queensland legislated for preference to ex-servicemen. In the city streets, the returned men demonstrated for jobs, sometimes clashing with trade unionists, and against the alleged menace of Bolshevism.

The immediate post-war years were buoyant: secondary industry expanded rapidly and building was booming. Mining, especially for metals, had suffered a loss of markets, but primary industry generally was doing well. Consumer prices were rising sharply, but unemployment, at about six per cent, was relatively low by the standard of the times. The unions moved to improve their position. During 1919, some 6.3 million man-days were lost in industrial disputes, for a total wage loss of nearly £4,000,000 – by far the costliest year for strikes since statistics had been kept. Building workers fought for and won, for a short time, the 44-hour, five-day working week. Seamen demanded higher wages and shorter hours, but the government, now a major shipowner, rejected their demands. The resulting strike lasted three months, and the seamen won. Metal miners at Broken Hill went on strike in May 1919 for a new three-year agreement, and the mines did not re-open until November 1920.

The men who came back found that many things had changed. Most returned to their families, but the long separation had strained many marriages: the number of divorced persons nearly doubled (from 4500 to 8500) between the censuses of 1911 and 1921, and for the first time there were more female divorcees than male. There was much concern about 'loose' sexual morals. Women's utility wartime clothing gave way to the post-war frivolity of low-cut blouses, short skirts, silk stockings and garter purses. There had been little dancing during the war; now 'flappers', smoking their cigarettes through fashionably long holders, played jazz tunes like 'Everybody's Doing

It' on the new 'Hornless Talking Machine' and danced the bunny-hug and the turkey-trot with their 'knuts'. Ladies' swimming costumes grew more revealing, and mixed bathing grew more popular, although it was still banned by some municipalities. Crowds flocked to the moving pictures to see the romantic dramas of Douglas Fairbanks and Mary Pickford, the torrid performance of Theda Bara (the 'scarlet vampire'), daring exposés of the white slave traffic and the dangers of venereal disease, and such home-grown productions as Raymond Longford's 'Sentimental Bloke' and 'On Our Selection'. The darkness of the cinema and the spread of the motor-car provided new opportunities for lovers. The epidemic of pneumonic influenza which swept Australia in the first half of 1919, leaving 11,500 dead behind it, was a brief interruption to the search for pleasure. Moralists tried, but with little success, to stem the tide. They campaigned for the censorship of films, a clean-up of the streets, the regulation of public behaviour, and the prohibition of liquor. Returned servicemen, encouraged by the liquor trade, formed a 'Liberty League' to combat the 'wowsers' – was this the freedom they had fought for?

In the last months of the war, C. E. W. Bean had expressed his hope that the agony through which Australia had passed would produce a new flowering of the Australian spirit. It was, he said, 'In Your Hands, Australians'. He asked his countrymen to ask themselves: 'What can I do for our nation, for our country, for Australia? . . . How can I help to make her the greatest, best, most beautiful, happiest country in the world, with the strongest people, the most brilliant arts, the healthiest and prettiest towns, the best laws?'[97] The war years themselves had given little evidence of a creative flowering. The diggers' democracy produced a vigorous literary and black-and-white journalism, which survived after the war in the *Bulletin* and *Smith's Weekly*. The popular verse of C. J. Dennis enjoyed a tremendous vogue. But there was little serious writing of quality – a handful of verses by Leon Gellert, Vance Palmer and 'Furnley Maurice' (Frank Wilmot) to put alongside the mass of anti-Hun bombast, including that of the best poet of the day, Chris Brennan; Harley Matthews' stories, *Saints and Soldiers* (1918), Leonard Mann's novel *Flesh in Armour* (1932), and Frank Dalby Davison's vignette, *The Wells of Beersheba* (1933). As the collection at the Australian War Memorial in Canberra reveals, most of the art inspired directly by the war was monumental-pedestrian; Will Dyson's wash and charcoal sketches, published in *Australia at War* (1918), were a notable exception. The black-and-white tradition, however, continued to flourish in David Low and Norman Lindsay of the *Bulletin*, Claude Marquet of the *Worker*, and Syd Nicholls of *Direct Action*, in C. J. Dennis' illustrator, Hal Gye, and, in the immediate post-war years, in two impressive newcomers – Percy Leason, whose 'Wiregrass' drawings were first published in 1919,

97 C. E. W. Bean, *In Your Hands, Australians*, London, 1919, pp. 16–17.

and J. C. Bancks who created Australia's most famous comic strip, 'Ginger Meggs', in 1921.

The war must also be held responsible for an outpouring of patriotic and sentimental songs, ranging from the early 'Australia Will Be There' to the later 'Take Me Back to Dear Australia'. None of these compared in quality with the soldiers' own creations, particularly that which enshrined the bitter comment of a front-line digger to a headquarters lance-corporal:

> ... we're just back from the shambles in France
> Where whizzbangs are flying and comforts are few,
> And brave men are dying for bastards like you.

Surprisingly, the war did little for science. The federal government in 1920 established an Institute of Science and Industry, the ancestor of C.S.I.R.O., but its concern was largely with industrial technology. The war inspired a number of inventions, but these were largely of immediate military interest – the periscope rifle, the 'Melbourne respirator' (or gas-mask), and an early design for a tank. There was little advance in fundamental research.

The hopes expressed by Bean, and later Leonard Mann, that social concern, and the arts and sciences and affairs of the intellect, might flourish in post-war Australia were disappointed. This may have been because of the overwhelming national preoccupation with the immediacies of war, or because, in the cliché of the time, the 'flower of Australian youth' had been killed in that war, or because men returned from the war to matters of immediate personal concern, or because of the deep-seated pragmatism of the Australian temperament. Or it may have been because, as D. H. Lawrence felt when he visited Australia in 1922, 'the instinct of the place was absolutely and flatly democratic, *à terre* democratic. Demos was here his own master, undisputed, and therefore quite calm about it'. Lacking caste distinctions and an élite of the 'responsible members of society', Australia offered poor soil for the creative intellect.[98] Or it may simply have been that the aspirations of most Australians were more mundane and sceptical:

> 'Beauty', sez Digger, sudden-like,
>   'An' love, an' kindliness;
> The chance to live a clean, straight life,
> A dinkum deal for kids an' wife:
>   A man needs nothin' less. . . .
> Maybe they'll get it when I go
> To push up daisies. I dunno.'[99]

98 D. H. Lawrence, *Kangaroo*, Harmondsworth, 1950, p. 27.

99 C. J. Dennis, *Digger Smith*, Sydney, 1918, p. 105.

9

1920-29

Heather Radi

*The paradox of the twenties—urbanization—the manufacturing
industries—suburbanization—land settlement and immigration—
the defence situation—Australia and the Empire—the Labor
Party—wages and arbitration—state politics in New South Wales
and Queensland—the power struggle within the Labor Party—
the formation of Country Parties—the fall of the Hughes Government—changing market conditions—'men, money and markets'—
assisted immigration—Commonwealth and state financial relations
—industrial employment—social conditions during the boom—
dead level culture—the Aborigines—women—industrial relations
and legislation—state Labor governments—declining economic
growth—arbitration and the fall of Bruce.*

In what way should the twenties be viewed: as an interlude between
the dramas of war and depression when Australians enjoyed ease and
prosperity beyond most previous experience and improvidently neglected to take heed against the morrow; or as a crucial phase in the life-
span of a young nation when the hope of shaping a destiny to one's
own pattern ended in the realisation that not all things are possible?[1]
How else can one explain the optimism at the beginning except in the
perspective of decades of nation-building? There was relief that a
terrible test had been passed. A high spirited people had shown their
fighting qualities. But there was also the confident belief that the
foundations for future greatness had been laid in the brief period of
nation-building before the war. The spirit of the Australian people had
found expression in a political and social system wherein individual
need and the good of all seemed reconciled. The measures taken then,
with so much deliberation about what was fair and reasonable and
necessary for the welfare and progress of the nation, had barely been
tested when the war intervened. The testing came in the twenties.

[1] See ch. 20 in *The Cambridge History of the British Empire*, VII, Pt. 1,
Cambridge, 1933: ch. 7 in G. Greenwood, Ed., *Australia: A Social and Political
History*, Sydney, 1955: ch. 3 in C. H. Grattan, *The Southwest Pacific Since 1900: A
Modern History*, Ann Arbor, 1963: ch. 3 in F. Alexander, *Australia Since Federa-
tion: A Narrative and Critical Analysis*, Melbourne, 1967: chs. 19 and 20 in R. M.
Younger, *Australia and the Australians: A New Concise History*, Adelaide, 1970.

The war behind them, the Australian people pursued progress. Their land, they believed, would support 100 million people, perhaps 200 million, in ever increasing prosperity. Governments resumed the task of development on an ambitious scale, encouraging closer settlement and continuing to do so, even when increasingly expensive measures were required to make the land productive. For the nation to be great industry was essential. Manufacturers were encouraged by extending the tariff. The methods were those worked out in an earlier period. Reliance on past measures was part of the optimism. The federal constitution left the states with the responsibility for one aspect of development and the federal government with the other – through its customs powers; but this division of powers was not questioned. With government so much involved in promoting development, there were obvious disadvantages in an arrangement which divided responsibility, yet the federal form of government continued to be considered appropriate to the Australian situation. The states were no longer financially autonomous. The federal division of industrial powers was a perennial irritant. Compulsory arbitration was both criticized and upheld: the presumption that it was the right way to settle disputes meant that reinforcement of the Court's authority became a central and abrasive issue. A nation convinced of its progressiveness failed to come to grips with the problems of its own times. The existing measures against poverty and want were admitted inadequate but on one ground or another objections were raised to the remedies proposed. There seemed both over-ready expectations that the established systems should work satisfactorily and ever-ready suspicion that changes were intended to advantage particular interests and must therefore be resisted. Optimism offset by sectionalism characterized the handling of public affairs. In the outcome the more complex problems remained unsolved – the problems of an urban industrial society developing within an economy still integrally part of the wider imperial trading area.

Whether measured by profits or social justice, the decade was disappointing. Possibly the legacy of distrust from the wartime dissension made suspicion of class interest a reason to oppose reforms, yet the slightly anachronistic nature of the twenties approach was also conducive to conflict. Country interests organized to reverse the trend towards city dominance. Labor was still attracted to the idea of state ownership, yet continued to expect, as it had before the war, that Labor governments could make the existing system work for labour. To the extent that they succeeded, industry felt threatened; and in the absence of improvements the blame was laid on the men in office rather than the system. Dissension within political parties, dissatisfactions sufficient to sustain new parties, minority governments (ineffectual or unduly susceptible to pressure), were features of the period, along with unsatisfactory and reckless administration.

While the enthusiasm of state governments to re-enter the business of settlement instanced both the optimism after the war and the return to traditional methods, it was also a measure of the way population continued to concentrate in a few urban centres.[2] In the interests of production and of population, more forceful government action seemed needed to counter the attraction of the cities. In 1921 Melbourne and Adelaide contained just over half the population of their states, Sydney and Perth only a slightly smaller proportion, Brisbane and Hobart about a quarter. The drift to the cities was not a new phenomenon nor unique to Australia; nor did it mean that rural population declined but that the cities absorbed most of the natural increase and the larger share of immigration. The cities offered modern amenities, better working conditions and more chance of employment. Possibly the decisive factor was employment. Work was irregular in the country. Tractors were replacing farm hands.[3] World markets were competitive and productivity and profits improved where farming was mechanized. Younger sons seeking new occupations had little chance of finding them in nearby towns. Industry had been moving from the country since railways brought competition from metropolitan manufactures; in the twenties road and rail together allowed primary produce to be processed in fewer centres.[4] Outback mining towns were dying as inefficient mining plants were caught between the relatively high cost of Australian labour and the low prices for minerals.[5] Together these changes brought a massive shift in population. Perhaps as many as a quarter of a million left the country and country towns during the twenties for the metropolitan centres[6] and the few cities which were truly industrial centres – Newcastle, Wollongong Port Kembla, Geelong, Ballarat and Ipswich. Between the censuses of 1921 and 1933 the metropolitan population grew by 37.41 per cent, the urban provincial by 7.71 per cent, and the rural by 19.66 per cent.

The larger cities were a natural location for manufacturing industry. Their increase marked the growing importance of manufactures.[7] The industrial workforce grew from 376,734 to 450,482; the value of production rose from £320m. to £420m. Though the newly opened steel

[2] F. W. Eggleston, *et al.*, Eds., *The Peopling of Australia*, (Further Studies) Melbourne, 1933.

[3] E. Dunsdorfs, *The Australian Wheat-Growing Industry 1788–1948*, Melbourne, 1956.

[4] Factories treating raw material, product of agricultural and pastoral pursuits, declined from 799 in 1919–20 to 615 in 1929–30. A convenient source of official statistics is the annual *Official Year Book of the Commonwealth of Australia*.

[5] G. Blainey, *The Rush That Never Ended: A History of Australian Mining*, Melbourne, 1963, pp. 283–93.

[6] C. Forster, *Industrial Development in Australia 1920–1930*, Canberra, 1964.

[7] C. B. Schedvin, *Australia and the Great Depression: A Study of Economic Development and Policy in the 1920s and 1930s*, Sydney, 1970: W. A. Sinclair 'Aspects of Economic Growth, 1900–1930', in A. H. Boxer, Ed., *Aspects of the Australian Economy*, Melbourne, 1965.

mills rarely worked at full capacity and were closed for thirteen months in 1922–3,[8] steel was the life blood of other industries. The motor body industry alone provided most of the growth in the manufacturing indices for South Australia. Production of motor bodies and accessories, electrical goods, chemicals, fertilizers, industrial gases, and textiles marked a major change in the economy even though the main expansion was still in light industry – the processing of rural produce, the supply of building materials, and the production of simple consumer items. Building the cities was once again a major undertaking, together with the provision of the services Australians had come to expect in their cities.

Improvements to the major cities had been commenced before the war.[9] Streets had been widened and some of the inner slums demolished. The electrification of suburban trains, the underground link to the city in Sydney, together with the proliferation of inter-suburban bus services relieved congestion in the centre and the conditions that had produced the noisome inner suburbs. These changes diluted an earlier concern about worker housing which had been one strand in a nascent town planning movement before the war. The cities were able to spread physically, far beyond limits previously set by transport to work; the areas between the radial tram and train lines could fill with the modest one-storey-home-and-garden which gratified most Australians. Only in Sydney in 1920 were tenants significantly more numerous than home owners; by the end of the decade even in Sydney home ownership predominated. Worker-housing schemes operated on a very modest scale except in Queensland, and there only 9000 new dwellings were built in the decade;[10] but readier access to credit and federal finance for ex-servicemen brought home purchase within the reach of the steady worker. Order and beauty, the other strand in the town planning movement, made little headway against the pressure of numbers. At best the movement achieved a few parks and playing fields, a little of the harbour foreshore in Sydney, some open space elsewhere, and a variety of building regulations setting minimum sizes for blocks which influenced decisively the shape of the cities. Bradfield's improvements to inner city transport in Sydney, and the creation of Greater Brisbane in 1925 owed something to the planners; but against that, Griffin's best design for Canberra was mutilated, and that of the Metropolitan Town Planning Commission

---

[8] H. Hughes, *The Australian Iron and Steel Industry 1848–1962*, Melbourne, 1964, pp. 88–108.

[9] A. Birch and D. S. Macmillan, *The Sydney Scene 1788–1960*, Melbourne, 1962: J. Grant and G. Serle, *The Melbourne Scene 1803–1956*, Melbourne, 1957: E. C. Fry, 'Growth of an Australian Metropolis', in R. S. Parker and P. N. Troy, Eds., *The Politics of Urban Growth*, Canberra, 1972.

[10] M. A. Jones, *Housing and Poverty in Australia*, Melbourne, 1972, pp. 116–8: C. A. Bernays, *Queensland – Our Seventh Political Decade, 1920–1930*, Sydney, 1931, pp. 226–33.

for Melbourne lapsed.[11] More realistically, or selfishly, the multitude of municipal authorities – forty-one in metropolitan Sydney – directed their efforts to paving streets and building roads[12] and urging state governments and statutory authorities to extend the other services, the water and electricity, sewerage and schools, which were the minimal requirements for urban living in the twentieth century. Such mundane matters were attended to. The result was a significant addition to the public debt, occasional abuse of position for personal profit,[13] but to a people still conscious of their pioneering past, little sense of achievement.

Schemes to water barren land and to create farms for settlers fitted more readily the Australian idea of what was worth doing and what was a suitable reward for the nation's heroes. The promise to servicemen that their jobs would be safe was not fully honoured after the war, but farms for heroes was an acceptable variant to governments eager to promote closer settlement.[14] To make this possible – for how else could a penniless soldier buy a settler's block – the federal government advanced money to the states. On the thin soil of the Granite Belt in Queensland, on the dusty eastern wheatlands in Western Australia and the Mallee in Victoria, on dry land watered from the Murray and the Murrumbidgee, the men who survived the hardships of the trenches tested again their physical endurance and their tenacity in adversity. For years, some struggled to clear blocks which were too small or too arid, to produce crops which the world valued little. From the inception of soldier settlement there was criticism of the land acquired. As the decade progressed, this grievance, along with others relating to pensions, war service homes and preference in employment, were taken up by the ex-servicemen's organization so that in the pursuit of redress, comradeship was transposed to the R.S.L., the most powerful pressure group in Australia for years to come.[15]

In the promotion of closer settlement, state rivalry was still an important factor. Each wanted its industries to grow, its population to increase. The vision of a nation of 100 million people drove them on

11 See G. Greenwood and J. Laverty, *Brisbane 1859–1959: A History of Local Government*, Brisbane, 1959: J. Birrell, *Walter Burley Griffin*, Brisbane, 1964: H. Stretton, *Ideas for Australian Cities*, Adelaide, 1970.

12 H. E. Maiden, *The History of Local Government in New South Wales*, Sydney, 1966, p. 128.

13 For examples see reports of royal commissions on conduct of aldermen of the Municipal Council of Sydney in regard to the construction of Bulwarra Rd., cartage contracts, the Bunnerong power house, and coal contracts, in *New South Wales Parliamentary Papers*, 1925, I; 1925, (2), I; 1928–29, I; 1929–30, I.

14 For the inception of soldier settlement see E. Scott, *Australia During the War*, Sydney, 1936. The mistakes are revealed in the Report by Mr Justice Pike in *C.P.P.*, 1929, (2), II.

15 See G. L. Kristianson, *The Politics of Patriotism: The Pressure Group Activities of the Returned Servicemen's League*, Canberra, 1966.

to get their share of that increase. The vision had additional appeal to national leaders. Population meant defence potential. Population drawn from Britain had the added advantage of strengthening the ties of empire. The immigration and settlement programme became identified as a national interest and, as such, a responsibility of the national government. Analysing the problems which Australia faced at the end of the war, Hughes placed considerable importance on increased production, as a means of countering inflation and of protecting the Australian standard of living, and also for Australia to become a great nation. Like most others, he assumed the land would be the basis of this expansion and new settlers the key to greatness. For Hughes the overriding consideration was national security but for his supporters and successor as prime minister, S. M. Bruce, increased production was an end in itself. As an inducement to the states to expand their work of settlement the federal government offered them cheap loan money. It was willing to bear the cost of the recruitment of migrants and, in conjunction with Britain, payment of their fares.[16] Britain had reasons of her own for supporting empire resettlement. British industry faced difficulties. The market for British manufactures would be enlarged by the transfer of part of the overlarge British workforce to the dominions. Australia wanted people, Britain needed markets, so the transfer appeared mutually beneficial.

The Australian government may not have fully appreciated the divergence of interests which nevertheless existed, or may have discounted it against the benefits of closer association with Britain. Rural labour was not noticeably in oversupply in Britain. The migrants came from the industrial cities, but if Britain's expectations were to be realised, they must become farmers in Australia. Too many lacked experience. But more significantly, Australia was poised on the threshold of industrialization, with the basis established during the war for further development of secondary industry. While the government on the one hand was eager to foster this development, and to that end had amended the tariff in 1920 to cover virtually everything that might be manufactured in Australia,[17] on the other hand it pursued a policy on development which required heavy capital investment in the rural sector. Not only did this intensify the conflict of interest between exporting industries and local manufactures, and the problem of overseas debt, but it left unresolved the fundamental issue of how to achieve a balanced national economy.

At the 1921 Imperial Conference the principles of the migration agreements were worked out, but it was the benefits of closer

16 See P. D. Phillips and G. L. Wood, Eds., *The Peopling of Australia*, Melbourne, 1928: F. W. Eggleston, *et al.*, Eds., *The Peopling of Australia*, (Further Studies) Melbourne, 1933; G. F. Plant, *Oversea Settlement: Migration from the United Kingdom to the Dominions*, London, 1951, Pt. III.

17 A. J. Reitsma, *Trade Protection in Australia*, Brisbane, 1960.

association with Britain that Prime Minister Hughes stressed to the
Australian people:

When the voice of Australia speaks as part of the British Empire, with its
500,000,000 of people, its mighty Navy, its flag on every sea, its strongholds
on every continent, its power and its glory shining and splendid, acknowledged by all, then she speaks in trumpet tones that are heard and heeded
throughout all the earth.[18]

The crude exaggeration was part of Hughes' political style but the
statement conveyed the essence of his view of Australia's post-war
situation. With one battlecruiser, three cruisers, four destroyers and
four submarines in commission, a part-time army, a population of five
and a half million, heavy industry undeveloped, Australia's defence
power was insignificant.[19] Alone, it was as nothing against Japan.
Lord Jellicoe advised in 1919 that for complete security an enormous
Pacific fleet was necessary.[20] Yet domestic economy made maintenance
of even the existing Australian fleet unacceptable. Unable to match
the nation it feared, Australia had a particular interest in resolving
problems of security through negotiation. It needed a foreign policy
and the diplomatic means for operating it.[21] Both Hughes and Bruce
held considerations of power basic to the conduct of foreign policy. In
his glorification of the British Empire, Hughes drew on the emotiona-
lism unleashed by war to cloak a practical intention of utilizing
British power and British diplomacy for Australian purposes.
  Australians no longer felt keenly the need to take an independent
stance. The 60,000 dead and the reputation of the Anzacs gave them a
pride in their own which was in no way diminished by accepting the
role Hughes proposed. There would be a special relationship with
Britain to provide reassurance against isolation. That at least seemed
the intention. How this special relationship would be established,
through what institutions and in what form, was the problem Hughes
faced in 1921. At Versailles, his presence amongst the leaders of the
great nations had ensured that he be heard. There, he had flam-
boyantly and obdurately rejected Japan's racial equality proposals and
mediation on her behalf. But at Versailles there was need to reach
agreement. The circumstances would not recur. In 1921 the international standing of the dominions had not been clarified. While the

18 *C.P.D.*, 30 September 1921, 97, p. 11632.

19 Of 127,960 men in the Army in 1921 (including all members enlisted for
active service in the war), only 3179 were permanent – T. B. Millar, *Australia's
Defence*, Melbourne, 1965, p. 174. See also 'Department of the Navy, Statement
Explanatory of the Estimates, 1921–22', in *C.P.P.*, 1920–21, *4*, p. 81 ff.

20 'Report on Naval Mission to the Commonwealth by Viscount Jellicoe', in
C.P.P., 1917–19, *4*, p. 471 ff.

21 For foreign policy and diplomacy see especially P. Hasluck, *The Government
and the People: 1939–1941*, Canberra, 1952, ch. 2: W. J. Hudson, *Australian
Diplomacy*, Melbourne, 1970.

extent of their autonomy troubled others, Hughes was less interested in the trappings of independence or the specification of status than in the use of imperial power, and to that end, the formulation of an imperial foreign policy by the whole empire in conference. So long as imperial policy incorporated Australia's aims as defined by Australia's representatives, implementation was best left to Britain. Britain had the power needed for successful diplomacy.[22]

The issue of particular interest to Australia was the Anglo-Japanese Treaty. Japanese and United States' rivalry made this Treaty distasteful to the United States and thereby to Canada. Australians knew of Japan's expansionist moves during the war and suspected, though they were not fully informed, that Britain's ability to restrain her ally was limited.[23] They were still nervous about Japan's reaction to the Australian policy of excluding all but British nationals from New Guinea. Possibly a desire not to arouse international interest was the reason for the slow development there.[24] Not until 1926–7 did the government dispose of ex-German properties and even then did little to encourage further settlement. Certainly in the handling of native affairs the Australian intention, if not the practice, was to avoid unfavourable notice. By itself, control of New Guinea afforded little protection to Australia. To the dilemma of Pacific security Hughes was prepared to accept the Anglo-Japanese Treaty as a possible restraint on Japan. His own suggestion of a conference where Japan and the United States could settle their differences was lost in the confusing interchange between Britain and the United States which culminated in all interested parties attending the Washington conference of 1921–2. Hughes, however, was not to have another chance to berate the great in conference. The British were prepared to support separate dominion representation at a preliminary conference in London, but did not pursue this when the Americans insisted on one conference in Washington.[25] Possibly neither party wanted to deal with Hughes' abrasive diplomacy a second time. Dominion representatives were included in the British delegation but Hughes' political position by then was too insecure for him to go in such a capacity.[26]

[22] See J. R. Poynter, 'The Yo-Yo Variations: Initiative and Dependence in Australia's External Relations, 1918–1923', in *H.S.*, *54*, April 1970, and the comment by W. J. Hudson in *55*, October 1970: M. R. Megaw, 'Undiplomatic Channels: Australian Representation in the United States, 1918–39', in *H.S.*, *60*, April 1973.

[23] D. K. Dignan, 'Australia and British Relations with Japan, 1914–1921', in *Australian Outlook*, *21*, 2, August 1967.

[24] H. Radi, 'New Guinea under Mandate, 1921–41', in W. J. Hudson, Ed., *Australia and Papua New Guinea*, Sydney, 1971.

[25] J. C. Vinson, 'The Problem of Australian Representation at the Washington Conference for the Limitation of Naval Armament', in *A.J.P.H.*, *IV*, 2, November 1958.

[26] For party strengths in Parliament see G. Sawer, *Australian Federal Politics and Law 1901–1929*, Melbourne, 1956, ch. 10.

The Pacific Pact and the agreement to limit naval forces, and above all, Japan's acceptance of the principle that the British Empire and the United States were 'two ocean' powers and thereby entitled to commensurately larger navies, provided the reassurance Australia wanted. Peace in our time, or at least for the next ten years, was the comforting conclusion from the Washington agreements.

For Australia, Washington marked the end of a short era of personal diplomacy. The Chanak crisis of 1922 and Britain's unexpected request for military support against Turkey revealed the hollowness of the imperial undertaking to keep the dominions informed. Guarded support was Australia's response.[27] Other dominions were more forthright in their condemnation of an arrangement whereby Britain acted on her own initiative but expected their unquestioning support. By the 1923 Imperial Conference it was readily apparent that any system of multi-consultation was unlikely to produce a unified policy for the empire. It followed that the special relationship that Australia sought would be with Britain herself, closer and more easily obtained because of the disparate aims of the other dominions. The form of the relationship was settled in 1924, when Bruce arranged for R. G. Casey to become Australia's liaison officer with the British cabinet. Through Casey, confidential information was passed to Australia and Australian diplomatic requirements were made known to Britain. It was the simplest solution to the problem of diplomacy and power, utterly dependent on the continuance of mutual trust, and so, ultimately on the existence of that spirit of community to which Hughes had appealed in 1921. Given those conditions, it was an arrangement which enabled Australia to be heard and heeded.

After Washington international tension eased. Australians did not need to look too closely to the conditions of their safety, nor to ask the hard questions about the nature and purpose of their defence forces. The Singapore base was the key to imperial Pacific strategy approved at the 1923 Imperial Conference.[28] Though work on the base stopped in 1924 and proceeded intermittently thereafter, the strategy continued to be accepted as adequate. This meant that the modest amount Australia was willing to expend on defence was concentrated on her naval force. The five-year construction programme announced in 1924 was of marginal importance within this strategic concept and totally inadequate outside it, yet with defence expenditure kept low, it encroached dangerously on provision for the other services. The air

---

27 P. M. Sales, 'W. M. Hughes and the Chanak Crisis of 1922', in *A.J.P.H.*, *XVII*, 3, December 1971.

28 For the proceedings of the Imperial Conference of 1923 see Cmd. 1987, 1988 in *British Parliamentary Papers*. See also J. M. McCarthy, 'Australia and Imperial Defence: Co-operation and Conflict 1918–1939', in *A.J.P.H.*, *XVII*, 1, April 1971: and J. M. McCarthy, 'Singapore and Australian Defence, 1921–1942', in *Australian Outlook*, 25, 2, August 1971.

force, Sir John Salmond found in 1928, was incapable of war operations of any kind.[29]

The presumption that security was not a pressing problem left
Australians free to stress the potential of the League of Nations or the
worth of the British Empire, depending mainly on their political
affiliations. Labor party members were too conscious of recent discomfort to take comfort from a special relationship with Britain.
When Bruce submitted the agenda for the 1923 Imperial Conference
to parliament, perhaps anticipating that the conference would formulate imperial policy, the future Labor prime minister, J. H. Scullin,
retorted:

We in Australia, so far removed from the centre of world politics cannot
control these things. We cannot go into the intrigues of Europe and change
its ways, but we can, in our own country, in our own day, and in our own
generation, do something to bring about reform ... We wish to extend the
hand of friendship and sympathy to the peoples of all lands, to acknowledge
our kinship with Britons across the seas, but politically, militarily, and
diplomatically we shall mind our own business.[30]

Where external security was concerned, Labor's varied heritage was
apparent.[31] One strand was utopian and socialist. Idealism born of the
hope of a socialist international order lingered on after hope died
early in the decade. If, as some Labor men held, Australia needed
only to mind its own business and avoid entanglements, the Singapore
base was not reassuring but provocative. The League of Nations they
would support in the hope that nations which accepted membership
of an international organization would agree to settle disputes by
arbitration. But their internationalism was not easily reconciled with
their deep belief in the superiority of their British stock and their
determination to keep Australia white. Labor was not unaware of the
offence this policy gave, nor altogether indifferent to the advantages
of British backing internationally. They were ready to concede the
Australian nation must look to Britain for immigrants, though they
were wary of encouraging immigration while there was unemployment
in Australia. But when Bruce established quotas for Southern Europeans,[32] so low as to be not much more than a gesture to those who
found the policy of exclusion odious, Labor objected on principle to
the admission of other races. Britons were kin. Labor tacitly accepted
that aspect of the special relationship but in other respects they wanted
no part in strengthening the ties of empire. In the wake of the wartime

[29] J. M. McCarthy, 'Australia and Imperial Defence: Co-operation and Conflict
1918–1939', in *A.J.P.H.*, XVII, 1, April 1971, p. 22.

[30] *C.P.D.*, 31 July 1923, *104*, pp. 1884–5.

[31] For an account of the federal Labor party see L. F. Crisp, *The Australian
Federal Labour Party: 1901–1951*, London, 1955.

[32] C. A. Price, *Southern Europeans in Australia*, Canberra, 1963, pp. 87–91.

divisions the party was pulled in contrary directions and the failure to develop a consistent attitude to foreign affairs was the result. Isolationism was an unrealistic stance, but neither internationalism nor overt support for Britain was possible for the party which held together socialists, eager to make the party over in their own image, and the Catholic Australian Irish who saw the party as their rightful inheritance. To socialists, Britain epitomized the evils of capitalism; to the Australian Irish, the evils of being British.

When a section of the Labor party hived off in 1916, the Irish Catholic influence was strengthened. Amongst the new leadership, Irish names were noticeable;[33] Catholic connexions became valuable. Poor Irish immigrants had long sought place and position in Australia, and the stage was now reached where Irish-Australians found not just acceptance but a powerful national party with which they could identify. With few exceptions, they looked on Labor as their party and on that party as the assurance that they were more truly Australian than others. For them, to be Australian, meant to be as acceptable, as worthy of consideration, as any other section of the community. In making Labor their party they infused this desire for equality into the party, twisting traditional egalitarianism to their own ends. They were not drawn to revolutionary doctrines while the machine to be used for that purpose was the party which was a symbol of their success. And, wanting to be as others and part of a wider movement to improve conditions for ordinary Australians, they were indifferent, or reluctant, to serve too narrowly a Catholic purpose. The Catholic vote stayed with Labor in 1920 and 1922 when a Democratic party, proposing state aid for church schools, stood candidates against Labor.[34] At most, one in six Catholics put their church's need before their party. When Labor debated the party's objective in 1921 the Irish and Catholics were noticeable amongst the opponents of socialization. Nevertheless the party's need to regain the support of militant unions held sufficient force for changes to be made which would satisfy militants. Conference altered the second part of the objective to read 'the socialization of industry, production, distribution and exchange' and defined the methods to be followed. Socialists had won a victory but the issue of whether the party was truly socialist was not finally settled. At the close of the conference those who wanted to be reassured the party was still one they could support pushed through with a simple majority the 'Blackburn gloss'.[35] It ended with the statement that

[33] L. F. Crisp and S. P. Bennett, *Australian Labor Party: Federal Personnel 1901–1954*, Canberra, 1954.

[34] P. J. O'Farrell, *The Catholic Church in Australia: A Short History: 1788–1967*, Melbourne, 1968.

[35] Quoted in full in L. F. Crisp, *The Australian Federal Labour Party: 1901–1951*, London, 1955, p. 281.

the party does not seek to abolish private ownership even of any of the instruments of production where such instrument is utilised by its owner in a socially useful manner and without exploitation.

The calmness with which Catholics accepted the new objective, when compared with their reaction to Labor's socialism in its early years, suggested new confidence on their part that the socialism of a party in which they had the numbers would not conflict with the church.

The temper of the war years was prolonged while Labor's loyalty continued to be suspect. Through socialists, it was associated with Bolshevik revolution, through the Irish, with rebellion. In 1920 and 1921 Labor leaders addressed mass rallies of Irish sympathizers. Protestant defence associations re-emerged[36] to sustain the virulent sectarianism of the war years to climax in 1924 in an abortive attempt in New South Wales to override the Catholic Church's requirements for Catholic marriage. Behind this there lay the old fear of a nation divided against itself. The Nationalists condemned their opponents for fomenting dissension even as they took advantage of the situation to strengthen their own position. Hughes had Hugh Mahon expelled from federal parliament in November 1920 for raging against 'this bloody and accursed Empire'.[37] He needed Mahon's seat to be secure against a solid Country party and Labor vote, and the Nationalists won the by-election. The question of Labor's loyalty was more significant because of the persistence of industrial unrest. In 1920, 3,587,267 working days were lost through industrial disputes. There were some who thought Bolshevism stalked the land.

As the postwar boom gathered momentum in 1920, the workers' struggle to maintain the value of their wages continued. Prosperity raised their expectations and encouraged them to use the strike. Public servants[38] and teachers sought redress by this method along with shearers, miners and factory workers. When so many had wage grievances, class interest was canvassed more widely, conveying the impression of militant class consciousness.[39] However, those who were fearful of Bolshevism gave too much importance to the actions of a minority, the militant unions who urged job control as a tactic to wring concessions from employers or advocated One Big Union to

---

[36] R. Rivett, *Australian Citizen: Herbert Brooks, 1867–1963*, Melbourne, 1965.

[37] *The Catholic Press*, Sydney, 11 November 1920 contains Mahon's speech: Hughes' speech in the House of Representatives is in *C.P.D.*, 11 November 1920, *94*, pp. 6382–9.

[38] F. T. de Vyver, 'The 1920 Civil Service and Teachers' Strike in Western Australia', in *Journal of Industrial Relations*, 7, 3, November 1965.

[39] P. J. O'Farrell, 'The Russian Revolution and the Labour Movements of Australia and New Zealand, 1917–1922', in *International Review of Social History*, *VIII*, 1963: M. Dixson, 'Reformists and Revolutionaries in New South Wales, 1920–22', in *Politics*, I 2, November 1966. See also D. W. Rawson, *Labor in Vain?*, Melbourne, 1966.

use the strike as a class weapon.[40] The failure of the arbitration system was at the root of the trouble. The award system was inflexible. The legalism which had crept into the system made hearings lengthy, costly and, in the uncertainty about the outcome, frustrating. Workers were impatient to get the 44-hour week and the better wages which they regarded as their right after the sacrifices they had been called upon to make, albeit at times unwillingly, during the war.[41] By whatever means available they pursued these aims disregarding rather than rejecting an arbitration process which failed to produce the desired results.

The operation of arbitration was a continuing problem throughout the decade[42] – partly because too much was expected of it. When arbitration did not work to the satisfaction of one side or the other, the dissatisfied party looked to its government to make changes in the system. Likewise, affection for federal or for state jurisdiction fluctuated according to which party was in power and how their supporters currently valued arbitration. In the final analysis, the advantage of the system to workers or to employers depended on the level of economic activity. In recessions, labour found that the award system provided a buffer against wage reductions; and employer organizations found arguments against the system. In prosperity, over-award payments assumed more importance and arbitration correspondingly less. Dissatisfaction tended to focus attention on how the unions could be made to abide by the court decisions, or how the courts could be reconstituted so as to ensure favourable results, rather than on the more basic problem of how to adjust wage levels to be fair to workers without placing such a burden on industry as to prevent that further expansion towards which so much of government programmes were directed.

The Nationalists were influenced by a number of considerations in their approach to the problem of industrial unrest. They were inclined to regard labour's demands as selfish and likely to endanger further industrial expansion; they were attracted by the idea of round table discussion or tribunals of employers and employees, a method currently in favour in England; they were opposed to any incursion on

40 I. Turner, *Industrial Labour and Politics: The Dynamics of the Labour Movement in Eastern Australia, 1900–1921*, Canberra, 1965: I. Bedford, 'The One Big Union, 1918–1923', in I. Bedford and R. Curnow, *Initiative and Organization*, Melbourne, 1963.

41 A five-day 40 hour week began to be canvassed in 1920 to support the case for a 44 hour standard week. See the 'Report of the Royal Commission on Proposed Reduction of the Standard Working Week from 48 to 44 Hours', in *New South Wales: Parliamentary Papers*, 1920, 2, p. 1221 ff.

42 For an introductory study see J. H. Portus, *Australian Compulsory Arbitration 1900–1970*, Sydney, 1971. See also G. Anderson, *Fixation of Wages in Australia*, Melbourne, 1929: O. de R. Foenander, *Towards Industrial Peace in Australia*, Melbourne, 1937, cf. B. Fitzpatrick, *The British Empire in Australia: An Economic History 1834–1939*, Melbourne, 1941, pp. 460–93: J. Hutson, *Penal Colony to Penal Powers*, Sydney, 1966.

the states' powers; but, above all, they feared the effect of industrial stoppages on their programme of development. The matter could not rest with the states. Having made production their foremost aim and also a national interest, they faced the problem of restoring harmony in industry without discouraging investment. For these reasons, the solution of the problem became a particular concern of federal government. In the immediate situation the Nationalists plumped for the system they knew as most likely to meet their dual purpose of ameliorating the discontent while keeping labour costs at a reasonable level. The imperfections of the system to secure either aim to their satisfaction was a continuing dilemma for Nationalist governments.

The changes made to the federal arbitration system in 1920 brought some benefits to the workers. The appointment of extra personnel expedited hearings. The need for flexibility was recognized in the provisions which enabled quarterly cost of living adjustments to be included in the new awards. A prosperity loading of 3s. a week was granted in 1921. The Piddington commission, set up in fulfilment of Hughes' election promise to investigate wages and prices, had reported in November 1920 that the Harvester equivalent was £5.17s.1d. As the Commonwealth basic wage then stood at £4.2s.0d. these concessions to labour were in proportions closer to what the government considered reasonable for industry rather than what unions regarded as fair to the workers.[43] However, by 1921 the boom had passed its peak. When prices began to fall the time-lag in adjusting wages was in the workers' favour. Also, with the unemployment at 12 per cent they had little spirit for industrial action.

There was another side to the changes made in 1920 to the arbitration system. Penalties were increased; the definition of a strike widened to include 'total or partial refusal ... to accept work if the refusal is unreasonable'; and a requirement that cases affecting standard hours be heard by a court of three. Higgins, who had granted the 44-hour week to engineers and timber workers, resigned in protest.[44] His successors restored the 48-hour week. The government's determination to exercise some restraints over labour costs, which was to become more apparent during the decade, was already evident in 1920. Though alternatives to arbitration had been widely canvassed, the measures taken by the government were in general directed more to shoring up the familiar system than to experimenting with any of the schemes which placed the onus for reaching agreement on the parties themselves.

Hughes understood labour's grievances better than most of his party

---

43 'Report of the Royal Commission on the Basic Wage', in *C.P.P.*, 1920–21, *4*, p. 524 ff. See also 'Report of the Royal Commission on Proposed Reduction of the Standard Working Week from 48 to 44 Hours', in *New South Wales: Parliamentary Papers*, 1920, 2, p. 1221 ff.

44 H. B. Higgins, *A New Province for Law and Order*, London, 1922, appendix B, Statement announcing resignation.

and he seemed more receptive to the idea of encouraging agreement between employers and employees. His influence perhaps explains the one major innovation, a proposal to create industrial tribunals on an industry basis composed of equal numbers of representatives of employers and employees. Hughes maintained, and perhaps this reflected his true feelings, that the intention was only to establish these tribunals for the militant minority who would not use arbitration, and therefore it was not an attempt to supplant arbitration but to extend some form of regulation where otherwise none existed. There were clearly some doubts about his intentions, though in practice this legislation was used only for the coal miners. If Hughes had hoped to develop acceptable alternatives to arbitration he was disappointed. In any case he was no longer in a position to dictate his party's policies.[45] At no stage in this parliament had he a reliable majority.[46] Labor waited for revenge; the newly-formed Country party had issues to press – in a session largely taken up in debate on the tariff, the party had to tread warily to avoid bringing the Nationalist government down; and amongst Hughes's own party there were some who hoped to see him replaced. He had to avoid a combination of all three. He continued to do things his way without much consultation with supporters, but there was less he could afford to do. The session was not very fruitful. Apart from winding up war activities and passing the new tariff, the main business was the industrial unrest.

Conditions of labour were more readily subject to state law than to federal arbitration. Even with the extension of the federal court's powers by judicial review, notably in the Engineers' case of 1920 which gave state employees access to federal arbitration, and in Cowburn's case in 1926, which held that a federal award over-rode state law, the workers still had more to gain from state governments. Understandably, Labor had most success in the states where the strong men of the party made their mark – E. G. Theodore in Queensland, and later in the decade, J. T. Lang in New South Wales.[47]

The absence of constitutional restraints on the states' industrial powers was somewhat offset for Labor governments by a need to fulfil state government's customary role as developer. There were limits to the benefits they could confer on workers set by their own budgetary needs, and their own labour costs, since public servants comprised a significant part of the workforce, and also, by the need to avoid making conditions for labour so favourable that overseas investment would be

---

[45] See L. F. Crisp, 'New Light on the Trial and Tribulations of W. M. Hughes, 1920–1922', in *H.S.*, 37, November 1961.

[46] For a summary account of all federal elections, party strength and programmes, and legislation see G. Sawer, *Australian Federal Politics and Law 1901–1929*, Melbourne, 1956.

[47] Both await critical biographies but see I. Young, *Theodore: His Life and Times*, Sydney, 1971: J. T. Lang, *I Remember*, Sydney, 1956, and *The Turbulent Years*, Sydney, 1970.

discouraged thus jeopardizing that development which Australians valued so highly. Since state enterprise was still important in Labor programmes, the difficulties were compounded. If Labor governments placed development ahead of reform, they lost the essential part of their programme for the working class; if they pushed too far the other way, they were beaten by hostile upper houses.[48] J. Storey led Labor to victory in New South Wales in March 1920, but he lacked control of the Legislative Council and had only an uncertain majority in the Assembly, and did not press controversial measures. A bill for equal pay for equal work never got to second reading. The 44-hour week was subject first to inquiry, then to the ruling of the Industrial Commission specially created for this purpose. With modest improvements to rent control and worker compensation this constituted almost the whole of the Storey-Dooley labour programme.[49] The sole consolation for radicals was the remission of sentences, following exoneration by Mr Justice Ewing, of most of the 'Wobblies'.

Theodore in Queensland seemed better placed to implement his programme, which was a mixture of radical and traditional developmental measures typical of Labor thinking of the time. In addition to an extension of the state's arbitration responsibilities – a living wage was declared for the first time in February 1921 – Theodore proposed a whole range of state enterprises to keep prices low and to provide employment, and since the state would be the employer, ideal employment conditions.[50] To meet the particular difficulties of large families and broken employment, he promised child endowment and unemployment insurance. He had a safe parliamentary majority. Smart use of a political Lt.-Governor in the absence of the governor gave him in February 1920, fourteen new councillors and control of the Legislative Council. But he was stopped by other means. For removing the prohibition on increasing pastoral rents, which had been written into the act earlier by a sympathetic government, Theodore encountered fierce opposition from pastoralists and their London financial connections. Pastoralists held their land at nominal rent. If Theodore had merely tried to redress that situation there might not have been such an outcry. Instead, the rent was to be sufficiently high to force sub-division. And the Legislative Council had blocked the measure for so long that in 1920 there was real danger of retrospective increases being ruinous. Theodore's opponents labelled it repudiation and sent a delegation to petition the Crown and to organize the London money market against him. In May 1920 he was denied the £9m. loan he needed for his programme. All he could get were small expensive

---

[48] K. Turner, *House of Review? The New South Wales Legislative Council, 1934–68*, Sydney, 1969.

[49] J. Storey died on 5 October 1921 and J. Dooley was elected leader on 8 October 1921.

[50] For earlier developments on these lines see D. J. Murphy, 'The Establishment of State Enterprises in Queensland, 1915–1918', in *L.H., 14*, May 1968.

loans from New York.[51] For four years the London financiers bided their time till Theodore, facing a conversion loan, had no choice but to capitulate on rents – a gift of £2.8m. to the pastoralists, the Brisbane *Courier* claimed.[52] A decade later when Lang provoked the cry 'Repudiation', Theodore must have heard echoes of 'Defeat Theodore'.

Defeated he was. Without loan money, Theodore's ambitious plans for state steel works and state coal mines were lost. Even projects traditionally expected of Australian governments, new railways and irrigation works, had to be abandoned. Unemployment insurance was introduced in 1923,[53] but on a scale so modest as to provide only for normal seasonal unemployment. Child endowment was postponed and later dropped. Without the stimulus of public works, Queensland suffered in the 1921–2 recession. Unemployment reached 21.8 per cent, nearly double that for all Australia. What mockery was this? Australia had become a nation amongst the world's nations and in Queensland men who dreamed of a new order waited for loan money.

Both these Labor governments had come under bitter attack from sections of the union movement. To some extent this was merely disagreement about how much in the way of better wages and shorter hours a Labor government should secure for the workers, and more especially for its own employees. But the failure to implement the radical side of Labor's programme revived the question of what the nature of Labor government should be. Was it an instrument to eliminate the exploitation of the working class? Was it socialist? In the aftermath of the recession, the prospect of militant class consciousness waned. Socialist hopes lay in the continuing power struggle within the Labor party. It was an extraordinarily complex struggle, between unionists and politicians, and between rival unions and, because of the federal structure of the Labor party, between state and federal parties. Position and power and ideology were at stake.[54] At one level it consisted of a challenge to A.W.U. hegemony from other unions resenting its power and its encroachments. The A.W.U. was the giant amongst unions, powerful enough especially in country electorates, for its officials to find the way into politics made easy. Their position was strengthened by overlapping membership with the Catholic section of the party. They had a community of interests with the politicians, wanting no radical changes, only a Labor party that could win elections. In the smaller rural states there was no real basis

51 B. Schedvin, 'E. G. Theodore and the London Pastoral Lobby', in *Politics, VI*, 1, May 1971.

52 *Courier*, Brisbane, 28 June 1924.

53 For details of Queensland legislation see C. A. Bernays, *Queensland – Our Seventh Political Decade, 1920–1930*, Sydney, 1931.

54 D. W. Rawson, 'Labour, Socialism and the Working Class', in *A.J.P.H., VII*, 1, May 1961: D. W. Rawson, *Labor in Vain?*, Melbourne, 1966: L. F. Crisp, *Ben Chifley*, Melbourne, 1961.

for opposition to this group. In Victoria corruption impeded the emergence of effective counter groups. But in the more industrialized New South Wales, and to some extent in Queensland, a basis for opposition existed in the Trades Halls which the A.W.U. could not dominate. Understandably, the unions which found the party too cautious, and too willing to abide by an arbitration system that was acknowledged to be imperfect, sought alternatives. Some withdrew from the party; others put their hopes in the Socialist Objective and sponsored politicians prepared to support it. A. C. Willis of the powerful Miners Union left to establish an Industrial Socialist Party.[55] J. S. Garden and other Trades Hall 'Reds' took the alternative approach. J. T. Lang was prepared to accept their sponsorship. To control the party the A.W.U.'s grip on the executive had to be broken. Though he had no inclination towards communism, Lang worked with Garden and the 'Reds'. His purpose was reform and his own supremacy, not socialism. In the complex manoeuvres by which he achieved this, he brought socialists in 1923 within grasp of control of the New South Wales party, and inevitably brought the state party into conflict with the federal party. In that the hegemony of the A.W.U. was one of the issues at stake, and the federal party was a politicians' party with no Trades Hall to exercise a countervailing influence, federal Labor stood with the A.W.U.

The other issue was socialism and, after the union of the rival Communist parties in 1922,[56] the relationship between the Communist party and the A.L.P. When Labor adopted the Socialist Objective in 1921, moderates controlled the state executives. The party had always managed to speak in socialist terms and yet retain its reformist character. Whether it would continue to do so if the industrialists and their Communist backers controlled the executive was the issue at stake in New South Wales after 1922. The 'Reds' wanted the rules altered to allow Communists to be members. Disagreement between politicians and the executive provided their opportunity. In March 1923 the A.W.U.-dominated executive replaced the party leader, J. Dooley, with its own candidate, dividing the party, bringing damaging counter charges of A.W.U. corruption, and an alliance at the June conference of Dooley's supporters and industrialists. Together they routed the A.W.U. and by a simple majority approved the affiliation with the Labor party of other working class parties, namely Communists. Shortly afterwards Lang became leader. A Lang-Willis alliance threatened the New South Wales federal politicians, whilst the association of the party with extremists endangered its electoral chances. On both grounds federal intervention was assured. In

---

55 I. E. Young, 'A. C. Willis, Welsh Non-conformist, and the Labour Party in New South Wales 1911–33', in *The Journal of Religious History*, 2, 4, December 1963.

56 See A. Davidson, *The Communist Party of Australia: A Short History*, Stanford, 1969.

October 1923 the New South Wales executive abandoned the Communists, and in 1924 federal conference ruled that all parties must accept the federal objective as paramount and binding; Theodore's motion that 'No member of the Communist party be admitted to the Labour party' was greeted with a chorus of support.[57] The Communist attempt to permeate Labor had failed.

In the course of this struggle several things became apparent: there was no widespread desire for the party to be anything but what it had always been, a machine for winning elections and safeguarding union interests; that the latter included protection of men who controlled votes at conference; that unity would be valued for its own sake, and a state party seeking to push a little further than others would find itself in conflict with the federal organization; and that federal intervention would tend to preserve the traditional reformist character of the party and the existing balance of forces within it. Running through the dispute was a conflict of interest, as old as the party itself,[58] between the city-based workforce and the country vote. The A.W.U.'s political position moved steadily to the right in step with opinion in the electorates which A.W.U. officials might hope to win. Concessions to country voters meant compromising the class nature of the party. On the other side, the urban craft and industrial unions, the railwaymen in particular, held to the view of a working class party, even though some were prepared to tread a moderate path. To gain office the party had to win country seats, and the difficulties of doing so were considerable. The drift to the cities weakened Labor. It was not farm owners but farm hands, old miners and factory workers who had to move. And in the Country party Labor faced a rival that claimed unique authority on country matters, and, furthermore, had built its following on deploring socialism.

Possibly the most significant political development of the period was the emergence to power of the Country party.[59] In 1920 there was still no federal organization, but Country party members sat in every mainland parliament (in New South Wales as Progressives until 1925). By 1923 the federal party, led by Earle Page,[60] a bustling country doctor turned businessman and politician, was a partner in the ruling coalition, having been instrumental in removing Hughes. In New South Wales Progressives kept Nationalists in power from 1922 to

57 See *Round Table, 15,* 1924-25, p. 392.

58 See N. B. Nairn, *Civilising Capitalism: The Labor Movement in New South Wales, 1870-1900,* Canberra, 1973.

59 For a detailed study see B. D. Graham, *The Formation of the Australian Country Parties,* Canberra, 1966. See also U. Ellis, *The Country Party: A Political and Social History of the Party in New South Wales,* Melbourne, 1958: U. Ellis, *A History of the Australian Country Party,* Melbourne, 1963: D. Aitkin, *The Colonel: A Political Biography of Sir Michael Bruxner,* Canberra, 1969: D. Aitkin, *The Country Party in New South Wales,* Canberra, 1972.

60 See his autobiography *Truant Surgeon,* Sydney, 1963.

1925, and held office in coalition with Nationalists from 1927 to 1930. In Victoria the party held the balance of power but lacked the solidarity needed for ministerial success. In the other states where rural industries predominated, a separate identity was not easily maintained, nor so important. In Western Australia, where the party first emerged in 1914, internal dissension weakened it and helped bring about the defeat of the Mitchell government in 1924.[61]

There had been various attempts to form a Country party before the war, but outside Western Australia the necessary cohesive force seemed lacking. Neglect of the farmer was not itself a claim of sufficient force to hold a party together. The claim gained weight during the war from compulsory marketing of primary products and mismanagement of some wheat pools. To specific grievances about prices and rail fares and interest rates, the extra factor needed to hold the movement together was added – detestation of 'government interference', readily convertible to anti-socialism. On other grounds an anti-Labor stance came naturally. Rural producers were especially sensitive about labour costs, more especially in the Australian situation where governments had provided other services – water, transport, credit – at low cost. Ex-servicemen were active in the new party. In addition to whatever suspicions they held of Labor's loyalty during the war, they brought Anzac pride in endurance and initiative to support traditional country contempt for the soft life of the cities, which translated into political terms meant antagonism to trade union demands for a shorter working week and better terms for labour. For much the same reasons the movement was imbued with suspicion of government extravagance.

The isolation which for so long had been the harsh reality of country life was disappearing as distance was offset by motor transport and surfaced roads. Yet, paradoxically, as this basic difficulty modified others loomed larger. Resentment about their lack of amenities helped generate amongst countrymen the sense of community needed for the party's survival. Complaints ranged from the trivial to the important, from the week-end excursion tickets provided for city workers, but not for them, to the shortage of telephones, entertainments, schools and hospitals in the country. Perhaps the country mother did value education more than her city sister, but generally education was not greatly prized. The majority of children spent the compulsory years to fourteen at school, then left. Except in the remotest districts, education to that level was available. Access to high schools and to the certificates which opened the way to employment in town was not so easy. Medical services did not match those of the city, but modern transport brought more people within reach of

[61] See B. K. Hyams, 'The Country Party in Western Australia 1914–1944', in *University Studies in History*, 1965. For parliamentary representation see C. A. Hughes and B. D. Graham, *A Handbook of Australian Government and Politics: 1890–1964*, Canberra, 1968.

treatment; infant mortality stayed lower in the country than in the city. There was a beggar my neighbour note to country grievances. Their own independence from the wage system and from the narrow routines of industrial society they discounted; the material comforts of others were made a grievance, and the tradition of government initiative to facilitate production was used to support government action to make country life more attractive. Economic uncertainty gave edge to the discontent as the rural industries began to feel that competitiveness which characterized world trade between the wars. But the reasons went deeper to a conflict between two ways of life and a desire to have the best of both.

Indirectly, by emphasizing the community of interests in their own regions, new states movements, in northern New South Wales and in the Riverina, aided the Country party.[62] The drive came not from farmers, but from country town businessmen, appalled by signs of stagnation in their towns. The Progressives responded by insisting on the appointment of a Royal Commission on New States, in 1924,[63] though there was little likelihood of new states being created. Yet, by bringing country town interests behind the Country party the prospects for decentralization improved, and, by the same process, the Country party was able to represent itself as the party for all interests outside the metropolitan area. Its organization had been provided by the farmers and graziers' associations but it neither wished to be a party based narrowly on interests, since it held sectionalism to be the fault of the existing parties, nor was it safe to rely on such a base when the interests of rural industries were so diverse. The over-riding concept of the rural community was essential for the party's survival. Interest, region and righteousness provided that wider basis the party needed. It saw itself in a reforming role as the watchdog of government. It deplored government intervention in producers' affairs, government extravagance and, in general, party politics.[64] Parties were too susceptible to sectional pressure, too hesitant handling difficult problems and too ready to spend money to reward supporters. How did a party with a disdain for party politics deal with the problem? M. Bruxner, from the 'right' social background, A.I.F. colonel and New England grazier, exemplified one approach. He held his Progressives aloof from other parties, thus avoiding loss of identity – a real danger for a new party – and contamination from parties less pure. Earle Page, a man more for getting things done, adopted the same tactics with Hughes, whom he distrusted, but not with Bruce.

[62] The New States Movement is examined in U. Ellis, *The Country Party: A Political and Social History of the Party in New South Wales*, Melbourne, 1958.

[63] 'Report of the Royal Commission into Proposals for the Establishment of a New State or New States', in *New South Wales: Parliamentary Papers*, 1925, (2), *II, III*.

[64] D. Aitkin, *The Colonel: A Political Biography of Sir Michael Bruxner*, Canberra, 1969, pp. 33–40.

Possibly he sensed Bruce's own distrust of party. Page's efforts to reform government were directed to watching expenditure, and deploring constitutional untidiness, especially where government finance was involved.

Fortunately for the Country party, its entrance into national politics coincided with the revival of demand for rural produce. So long as the industries for which it held a special brief were assured of good returns, it was relatively free from the difficulty of reconciling its obligations to its supporters, with its concept of 'good government'. It faced occasional embarrassment in its first parliament when, for example, in the winding-up of wartime marketing schemes there was commercial advantage in continuing controls – to dispose of the wartime stocks of wool, to market the 1920–21 wheat crop, and to meet Britain's bulk purchase of butter in 1920. The tariff, which it had so roundly condemned in elections likewise posed problems. Some rural industries wanted tariff protection. Reasonable protection all round provided the solution. This allowed the party to give general support to the government without prejudicing the claims of its own supporters. It could criticize the 'feather-bedding' of industries, which would be better for some competition, while objecting to duties being placed on items used by rural producers, notably fertilizer, agricultural machinery, and wire netting. Likewise, on the arbitration issue, the party had to balance dislike of government intervention against the advantages of regulation. Conciliation rather than arbitration seemed implied by the former; but there were advantages when dealing with a powerful union, such as the A.W.U., in having the court's award to hold to. There were reasons therefore for retaining compulsory arbitration and, if anything, strengthening the court's disciplinary powers. It might be 'inept, ineffectual and an excrescence on our industrial life',[65] as one Country member stated in the debate on the 1920 amendments, but the party voted to support government policy. At the state level, however, their aim was to limit the operation of arbitration, in particular the extension of a standard working week to agricultural labourers. These workers were alternatively granted and denied access to the New South Wales court as Labor governments moved in and out of office. The Country party could do little about the imperfections of a federal system which allowed the A.W.U. to shop around between federal and state arbitration. A constitutional convention had been promised but agreement on how it should be constituted was not forthcoming.

Uncertainty about Country party support was a constant threat to Hughes. The new party rarely voted solid and constantly criticized the government's administration. A censure motion on the 1921–2 budget nearly brought the government down and led to negotiations for a coalition. Hughes' terms were not attractive and negotiations broke down. In any case the Country party was unlikely to find a Labor

65 W. J. McWilliams, in *C.P.D.*, 20 August 1920, *93*, p. 3735.

party recently committed to socialization a satisfactory partner. The coalition tactic was still suspect, as was Hughes himself, amongst other things for his continuing 'socialism'. His experiments in state enterprise included a shareholding for the government in Amalgamated Wireless and partnership with Anglo-Persian Oil in Commonwealth Oil Refineries. To safeguard his position against critics, amongst Nationalists as well as the Country party, he brought Bruce into the government as treasurer.[66] Bruce was the opposite of Hughes. Where Hughes was hasty, dominating, secretive, imaginative, difficult and beloved of the diggers, Bruce had served honourably as an officer in the British army, his education had been finished in Cambridge and the London Inns of Court, he was reserved, cautious, systematic, and a man of business with reassuring connections for those who distrusted Hughes with Paterson Laing and Bruce, Melbourne wholesalers. As treasurer he provided a balanced budget for 1922–3 using the reserve to reduce taxation and applying systematically the principle of borrowing for public works.

In the 1922 election Labor won more seats than the Nationalists, but the Country party benefited. In February 1923 the Bruce-Page ministry was formed.[67] The Country party's price had been the removal of Hughes, together with the deputy prime ministership for its own leader, and five of the eleven cabinet posts, including that of treasurer, postmaster-general and works and railways. The bargain was better than Hughes had offered. Also Bruce was the kind of leader the Country party trusted. Coming late to politics, cultivating aloofness, and evincing none of Hughes' hunger for power, Bruce symbolized reliability and good management. This gave the coalition solidity. Control of key portfolios for the redress of country grievances provided the tangible evidence of the political effectiveness that a minority party needs: telephones were more readily available to country subscribers; the tax on leaseholds was abolished; some £20m. of federal money was made available for roads; and the Tariff Board was enlarged to include a representative of rural interests. The concessions and assistance rural producers began to seek as the world market became more competitive were more easily obtained by ministers in office than by pressure from the corner benches, where requests were exposed to attack from either side of the house.

Attitudes of producers and party changed with market conditions. As prices tumbled in 1921 wheat growers became more interested in compulsory pools, small graziers looked back wistfully to the wartime marketing arrangements, dairy farmers lost enthusiasm for a free market, and fruit growers wanted subsidies. Farmers began to claim a right to a fair living; and freedom from government interference

66 See C. Edwards, *Bruce of Melbourne: Man of Two Worlds*, London, 1965. See also P. Heydon, *Quiet Decision: A Study of George Foster Pearce*, Melbourne, 1965.

67 B. D. Graham, 'The Country Party and the Formation of the Bruce-Page Ministry', in *H.S.*, 37, November 1961.

became a subordinate, though still necessary, consideration to government's responsibility for the farmer's fair return. As prices levelled and then improved a little it was clear that not all industries were in difficulties, but some of the closer settlement industries were. Orderly marketing was the policy formulated by the Country party to deal with the situation, which, in effect, meant some kind of pooling arrangement or common marketing authority to regulate supplies to the market and to negotiate with shippers for freight concessions. The organization was the producers' responsibility; the government's role was to guarantee the necessary finance, from the treasury under the Export Guarantee Act of 1924, later from the Commonwealth Bank following the creation of a special Rural Credits Department in 1925. This approach had a theoretical nicety which was disregarded in a situation of need. Assistance to primary producers was a well established practice and the Bruce-Page government, in fact, acted in an *ad hoc* fashion to support industries in need. It renewed a bounty on meat exports, offered wheat pools a 3s. 8d. per bushel guarantee for the 1923–4 crop, appointed export control boards for dried fruits and dairy produce in 1924 and empowered the former to make advances to needy producers, most of which had later to be written off. There were two main approaches. Where the home market was small, a direct subsidy on exports was paid. Where it was of sufficient quantity for higher domestic prices to offset export losses, the subsidy was indirect. Export bounties, for instance, were paid on canned fruit and fortified wines. On the other hand, the embargo on imported sugar was renewed in 1925 and 1928, and an import duty placed on butter, as an essential feature of the Paterson scheme of 1926. Under this scheme the home consumption price rose by the amount needed to cover the gap between the return on exports and what was deemed a reasonable return to the producer.[68] The Australian consumer subsidized the British breakfast and the Australian dairyfarmer.

The industries in greatest difficulty in the mid-twenties were amongst those promoted by closer settlement. At best, there was a doubtful element in these schemes since they involved the application of increasingly large amounts of capital to unproductive land. Even when brought into production, this land often returned less than that already cultivated. Yet the worthiness of the undertaking was so taken for granted, that profitability seemed a subordinate consideration. Costs, if calculated at all, were based on the exceptionally high prices at the end of the war. Market prospects were hardly considered. The danger of over-production had been dismissed by an official inquiry in New South Wales in 1921 as 'quite groundless'.[69] Australians seemed

---

[68] More information on marketing is available in the *Economic Record*, especially the Supplement of February 1928.

[69] 'Report of the Select Committee of the Legislative Council on Conditions and Prospects of the Agricultural Industry and Methods of Improving the Same', in *New South Wales: Parliamentary Papers*, 1921, *I*, p. 68.

bewitched by the vision of water flowing in their dry land. South Australia 'over-prepared' for soldier settlement;[70] New South Wales and Victoria vied with each other, building the Burrinjuck dam on the Murrumbidgee, the Eildon on the Goulburn and the Glenmaggie in Gippsland. The mighty Hume on the Murray grew higher throughout the decade.[71] Unfortunate Queensland had ambitious plans for the Burnett but only managed a pilot scheme on the Dawson. Costs were raised further by railways, still seen as a necessary ancillary to settlement. While federal subsidies were pushing the states into building roads,[72] the states extended their railways, spreading branch lines through settlement areas to make this the last great age of railway building in Australia.[73] South Australia re-equipped its run-down railway system importing an American expert and on his advice, new engines powerful enough for the Rockies but too heavy for much of the existing track.

Big engines and big projects had an irresistible appeal to Australians still driven by state pride to outdo one another. New South Wales pushed ahead with the irrigation of the Riverina to match Victoria. Western Australia established a dairy industry to be independent of eastern Australia.[74] In the heavily timbered southwest of the state groups of settlers worked together to clear land, which was then to be allocated amongst them, along with their share of the cost of clearing. Communal settlement had not been notably successful in the east when tried in the 1890s. Nor was it in the west in the 1920s. Every possible difficulty was encountered.[75] There was a rush of inexperienced settlers. The work began without proper preparations. Living conditions in the clearing camps were appalling. Suitable supervisors were hard to find and unnecessary expense was incurred – dynamite was used to fell small trees. Not all settlers were fitted for, or willing to do, their share of the heavy work of clearing. Some of the soil proved unsuitable for dairy pasture. Western Australia got its dairy industry at great public cost and much personal suffering.

[70] Report of Mr Justice Pike, in *C.P.P.*, 1929, (2), 2, pp. 1910–13.

[71] For more information on irrigation see B. R. Davidson, *Australia: Wet or Dry?*, Melbourne, 1969.

[72] By special grants, initially on a £1 for £1 basis, later £1 for 15s. See *C.P.D.*, 27 July 1926, 114, pp. 4590–99.

[73] For examples see S. Glynn, 'Government Policy and Agricultural Development: Western Australia, 1900–1930', in *A.E.H.R.*, *VII*, 2, September 1967: S. Glynn, 'The Transport Factor in Developmental Policy: Pioneer Agricultural Railways in the Western Australian Wheat Belt, 1900–1930', in *A.J.P.H.*, *XV*, 2, August 1969.

[74] F. K. Crowley, *Australia's Western Third*, London, 1960, pp. 211–12: G. C. Bolton, A *Fine Country to Starve In*, Perth, 1972.

[75] See G. Taylor, 'Group Settlement in Western Australia', in P. D. Phillips and G. L. Woods, Eds., *The Peopling of Australia*, Melbourne, 1928: I. L. Hunt, 'Group Settlement in Western Australia: A Criticism', in *University Studies in Western Australian History*, 1958.

Victoria developed its brown coal, also at great cost, and also to be independent in its case of New South Wales and the miners' union. Strikes had interrupted coal supplies. The technical difficulties in utilizing brown coal were considerable and the machinery first installed for pressing and drying proved inefficient. Despite this, the scheme's forceful manager, Sir John Monash, was able to get £50,000 in 1925, virtually to start again.[76] And in New South Wales coal mines worked below capacity. Monash was a rule to himself, but it was difficult to make semi-independent authorities accountable to higher authority, and even more difficult not to continue a project once work had commenced.[77]

The spirit in which development had been undertaken, the scale of the projects, and the carelessness in calculating returns on investment brought a rapid increase in state debts and some hesitation about new projects. Yet at this stage in the early 1920s when a careful stocktaking seemed needed, the federal government encouraged the states to go ahead.[78] The states' settlement schemes were the key to its immigration programme. There had been no shortage of intending settlers,[79] but the arrangements made in 1920 gave the states the right to specify the numbers and categories to be assisted. Despite initial enthusiasm their response to the federal government's inducements was poor. When the Bruce-Page administration assumed office, only Western Australia, New South Wales and Victoria were participants. Western Australia's group settlement was the largest scheme. In contrast, New South Wales had used £100,000 of a possible £6m.[80] Other state governments had reservations about placing British immigrants on the land in preference to their own citizens. Queensland refused to accept this aspect of the agreement and had its plans for the Burnett rejected. Possibly there were other reasons in its case since Theodore's government was still in disfavour with London financiers.

'Men, money, and markets' was the catchcry of the Bruce-Page administration. Seen in the context of the states' flagging efforts, it did not signify any particular success in obtaining migrants or in finding markets, only that this administration, in an effort to revitalize the states' programmes, brought the federal government more forcefully behind the states and into activities which had been primarily state

[76] See A. D. Spaull, 'The Rise of the Victorian Briquette Industry, 1895–1935', in *A.E.H.R.*, IX, 1, March 1969.

[77] For a critical examination of the administration of development see F. W. Eggleston, *State Socialism in Victoria*, London, 1932.

[78] 'Report of the Commonwealth and State Ministers' Conference of 1922' in *C.P.P.*, 1922, 2, pp. 1525–62.

[79] 'Report of the Oversea Settlement Committee for 1923', *British Parliamentary Papers*, Cmd. 2107, 1924.

[80] 'Second Annual Report of the Development and Migration Commission' in *C.P.P.*, 1929, (2), 2, p. 1567.

matters, before the war. On evidence of hardships, the federal government came to the settlers' aid, even when the responsibility lay more properly with the state authorities who had provided blocks too small to bear the debt incurred or encouraged production of crops on which the return was insufficient to service the debt. Home consumption price schemes and subsidies on exports provided the relief that was necessary for the continuance of the settlement programme. 'Men, money, and markets' proclaimed new confidence in old policies. The illogicality of providing piecemeal relief only to proceed along the same lines in more ambitious fashion was not noticed, or perhaps was discounted against the prospect of imperial preference. In proposing a further £20m. to bring the total sum available for immigration and settlement to £34m., Bruce seemed at the 1923 Imperial Conference to be adopting a more ambitious approach in the hope that a larger British commitment to empire settlement would provide leverage for trade preference.[81] There was overall merit in the strategy of trying to enlarge the scheme to the dimensions that would warrant concessions from Britain, but it had one serious flaw. Domestic politics in Britain did not allow tariffs for the benefit of dominion producers. Neither a substitute British commitment of £1m. to promote empire trade, nor the preference finally granted in 1925 to a limited range of empire produce, guaranteed the necessary markets. Australia became a party to the £34m. agreement without assured markets for the additional production presaged by that agreement. In his handling of this issue, Bruce revealed both his strengths and weaknesses. He liked big projects and liked to present policies which dovetailed neatly into each other. He pursued the logic of the situation, and his analysis of problems was usually sound. But politics is not a neat business. Bruce lacked the ability to extemporize when the ideal solution eluded him. He had no flair for reshuffling the pieces to produce new solutions. If a piece was missing he could only proceed in disregard of it, as he did in this instance, or niggle away at it, as he did with industrial relations, never getting the hoped-for results.

New migration agreements were signed in 1925 with Western Australia and Victoria, in 1926 with South Australia, Queensland, and Tasmania, and in 1928 with New South Wales. Ironically these new agreements were made about the time that old projects were shown to have failed. Western Australia's group settlement was suspended in 1924, and, following trenchant criticism by a royal commission, the use of groups was abandoned in 1925. Salvaging the wreckage involved extending credit to the full value of blocks, which placed a hopeless burden on the settlers, reconstructing blocks, which reduced the number of settlers, and the writing off of huge losses. Less than 2000 were settled at a cost of £9m. At the same time soldier settlers were in difficulties. £5m. was made available by the federal government

81 For Bruce's own account see 'Imperial Conference 1926', Appendices to the Summary of Proceedings, in *British Parliamentary Papers*, Cmd. 2769, 1926.

in 1925 for writing down their debts. In 1926 Victoria's closer settlement scheme was suspended. The appointment in that year of a Development and Migration Commission to plan migration and development suggested that the Bruce-Page government was determined to avoid a repetition of earlier mistakes. In its advisory role to the government on all projects under the agreements, the Commission was cautious. A number of minor undertakings were approved, mostly works subsidiary to existing projects. The only one to exceed £1m. was a pilot scheme for irrigation on the Lachlan. The dimensions Bruce envisaged were never reached, but as much for reasons inherent in the undertaking as to any scrutiny by the Commission.[82] In so far as the mistakes had stemmed from the basic nature of the undertaking not much changed. The problem remained that of the high capital costs of opening new land and the undercapitalization of individual farms.[83] Small-scale farming was not the most efficient but the concept of the minimum living area was inherent in the idea of increasing population by further settlement. The difficulty of calculating the minimum living area was a subsidiary, though intractable, problem. Both needed to be related more directly to market prospects.

The terms of the migration agreements were liberalized in 1925 to allow equal numbers of Australian and British settlers, and to increase to £1500 both the amount per farm on which a contribution to interest would be paid, and the maximum capital which an immigrant seeking an assisted passage could possess. Britain suggested in 1927 that efforts had been directed too narrowly to creating farms rather than to agricultural development generally. The alternatives were not spelt out and the overall conception stayed virtually unchanged. Only in Queensland did land policy gradually modify to give more weight to the economic unit rather than the living block. Elsewhere efficient operation remained a subordinate consideration to greater numbers. The bitter lesson of the heavy capital cost of closer settlement was slowly driven home in this decade. At the end of it, the states claimed losses of £27.8m. on soldier settlement; a Commonwealth commissioner, Mr Justice Pike, found the loss to have been £23.5m.[84] Private rural indebtedness also increased enormously. Only part of this was the debt which new settlers had unavoidedly incurred. Credit had been fairly readily available to farmers throughout the decade. Some borrowed to improve properties. When prices began to fall towards the end of the decade, the existing high level of rural indebtedness made the farmers' position especially precarious.

Australia obtained 260,927 immigrants from Britain in the period 1921–30, some 80 per cent of whom were assisted. Nomination by

[82] Cf. G. Greenwood, Ed., *Australia: A Social and Political History*, Sydney, 1955, pp. 307–23.

[83] See S. M. Wadham, *Australian Farming, 1788–1965*, Melbourne, 1967.

[84] His Report is in *C.P.P.*, 1929, (2), 2, p. 1901 ff.

friends or employers qualified an intending migrant for an assisted passage and the majority came under this category. Only a small proportion of the total settled on the land. The rest were absorbed into the workforce undoubtedly providing some of the skilled labour needed for industrial expansion and some of the unemployed. The latter gave Labor arguments to use against the Bruce-Page government even though state Labor governments signed the agreements. Only Lang in New South Wales stood out, and possibly his abstention owed as much to his general indifference, and at times hostility, to the rural wing of his own party as to any Labor fear of immigration.

The federal government's initiative on immigration and settlement was one of the earliest, if least successful, instances of its superior financial resources being used to induce the states to adapt their programmes to what it thought best.[85] The federal government did not lack revenue. Because of the war debt it continued to collect income tax, even when its customs revenue regularly outdistanced estimates.[86] On the other hand the states' financial position steadily deteriorated. Inflation had reduced the value of the 25s. per capita paid to them from federal 'surplus revenue'. Their own taxing powers were limited by the Commonwealth government's prior right to income tax. Against this, the burden of state debts increased, due in part to mismanagement,[87] and in part to the need to supply services for the growing urban industrial complex concurrently with those undertaken for the purpose of accelerated rural development. About a quarter of state revenue went to servicing this debt; in Tasmania, with a nearly static population, about two-fifths. The desirability of all states being able to maintain comparable services was partially recognised in the increased special grants for Western Australia from 1925 and Tasmania from 1926,[88] but the general problem of state finance proved more intractable.

Page, as treasurer, deplored the anomaly of his government collecting taxation then passing some of it over to the states. But his 1923 offer to substitute for per capita payments a division of the income tax field which would give the federal government the right to tax companies, a likely growth area, and the states the right to tax individuals, the hazardous area electorally, was not to the premiers' liking.[89] He did not press the proposal. With its swollen customs

85 Cf. A. J. Davies, 'Australian Federalism and National Development', in *A.J.P.H.*, *XIV*, *1*, April 1968.

86 For a summary of the budgets see G. Sawer, *Australian Federal Politics and Law 1901–1929*, Melbourne, 1956, pp. 205–7, 240–3, 282–4, 312–3.

87 For examples see 'Report of the Commonwealth Grants Commission for 1933', in *C.P.P.*, 1932–4, *4*, p. 587 ff.

88 R. J. May, *Financing the Small States in Australian Federalism*, Melbourne, 1971.

89 'Report of the Commonwealth and State Ministers' Conference of 1923', in *C.P.P.*, 1923–4, *2*, p. 348.

revenue the federal government was in the happy position of being able to reduce income tax, undertake new activities, add a little to old age pensions to bring these to £1 a week in 1925, and to continue per capita payments while negotiating an alternative. The states insisted they had a moral, if not a legal right, to 'surplus revenue' and thereby were manoeuvred into fighting to retain the arrangement under which their finances continued to deteriorate. A solution which would encompass state debts and future borrowing, became the federal government's aim. Conversion activity on its own enormous debt, and on those of the states, along with the new loans which the federal and the states governments were seeking, meant one or other Australian government was almost continually in the market for loan money. Better placement of loans, it was hoped, would result in better terms. When £15m. had to be borrowed in New York in 1925–6 because the London money market could not meet Australia's requirements, machinery for coordinating borrowing acquired greater urgency. A voluntary loan council had operated since 1923 but New South Wales refused to join. Finally, by threatening to stop all per capita payments in 1927, the federal government forced the states to accept its terms, confirmed by constitutional amendment in 1928. The Commonwealth took over responsibility for state debts, agreed to make an annual contribution to the interest on those debts equal in amount to the per capita payments, and in return obtained the states' agreement that the loan policies of all governments would in future be decided by the Loan Council.[90] This Financial Agreement of December 1927 left the states' financial position much as it was, though by conceding two votes and a casting vote to the federal government in the Loan Council and giving it the responsibility for state debts, it significantly impaired their independence.

In the long term the most important feature of the Loan Council was its power to set a limit to the total amount to be borrowed by Australian governments, but at the time of its formation the primary objective was not so much a limitation of borrowing as the coordination of loan policies to put an end to competing approaches to the money market. The spiralling effect of unlimited borrowing was not fully appreciated. Monetary policy followed orthodox lines. In 1920 the note issue was transferred from the treasury, on the grounds that it had subordinated sound monetary principles to its own requirements during the war, to a Notes Issue Department of the Commonwealth Bank, which in turn was blamed for causing financial stringency. Partly to redress that situation, the Commonwealth Bank was reconstituted in 1924 to be a 'central bank'. It was given discounting powers and control of the note issue and placed under a board consisting largely of representatives of industry.[91] Labor protested that

90 S. R. Davis, 'A Unique Federal Institution', in *Annual Law Review, II,* 2. December 1952.

91 See L. F. Giblin, *The Growth of a Central Bank,* Melbourne, 1951.

the enemies of their 'people's bank' had been given control of it. Neither side understood central banking. With the inflow of capital and the heavy spending on public works coinciding in the mid-twenties with good seasons, a minor boom developed. There was a record wheat harvest in 1924–5 which averaged 6s. 6d. a bushel. Wool production increased by 50 per cent between 1923 and 1926. Money seemed plentiful in mid-decade but there were underlying problems.

Industrial expansion was uneven, constricted in various ways by the heavy demands of governments on capital.[92] This was somewhat obscured by the general air of prosperity, but it was apparent that the existing tariff had failed to stem the flow of imports. The Tariff Board had been established in 1921 as a precautionary move against over-protection and country discontent. It had been charged to review all applications for protection and the overall effect of the tariff.[93] It found itself fully occupied handling a flood of requests for extra protection, and driven to recommend higher duties. How else could industry be protected if wages rose? And when the signs of prosperity were all around was the worker not entitled to his share? Protection by instalment brought unevenness in industrial expansion, which in turn was a cause of unemployment. The just wage was the central concept in arbitration. Whether this subsumed a right to higher wages when industry prospered, remained contentious. Attempts to prove or disprove increased productivity were unconvincing[94] and, lacking adequate measurements, interested parties were chary of pursuing the principle. In practice, the courts adjusted their established criteria to the new circumstances, passing on to labour a share of the prosperity. Wages edged higher and the working week shortened. By 1927 the 44-hour week was the standard. Yet the advantages were offset by disadvantages: the benefits of protection by higher wages, the improvements in wages by persistent unemployment. How to adjust these operations to prevent arbitration and protection countering each other was a problem which worried the Tariff Board but the solution was not in its hands.

While the boom lasted there was the prospect of tangible gain for all ranks in society. Perhaps this helped sustain the myth of an egalitarian society. 'Society in Australia is not yet fixed and formalised. Men do not find it difficult to change their house or town or class. There *is* no class except in the economic sense', W. K. Hancock could write at the end of the decade.[95] Yet he also noted the 'permanence of economic barriers'. Lacking some of the marks of class evident in

92 See C. B. Schedvin, *Australia and the Great Depression: A Study of Economic Development and Policy in the 1920s and 1930s*, Sydney, 1970.

93 See R. C. Mills, 'The Tariff Board of Australia', in *E.R.*, *3*, 4, May 1927.

94 For example see A. B. Piddington, *Report on Productivity of Queensland and the Remuneration of Labour*, Brisbane, 1925.

95 W. K. Hancock, *Australia*, London, 1930, p. 270.

other societies, Australians were inclined to discount the existence of class and were especially drawn to do so in this period when superficial differences in life styles were modifying as greater numbers were drawn into the common pattern of suburban life. What changed was superficial rather than fundamental. The need to find employment still pressed on the working class; that was a condition of class that few indeed could hope to exchange for the independence that allowed change of house or town to be a matter of choice. Recorded unemployment ranged from 5 to 9 per cent even in good years. At the lower level skilled labour was probably in short supply, but many of the unskilled must have experienced intermittent employment.[96] There was not much large-scale industry with long production runs and stability in employment; there was no certainty of employment where firms were small or jobbing was the basis of business; and in the rural and associated processing industries, demand for labour was seasonal. Uncertainty in employment faced many workers. On the other hand, as the demand for labour was still predominantly in the unskilled and semi-skilled categories, the workforce had a high degree of occupational mobility. Probably, not many were unemployed for long periods. In that case unemployment brought a reduction in earnings, but as wages edged higher this still gave most of the working class a level of comfort beyond their previous experience. By the same token that comfort was more precious because there was no way past the economic barriers. Despite unemployment, in the country districts where employers had little regard for their labourers' comfort, a scarcity of labour was reported.[97]

Something of the condition of the working class is revealed through the pages of the *Labor Daily*. In 1924 it advertised phonographs and motor cycles, by the end of the year, motor cars and pure silk hose. Its women's page displayed fashions to grace the most elegant occasions. It published the programmes of one of the radio stations and some of the cinemas, admission to matinees being 6d. Radio and cinema, the new entertainments, were not beyond the workingman's means. If only 1400 licences were held in 1924 the simple crystal set could be made at home. Radio's commercial success followed the change in 1928 from sealed sets, which picked up only the station for which a licence was held, to open licences and two classes of stations, one accepting advertisements. By 1929 300,000 listeners held licences.[98]

96 See C. Forster, 'Australian Unemployment, 1900–1940', in *E.R.*, *41*, 95, September 1965: 'Report on Unemployment and Business Stability in Australia', by the Development and Migration Commission, in *C.P.P.*, 1926–8, p. 645; 'Report of the Royal Commission on National Insurance: Second Progress Report: Unemployment', in *C.P.P.*, 1926–8, *4*, p. 1411 ff.

97 'Report of the Royal Commission on National Insurance: Second Progress Report: Unemployment', in *C.P.P.*, 1926–8, *4*, p. 1421.

98 I. K. Mackay, *Broadcasting in Australia*, Melbourne, 1957: R. Curnow, 'The Origins of Australian Broadcasting, 1900–1923', in I. Bedford and R. Curnow, *Initiative and Organization*, Melbourne, 1963.

As there was no A.B.C. to purvey 'culture', stations provided music, serials and sporting news, setting the level of programmes to reach the widest audience and shaping taste to a middling standard. More rapidly the cinema established its ubiquitous presence, reaching also to popular taste. As the medium that transported workingman and socialite alike into other lives and other lands, the movie provided them with new experiences to transcend the separate experiences that made life styles different; and as U.S. production interests gained control of distribution, the world opened to them was the go-getting, unreal world of American movies. Facing distribution problems and, after 1929, the greater technical difficulty of making talkies, the promising indigenous film industry languished.[99] Admiration for British culture survived, but at a low level, in part because the form in which it survived was rapidly becoming outmoded, in part because the admiration had been so largely pretence and pretentiousness – a defence against the overweening superiority of the British and a way to demonstrate social standing. The British were no longer the self confident masters of the world and their own culture was subject to Americanization. The British immigrants in the period were predominantly 'assisted' and unlikely to be of the class that valued traditional culture. The utility of that culture depreciated. Its desuetude was not directly the result of Americanization, nor had the latter proceeded far enough for one simply to replace the other. If anything, these were countervailing influences enabling the dead level Australian culture to reach its apogee.

The dead level culture probed not the problems of existence, but provided new styles and diversions, and reassurance that Australians retained the qualities of their fathers. Its shallowness gave it a curiously classless quality. Neither middle class nor working class found much need to elucidate or justify or analyse the conditions of their existence. The middle class had capitalized on these when necessary. The working class had not found need, having risen to comfort and leisure without great effort on the part of individuals – neither the thrift that in harsher circumstances was necessary to lift oneself out of want nor the organization required to battle an oppressive establishment. In the absence of other traditions, middle class and working class alike sought diversion in their leisure. They found it in the cult of sport and heroes. They gave devotion to those who challenged the elements or proved their physical prowess. The air was the last element to be conquered, the one remaining area in which Australians could be pioneers. For the men who in light planes bridged the great distance surrounding Australia, adulation was unlimited. When C. E. Kingsford Smith crossed the Pacific in 1928, the nation followed his progress

99 'Report of the Royal Commission on the Moving Picture Industry in Australia', in *C.P.P.*, 1926–28, *4*, p. 1372 ff. See also R. Megaw, 'The American Image: Influence on Australian Cinema Management, 1896–1923', in *R.A.H.S.J.*, 54, 2, June 1968.

and shared his triumph. The nation shared other triumphs vicariously through the exploits of sporting champions and life-savers, each symbolically Australian. The life-saving club – there were seventy-two in New South Wales in 1930 – was the key to the emerging beach cult. Against the tameness of urban existence, life-saving had glamour and, in shark-infested waters, an element of danger that made it something of a peacetime substitute for that awful test of national masculinity that war had provided so recently and so satisfyingly.

In organized sport the role of the champion was somewhat similar; though to the individual, and to the country boy in particular, it meant a chance of status and fame. The youthful Bradman practising day after day in a Bowral backyard was the archetype of a generation of Australians who found sport glorious. He perfected his judgement of speed and direction by batting a golf ball off a corrugated tank using a stump for a bat. Many of the champions were country-bred. Possibly sporting prowess came more naturally in that environment, but the champion was the creation of the cities, their substitute for the real challenge of the bush. In the country, organized sport declined as the best sportsmen were attracted away by the crowds and publicity the cities offered. Newspaper empires were forming in this period and in the fierce competition for circulation a few major dailies developed further the technique of presenting sensation as news.[100] When journalism featured eye-catching headlines, stunts, and bathing beauties, the record-breaking sportsmen were certain of news coverage. The great had enormous following: W. A. Oldfield, J. M. Gregory and A. A. Mailey in cricket; Tim Banner and Tom Miles in foot-racing; Andrew 'Boy' Charlton in swimming, who at sixteen won the 1500 freestyle at the 1924 Olympics. In cricket, football, foot-racing and horse-racing there were heroes and followers and wherever there were playing fields, players. The churches, especially the Protestant churches, inveighed against gambling, but their exhortations on this matter were little regarded. Probably, the faithful were no fewer than before, but gambling was part of the sporting life.

The abandoned gaiety that was a phenomenon of the post-war period elsewhere was not very noticeable in Australia. Perhaps the absence of a clearly distinguishable propertied class to feel threatened or disillusioned, or the lack of an intellectual tradition to be discredited, left Australians less susceptible to the frenetic pleasure-seeking of the Jazz Age. Not many in Australia had great wealth and few had the class pretensions which the coincidence of wealth and power supports. In general this did not change, though the number of the wealthy increased a little as ownership became more concentrated, notably in industrial enterprises and newspapers.[101] B.H.P. extended

[100] For examples see journalists' memoirs including C. McKay, *This is the Life*, Sydney, 1961: E. Baume, *I Lived These Years*, London, 1941: G. Blaikie, *Remember Smith's Weekly?*, Adelaide, 1966.

[101] H. Mayer, *The Press in Australia*, Melbourne, 1964: R. S. Whitington, *Sir Frank: The Frank Packer Story*, Melbourne, 1971.

its control from the raw materials needed for steel production to the mills that used the steel. Australian Glass Manufacturers (Australian Consolidated Industries from 1939) absorbed its major rivals and expanded to associated products; cement companies merged when competition threatened profits. This sort of concentration was a natural outcome of growth in firms which succeeded in newly-established industries, speeded perhaps in Australia by the smallness of the protected market. In the process a few families became very wealthy. Their wealth gave them social standing but not a life style vastly different from that of other Australians. Three manufacturing complexes grew from the Grimwade family firm to become Drug Houses of Australia, Commonwealth Industrial Gases and Australian Consolidated Industries. This made Russell Grimwade one of the wealthiest of Australians.[102] In the twenties he chaired directors' meetings, supported a number of public concerns, collected Australiana, enjoyed motoring and expensive cars – as did Bruce who was his friend – and in his spare time made furniture. He patronized Australian artists and had scientific interests which marked him out somewhat from his class, but there was a practical purpose to the latter which was characteristically Australian.

There were no traditions in Australia to support the contemplative life against the practical. Education was still imbued with utilitarian considerations and public policy favoured one kind of education for all citizens.[103] What changes there were in this decade were towards uniformity in post-primary education, towards more state high schools offering a standard range of academic subjects.[104] In New South Wales this meant up-grading and transforming junior high schools, given originally a commercial or technical orientation, into the standard high school. An experiment with rural super-primaries, with a curriculum especially designed for country children, survived only from 1923 to 1925. In Victoria, an earlier aim of freeing schools from the tyranny of external examinations proved unavailing as very few of the registered secondary schools showed interest in being 'exempted'. The pressure for extending secondary education came from parents looking to the public examinations for the useful certificates for white collar jobs; or for technical education, inadequately provided, despite greater demand.[105] The Fuller government in New South Wales reimposed

[102] J. R. Poynter, *Russell Grimwade*, Melbourne, 1967.

[103] B. K. Hyams and B. Bessant, *Schools for the People?*, Melbourne, 1972: J. F. Cleverley and J. Lawry, Eds., *Australian Education in the Twentieth Century*, Melbourne, 1972.

[104] A. M. Badcock, 'The Vocational Fallacy in State Education in Victoria, 1900–1925', in *Melbourne Studies in Education*, 1965: A. R. Crane, 'Changes in the Secondary School System of New South Wales under the Directorship of S. H. Smith (1923–1930)' in *Australian Journal of Education*, I, 2, July 1957.

[105] C. Forster, *Industrial Development in Australia 1920–1930*, Canberra, 1964, pp. 185–94.

fees for high schools in 1923. Its justification, that high schools provided culture, a luxury which parents could not expect the state to provide for nothing, was both a misrepresentation, since the curriculum was too influenced by university entrance requirements to have much cultural content, and a revelation of the utilitarian concept of education. Except in a few private schools, not much was done to transmit the full intellectual heritage in the humanities. Nor was it in the universities. If anything, the universities' role as vocational training centres was reinforced. The McCaughey bequest helped enable the University of Sydney to establish separate faculties for engineering, dentistry, veterinary science, agriculture, economics and architecture in 1920; yet the enrolment for the whole university stayed almost stationary throughout the decade.[106]

Nor was there an indigenous literary tradition which the cultivated Australian could take as truly his own. Earlier nationalist writers, intent on marking their difference from the British, decried the refinements of the cultivated Englishman. In doing so they shaped an Australian literary tradition antipathetic to the intellectual life. Without supporting traditions and institutions, intellectual life withers. This had happened in Australia by the 1920s. It was not the result of any deliberate levelling down, but of atrophy. The outcome was not the egalitarianism envisaged by earlier idealists based as that was on respect for the autonomy of other individuals, but a narrowness in men's conception of human potential which could justify the claim that this was the 'mean' decade.[107] Parkes wrote bad poetry, Deakin assayed theology, Lane used fiction to expound socialism, and even Hughes produced some poor political theory. The men of the twenties applied themselves to the tasks in hand. Significantly, the use of science to solve problems of industry was the one major innovation in learned institutions. Mainly at first against natural difficulties and the pests which plagued rural Australia, the government sponsored scientific research, initially in the Institute of Science and Industry, after 1926 through the Council for Scientific and Industrial Research (later C.S.I.R.O.).[108] A national Forestry School established in Canberra in 1926 was in the same pattern.

Australian artists and writers lamented their failure to impress their Australian public, looked longingly for recognition overseas, and generally failed to find it.[109] In theatre, Louis Esson and the Pioneer Players, 1922–6, hoped that Australian plays would find a public but could not compete against movies, vaudeville and imported successes,

---

[106] A. Barcan, *A Short History of Education in New South Wales*, Sydney, 1965.

[107] R. M. Crawford, *An Australian Perspective*, Melbourne, 1960, p. 61.

[108] G. Currie and J. Graham, *The Origins of C.S.I.R.O.*, Melbourne, 1966.

[109] For literature see H. M. Green, *A History of Australian Literature*, 2 vols, Sydney, 1961. For art see B. W. Smith, *Australian Painting, 1788–1960*, Melbourne, 1962.

mostly English comedy and American melodrama. In art, imports were subject to heavy duty, which artists complained isolated them from new developments. They were, nevertheless, drawn into controversy over modernism, but mainly to resist an aesthetics they did not understand.[110] The exuberance of discovering the sun-drenched Australian scene had subsided into convention, with stifling effects on creativity. Something comparable had happened to the national literary tradition. 'Verse about shearers and horses' was the derisive, and partly inaccurate, description given it in *Vision*, 1922–4.[111] The writers associated with *Vision* – Jack Lindsay, Kenneth Slessor, R. D. FitzGerald – proposed an infusion of sensuous joy, encouraged by that maverick Norman Lindsay, who, in the seclusion of a holiday resort propounded the irrational nature of creative genius and painted the masses of female flesh which shocked and repelled the Australian public. *Vision* had a curiously *fin de siècle* quality infused with youthful zest. Its eclecticism was inadequate to sustain a literary tradition, but aspects of *Vision*'s credo echoed in the works of other poets – something of the gusto in Hugh McCrae's *Satyrs and Sunlight* (1928), the longing for pure beauty in Shaw Neilson's poems, and a gentler lyricism in Furnley Maurice's *The Gully and other Verses* (1929). And despair about the way of life that was now Australian:

> The towns are full of wandering haunted men
> No hidden waters call; their gain and loss
> Have trapped them, they will never see again
> The old logs mouldering in their cloaks of moss
>
> . . .
>
> Comes fear upon these people for sweet things
> So peaceably forgotten, calm unknown?
> Comes a bush fear on their mad wanderings
> That their cars thrash the roads from town to town?[112]

Perhaps a similar disquiet can be detected behind the preoccupations of other writers with the pioneering era and the country.

In that the outback continued to provide the setting for Australian writers, the national literary tradition changed little, but within that tradition the relationship between man and his environment was handled more subtly. Expatriates showed greater facility in this than the more truly Australians. Henry Handel Richardson, with only a brief visit to refresh memories, completed the Richard Mahony trilogy with *The Way Home* (1925) and *Ultima Thule* (1929). She was as

---

110 See *Art in Australia*, Sydney, in particular *8*, 1921. Cf. B. S. Smith, *Australian Painting, 1788–1960*, Melbourne, 1962.

111 J. Lindsay 'Australian Poetry and Nationalism', in *Vision*, Sydney, *1*, May 1923. See also J. Tregenza, *Australian Little Magazines 1923–1954: Their Role in Forming and Reflecting Literary Trends*, Adelaide, 1964.

112 Furnley Maurice (Frank Wilmot), 'Town Folk', in *The Gully and Other Verses*, Melbourne, 1929, p. 23.

Australian as any *Bulletin* writer in her concern about the influence on man of the Australian environment. Yet the relationship she presented was not any simplistic mateship. Her account of Mahony's gradual degeneration was a study of the mind of man, the colonial society and the forces that create and destroy civilization. Other expatriates such as Martin Boyd, in his family novel *The Montforts* and Vance Palmer in his early romantic phase,[113] explored the development of character using the experience of pioneering and the frontier. So also did Katherine Susannah Prichard in *Working Bullocks* (1926), and *Coonardoo* (1929) and M. Barnard Eldershaw, *A House is Built*, (1929). Why a writer like Prichard, who later wrote self-consciously as a social realist, should make the outback her subject, is a curiosity of the period that ultimately can only be explained in terms of the relatively simple conception of the condition of man the national literary tradition had fostered. Its epic quality came not from man's struggle within himself and his triumph over his own nature, but in his battle with the elements. Pioneering provided superb material for this – fire and flood and perennial drought – and evidence also of man's triumph. Against that, the possibility that man's tragedy might lie in his own nature, held little appeal. Life in suburbia had no such epic proportions. Most serious writers ignored it. Those who lived it liked to be reminded that they came of heroic stock. The simpler forms of the bush tradition still held the popular imagination: Mary Grant Bruce's Billabong series for children, Steele Rudd's stories of cocky-farmers-grown-prosperous, and the bush ballads. Lawson died in 1922 and Paterson was writing little, but their earlier verse was republished.

Confirmation that they came of heroic stock was provided by historians, beginning in this period to interpret their nation's early experience. In what they emphasized they revealed what mattered to them as Australians: Ernest Scott and A. G. Price, the fortitude of their founding fathers; S. H. Roberts, the romance of land settlement; Myra Willard, the fundamental importance of a white Australia; Edward Sweetman, self-government and political freedom. V. G. Childe showed an idealist Labor party betrayed by placemen; E. O. G. Shann, a land made productive by sturdy pioneers.[114] Here was the flavour of Australian nationalism and the works that paved the way for the young Hancock's brilliant interpretative *Australia* at the end of the decade. In the official history of the war, C. E. W. Bean revealed both his own intense pride in being Australian and the qualities Australians valued.[115] His excellent military history reconstructs the battles and

---

113 Vance Palmer was in Australia during the 1920s but earlier had spent a number of years overseas. See H. Heseltine, *Vance Palmer*, Brisbane, 1970.

114 For a more detailed survey of historical writing see J. M. Ward, 'Historiography', in A. L. McLeod, Ed., *The Pattern of Australian Culture*, Melbourne, 1963.

115 K. S. Inglis, *C. E. W. Bean, Australian Historian*, Brisbane, 1970.

the way the men faced the terror and ghastliness and challenges of war. The legendary Anzac was proof of Australian character, proof that Australians as a people were vigorous, valiant, independent, disrespectful of authority, reliable, inventive, comradely, and the best fighting men in the world. The Anzac bridged the gap between pioneering and the present, by giving to the people of the city the right to the qualities of the outback.[116]

Intent on their own fortunes Australians noted little what happened to the other Australians whose land they had taken as their own. Perhaps in the folklore of the elders something survived of the history of the original Australians in this period, but the other Australians recorded what happened to them only if exceptional. Headlines occasionally proclaimed some massacre in the remoter regions, outrageous enough to feature in a sensation-hungry press and to disturb the very small liberal conscience. Slaughter of tribal Aborigines in retaliation for cattle spearing in the Kimberleys in 1926 produced an official enquiry; famine in the centre, an investigation in 1928 – sufficiently delayed to report reassuringly. The administration of Aboriginal affairs continued negligently and haphazardly along lines set down at the turn of the century.[117] The national government helped endow a chair of Anthropology at the University of Sydney, later filled with distinction by A. P. Elkin, but this was done for the better administration of New Guinea not for greater understanding of the problems of a people dispossessed. However, in the activity Australians admired above all others, Aborigines could 'make it'. As champions they were acclaimed and then accepted: Lynch Cooper in foot-racing, Doug Nicholls on the football field.[118]

In a society which held obvious masculinity in high regard, women were neither expected nor encouraged to be active in public life. Home and family were woman's domain. If she shared the comfort of the period, it was by reducing the drudgery of housework with the new electrical gadgets, and by limiting the size of her family. From 1925 the birthrate fell more noticeably. In the war, men rather than industrial production had been required from Australia, so in contrast to what happened where production was essential, woman's role had been to keep the homes going. Not enough had been drawn into the workforce to upset the occupational pattern. Nor was there noticeable change in the following decade. Women made up about a third of the workforce in the industrial states, as little as a sixth elsewhere. Perhaps they only found their place was in the home because prejudice

[116] See K. S. Inglis, 'The Anzac Tradition', in *Meanjin Quarterly*, *24*, 1, March 1965: G. Serle, 'The Digger Tradition and Australian Nationalism' in *Meanjin Quarterly*, *24*, 2, November 1965.

[117] C. D. Rowley, *Aboriginal Policy and Practice, I, The Destruction of Aboriginal Society*, Canberra, 1970, pp. 230–90. See also E. W. Docker, *Simply Human Beings*, Brisbane, 1964.

[118] M. T. Clark, *Pastor Doug*, Melbourne, 1965.

about what constituted women's work denied them alternatives. Yet if that was so, they accepted the situation and the prejudice – and 55.6 per cent of male pay[119] without obvious discontent. A few women stood for parliament just before the war, the first to be elected was Edith Cowan to the Western Australian parliament in 1921, but by the end of the decade only three had followed suit.[120] If anything, women's role in public affairs contracted during this period. Before the war a minority had been active politically, active in associations whose aims presaged political solutions, notably the temperance groups, active in trade unions and moving into the professions. Against an almost solid wall of disapproval in the twenties they seemed to give up. Even the temperance cause, which had been peculiarly the women's, faltered.[121] It could perpetuate six o'clock closing and 'the six o'clock swill', but had near universal failure with local option and referenda. This was not because women themselves wanted the pubs open – their exclusion from the bars went unquestioned – but having accepted the limitations on their domain, they ceased to organize as actively on issues of public interest.

The concept of public interest had in any case become blurred or debased. Nowhere was there a challenge of any weight to the belief that the fundamentals of a good society had already been established by democratizing the political and social system. Politics could proceed on narrow calculation of retaining support and counting numbers. No alternative was propounded with sufficient force to make reconsideration necessary. The churches spoke with authority on moral issues but their right to do so was narrowly circumscribed by tacit acceptance, on their part and by the rest of the community, of the danger of their interference in public affairs. Any but the most general pronouncement of Christian principles could be misconstrued as a statement of partisan intent. The issues they addressed tended to be those of private morality. Their influence reinforced the censorious element in the community, extending in this period to literary censorship,[122] but their guidance on what properly was public interest, was minimal. In the prosperous years, hardship was rarely obtrusive enough for the appeal to public interest to be made on behalf of others, or alternatively, to preclude facile identification of public and private interest. Superficial social congruities, the fuzziness of party ideologies and

119 The Amalgamated Clothing and Allied Trades Union of Australia *v*. D. E. Arnall and others, 1 March 1928, in *Commonwealth Arbitration Reports*, 26, pp. 76–9.

120 K. Sherrard, 'The Political History of Women in Australia', in *A.Q.*, XV, 4, December 1943: J. Williams, 'Women in Queensland State Politics', in *Refractory Girl*, 4, 1973.

121 G. T. Caldwell, 'From Pub to Club', in *Australian National University Historical Journal*, 9, 1972.

122 P. Coleman, *Obscenity, Blasphemy, Sedition: Censorship in Australia*, Brisbane, 1962.

the encompassing national myths all tended to make public interest a nebulous concept, but nevertheless one of considerable political force. By default the accepted and established was sanctioned as public interest. This meant on the one hand a premium on conformity and on the other a sharpened response to activities contrary to what was thus upheld. 'Public interest' cloaked conservatism enabling those who wanted no change to impose on their opponents a comparable conservatism or risk denigration for association with 'irresponsibles'. Nowhere was this more apparent than in the official and community attitudes to strikes and trade unionism.

In the years of apparent prosperity most unions were prepared to put their trust in Labor government and their efforts into getting the most from arbitration, but a few unions, notably the miners,[123] the seamen and the waterside workers, were not prepared to forgo industrial action. In each case their working conditions were hard and their grim struggle over many years had not markedly improved these. The issues were industrial, and political only to the extent the workers' right to choose their methods for redress of grievances was involved; but the latter was made the overriding issue, the grievances themselves relegated to second place, by those who asserted public interest. Strikes did cause loss and inconvenience. Strikes on the waterfront, especially, affected profits of shipowners and producers, and where perishables were involved sometimes caused serious loss. By identifying production and the interests of producers with those of the nation, the government had only to point to the losses to justify action against strikes. The existence of an arbitration system became in itself the reason for requiring unions to abide by arbitration. The arguments were such as to place Labor in the position where it was required, in the public interest, to condemn strikes, but was unable to do so unreservedly without denying that the union was primarily an industrial organization and functioned as such only if its members could act in combination in defence of their interests. The right to strike was integral to the union's purpose. During the boom, when wages were improving and Labor was in a commanding position in the states, it could prevaricate on this issue without great embarrassment. But failure to resolve the dilemma left state Labor governments vulnerable. As the boom subsided, one after the other these governments floundered. Shown to be ineffectual, they were defeated. Their ambivalence on the question of strikes was sign not cause of their ineffectualness, but when Labor no longer held office, the workers' only defence was their industrial organization, the union. And that proved equally ineffectual against the mounting pressure to reduce wages. The worker's right to offer or refuse his labour in combination had been slowly undermined, and with it, the support he might expect from his own class. In the major strikes at the end of the decade the

---

[123] See R. Gollan, *The Coalminers of New South Wales: A History of the Union, 1860–1960*, Melbourne, 1963.

unions were defeated by the readiness of other workers to replace the men who went out. The defeat was doubly disastrous: for individuals it meant unemployment, futile resistance, violence and suffering; and for the movement that had put its trust in the organization of union and party, a helplessness more subtly incapacitating than any of the legal restraints devised by its opponents.

That outcome was not foreseen in 1925 when the Bruce-Page government, tired of the repeated delays to shipping, decided the government must act to end this trouble. Late in 1924 the waterfront had been in turmoil. To be rid of the hated Overseas Shipping Bureau, which originated as a strike-breaking agency during the war and continued thereafter to give preference in employment to 'non-union' labour, the watersiders banned overtime. Abetted by the guerrilla tactics of the seamen, they so delayed shipping as to induce Lord Inchcape himself to urge the practices of the Bureau be stopped.[124] Other stoppages followed, over the use of non-union labour and the pick-up place for seamen. The arbitration court made the hearing of the union's case conditional on an assurance that the union would abide by the terms of its award, but members disregarded those assurances and continued to delay ships to get conditions improved. In a showdown partly engineered by the government the seamen's union was deregistered. When shippers refused to renew the seamen's articles in the terms of the old agreement, and the union began tying up shipping, Bruce rushed special legislation through parliament. By amending the Immigration Act to allow the deportation of immigrants for offences under federal commerce or arbitration laws, he threatened the union's officials, T. Walsh and J. Johnson, with deportation; and by amending the Navigation Act to permit its suspension, he threatened the seamen themselves with competition on the coastal run from cheap-labour overseas shipping.

These measures were significant not so much for what followed but for what was revealed as government intention. The strike was settled fairly quickly; the owners, possibly fearing for their coastal monopoly, conceded most of the union's demands. A month later the seamen's union was supporting the British seamen's strike. Efforts then to deport Walsh and Johnson failed: the High Court held they were not immigrants, having been in Australia 32 and 15 years respectively.[125] In the strike the Commonwealth Line had avoided confrontation. It had been placed under a board in 1923 as a way of avoiding competition between government and private enterprise. By 1925 the government was already considering terms of sale, and did dispose of it in 1928 at a fraction of the purchase price,[126] satisfied that accumulated

---

124 See C. Edwards, *Bruce of Melbourne*, London, 1965.

125 B. C. Fitzpatrick, *The Australian Commonwealth: A Picture of the Community 1901–1955*, Melbourne, 1956, pp. 255–6.

126 K. Burley, *British Shipping and Australia: 1920–1939*, Cambridge, 1968.

losses provided reason to withdraw from such an undertaking. The government had not been involved as a party to the dispute. It had intervened to help the party it considered in the right, disregarding criteria established over the years for determining the illegality of a strike – these could not apply to a union no longer registered with the arbitration court – and showing in the attempted use of its immigration powers that it had assumed to itself the responsibility for judging a union's right to strike.

The Bruce-Page government seems indeed to have acted in the belief that the seamen had been misled by 'Communist' officials, and that against foreign doctrines, exceptional measures were justified. Ignoring the question of whether, in the absence of grievances, the seamen would have followed such leaders, the government armed itself with deportation powers wide enough to threaten others. The Labor party, which had reiterated its objections to Communists only eight months previously, found its suspicions of the Bruce-Page government confirmed. Were not immigrants Australians? Why was this power needed in addition to existing laws? How many unionists might be deported? The government had forged a sledgehammer to crack a nut. There was no widespread support for Walsh and Johnson, not even agreement between them. A sledgehammer seemed destined for tougher work. Unionism itself seemed the likelier target. Labor challenged Bruce to take the issue to the people. Bruce did and won the November election on the issue of law and order:

an attempt has been made to subvert democracy to domination by a few extremists. At the period of our greatest prosperity and most glowing opportunity there are wreckers who would plunge us into the chaos and misery of class war.[127]

Labor failed to convince the electorate that the government's measures were oppressive and partisan, perhaps because it had hesitated to press such charges in fear of being identified with 'wreckers'.[128]

Even allowing for the exigencies of electioneering, the image Bruce created of a Labor movement about to succumb to revolutionary violence was the reverse of what was actually occurring. There were other strikes in 1925, notable amongst them a six-day stoppage by Queensland railway workers for restoration of the 5s. taken from the living wage during the 1921–2 recession, and a transport strike in north Queensland originating from action against the iniquitous 'bull' system of recruiting waterside labour. But, compared with the years at the beginning of the decade, or with other industrial countries, England for instance, the situation was not exceptional. Strikes were usually limited in nature, limited to redress of specific grievances and

---

127 *Sydney Morning Herald*, 6 October 1925.

128 See for example Charlton's speech in *Sydney Morning Herald*, 10 October 1925.

of short duration. There is an oral tradition the word was 'Don't let them stampede you into another 1917'. Close to a million working days were lost each year but regularly coalmining provided about half the total. Since miners were on short time for much of the twenties, many of the days lost in strikes would have been lost anyway.[129] When Bruce made the menace of industrial warfare the principal election issue, he found an issue which both partners to the coalition could make their own. The parties had agreed not to contest seats against each other. As that put limits to Country party ambitions and to its pretensions to independence and political purity, it had particular need of an issue which aligned Nationalists behind producers. In addition, law and order provided a simple emotional issue to attract the 40 per cent of the electorate, which if the previous election was any guide, voted only because voting had become compulsory.[130]

By making the industrial problem and the 'Red' menace the election issue and finding it such a winning issue, the government committed itself spectacularly and unreservedly to eliminating strikes, which it could not do. It was driven on from measure to measure, trying one approach then another, until finally its proposal to abolish the Commonwealth Arbitration Court brought about its defeat. First the Crimes Act was amended so that, on proclamation of a serious industrial disturbance, to strike, or even to advocate a strike, became an offence.[131] The penalties for doing so included deportation in the case of immigrants. Next the Arbitration Act was amended to give the court power to police its awards. Later in 1926, Bruce initiated constitutional amendment to obtain wider industrial powers for the Commonwealth.[132] His extraordinarily complex proposals – designed for instance to allow Commonwealth 'authorities' but not a future Labor government to regulate industrial employment – were too confusing for the electorate, divided already on the merits of centralism. It rejected them. The inclusion of an ill-defined power over essential services was in the immediate situation so menacing as to antagonize the traditionally centralist Labor party; and, in conjunction with the other more carefully defined proposals, was so odd as to raise questions about the underlying purpose of these amendments. Were they designed to remedy deficiencies in the constitution, or to re-shape the constitution to hamper Labor, not only in federal government but

---

[129] See R. Gollan, *The Coalminers of New South Wales*, Melbourne, 1963, pp. 157–8. Cf. A. G. L. Shaw and G. R. Bruns, *The Australian Coal Industry*, Melbourne, 1947.

[130] N. Gow, 'The Introduction of Compulsory Voting in the Australian Commonwealth', in *Politics*, VI, 2, November 1971.

[131] For details of the legislation and party response see G. Sawyer, *Australian Federal Politics and Law: 1901–1929*, Melbourne, 1956, pp. 275–7.

[132] A. Wildavsky, 'The 1926 Referendum', in A. Wildavsky and D. Carboch, *Studies in Australian Politics*, Melbourne, 1958.

also in the states? Circumstantial evidence suggests the latter. The contentious issue in 1926 was the 44-hour week. What state Labor governments might do, or had already done, to hours and wages had more immediate import for industry than the prospect of a federal Labor government. By mid-decade Labor once again dominated state politics, and Labor governments were willing to enact the 44-hour week. The High Court had ruled that Commonwealth awards prevailed over state law, but even so the longer week could be enforced only for unions under federal awards.[133] That proved impracticable in some instances, impossible in others. Engineers under a federal award which specified a 48-hour week, refused to work the longer week where state law prescribed 44 hours.[134] In May 1926, the month in which Bruce announced the government's intention of seeking constitutional amendment, they began taking the 44 hours and 44-hours' pay. In the light of this, the government's pursuit of greater industrial powers seems but another move to restrain the unions, the result in turn of its inability to keep Labor out of office in the states, and its fear that the unions ran these governments.

The rapidity with which the fortunes of state Labor were repaired suggests that the self-destruction of the war years had been less serious than at first appeared. Labor stayed in power in Queensland until 1929, won South Australia and Western Australia in 1924, New South Wales and Tasmania in 1925, and formed minority ministries in Victoria in 1924 and 1927–8. To win Victoria, where country votes had a three to one weighting, Labor needed a miracle.[135] Possibly prosperity favoured Labor, its image as the party of reform serving to identify it with the improved conditions after 1923 for worker and producer alike. However, the basis of its success was a new-found caution and a courting of the farmer's vote. State parties avoided the issue of socialization, and slanted programmes to small producers to take advantage of the political instability that followed the formation of the Country party. State Country parties were slower than their federal counterpart to adopt the coalition tactic.[136] They split the anti-Labor vote and raised, but failed to satisfy, the small farmers' hopes of compulsory pools. However Labor believed that the elimination of the middleman would result in lower prices for consumers and in better returns for producers, so it was willing to introduce compulsory

[133] Clyde Engineering Co. Ltd *v* Cowburn, March-April 1926, in *Commonwealth Law Reports, 37,* p. 466.

[134] J. Hutson, 'The Amalgamated Engineering Union and Arbitration in the 1920s', in *L.H., 14,* May 1968.

[135] Country votes had a 100 : 37 weighting in 1924 and 100 : 47 in 1926. See S. R. Davis, Ed., *The Government of the Australian States,* Melbourne, 1960, p. 223. Cf. J. Rydon, 'Victoria 1910–1966: Political Peculiarities', in *H.S., 50,* April 1968.

[136] See B. D. Graham, *The Formation of the Australian Country Parties,* Canberra, 1966.

pooling and prepared to allow grower control. The prototype legislation was enacted in Queensland in 1922.[137] For any commodity where 60 per cent of producers approved, compulsory pools would be established with management controlled by producer representatives. With little else going for it in 1923, the Queensland Labor government increased its majority. Its programme by the end of the decade had become so oriented to rural needs as to be little distinguishable from that of its opponents.

While the rural vote was essential for Labor to get into office, the more crucial issue in office was what its labour supporters expected of a Labor government. Again, it was Queensland Labor which first confronted this problem, complicated there by the prolongation of the recession, the range of business undertakings initiated by earlier Labor governments, and the special expectations of those employed in these works.[138] Quite simply they required a Labor government to be a model employer. Their insistence that conditions for them be better than for others was a contradiction of whatever socialist ideals had been embodied in 'consumer socialism', but, in making that demand, the employees of the state were merely presenting, in exaggerated form, the working class expectation of better conditions under a Labor government. Theodore resisted both demands on the grounds that the unfavourable economic conditions made wage increases impossible; and he buttressed that decision with a requirement that the business undertakings be run on business lines. In effect, he made profitability the prime criteria. On that basis what special purpose remained for the state to be in the business of selling meat or fish or other 'essentials'? The gradual abandonment of its business undertakings followed inexorably.[139] The pressure for a general wage rise was not easily resisted. As political careers were endangered by union opposition, Theodore faced rebellion in the party room. By October 1924 he had either to resign or capitulate. He chose the latter, approved of the introduction of the 44-hour week in lieu of higher wages, but was noticeably absent when the legislation was passed. In February 1925 he resigned as premier. In the course of this struggle the question of whether productivity had increased was canvassed by both sides, but Theodore's efforts to make this a prerequisite for higher wages failed. The adjustment, when made, was precipitated by the railway strike of September 1925 which persuaded W. N. Gillies, Theodore's more pliant successor, to raise the living wage to £4. 5s. od. by

137 See C. A. Bernays, *Queensland – Our Seventh Political Decade, 1920–1930*, Sydney, 1931.

138 See E. M. Higgins, 'Queensland Labor: Trade Unionists versus Premiers', in *H.S.*, *34*, May 1960: A. A. Morrison, 'Militant Labour in Queensland, 1912–1927', in *R.A.H.S.J.*, *38*, 5, 1952.

139 C. A. Bernays, *Queensland – Our Seventh Political Decade, 1920–1930*, Sydney, 1931. See also J. B. Brigden, 'State Enterprises in Australia', in *International Labour Review*, *16*, 1, July 1927.

legislation. Yet Gillies in his short term as premier transformed the Arbitration Court into a Board of Trade and Arbitration with wide investigatory and administrative powers, thereby creating a more effective buffer between government and unions. Here was some support for Bruce's claim in September 1925 that the unions had brought state governments to heel, but also evidence that Labor governments were not mere tools of the unions. W. G. McCormack, who succeeded Gillies in October 1925, was a tough ex-miner, impervious to union pressure and ruthless in handling labour disputes.

As Theodore's ambitions transferred to federal politics and a New South Wales electorate, the other ambitious Labor man, J. T. Lang, had reason to study Theodore's career. The militants had forced concessions from Theodore; Lang became their champion.[140] Perhaps it was mere coincidence that the rivals took different stances, yet the moderation Lang showed during the 1925 election disappeared almost overnight. Possibly Lang's moderation was partly assumed. In this election there was a greater than usual need to appear moderate. The Communists stood candidates, and Labor had nothing to gain from a programme which could be confused with the Communists'. They polled 831 votes in all. Whereas, the sectarian squabble which surrounded the anti-Catholic marriage bill of the previous parliament would produce a solid Catholic vote for Labor, provided the socialist issue did not intrude. After he had won, Lang showed himself willing to oblige the militants. He restored seniority to the 1917 strikers – reversed by Bavin in 1929[141] – refused Bruce the services of the New South Wales police and threatened to establish a state shipping line during the 1925 seamen's strike, made the 44-hour week mandatory, transformed the Arbitration Court into an Industrial Commission and charged it to set a living wage for rural workers, abolished fees for high schools, amended fair rents and introduced widows' pensions. Having obtained, in December 1925, twenty-five nominations to the Legislative Council, not all of whom showed their gratitude in the manner intended by following the Queensland example of 1922 of voting their own demise, Lang pressed on with a Rural Workers' Accommodation Act, adult suffrage for local government, compulsory insurance of workers at the employers' expense, establishing the Government Insurance Office to stop insurance companies profiting unduly from this, and a family endowment scheme. By then Langism was a term of abuse and a phenomenon to be feared. The Victorian Country party leader, contrary to all his party professed, suggested merger with the Nationalists to stop Langism spreading to Victoria.[142]

140 Cf. M. Dixson, 'Ideology, the Trades Hall Reds and J. T. Lang', in *Politics*, *VI*, 1, May 1971.

141 L. F. Crisp, *Ben Chifley: A Biography*, Melbourne, 1961, p. 28.

142 B. D. Graham, *The Formation of the Australian Country Parties*, Canberra, 1966, pp. 263–5.

Little of Lang's impressive legislative record owed anything to the various notions of socialism which from time to time had captured the imagination of Australian Labor. Any part of it, viewed separately, belonged logically with the earlier 'Lib-Lab' reforms. The shorter working week could be seen as a further instalment of what was 'fair and reasonable'; likewise access to arbitration for agricultural workers and compulsory insurance of workers. The family endowment of 5s. a week for each child, paid only to those on or below the basic wage, rectified the deficiency in a minimum wage calculated on the basis of a standard family unit; the £1 a week and 10s. for each child, paid to widows with dependent children and limited means, extended the principles already established in regard to the aged. Nothing in this programme was based on a new analysis of the problems of industrial society. None of the fundamental relations in society were changed. Yet Lang met bitter opposition. Some of it came from a narrow concern about costs – good accommodation for seasonal workers was not every farmer's idea of a good investment – and some from old-fashioned fears about undermining individual initiative. And what widows would marry in preference to a pension and union unblessed by the church?[143] But the overriding objection to Lang's programme was that, taken as a whole, it too blatantly conferred benefits on one class while making the other pay. Lang was a demogogue. He liked to appeal to the people and did so in simple terms of their interests against the bosses, and he as their protector. Inevitably, he stirred class enmities, and his association in the extra-parliamentary party with the remnants of the socialists convinced his opponents that he too was a socialist.

While the tiny Communist party spoke in class war clichés and did little, the declining band of socialists still hoped that the existing political system, through the instrument of the Labor party, could transform society. In the faction struggle within the party, Lang had become dependent on the support of the militant industrialists. Labor members from country electorates were worried by measures for workers' compensation, manhood suffrage in local government and better accommodation for rural workers. In October 1926, P. F. Loughlin challenged Lang, unsuccessfully, for leadership. In November, Lang resorted to conference to have himself declared leader of the party. In these manoeuvres, Lang's supporters in the Executive sponsored new rules – the 'Red' rules. These were designed to limit the power of individual unions to strengthen the leader's position, but the 'Reds' stood to gain from a reduction in A.W.U. numbers at conference, and from a new rule allowing Communists to be delegates provided the party did not run candidates against Labor and the delegate had been an A.L.P. member for a year, which indeed should

143 For denunciation of the Act as an encouragement to immorality see *New South Wales: Parliamentary Debates*, 26 November 1925, *103*, pp. 2588–91. (Mr J. H. Hill, M.L.A. Oxley.)

have been impossible under the 1924 party ruling. When a chance vacancy gave the A.W.U. a majority on the executive, rival executives emerged each claiming legitimacy. Lang had one supporter in cabinet and it ceased to meet.[144] In 1927, for the second time in a decade, federal Labor intervened to bring unity in New South Wales and, as before, did so by largely restoring the old balance.[145] Lang remained leader; metropolitan unions and miners controlled the executive; Communists were barred from the party. The A.W.U., finding its power again limited, disaffiliated. Belatedly Lang wooed the country voters with marketing legislation modelled on that of Queensland, and a redistribution increasing the number of country electorates. But his systematic elimination of opponents in the party – carried through to preselection – so weakened his position that he was forced to an early election in October 1927 which he lost.

Elsewhere the party was not so torn by dissension or so effective.[146] Possibly the one was the result of the other. Inability to get contentious measures through the Legislative Councils may have so dampened expectations as to exert a moderating influence on party conflict. More likely pressure for political initiative was less because of the character of the union movement. The febrile atmosphere of industrial unionism did not extend much beyond New South Wales. Where that was lacking, party and politicians could better absorb the shocks that a party, which believed in its reforming role, received when its measures were consistently rejected. Taxation reform in Victoria and South Australia, the 44-hour week in Western Australia, workers insurance and rent control in Victoria were amongst the measures blocked by Legislative Councils.[147] The second Labor ministry in Victoria managed to stiffen the Factory and Shops Act and reform apprenticeship, but not much else.

Attempting little and achieving less, these Labor governments were not much more entitled to the mantle of reform than their opponents. Their perception of labour's problems was narrow; their measures on behalf of the working class were of the kind that redistributed income. Transformation of the organization of production was not their intention. Indeed, critical analysis of the productive system had become something to avoid, a dangerous activity associated with foreigners and Communists. The methods for socialization were removed from the party's platform in 1927. The modest 'reform'

---

[144] G. N. Hawker, *The Parliament of New South Wales, 1856–1965*, Sydney, 1971, p. 233.

[145] L. F. Crisp, *Ben Chifley: A Biography*, Melbourne, 1961, pp. 66–8: M. Dixson, 'Ideology, the Trades Hall Reds and J. T. Lang', in *Politics*, VI, 1, May 1971.

[146] P. R. Hart, 'J. A. Lyons, Tasmanian Labour Leader', in *L.H. 9*, November 1965: D. Black, 'The Collier Government 1924–1930', in *University Studies in Western Australian History*, 1959: D. Hopgood, 'The View from the Head Office: the South Australian Labor Political Machine, 1917–1930', in *Politics*, VI, 1, May 1971.

[147] G. Serle, 'The Victorian Legislative Council, 1856–1950', in *H.S.*, 22, May 1954.

programmes served as a substitute, and as a way of evading basic questions about the organization of production, even of the conditions under which the system as it existed could operate successfully. That it would continue to do so was implicit in all that Labor proposed. The other side of this was that, by avoiding such questions, Labor devised no solutions to deal with a downswing in the economy. Against that adversity Labor government could afford the worker no security. At the same time, by continuing to press labour's claims without regard to economic circumstances, their opponents could argue more convincingly the selfish and irresponsible nature of those measures. Lang exacerbated this antagonism. He pushed ahead in the 'Lib-Lab' tradition, seeking out the especially disadvantaged to be beneficiaries of income redistribution, but he twisted that tradition to fit the paridigm of class conflict by requiring wherever possible the cost be a direct charge on industry.

It was clear by 1927 that economic growth was tapering off. Export earnings had stabilized at about £145m. a year; manufacturing output, £400m. for 1925–6, rose a little, but only with extra doses of protection in 1926 and 1928, and then at a slower rate than previously. Unemployment, under 6 per cent in the first quarter of 1927, exceeded 10 per cent at the end of the year. Bruce still sounded sanguine about the economic future in July 1927 when he delivered the Joseph Fisher Memorial Lecture[148] on the theme Australia's credit was sound, much as Bent might have done in the 1880s or Robertson in the 1870s; but his subsidiary theme was the need to watch costs as 'we will have to increasingly rely on overseas markets'. This was repeated with greater insistence in the following years. Five months previously the Commonwealth Arbitration Court had begun to bring its awards into line with state practice. It had granted the A.E.U. the 44-hour week and foreshadowed similar conditions for other industries. The Tariff Board had been protesting since 1924 that high labour costs could negate the benefits of protection. In 1925 it had drawn the government's attention to 'the growing tendency of employers and employees to pass from the Arbitration Court, where wages may have been increased, to the Tariff Board, whence a recommendation for an increase in duty may be made'.[149] By 1927 the situation was 'even more ominous'.[150] The list of industries seeking increased protection was longer; likewise the list of unions with cases before the Court. The Board, in fact, identified a vicious circle of rising wages, higher tariffs and support schemes for primary producers which together created an 'artificial price level'. This concept was used both in explanation of the difficulties of manufactures and therefore as the reason why

148 S. M. Bruce, *The Financial and Economic Position of Australia*, Adelaide, 1927.

149 'Report of the Tariff Board for 1925', in *C.P.P.*, 1925, 2, 2, p. 1880.

150 'Report of the Tariff Board for 1927, in *C.P.P.*, 1926–28, *4*, p. 1638.

future economic growth was dependent on primary production; and also as the reason why, in the interests of exporters, costs must come down. The Bruce-Page government, faced with the disappointing results of its efforts to force the pace of development, was drawn to the same conclusion. Costs must come down. Bruce seems to have confused the particular problem of the exporting industries, that of being unable to pass on increased costs, with the more general problem of how to sustain economic growth. Exporters would clearly benefit from any reduction in costs. But the issues were not simply those of exporters. A group of economists calculated in 1928 – they were already assuming the role of adviser to government[151] – that the same average income for the same population could not have been sustained without protection.[152] They found the general price level had risen by about 10 per cent and that there were instances where the tariff was not justified, but that the assistance given to industry, some £26m. to secondary industries, £22m. to primary industries, had, by the effect of pooling national income, enabled a higher standard of living to be maintained than would otherwise have been possible.

Bruce's increasing preoccupation with costs and markets and additional production, when world prices had fallen slightly but no drastic change had occurred in the position of the major rural industries, signified a reordering of the priorities which the Deakinite Liberals had adopted in nation-building. Under Deakin, encouragement to individual industries was conditional on their ability to sustain a better living standard for those at the bottom of the income scale. The Nationalists were placing maximization of production ahead of any further redistribution of income or additional assistance to the needy. The cost to industry became a stock argument against higher wages, attempts to restructure the wage system to provide more adequately for large families, and new measures in relief of hardship. A national insurance scheme to provide for the sick, for widows, for the aged and the unemployed was discussed throughout the decade, promised at election after election, investigated by a royal commission for four years, aired in parliament in 1928, but never enacted.[153] The Bruce-Page government would not place the burden squarely on industry, as Lang did with child endowment and workers' compensation, but it baulked at making it a charge on revenue, even in the good years when it was salting away surplus revenue in special reserves. Likewise, child endowment was discussed throughout the decade. With

[151] N. G. Butlin, 'Economic Enquiry in Australia', in *A.E.H.R.*, *VII*, 2, September 1967.

[152] J. B. Brigden *et al.*, *The Australian Tariff: An Economic Enquiry*, Melbourne, 1929. See also L. F. Giblin, 'The Tariff – its Costs and Effects', in *Annals of the American Academy of Political and Social Science*, *158*, 1931.

[153] For more detail on national insurance and child endowment see T. H. Kewley, *Social Security in Australia*, Sydney, 1965, and T. H. Kewley, *Australia's Welfare State*, Melbourne, 1969.

a wage structure devised around the needs of a standard family unit, grossly discriminating against women on those grounds, child endowment was a logical next reform.[154] Only after Lang's Act had finally passed in April 1927 did the Commonwealth take the matter up at a premiers' conference, in June 1927,[155] and then, it seemed, less from concern about the welfare of the family than from fear that industry would be burdened by providing twice for some children. A family unit of five was the basis for federal and state basic wages; Lang had altered this to a unit of two in New South Wales. So unless there was agreement on a family unit for wages, a uniform endowment scheme would provide for some children already covered by wages. Bruce proposed a two-unit family. The implications of that were unwelcome and he was manoeuvred into appointing another royal commission. As wage levels had not changed in New South Wales, despite the new unit, Bruce's insistence on a standard family unit suggests either pedantic concern about formal consistency, or an intention of using the issue to secure agreement for a smaller unit which would justify a reduction in wages. Viewed less unkindly, the former might seem no more than being systematic, in line with the government's increasing use of commissions and enquiries with varying degrees of expertise.[156] It also commissioned, in 1927, a report on the constitution,[157] which was appropriate both for the year in which the federal parliament finally met in Canberra and from a government which helped tip the constitutional balance further towards the Commonwealth. As with many of the commissions, nothing came of this. But the contention that Bruce's purpose was wage reduction, at best wage restraint, is supported by the action his government did take in regard to arbitration.

The provisions of the Conciliation and Arbitration bill introduced in December 1927 were complex but the purpose was simple: it was to put an end to the situation where the movement of wage levels was contrary to that desired by the government and beyond its direct control. The crucial innovation was a requirement that before making any award or certifying any agreement the court should

take into consideration the probable economic effect of the agreement or award in relation to the community in general and the probable economic effect thereof upon the industry or industries concerned.

In reply to Labor's outcry, the government denied its intention was to reduce wages, and, in token of that, exempted the basic wage from

---

[154] A. B. Piddington, *The Next Step: A Family Basic Income*, Melbourne, 1921.

[155] 'Report of the Commonwealth and State Ministers' Conference of 1927', in *C.P.P.*, 1926–28, (5), *1*, p. 373 ff.

[156] Cf. G. Greenwood, Ed., *Australia: A Social and Political History*, Sydney, 1955, pp. 304–23.

[157] 'Report of the Royal Commission on the Constitution', in *C.P.P.*, 1929–31, 2, p. 897 ff.

this directive. Nevertheless, when local manufactures were asserting their inability to survive under existing tariffs and exporters were protesting about costs, the only possible outcome was wage cuts for some workers. There was a ruthless logic to the proposals, given the reordering of priorities. Wage levels would no longer be set by the bargaining power of labour and industry, nor by any abstract notion of the just reward for labour; but by a government authority charged to consider the economy. The just wage had always been an elusive concept, but the supposition that wages were not dependent on the ability of industry to pay had given the court's decisions credibility. When that assumption could no longer be made, when a court not especially equipped to make economic judgements was required to act on the new criteria, what grounds existed then for the unions to accept arbitration? As a result, what had always been a subsidiary problem in compulsory arbitration, that of securing compliance from the unions, became itself the major problem. Wage restraint and the elimination of stoppages were two sides of one policy. Penalties were increased; the union became liable to fines incurred by branch officials or through unauthorized strikes, and, since the aim was to rid the unions of militant leaders, fines could be remitted if the responsible official was dismissed. But in addition, in the power given the court to supervise union affairs, a significant new approach to the problem emerged. The court could inspect a union's books, disallow its rules, order and supervise secret ballots, and on the request of any ten members of a union require a ballot be held.[158] A.W.U. officials, long suspected of rigging ballots, were especially outraged, but in part at least from fear that their union with its 150,000 membership faced financial ruin if members persistently exercised this new right.

These measures were doubly offensive to Labor, involving as they did, an overt attack on the union's autonomy and a covert attempt to undermine the solidarity of the union movement. The value placed on autonomy had but recently been demonstrated in the constitution of the Australasian Council of Trade Unions (A.C.T.U.). Its creation in 1927 was the culmination of a decade of attempts to establish a federal organization, mainly to provide coordinating machinery for industrial action.[159] The problem had been the reluctance of individual unions to surrender the management of their disputes to any superior body and the new council was empowered to deal only with matters referred to it by constituent members. Even so not all unions were prepared to join. The A.W.U. remained outside. That the court was given power over union affairs such as the unions were unwilling to confer on their own council, was resented; that those powers could be used by the

[158] For a more detailed analysis of the Act see G. Anderson, 'The Commonwealth Conciliation and Arbitration Act, 1928', in *E.R.*, *4*, 7, November 1928.

[159] See *Labor Call*, 9 August 1945: F. R. E. Mauldon, 'The Australasian Council of Trade Unions', in *E.R.*, *4*, 6, May 1928: P. W. D. Matthews and G. W. Ford, Eds., *Australian Trade Unions*, Melbourne, 1968.

narrowly self-interested to frustrate or remove union officials who were prepared to use the strike, was intolerable. Yet that seemed the underlying purpose of some of the innovations. The encouragement of secret ballots, the remission of fines if officials were dismissed, the power given the court to legalize a lockout if a strike existed, were these not based on the hope that self-interest would induce the majority of workers to refuse support to officials, or to other unions, if there was risk to their own pay packets? What other reason could there be for widening a strike by legalizing a lockout?

From the back benches, Hughes warned that the result of legalizing a lockout would be 'industrial civil war'.[160] His loyalty to his party rested on nothing more substantial than his inability to dislodge Bruce. As if anticipating the coalition's narrow victory in the election later in 1928[161] and the chance that would give him to destroy the government, Hughes began to speak out against it on this issue. The government may not have intended a blow at unionism, but it did not understand the situation; the results would be contrary to what Bruce and his attorney-general, J. G. Latham, anticipated. In short, Hughes judged some of the new provisions to be useless, others to be provocative. In 1928, with unemployment around 10 per cent, the workers were ill-placed for direct action. Fewer working days were lost through disputes than in any other year in the decade. With state governments in financial difficulties and public works programmes under review, with manufactures languishing and drought widespread in the outback, jobs were scarce. Employers seeing the balance tip again in their favour were asking that compulsory arbitration be abolished. There were good reasons for the unions to cling to arbitration. Nevertheless within months of the new arbitration act, the industrial scene erupted. Not into war, as Hughes had predicted, but into lawlessness – defiance of the arbitration court's authority and defiance of the law by men left unemployed when others had taken their jobs. In a series of strikes in 1928–9, the new act proved of no avail but the unions were defeated. In adversity these workers were made conscious of class as they had not been in prosperity, but the structural means for harnessing class consciousness to action did not exist. With the A.C.T.U. incapable of providing direction – it proposed boycott of the court was futile in itself and still-born – and state Labor governments of their own making ineffectual, this consciousness, deprived of direction, floundered into violence.

Earlier in Queensland, ironically under the Labor government of the tough ex-miner McCormack, a strike which hinged on the rights of unionists had taken a similar course. After the dismissal of union labour from the South Johnston mill in 1927 unionists and non-unionists clashed. In the following months cane-trucks were stoned,

160 *C.P.D.*, 18 May 1928, *118*, pp. 5052–9.

161 For the election campaign see F. W. Eggleston, 'Australian Politics and the Federal Elections', in *A.Q.*, *I*, 1, March 1929.

farmers threatened, a picket mysteriously shot. But the union could not stop the mill using non-union labour. When other unions, including the militant railwaymen, finally went out in support, McCormack ruthlessly dismissed all railway employees to break the strike. His actions exacerbated the tensions in the Labor movement without improving his political position. He lost the next election. The immediate sequel was a declaration from the Queensland Trade Union Congress that 'recognition of the class struggle and active participation on behalf of the workers must be the basis of working-class politics'.

But it was lack of class solidarity which was revealed in the major strikes in 1928–9, on the waterfront, amongst timber workers and on the northern coalfields of New South Wales. When employers sought non-union labour, men were available. Each instance involved resistance to an award or an agreement which imposed harsher conditions or provided lower wages, and in each case resistance was futile. In a series of moves to reorganize the waterfront Mr Justice Beeby introduced into the watersiders' award, of September 1928, a requirement for attendance twice daily at pickups.[162] Though the union had already indicated it would reject such terms, it was clearly divided over whether to strike or not. Some ports went out, some did not. Bruce had always been sensitive to any interruption of shipping. Without waiting to see which response would prevail, he rushed through a Transport Workers Act to authorize licensing of waterside labour. In fact, his purpose was to secure preference in employment for the non-unionists already being recruited. They had no objection to being licensed. To unionists this was 'dog-collar' labour and the act the 'dog-collar' act, but when the strike finally collapsed, watersiders who had resisted licensing found they got last call at pickups. In the year following the strike, not many of them worked regularly. Those who were replaced harried their replacements; protest meetings were unruly; and on 2 November a man was killed when police opened fire on demonstrators.[163] For months the 'volunteers' worked under police protection. Amongst them were a noticeable number of Italians and Maltese and their homes became the target of mysterious bomb attacks. The Labor government in Victoria was unable to extricate itself from the awkward position of no control over the issues in dispute but was responsible for the police and so for the protection of the strike-breakers. It failed to retain the confidence of either side and was defeated in parliament on the issue of law and order. The timber workers' strike which followed Mr Justice Lukin's new award, of January 1929, brought similar disorder. Shots were fired, 'volunteers' were bashed and mills went up in flames. Lukin's award confirmed

162 W. J. Brown, 'The Strike of the Australian Waterside Worker; a Review', in *E.R.*, 5, 8, May 1929.

163 L. J. Louis and I. Turner, Eds., *The Depression of the 1930s*, Melbourne, 1968, pp. 24–31.

Labor's worst fears about the new arbitration act. Wages were cut, the 48-hour week restored, the ratio of youth to men increased. Though support from other unions was more conspicuous – the A.C.T.U. showed its first signs of effectiveness by organizing a £122,000 strike fund – the mills found other labour.[164] The 'strike' dragged on until the strikers were merely the unemployed.

In the lockout on the northern coalfields of New South Wales, the miners held on tenaciously from March 1929 to June 1930, stubbornly refusing to give in until long after the depression had swept away any possibility of victory.[165] They had been locked out for refusing to accept a wage cut. The industry had been in difficulties for several years as demand fell away, partly as a result of increasing use of oil, partly because the coalfields of the Ruhr were being exploited to pay reparations. But miners refused to believe the mineowners could not continue to pay current rates and, lacking proof, they refused government offers to match a shilling off wages and a shilling off profits with a two-shilling-a-ton subsidy on rail freight plus a one-shilling bounty from the Commonwealth for coal shipped interstate. In April, Bruce intervened personally in an endeavour to bring the parties together. Regrettably, he was persuaded that proceedings under the Commonwealth Industrial Peace Act against John Brown, for locking out his miners, were the barrier to fruitful negotiations and, disregarding Latham's warnings, he had the prosecution withdrawn. The only result was an outcry that union after union had been prosecuted and heavily fined, and the bosses got off. For the miners such injustice stiffened their resolve. Mass pickets followed. A later compromise was rejected. When the Rothbury mine was re-opened with non-union labour under police protection, on 16 December, another man was killed by police fire in defence of strike-breakers. By the close of the year the coalfields were in turmoil. For Bruce, the futile intervention earlier had been the beginning of the final reckoning. He had tried one approach after another but he could not eliminate strikes. Neither the penalties in the new arbitration act nor the supervisory powers given the court had provided a sufficient deterrent. The watersiders had been fined within days of going out but the strike went on. The timber workers had been fined. A court-ordered ballot had been a farce. Timber workers ceremoniously burnt the ballot papers and an effigy of Judge Lukin. The new arbitration act was worse than useless. Strikes had been broken but not prevented. Bruce's aim had been prevention, to spare industry loss from disruption of work.

164 See M. Dixson, 'The Timber Strike of 1929', in *H.S.*, *40*, May 1963: B. Fitzpatrick, *A Short History of the Australian Labor Movement*, Melbourne, 1944, pp. 153–71.

165 M. Dixson, 'Stubborn Resistance: the Northern New South Wales Miners' Lockout of 1929–30', in J. Iremonger, *et al.*, Eds., *Strikes: Studies in Twentieth Century Australian Social History*, Sydney, 1973: R. Gollan, *The Coalminers of New South Wales*, Melbourne, 1963, pp. 177–99: K. F. Walker, *Industrial Relations in Australia*, Cambridge, Mass., 1956.

By 1929 Bruce knew that Australia was facing difficulties with its overseas debt and that the problem was not just the size of the debt, nor the shortage of new money for further expansion, but the more pressing need for conversion of the alarmingly high and steadily mounting short term debt.[166] Earlier Bruce had arranged for a British Economic Mission to visit Australia ostensibly to study matters of mutual economic interest to Australia and Britain but in fact to examine Australia's 'fiscal and economic policies'. Perhaps he had counted on a reassuring report to be an open sesame to the financial world of the City of London, perhaps his intention had been to take advice from Mother England, but what he received, in January 1929, was criticism of nearly every aspect of the recent development and seemingly unsolicited advice that the system of arbitration had failed, that the practice of adjusting wages to cost of living was open to the 'gravest criticism' and that the faults of arbitration were intensified by the over-lapping of state and federal jurisdictions.[167] It was the latter that Bruce emphasized at the Premiers' conference in May when he issued an ultimatum to the states that either full industrial powers be transferred to the Commonwealth or the Commonwealth would withdraw from the field of arbitration.[168] There is no reason to conclude he was unduly influenced by British advice for equally he may have been trying to use that advice in a final attempt to induce the states to transfer to the Commonwealth the industrial powers which he had failed to secure by referendum in 1926. A week previously the premiers had met in Sydney and issued their ultimatum that the Commonwealth withdraw from arbitration.[169] Western Australia, the only surviving Labor government, had not attended. What lay behind the moves by Nationalist against Nationalist remains obscure. The burden of maintaining the peace fell on the states, and that of maintaining the unemployed. Perhaps the premiers had tired of policing troubles which seemed to originate in federal arbitration. But if Bruce hoped to bluff them into withdrawing in favour of the Commonwealth – and his increasing preoccupation with, and personal involvement in, industrial relations suggests he may have tried a bluff – he lost. In August, when the necessary legislation was introduced, a deceptively-named Maritime Industries bill which made special arrangements for maritime industries and repealed all other federal arbitration legislation, Hughes found the issue which could bring the

---

[166] See C. B. Schedvin, *Australia and the Great Depression*, Sydney, 1970.

[167] 'Report of the British Economic Mission', in *C.P.P.*, 1929, (2), *I*, p. 1231 ff.

[168] 'Report of the Conference of Commonwealth and State Ministers of 1929', in *C.P.P.*, 1929, (2), *I*, p. 1421.

[169] The Premiers excluded shipping and shearing; Bruce's legislation proposed that the federal parliament and government should retain responsibility for the maritime industries only. See 'Report of the Conference of Commonwealth and State Ministers of 1929', in *C.P.P.*, 1929, (2), *I*, p. 1421, and *C.P.D.*, 23 August 1929, *121*, pp. 280–91.

government down. Protesting against the dismantling of 'that temple of industrial legislation slowly and painfully reared by successive governments'[170] he rallied dissidents in the party against Bruce.[171] Not for the first time Hughes misrepresented what was at issue. It was not a question of scrapping arbitration, but of restoring to the states the full responsibility for the regulation of working conditions and wages which arbitration subsumed. Under state control, with Nationalists in power, wage regulation was unlikely to favour the workers. If Hughes hoped that Labor would forgive him for this last service to the workers, he reaped as he had sown. Not even those who turned on Bruce would accept Hughes as a leader. Bruce had made wage regulation the key to all the difficulties which beset his government's programme for development. All that he stood for politically was in eclipse. Neither that unlimited progress which he had promised nor the harmony between classes which he regarded as fundamental to a good society had resulted from his neat analysis of national needs and his persistent pursuit of right as he saw it. He was defeated in the House, defeated in the October election, defeated even in his own electorate.

[170] W. M. Hughes in *C.P.D.*, 5 September 1929, *121*, pp. 596–605.

[171] D. Carboch, 'The Fall of the Bruce-Page Government', in A. Wildavsky and D. Carboch, *Studies in Australian Politics*, Melbourne, 1958.

10

1930-39

J. R. Robertson

Population growth—the Great Depression—weaknesses in the economy—the employment situation in 1929-31—mass destitution —the battle of the plans—Scullin and Theodore—parliamentary situation—Scullin's early measures—the financial situation in 1930—the Melbourne Agreement—caucus crisis—East Sydney by-election—the Lang Plan—Lang defaults—the Senate obstructs— the Premiers' Plan of 1931—the fall of the Scullin government— the fall of Lang—political oddities—separation and secession movements—political longevity after the crisis—public works— political innovations—the Lyons government rehabilitates the economy—the rural industries—mining and manufacturing— motor vehicles—steel production—gross domestic product—political instability returns—Menzies appointed prime minister—the standard of living in the thirties—transport and communications—airways and railways—broadcasting—religion and education—the arts—popular culture—censorship and subversive tendencies—demographic pessimism—sport—foreign affairs— Manchuria—Abyssinia—trade diversion—Spain—the British shield—the threat from Japan—Munich—Czechoslovakia and Poland—war.

In the 1930s Australia's population growth rate was less than 1 per cent per annum, the lowest, by a significant margin, in the nation's history. For over a century the continent had excelled in providing the good life for the ordinary man and woman, so attracting a high rate of immigration from Britain and Europe. But in a few bleak years of economic catastrophe this trend was reversed; there was a net migration from Australia in the early 1930s. Only in 1936 was the old pattern beginning to re-establish itself, though very slowly. Over the decade Australia gained fewer than 20,000 settlers from Germany, Italy and Greece, and lost people to Britain. The birth rate, too, was the lowest in the country's history. Australia's population had increased by over one million in the 1920s but only rose half a million in the 1930s. This is often thought of as a 'mean' decade. Compared with others, it was; yet even the dismal thirties were not completely unproductive and not wholly without beneficial effects on Australia's subsequent development.

415

The 1930s take much of their character from the great depression. Unlike a war, a depression is a catastrophe of which beginning and end can never be pinpointed to the day nor, perhaps, even to the year. Not until 1930 did Australians who lived through it commonly talk of a 'depression'; nowadays many think of it as dating from 1929. In fact, it was in 1927 that unemployment began its unbroken rise to the peak of 1932, and in 1928 that the level of manufacturing activity in the eastern states began to decline. The economy reached its nadir in 1932–33. Thereafter things improved, though it is not easy to determine when the depression had run its course. Estimates of the gross national product show that it was not until 1938 that Australia significantly exceeded its pre-depression productivity, after the G.N.P. had fallen by over 25 per cent from 1928 to 1932. By another measure the depression could be said to have continued throughout the 1930s, for the rate of reported unemployment never fell below 8 per cent. By this indicator Australia at no stage of this decade matched the best years of the 1920s. Other economic indices give a different picture. By 1937 manufacturing output was running at a higher level than before the depression and building activity had regained pre-depression levels.[1] Throughout the decade the mining industry enjoyed much greater prosperity than in the 1920s. Though, with unemployment running at 25 per cent, Australia scarcely was out of the depression, 1933 was a significant turning point in the psychology of the nation. By then the economy was obviously improving. Australians were aware that the worst was over. Factory gates began to re-open, and the dole queues began to shorten. The great depression had made its impact on the Australian community. No experience so searing marred Australia's domestic history during the remainder of the 1930s.

Some indication can be given of the major weaknesses developing in the Australian economy during and after 1929.[2] First, the prices of her main exports fell. Wool had accounted for nearly one-half and wheat for nearly one-quarter of Australia's merchandise exports over the six-year period ending on 30 June 1929.[3] The average price for one pound of greasy wool fell from 20d. in 1927–8 to 9d. in 1931–2. Wheat fell from an average of 5s. 6d. a bushel in 1927–8 to 2s. 6d. in 1930–31. As well, a drought in 1929 led to smaller shipments of both

---

[1] N. G. Butlin, *Australian Domestic Product, Investment and Foreign Borrowing 1861–1938/39*, Cambridge, 1962, pp. 148–50, 168–70.

[2] For a general account of the depression see C. B. Schedvin, *Australia and the Great Depression: A Study of Economic Development and Policy in the 1920s and 1930s*, Sydney, 1970: E. R. Walker, *Australia in the World Depression*, London, 1933: D. B. Copland, *Australia in the World Crisis 1929–33*, Cambridge, 1934: W. R. Maclaurin, *Economic Planning in Australia 1929–1936*, London, 1937: L. F. Giblin, *The Growth of a Central Bank*, Melbourne, 1951. See also the articles in R. Cooksey, Ed., *The Great Depression in Australia*, Canberra, 1970, being No. 17 of *Labour History*.

[3] Excluding gold exports and invisible items such as earnings from insurance.

commodities. Under these influences the value of Australia's merchandise exports almost halved from 1928–9 to 1931–2.

For most of the 1920s Australia had been importing more than it exported. It had been financing this excess of imports and conducting a large public works programme by means of loans raised on the London market. In January 1929, shortly before Australian exports began to contract, the London money market's lending terms became too expensive to suit the Australian Loan Council. The in-flow of long-term loans came to an abrupt halt, quickly leading to a severe cut in public works expenditure, and accentuating Australia's external payments problem. In order to pay for imports, large quantities of gold were exported during 1929. If allowed to continue, this outflow of specie would have left Australia's supplies badly depleted, with serious implications for the internal monetary structure, because of the statutory provision requiring a minimum gold reserve equivalent to 25 per cent of the Commonwealth Bank note issue.

By November 1929 Australia's financial position in London, where she had run up large debts, was critical. There was doubt as to the country's ability to pay all its interest bills, and to redeem maturing loans. Particularly dangerous was that part of the external debt which was short-term, or floating, in the form of Treasury Bills or overdrafts. By the end of 1929 Australia's floating debt was £23m., a formidable sum. Much of the overdraft was with the Westminster Bank, which often put pressure on the commonwealth government to reduce its borrowings. During 1930 and 1931 commonwealth government Treasury Bills fell due every few months. They were renewed by London financial institutions, but only after frenzied appeals from an Australian government facing the threat of national insolvency. Late in 1929 another reason for apprehension lay in the fact that 1930 happened to be a year of abnormally high domestic loan maturities. In the event, the commonwealth government experienced no difficulty in having its internal conversion loans fully subscribed. Because opportunities for profitable investment in the private sector were so limited, maturing government bonds were readily renewed. Another danger facing public finance was the accumulated commonwealth government deficit, which by the end of 1929 had reached £5m. The state governments were experiencing somewhat similar budgetary difficulties. These deficits were to grow, and great argument was to rage over the manner of dealing with them.

Australia's economic prospects were held in low regard by financiers in London, as indicated by the downward trend in the price of commonwealth bonds. As well, the years of adverse trade balances had ended Australia's exchange parity with Britain. By the end of 1929 the Australian pound was worth less than the English pound in international commercial transactions. The drift continued, quickening during the summer of 1930–31, when the exchange rate fell to £A130 = £E100. In December 1931 the rate was stabilized at £A125 = £E100, which remained for almost thirty-six years.

Though some benefited, and others suffered little, for the Australian community generally the steady deterioration in the economy meant unemployment, or short-time employment, or lower wages.[4] Many wives and mothers aged rapidly because of the worry and hardship of the depression. The more fortunate householders who retained remunerative jobs did not escape personal contact with the depression, for disconsolate hawkers knocked at their doors, while beggars asked them for charity or work. At its peak the army of unemployed exceeded half a million, according to the most reliable estimates. For most men, a short period without a job was sufficiently unpleasant. Worse still was the fact that so many were unemployed for years at a time. The 1933 census revealed that as at 30 June about half the unemployed males had been without a job for over two years, about one in ten for four years or more. Particularly sad was the effect on school-leavers who had to wait years for their first job. Professional people, the self-employed and the small business-men suffered a cut in income. The landlord received less rent, the company director fewer fees and the shareholders lower dividends, or none at all. Apart from the unemployed, primary producers were the hardest hit, particularly wheat farmers. They changed their farming methods to cut expenses, replacing tractors with horses, and using less superphosphate. Boiled wheat and treacle, or 'cocky's joy', became an important food item. Despite the furore about their sacrifices, the old age and invalid pensioners were amongst the least hurt. In fact, until June 1931 they benefited, as they enjoyed a fixed income while prices were dropping. Then the pension was cut from £1 to 17s. 6d. a week, leaving the recipient no worse off than in 1929, in terms of purchasing power. At the outset of the depression the fall in commodity prices generally outstripped reductions in wage rates; a man who did a full week's work, receiving the minimum wage legally due to him, would probably have been better off in 1930 and 1931 than in 1928 or 1929. There is no means of knowing how many men were in this category. Almost certainly, the proportion was small.

Australia, the so-called 'working man's paradise', was almost completely without machinery to relieve mass destitution. Only Queensland had an unemployment insurance scheme, in operation since 1923. Other states had to devise emergency measures. Though it had obvious political and moral responsibilities, the commonwealth government had no clear constitutional obligation to participate in unemployment relief. Except in federal territory it did not set up its own machinery. Instead, it provided limited sums of money to the states, who organized their own aid schemes. There were some instances of private charity, the R.S.L. being notable for its well

4 See C. Forster, 'Australian Unemployment, 1900–1940', in *E.R.*, *XLI*, 95, September 1965. For contemporary documents on the economic and social aspects of the depression see L. J. Louis and I. Turner, Eds., *The Depression of the 1930s*, Melbourne, 1968: F. K. Crowley, *Modern Australia in Documents*, *I*, 1901–1939, Melbourne, 1973.

organized scheme, made available to all needy ex-servicemen or dependants. For the most part, however, agencies of the state governments controlled and administered assistance to the poor. New South Wales set up an Unemployment Relief Council, which gradually brought order to an initially confused distribution system. In all states the unemployed could be assisted through gifts of money, clothes, fuel or food; some were allotted a few hours' work at a time on a government relief project. Help was given only to those who could prove their poverty. To do this a man had to answer personal questions which further reduced his chances of retaining his self-respect. Having satisfied the authorities that he was destitute, a man was entitled to join one of the long dole queues which came to be an accustomed part of the Australian scene.

Many poverty-stricken families had to leave their homes, some having been forcibly ejected because they could not pay the rent. Sydney Domain became a refuge for hundreds of men, sleeping on benches or bare ground, wrapped in woollen garments or in newspapers. At various localities in the big cities there were shanty towns in which families lived in huts made of hessian and corrugated iron. Floors were sand, smoothed out and sometimes covered with bags. Conditions were unsanitary; myriads of insects swarmed; it was often hard to find fuel for cooking. Storms created havoc, demolishing shanties and leaving the surrounds a quagmire. Some men preferred to leave the city and go 'on the track' or else 'jump the rattler' to a country town. Some swagmen were accompanied by their wives. They did not have to travel far to come across a small shanty town where they could settle down for a few days, perhaps supplementing their diet with rabbits or fish from a nearby river, before being moved on by the police to the next town. In less harrowing ways the depression modified social patterns. Consumption of alcohol and tobacco fell. The crowds at race courses thinned out; attendances fell away at Melbourne football matches, some clubs finding themselves in financial difficulties. In some districts cricket declined considerably because men could no longer afford to play. Cinema audiences were almost halved, and patrons sat in cheaper seats. Because of the depression there were 30,000 fewer telephone subscribers and 50,000 fewer cars on the road.[5]

Many economists felt that a reduction in the size of the vast army of unemployed, and a lessening of the sum total of human misery, depended largely on factors beyond Australia's control, such as an improvement in world trade, particularly a rise in the prices of wool and wheat. Few, however, denied that the Australian government could and should adopt its own domestic anti-depression policy. The search for the most effective measures proved immensely difficult. As J. H. Scullin, prime minister during the worst of the depression, put it on 8 May 1931: it was necessary to 'balance budgets so as to restore

[5] See G. C. Bolton, *A Fine Country to Starve In*, Perth, 1972: A. Walker, *Coaltown, A Social History of Cessnock*, Melbourne, 1945.

confidence; restore confidence so as to provide employment; and provide employment so as to balance budgets'. The problem was to find the point at which to break the cycle.

A fierce controversy developed between proponents of rival plans for economic rehabilitation. Three inter-related issues dominated this argument. First, how great an effort should the seven Australian governments make to balance their budgets? Conservative financiers asserted that governments should live within their means, like private citizens. If receipts fell it was necessary to adjust expenditure accordingly. This would entail cuts in the salaries of public servants, reductions in pensions and other social service payments, and administrative economies, including retrenchments. Only, it was argued, by balancing their budgets would governments engender in the business community that confidence in public finance which was an essential prerequisite for an economic revival. Radicals strongly resisted such cuts. They claimed that the times justified governments running their budgets at a deficit for, they reasoned, to economize would be to reduce consumption and thereby accentuate the depression.

Second, how much use should be made of credit expansion? In practice, all significant sections of the community acquiesced in some loosening of credit to finance government deficits. Beyond that, there were violent disputes over the extent and form of credit expansion. Orthodox economists approved if it was limited and controlled by the Commonwealth Bank, taking the form of bank overdrafts and Treasury Bills. Radicals wanted much more extensive credit, by means of a special printing of banknotes, outside Commonwealth Bank control. The third issue aroused even more anger than the first two. Some men argued that, while in financial trouble, Australian governments should refuse to pay part of their overseas debts, by defaulting on interest payments. Conservatives and moderates maintained that Australia must meet all her debt commitments, because it would be both immoral and unwise not to do so; unwise because Australia, whose future development would depend heavily on external loan raisings, must maintain its reputation as a credit-worthy borrower.

During the onset of the depression the prime minister was James Henry Scullin, a slightly-built man of fifty-three years of age, the son of a Victorian railway worker and a devout Catholic.[6] His first forty-five years had been spent in and around Ballarat. In 1922 he moved to Melbourne, as member in the House of Representatives for Yarra, one of the safest Labor seats in the commonwealth. Six years later he

[6] For Scullin's government see J. R. Robertson, 'Scullin as Prime Minister: Seven Critical Decisions', in R. Cooksey, Ed., *The Great Depression in Australia*, Canberra, 1970: W. Denning, *Caucus Crisis: The Rise and Fall of the Scullin Government*, Parramatta, 1937: L. F. Crisp, *Ben Chifley*, London, 1961, chs. 5 and 6: L. F. Crisp, *The Australian Federal Labour Party*, London, 1955. For information on cabinets and legislation in this period see G. Sawer, *Australian Federal Politics and Law 1929–1949*, Melbourne, 1963.

was elected leader of his party, and in October 1929 he was sworn in as Australia's prime minister. He was to prove unequal to the task of coping with the depression. As a result, he has been adjudged weak. The verdict is rather unfair. Australia has produced stronger prime ministers, but it may be doubted whether any of them would have succeeded in the conditions of 1930–31. Scullin's hair turned white and his face became deeply lined during two years of grappling with a series of crises which would have baffled any man. From the beginning he was not politically well placed to cope with economic and financial problems. The elections held on 12 October 1929 were for the House of Representatives only, and resulted in a record majority for Labor. This was a mixed blessing, for an unwieldy parliamentary majority frequently proves an embarrassment to its leader, as it allows too much scope for the growth of factions. Labor's *raison d'être* was the improvement of the lot of the working man, the ordinary Australian. While a depression was raging it was impossible to move towards this objective, or even to maintain existing standards. Frustrated in this direction, the Labor party turned to internal quarrels over the extent of the sacrifice to be asked of certain under-privileged sections of the community, such as pensioners and those on the basic wage.

One disruptive influence within the Labor party lay in the person of the new treasurer, Edward Granville Theodore, a big and tough man, who was as effective an orator as his leader.[7] While he was premier of Queensland (1919–25) Theodore had participated in some questionable transactions involving mines at Mungana, in the north of the state. The non-Labor parties vowed that when they became the government they would institute a full inquiry into his dealings. Labor was defeated at the Queensland general election of 11 May 1929, and the new government honoured its promise; a royal commissioner began his inquiry on 30 April 1930. Theodore also threatened to be an embarrassment to the federal cabinet because, during the 1929 election campaign, he had promised that a Labor government would re-open, on the men's terms, the coalmines in the northern fields of New South Wales where for months the miners had been locked out by owners seeking to reduce the hewing rate. Moreover, Theodore had transferred to federal politics in 1927, not through a Queensland seat, but *via* the Sydney suburban seat of Dalley. In his new surroundings the able and ambitious man from the outback threatened the supremacy of the local strong man, Sydney-born and bred John Thomas Lang, a party boss at the head of a powerful, but brittle, political machine. Since his defeat in the 1927 New South Wales elections, Lang had been leader of the state opposition. He and Theodore were soon contesting the right to speak for the Labor movement in New South Wales. Lang's attacks on Theodore were to have their repercussions on federal cabinet. Much of the Scullin government's worries were caused by its being sucked into internecine party

7 See I. Young, *Theodore: His Life and Times*, Sydney, 1971.

strife in New South Wales. Besides these considerations, the fact that not one of Scullin's ministers had had any previous experience in federal office, and that one or two of them lacked ability, was of minor consequence.

Two other obstacles facing the Scullin government were especially important. In the Senate, half-elected in 1925 and half in 1928, seven members of the A.L.P. faced twenty-nine opponents. At first, it was assumed that it would only be a matter of time before Scullin resolved this situation by forcing the Senate to a double dissolution, as Cook had done in 1914. However, in the first few months of Scullin's prime ministership the Senate was not obstructive, though it became so when Labor lost ground in the electorate. From mid-1930, as the upper house began to wreck much of the government's legislative pro-gramme, there was increased speculation on the possibility of a double dissolution. Scullin often threatened this action, but never implemen-ted it. As Labor steadily declined in popularity it became increasingly likely that a double dissolution would result in Labor losing control of the lower as well as of the upper house. If Scullin had initiated steps for a dissolution immediately on winning the October 1929 election he would have had no better than an even chance of bringing both houses to the people in time to catch the electorate still in a mood favourable to Labor. It could be argued that it would have been better for both Scullin and the Labor party if they had fought an election in August 1930, and lost it, leaving the Nationalists to suffer the obloquy of failing to cope with the depression. However, Scullin felt that he could not patently shirk responsibility, because to do so would be to destroy Labor's credibility with the electors for years to come. The second obstacle was the chairman of the Commonwealth Bank Board, the elderly Sir Robert Gibson, a man of orthodox views on public finance. Under the Commonwealth Bank Act of 1924, Gibson was not required to take orders from the prime minister. He was answerable only to the Bank Board, which elected the chairman for annual terms.

Immediately after his appointment as prime minister, Scullin caused a stir by refusing to live in the prime minister's lodge. He then placed a ban on the export of merino rams, and began dismantling the scheme for assisting immigrants to sail from Britain. With other ministers, he expended much energy in vain efforts to honour Theodore's promise to the coalminers. In the autumn of 1930 he proceeded with legislation to alter the arbitration system, to amend the constitution, and to establish a genuine central bank. On the economic front he took Australia off the gold standard in December 1929, by prohibiting the export of gold except with government approval. A long-standing high protectionist, he placed great faith in plans to make Australia less dependent upon imports. Beginning with his schedule of 21 November 1929, he raised tariffs to an unprecedented level. In April 1930 he completely prohibited the import of some commodities. He tried to increase Australia's export earnings by successfully exhorting farmers to grow more wheat. As well, he raised income tax on companies and individuals and effected a number of small economies, such as stopping work on the War Memorial and abandoning the decennial census, due in 1931. The Defence Department also suffered through the abolition of compulsory military training, the removal of the Royal Military College from Duntroon to Sydney, and a reduction in the number of ships in the sea-going squadron.

By the winter of 1930 Scullin was forced to concede these measures had failed. Australia now obviously faced 'a financial depression without parallel in the thirty years' life of the Commonwealth'.[8] The state of the economy took nearly all of his attention. In June, he and the Bank of England agreed that Sir Otto Niemeyer should conduct an inquiry into Australia's public finances. Meanwhile, the federal government sustained more blows. At the beginning of June the coalminers were forced back to work on the owners' terms; some unionists were furious with Scullin for failing to honour Theodore's election promise. The Senate obstructed important government legislation. On 28 May it rejected the three bills to increase the constitutional power of the commonwealth parliament; on 4 July it defeated a bill to establish a compulsory wheat pool with a guaranteed price of 4s. a bushel; and it referred to a select committee Labor's proposed central banking scheme. On 9 July Theodore resigned from cabinet because the enquiry instituted by the Queensland government had cast grave doubt on his probity in the Mungana affair. Scullin took the treasury portfolio. A few hours after being sworn in he presented his budget, the professed aim of which was to balance revenue against expenditure for the financial year 1930–31. Government receipts were to be raised by still higher income and company taxes, as well as by increased postal charges, and through various innovations, most important of which was a sales tax, to be levied for the first time on 1 August 1930. By contemporary standards, this was a harsh budget, which added to Scullin's unpopularity. Moreover, conservative critics claimed that the budget would not balance, despite the higher taxes. They urged Scullin to reduce expenditure.

Early in August Scullin, with Theodore's concurrence, persuaded cabinet to renew Sir Robert Gibson's term as a director of the Commonwealth Bank Board, due to expire on 10 October 1930. After this became public knowledge Scullin's act was sharply criticized by trade unionists, on the ground that Gibson's policy was opposed to Labor's. Scullin justified himself by pointing out that Gibson, whatever his views, was more capable and experienced than any other man on the Board. He had the confidence of English financiers and his advice was needed in the delicate loan negotiations in which Australia was then engaged. Australia's credit in London would be harmed were Gibson not re-appointed. By refusing to renew Gibson's directorship, the government could have ended his chairmanship of the Board, but

---

8 *C.P.D.*, 9 July 1930, *125*, p. 3888.

it could not have nominated another man to the latter position; the chairman was selected by the directors from amongst themselves, and a majority of them were supporters of the Nationalist or Country parties.

Later in August the deepening financial crisis was analysed at a Premiers' Conference in Melbourne. Scullin, suffering from a bronchial cold and pleurisy, could not attend all its sessions; he even presided over one cabinet meeting from his sickbed. The premiers listened carefully to Sir Otto Niemeyer's views. He echoed Australian conservatives in advising that Australia's living standards had been pushed too high relative to her competitive position in world trade. Costs had to be lowered, and this meant wage reductions. The federal government's receipts were below Scullin's estimates of July, so that expenditure would have to be reduced in order to balance the budget. On this point Scullin professed to agree in principle. However, in practice he was not ready for cuts in pensions and public service salaries, because they would be extremely unpopular in most Labor circles. Nevertheless the government representatives at the Melbourne Conference agreed to try to balance their budgets, as well as to refrain from borrowing overseas and spending money on 'unreproductive' public works, a decision which was strongly attacked by trade union leaders and labour journalists.

Shortly after the meeting Scullin left Australia to attend the Imperial Conference in London, which was scheduled to meet in October 1930. He sailed from Fremantle on 25 August, and did not return until 6 January 1931. During his absence J. E. Fenton acted as prime minister and J. A. Lyons as treasurer. Scullin's decision to leave Australia at this stage was strongly criticized, but, on balance, was probably wise. Perhaps another minister, such as J. A. Lyons or Frank Brennan, could have deputized for Scullin in London, but the 1930 Imperial Conference held important constitutional and economic sessions at which Australia needed to be represented by its leader. Scullin also recovered his health, and took advantage of his visit to London to persuade King George V to accept the Australian-born Sir Isaac Isaacs as the next governor-general. However, he had left the commonwealth government's budgetary problems unresolved, and whilst overseas, his parliamentary party began to crack. Tensions which had been building up ever since the election were brought to breaking point by two events; the first was the New South Wales election campaign of September-October, and the second was the emergency sittings of federal parliament in November-December. At the poll on 25 October 1930 the New South Wales Nationalist premier, T. R. Bavin, who had advocated the economies proposed in the Melbourne Agreement, was soundly defeated by J. T. Lang, who had denounced them. Lang's victory embarrassed Scullin, and gave a great fillip to the radicals within the federal Labor caucus. On 30 October the federal parliament began special sittings to reduce the budget deficit. While caucus argued over what should be done, from London

Scullin gave what support he could to Fenton and Lyons, who were partly successful in their attempt to impose economies. The distant prime minister also helped force caucus radicals to drop proposals envisaging a form of repudiation and inflation of the note issue. But against his will the party appointed two Labor politicians to the High Court – H. V. Evatt and E. A. McTiernan.

When Scullin returned home his party was still nominally united. However, on 26 January he persuaded caucus to reinstate Theodore as treasurer, even though he had not been cleared of the Mungana charges, and this led to much dissension. As a back-bencher since July, Theodore had been very quiet in parliament, but active in caucus behind the scenes. He had played an influential role in guiding the party's radical section in opposition to the orthodox policies of Fenton and Lyons. Scullin's action in reinstating Lang's rival in the cabinet antagonized Lang and his supporters in the federal caucus; the reinstatement also offended Fenton and Lyons, who resigned their portfolios on 4 February 1931. Next day the member for East Sydney died; he represented a safe Labor electorate. The ensuing by-election meant that the differences within the Labor party over economic policy, and the power struggle between Theodore and Lang, were both brought to the hustings. Lang and the federal ministers fiercely contested the right to speak on behalf of their party in the by-election campaign, and this conflict was sharpened because it coincided with a Premiers' Conference in Canberra on the economic crisis. At the conference Theodore and Scullin presented a radical financial plan which Lang at first appeared ready to accept. But a weekend trip to Sydney convinced him that to approve of the federal government's scheme would be to compromise himself in the eyes of the East Sydney militants. He therefore needed to devise something more radical. In such a fashion was born the three-point Lang plan.[9] This plan proposed first, that Australian governments should pay no further interest to British bondholders until Britain had extended the same concessions to her Australian debtors as she herself had obtained from her creditors in the United States. The second proposal was to reduce to 3 per cent all interest payable on government loans held in Australia. The third proposal demanded that immediate steps be taken by the commonwealth government to abandon the gold standard in favour of 'a currency based upon the wealth of Australia, to be termed "the goods standard" '; this was a meaningless catchcry included for propaganda purposes, as Australia had been off the gold standard since 1929. For the most part Lang's plan did not commend itself to

[9] The rival plans for economic rehabilitation, together with other documents on economic policy, may be found in E. O. G. Shann and D. B. Copland, Eds., *The Battle of the Plans: Documents Relating to the Premiers' Conference, May 25th to June 11th 1931*, Sydney, 1931: E. O. G. Shann and D. B. Copland, Eds., *The Crisis in Australian Finance 1929 to 1931: Documents on Budgetary and Economic Policy*, Sydney, 1931.

economists, but it made good sense politically, and his organization won the fight to represent Labor in East Sydney; his candidate, E. J. Ward, won the election and entered the House of Representatives.

In Canberra, Scullin ruled that Ward could not sit in caucus, because he had not been elected on a federal Labor platform. But Ward's exclusion on 12 March 1931 provoked the secession of six other members of Scullin's party, who formed a separate group, led by J. A. Beasley, and owed allegiance to Lang. Next day the 'Lang Labor' group helped Scullin to defeat a no-confidence motion, when Fenton, Lyons and three other former Labor men voted with the Nationalists. From this time onwards the Beasley group held the balance of power in the House of Representatives. Its members all disliked Scullin, but disliked the Nationalists even more, and hence for the next eight months kept Scullin in office. On 27 March 1931 a special federal conference of the A.L.P. expelled Lang's New South Wales branch and then formed a new Labor party in that state. Meanwhile the Fenton-Lyons group had been moving steadily to the right, and in the autumn the Nationalist party merged with six former members of the A.L.P. to create the United Australia party (U.A.P.). On 7 May Lyons announced that he was leader of the newly-formed party. This completed the third political fusion amongst non-Labor politicians in federal politics.

The reinstatement of Theodore had thus led to the loss of both the right and the left wings of Scullin's party. This suggests that Scullin may have blundered in forcing his former treasurer upon a reluctant caucus. On the other hand, the alternative had serious disadvantages. To have retained the portfolio himself on a permanent basis would have imposed great strains on his health. Furthermore, Lyons had not wanted the job, and had admitted that he was no financial expert; and apparently no one else in the party was deemed to have sufficient ability. Despite all his handicaps, it is likely that Theodore was Labor's best man for the task. And his reinstatement might not have caused such disruption had it not been immediately followed by the East Sydney by-election, which forced Theodore and Lang into open conflict. In March Lang had added to the political turmoil by repudiating interest payments due on state loans raised in London. The federal government paid the amounts due, and then began legal proceedings to recover the sums from the New South Wales government. Many depositors in the Government Savings Bank of New South Wales then feared for the safety of their capital and interest, so long as Lang pursued these policies, and a run developed on the bank, reaching such dimensions that it was forced to close its doors on 23 April. In December, after lengthy negotiations, it was taken over by the Commonwealth Savings Bank.

Federal cabinet, reconstructed on 2 March, spent the ensuing three months pushing ahead with a radical financial scheme largely inspired by Theodore. Its lynch-pin was the Fiduciary Notes Bill, designed to expand the note issue by £18m.[10] Other bills sought to reduce government and private interest rates, and to ship gold to London as the only means of redeeming Treasury Bills falling due there on 30 June. Scullin must have realized that the Senate would not agree to these proposals. Possibly he espoused the tactic as window-dressing, in order to give his followers an impression that he was radically-inclined. But meanwhile, on 2 April 1931, Gibson had delivered an ultimatum; unless the seven Australian governments reduced their deficits he would not allow them any further short-term accommodation. On 17 April the Senate rejected the Fiduciary Notes Bill. On 13 May it defeated the gold shipment bill, after Sir Robert Gibson had been called to the Bar of the House. Many a time Scullin had announced he would not default. Now it seemed that he would be forced to do so, unless he came to terms with the opposition and the Commonwealth Bank Board by cutting expenditure.

The bargaining between government, opposition and the banks, with university economists as influential advisers, took place at a three weeks' Premiers' Conference, beginning in Melbourne on 25 May. From this emerged the Premiers' Plan, an agreement by all governments to reduce by 20 per cent 'all adjustable government expenditure as compared with the year ended 30 June 1930'. This meant cuts in pensions, other social services and civil servants' salaries. Also, there was to be an internal public debt conversion, bondholders having to accept a cut of $22\frac{1}{2}$ per cent in interest. As part of the bargain, the Senate passed a bill authorizing the shipment of £5m. worth of gold reserves to meet the maturing Treasury Bills. Professedly, the underlying principle of the Plan was 'equality of sacrifice'. The Premiers' Plan passed federal parliament with comfortable majorities. The opposition unanimously supported it. Two of Scullin's ministers opposed it, and so resigned. Half the parliamentary Labor party voted for it, half against, but the threatened permanent split did not eventuate. In the extra-parliamentary Labor movement there was much criticism of the federal cabinet for adopting the Premiers' Plan. On 18 June the federal executive approved of it by a narrow majority, reluctantly conceding that the only alternative was 'a Nationalist Ministry' which 'would be abhorrent to the workers and disastrous to the country'. At the end of August a special federal conference approved of Scullin's economies. At Labor's grass roots level the federal government had less success in selling the Plan. The Australasian Council of Trade Unions arranged an interstate campaign against it. Scullin's own Victorian state branch refused to support him. Lang signed the Plan and on some issues co-operated with Scullin;

---

[10] The average total note issue in 1931 was £50.2m., of which £25.2m. was in the hands of the public. This and other statistical information cited in this chapter came from relevant issues of *The Official Year Book of the Commonwealth of Australia* and the *Quarterly Summary of Australian Statistics*.

but he was slow to put the Plan into effect in New South Wales, and his supporters in federal parliament continued to denounce the government.

There were some bright patches amongst the gloom in the last months of 1931. Partly this was attributable to the Premiers' Plan, if only because the existence of a definite policy instilled some sense of purpose into the community. Government budget deficits, much lower than in 1930, were within the Plans' guidelines. The commonwealth began to benefit from the moratorium on certain inter-governmental debts, which had been suggested by President Hoover of the United States. Australia was now enjoying a favourable trade balance. The conversion loan was a resounding success. Promising, though short-lived, upturns in wool and wheat prices, a marked increase in gold production and good seasonal prospects helped restore a little confidence, reflected in a stock market rally early in November. On the other hand, the army of unemployed was growing, and the problem of the London floating debt had not been solved.

After the adoption of the Premiers' Plan some important differences remained between the federal government and the Bank Board. The government gradually forced a scaling down of bank interest rates on private transactions, so that by the end of the year they had been cut rather more than the rates on the public debt. The Bank Board, under government pressure, allowed credit of £3m. for wheatgrowers, which was used to provide a bounty on production in the 1931–2 season; but it would not grant credit of £5m. for unemployment relief works. Gibson's stubbornness provoked a major crisis in caucus in September. E. J. Holloway, who had resigned from cabinet in June, headed a demand that Scullin reintroduce the Fiduciary Notes Bill. For a time yet another split in the Labor party seemed inevitable. This crisis blew over, partly because Gibson relented slightly, granting some funds for the unemployed.

In November Lang decided that he would no longer keep Scullin's federal government in office. On the 25th his spokesman, Beasley, moved for a select committee or royal commission to investigate Theodore's alleged corruption in the distribution of unemployment relief funds in the Dalley electorate. Scullin accepted this as a question of confidence in his administration. The Beasley group crossed the floor to vote with the U.A.P., so defeating the government. Lang's motives are not clear. Perhaps he judged the time ripe to destroy Theodore. If so, his judgement was proved right. But perhaps he feared that some of Beasley's group might drift back to Scullin unless they were forestalled. The governor-general granted Scullin's request for a dissolution and, after a short campaign, a general election for both houses of parliament was held on 19 December 1931. This was a confused, multi-party affair, but from it emerged a triumphant Lyons, leading a party which held more than half the seats in the lower house. The Country party won sixteen seats, the federal Labor party only thirteen.[11] Lang Labor won four seats.[12] Within New South Wales state Labor had gained the upper hand in its bitter contest with federal Labor. Theodore lost Dalley, never to return to parliamentary politics. In Australia as a whole Scullin's followers fared better, polling over two and one-half times as many votes as Lang's.

Lyons was much more fortunate than Scullin in the timing of his entry into office. Though the depression was to get worse under Lyons before it got better, the shock of its impact would be linked with Scullin's name. The U.A.P. had every incentive to work together harmoniously, with the example of the Labor party fresh in its memory. One of Lyons' first problems was the inherited conflict with Lang. On 29 January 1932 the New South Wales premier again defaulted. The conservative elements in the federal cabinet were determined to deal harshly with him. Urged on by them, Lyons allowed the bondholders to go unpaid, so underlining the seriousness of Lang's action. Parliament was then called for a brief, emergency session to pass legislation which instituted a new procedure whereby the commonwealth could collect money from a defaulting state. Lang countered with increasingly controversial tactics. Finally, he directed state civil servants to handle public money in a manner contrary to that decreed by federal legislation. As a result, on 13 May 1932 he was dismissed by the state governor, Sir Philip Game, on the ground that he was behaving unconstitutionally. For a governor to dismiss a premier was an astounding act. Many feared serious disturbances would follow. Somewhat to their surprise, Lang stepped down quietly: possibly he was rather anxious to be relieved of the cares of office; probably he realized that he had manoeuvred himself into an impossible position.[13] He lost the ensuing election, fortunately for the governor. B. S. B. Stevens became head of a U.A.P.-Country party coalition ministry which undertook to pay the state's interest bills.

Though Lang lived for decades after his dismissal, and remained a member of state parliament until 1946, he never again held cabinet rank.[14] His hold on the New South Wales Labor party, so strong in the early and middle 1930s weakened thereafter. In 1939, after complicated manoeuvres in the inimitable Labor style, he was supplanted

---

[11] Plus the Northern Territory, the member for which did not have full voting rights. For statistics of state and federal elections see C. A. Hughes and B. D. Graham, *A Handbook of Australian Government and Politics 1890–1964*, Canberra, 1968.

[12] A fifth was added, at the expense of the U.A.P., at a by-election before parliament met.

[13] See I. Young, 'J. T. Lang and the Depression', in *L.H.*, 5, 1963: R. Cooksey, *Lang and Socialism: a Study in the Great Depression*, Canberra, 1971: B. Foott, *Dismissal of a Premier: The Philip Game Papers*, Sydney, 1968: J. T. Lang, *Why I Fight*, Sydney, 1934.

[14] He was elected M.H.R. for Reid, 1946–9.

as leader by W. J. McKell.[15] Probably no Australian politician has inspired such extremes of admiration and hatred as Lang. Many regarded him as a dangerous leftist. To be sure, he made many inflammatory remarks, but he was bitterly anti-Communist and had 'very little time ... for ... high sounding theories of social reform'.[16] In many of his less responsible actions he was not behaving as a leftist, but as a provincial 'states-righter'. He was quick to appeal to New South Wales sentiment, and to follow policies which paid scant regard to the interests of the other five states. By withdrawing from the Loan Council, by repudiating interest payments and by delay in applying the Premiers' Plan he set New South Wales apart from the rest of Australia, taking credit for the fact that his state was following an independent line.[17] Voting figures support the contention that Lang was not an all-Australian so much as a local phenomenon. At the 1931 federal election over 75 per cent of his votes came from Sydney and Newcastle. Outside New South Wales he was well known, but he failed to enlist widespread support. Lang Labor candidates never obtained more than 15 per cent of the Australian vote.

With Lang's fall a great depression phenomenon had run its course. Others, though less dramatic, were longer-lived. There was, for example, the Social Credit party whose policy was based on the writings of Major C. H. Douglas, an eccentric Englishman who held that poverty could be abolished if the state used and distributed its credit to equalize consumption and production.[18] Thirty-six Social Credit candidates stood in the 1934 federal elections, polling 4.69 per cent of the votes. Their significance halved at the next election and the party put up no candidates in 1940. Social Credit candidates only contested state elections in Queensland, and then only in 1935 and 1938. The Communist party first appeared at a federal election in 1931.[19] It received well under 1 per cent of the total votes cast, polling a little better in 1934 and 1937. The number of card-holding members of the party grew from about 300 in 1929 to 3000 in 1935, the rate of increase levelling off thereafter. During these years nothing came of various threats to suppress the movement. It formed or permeated some 'front' organizations which attracted wider support, such as the Friends of the Soviet Union and the Movement Against War and Fascism. Until

[15] See J. Jupp, *Australian Party Politics*, Melbourne, 2nd ed., 1968, p. 79.

[16] J. T. Lang, *The Great Bust: The Depression of the Thirties*, Sydney, 1962, p. 401.

[17] Lang's initial default did not mean that bondholders lost their interest, only that for a time other Australians paid New South Wales' bills.

[18] See J. McKellar, 'The Douglas Analysis of the Economic System', in *A.Q.*, *4*, 13, March 1932: B. Berzins, 'Douglas Credit and the A.L.P.', in R. Cooksey, Ed., *The Great Depression in Australia*, Canberra, 1970.

[19] See A. Davidson, *The Communist Party of Australia: A Short History*, Stanford, 1969.

December 1935 the party counted the A.L.P. amongst its enemies. But when the Communists switched to a 'united front' policy, the A.L.P. rejected their approaches. Early in the decade the party gained control of several trade unions, so beginning the strategy which led to its only real strength in the Australian community. By the end of the 1930s a significant contribution to this strength had resulted from the prestige of Communist leaders in some unions. The Nazi-Soviet Pact of 23 August 1939 threw the local party into confusion, some members resigning, others rationalizing Soviet policy.

At the opposite political extreme were the Sane Democracy League, the Soldiers and Citizens party, the Empire party and, in South Australia, the Emergency Committee. The Sydney-based All for Australia League, representative of 'the extreme Right Wing of respectable and law abiding conservatism' merged with the U.A.P. in the middle of 1932, after an independent existence of about eighteen months.[20] In February 1931 a more militant body appeared called the New Guard.[21] This was an extreme conservative answer to the supposed left-ward drift of the community. Formed on the initiative of eight Sydney businessmen, five of them ex-A.I.F., the strongly anti-Communist New Guard, led by Eric Campbell, aimed at assisting the police to maintain law and order in the event of social disturbance. For their part, the police were worried that disorder would result from the activities of the New Guard, as it organized itself on para-military lines throughout much of New South Wales. New Guards and Communists attacked each other at Sydney political meetings, but fortunately in a mild version of the type of disorder then occurring in other parts of the world. A great rally in Sydney Town Hall in July 1931 demonstrated the size of the New Guard's following. Its audacity was revealed when, before the baffled Lang's eyes, Captain de Groot's sword prematurely slashed the ribbon at the official opening of Sydney Harbour Bridge. This was its most celebrated *coup*; but its most splendid achievement was to defeat a bushfire at Cobar. The New Guard was short-lived. It faded away during 1933, many resigning because they objected to Campbell's dictatorial-style leadership.

Conservatives in country New South Wales who objected to Lang's attitude during the depression could adopt a programme barred to their city brethren: they could agitate for separation from the mother-state.[22] This was the stated aim of a movement in the Riverina, led by Charles Hardy, a Wagga Wagga timber merchant who in 1931

20 See T. Matthews, 'The All for Australia League' in R. Cooksey, Ed., *The Great Depression in Australia*, Canberra, 1970.

21 See E. Campbell, *The Rallying Point: My Story of the New Guard*, Melbourne, 1965: P. Mitchell, 'Australian Patriots: A Study of the New Guard', in *A.E.H.R.*, *IX*, 2, September 1969.

22 See U. Ellis, *The Country Party: A Political and Social History of the Party in New South Wales*, Melbourne, 1958, pp. 130–65, *passim*: D. H. Drummond, *Australia's Changing Constitution: No States or New States*, Sydney, 1943.

became a Country party senator. On the banks of the Murrumbidgee at Wagga Wagga on 28 February 1931 a crowd of 10,000 enthusiastically endorsed the aim of separating from New South Wales. Of somewhat more significance was the New England New State movement, given a new lease of life by the depression and the reaction against Lang. The movement drew up a constitution in April 1931 for the proposed state, and asked the commonwealth government to put the issue to a referendum. The commonwealth government refused but the state government appointed a royal commissioner, H. S. Nicholas, K.C., to consider a re-drawing of New South Wales' boundaries. In 1935 Nicholas suggested that the state be divided into three areas, each to express its opinion through a referendum. The government ignored the suggestion and, as economic conditions improved, the New State movement became quiescent. Some suspect that the fluctuations in its activities were partly attributable to the machinations of leading Country party parliamentarians, particularly Dr Page, who used it to his own advantage while in opposition, only to lose interest in it when he returned to office.

In the early 1930s Western Australia produced the only significant attempt to reverse the decision of 1901, with a proposal that the state leave the commonwealth.[23] Anti-federal sentiment had long existed in Western Australia. It had an emotional basis in, for example, antipathy to the remote, big cities of the east, and was nourished by federal policy which sometimes ran counter to Western Australian interests. Particularly was this so of Australia's policy of high protection for secondary industries. The federal government's aim of fostering the manufacturing component in Australia's economy was advisable from the viewpoint of the nation as a whole. But Western Australia saw itself hindered, not helped, by a policy which increased the burden on its primary industries, without the compensation of diversifying the state's economy, for it had little chance of establishing factories in the face of competition from the larger units in the east. Census figures showed that in 1901 the proportion of Western Australia's population engaged in manufacturing was about the national average; by 1933 a steady decline had made Western Australia the least industrialized of any state. The vulnerability of Western Australia's economy was amply demonstrated during the depression. Separatist sentiment was increased by Scullin's ever higher tariffs.

In May 1930 the Dominion League of Western Australia was formed, aiming at secession, the state to become a self-governing member of the British Commonwealth. The Country party was almost unanimous in favour of secession. The two other parties were divided, with the Nationalists on balance secessionist, and Labor anti-secessionist. The non-Labor Mitchell government agreed to a referendum,

[23] F. K. Crowley, *Australia's Western Third*, London, 1960, pp. 271–7: E. D. Watt, 'Secession in Western Australia', in *University Studies in Western Australian History*, 1958.

held on 8 April 1933, the day of the state general elections. Voting at the referendum was compulsory; at the elections it was not. By a two-to-one majority the electorate supported secession. The only significant area in favour of the *status quo* was the prosperous gold-mining belt. The newly-elected Labor government somewhat un-enthusiastically agreed to appoint a deputation, which asked the British parliament to give effect to the referendum vote by amending the Act which had created the federation of Australia. The delegates met the British authorities in November 1934; but in May 1935, a committee of the British parliament decided that Western Australia's petition was not proper to be received, so vindicating the long-expressed opinion of some of the state's best legal experts. The rejec-tion of the petition, aided by returning prosperity, killed secession. Grievances were allayed by the establishment in 1933 of the Common-wealth Grants Commission, with its recognition that Western Australia and the other two less populous states needed special consideration. The three-man commission received applications for financial assis-tance, and by 1939 had recommended grants totalling £14m. to South Australia, Tasmania and Western Australia.[24]

In their different ways, both Western Australia's secession and Lang's state-rightism could be regarded as having similar origins in the centrifugal tendencies at work in the Australian community. Both New South Wales and Western Australia were unhappy with Can-berra's management of their affairs. Because of its remoteness and political weakness, Western Australia could not hope to influence national policy to any significant extent, and so registered its dis-content by attempting to secede. Because of its geographical situation, New South Wales could not hope to secede, but its economic and political importance gave it the opportunity to go its own way within the federation, even to attempt to determine national policy.

The six years after the fall of Lang's government saw comparative political calm throughout Australia, a calm partly the result of the battering sustained by those parties which happened to be in office during the worst of the depression. In October 1931 each of the seven governments in Australia had been on the treasury benches for the preceding twelve months or more. Each was defeated when next it met the electors. On 11 June 1932 Lang's government was defeated in New South Wales, and a non-Labor government was defeated in adjoining Queensland.[25] Whichever party won the first contest after October 1931 enjoyed a long period in office, ranging from almost ten years in the Commonwealth and New South Wales, to over thirty years

24 J. A. Maxwell, 'Problems of the Commonwealth Grants Commission', in *E.R.*, *14*, 27, December 1938: A. H. Birch, *Federalism, Finance and Social Legislation in Canada, Australia and the United States*, Oxford, 1955, pp. 129–37.

25 However, on 9 May 1931 the McPhee Nationalist government of Tasmania had won a general election, being the only administration in Australia to achieve such a feat between November 1928 and September 1934.

in South Australia and Tasmania. In some cases, notably the Commonwealth, New South Wales and Victoria, the victors had their disagreements; but not until 1939 did political clamour begin to rival that of 1931. Stevens in New South Wales, Dunstan in Victoria, Forgan Smith in Queensland, Butler in South Australia, Willcock in Western Australia and Ogilvie in Tasmania each had a long, unbroken spell as premier. A like feat was accomplished in the federal parliament by Lyons, first as head of a solely U.A.P. government, and from November 1934 as leader of a U.A.P.-C.P. coalition. Though of limited ability, his qualities were what the times needed. Hard-working, honest, kindly, unadventurous, and a devoted family man, Lyons was more capable than any other contemporary federal politician of offering Australians a sense of security, a haven from the recent bewildering disasters.[26]

The work of the federal and state governments was very different from the social experimentation of pre-1914 administrations, nor was there any encouragement of land settlement on the 1920s pattern. 'Economy and careful management', Dunstan's self-expressed guidelines, seemed to apply to all other states. Net loan expenditure by the states on public works and services in the five years to 30 June 1939 was less than half that of the corresponding period to 30 June 1929. There were no additions, though some significant modifications, to the nation's railway network. The Sydney Harbour Bridge, begun in 1926, was duly opened in March 1932, but the planned city underground railway system was not completed during the decade. Expenditure on other public facilities, such as telegraph and telephone installations, and electricity undertakings, ran at levels well below those of the 1920s.[27]

On the other hand, loan funds, though smaller, were put to better use than during the 1920s. Ogilvie's administration intervened in Tasmania's economic life, devoting nearly 30 per cent of government revenue to developmental projects, including hydro-electric power and re-afforestation. The government of South Australia, whose economy had been particularly vulnerable to the fall in world prices for primary products, pursued a fairly successful policy of encouraging the growth of manufacturing industries within the state's boundaries.[28] In Queensland, where unemployment was lower than anywhere else in Australia, Forgan Smith was more venturesome than other premiers in using

---

[26] See P. R. Hart, 'Lyons: Labor Minister – Leader of the U.A.P.', in R. Cooksey, Ed., *The Great Depression in Australia*, Canberra, 1970. See also Enid Lyons, *So We Take Comfort*, London, 1965, pp. 184–277. The period of Lyons' administration is covered in G. Sawer, *Australian Federal Politics and Law 1929–1949*, Melbourne, 1963, chs. 2–4.

[27] N. G. Butlin, *Australian Domestic Product, Investment and Foreign Borrowing 1861–1938/39*, Cambridge, 1962, p. 391.

[28] T. J. Mitchell, 'J. W. Wainwright: The Industrialisation of South Australia, 1935–40', in *A.J.P.H.*, VIII, 1, May 1962.

public works programmes as a means of providing jobs. Various other state governments carried through important irrigation and drainage works, of lasting benefit to the country. The Hume Dam was completed in 1936.

There were a few political innovations. In 1933 voters at a referendum approved the New South Wales government's scheme replacing the nominated Legislative Council with one chosen by the Assembly and Council acting together as an electoral college. The same administration, although non-Labor, began replacing Sydney's private bus service by a government-owned monopoly.[29] Western Australia followed other parts of Australia by adopting compulsory voting in 1936. In the federal sphere several much-discussed plans proved still-born. Lyons proposed a constitutional amendment to confer upon the commonwealth parliament power to implement marketing schemes, free of any hindrance from section 92 of the constitution. He also sought power to control air transport. Both proposals were rejected at a referendum on 6 March 1937.[30] The role of government and private trading banks in economic planning was put before a royal commission, which insisted that the federal government must have ultimate control over monetary policy; but its far-reaching proposals were not adopted during the decade. In 1938 the government enacted a scheme for compulsory health and social service insurance on a contributory basis, but it was bedevilled by political disputes, and was never implemented.

The main concern of Australian governments after 1932 was that of rehabilitating the economy. Their initial response was to continue the policy of the Premiers' Plan, enforced a little more strictly. Thus Lyons made further reductions in public service, parliamentary and ministerial salaries, and in social service benefits. The former prime minister, S. M. Bruce, became a special minister in London in September 1932, where he began delicate negotiations aimed at reducing Australia's interest payments to British holders of Australian bonds. From 1932 to 1939 loans worth £22m. were converted in London on terms which, on the average, meant that the British investor accepted a cut of over 25 per cent in his interest receipts. By 1937 the annual savings consequently accruing to the federal treasury were over £4m.[31] Lyons reduced import duties, and removed various other restrictions which Scullin had placed on external trade. Some of these relaxations were in line with the Ottawa agreement, negotiated in July and August 1932 in an effort to increase trade between Empire countries.

29 See D. Aitkin, *The Colonel: A Political Biography of Sir Michael Bruxner*, Canberra, 1969, pp. 156-9, 180-88.

30 There is a useful analysis of the voting in *Round Table*, London, 27, June 1937, pp. 651-7.

31 *Official Year Book of the Commonwealth of Australia*, 1938, p. 898 and 1940, p. 875: C. Edwards, *Bruce of Melbourne: Man of Two Worlds*, London, 1965, pp. 213-22.

Australian producers of fruit, wine and butter welcomed the preferential treatment they were given in the British market. Labor criticized the agreement claiming, unfairly, that it sacrificed Australian secondary industries. The party also condemned Lyons' later and slight reductions in tariffs. Other critics, mainly in the Country party, denounced Lyons because he allowed some of Scullin's tariffs to remain.[32] In a gesture towards free trade the Lyons government negotiated treaties which slightly lowered trading barriers with Belgium, France and Czechoslovakia. These came into operation on 1 January 1937.

By November 1932 a steady excess of federal revenue over expenditure enabled Lyons to reduce some of the emergency depression taxes. This process was continued a year later under what its supporters hailed as the 'restoration' budget of 1933–4, for it also marked the first step along the return path to pre-1930 rates of government expenditure. Labor was furious with the ministry, however, because it allowed tax cuts to take precedence over restoration of pensions and public service salaries. It was equally incensed by the government's imposition in December 1933 of a tax on flour, in order to finance a subsidy to wheatgrowers.

In 1933 occurred the first fall in the numbers of workless since the onset of the depression. Australia now entered a five-year period of economic recovery. Unemployment fell steadily to 8 per cent in March 1938, which would have been a middling rate for the 1920s. Each year the commonwealth government easily balanced its budget, and the state governments reduced their deficits until, in 1937–8, the six state budgets, *en bloc*, virtually balanced, for the first time in the thirties. Although export prices did not regain pre-depression levels, from 1931 to 1939 Australia's external trade in 'visible' items continued to provide a healthy excess of exports, enabling overseas liabilities to be met with little trouble. Thereby Australia restored her credit on the London money market, but in fact it was not until 1938–9 that fresh funds were borrowed from that source. By 1935 share prices had returned to their pre-depression levels. Two more years elapsed before pensions were restored to the 1930 rate of £1 per week. Signs of increased economic activity were everywhere apparent, although revival was more marked in some sectors than in others.

The rural industries, which had suffered so much during the depression, did not fully recover their prosperity during the 1930s, agriculture showing less resilience than the pastoral industry. Average wheat production between 1933 and 1939 exceeded that of the 1920s. But lower prices meant the crop was worth less. Wheat's share of total export earnings tended to fall after 1932, and the area sown to wheat averaged about 13m. acres in the period 1935–40, compared with a planting of over 18m. acres in 1930–31. One of the main reasons for

---

[32] F. S. Alford, *The Greater Illusion: A Critical Review of Australia's Fiscal Policy*, Sydney, 1934: *Round Table*, London, *23*, September 1937, pp. 895–904.

the industry's sufferings was the accumulation of debts incurred by growers during the twenties. When prices fell more than half of the farmers' income had to be paid to creditors. Between 1929 and 1932 the four main wheat-producing states legislated for the relief of debt-burdened farmers. This, together with various forms of commonwealth government assistance, such as the 1931 bounty and the 1933 flour tax, merely alleviated the situation. In 1934 a royal commission on the Wheat, Flour and Bread Industries began its work, publishing five reports over the following two years. It recommended debt adjustments. The resulting commonwealth legislation, despite the high hopes it engendered, reduced growers' debts only marginally, by some 8 per cent. Of more benefit was the introduction by federal parliament in 1938 of a guaranteed home consumption price, initially fixed at 5s. 2d. a bushel. The industry also profited from the expansion of the bulk-handling system, at the instigation of the government in New South Wales and of the growers in Western Australia.[33]

The pastoral industry was in a less serious plight. Wool prices remained lower than during the 1920s but demand did not fall away so as to cause a great build-up of stocks. At times, such as the summer of 1933–4, the market was in sellers' favour. Sheep numbers remained fairly stable and production held up well, though there were seasonal fluctuations in the size of the clip. Wool, unlike wheat, did not need direct government assistance. Even so, by 1938–9, years of indifferent returns had caused growers' organizations, traditionally opposed to government intervention in marketing schemes, to flirt with the idea.[34] In Queensland, production in the heavily protected sugar industry steadily increased, until by the end of the decade it was almost twice the 1920s average. The dairying industry was hit hard in 1933 by the collapse of the British market for butter. Thereafter, recovery was hampered by the conservatism of many dairy farmers, who were slow to use new methods and new machinery which would have increased their efficiency. Despite constitutional difficulties, the commonwealth and states were able to implement a domestic butter price-stabilization scheme, in place of the Paterson Plan of 1926–34. Generally, the depression produced some long-term benefits to the agricultural industry by stimulating research and its application to practical farming.[35]

---

[33] L. F. Giblin, 'Farm Production and the Depression', in *E.R.*, XI, (Supplement), March 1935: K. O. Campbell, 'Australian Agricultural Production in the Depression', in *E.R.*, XX, 38, June 1944: E. Dunsdorfs, *The Australian Wheat-Growing Industry 1788–1948*, Melbourne, 1956, ch. 6.

[34] S. J. Butlin, *War Economy, 1939–1942*, Canberra, 1955, p. 61: R. C. Wilson, 'The Wool Market', in *A.Q.*, 27, September 1935.

[35] See R. S. Maynard, 'The Problems of the Dairying Industry', in *A.Q.*, 27, September 1935: S. M. Wadham, *Australian Farming, 1788–1965*, Melbourne, 1967, pp. 54–7.

Coal excepted, the mining industry, which had begun to pick up when the depression was at its worst, prospered during the 1930s, doubling the value of its production between 1931 and 1936. The improvement continued thereafter. Very few valuable new fields were found, but changed economic conditions made known deposits more profitable. Production of silver-lead, tin and copper all recovered quickly from the depression, to rival the 1920s in value, but the most spectacular advance was made in goldmining, particularly in Western Australia, where value of production increased seven-fold from 1930–40. A well-known machinery magnate and company promoter, Claude de Bernales, made a fortune from reviving abandoned gold mines in Western Australia, several of which weathered the collapse of his investment empire in 1939. Prospecting and employment in gold mines saved many families from lingering poverty.[36]

Contemporaries were impressed by the upsurge in manufacturing industry, particularly after 1934, when 'truly remarkable' progress was made.[37] The shock of the depression stimulated many industries into a drive for greater efficiency. At the same time the domestic market was made more secure by higher protective tariffs and by the temporary inability of Australians to pay for imports on the former scale. Import replacement, therefore, gathered pace during the decade. By 1939 Australia was manufacturing a whole range of products which ten years earlier had been imported. Increased munitions production was important. For example, manufacture began of 3.7 inch anti-aircraft guns. Some other new industries are worth particular mention. By the outbreak of the war, though nothing had come of plans to produce engines locally, significant advances had been made in the vehicle industry. Many chassis parts were made in Australia, while local assembling increased. Since the 1920s local assembly plants had been operated by the American enterprises, Ford and General Motors Corporation. The latter, in 1931, bought out Holden's Motor Bodies Ltd of Adelaide to form General Motors-Holden's Pty Ltd. Initial differences between Americans and Australians on its staff did not prevent its emergence as one of Australia's biggest industrial undertakings. In September 1936 it opened the first factory on the sandy wastes of Fishermen's Bend, two miles from Melbourne's G.P.O. At about the same time it began producing the utility, a type of vehicle peculiarly suited to Australian rural needs. In 1939 another American motor giant, Chrysler, decided to begin production in

36 G. Blainey, *The Rush That Never Ended: A History of Australia Mining*, Melbourne, 2nd edition, 1969, pp. 209–23: M. H. Ellis, *A Saga of Coal*, Sydney, 1969, pp. 204–9.

37 F. R. E. Mauldon and J. Polglaze, 'Australian Manufacturing in the Depression', in *E.R., VI*, (Supplement), March 1935. See F. G. Davidson, *The Industrialization of Australia*, 4th edition, Melbourne, 1969.

Australia. By this time practically all the motor bodies bought in Australia were locally made.[38]

Australian businessmen combined with the government to bring six companies into a consortium to form the Commonwealth Aircraft Corporation in October 1936, which established a factory at Fishermen's Bend where it began building the Wirraway, an advanced training aeroplane.[39] Increased manufacturing had a marked effect on the output of steel, which was one of the first commodities to feel the revival of demand after the depression. Production rose rapidly during the thirties to a volume three times that of the 1920s. Broken Hill Proprietary carried out important plant extensions at Newcastle in 1934 and 1935, and it was in this decade that it made Port Kembla an important steel centre; it had acquired an industrial monopoly in October 1935 by absorbing its only rival, Australian Iron and Steel Ltd. By 1939 B.H.P., enjoying unprecedented prosperity, had improved its efficiency so that it was producing steel as cheaply as anywhere else in the world.[40]

The swing to manufacturing should not be exaggerated. As was demonstrated in 1938, the economy was still vulncrable to fluctuations in the wheat and wool industries. During the 1930s the manufacturing share of the gross domestic product was only marginally greater than it had been during the 1920s.[41] From 1930 to 1939 the gross product of rural industries, excluding mining, exceeded that of the manufacturing sector by a substantial margin. Australia still made its way in the world by selling raw materials. In 1939 less than 5 per cent of export income was derived from the sale of manufactured goods. Of this fraction, over half comprised iron and steel products. Nevertheless these cautionary words should not obscure the fact that in the 1930s there was a turning point of significance in Australia's economic history. The manufacturing share of the national product was slowly increasing, reaching a record in 1938–9, whilst the share of the rural sector was diminishing, albeit with fluctuations. After 1932 recorded factory employment showed a rapid and unbroken rise, exceeding the twenties peak by 1935. In 1929 Australia's factory workers numbered 450,000, ten years later 560,000. They produced a wider range of products, they used more sophisticated machinery, and they possessed new skills. For all its limitations, the painful re-adjustment of the

38 For the motor industry see L. J. Hartnett, *Big Wheels and Little Wheels*, Melbourne, 1964: S. A. Cheney, *From Horse to Horsepower*, Adelaide, 1965: G. Maxcy, 'The Motor Industry', in A. Hunter, Ed., *The Economics of Australian Industry: Studies in Environment and Structure*, Melbourne, 1963.

39 See G. Odgers, *The Royal Australian Air Force*, Sydney, 1965, pp. 64–5.

40 See H. Hughes, *The Australian Iron and Steel Industry, 1848–1962*, Melbourne, 1964.

41 N. G. Butlin, *Australian Domestic Product, Investment and Foreign Borrowing, 1861–1938/39*, Cambridge, 1962, p. 13.

depression decade had created an industrial base which soon was to serve Australia well.

In 1938 lower wheat and wool prices and indifferent seasonal conditions caused a reduction in overall economic activity. Although output of manufactures increased, unemployment rose slightly and share prices drifted. Other features of the economy bore an uncomfortably close resemblance to the eve of the great depression. In February 1939 concern was expressed at the fall in Australia's London funds, and the possibility of imposing import licensing was discussed. An additional worry was derived from the heavy strain being put on the commonwealth budget by defence spending.

As if in sympathy with an ailing economy, politics entered a new phase of instability. In 1938 the ruling parties in south-east Australia began to be afflicted by internal dissension reminiscent of Labor's troubles in 1931. The Country party leader, Albert Dunstan, clashed with fellow Victorian, John McEwen, who had entered federal cabinet in 1937. In New South Wales personal jealousies and ambitions eventually led to the overthrow of Stevens in August 1939. Lyons, too, had to contend with factious men in his cabinet. Prominent amongst these was an ambitious Victorian in his mid-forties, Robert Gordon Menzies, who, after three years as a minister in Victoria, had entered federal cabinet in October 1934. In October 1938 he appealed for 'inspiring leadership' in the event of war in Europe, which his colleagues construed as an attack on Lyons. In March 1939, probably seeking to weaken Lyons' hold on the prime ministership, Menzies resigned both his portfolio and his deputy-leadership of the U.A.P. Then, on 7 April 1939, Lyons died suddenly, his death hastened by the strain of trying to keep together his discordant ministry.

The selection of his successor caused three weeks' most intense manoeuvring for position.[42] Earle Page, leader of the Country party and deputy to Lyons, succeeded as interim prime minister, until the major party in the coalition could choose its new leader. For this post an obvious contender was Menzies. His most significant potential rival, Charles Hawker, had been tragically killed in an air crash in October 1938; but others remained. R. G. Casey, then treasurer, had been singled out as a likely prime minister. W. M. Hughes, too, was in the running. Menzies had also to contend with the opposition of Page. At that time Page disliked Menzies, probably because he felt that Menzies had treated Lyons very poorly towards the end of his life. Page indicated that he would not serve under Menzies.

[42] This jockeying, and federal politics in 1939 generally, are well documented. See G. Fairbanks, 'Menzies Becomes Prime Minister, 1939', in *A.Q.*, *40*, *2*, June 1968: C. Edwards, *Bruce of Melbourne: Man of Two Worlds*, London, 1965, ch. 24: E. Page, *Truant Surgeon: The Inside Story of Forty Years of Australian Political Life*, Sydney, 1963, pp. 262–82: U. Ellis, *A History of the Australian Country Party*, Melbourne, 1963, pp. 236–49: K. Perkins, *Menzies: Last of the Queen's Men*, Adelaide, 1968, pp. 72–86: D. Pike, *Charles Hawker*, Melbourne, 1968.

In a last-minute bid to deny Menzies the leadership Page tried to induce Bruce, then High Commissioner in London and at the time in the United States, *en route* to Britain from Australia, to re-enter politics as prime minister. Though Lyons had made a similar proposal to Bruce a fortnight before he died, and though Casey supported Page, Page's action remains one of the most bizarre episodes in the commonwealth's political history. In response, Bruce set such impossible terms as to suggest that he had no desire to become prime minister. Most members of the U.A.P. resented Page's initiative. On 18 April they selected Menzies as their new leader, by a slim majority over Hughes.

Page was still determined to stop Menzies becoming prime minister. He became obsessed with the notion that he could do this by accusing Menzies of cowardice. In 1915 Menzies had resigned his commission in the Australian Military Forces, and had not served overseas. Page intended to use this incident in public support of his belief that Menzies was not fitted to lead his country when war, once again, seemed imminent. Horrified friends tried to dissuade Page, without success. Even an afternoon trip to the tranquillity of Brindabella Mountain failed to make him more clear-headed. Page, usually a shrewd politician, was temporarily ruled by a passion which completely upset his judgement. Next morning, 20 April, a shocked House heard his speech, in which he also touched on allegedly unsavoury episodes in Menzies' more recent career.[43] Menzies' reply was dignified, and he became prime minister. Far from destroying Menzies, Page, as his friends had foreseen, destroyed his own immediate prospects and damaged his party. Two of his followers resigned immediately. Six months later he was forced from the leadership of the party he had been largely instrumental in forming, and which he had led for nearly twenty years. He also wrecked the U.A.P.-C.P. coalition government for a year, though the Country party still voted with Menzies in the House.

The 1930s has been assessed as a mean decade. All things considered, it was far from glittering, paling by comparison with the obvious material advance in the 1920s. The depression checked for years the trend towards improved standards of living. Wage rates fell, so that from 1931 to 1936 the purchasing power of the earnings of an average employee on full-time steadily declined.[44] Yet these men were luckier than many of their fellows. In 1936, probably half of the thousands unemployed had been without a job for at least three years. In 1938 New South Wales' system of unemployment relief gave part-time employment to 19,000 men; yet this was the lowest number since the depression. They received half the basic wage. A greater number, less fortunate, were on the dole, the combined value of which equalled one-quarter of the basic wage, which had once been declared to be the

[43] *C.P.D.*, 20 April 1939, *159*, pp. 16–17. Menzies' reply is on p. 19.

[44] *Official Year Book of the Commonwealth of Australia*, 1942–43, p. 468.

minimum necessary for a man to live in a civilized community. Thus those on relief had been reduced to living in uncivilized conditions, a verdict which would have been supported by most who saw their shabby settlements. Till the outbreak of the war, 'bagmen' could be seen tramping country roads, rarely living in the comfort of a substantial building. Owing to that post-1914 'slump in alertness about social matters', noticed by the astute American scholar, C. H. Grattan, Australia's system of social services was no longer an example for the rest of the world to follow.[45] There was some talk of slum clearance in Sydney and Melbourne, and of a national housing policy aimed at improving living conditions for people on low wages, but little was done.[46] Expenditure on housing during the thirties was well below the level of the preceding decade. Little general awareness was shown of the Aborigines' plight, though the publication of works by S. D. Porteus and W. L. Warner, followed in 1938 by A. P. Elkin's *The Australian Aborigines*, pointed to the informed interest being taken in their social organization.[47]

For all its dreariness, the decade cannot be dismissed as one of complete stagnation.[48] Some honest, unspectacular groundwork was performed, laying the foundations which, in the forties, enabled the nation to play a sizeable part in defending itself against the threat of invasion. Material development did not come to a dead stop; the creative arts did not go into hibernation; even the average man's style of living was made more comfortable, albeit only at the end of the decade. By 1938 the average purchasing power of a fully-employed man had recovered sharply from 1936, to exceed pre-depression levels. An important breakthrough came in 1939, when the principle of paid annual leave was introduced into the award of a significant section of wage-earners, B.H.P.'s. iron-workers. Despite the setback of the early thirties, a few years later Australia's standard of living was one of the highest in the world, though behind that of New Zealand, Canada and the United States.

Amongst the most remarkable improvements during the 1930s were those in means of transport and communication.[49] Their significance was not confined to material benefits, having important repercussions on political and social life, and on the strengthening of Australia's

[45] C. H. Grattan, 'The Future of Australia', in *A.Q.*, X, 4, December 1938, p. 28: A. G. Colley, 'Unemployment Relief in New South Wales', and 'Living Conditions of the Unemployed', in *A.Q.*, XI, 2, June 1939.

[46] N. H. Dick, 'Housing and Slum Clearance in New South Wales', in *A.Q.*, 28, December 1935.

[47] See S. D. Porteus, *Psychology of a Primitive People*, London, 1931: W. L. Warner, *A Black Civilization*, New York, 1937.

[48] A sympathetic view of the late 1930s is given in R. M. Crawford, *An Australian Perspective*, Melbourne, 1960, pp. 68–70.

[49] See S. Brogden, *The History of Australian Aviation*, Melbourne, 1960: D. M. Hocking and C. P. Haddon-Cave, *Air Transport in Australia*, Sydney, 1951.

sense of community. The most spectacular progress was made in aviation. By 1930 most of the epic pioneering flights were over, but the public imagination was still fired by such exploits as that of Amy Johnson in 1930, who was the first woman to fly from England to Australia. Heroism was inseparable from early commercial flying, as both pilot and passenger risked their lives when, with the most rudimentary navigational aids, they took off on a long journey. During the twenties airlines relied heavily on subsidies from a government anxious to provide mail services for the outback districts and to foster aviation because of its military implications. The first unsubsidized regular air service opened on 1 January 1930, between Brisbane and Sydney. Thereafter, there was steady growth, despite the depression. By the mid-1930s airlines had proved their ability to operate services as regular as shipping lines. Route mileage quadrupled over the decade. By 1939 an extensive network embraced Australia, the eastern section being best served; navigational and safety aids had been installed by the Department of Civil Aviation. Mails were no longer more important air traffic than passengers; the decade saw more than a ten-fold increase in passenger-mileage.

Many airlines had come and gone. The most successful of those remaining was Australian National Airways, founded in 1936, being a merger of two of the leading airline firms; it subsequently took over Airlines of Australia Ltd, and by then had an Australia-wide network from Cairns to Perth. In 1931 R. M. Ansett had set up in the transport business, with a second-hand Studebaker which conveyed passengers by road between Ballarat and Hamilton in Western Victoria. In 1936 he founded Ansett Airways Pty Ltd and began regular air services between Hamilton and Melbourne; twenty years later Ansett Transport Industries Ltd absorbed Australian National Airways. During the 1930s C. A. Butler was building up his services in New South Wales. In 1938 E. J. Connellan surveyed the Northern Territory and the Kimberleys, preparatory to founding an airline which was still operating over thirty years later. Less happily, it was in the mid-thirties that Norman Brearley, Western Australia's leading aviation pioneer, had handed over West Australian Airways to Australian National Airways.

At about the same time regular air services were established between Australia and Britain. As an experiment, in 1931 air mail was carried between the two countries. The prize of the long-term contract provoked a 'bitter life and death struggle', in which the major contenders were West Australian Airways and Queensland and Northern Territory Aerial Services Ltd (QANTAS).[50] The latter won and, partnered by a British company, Imperial Airways, commenced Australia's first overseas air service in December 1934, Darwin being the point of entry: the service was weekly using land-based aircraft. By 1938 the air journey from London to Sydney took only nine or ten days, about

---

[50] See H. Fysh, *Qantas Rising*, Sydney, 1965, p. 223.

one-third the time taken by ship. International air travel had had little direct impact on the ordinary man, but it was beginning to modify the basis on which statesmen made their calculations. Scullin's trip to England in the summer of 1930–31 involved two months' travelling time. The course of Australia's political history might have been altered had he been able to board a plane for the journey. Australia's last substantial ministerial delegation to set off by sea was led by Page in 1938.[51]

Rail communications were also improved. In the early 1930s the summer rail trip from Perth to Adelaide was very hot and dusty. By the end of the decade air-conditioned coaches were in use, and a few hours had been clipped off travelling time. The completion in 1930 of a standard gauge track from Grafton to Brisbane, and the opening in 1937 of new lines between Port Augusta and Red Hill in South Australia reduced the changes of gauge between Brisbane and Perth from five to three. New South Wales, Victoria and South Australia improved facilities for long-distance passenger traffic. Most noteworthy was Victoria's Spirit of Progress, which began running in 1937. Unfortunately for railway finances, this improved system was meeting increasingly strong competition from road transport.

In April 1930 a wireless telephone link was opened between Australia and England, and in December a telephone service was inaugurated between Western Australia and the eastern states. For the first time a prime minister in Canberra could talk to a prime minister in London, and people in Sydney could talk to friends in Perth, without leaving home. Wireless broadcasting also developed very rapidly, and by the end of the thirties had become one of the important influences on Australian life. In 1932 the Australian Broadcasting Commission was established to take over Class A stations: Class B stations were operated by private enterprise and did not receive a share of revenue from listeners' licence fees.[52] By 1935 all states had been linked by landline or cable so that a programme originating in Sydney could be heard in Perth or Hobart. Scullin was the first prime minister to use the wireless for talks to the nation, a practice which helped bind his listeners more closely together in common awareness of the problems facing their government. Radio was first used extensively in a general election campaign in 1931.

In some fields, such as public health and medical practice, little of note happened, though Tasmania effected improvements in its health services. Education was little better, being short of both money and

---

51 E. Page, *Truant Surgeon: The Inside Story of Forty Years of Australian Political Life*, Sydney, 1963, p. 250.

52 See G. C. Bolton, *Dick Boyer*, Canberra, 1967, pp. 97–9: B. Tildesley, 'The Cinema and Broadcasting in Australia: Reports Presented to the Pan-Pacific Conference of Women, 1934', in *A.Q.*, *24*, December 1934.

ideas.[53] Syllabus, textbook and teaching methods scarcely changed, and universities were badly understaffed. In July 1930 teaching began at the University of Western Australia's new campus at Crawley, and in 1938 the first rural university was established at Armidale in northern New South Wales, but only a small proportion of Australia's population was thereby affected. In 1934 the Munn-Pitt survey underlined the deficiencies in Australia's libraries. In contrast to the previous decade, the 1930s did not see the appearance of any literary or scholarly journal of permanence.

Except that congregations were less well dressed and stipends lower, the Protestant churches were little affected by the depression. Clergymen were more anxious to denounce the traditional sins of gambling, drunkenness and sexual vice, than to expatiate on means of reducing unemployment. Some church gatherings seriously criticized an economic system which produced so many poor; and there were notable clerics, such as John S. Moyes, Anglican Bishop of Armidale, and E. H. Burgmann, Anglican Bishop of Goulburn who expressed deep concern over the depression. They could not enlist support in a crusade against poverty, and Burgmann denounced his church for its conservatism. Despite the humble origins of most of its adherents, and despite its distinctive social doctrine, the Catholic church differed little from the Protestants in its failure to come to grips with the unpleasant problem of a malfunctioning economic system. Michael Kelly, Archbishop of Sydney, was more given to proclaiming the folly of mixed marriages than to denouncing the injustices which forced men on to the dole. Some younger Catholics, probably out of compassion for the poor, advocated a more even distribution of property and the establishment of a co-operative commonwealth. By 1940 Catholic social thinking was becoming pre-occupied with the menace of communism. These years saw the emergence of Catholic Action, its monthly *Catholic Worker* beginning publication in January 1936 under the editorship of a young law student, B. A. Santamaria.[54]

If the crisis of the 1930s produced no great culture, at least the period can stand comparison with others. The novelists were in form, as is indicated by a list which includes Brian Penton's *Landtakers* and *Inheritors*, Christina Stead's *The Salzburg Tales*, Xavier Herbert's *Capricornia*, Leonard Mann's *Flesh in Armour*, together with titles by Kylie Tennant, Vance Palmer, Norman Lindsay, Frank Dalby Davison and Patrick White. Historical scholarship was of unprecedentedly high quality. This was also the most fruitful period of Australia's only

---

[53] See R. Goodman, *Secondary Education in Queensland: 1860–1960*, Canberra, 1968: A. Barcan, *A Short History of Education in New South Wales*, Sydney, 1965: D. Mossenson, *State Education in Western Australia: 1829–1960*, Perth, 1972: K. S. Cunningham, *et al.*, *Review of Education in Australia, 1938*, Melbourne, 1938.

[54] P. J. O'Farrell, *The Catholic Church in Australia: A Short History, 1788–1967*, Melbourne, 1968, pp. 260–64: J. G. Murtagh, *Australia: The Catholic Chapter*, Sydney, revised edition, 1959, pp. 173–8.

noteworthy essayist, Walter Murdoch. Apart from the work of Kenneth Slessor, little poetry of lasting merit was written in Australia during the 1930s; a noted poet, R. D. Fitzgerald, spent nearly all the decade in Fiji. In 1938 Rex Ingamells founded the Jindyworobak Club, stressing the need for Australian poets to write in the Australian idiom. Other writers shared his hope that a more vigorous nationalism might pervade Australian culture.[55] The art world was ruffled by a controversy between the traditionalists, who numbered R. G. Menzies among their spokesmen, and the modernists. The latter in 1938 founded the Contemporary Art Society – one of whose luminaries was H. V. Evatt. In the second half of 1939 an exhibition of paintings by overseas masters of the modern movement created great public interest and did much to influence Australian taste. Local artists did not react to the depression. Norman Lindsay notwithstanding, the decade's work was undistinguished compared with that of the forties.[56] In music the story was happier. The A.B.C.'s broadcasts of recorded music greatly heightened musical appreciation, whilst its establishment of symphony orchestras in the major cities brought an improvement in Australia's cultural life.[57]

Popular culture also substantially changed in character during the decade, the new technologies of radio and cinema making a big impact on the life of the ordinary man. Throughout the depression, sales of wireless sets forged ahead. It seems that the family man attached a high priority to a radio as offering some solace in dismal times. In the ten years till the war's outbreak the number of licensed wireless sets in use almost quadrupled; there is no way of estimating the number of home-manufactured crystal sets owned by schoolboys. Radio began to challenge the press as a disseminator of news, especially about cricket and sport generally, in an era that produced Donald Bradman, the batting machine, and Phar Lap, the wonder horse. The A.B.C. talks division raised critical standards, though one commentator deplored the Australian public's readiness to take its opinions 'from the new race of dons who frequent the national airwaves'. Commercial radio's influence was all pervasive.[58] Advertisers sponsored pro-grammes calculated to appeal to the largest possible audience, and the result was Australian-type serials of the Dad and Dave genre, 'soap operas' and variety shows, which were harmless enough, though they did nothing to raise cultural standards. In Sydney a young radio

[55] R. C. Ingamells, *Conditional Culture*, Adelaide, 1938: P. R. Stephensen, *The Foundations of Culture in Australia*, Sydney, 1936: J. K. Ewers, *The Great Australian Paradox*, Perth, 1939.

[56] B. W. Smith, *Australian Painting 1788–1960*, Melbourne, 1962.

[57] H. Bainton, *Remembered on Waking*, Sydney, 1960, p. 66: B. Tildesley, 'The Cinema and Broadcasting in Australia: Reports Presented to the Pan-Pacific Conference of Women, 1934', in *A.Q.*, 24, December 1934.

[58] See W. M. McNair, *Radio Advertising in Australia*, Sydney, 1937.

entertainer, Jack Davey, who arrived from New Zealand in 1931, was attracting a large following. Davey probably was foremost amongst those who used the new medium to add greatly to the average Australian's enjoyment of life.[59] Picture theatres flourished as silent films gave way to talkies. The American industry dominated the Australian scene, with British films a bad second. Few films from the European continent were screened; there was a flourishing local film industry.[60] America's output, though of indifferent quality, did cater for existing tastes. A weekly outing to the 'flicks' became an established routine for those thousands of families who could afford the expense. In fact, many poor people probably welcomed the cinema as a cheap means of escape from everyday tribulations. Films were seriously reducing support for the big commercial live theatres but, by way of compensation, this very process spurred the growth of amateur theatrical groups, specializing in more serious plays with limited box office appeal.[61]

The cinema and radio did not cause a fundamental change in community attitudes. Australia was still regarded by some as 'wowserland', even though its citizens were renowned for their strong language, their heavy beer drinking and their propensity to gamble, betting on horse races being facilitated by the wireless. Australian boastfulness impressed some visitors, while others saw no lessening in the national inferiority complex. To some critics Australia seemed an intolerant society, while others thought it as easy going as ever. The 'White Australia policy' remained 'the indispensable condition of every other Australian policy' though in 1934 a government mission to China led to an easing of restrictions applying to the eight thousand Chinese living in Australia.[62]

If a tightening of censorship is any guide, there was a slight move towards puritanism during the thirties. Films were censored more strictly than in other countries. Censorship of books became more severe, sometimes leading to controversy, as happened following the banning of Norman Lindsay's *Redheap* in 1930. By 1936 the list of banned books numbered about 5000. Most had been suppressed on grounds of indecency, a few because of the political opinions expressed. Huxley's *Brave New World* was banned for a few years, as were works by Lenin and Stalin.[63] The government's fear of 'subversive tendencies' also led to the celebrated case centring on Egon Kisch. Kisch, a Czechoslovakian and a Communist sympathiser, came to Australia to

59 L. Wright, *The Jack Davey Story*, Sydney, 1965.

60 See J. Baxter, *The Australian Cinema*, Sydney, 1970.

61 G. V. Portus, *Free, Compulsory and Secular*, Oxford, 1937, pp. 62–4.

62 W. K. Hancock, *Australia*, Sydney, 1945, p. 66: A. C. Palfreeman, *The Administration of the White Australia Policy*, Melbourne, 1967, pp. 8–9.

63 *Round Table*, London, June 1935, 25, pp. 614–17: S. Murray-Smith, 'Censorship and Literary Studies', in G. Dutton and M. Harris, Eds., *Australia's Censorship Crisis*, Melbourne, 1970: P. Coleman, *Obscenity, Blasphemy, Sedition: Censorship in Australia*, Brisbane, 1962.

address an anti-war congress in Melbourne in November 1934. The government tried, unsuccessfully, to use a dictation test in Gaelic to stop him landing. Though prevented from addressing the congress, he spoke at other meetings and attracted a great deal of attention. In this he was aided by his novel method of entering the country: he jumped from ship to wharf at Melbourne, fracturing his leg. A protracted legal battle ended with an embarrassed government agreeing to drop procedings and pay Kisch's court costs provided he left Australia promptly, which he did in March 1935. Despite the protests, a majority of the public supported the government's aim in denying Kisch freedom of expression.[64] In 1936 the dictation test was used to exclude an Englishwoman, Mrs M. Freer, on the ground that her entry might lead to the dissolution of 'a perfectly good Australian marriage'. After protests the government gave way and she was permitted to land in July 1937.

Understandably, the public mood was more pessimistic than it had been during the twenties. The refusal of the rest of the world to pay satisfactory prices for Australia's wool and wheat, and the country's unprecedented inability to provide the good life for all, raised a question mark over the nation's prospects. Some gloomily wondered whether Australia would be able to maintain its European civilization inviolate 'amidst Asian seas'. Those who decried the idea of trying to develop Australia's 'miserable tropic realm' received a favourable hearing: no attempt was made to use the north's resources.[65] Talk of abandoning Canberra was another manifestation of defeatism. Most indicative of the prevailing mood, however, was the discussion over the eventual size of Australia's population. Griffith Taylor, a geographer who had lived for years in Australia but who, during the 1930s occupied a chair in North America, affronted many by asserting that Australia would never be able to support more than sixty million people, and that only at living standards well below those enjoyed in Europe. Some economists and demographers were much less sanguine, holding that the Australian community would never be anything more than a handful of lonely people lost in a vast continent with limited natural resources. Many of them believed that Australia would not in future depart from her 1930s experience of a low birthrate and little, if any, gain from migration. It followed that Australia's population would only increase by a further million or two, a slow decline to begin about 1950, or in the 1970s according to other forecasters.[66] Undeterred by the pessimists, the Lyons government in April 1938

64 See E. E. Kisch, *Australian Landfall*, Melbourne, 1969: *Round Table*, London, March 1935, 25, 98, and June 1935, 25, 99.

65 W. W. Williams, 'Northern Australia: The Bogey of the Empty Spaces', in *A.Q.*, IX, 1, March 1937.

66 G. Taylor, *Australia: A Study of Warm Environments and their effect on British Settlements*, London, 1940, pp. 440–48: G. V. Portus, Ed., *What the Census Reveals*, Adelaide, 1936, pp. 1–54. See also F. W. Eggleston, *et al.*, Eds., *The

reinstituted the system of assisted passages for British migrants. Labor barely tolerated this resumption; it was strongly critical of 'wholesale migration from southern and central Europe as a menace to Australian standards of working and living'.[67] It really had little to fear. Net immigration in 1939 was less than 14,000 but this was easily the biggest intake of the decade. Over 3000 migrants came from Britain, nearly 5000 from Germany, most of them refugees from Nazi rule. The most serious affray between Australian-born and immigrants from southern Europe occurred in January 1934 in Kalgoorlie, several men being killed, scores injured and much property being damaged.[68]

Despite their tribulations, Australians did not become too despairing. Some geographers still envisaged a nation of two hundred million. Others, including experienced businessmen, enthused over Australia's grand destiny. Developmental projects were canvassed. In 1938 John Bradfield, the engineer who had prepared the general design of the Sydney Harbour Bridge and who supervised its construction, submitted to the Queensland government a report in which he advocated turning the waters of the coastal North Queensland rivers into the interior. An even more ambitious scheme to create a vast inland lake in Central Australia was being propounded by the popular author, Ion Idriess. Enthusiastic private citizens and calculating officials also considered a long-mooted plan to use the waters of the Snowy River for irrigation and power.[69]

Sport, a traditional area of Australian prowess, produced several champions. Kalgoorlie-born Walter Lindrum dominated world billiards, achieving most of his great feats during the 1930s. Though past his prime, Hubert Opperman was still capable of winning overseas cycling events. Australians occasionally won an Olympic gold medal, and two Wimbledon titles; Adrian Quist and John Bromwich won the Davis Cup for Australia on the eve of the war. In cricket, Australia was defeated only in the famous 'bodyline' tour of 1932–3. The champion batsman, Don Bradman, was at the peak of a career which spanned 1928–48, and Australians boasted of the latest feat of 'our Don'. Such men who helped to boost the national ego when it needed bolstering were assisted by a new generation of travellers, who saw the country through rose-coloured spectacles. In July 1930 Ernestine Hill, a journalist not ashamed to flaunt her patriotism, set off with her 'swag

---

Peopling of Australia, (Further Studies), Melbourne, 1933: W. G. K. Duncan and C. V. James, Eds., *The Future of Immigration into Australia and New Zealand*, Sydney, 1937.

[67] *Round Table*, London, December 1938, 29, p. 170.

[68] R. Gerritsen, 'The 1934 Kalgoorlie Riots: A Western Australian Crowd', in *University Studies in History*, 1969: G. Casey and E. Mayman, *The Mile that Midas Touched*, Adelaide, 1964, ch. 18.

[69] L. J. Hartnett, *Big Wheels and Little Wheels*, Melbourne, 1964, p. 105: I. L. Idriess, *The Great Boomerang*, Sydney, 1941: L. Wigmore, *Struggle for the Snowy*, London, 1968.

and typewriter to find what lay beyond the railway lines'. For years she journeyed through the sparsely inhabited outback. The book which resulted, *The Great Australian Loneliness,* ran through many editions in the ensuing thirty years. English visitors such as Arnold Haskell and Thomas Wood, settlers such as William Hatfield and native-born writers such as Paul McGuire, also wrote morale-boosting travel books which increased Australians' awareness of their own continent.[70] A sense of opportunity returned, dispelling the gloom generated by the depression.

During the 1930s Australian attitudes to foreign affairs underwent a dramatic reversal. In 1930–31 the public was too preoccupied with the depression to worry about disturbances in distant parts; but as the decade progressed international crises increasingly affected Australia, culminating in the outbreak of war on 3 September 1939. Throughout the thirties Australia hardly had an independent foreign policy, being a small, weak nation which relied upon a powerful Britain for protection. The relationship between the two countries was of a very special nature. Any doubts remaining as to Australia's constitutional independence of Britain were held to have been removed by the Statute of Westminster (1931); but this was not ratified by Australia until 1942, and throughout the thirties most Australian political leaders handled foreign affairs as if Britain had never enacted the Statute. Australia's relations with foreign countries were in the hands of the British Foreign Office. In 1934, two men in a nook of the prime minister's department constituted Australia's department of External Affairs. True, in the following year it was made a separate department with its own ministerial head; but only small additions were made to its staff, and when the decade ended Australia had no diplomatic mission in any foreign country. Such information as Canberra received on international relations came from British sources. The voice of Australia was not heard by the world's governments, save that of the United Kingdom, and British policy-makers took little notice of advice or criticism from Australia. The Australian proposal for a Pacific Pact, aired in federal parliament in August and September 1936, and placed before the 1937 Imperial Conference by Lyons, indicated a readiness to take the initiative in regional affairs; but the suggestion was killed almost as soon as it was made. Though significant as a pointer to the future, it hardly answered the complaint of some Australians: 'in practice Australian foreign policy is decided in London, not in Canberra'.[71]

[70] A. L. Haskell, *Dancing Round the World,* London, 1937: T. Wood, *Cobbers,* London, 1934: W. Hatfield (Ernest Chapman), *Australia Through the Windscreen,* Sydney, 1936: W. Hatfield, *I Find Australia,* London, 1937: P. McGuire, *Australian Journey,* London, 1939.

[71] W. Macmahon Ball, *Possible Peace,* Melbourne, 1936, p. 117. Much of the information in this section is taken from P. Hasluck, *The Government and The People, 1939–41,* Canberra, 1952, pp. 37–108: A. Watt, *The Evolution of Australian*

Despite the handicaps, there was an informed Australian opinion on foreign affairs, which assisted the subsequent growth of a more sophisticated system of external contacts. As the decade progressed, argument focused on the rise to power of the aggressive military dictatorships of Germany, Japan and Italy. Some attention was paid to a change of fundamental importance, the decline in Britain's strength east of Suez; but its implications were not properly debated, perhaps because they were too unpleasant to contemplate. By 1939 Australians were beginning to realise that their security might depend upon the friendship of the United States, but of this there was little formal recognition.

In October 1929 Scullin himself took the portfolio of External Affairs, allocating it only a small fraction of his time. Hating anything which savoured of militarism, his foreign policy centred on the desirability of universal disarmament. This suited a penurious treasury, and matched the stated professions of leaders in other English-speaking countries. On 31 October 1929 he announced the abolition of compulsory military training. The economies enforced throughout his administration bore heavily on the Defence Department. The Lyons government made further cuts, and by the beginning of 1933 the Australian defence system had reached its lowest point for twenty years. Defence and related issues were virtually ignored at the federal election campaigns of 1931 and 1934.

Even the opening in September 1931 of the Japanese offensive in Manchuria prompted no definite reaction from the Scullin government and awakened little interest in foreign affairs, outside a few small groups. Some opinion, such as the *Sydney Morning Herald*, supported Japan; others simply wished to keep out of the conflict. A left-wing Labor attitude was expressed by E. J. Ward, who demanded that in no circumstances should 'Australian lives be sacrificed in the event of a war for Chinese markets'.[72] Another group deplored the move as naked aggression and feared that the League of Nations' inability to restrain Japan seriously weakened that system of collective security upon which Australia's safety partly depended. Those who condemned Japan's actions were divided over its implications for Australia. Some thought Manchuria was the first victim in a list on which Australia appeared. Others hoped that Japan might become so embroiled with China as to prevent its southward advance. Nor was there general agreement that Japan's rise had swung the centre of gravity in global politics from Europe to the Pacific. Some thought that it had. However, in the winter of 1932 R. G. Casey, then a new recruit to the U.A.P. in federal parliament, could give an address on 'The International Situation' in which he did not mention Japan,

---

Foreign Policy 1938–1965, Cambridge, 1967, pp. 1–32: W. J. Hudson, Ed., *Towards a Foreign Policy: 1914–1941*, Melbourne, 1967. See also W. Levi, *Australia's Outlook on Asia*, Sydney, 1958.

72 *C.P.D.*, 14 October 1931, *132*, p. 709.

and in which he described 'the triangle formed by Britain, France and Germany' as 'the centre of the world'.[73]

The next major world crisis caused more anxiety in Australia. In October 1935 a series of incidents culminated in Italy invading Abyssinia. Attempts to restrain the aggressor brought to the fore the dilemma facing Australia and other peacefully-inclined nations. Initially, local opinion favoured Britain's support of the League of Nations against Italy. In September realization spread that this hard line might result in war. So the major political parties softened their attitude. The government applied sanctions which did Italy no harm. Even these mild admonitions were opposed by a Labor party frightened they might lead to war. As the Italian army conquered Abyssinia an Australian cabinet minister, W. M. Hughes, drew some unpalatable conclusions from the state of world tension. He wrote *Australia and War Today: The Price of Peace* 'to arouse the people of Australia to a realization of the danger to which this country is exposed through the utter inadequacy of its defences'. He added: 'In a world armed to the teeth or feverishly increasing its armaments Australia's defences are at a lower ebb than at any time during the last quarter of a century.'[74] The truth of this assertion did not alter the fact that it was a severe criticism of the government of which Hughes had been a member for a year. Lyons properly demanded his resignation, which took effect on 6 November 1935. Within four months Hughes was back in cabinet.

Shortly afterwards the Lyons government, in one of its few moves impinging on foreign policy, showed that it, too, was capable of contributing to world ill-will. On 22 May 1936 it announced its trade diversion policy, which in part flowed from the conservative tradition of cementing ties with Britain.[75] Its twin aims were to reduce the swelling torrent of Japanese textile imports, diverting the market to British exporters, and to lessen the intake of American motor vehicles, in order to promote their local manufacture by British-owned firms. The government defended its innovation with some confused reasoning, and fierce controversy developed, probably more active and informed outside parliament than within, where the three major parties were divided on the scheme's merits. Retaliation from both Japan and

[73] P. D. Phillips, 'The Far Eastern Situation: Some Aspects', in *A.Q.*, 20, December 1933: R. G. Casey, 'The International Situation', in *A.Q.*, 15, September 1932: F. M. Cutlack, *The Manchurian Arena; an Australian View of the Far Eastern Conflict*, Sydney, 1934.

[74] W. M. Hughes, *Australia and War Today: The Price of Peace*, Sydney, 1935, p. vi. For the change of attitudes by the New South Wales branch of the Labor party in August 1935 see E. Andrews, 'The *Labor Daily*'s Volte Face on the Abyssinian Crisis, 1935', in *Australian Outlook*, August 1965.

[75] J. Shepherd, *Australia's Interest and Policies in the Far East*, New York, 1939, pp. 43–66: H. Burton, 'The Trade Diversion Episode of the Thirties', in *Australian Outlook*, 22, 1, April 1968: I. M. Cumpston, 'The Australian-Japanese Dispute of the Nineteen Thirties', in *A.Q.*, 29, 2, June 1957.

the United States was prompt. As early as July 1936 the former forced Australia to begin negotiations, while by the end of the year America was enlisting British aid to end trade diversion. Early in 1937 many restrictions on commerce between Australia and Japan were removed, but quotas remained on the two most important commodities, wool and textiles, limiting shipments to pre-1936 levels. With America, the dispute formally came to an end on 1 February 1938. It seems that the government had harmed Australia's trading interests, for by 1938–9 Japan and the United States were exporting to Australia at roughly the pre-1936 rate, while taking much less Australian produce.

Probably most significant of all, the government had antagonized the two most powerful nations in the Pacific, scarcely a prudent policy when world disharmony was rapidly increasing.[76] Under Adolf Hitler Germany was rearming, in violation of the Versailles Treaty. In March 1936 it occupied the Rhineland. A year later S. H. Roberts, Professor of History at Sydney University, published *The House that Hitler Built*, in which he warned of 'the inevitability of war' unless Hitler modified his teachings.[77] Others suggested that Germany could be mollified by returning its former colonies, among them north-east New Guinea. Often discussed, this proposal found little support in Australia.[78] The outbreak of the Spanish Civil War in July 1936 increased Australia's interest in external affairs, though the very fact that the issue was so explosive inhibited full discussion. The Labor party divided into three.[79] Traditionalists objected to Australia having anything to do with distant quarrels; the Catholic component became greatly exercised, viewing the Republicans as a threat to the Catholic church, and so supporting Franco; the left-wing was anxious to see the Republicans win. Curtin, who in 1935 had succeeded Scullin as leader of the opposition, realized that one false step could split the party which he had been painstakingly reassembling after the depression fiasco. Accordingly, he was extremely reticent on the war. The government's policy was one of strict refusal 'to interfere in the internal disputes of any foreign country'. It appealed to Australians not to take sides. Lyons also realized that the war had wider, more dangerous, implications as German and Italian forces were assisting Franco, while the U.S.S.R. was helping the Republicans. The cabinet showed its impartiality in 1938 when it appropriated £3000 for the

---

[76] See E. M. Andrews, *Isolationism and Appeasement in Australia: Reactions to the European Crises, 1935–1939*, Canberra, 1970.

[77] S. H. Roberts, *The House That Hitler Built*, London, 1937, p. 363.

[78] *Round Table*, London, September 1936, *26*, pp. 848–50; September 1937, *27*, pp. 850–53; March 1939, *29*, p. 413.

[79] See J. A. McCallum, 'The Australian Labour Party', in *A.Q.*, *29*, March 1936: E. M. Andrews, 'Australian Labour and Foreign Policy, 1935–1939', in *L.H.*, *1*, November 1965.

relief of war victims of both sides. Some Australians joined the International Brigade, a few being killed in the fighting.[80]

From 1933 defence expenditure had been steadily growing, though it was not till 1937 that pre-depression levels were regained. Thereafter the upward trend was accelerated under pressure of events in Europe and Japan's further aggression in Asia. Foreign policy was one of the main issues at the 1937 federal election. Lyons stressed the importance of active co-operation with the United Kingdom, Curtin propounded Labor's isolationist views. Then, and at other times, there was some informed discussion on Britain's role in Australian defence. Some, principally among the government parties, held that the best way of maintaining peace and protecting Australia was by full co-operation with Britain. Others, mainly in the Labor party, preferred a more self-reliant policy. They perceived the hazards in too close a link with Britain, for thereby Australia would run the risk of being dragged into a European war, while there was growing doubt as to Britain's willingness and ability to aid an Australia threatened by invasion. Britain, commented the *Round Table* in December 1935, no longer ruled the waves. Faced with the threat of Hitler's Germany, could the United Kingdom divert any significant proportion of her resources to the Far East? 'No', answered many, including leaders of the armed services; and Britain did not allay these doubts at the 1937 Imperial Conference.

Towards the end of his life Lyons came to believe that in the event of war Australia could expect no help from the United Kingdom, though he did not express his fears in public. Menzies was another U.A.P. leader who partly perceived Britain's weakness, but apparently the full implications were so unpalatable that he shrank from facing them squarely. Australian defence policy still relied heavily on Britain for technical advice. In 1939 all three services were commanded by Englishmen. It has been argued that Australia was far too reluctant to assert its own interests in opposition to those of Britain.[81] The most tangible evidence of Britain's involvement in a defensive perimeter around Australia was the supposedly impregnable fortress at Singapore, officially opened on 14 February 1938. Some Japanese strategists respected its potential to protect Australia. Amongst Australians there were some military personnel who thought that Singapore was not well sited to protect Australia, particularly the east coast. Others feared that Britain would be too weak to send an effective fleet to Singapore, and without a powerful fleet, the famous base would rather lack its punch. In the public estimation, however, Singapore was the lynchpin of Australia's defence. Yet successive Australian governments scarcely lifted a finger to ensure that the base was equipped to fulfil

---

80 *Sydney Morning Herald*, 12 September 1936: *C.P.D., 151,* p. 57.

81 J. M. McCarthy, 'Australia and Imperial Defence: Co-operation and Conflict, 1918–1939', in *A.J.P.H., XVII,* 1, April 1971.

its allotted role. The whole question of Australia's defence relationship with Britain was intertwined with an important debate on the
respective merits of sea and air power. Pearce and Parkhill, Lyons'
first two defence ministers, desirous of maintaining close ties with
Britain, concentrated on building up the navy, the better to equip it
for its role as an adjunct to the Royal Navy. Those, such as Curtin,
who did not think the British connection would be of much use to
Australia in an emergency, wished to develop the air force as the
first line of defence. After 1933 the government spent more on the
navy than on either of the other two services, but by 1938 the air
force's share of the defence vote had increased greatly.

Australia's awareness of the decline in Britain's power east of Suez
was sufficient to prepare the ground for a more friendly attitude
towards its only possible alternative protector, the United States.[82] At
the beginning of the 1930s such relations as existed with that power
were not particularly cordial. The depression accentuated tensions, as
each nation followed a policy of economic autarchy. Australia was the
main offender, the trade diversion policy being only one of a series of
actions which offended United States trading interests. After 1936
relations improved, Australia taking the initiative. In 1937 F. Keith
Officer was appointed to the newly-created post of Australian Counsellor to the British embassy in Washington. After the end of trade
diversion it was decided, in 1939, that Australia's first legation to a
foreign country would be opened in Washington. These efforts at
friendliness had probably removed most of the ill-will engendered by
Australia's earlier policy, though they had not gone far towards
fashioning an alliance. Meanwhile, events in the Pacific suggested that
Australia would soon need a powerful friend.

In July 1937 hostilities between China and Japan entered a new
and more serious phase when Japanese troops fired on Chinese units
at the Marco Polo bridge near Peking. Thereafter Japanese armies
steadily penetrated further into China. This aggression, unlike that in
1931, was almost universally condemned in Australia. The government, however, was frightened into a reversal of its provocative policy
of 1936, and decided to do nothing which might offend Japan. It
scotched several attempts by various groups to impose private boycotts
on exports to Japan. Most celebrated was the refusal, in the summer
of 1938–9, of the watersiders at Port Kembla to load pig iron, saying
it might return in the form of Japanese bombs. The Lyons government
hoped to earn Japanese goodwill by dealing firmly with the Port
Kembla lumpers.[83] Still, in May 1938 it had annoyed Japan by

---

[82] On Australia's relations with the U.S.A. during the 1930s see R. A. Esthus,
From Enmity to Alliance: U.S.-Australian Relations, 1931–41, Melbourne, 1965.

[83] See L. Richardson, 'Dole Queue Patriots: The Port Kembla Pig-Iron Strike
of 1938', in J. Iremonger, *et al.*, Eds., *Strikes: Studies in Twentieth Century Australian Social History*, Sydney, 1973.

refusing to allow it to import iron ore from Yampi Sound in the north of Western Australia.

It may be doubted whether, at this stage, Japanese policy was likely to be influenced by Australian provocation, real or imagined. Many contended that it was only a matter of time before Japan would take the opportunity to strike south, with Australia her ultimate objective. That opportunity would come when war broke out in Europe, tying up Britain's military resources so that she would have none available to face Japan in the Pacific. If, or when, Japan struck, it was expected that Australia would fight her in Australia. Though some advocated the sending of an Australian battalion to Singapore, there were no plans to face the Japanese in Malaya or New Guinea, despite the latter's obvious strategic significance. The small regular army, essentially little different from its predecessor of 1914, was not trained in jungle fighting. Its envisaged role was to man the coastal forts at the outbreak of war, and await the invader.[84] Amateurs turned their hand to defence planning. Between 1935 and 1939 more books and pamphlets were written on this subject than in the previous thirty-four years of the Federation's history. Like the professionals, most of the armchair strategists described means of resisting a Japanese invasion of Australia. In 1939 the young W. C. Wentworth published a defence plan for Australia in case of a Japanese attack within the ensuing three years. He proposed very heavy expenditure on coastal batteries, and thoroughly described methods of repelling a Japanese advance in the 'Sydney Base Area'. The popular writer, Ion Idriess, though less detailed in his tactical and strategic planning for Australian regular and guerrilla forces, gave useful advice on how to make dugouts, how to dodge shell-fire and like matters.[85]

In 1938 it became increasingly apparent that Hitler would create in Europe the very conditions Japan desired. In March he occupied Austria; in April Lyons announced extra expenditure on defence. Five months later, as had been predicted by the Department of External Affairs, Hitler demanded that Czechoslovakia cede part of its territory, the Sudetenland, to Germany. He got his way after a diplomatic crisis culminating in the Munich agreement of 30 September 1938. Canberra's wish to avoid war was so intense that it urged Britain to persuade Czechoslovakia to offer the most generous concessions to Hitler.[86] Curtin, too, supported the Munich appeasement. In both country and cabinet a minority criticized the agreement. Hughes, by this time Minister for External Affairs, hated appeasing the Nazis,

---

[84] G. Long, *To Benghazi*, Canberra, 1952, p. 32.

[85] W. C. Wentworth, *Demand for Defence: Being a Plan to Keep Australia White and Free*, Sydney, 1939: I. L. Idriess, *Must Australia Fight?*, Sydney, 1939.

[86] A. Watt, 'Australia and the Munich Agreement: Underlying Assumptions and Operative Methods of Australian Foreign Policy (1938)', in *Australian Outlook, 17*, April 1963.

though he did not go so far as to resign his portfolio in protest. In November the government revealed how little reliance it placed on Munich as a guarantee of peace when it further increased spending on defence, to the highest level in Australia's peacetime history. The economy's capacity to produce munitions was expanded. Plans were laid to switch the workforce to a wartime footing. The Labor party in Tasmania even advocated the re-introduction of compulsory military training. Despite these preparations, the re-arming of Australia, by the winter of 1939, was running badly behind schedule.

The news from Europe became even more alarming. On 15 March 1939 Hitler seized the Czechoslovakian capital, Prague. Lyons' reaction mirrored that of the British prime minister. After a few days' delay Chamberlain abandoned appeasement. Instead, he gave guarantees to the eastern European states thought likely to be Hitler's next victims. Although Britain did not consult Australia before making this radical change in policy, Lyons promptly accepted it. Towards the end of March he declared his new belief that appeasement would not bring peace; security required that the aggressor nations be halted. These fine, resolute speeches were amongst Lyons' last political acts, for he died on 7 April 1939. In the contest for the vacant prime ministership Hughes, who regarded Hitler's occupation of Prague as final proof of the futility of appeasement, was narrowly defeated by Menzies, one of the warmest defenders of Munich, who still favoured reconciliation with Germany.

Events proved Hughes right. On 1 September German troops invaded Poland. Pursuant to her March guarantees, Britain declared war on Germany. On the evening of Sunday 3 September Australia entered the conflict. 'Great Britain has declared war', said the prime minister, and 'as a result, Australia is also at war'. These carefully chosen words were wholly consistent with Menzies' attitude in a long-standing controversy over Australia's right to decide for herself whether she could opt out of a war involving Britain. Little exception was taken to Menzies' terminology, because its constitutional implications were swamped in the wider issues of policy. Some might want Australia to frame its own foreign policy; others might have been increasingly aware that distance prevented their national objectives from coinciding with Britain's; but when the question arose of resisting a dictator's military aggression, Australians were still in heart and mind very close

II

1939-51

G. C. Bolton

Review of period—economic planning for the war—secondary industry—the situation in federal politics—the second A.I.F. in action—Menzies resigns—Curtin leads a Labor government—Japan attacks—organizing a total war effort—the American alliance—The Battle in the Coral Sea—overseas military service—American influences on Australia—Australia's new foreign policy —the role of Evatt—Australia and the United Nations—Australia and Japan—India—Indonesia—the Cold War—federal-state financial relations—Labor and the elections of 1943—the 1944 referendum—full employment—dual enterprises—the role of the Commonwealth Bank—rehabilitation—formation of the Liberal party—social services of the Chifley government—post-war immigration policy—contributions of immigrants—a cultural cause celebre—intellectual trends—the media—the primary industries—wool—mineral industries—manufacturing and building —Snowy Mountains Scheme—international trade—the Commonwealth—bank nationalization—communism and communists—industrial unrest—'the Movement'—the 1949 election—economic and social policies of the Menzies government—the aborigines—foreign policy—the Korean War—the ANZUS treaty—compulsory military training—attempts to ban the Communist party —the 1951 double dissolution—inflation—the Australian Federal Jubilee.

War is a powerful agent of social change, yet few seem to have understood at the time the great social, economic, and political changes that would come of Australia's participation in the Second World War. In part this was because the changes were not sudden, and took place within the existing framework of Australian society and institutions. Moreover, the changes were often launched by people who did not fully understand the implications of what they were doing. Even in the post-war years after 1945 the immediate attention of most politicians was fixed on solving problems or continuing arguments or promoting developments which concerned Australians during the depression years of the 1930s. Yet in the years between the outbreak of the Second World War in 1939 and the formal signing of peace with

Japan in 1951 three stages in an accelerating process of change can be noted. The first two years of the war, from September 1939 to December 1941, were in many ways a re-run of the experiences of the First World War. Military campaigning took place in the same distant Mediterranean theatres, and although the war effort was gradually tooled up, life on the home front was not unlike peace-time, only more prosperous. This phase ended when Japan entered the war in December 1941. From then until August 1945 was the period of maximum war effort, when the Australian government was able to command unusually great powers in mobilizing the human and economic resources of the nation, and so to set precedents which might be applied to peace-time uses. And from then until 1951 came the period of post-war reconstruction, when the great debate in politics was over objectives. Was Australia's first priority to seek security for all through government planning, or to create the best conditions for private enterprise to generate economic growth? This debate was more apparent than real, since nearly all politicians were in agreement about the basic requirements for controlling and developing the Australian economy. The really important decisions of the 1945–51 period were taken in the fields of social planning and to a lesser extent foreign policy. Here it was that Australians committed themselves to new departures in the future.

Australian dependence on precedent and the experience of the past was strongly in evidence when the Australian government took the view on 3 September 1939, that as Britain was at war, so also was Australia. Nor was there much to show that official thinking on war planning had advanced beyond the lessons of the First World War. Even some of the individuals concerned were the same. W. M. Hughes was once more attorney-general responsible for war legislation, and General Brudenell White was Chief of the General Staff of the Australian Military Forces. The 'citizen army' tradition still prevailed, and compulsory military training was re-introduced for home defence. Few adequate preparations had been made for putting the economy on a wartime basis, and where clear guidelines existed, they were founded mainly on British precedent or on the experience of the war of 1914–18.[1] The Australian government was too insecure to run far ahead of public opinion in planning the wartime economy, and its attempts to set up a Canberra-centred 'economic cabinet' were half-hearted and ineffectual. Several important steps were taken, nevertheless. In August 1939 the Commonwealth Bank was authorized to control foreign exchange. In December, faced by a deteriorating balance of payments, the government brought in import licensing. The Wheat Board was empowered to acquire and market the Australian crop, and although over-production continued to worry growers for some months, it soon became apparent that the war would increase

[1] S. J. Butlin, *War Economy: 1939–1942*, Canberra, 1955, pp. 24–5: P. Hasluck, *The Government and the People: 1939–1941*, Canberra, 1952, ch. 3.

demand. At the same time an agreement similar to the BAWRA agreement of the First World War ensured that Britain would be the purchaser of the entire Australian wool clip at an agreed price for the duration of the war. The governments of the states were empowered to impose rent control, but this did not entirely stamp out such practices as illicit sub-letting and demands for 'key money'. To protect consumers, a federal system of price control was set up. This checked, but could not entirely halt profiteering or legitimate price rises because of wartime shortages. Between September 1939 and June 1942 the Australian price index rose by 18 per cent.

Wage increases and falling unemployment blunted the impact of rising prices. The war soon boosted secondary industry. With much of Europe under Nazi control, Britain embattled, and the sealanes hazardous, Australia was cut off from many of her usual sources of imported manufactures. Local alternatives had to be built up quickly. This was not always easy, because the depressed 1930s left Australia with a shortage of skilled manpower. On the other hand, at the cost of some hardship to consumers, the high tariff policy of the pre-war years had built up Australian manufacturing industries, most of which weathered the depression, and Australia entered the war with a healthy iron and steel industry, and with foundations laid for the production of munitions and light aircraft. Shipbuilding was also encouraged: from 1940 Whyalla in South Australia became a centre for this industry. Much was achieved by the Department of Munitions, set up in 1940 under a director-general, the veteran industrialist, Essington Lewis, who before the war had seen the need to prepare for a demand for munitions.[2] The production of machine tools, armaments, drugs, and chemicals made great strides. New industrial complexes came into being which could later be converted for peace-time uses. Australian industry began to gain an experience, confidence, and technical knowledge which would provide a firm basis for expansion and diversification after the war.

Politically the break with pre-war attitudes came more slowly. Federal politicians kept up their old zest for feuding as if there was no war. Early in 1940 the Lang faction split once again from the main body of the A.L.P. The government parties were equally rent with squabbles, even after the Country party rejoined the Menzies government in 1940 and found a new leader in the down-to-earth Queenslander, Arthur Fadden.[3] Nor was the Australian public ready for wartime sacrifices. In August 1940 the government announced its intention of introducing petrol rationing, at a time when Britain's survival depended on a narrow margin of merchant seapower. Interested pressure-groups at once mounted a campaign of newspaper advertisements against this move, and this may have contributed to

[2] See G. Blainey, *The Steel Master: A Life of Essington Lewis*, Melbourne, 1971.

[3] See A. W. Fadden, *They Called Me Artie*, Brisbane, 1969.

the Menzies government's loss of support at the elections in September. The government coalition and the Labor opposition each emerged with thirty-six members in the House of Representatives, so that the survival of the Menzies government depended on the support of two independents. The government was further weakened by losing three experienced cabinet ministers in an aircraft crash shortly before the election; it was hardly a compensation that one or two of its least competent ministers were defeated at the polls. After this rebuff the government confined itself during the next few months to minor initiatives on the home front, such as the harassment of Communists and Jehovah's Witnesses, two fringe groups which for widely different reasons withheld support from the war effort. Menzies, often stung to his most constructive efforts by adversity, tried to win back public support by extending social services. The national insurance scheme about which he had made such an issue in 1939 was never revived, then or later. But early in 1941 his government introduced a federal scheme for child endowment.

Menzies nevertheless failed to gain ground. He was away from Australia a good deal of the time, too much for the good of his contact with the mood of the nation or his own back-benchers. He saw Australia's international role much as it had been during the First World War; as one of close consultation with Britain, with provision for Dominion prime ministers such as himself to sit in the British war cabinet. Australia, according to this view, could exercise greater influence as the respected consultant of the Mother Country than through any wayward and overweening aspirations to blow her own trumpet. 'I am one of those old-fashioned Australian politicians,' Menzies wrote later, 'who think that our nation's foreign policy should not be aimed at noisy demonstration or assertion. A little man waving a big stick is not only faintly absurd, but liable to lose his balance.'[4] Menzies also hoped that Australia would have a wartime coalition government, like Britain in 1915 and 1940, but the Labor party consistently refused his overtures, although its leaders consented to join an all-party Advisory War Council set up in October 1940. On the war front Australia's role was seen as that of an auxiliary, providing troops and warships to fight battles for her allies on fronts far removed from her own shores. It was assumed that, as during the First World War, the main fight for freedom would be waged in Europe, and that it was in Australia's interests to prove herself a staunch ally, deserving of Britain's shield, by taking part wholeheartedly even when her own shores were not in immediate danger.

Given these assumptions, the first call was for recruits to the A.I.F.

[4] R. G. Menzies, *The Measure of the Years*, Melbourne, 1970, p. 44. For his account of the 1939–41 period see R. G. Menzies, *Afternoon Light*, Melbourne, 1967, ch. 3. Menzies produced a good impression on the upper-class Englishmen who met him at that time; see for instance, Sir H. Nicolson, *Diaries and Letters, Vol. 2, 1939–45*, London, 1967, and R. R. James, Ed., *Chips: The Diaries of Sir Henry Channon*, London, 1967.

to form the Sixth and Seventh Divisions for training in Palestine.[5] There was no lack of volunteers. Some cynically explained this by reference to the high unemployment rate of 1939, but there can be no doubt that, among a generation brought up at school and at home to the Anzac traditions of their fathers, there were many who thought enlistment an inescapable patriotic duty.[6] Few saw action until the fall of France and Italy's entry into the war on Germany's side in June 1940. Later that year Australians played a prominent part in Wavell's push out of Egypt against the Italians in Libya, and early in 1941 had the satisfaction of chasing their enemy west beyond Benghazi. The Royal Australian Navy, comprising four cruisers and several destroyers, also scored triumphs in the Mediterranean. The cruiser *Sydney* sank the *Bartolomeo Colleoni* in July 1940, and in March 1941 the elderly destroyer *Stuart* figured gloriously in a combined action against a numerically superior Italian force off Cape Matapan. But early in 1941 fortunes shifted against the Allies in North Africa. In March the arrival of Rommel's *Afrika Korps* toughened the opposition, and at the same time the Allied forces were called to other fronts. Since November 1940 Italy and Greece had been at war along the Albanian border; when the Germans invaded Greece and Yugoslavia on 6 April 1941, the Australians were among the reinforcements thrown in to stem the advance. Against German superiority in armour the task was hopeless. After evacuating Greece the Australians and other British Commonwealth units were forced out of Crete in May. Meanwhile, Australian forces were among those in action against the pro-German French in Syria, a campaign which ended in Allied victory. During these important campaigns the Germans and Italians in Libya launched a counter-attack, hustling the Allies back across the Egyptian border. The only Allied outpost left in Libya was a besieged garrison in the port of Tobruk, soon famed as the 'Rats'. As many as two-thirds were Australians.

These battles awoke most Australians to a more lively sense of danger, increased after June 1941 by Hitler's advance into Russia, and confirmed by Japan's increasing belligerence. This led Australia to commit its Eighth Division to garrisoning Malaya. On the home front air raid precautions were improved – the first blackout tests were in July 1941 – and a payroll tax was introduced. Intended originally to raise extra finance for the war, it was to prove too useful a source of revenue for later governments to discard in time of peace. No sense of emergency showed itself among the squabbling politicians of Canberra. Within the United Australia party intrigues continued against Menzies until at the end of August 1941 he resigned the prime ministership. He was replaced by Fadden, the Country party leader; a few weeks later the seventy-nine-year-old W. M. Hughes became

5 See G. Long, *To Benghazi*, Canberra, 1952, chs. 2–3.

6 G. Johnston, *My Brother Jack*, London, 1964, is a beautifully observed semi-fictional portrayal of these attitudes.

leader of the U.A.P. In his first weeks of office Fadden made a pur-
poseful start, particularly in his dealings with the British government.
Never having visited the Old Country, he lacked Menzies' respect for
Downing Street. At the instance of General Blamey, he demanded the
relief of the Ninth Division in Tobruk, and he thereby showed a
blunt regard for Australian interests which anticipated the nationalist
self-awareness of Curtin and Evatt.[7] Yet Fadden's days were numbered.
The disunity of the government parties contrasted too keenly with the
discipline of the Australian Labor party, now reaping the benefit of
the reunion which Curtin had painstakingly negotiated with the Lang
Labor faction during the previous year. At the next sitting of parliament, in October 1941, the two independents switched their support
from the government to the A.L.P., Fadden's ministry was outvoted
on the budget debate, and resigned.

Curtin took office, initiating eight years of Labor rule. This was to
be the first occasion in Australian history when Labor won two
successive federal general elections, and the only one since 1916 when
Labor commanded a majority in both houses of parliament. Since the
A.L.P. split during the war of 1914–18 over conscription and other
issues, the party had been too narrowly based on the trade union
movement and the working class to appeal often to the majority of
Australian voters, who usually identified themselves with, or aspired
towards, the ranks of the urban and rural property-owning bourgeoisie.
Labor spokesmen, viewing the common man as the dupe of private
interests, tended to blame their long periods out of office on the
hostility of the press and the superior resources of the big business
interests backing their opponents. But at the state level Labor governments at that time held office for long spells, often in the less industrialized parts of Australia (Queensland, 1915–29, 1932–57; Western
Australia, 1924–30, 1933–47; Tasmania, 1923–8, 1934–69; New South
Wales, 1941–65). In those states the A.L.P., although grounded in
theory on a militantly working-class and socialist base, pursued policies
which won support from other elements in the community, such as
small farmers and white-collar workers. At the federal level, particularly after the schisms of 1916 and 1931, Labor was under greater
pressure to define and preserve its traditional principles, even when
these were no longer wholly appropriate in a socially mobile Australia.[8] Searching for its own soul, Labor was apt to neglect the task of
courting the uncommitted voter, who was thus only drawn in times
of unusual emergency to the federal A.L.P. Such an emergency arose
at the onset of the 1929 depression, when the Bruce government

---

[7] P. Hasluck, *The Government and the People: 1939–1941*, Canberra, 1952,
appendix 10: W. S. Churchill, *The Grand Alliance*, London, 1950, pp. 367–71.

[8] A more sophisticated analysis of the A.L.P.'s failure to win elections may be
found in D. Rawson, *Labor in Vain?*, Melbourne, 1966. This passage was written
before December 1972, but it has yet to be seen whether events will falsify this
analysis.

appeared to be scrapping the shield of the arbitration system. Such another was 1941, when Labor was thought to reflect the Australian consensus in time of war more truly than its squabbling opponents.

The new prime minister, John Curtin, was fifty-six years old, reserved, and lacking in showmanship.[9] Like Attlee in Britain, he came from the second ranks of his party to rebuild it after its top men were engulfed in the controversies of the depression. There he developed the qualities of patience, subtlety, and a selfless sense of duty which enabled him to carry the leadership of Australia through its moment of greatest crisis. Among his cabinet two men came to stand out, and later followed him in turn to the leadership of the A.L.P. One was J. B. (Ben) Chifley, a gravelly-voiced former engine-driver from New South Wales, who became treasurer;[10] the other was the ambitious idealist, Dr H. V. Evatt, who resigned from the High Court bench to enter politics, and now became attorney-general and minister for external affairs.[11] For a time of war it was an inexperienced cabinet. Only Chifley and the deputy prime minister, F. M. Forde, had held portfolios in the past, although the Advisory War Council had provided one source of expertise and continuity.

The new ministry scarcely had time to settle into office before it was confronted by crisis. On 7 December 1941 the bombing of Pearl Harbour signalled Japan's entry into the war as an ally of Germany and Italy. Japanese troops also invaded Malaya, and the British soon lost two of their best warships, the *Prince of Wales* and the *Repulse*, in Malayan waters. These calamities followed only a few days after Australia's *Sydney* was lost with all hands on 19 November 1941, after an engagement with the disguised German raider *Kormoran*, which was itself destroyed in the action, fought 150 miles south-west of Carnarvon. So, suddenly, a very old Australian nightmare came to life. Throughout their history Australians had been given to bouts of fear that their remote, underpopulated coastline would tempt a foreign aggressor, probably Oriental, but this terror had been kept at bay by the naval supremacy of the British Empire.[12] After December 1941 that supremacy was no more. Posters designed to spur the Australian war effort warned the reader: 'He's coming south', and there was no need to spell out who 'he' was. By Christmas the Japanese were masters of Hong Kong. During the early weeks of 1942 they thrust irresistibly through Malaya, sealing their victory on 15 February by

9 See A. Chester, *John Curtin*, Sydney, 1943: I. Dowsing, *Curtin of Australia*, Melbourne, 1968.

10 See L. F. Crisp, *Ben Chifley*, London, 1961.

11 For conflicting views of Evatt's performance see K. Tennant, *Evatt: Politics and Justice*, Sydney, 1970: A. Watt, *The Evolution of Australian Foreign Policy, 1938–1965*, Cambridge, 1967, pp. 44–105. See also A. Dalziel, *Evatt the Enigma*, Melbourne, 1967.

12 Some shrewd comments on this neurosis are made in H. McQueen, *A New Britannia*, Melbourne, 1970, pp. 56–79.

the capture of the great naval base of Singapore, previously thought impregnable.[13] Next they overran the Philippines, Indonesia, Burma; by the beginning of April the centuries-old European domination of South-East Asia was at an end, and European refugees were fleeing for the uncertain sanctuary of Australia. Grim accounts circulated of beheadings, bayonetings, rapes, and other atrocities committed by the victorious army. For the first time Australia's mainland tasted enemy action, as Japanese aircraft struck at Darwin, Broome, and other points along the northern coast. The year 1942 saw the greatest crisis in the nation's history.

As the threat to Australia mounted, civilian morale remained on the whole resolute, though the bombing of Darwin on 19 February 1942, when 8 ships were sunk, 23 aircraft were destroyed, and 243 people were killed, was accompanied by a stampede into the surrounding bush. The censorship authorities thought they discerned in private letters a sharply increased questioning of Britain's capacity. Preparations intensified. Public air-raid shelters were constructed after December 1941 and in innumerable backyards and school playgrounds householders and youths dug slit trenches, while shopkeepers boarded up their windows against flying glass. Happily these precautions were hardly put to the test. Outside Darwin and Broome Japanese action against Australian civilians was limited to stray bombs in North Queensland, an evening of great confusion when three miniature Japanese submarines entered Sydney Harbour on 31 May 1942 and sank a ferry boat; and a few shells which a week later burst harmlessly in seaside suburbs of Sydney and Newcastle, presumably fired from Japanese submarines. During the rest of the war Japanese submarines sank twenty-nine merchant ships off the Australian coast, with the loss of 577 lives, and nearly 300 were killed when the hospital ship *Centaur* was sunk off the Queensland coast in May 1943.

Other measures temporarily adopted on the home front included daylight saving and a 'brownout' restricting the use of lights by night. Rationing was extended during 1942 to tea, sugar, butter, meat, and clothing. Although the level of hardship never came anywhere near that experienced in Britain or Europe, these controls were the most stringent to be introduced in Australia since the early years of the Botany Bay penal colony. The Australian government likewise had greater powers over money and manpower than any Australian authority since Governor Macquarie. It took over the whole responsibility for collecting income tax in 1942, thereby depriving the state governments of their main source of revenue; thereafter they received fixed annual sums which made them dependent on the federal treasury. The government also used the national security regulations to control banking. The rate of public lending for war loans was stepped up, and fourteen campaigns – variously called liberty loans,

13 J. M. McCarthy, 'Singapore and Australian Defence, 1921–1942', in *Australian Outlook*, 25, 2, August 1971.

austerity loans, and victory loans – raised over £950 million. The director-general of manpower, W. C. Wurth, a seasoned civil servant from New South Wales, headed a department which classified and allocated the jobs of every Australian. Except in posts deemed essential for the war effort, all able-bodied young men were now called up for armed service. Older civilians were encouraged to take on extra responsibilities as air-raid wardens or members of Australia's home guard, the Volunteer Defence Corps. The old taboos against the employment of married women were swept aside for the time being, in order to staff hospitals, munition factories, and many jobs from tram conducting to farmwork. The home front showed a rare unanimity, and few were found to sympathize with the incautious nationalists of the 'Australia First' movement, who, by questioning Australia's close ties with the Anglo-American alliance, earned themselves internment and – for four of their associates in Western Australia – trial and conviction for what were really flimsy accusations of sedition.[14]

Yet the knockout to British naval power in South-East Asia made it clear that Australia could no longer count on her traditional guardian. Curtin spelt this out in a press statement at the end of 1941 when he stated: 'Australia looks to America, free of any pangs as to our traditional links or kinship with the United Kingdom'.[15] This displeased many traditionalists, but was irrefutable considering the numbers at Australia's disposal. Most of the 8th Division became prisoners-of-war when Singapore fell, and spent the next three years in hardship at Changi or on the Burma 'death railway'.[16] It was decided to call home the 6th and 7th Divisions who were with the British Ninth Army in Syria. This brought the Australian government into head-on collision with Winston Churchill, who wished to throw these divisions into the shaky Burma campaign, for which the Australians were the only available reinforcements. Curtin firmly refused, wisely, as it was improbable that the Australians could have stemmed the Japanese advance, and it was essential to find seasoned troops for New Guinea. Churchill gave way, though with a bad grace, and only after America's president Roosevelt had also tried unsuccessfully to shift Curtin. This clash was almost immediately followed by another when the British government invited R. G. Casey, Australia's representative in Washington, to accept appointment as British minister of state in Cairo. Casey accepted, but the Australian government gave publicity to its

14 This episode is well described in B. Muirden, *The Puzzled Patriots*, Melbourne, 1968.

15 *Herald*, Melbourne, 27 December 1941. The full text is reproduced in F. K. Crowley, *Modern Australia in Documents*, 2, 1939–1970, Melbourne, 1973, pp. 49–52. For contemporary criticisms see G. Long, *The Six Years War*, Canberra, 1973, p. 137.

16 Two first-hand accounts of life as a prisoner-of-war in Malaya are R. Braddon, *The Naked Island*, London, 1951, and W. S. Kent Hughes, *Slaves of the Samurai*, Melbourne, 1946.

protests against the British poaching a man who could usefully serve Australia's interests. These episodes, following Fadden's earlier brush over the Tobruk garrison, showed a growing independent-mindedness in Australia. It was not surprising (though there were also other legal and constitutional reasons) that later in 1942 the Australian parliament decided to adopt the Statute of Westminster of 1931, thus spelling out Australia's autonomy in a way which previous governments had not chosen to stress.

If the American alliance was now essential to Australia, Australia because of its location and its industrial and agricultural capacity became scarcely less important to the Americans as a base. Once the Philippines were in danger of conquest, the Americans quickly decided to defend Australia. In April 1942 General Douglas MacArthur of the U.S. Army was appointed supreme commander for the South-West Pacific, with authority over all Allied personnel. His first headquarters were in Melbourne, but were soon transferred to Brisbane. Australia's General Sir Thomas Blamey was in charge of all land forces in the area, but Americans commanded the naval and air forces. This was appropriate, as although it was American superiority by air and sea that turned the scale in this area, it was for the Australians to bear the brunt of fighting during 1942 until enough American soldiers could be trained and sent to the front. The Japanese strategy appeared to involve the isolation of Australia by gaining command of the sea and, after capturing Midway Island, invading New Caledonia, Fiji and Samoa.[17] Three weeks after MacArthur had assumed command, on 4–8 May 1942, occurred the battle of the Coral Sea. American warships and aircraft fought a Japanese convoy preparing a sea attack on Port Moresby which resulted in heavy casualties on both sides. In June Japanese seapower suffered a major defeat at Midway which saved Sydney and other Australian cities from bombing attacks by Japanese carrier-based aircraft. Danger persisted nevertheless in New Guinea, where the Japanese army thrust south until at one stage in August 1942 its advance units were within fifty miles of Port Moresby, and were launching a seaborne attack on Milne Bay at the southeast tip of the island. They were repulsed, and counter-attack followed: the Australian victory at Milne Bay was the first defeat inflicted on Japanese land forces during the war. Between September 1942 and January 1943 the Japanese were forced back along the Kokoda Trail over the Owen Stanley Range, in desperately laborious fighting which at its height absorbed 54,000 Australians and 30,000 American servicemen, as well as much valuable support from the local inhabitants. It would take another two years of dour campaigning to dislodge pocket after pocket of fanatically determined Japanese troops, but by the end of 1942 the threat to Australia was over. And greater victories were reported elsewhere on the world's war

[17] See L. Turner, 'The Crisis of Japanese Strategy, January–June 1942', in *The R.M.C. Historical Journal*, March 1972.

fronts: Guadalcanal, Alamein – in which the 9th Australian Division took a conspicuous part – and Stalingrad.

This lifting of danger confronted the Curtin government with a moment of political crisis, since the question now arose of the liability of men conscripted for the militia to serve outside Australian territory. Until the Vietnam action of 1964 it was a settled Australian tradition that, although volunteers might be called for overseas service with the A.I.F., it was right to conscript men only for the defence of their own country. New Guinea, as an Australian trust territory, counted as Australian soil, and the C.M.F. performed there well enough to disprove the old sneer that they were only 'chocolate soldiers'. But as the tide of war swept beyond eastern New Guinea, were they to be withdrawn from action at some invisible boundary-line, leaving the fighting to the A.I.F. and the Americans? Knowing the strength of feelings within the A.L.P. about the conscription issue which split the party in 1916, Curtin had to move with finesse. By the beginning of 1943 he had managed to persuade his party to extend the C.M.F.'s area of responsibility to the Equator in the north and the enemy-occupied Solomons in the east, and this became Australian policy for the rest of the war. This meant that by April 1943 there were 466,000 Australians and 111,000 American troops serving in the South-West Pacific. From then on the buildup was nearly all on the American side, so that by the latter part of 1944, of almost a million servicemen in the area, over half were American. MacArthur deployed American forces in a strategy of 'island hopping', moving from one carefully chosen advance base to the next to northward, leaving behind large pockets of Japanese to be dealt with at leisure. Blamey preferred a more thorough but perhaps more wasteful system of mopping up, because the Japanese were entrenching themselves in the South-West Pacific Islands, even to the extent of cultivating crops. Japanese tenacity persisted even among the prisoners-of-war in Australia in 1944, when 1100 of them armed with baseball bats, fenceposts, staves, and similar weapons, broke out of the Corowa camp and were only suppressed after over 200 were killed. So while the Americans spear-headed the thrust towards Japan, and made headlines, and while General MacArthur treated the Australian government and army with contemptuous superiority, the Australians found themselves in the slow and gruelling business of ousting the Japanese from New Guinea, New Britain, Bougainville, and Borneo. These tasks still occupied them when the war ended on 8 May 1945 in Europe and on 15 August 1945 in the Pacific. By then 33,826 Australians had been killed on active service, 10,264 in the Royal Australian Air Force: Australian airmen had continued to fight in the Mediterranean and in Europe, as well as in the Pacific, until the end. 180,864 servicemen and service-women had been wounded or injured, and more than 23,000 had been prisoners-of-war. At the end of the war more than 500,000 Australians were in uniform and their demobilization posed a major problem.

Australia's war in the tropics had several notable consequences on the civilian front. Medical research was advanced through the discovery of antidotes for scrub typhus and malaria. Of more general use was the introduction of the sulfa drugs and penicillin, the latter developed in England by the Australian Sir Howard Florey: their production was undoubtedly stimulated by wartime needs, and their long-term value was partly reflected in the falling civilian death-rate of the middle and late 1940s. The American contribution to Australia's future development was not confined to the introduction of coca-cola and the provision of profits for the nightclubs, bars, taxi-drivers, and other service industries which sprang up in Australia's cities to cater for warriors on leave. Of more lasting importance was the development of bulldozers, four-wheeled drive vehicles, 'ducks', and light aircraft, all of which would greatly facilitate the development of Australia's outback after the war. Wartime experience provided the technical know-how for crop-dusting, the use of radar in civilian aircraft, rainmaking experiments through cloud-seeding with 'dry ice', and the large-scale earthmoving on which Australia's major postwar irrigation projects depended.[18] All these developments owed something to American technological ingenuity as shown in the South-West Pacific campaign. It was particularly significant that many Australian and American servicemen were stationed in the Northern Territory. With the construction of airstrips, army camps, and meat-works the neglected North sprang into unwonted activity; the 750-mile bitumen strip which connects Darwin to Alice Springs is a memento to American hustle and efficiency in that critical year 1942. Not only was interest revived in northern development, but in the whole vexed question of decentralization and the right use of Australia's open spaces.

By turning Australia from her traditional dependence on the British Empire and cementing the American-Australian alliance, the war produced a favourable climate of opinion for future American interest and investment in Australia. And by forcibly reminding Australia of the existence of her Asian neighbours, the Japanese thrust may have kindled interest in the possibility of trade and other contacts with the Near North once peace was restored. These new developments in Australian foreign policy had been foreshadowed in the early years of the war. Until 1940 Australia had been slow to expand the scope of her Department of External Affairs by the recruitment of career diplomats and the appointment of overseas envoys. In that year the Menzies government broke new ground by appointing a senior cabinet minister, R. G. Casey, as Australian representative in Washington; the United States reciprocated by the appointment of a career diplomat to Canberra, Mr Clarence Gauss. During the next twelve months two more distinguished Australians, Sir John Latham and

18 A good account of the impact of the war on technology is D. P. Mellor, *The Role of Science and Industry*, Canberra, 1958.

Sir Frederic Eggleston, were appointed to Tokyo and Chungking respectively.

It was significant that the United States and East Asia were chosen as the first three postings, since these were the quarters which Australia most needed to cultivate. Casey at Washington did much to promote the role of Australia as a bridge and mediator between Great Britain and the United States.[19] Although this role was thought promising, it was rather lost sight of during the later stages of the war. Instead, Australia's attitude towards the United States was oddly ambivalent. Profoundly grateful for American help in repelling the Japanese, the Australian government was yet rather suspicious of 'dollar imperialism', and showed considerable wariness about encouraging a continued American presence in the South-West Pacific after the war. There was even a tendency, particularly after the victory of a Labor government in Britain in 1945, to draw closer once more to the British Commonwealth in any issue which raised a potential clash of interests with the United States. Instead of pushing her claims as a bridge between Britain and America, Australia in the years between 1944 and 1949 seemed to concentrate on playing the role as a bridge between the Western powers and the newly emerging nationalist movements of South-East Asia, especially India and Indonesia. There were even times when Australia seemed desirous of figuring as a 'middle power' between the Soviet Union and the West in the 'cold war' which developed after 1945. It was certainly Australia's aim in those years to stand apart from any of the great powers, and to star as a spokesman for the smaller nations of the world whose numbers in the new United Nations Organization might make up for their lack of military strength. This marked an unusual departure from Australia's customary reliance on close ties with a great and powerful ally, such as Britain or the United States. It was only possible because for a few years Australia was relatively free from any menace, real or imaginary, from the Near North. Between 1945, when Japan was defeated, and 1949, when China went Communist, it was hard to envisage the possibility of menace from an Asian power, and easy for Australia to overrate her ability to stand on her own feet in world affairs.

The architect of Australian foreign policy in those years was Dr H. V. Evatt, minister for external affairs from 1941 to 1949. Prodigiously self-confident and hard-working, Evatt knew few restraints. He might ultimately defer to the guidance of Curtin or Chifley, but most of the time his colleagues were glad to leave foreign affairs to his restless ambition. The permanent officials of his department were few in number, though a vigorous programme of recruitment was begun during the war, and lacked a strong civil service tradition that might have tempered his enthusiasms. Indeed, between 1947 and 1950 the permanent secretary of the department was John Burton, a very young protegé of Evatt's who naturally reflected many of his views. Evatt's

19 See R. G. Casey, *Personal Experience 1939–1946*, London, 1962.

policies were thus seldom subjected to informed criticism before they were translated into action. Since he relied heavily on his own energy and capacity for mastering detail, his judgements were sometimes questionable; but Australians enjoyed seeing one of their number cutting a prominent figure in international politics, and in London *The Times* later discerned an irony in the fact that it was Evatt who gave Australia the international standing which provided so effective a platform for his great rival, Menzies.[20]

Evatt's first essay in external affairs was the conclusion of an agreement with New Zealand in 1944. This agreement asserted the right of Australia and New Zealand to be consulted on any measures affecting the South-West Pacific after Japan's defeat. It sought the creation of a common trusteeship policy for the advancement of the Pacific Islanders – the South Pacific Commission formed in 1947 answered that need – and called for a regional defence policy based on Australia and New Zealand. Australia would also have liked to stake a claim to administer the Solomons and the New Hebrides, but the New Zealanders would not go along with this naïve imperialism; this was just as well, since postwar Australia had the heavy responsibility of looking after New Guinea. Most offensive of all to the Americans, the Australia-New Zealand agreement made a point of stating that the possession of bases in the South-West Pacific should not constitute a claim to sovereignty. The Australians seem mostly to have had in mind the case of Manus Island, north-east of New Guinea, where the United States had a strong base which it contemplated maintaining after the war as one end of a line of defence in the western Pacific. As it was, after a few years of lukewarm negotiation, the Americans pulled out of Manus. Australia's sensitivity on this point was not well timed, as nobody could foresee the extent of American involvement in world politics after the war, and there was a real risk that the United States might retreat into isolationism, as she had done after the First World War. Australia for her part was unwilling to leave the Americans on Manus without a reciprocal arrangement giving Australian forces access to other American bases in the western Pacific. There was, too, a risk that if the United States had unconditional use of bases on Australian soil, Australia in the eyes of her neighbours would be tied too closely to American foreign policy. But it was also true that some members of the Labor government were unthinkingly and instinctively anti-American. This emerged quite forcibly between 1944 and 1946, when the party's leaders had great trouble in securing acceptance of the Bretton Woods agreement, under which Australia became a participant in the World Bank set up on largely American capital to tide member-nations over periods of financial instability. A depression-bred fear of 'Wall Street capitalism' easily spilt over into anti-Americanism, and this was a factor which Evatt could never entirely escape.

20 *The Times*, London, 3 November 1965.

Evatt came notably to the fore at the San Francisco conference of April 1945 setting up the United Nations Organization. Eclipsing Forde, nominally the senior member of the Australian delegation, Evatt showed such activity that, as one of his biographers rather un-critically comments Australia sponsored many more amendments to the United Nations Charter than any other nation.[21] Evatt's main aim was to strengthen the United Nations as a curb upon the great powers, whose rivalries he saw as the main threat to world peace. The dis-couraging history of the League of Nations had not damped his faith in collective security, and it was not then apparent that Russia and the United States could achieve a 'balance of terror', so that the stubborn wrangling of smaller powers would prove the greater risk in the 1960s and 1970s. Australia under Evatt's guidance sought to limit the power of veto which the U.S.A., the U.S.S.R., Britain, France, and China could exercise on United Nations resolutions, and to strengthen the powers of the General Assembly, which was the main forum of the smaller nations. This campaign was largely unsuccessful, except for ensuring that the veto could not kill discussion of any issue. Australia was somewhat more fortunate in promoting her own special concerns. The United Nations agreed to adopt the principle of fostering full employment policies, and undertook to refrain from interfering in matters which came under the domestic jurisdiction of its members. The main effect of Australia's performance at San Francisco was psychological. For the first time Australia, rather than Canada or South Africa, was foremost among British Commonwealth countries in pursuing a distinctively independent foreign policy. This may have been at times inconvenient for Britain and America, but Australia's prestige was almost certainly greater as a consequence.

After Japan's surrender in August 1945, Evatt threw himself into the task of designing the future in South and East Asia and the western Pacific. He urged a tough line with Japan, even calling – though he later disclaimed it – for the trial of the emperor Hirohito as a war criminal. In this Evatt reflected popular feeling in Australia. Fed on stories of Japanese wartime atrocities and on newspaper cartoons depicting the Japanese as ugly apes in morning dress, the Australian public felt little pity for the victims of the first atomic bombs, and nourished an unusual hatred which could be wiped out only by the recovery of Japan as a trading partner with capital to invest in Australia. A senior Australian judge, Sir William Webb, presided over the international military tribunal which passed sentence on prominent war criminals in the Far East. An Australian, Professor Macmahon Ball, became the British Commonwealth representative on the Allied Council advising the Supreme Commander of the Allied

21 A. Dalziel, *Evatt the Enigma*, Melbourne, 1967, p. 8. For another view of this period see P. Hasluck, 'Australia and the Formation of the United Nations: Some Personal Reminiscences', in *R.A.H.S.J.*, *40*, 3, December 1954, and *41*, 5, January 1956.

occupation force in Japan, General MacArthur. It was MacArthur's autocratic personality that created problems for Australian interests in Japan, rather than his bold experiment in guiding the Japanese into the paths of parliamentary democracy; but where the Americans concentrated on building up Japan as a reliable bastion of anti-Communism in case Chiang Kai-shek's China failed to hold, Australia was still conscious of her narrow escape from invasion and viewed Japan's rapid recovery uneasily. To Australia it seemed good sense, as well as good international morality, to build up friendships in the regions between Japan and Australia. This made her particularly sympathetic to nations such as India, Pakistan, and Indonesia which were emerging from colonial status and seeking a place in the world as independent states. Because the Attlee government in Britain accepted India's desire for independence, Australia's role was mainly that of a sympathetic friend, whose support was of value on such occasions as the Commonwealth Prime Ministers' conference of 1949, when it was decided that India could become a republic without losing membership of the British Commonwealth. Australia's standing in the Indian sub-continent was attested in 1949–50 by the appointment of the distinguished judge, Sir Owen Dixon, as mediator in the dispute between India and Pakistan over the ownership of Kashmir.

But it was the cause of her nearest neighbour, Indonesia, which stamped Australia most clearly as the friend of new Asian nations. When the Indonesian nationalists refused to accept the resumption of Dutch rule after 1945, Australia showed a consistent bias in their favour. Even the waterside workers, whose job gave them an occasional interest in foreign policy, refused to handle cargoes which might be used against Indonesian interests. So it was no surprise when in 1947 Australia was the power nominated by the Indonesian nationalists to sit on a three-nation good offices committee appointed by the United Nations to try to resolve the Indonesian question. Conciliation failed at first. Two years of civil war followed before the Dutch and the Indonesians were brought to the negotiating table in 1949. Encouraged by the United Nations commission, the Dutch at length recognized Indonesian independence. Australian support for the Indonesians was of course not the only factor which caused the Dutch to agree, but it was largely due to the Australians that the war of independence never entirely took on the character of a racial conflict between Europeans and Asians. So Australia earned considerable goodwill in Indonesia, but the peace settlement contained one item which would eventually threaten that goodwill. Dutch New Guinea, racially distinct from the rest of Indonesia, remained for the time being under the Netherlands government, although the Indonesian authorities made no secret of their claim to inherit it. This unresolved question was a potential trouble-spot in which Australia, as the neighbouring power in eastern New Guinea, would of necessity be involved.

In the short run, Evatt's policies laid a firm foundation for good relations between Australia and her Asian neighbours, and did much to make up for any unpopularity arising from Australia's immigration laws. At a time when nations such as India and Indonesia were looking for friends, Australia's quick response carried conviction: Australia was not to be regarded as the lackey of the old colonial powers. Outside the Near North, Evatt's interventions in international affairs were less fortunate. More willing than the British to recognize Israel's independence in 1948, he nevertheless risked alienating Israeli friendship by flirting with a scheme to internationalize Jerusalem. And during his term as president of the United Nations General Assembly, late in 1948, he displeased the Americans by failing to support their stand warmly enough at a critical point in the 'Cold War', when the United States and Britain were confronting the Soviet Union over the blockading of Berlin. Evatt never appreciated the 'Cold War'. To him it was largely a matter of great-power brinkmanship, jeopardizing the peace of the world for the sake of prestige. Russia might bluff and bully, but she had been too greatly injured in the Second World War to wish to launch a third. This view was of course anathema to the very strong anti-Communist groups in Australia, especially after the events of 1948–9 when the Communist leader Mao Tse-tung drove Chiang Kai-shek out of China. Once China fell to the Reds, the United States intensified its efforts to build up a stable anti-Communist grouping in South-East Asia. Australia, still anxious for a hard peace with Japan, was slow to change its policies. At the end of 1949 the Australian government was considering recognition of the new régime in China, assuming that Great Britain did likewise, rather than follow the American line of non-recognition. But because their opponents were doing their utmost to tar the Labor government with the Communist brush, it was decided to put off recognizing Mao's China until after the elections.[22] Labor lost, and China remained unrecognized until 1973. Even if Evatt had remained minister for external affairs, Australia would almost certainly have been obliged to draw nearer to the United States after 1950, because the Korean War exposed the dangers of Australian isolationism. Maybe in Asia and Africa the ideal of a 'third world' of neutral powers mediating between the Russian and American giants was not yet dead. But it was no longer a realistic vision for Australia.

Evatt's performance as minister for external affairs, although controversial, probably did his party no harm in the eyes of the Australian public. One must look to the home front to understand how and why the voters passed an adverse judgement on the Labor government. Most members of that government gave first priority in their post-war planning to ensuring that there would be no repetition of the hardships of the 1930s depression: as Chifley said, 'The ordinary people of Australia ... wonder what sort of democracy it is which is unmindful of their interests in peacetime, yet in wartime says to them, "Give us

22 H. S. Albinski, 'Australia and the China Problem Under the Labor Government', in *A.J.P.H.*, X, 2, August 1964.

of your best in the factory or the field; give your lives for your country". What happened previously must never occur again'.[23] Probably the most significant weapon for the Curtin government was one possessed by no previous federal ministry: uniform income tax. Although since the First World War both the federal and the state governments had collected income tax, the federal government, having taken over the whole responsibility as a wartime measure in 1942, showed no disposition to give it up; and the High Court ruled, on challenge from several of the state governments, that the new system came within federal powers. The federal government then further simplified the taxpayers' life by introducing pay-as-you-earn deductions, so that the public readily accepted uniform taxation. Holding the purse strings, the federal government's position was greatly strengthened, as the state governments came to rely more and more on the annual premiers' conference for handouts from the federal treasury. Because the war called for planning on a national scale in a way which had never before been necessary, the logic of events would have thrust the federal government to the fore at the expense of the state governments, no matter what political party was in power. A Labor government, traditionally centralist, was more willing to defend these initiatives and accept the praise or blame which ensued.

During the crisis months of 1942 party strife was restrained in the federal parliament, only to revive with the waning of the Japanese threat and the prospect of elections in the spring of 1943. Curtin's government had gained great prestige from its handling of wartime affairs, but its critics thought it over-zealous in using national security regulations to build up Canberra's control of the economy in order – it was alleged – to promote socialist policies when the war ended. In June 1943 the government survived a motion of no confidence with the support of the independents, but was almost immediately plunged into bitter controversy through one of its own cabinet members, E. J. Ward, who, although a hard-working and not incompetent minister, suffered from an inability to distinguish between manly forthrightness and loud-mouthed larrikinism.[24] Ward asserted, on an authority which he was never prepared to name, that if a Menzies government had remained in power it would have responded to a Japanese threat to northern Australia by withdrawing all forces to a line running approximately from Brisbane to Adelaide. Such a story was not calculated to appeal to the inhabitants of Queensland and Western Australia, who would have been abandoned to the Japanese whilst Sydney and Melbourne were defended. Strategically there was some logic in the concept of the 'Brisbane Line', and it was probably discussed in outline as the basis of a last stand if events went to that extremity; but there is no evidence that either the Menzies or the

---

[23] Quoted in L. F. Crisp, *Ben Chifley*, London, 1961, p. 183.

[24] See E. Spratt, *Eddie Ward: Firebrand of East Sydney*, Adelaide, 1965.

Curtin government found themselves called upon to give the plan any specific authority. Ward's charge gave rise to a good deal of accusation and denial, and he was suspended from office during an enquiry into his allegations. Nothing substantial resulting, he was demoted to a junior position in cabinet, and the uproar subsided. It may simply have been coincidence that at the ensuing federal elections Queensland and Western Australia registered an unparalleled vote in favour of Labor.

The 1943 elections were a triumph for Labor throughout Australia. Going to the polls with a majority of one, Curtin's government returned with forty-nine seats in a House of Representatives of seventy-four members, and a comfortable majority in the Senate. Among the causes of the landslide were the continued bickering of the other parties, and Curtin's canniness in drawing the teeth of the socialist bogey by announcing in August 1943 that his government would nationalize no new industries during the war. The Sydney *Bulletin* claimed that the A.L.P. benefited because Australian wives and mothers feared that their opponents would extend military conscription for overseas service. Beyond all else the Australian voters, who tend to judge politicians for their managerial skills, were expressing a vote of confidence in the Curtin government's administration of the problems of wartime, and giving them a mandate to plan for peace.

But had the Curtin government the power? Nearly forty years of interpretation by the High Court had left federal-state relations bedevilled with complexities, of which Section 92, providing for absolutely free commerce between the states, was the biggest obstacle in blocking the federal government's exercise of powers. Although uniform taxation and the federal government's increased financial powers had strengthened Canberra's hand, it was evident that any major increases in social services could only be made at the expense of state rights. Moreover, the Curtin government sought a more effective control of banking, as well as of price and wage stabilization. It was not only the depression of the 1930s that suggested the need for such powers, but also the likelihood of inflation after the war on a scale which might price Australia's staple exports off the world's markets. Unless controls were imposed, prices would surely spiral because of the war-caused boom in productivity and employment, together with inevitable shortages in civilian consumer goods. Of course it was possible for the six state parliaments to pass wage and price-fixing legislation, but there was no way of guaranteeing that all would pass the same legislation, or any at all – except Queensland – as all of them had non-Labor dominated Legislative Councils. For the time being the federal government could claim authority under the defence powers in these fields, as in banking. But the defence powers were valid only during the war and for as long afterwards as the High Court was prepared to rule. A referendum could give the commonwealth full powers for the work of post-war reconstruction. Hence, in October 1942 Evatt brought forward a bill for such a referendum, but withdrew it after an all-party conference with state parliamentary leaders, when it was agreed to refer the necessary powers to the federal parliament for a five-year period after the war. When several of the state parliaments failed to honour this undertaking, the Labor government decided to go ahead with a referendum. Held in August 1944, the referendum requested the voters' consent to giving Canberra a list of fourteen powers on an all-or-nothing basis, with no provision for picking and choosing. This was too big a mouthful for the public to swallow, even without the influence of such opposition politicians as Fadden, with their alarming forecasts that, if they voted 'Yes', 'in peace-time you will work under government compulsion; you will eat what the bureaucrats ration out to you; you will live in mass-produced government dwellings; and your children will work wherever the bureaucrats tell them to work'.[25] The 'Noes' had it by a margin of 2.3 to slightly under 2 million votes. Had the government asked for fewer powers in separate questions – over social services, civil aviation, organized marketing, and price control, to name the more important – it might have been partly successful. As it was, not for the only time, it lost everything by poor tactics.

So the government had to proceed by piecemeal legislation. Some of its members foresaw the worst; Arthur Calwell,[26] for instance, thought that without such powers no government could prevent the stagnation of Australia's economy and population, followed in time by an Asian takeover.[27] This gloom did not prevail in government thinking. Instead the government soon spelt out its intention of securing full employment for Australians after the war. This was a bold assertion, as high unemployment had been accepted as normal in the period between the wars, and even so eminent an expert as Professor Douglas Copland[28] forecast that between 5 and 8 per cent of Australia's postwar workforce would lack jobs. Among politicians only Menzies seems to have expected the high demand for labour which in fact occurred. But the Curtin government made a start to provide social security with the means at its disposal. Price and wage-fixing were left to the states, backed by the national security regulations while their validity lasted. Welfare improved; by 1945 the Curtin government had extended the scope of maternity and hospital benefits, and entered for the first time into the payment of unemployment, sickness, tuberculosis, and funeral benefits. But moves in 1944–5 to pay for the medicine and care of the needy through pharmaceutical and hospital benefits, met with strong opposition from the medical

25 *Sydney Morning Herald*, 25 July 1944. See W. J. Waters, 'Australian Labor's Full Employment Objective, 1942–45', in *A.J.P.H.*, XVI, 1, April 1970. See also W. J. Waters, 'Labor, Socialism, and World War II', in *L.H.*, *16*, May 1969.

26 See A. A. Calwell, *Be Just and Fear Not*, Melbourne, 1972.

27 *C.P.D.*, 10 March 1944, *177*, pp. 1211–13.

28 See *Essays in Honour of Sir Douglas Copland*, in *E.R.*, *36*, 73, March 1960.

profession. They feared it was the thin end of the wedge for nationalization, and encouraged the state of Victoria to challenge this legislation successfully in the High Court. The Labor government had better
luck with its aviation policy. Having been prevented by the High
Court from nationalizing all private interstate air services, in 1946 it
set up its own service, Trans-Australia Airlines. This competed with
the only other major private company – Australian National Airways –
under a careful system of regulations which gave equal opportunities. In
1947 the government also nationalized the long-established QANTAS
airline, thus entering the international field; it did so by acquiring the
50 per cent of the shares in the company which it did not already
own, having bought the other 50 per cent from the U.K. government.
Thus in aviation as in education, broadcasting, and a number of other
fields, the Australian solution has been neither complete government
control nor complete private enterprise, but a carefully worked out
compromise in which private operators get their opportunity to seek
profit, but standards are regulated and competition provided by a
government agency.

A similar arrangement eventually emerged in the area of banking,
but only after a controversy which was to have fateful after-effects
for the Labor government. Since the events of 1931, when the Commonwealth Bank Board had laid down the law to the Scullin government, Labor leaders were resolved that never again would their
policies be thwarted by a government's inability to control banking.
Chifley, the tough-minded treasurer, had a brush with the bankers as
early as 1942, when he invoked National Security regulations in order
to override the Commonwealth Bank Board and ensure that a limit
of 5 per cent was set as interest on advances. In 1943 a government
mortgage bank was set up, and attached to the Commonwealth Bank.
Early in 1945 a number of important amendments to the Commonwealth Bank Act were brought forward. The Board, largely a collection
of private bankers and businessmen, was dissolved. In its place was
created a governor and advisory council nominated by the government;
the governor was the very able and energetic economist, Dr H. C.
Coombs. The Commonwealth Bank received a charter defining its
main tasks as ensuring the stability of the currency, full employment
for Australians, and the economic prosperity and welfare of the
nation. The Commonwealth Bank would compete fully with the
trading banks, extending its operations to housing loans and other
new ventures. The trading banks had to operate under licence and
to keep a stated quantity of their reserves under the Commonwealth
Bank's control. The Commonwealth Bank would control interest rates.
These powers were seen as insurance against inflation or depression.
Finally, authority over banking would be vested in the government
and not, as previously, in parliament which might be dominated by a
hostile Senate. The effect of these amendments was to consolidate the
Commonwealth Bank's position as Australia's central bank, and to
ensure that the Bank could not act in defiance of government policy.

These measures were essential for strong government handling of economic affairs. They were attacked by the government's opponents as 'creeping socialism', but the legal attack was confined to the weakest feature of the legislation, a provision that henceforth all local authorities and semi-governmental corporations must bank with the Commonwealth. This was not essential to the main purposes of the Banking Act, but the government nevertheless rose to the challenge when the Melbourne City Council decided to go to law over it. The government's subsequent defeat in the court had long-lasting political consequences.

Meanwhile, as the war drew to a close in 1945, the government felt a particular responsibility for the rehabilitation of ex-servicemen and women, many of whom had been forced to cut short their education in the hard times of the 1930s. A reconstruction training scheme was brought into being to provide grants for veterans to train for civil occupations at all levels from technical school to university. This was soon supplemented by a scheme to extend university scholarships to students who had not been ex-servicemen. This legislation had a profound effect on Australian society. It was not simply that it filled the universities with students of a more mature and determined cast than usual, nor even that it stimulated a demand for the extended teaching of such subjects as medicine, dentistry, economics, and psychology. These effects might have been foreseen by anyone who noted the response to the adult education movement in the armed services. What was less readily predictable was the effect of opportunity on the social aspirations of the ex-servicemen. Previous generations of Australians moved more slowly out of their class, and since the 1920s the opportunities for moving out of the working class had been fewer. Now many more Australians had access to white-collar jobs and white-collar attitudes. It was debatable whether the A.L.P., with its sturdily working class image, would be able to keep their loyalties. The leading members of the Curtin government do not seem to have been aware of this problem. J. J. Dedman, minister for postwar reconstruction from early 1945, was a dedicated administrator who built up a much-needed scheme through which the commonwealth helped the states to finance the building of war service homes; but he is also remembered for the tactless comment that the government should not give too much help to homebuyers because it did not want the workers to become little capitalists.[29] What the Australian people wanted above all was to become little capitalists. They would support the politicians who best helped this objective.

Still squabbling and divided, the non-Labor opposition was in unimpressive shape after their rout in 1943. During that election the U.A.P.'s loss of credibility was shown by the growth of several mushroom anti-Labor parties, such as the One Party for Australia group

[29] *C.P.D.*, 2 October 1945, *185*, p. 6265.

sponsored by a prominent sausage manufacturer. None provided lasting competition, but their activities were an unhealthy symptom. The rot spread further in February 1944, when the U.A.P. members left the Advisory War Council, except for W. M. Hughes, who was thereupon for the last time in his long life expelled from his party. The Country party stayed with the Council; more cohesive and better disciplined, it seemed to have a good chance of surviving to become the senior opposition party. It was at this low point in his party's fortunes that Menzies staged a remarkable political comeback. Realizing that the U.A.P. was discredited beyond redemption, he found support for the idea of establishing a new party which would revive the old name of 'Liberal', the party of Barton and Deakin and many other giants of the federation era. Having found financial as well as political backers, Menzies launched his new party in October 1944. It may have been hoped that all the non-Labor groups would merge under the Liberal banner, but the Country party soon made it clear that it would not sink its identity. The U.A.P. came over in a body to the new party, as did a number of separated brethren such as Hughes. This gave rise to comments that new Liberal was but old U.A.P. writ large, but in fact Menzies wished to give the new party a different emphasis. Where the U.A.P. had been too obviously the party of city businessmen, the Liberals aimed to present a wider appeal, identifying themselves with less prosperous citizens in search of opportunity, and winning voters from both the Labor party and – though this was not too openly avowed – the Country party. During their first year or two the Liberals were only moderately successful. Although they gained several seats from Labor at the 1946 elections, and emerged as the senior partner in the opposition coalition, this was hardly more than the normal swing of the pendulum. Menzies and the Liberals had yet to prove themselves.

By contrast the A.L.P. appeared to emerge from the war in good order, although several of its leading members disappeared from the scene in 1945–6. Curtin died in July 1945, a victim of wartime strain. He was replaced as prime minister and Labor leader by Chifley, a tougher and more contentious figure, homespun, intelligent, a superb administrator, and yet at times insensitive to the mood of the public. Forde lost his seat at the 1946 elections, and was appointed high commissioner to Canada. Beasley had gone a year earlier to Australia House in London; in 1946 his old leader, Lang, turned up in the House of Representatives as a one-man party whose attacks on his old Labor associates were often more damaging than those of the official opposition. But with a good majority in the House and a near-monopoly of the Senate, Labor had no real worries in 1946. The government's hand was strengthened somewhat in 1946, when a referendum gave it specific power to legislate for social services – but it was notable that even for so beneficent an extension of federal power, over 45 per cent of the electors voted 'No'; a revealing commentary on the alleged tendency of Australians to look to the government for aid at every turn. Given this authority, the government in 1947 brought in another pharmaceutical and medical benefits scheme. Once again the doctors put up such strong opposition that the national health scheme was not operating when the Chifley government left office in 1949. Partly the doctors were concerned for their professional standards, partly they were alarmed by tales of too much bureaucracy in Britain's new national health service, but in terms of the public good their stand was irresponsible and selfish, and goes far to explain why the Chifley government sometimes tended to see itself as the only righteous body among a horde of self-seeking pressure groups.

Despite this feud the government remained convinced of the value of medical research. In this it reflected community attitudes. Even Australians who appreciated no other form of academic enquiry could see the value in medical research, particularly where it affected children. This concern explained the public excitement over the claims of Queensland's Sister Elizabeth Kenny to have developed new techniques for the treatment of poliomyelitis. Rebuffed by the Australian medical profession, Sister Kenny kept the confidence of many who hoped to see the amateur confound the professionals, and from 1941 she was finding acceptance in academic circles in the United States. No such controversy surrounded the work of Dame Jean Connor, also on poliomyelitis, or the identification by (Sir) Norman Gregg in 1941 of German measles in pregnant women as the cause of certain ante-natal abnormalities; but despite such solid achievements, Australia was slow to support medical research systematically. It was only in 1937 that a Medical Research Council had been set up with federal financial backing. Now, in 1946, it was to some extent the claims of medical research which prompted the Chifley government to set up the Australian National University in Canberra, Australia's first entirely postgraduate institute of advanced research. Of its four research schools only one was named after an individual – the John Curtin school of medical research – and he was a hero of the A.L.P. rather than the A.M.A.

Probably the Chifley government's most significant contribution to Australia's future was its immigration policy. For years politicians had preached that Australia's open spaces were an invitation to invasion, and the threat had at last materialized with the Japanese thrust. More people were required for Australia's development, but natural increase was not enough. Although during the 1940s the birthrate recovered from the fall-off during the depression, there were only 7½ million Australians at the 1947 census. Potential migrants were not hard to find. After the downfall of Germany and a series of Communist takeovers in eastern Europe it was known that a large number of displaced persons and refugees were in search of new homes. In deciding to set up a department of immigration in 1945, the federal government hoped to make its harvest among these Europeans. This required political courage in an Australia which prided itself on being 98 per cent British in origin.

In the Labor movement the feeling was especially strong that foreigners would deprive Australian trade unionists of jobs by working for low wages. The roots of anti-foreign prejudice went further. A Melbourne survey of 1948 found that the majority of those interviewed were prepared to welcome only unrestricted English migration, although the Irish would be tolerated also. Germans, although wartime enemies, were preferred in limited quantities to Southern Europeans. Nearly half those interviewed favoured a total ban on Italians, and more than half wanted to keep out all Jews and Negroes. Possibly the activities of terrorists such as the Stern Gang in Israel made for an unusual amount of anti-semitism in 1948; but it was odd, so soon after the war, that Jews should be nearly twice as unpopular as Germans. The one surprising sign of racial tolerance was that only 24 per cent sought the total exclusion of Chinese, and nearly as many thought they should be actively encouraged as migrants; China, of course, was not yet Communist.[30] On the evidence, even when mass unemployment no longer existed, the average Australian still had some murky prejudices against foreigners. It must have required considerable political courage and skill to introduce such a marked change in immigration policy.[31]

These qualities were found in Arthur Calwell, who as minister for immigration showed somewhat unexpected qualities of statesmanship. Only one major criticism could be levelled at him. While taking considerable pains to educate Australian opinion into acceptance of Europeans, he upheld the White Australia policy against individual Asian migrants as callously as any petty bureaucrat. Perhaps he felt that Australian working-men would more readily accept Europeans if they could be sure the line would be held against those with the wrong racial background. Certainly his plans for attracting European migrants were boldly imaginative. Under a 1946 agreement with Britain migrants were brought out at a purely nominal payment. Until 1955 ex-servicemen and their families received free passages. Over half a million British migrants have since come to Australia under these arrangements. In 1947 an agreement was negotiated with the International Refugee Organization, under which many displaced persons in Europe would come to Australia at the Australian government's expense. On arrival they were required to work for two years at jobs to which they were allotted to the requirements of the Australian workforce. Professional skills were often disregarded. There were tales of surgeons working as hospital cleaners, and musicians

[30] Details of this survey will be found in O. A. Oeser and S. B. Hammond, *Social Structure and Personality in a City*, London, 1954, p. 55.

[31] For the origins and working of Australia's post-war migration policy, consult R. T. Appleyard, *British Emigrants to Australia*, Canberra, 1964: J. Jupp, *Arrivals and Departures*, Melbourne, 1966.

milking cows in Gippsland. It is certainly the case that one highly regarded philosopher began his academic career as a gardener at the University of Western Australia. For most, the advantages eventually outweighed the hardships. Under this scheme more than 200,000 newcomers were introduced into Australia, about 85 per cent of them between 1947 and 1951. Meanwhile there was a drive to recruit migrants from elsewhere in Europe, so that by the time Calwell left office in 1949 over half a million migrants had reached Australia, of whom only about one-third were of British or Irish origin.

Considerable efforts were made to ensure a welcome for these migrants. Official propaganda discouraged the use of such epithets as 'Pommy', 'Dago', 'Balt', or 'Reffo'. The newcomers were to be 'New Australians', cared for by Good Neighbour Councils. School programmes and radio broadcasts were devoted to easing their assimilation. And if there were lingering pockets of prejudice among the older generation, on the whole Australians accepted the newcomers easily, to the benefit of their society and culture. The migrant impact on the Australian way of living was at times unexpected. That Australian food and wine should improve as a result of migrant interest was neither surprising nor unwelcome. Nor was it unexpected that the migrants' children should turn out to include some outstanding athletes among their number, although soccer continued to be an interest for devoted ethnic minorities rather than a serious rival to rugby and Australian rules. If the migrants increased the proportion of Roman Catholics in the community, they also diluted the Irish bias of that church. But the Chifley government cannot fully have foreseen that the migrant influx would in time increase the anti-Labor element in Australia. Many of the newcomers came from countries where the Social Democrat parties – with whom they equated the A.L.P. – had not been strong enough to stand up to Communist subversion. Driven from their homelands by the Reds, and unsure of the strength of Australian parliamentary traditions, they would prefer those politicians who made the most convincing show of combating the extreme Left in Australia. The A.L.P. did not pay enough attention to this factor.

A most impressive contribution of the postwar migrants came in the field of culture and the fine arts. Their influence could be discerned not so much in a roll-call of big names – though Judy Cassab and Louis Kahan among the artists, David Martin as novelist, Gustav Nossal as research scientist, and Frank Knopfelmacher as controversialist come readily to mind – as in the effect which they had on middle class attitudes towards such activities as theatre and concert-going. There was still a rather philistine streak among many Australians, and it had been encouraged by two major controversies of 1944: the Archibald Prize row and the Ern Malley hoax. The former episode arose when the annual prize for Australia's finest portrait was given to William Dobell for a rather cadaverous picture of his friend, Joshua Smith. Those who disliked the portrait felt so strongly that they instituted a lawsuit to prevent the award of the Archibald Prize to Dobell, and the lay public gained great amusement from the attempts of the artistically learned to define good art in a way that would satisfy a court of law. In comparison, the Ern Malley hoax was good clean fun. Max Harris, editor of an avant-garde literary periodical called *Angry Penguins*, having received the posthumous poems of a young telegraph linesman named Ern Malley, was so impressed by them that he devoted a special issue to their publication. It then emerged that the poems were a spoof, concocted as deliberate nonsense by two fellow-poets one afternoon, using amongst several books to hand a pamphlet on malaria control as their raw material. Harris survived this experience to become a leading Australian man of letters, but for years afterwards, any experimental or unorthodox literary group in Australia exposed itself to sneers of 'Ern Malley'.

Such debunking was less unhealthy than the ever-present grundyism of the censorship laws, which in the 1940s tended to concentrate on guarding Australian ears from the sort of profane language which might be heard freely in every army camp and football field. Thus Sumner Locke-Elliot, author of Australia's only significant contemporary play about the Second World War, *Rusty Bugles*, experienced trouble over the staging of his play because his soldiers talked like soldiers. Robert S. Close, author of *Love Me Sailor*, was prosecuted for causing a hardened Sydney detective-sergeant offence and shame through reading the commonest Australian adjective frequently in the book. It was curious that the wowsers were so influential in cultural affairs, since during these years they had little success in such other matters as the high consumption of beer or the diminishing size of women's bathing costumes.

Yet it would be wrong to assume that Australia was a cultural desert. On the contrary, the movements of the 1930s flourished, and stimulated the appearance of new talents. The ferment of ideas was seldom livelier at any point in Australia's cultural history. The nationalist Jindyworoback movement produced a number of competent poets, notably Ian Mudie and Rex Ingamells.[32] 1940 saw the beginnings of *Meanjin*, which, published first in Brisbane but before long under the auspices of the Melbourne University Press, soon established itself as Australia's leading literary and critical magazine. *Meanjin* belonged to no particular coterie, and if its overall tone suggested a left-of-centre view about society and politics, this was no more than a reflection of contemporary intellectual trends. Not that the poetry of the 1940s was written from any marked ideological position. A. D. Hope and Judith Wright, probably the finest poets to emerge during this decade, showed a capacity, new in Australia, for the

[32] For details of the writers discussed in this paragraph see H. M. Green, *A History of Australian Literature*, 2, 1923–1950, Sydney, 1961. See also G. Serle, *From Deserts The Prophets Come: The Creative Spirit in Australia: 1788–1972*, Melbourne, 1973.

subtle exploration of private emotions and relationships. Yet this maturing of insight meant no divorce from their Australian origins. There is as keen an awareness of environment in Hope's sardonic 'Australia' as in Judith Wright's evocations of the New England background. John Manifold, Douglas Stewart, Kenneth Slessor, and James McAuley spanned the political spectrum, but all sought their subject matter from the great myths of the Australian past: Ned Kelly, Captain Cook, Quiros. A lively sense of Australia's history, perhaps stimulated by the 1938 anniversary celebrations for New South Wales, also inspired the work of several novelists. Eleanor Dark in the *Timeless Land* trilogy went to Australia's first decades for her material. Dark was also one of several novelists, such as Dymphna Cusack and the longer established Katharine Susannah Prichard, who wrote novels of contemporary life in which an admirable sense of social concern hobbled them to a rather naïve and one-sided view of working class virtue and bourgeois unpleasantness. Taken all round, it was a decade in which Australia could boast more of its poets than its novelists, and perhaps more of its artists than either. For a decade in which the young Sidney Nolan and Arthur Boyd followed hard upon the heels of William Dobell, Albert Tucker and Russell Drysdale was important even by international standards, even though all five perfected their craft through attempts to interpret the peculiar character of the Australian landscape and people.

These achievements passed by the majority of Australians for the time being. The time had long gone by when the *Bulletin* bards appealed to literary coterie and laymen alike. The last survivors from the nineties were dying off – 'Banjo' Paterson in 1941, O'Dowd and Ogilvie in 1952 and 1953 respectively – and their successors in popular estimation tended to be novelists who carried on the tradition of bush writing and telling a good, straightforward yarn. Such authors were Ion Idriess, with his tales of Australia's north, or Arthur Upfield, creator of the part-Aboriginal detective, Napoleon Bonaparte. Even more than in the 1930s, however, the novel was yielding ground to other media such as film and radio. The films were almost all imported from Britain or, far more often, from the United States. It was only after about 1947 that a small flow of European films with English sub-titles began to reach Australia, and then it was left to adult education boards and non-commercial cinemas to screen them. As for the Australian film industry, it had fallen on meagre days. Apart from newsreels, it was largely kept alive by one man, Charles Chauvel, whose *Forty Thousand Horsemen* was staple fare of Anzac Day afternoons;[33] *Smithy* and *Bush Christmas* were films by other producers which also enjoyed some popularity, but the finance for expansion was not forthcoming.

Radio on the other hand was at its zenith. These were the great

[33] Amongst his other films were *In the Wake of the Bounty*, *Rats of Tobruk*, *Sons of Matthew*, and *Jedda*.

days of audience participation in talent shows such as 'Australia's Amateur Hour', or in quiz contests, notably those compered by Jack Davey and Bob Dyer. By 1950 over 2 million radio licences had been issued, and it was estimated that about six-sevenths of the listening public preferred the diet of swing, serials, and advertisements offered by the commercial stations to the more varied fare attempted by the Australian Broadcasting Commission. The A.B.C. operated under a number of handicaps. Politicians attempted pressure on its programme content. It was obliged to find time to broadcast long stretches of the federal parliament's debates, a programme with little sparkle except for occasional moments of rough comedy. Programme policy in general was a constant compromise between the pressure to compete for listeners with the commercial stations, and the duty of catering for minority tastes, or actively promoting educational and cultural items of a kind ignored by the commercials.

Because of the system of tying A.B.C. income to a percentage of listeners' licence fees, finance was always uncertain until 1948, when the federal government assumed direct responsibility.[34] Despite these problems the A.B.C. had three major achievements to its credit. It promoted the establishment of a symphony orchestra in each state capital, and organized regular visits by overseas musical celebrities. It succeeded, after considerable opposition from newspaper owners, in establishing a news broadcasting service which won favour because of its immediacy and its attempts at objectivity. And it led the commercials in its coverage of sporting events. Racing and football commentators developed a machine-gun speed and precision, which gave Australian suburban Saturday afternoons a specially characteristic background noise. And the 1940s were a satisfying decade for Australian sport. Bradman and his disciples thrashed the English cricketers with merciless regularity. Football and racing were quickly back to normal after the war; Bernborough was even comparable to Carbine and Phar Lap.

Such, then, was the culture shared by old and new Australians. It reflected an ample leisure born of a flourishing economy. Despite minor setbacks, Australia was about to enjoy a quarter-century of prosperity rivalling, and perhaps surpassing, the long boom of the later nineteenth century. Between 1945 and 1950 the roots of this prosperity lay still, as in the past, in good export prices for primary products. Europe, its economy dislocated by the war, had to be fed and clothed from overseas. Wheatgrowers enjoyed a period of unnaturally keen demand for their harvests. The price of wheat rose from 24.37c. a bushel in 1938/9 to 131.77c. in 1946/7, never dropping below that figure in later years. At the outbreak of war in 1939 a Wheat Board was set up to stabilize prices, and during the war wheatgrowers received a guaranteed minimum price for their output.

---

[34] These problems are discussed in G. C. Bolton, *Dick Boyer*, Canberra, 1967.

In 1948 the board was made permanent, and reconstituted for peace-time purposes. The guaranteed minimum price continued. In good years the excess profits from overseas sales would be pooled to help provide a subsidy for lean years, with the commonwealth contributing whatever extra subsidy was required to keep up payments to wheat-growers. Security prompted expansion. Crop production, which stood at 142 million bushels in 1945/6, went to 184 million in 1950/51. This was due partly to greater use of superphosphate and other fertilizers, but mainly to the expansion of wheatgrowing into 'light' lands previously thought unsuitable, but now brought into production by supplementing deficiencies in trace elements. New South Wales remained in these years the leading wheatgrower among the states, but was being steadily overtaken by Western Australia. It was not yet foreseen that, since the other wheatgrowing nations of the world were also expanding the European market might before long be satisfied, and Australia would be hunting for custom – even in Communist China.

Most primary producers benefited in these years from preferential trade agreements with Britain, either dating from the Ottawa arrangements of the thirties, or newly negotiated to help Britain over an acute period of postwar rationing. The dairying industry, further fortified by government subsidies on the production of butter and cheese, kept its place on the British market; but although production increased with greater efficiency, there was no obvious incentive for expanding the industry, and the number of dairy cattle in Australia remained constant at about 3.2 million. Sugar, the mainstay of tropical Queensland, faced problems in overseas markets through competing with other producers where labour costs were low. Yet the Australian home market took only between 500,000 and 600,000 tons in any one year, and average production already exceeded 800,000 tons in the years between 1935 and 1939. With increasing efficiency, the surplus grew greater each year, and it was not until 1953 that some security came when Britain signed a 21-year agreement giving preference to Australian sugar up to a maximum of 600,000 tons. Since export prices seldom exceeded home consumption prices, a government subsidy to growers was usually necessary. In return for secure prices, the sugar industry submitted to a more detailed amount of regulation than any other. Not only prices, but the areas to go under cane and the types of cane to be preferred were laid down by consultation between the Australian government, the Queensland government, and the major refining company. The justification for the sugar subsidies, as for dairying and the dried fruits industry of the Murray-Murrumbidgee irrigation areas, was that they promoted decentralization and the settlement of rural districts. In the years of European shortage after 1945 this policy looked more than usually plausible.

Wool nevertheless remained the most important of Australia's staples. In 1938/9 Australia pastured just under 120 million sheep, whose annual woolclip averaged almost 1000 million pounds weight and sold at an average f.o.b. price of only 8.88c. a pound. Production was retarded because years of low prices discouraged investment in pasture improvements, fencing, watering, and other sound management policies. Between 1940 and 1945 prices gradually improved – to 15.84c. in 1945/6 – and wool provided between 25 and 32 per cent of Australia's annual export income. Still the pastoral industry could not expand because of wartime shortages of labour and material. Instead, following the bad drought of 1944/5, sheep numbers dropped to 96 million in 1946. Even so, a considerable stockpile of wool had accumulated by the end of the war, and in order not to glut the market Australia in 1945 joined with Great Britain, South Africa, and New Zealand in forming a joint disposals organization to ensure the orderly marketing of the surplus. This organization was wound up in 1951, its task successfully completed. During those years wool was strongly in demand from the war-damaged countries of Europe, and a sharp rise in prices was pushed far higher by stockpiling at the outbreak of the Korean War in 1950. During the 1950/51 season the price of wool soared to an all-time maximum of 120.2c., and wool came to constitute 67 per cent of Australia's export income. These unexpected overseas earnings, and free spending by pastoralists making up for lost years, did much to trigger an inflationary spiral between 1948 and 1951.

The number of men employed on the land dropped sharply during the 1940s, and farmers and graziers were turning eagerly to mechanization and the provision of long-delayed improvements. Wool and wheat seemed to most minds to offer more for the future than mining. It is ironic at a distance of twenty years to read the rather disparaging comment in the *Commonwealth Year Book* for 1951 that 'the value of production from the mineral industry is now considerably less than that returned by the agricultural, the pastoral, and the dairying industry'.[35] Yet such a comment was justified then. The war brought an end to the revival of goldmining. International gold prices were pegged during and after the war in order to ensure currency stability. This discouraged prospecting and development in Australia. From $1\frac{1}{2}$ million fine ounces in 1941 annual production dropped to beneath the million mark during the early 1950s. Nor, despite the world's demands for raw materials, was there a marked increase in base metal output. Copper production fell by 10 per cent between 1941 and 1952. Silver-lead and zinc production failed to grow significantly. Iron ore mining was deterred by a ban on exports. These were Australia's traditional base metals, and during the forties no newcomers supplemented them. The Australian government provided some stimulus by setting up a Bureau of Mineral Resources under the directorship of H. G. Raggatt. Geophysical surveys for uranium and oil were commenced. The government also found most of the finance for an aluminium

35 *Official Year Book of the Commonwealth of Australia, 38*, 1951, p. 846.

plant at Bell Bay in Tasmania, in the hope of encouraging Australian bauxite production. These initiatives bore results only in the 1950s. During the 1940s 'the rush that never ended' was at its slowest dawdle.

So far the picture of the Australian economy was etched on traditional lines. Primary production was dominant as the major contributor to export income. Britain remained Australia's best customer and biggest source of imports, though her performance in both respects already showed the decline that would set in strongly during the 1950s and 1960s. Western Europe took up most of the slack in those years. The United States' trade with Australia had not yet recovered since the trade diversion policies of the later 1930s, particularly since Australia took seriously its membership of the sterling area, and imposed limits on dollar expenditure. South and East Asian trade, although growing, was still relatively small. Yet changes were also taking place in the Australian economy, so that there are good grounds for the verdict that 'the Second World War makes a critical break in Australian economic development'.[36]

Perhaps the war's most obvious effect was its boost to manufacturing. The early 1940s saw unprecedented growth in engineering, metal industries, explosives, and chemicals. Between 1939 and 1946 Australia's factories increased in number by over 15 per cent but the maximum advantage was not taken of the foundations laid by war production. For a few years after 1945 investment in secondary industry declined. The production of machine tools was allowed to fall off to some extent, and the conversion of munitions factories to peacetime purposes was at times slow and ill-planned. Fears of a postwar slump combined with labour troubles to inhibit bold management. Above all, growth was hampered by shortages of raw materials, especially fuel. These difficulties were offset by a very strong consumer demand, the product of high employment and shortages of overseas goods. Established lines of production such as footwear, clothes, plastics, and agricultural machinery, all continued to expand satisfactorily. The later 1940s saw new ventures, particularly the production of paper pulp and motor cars. When production began on the Holden at the end of 1948 demand was so keen that for many months recent second-hand models sold above the price of new cars. Not surprisingly, one of the greatest areas of growth was the building industry. Because of the depression and the war there was a great backlog of demand for private housing, to say nothing of schools, hospitals, factories, shops, and office buildings. Between 1948 and the peak year 1951 between 100,000 and 120,000 Australians found employment in the building trade. Even this could not meet the demand, especially as many homeowners sought to introduce such innovations as indoor plumbing, coloured wall paints, and the use of louvres for

---

[36] N. G. Butlin, 'Some perspectives of Australian economic development, 1890–1965', in C. Forster, Ed., *Australian Economic Development in the Twentieth Century*, London, 1970, p. 319.

enclosing verandahs and sleepouts. A great boost was given to the cult of the do-it-yourself handyman. Although new houses were erected at the rate of about 75,000 a year, the quality was often inefficient and almost always unimaginative, because most building firms operated on a very small scale, and materials were often short. Many of the new suburbs developed at this time were dreary, treeless, and lacking in amenities for the mothers and young children who would spend nearly all their time there. And the needs of these new suburbs placed an unexpectedly heavy call on the public purse.

Government spending during the 1940s swung markedly from rural enterprises, such as railways and irrigation, to expenditure in the cities. Since the farmers for the first time in many years were enjoying liberal access to their bankers, they raised little outcry when federal and state governments stepped up their outlay on domestic water supply schemes, schools, roads, and above all electricity. The importance of fuel and power among Australian priorities was never more apparent than in the late 1940s, when power cuts were frequent because of outmoded equipment and industrial unrest. The most notable government enterprise of these years was the Snowy Mountains hydro-electric and irrigation scheme, which involved co-operation between the governments of Victoria, New South Wales and South Australia, and the Australian government. This scheme involved a major feat of engineering: the diversion of the headwaters of the Snowy through a series of tunnels and dams into the Tumut-Murrumbidgee system. The Murrumbidgee and Murray irrigation areas would thus be provided with controlled water supplies, but the main object of the scheme was to generate power for Canberra, Victoria, and New South Wales. Few were persuaded by critics who pointed out that the same amount of electricity – less than one per cent of the total needs of Victoria and New South Wales – could have been provided more cheaply by other means.[37] To some extent criticisms based on purely economic factors missed a significant point. Australians have been so much as the mercy of their environment in planning economic development that their morale and self-confidence are lifted by major co-operative engineering feats such as the Snowy scheme. Soon the opening up of the Australian Alps led to a growing tourist traffic, who found much to admire in a great work of construction co-ordinating the work of men of many nationalities. The Snowy operation represented a defeat for the parochialism and federal-state rivalry which had long got in the way of economic progress; it was also an example of co-operation between Labor governments in Canberra and Sydney and Liberal governments in Melbourne and Adelaide.[38] The importance of these psychological factors in economic

[37] See *Current Affairs Bulletin*, Sydney, *31*, 13, May 1963, and *32*, 7, August 1963.

[38] For an example of an enthusiastic private observer, see G. Johnston, *Clean Straw For Nothing*, London, 1969, p. 99.

decision-making was to be seen a number of times in postwar Australia, notably in the field of northern development.

Most government enterprise was financed from within Australia; between 1939 and 1950 the domestic share of Australia's public debt rose from 50 to 77 per cent.[39] Where in earlier years the federal and state governments were major borrowers of overseas capital, the quest for capital imports now fell more and more to private enterprise. Britain, despite its postwar financial difficulties, remained the chief source of capital. Australia as a member of the sterling bloc had an interest in promoting Britain's economic recovery, and therefore, like Britain, cut back her spending and her search for capital outside the sterling area. This put a limit to the import of dollar commodities, such as cars, petrol, and machinery, and may have discouraged a certain amount of American investment.[40] This policy was challenged by the economist Sir Douglas Copland, who argued that loans should be sought in the United States because the sterling area could not provide Australia with adequate capital imports.[41] This provoked the rejoinder from the British economist, Sir Sidney Caine, that Britain had curbed home investment during the postwar years in order to remit capital to Australia and South Africa for such non-essentials as milk-bars and cinemas. But the Australian government, at any rate under Chifley, preferred to stick with sterling. This may have been partly through distrust of Wall Street, reinforced by the fact that many American manufacturers and bankers were pressing for the abandonment of British Commonwealth preferential tariffs and quotas as a reward for American economic aid for Britain. These powerful interests prevented America from joining an international trade organization proposed under United Nations' auspices by the Havana Charter of 1948, and although the Americans adhered to the General Agreement on Tariffs and Trade of the same year – as did Australia – it was hardly surprising that the Australian government was cautious about inviting American economic influence. So, at the risk of holding back some sectors of Australia's economic growth, the Australian government kept in line with the British. When the pound sterling was devalued in 1949 in order to improve British competitiveness on export markets, the Australian pound followed suit. These policies were to have their impact on Australian politics.

The Chifley government held to the sterling bloc in these years not only because of its view of Australia's best interests, but also because of natural sympathy with a British government of the same

39 N. Cain, 'Trade and Economic Structure at the Periphery: The Australian Balance of Payments, 1890–1965', in C. Forster, Ed., *Australian Economic Development in the Twentieth Century*, London, 1970, p. 115.

40 D. T. Brash, *American Investment in Australian Industry*, Canberra, 1966.

41 D. Copland, 'The dollar gap and the Commonwealth', in *Foreign Affairs, 28*, 1950, pp. 671–5: B. Thomas, 'The evolution of the sterling area and its prospects', in N. Mansergh, *Commonwealth Perspectives*, Durham, N. C., 1958, pp. 175–207.

reformist Labor outlook as its own. At commonwealth prime ministers' conferences Chifley was likewise more forthcoming than most of his colleagues in insisting that Australia and the other major dominions should bear their share of commonwealth defence burdens instead of leaving everything to Britain.[42] Such actions did not speak loudly enough for the more demonstrative anglophiles among the opposition, such as Menzies and T. W. White. Loud criticisms were voiced early in 1947 when, on the retirement of the Duke of Gloucester as governor-general, the Chifley government nominated an Australian as his successor. Admittedly the government was provocative in choosing W. J. McKell,[43] then active in politics as the Labor premier of New South Wales, and notable as an old associate of Chifley's in the Labor faction fights of that state in the 1930s. The opposition seemed to feel that no Australian, whatever his background, was fit to follow a royal duke; but McKell turned out, despite repeated insults from some non-Labor politicians, to be a competent and dignified governor-general, able to sink his former political allegiances when a question of constitutional principle arose; as it did in 1951, when the Menzies government requested a double dissolution of the federal parliament. The main importance of this controversy was that it illustrated a growing tendency among the Chifley government's opponents to portray it as disloyal to the British connexion and careless of its ties to the non-Communist world in general. The government was luridly portrayed as bent on curbing the Australian people's liberty by the imposition of socialist policies which, if carried to an extreme, would differ only in degree from Communist dictatorship.[44]

Confident of its own good intentions, the Chifley government did not take such criticisms seriously enough. Instead, with a poor sense of timing and tactics, it suddenly announced in August 1947 its intention of nationalizing all the private banks. This followed a High Court decision upholding the Melbourne City Council's challenge to that part of the 1945 banking legislation which required all local authorities to transfer their accounts to the Commonwealth Bank. Although this made no difference to the government's powers over central banking, Chifley and his ministers feared that more vital sections of the Commonwealth Bank Act would next be challenged. Uncertain of their legal grounds, the government over-reacted, announcing its plans impulsively and bluntly to an unprepared public. The private banks, their worst fears confirmed, threw their wealth and power behind the strongest and most successful campaign

[42] L. F. Crisp, *Ben Chifley*, London, 1961, ch 18..

[43] See V. Kelly, *A Man of the People*, Sydney, 1971, and B. Nairn, 'Sir William McKell and Labor History', in *Labour History, 20*, May 1971.

[44] See, for example, Australian Country Party, *The Red Twins – Communism and Socialism*, Sydney, 1949, or many of the speeches of Eric Harrison, J. P. Abbott, H. L. Anthony, and A. G. Cameron in *C.P.D.*, 1946–49.

of anti-government lobbying ever mounted in Australia's history.[45] The banks found allies not only among the wealthy, but among farmers who owed their survival through the depression to a sympathetic bank manager; among bank clerks who valued their white-collar status and saw their careers threatened by relegation to the standing of civil servants; and among many swinging voters who were tired of government regulation with its overtones of wartime, and saw the banking legislation as yet another piece of unwarranted bureaucratic interference. The government showed little insight into these reactions, or in planning its tactics. For the whole showdown was probably unnecessary. The High Court ruled in 1948 that nationalization was beyond the Australian government's powers, and this was confirmed in 1949 by the Privy Council. The private banks were growing to accept the necessity for a strong central bank and might not have faced challenging the 1945 legislation.[46] Even if they had, the High Court, judging by its comments in the 1948 case, would have confirmed the government's rights to quite substantial powers. Evatt, as attorney-general, could not bring himself to trust the judgement of his former colleagues on the High Court, but insisted on prolonging the controversy by the appeal to the Privy Council. His addresses to both courts were too lengthy to help the government's case. Yet, with all these miscalculations, the Chifley government apparently did itself no harm by its attempt at bank nationalization. Public opinion polls showed that although it lost majority support at the end of 1947, the Chifley government regained a lead of up to 4 per cent over the Liberals and Country party during 1948 and the first half of 1949.[47] Although during 1947 the Liberal-Country party coalition defeated Labor governments in Western Australia and Victoria, it was by no means certain that Menzies and Fadden could copy this success at the federal level. Perhaps because of this uncertainty, the opposition intensified its efforts to tar the A.L.P. with the brush of Communism.

Communism at first sight seemed an unlikely menace for Australia, with its high living standards, virtually full employment, and the strong bourgeois principles which might be expected of a people with perhaps the highest percentage of homeowners in the world. Fears grew nevertheless. After the war ended, country after country in eastern Europe was sucked into the Soviet orbit through the threat of Russian military might, the subtle infiltration of governments, and the ruthless suppression of opponents. By 1948, with the overthrow of democracy in Czechoslovakia and the first Berlin crisis, the Red advance seemed almost irresistible. Within Australia, Communists were achieving a publicity out of proportion to their numbers. In the

45 A. L. May, *The Battle for the Banks*, Sydney, 1968.

46 'Sir Leslie McConnon' in C. D. Kemp, *Big Businessmen*, Melbourne, 1964, pp. 141–64.

47 Quoted by L. F. Crisp, *Ben Chifley*, London, 1961, p. 339.

bitter aftermath of the depression, Communist spokesmen won approval in some trade unions as effective and militant fighters for their grievances. During the late 1930s and early 1940s several trade unions, among them the ironworkers, coalminers, sheet metal workers, seamen, and waterside workers, elected Communist officials. They were chosen more for their efficiency than their principles, and their influence, surviving an ineffectual ban on Communism in 1940–41, probably strengthened as a result of Russia's sacrifices in the Second World War. The exact extent of Communist influence in the Australian trade unions was hard to gauge, because conservatives unfriendly to the Labor movement tended to label any militant left-winger as an out-and-out Communist. The most generous calculation was that Communists controlled four of Australia's five Trades and Labour Councils in 1945, and influenced half a million union members among Australia's workforce of 2,114,000.[48] To keep such estimates in perspective, it must be remembered that Communist candidates never gained more than $1\frac{1}{2}$ per cent of the total vote cast at federal elections in the 1940s, and that the only Communist who ever sat in an Australian state parliament – Paterson, a former Rhodes scholar, in Queensland between 1944 and 1950 – never got a majority vote in his electorate, but owed his success to the absence in that state of preferential voting. Nor were Communist sympathizers of importance in the Labor party, whatever its opponents alleged.

Politically the Communists were never important. Industrially they were enough of a nuisance to give credence to the anti-Communists, particularly since strikes frequently happened in the sectors of industry that hit the public. Late in 1945 the coalminers, ironworkers, and seamen were all on strike. During the next two years meatworkers, metalworkers, ironworkers, railwaymen, and the Melbourne public transport workers all staged important strikes. In 1948 there were further disputes among miners and railwaymen. In both Sydney and Melbourne strikes by gas and electricity workers and coalminers caused breakdowns in the city power supplies, disrupting public transport, heating, refrigeration, and light. Since the railways and electricity services were already subject to breakdowns because of obsolete equipment, the public built up a considerable sense of irritation. Many people shared with their newspapers the view that the trade unions were selfishly irresponsible, and that the Labor movement was not doing enough to discipline their activities. The unions, still scarred by the bitter years of depression, thought it

[48] B. A. Santamaria, *The Price of Freedom*, Melbourne, 1964, ch. 2. Strongly anti-communist, this account may be compared with H. E. Weiner, 'The Reduction of Communist Power in the Australian Trade Unions', in *Political Science Quarterly*, 69, 1954, and J. W. Kuhn, 'A note on communists and strikes in Australia', in *Political Science Quarterly*, 70, 1955, which attributes communist success to a lack of adequate grievance procedures in the trade union movement. A. Davidson, in *The Communist Party of Australia*, Stanford, 1969, agrees with Santamaria's estimate.

natural enough to put their own ends first, and even Chifley found it hard to spur the coalminers to greater productivity and public-spiritedness. Yet it was precisely in the area of fuel and power that some of Australia's biggest problems of economic growth were to be found. While coal and electricity supplies remained erratic, and the import of oil fuels from dollar areas was restricted, investors were deterred from planning expansion in secondary industry. Questions of fuel and power had a great bearing on the outcome of the 1949 elections.

The showdown with the unions came in the middle of 1949, when the coalminers of New South Wales and Queensland once more came out on strike. Concerned for the economic effects of the strike, the Chifley cabinet and the Labor governments of the two states stood firmly against it. Eventually the strike was broken when troops were sent in to man the open-cut mines. Only a Labor government could have got away with such a move, without causing lasting resentment in the trade union movement. As it was, the strike and its aftermath caused a temporary rise in unemployment which may have told against the Chifley government.[49] Meanwhile, other forces were organizing against the Communists. Since 1937 a group of young Melbourne Roman Catholic laymen had been perturbed by the spread of Marxist sympathies in Australia. Between 1942 and 1945 some members of this group, the Catholic Social Studies Movement, among whom B. A. Santamaria was prominent,[50] determined to fight Communist influence in trade unions by imitating their methods and determination. Such was the genesis of 'the Movement'. For a few years it worked unpublicized, and was a main force behind the setting up of 'industrial groups' within Communist-influenced trade unions. By no means entirely Catholic in membership, these industrial groups challenged and exposed the tactics of left-wing union officials in rigging meetings and ballots, and by 1949 their activities were bearing fruit. In that year Communist officials of the Ironworkers' Union were defeated by moderates, a change for which 'the Movement' claimed some credit. It was at least symbolic that in the same year, for the first time since the war, the Students' Representative Council of Melbourne University, the most ideologically active Australian campus, had as its president not a left-winger but the future Liberal cabinet minister Ivor Greenwood. The extent of 'the Movement's' influence in turning the tide against Communism has been belittled by its enemies and exaggerated by its friends. In some ways 'the Movement' had easy going, since strikes at home and Stalinism abroad helped to make Communism unpopular. Yet it could not be denied that by 1949 'the Movement' was rising in power and confidence among the counsels

[49] L. Haylen, *Twenty Years' Hard Labor*, Melbourne, 1969, p. 89.

[50] See J. D. Pringle, *Australian Accent*, London, 1958, ch. 4: F. G. Clarke, 'Labour and the Catholic Social Studies Movement', in *L.H.*, 20, May 1971: P. Ormonde, *The Movement*, Melbourne, 1972.

of the A.L.P., and that the left wing, both within and outside the Labor movement, was on the defensive.

But the 'Red menace' was far too good a political cry to be abandoned by the non-Labor parties with a federal election in the offing. Throughout 1949 lavish propaganda warned the voters that the return of the Chifley government would cost them a good deal of liberty. Much of this propaganda was so extravagant as to be self-defeating, but some of it may have stuck. Other factors probably caused the loss of popularity registered by the Labor government in public opinion polls during the latter half of 1949. One was simply a question of image. Although the Chifley government generated idealism and enthusiasm among the young intellectuals in the federal public service, to many of the younger generation outside Canberra its members seemed a group of opinionated old bores in austerity suits, preoccupied with a depression that was now part of the past. Of greater substance was the problem of inflation. Denied power over price control – a 1948 referendum on the issue fared no better than its predecessors – the government, after holding price levels almost steady between 1942 and 1947, was unable to check an 18 per cent increase in the cost of living between 1947 and 1949. Wages kept pace with this rise, thanks to a series of generous arbitration court judgements, so that a consistently high level of consumer spending seemed likely to trigger further inflation. The devaluation of the Australian pound in 1949 was a further inflationary pressure, especially in view of the keen demand for wool and other Australian primary produce.

While Chifley hesitated to promise easy solutions, Menzies had no qualms about stumping the country promising to put value back into the pound. Menzies must have known that this was economic nonsense, but it was the nonsense the voters wanted to hear. Tired of regulations and restrictions, they wanted to enjoy the fruits of prosperity. This feeling crystallized after June 1949, when the High Court ruled that the Australian government no longer had the power to impose petrol rationing, and the government asked the states to re-impose it on the grounds that unrestricted petrol imports would drain Australia's dollar reserves. To the opposition this was a prime example of the Chifley government's fondness for unnecessary controls. Adequate supplies of petrol, they claimed, could be found from non-dollar sources.[51] In denying this, the government accused the opposition of irresponsibility towards Australia's financial standing and cynicism in appealing to the selfish instincts of motorists for votes. In the event, neither side was right. There was probably not enough petrol available from non-dollar sources, but because of the boom in Australia's export income due to devaluation and rising wool prices, it was possible to abolish petrol rationing without harmful economic consequences – in fact, to Australia's benefit in that it stimulated investment in oil

[51] A. W. Fadden, *They Called Me Artie*, Brisbane, 1969, pp. 107–8, gives the background of the opposition's case.

refineries, the manufacture of motor-cars and spare parts, and allied industries. Not that it would be just to infer that the Liberals and the Country party appealed solely to the self-interest of the voters. Fearful of Communism, they proposed measures of self-discipline: the re-introduction of compulsory military training, and the outlawing of the Australian Communist party and its sympathizers. It was hard to predict which of the opposition's policies would prove vote-winners, or whether the public would prefer to stay with a Labor government which relied on its record in providing full employment. Apart from the natural uncertainties of an election, there was a major redistribution of parliamentary seats under an Act of 1948, enlarging the House of Representatives from 74 to 121. At the same time the Senate increased from 36 to 60, and its method of election was altered to proportional representation – a device which more than any other secured an accurate reflection of Australian party allegiances, but made it hard for governments to secure an absolute Senate majority in their own right, and easy for comparatively small minority parties to hold the balance of power there. This was unforeseen in 1949. Minor parties were not a factor in the election.

'Give thanks and rejoice this day for the deep, quiet sanity of the British Empire', wrote the London *Daily Express* on the Monday after the election.[52] Mouthpiece of Lord Beaverbrook, it had a con-servative victory to boast of: 74 seats in Australia's House of Repre-sentatives went to the Menzies-Fadden coalition, and only 47 to their opponents. Worse for the A.L.P., the members who lost their seats were mostly among the younger and more dynamic elements in the party. Their only consolation was that they still retained control of the Senate. To some commentators the 1949 elections marked a notable watershed in Australian history, when Australians turned their faces from 'the light on the hill, the hope of a better society which sustained radicals and optimists in the past, and devoted the remnant of their energies to being "the lucky country".'[53] No doubt many thought in 1949 that the replacement of Labor by a 'free enterprise' government was a momentous change. In most important respects it made very little difference at all.

Menzies and his colleagues did not put the value back into the pound. Instead, inflation continued faster than ever during 1950, as both export and import figures reached record heights. If the Menzies government did little to check this boom, this was not because they were abandoning the financial controls won for them by their Labor predecessors. Although they resurrected the Commonwealth Bank Board, it was still with Coombs as governor and the treasury in un-doubted control. The central banking system as renovated in 1945

[52] *Daily Express*, London, 12 December 1949.

[53] J. Young, 'Dowsing the Light on the Hill', in *Australian Book Review, 8*, 2–3, 1968, p. 42.

was too valuable for any modern Australian government to discard. In other ways the Menzies government followed many of the Chifley government's more creative initiatives. Immigration was fostered just as carefully by the Liberal Harold Holt as by Labor's Arthur Calwell. Work continued unabated on the Snowy scheme, the Australian National University, and the Bureau of Mineral Resources. Nor was there any cutback on social services. The proportion of government expenditure on social welfare in fact increased from $4\frac{1}{2}$ per cent in the last year of the Chifley government to $5\frac{1}{2}$ per cent in 1953–4. The scope of social services was not greatly extended, however; the main innovation of the early 1950s was the payment of child endowment to the first child in a family, previously ineligible. Moreover, the new government succeeded in putting through a national health scheme acceptable to the medical profession. Piloted by the veteran minister for health, Sir Earle Page, the new scheme did not provide for free medicine, but certain expensive drugs could be had for a standard fee of five shillings. Hospital and medical benefits were confined to those who subscribed to a registered contributory fund, the amount of benefit varying with the contributor's input. Because of the number of separate administrative programmes among competing benefit funds, this scheme proved expensive to run, but at least succeeded in securing Australians against many of the expenses of illness.

Greater attention was also paid to the welfare of Australia's Aboriginal minority. This was a critical moment for them, because for the first time since the coming of the white men their numbers ceased to dwindle and, for reasons which are not entirely clear, the Aboriginal birth-rate started to show a continuous upward swing. Under the stimulus of the anthropologist A. P. Elkin and the administrator E. W. P. Chinnery, the government committed the Northern Territory administration as early as 1939 to 'the raising of their status so as to entitle them by right and by qualification to the ordinary rights of citizenship'.[54] During the 1940s the more progressive state administrations had been abandoning the old concept of segregating the Aborigines in reserves, and had begun to grope towards an ideal of assimilation. The war created wider employment opportunities for the Aborigines of the North both in the pastoral industry and through military activities. The first important portent of changing social attitudes among the Aborigines arose in 1946 in the Pilbara district of Western Australia. Here, under the influence of a white man, Don McLeod, many Aborigines stopped working for the pastoralists in order to form co-operative settlements making a living from livestock and alluvial mining. Despite many vicissitudes these co-operatives survived for more than two decades. At the level of official policy, however, the government remained relatively inactive until 1951

[54] C. D. Rowley, *Aboriginal Policy and Practice, Vol. I, The Destruction of Aboriginal Society*, Canberra, 1970, pp. 328–9; and see ch. 17 for an appraisal of federal policy in this period.

when one of the new intake of 1949 Liberals, Paul Hasluck, convened a conference of federal and state ministers affirming the responsibility to give Aborigines access to citizen rights. It was not yet foreseen that Aborigines might come to prefer a separate but equal status. The immediate task of putting assimilation into practice was formidable enough.

In foreign policy the Menzies government departed in some ways from Evatt's line, but to a large extent the changes were in the style, not the content, of Australian diplomacy. Under two highly competent ministers for external affairs, first Percy Spender[55] and after 1951 R. G. Casey, the Australians continued and in some ways extended their commitments towards Asia. Spender was the author and main driving force behind the adoption in 1950 of the Colombo Plan, an agreement between a few highly developed countries such as Australia and a number of the less prosperous new nations of Asia. Under the Colombo Plan Australia undertook to admit regular intakes of Asian students into her universities and technical colleges, and to donate technological aid and the services of experts to modernize and diversify the economies of such countries as India, Pakistan, and Indonesia. Although Australia's main expenditure on under-developed nations was to be concentrated in Papua-New Guinea, the Colombo Plan earned considerable goodwill as a practical gesture of concern, particularly since it was aimed at developing the recipients' capacity for self-help.

At another level of diplomacy, the two Asian issues which most preoccupied Australian politicians between 1949 and 1951 were the Japanese peace treaty and the rise of Communist China. These two developments were inter-related, in that it was the growth of Communist power in East Asia which prompted the United States to seek a speedy peace with Japan, and made her more ready to mollify Australian doubts and fears about Japan's conduct in the future. Even during Evatt's time, Australia had intimated that she would welcome a regional security pact in the South-West Pacific which included the United States. The more warmly pro-American Menzies government pressed these initiatives during the early part of 1950. One obstacle to American involvement in the region was removed at the end of 1949, when the Dutch recognition of Indonesia lowered the international temperature. But matters were not clinched until after the outbreak of the Korean War in June 1950, when the Communist North Koreans invaded the pro-American South. The United Nations denounced this aggression and called for a task force to repel the invaders. The main response came from the Americans, but Australia also sent regular troops: it was one of the few occasions when Australians have participated in a United Nations peace-keeping operation. The war swept back and forward across Korea, first the North Koreans and then the United Nations forces gaining the upper hand. Then, as the

55 See P. C. Spender, *Politics and a Man*, Sydney, 1972.

front line rolled back towards China, Communist 'volunteers' from that country once more turned the tide in favour of the North Koreans. Eventually the war ground to a stalemate near the original frontier between North and South, and petered out in a marathon of armistice talks. These events moved the Americans to hurry on the conclusion of peace with Japan's new parliamentary government which, lacking a regular army, was thought to constitute no threat to the security of its neighbours.

Even in these circumstances Australia was not happy about falling into line until the United States was pledged to sign a regional security pact, the ANZUS treaty of 1951.[56] Although it fell short of committing the Americans to come automatically to the defence of Australia and New Zealand if they were victims of aggression, the ANZUS treaty was seen as a necessary insurance. In its frank recognition of Australia's dependence on American might in the Pacific, it was the logical outcome of Curtin's wartime policies. Although Evatt condemned the treaty, as is the way of oppositions, Australian fear of China must have brought a closer alliance with the United States into being. The most notable feature of the treaty was the exclusion of Britain, despite the Menzies government's reputation for pro-British feelings, and despite the known wish of the United Kingdom government to be included in the pact. The old ties were gradually loosening.

Within Australia the Korean war had several noteworthy effects. It made for greater public acceptance of the re-introduction of compulsory national service. This consisted of no more than a basic training course of between four and six months for eighteen-year-olds – a surprisingly modest programme at a time when the Menzies government believed that a third world war would break out within three years;[57] and yet it was not thought necessary to send conscripts to Korea as it was later thought necessary to send them to the more limited war in Vietnam. Any greater intake of national servicemen in 1950–51 would have placed strains on the economy and manpower reserves of Australia, and the government deemed it unwise to risk these consequences. This sense of an imminent showdown with the Communist world may also have spurred the Menzies government in its attempts to outlaw the Australian Communist party, a measure to which Menzies himself was a late convert, although the Country party and right-wing Liberals had been urging it for years. The A.L.P. was thought to be in some danger of splitting over this issue, but eventually, strongly influenced by 'the Movement' and the industrial groups, came down in favour of the ban. But the Labor opposition (and many others) could not swallow some of the enforcement measures which

56 For this treaty consult T. R. Reese, *Australia, New Zealand, and the United States*, London, 1969, and P. C. Spender, *Exercises in Diplomacy*, Sydney, 1969. The text is reproduced in F. K. Crowley, *Modern Australia in Documents*, 2, 1939–1970, Melbourne, 1973, pp. 248–50.

57 *Sydney Morning Herald*, 3 March 1951.

the Menzies government thought essential for the operation of the ban, in particular a clause placing the onus of proof for any person accused of illegal Communist practices not, as is usual in British justice, on the prosecution, but on the accused. Given the propensity of some Australian politicians to accuse anyone with unorthodox or radical views of being a Communist, this was a very sweeping power for the government to exercise, and provided the main plank for opposition to the bill.

After a stormy passage through parliament, the legislation outlawing Communism was brought before the High Court, who ruled that the federal parliament had no power to pass such an act. The Menzies government then prepared to seek the necessary authority from the voters through a referendum. Although the government parties and some Labor members supported a 'Yes' vote, at the referendum in September 1951 the proposal was rejected only by a very narrow margin; Queensland, Western Australia and Tasmania voted in favour and the overall 'No' majority was less than the total of informal votes. Almost certainly it was the doubt raised by the onus of proof clause that turned the balance.[58] Although Menzies represented the measure to be essential to Australia's security, it was never revived subsequently. Perhaps the situation was sufficiently controlled by the Australian Security Intelligence Organization, which the Chifley government had established in 1949; perhaps Menzies may have felt that the Communist controversy had served its turn in dividing the A.L.P., although the full repercussions were not apparent for some years.

This rebuff did not mean that the voters had lost confidence in the Menzies-Fadden coalition. On the contrary, their authority was confirmed at a general election in April 1951 when the Menzies government, in order to get rid of a hostile Senate which persistently rejected or altered its legislation, advised the governor-general to make a double dissolution of parliament.[59] Although the A.L.P. recovered five seats in the House of Representatives, the outcome was a majority for the Menzies-Fadden coalition in both houses. Shortly afterwards, during the celebrations for the fiftieth anniversary of Australian Federation in June, Chifley died. He was replaced as leader of the Labor party and the opposition by Evatt, who despite his superb intellect, was too impulsive to be a good political tactician, such as was then needed to control the diverse elements in his party. Yet it seemed likely that before long he would be prime minister, as Menzies had won his election only in the nick of time.

The problem of inflation, which had gathered momentum all through the wool boom of 1950, was getting out of hand during the early months of 1951 as wool prices receded without any corresponding drop in Australia's swollen volume of imports. Severe and unpopular

58 L. C. Webb, *Communism and Democracy in Australia*, Melbourne, 1954.

59 R. G. Menzies, *The Measure of the Years*, Melbourne, 1970, ch. 5.

corrective action would soon be unavoidable. And in contemplating remedial measures, it was remarkable how in some ways the government's thinking and its cohesion had improved very little since the late 1930s. Even during the wool boom the coalition between the Liberals and the Country party was severely strained over financial policy. Menzies and most of the Liberals were in favour of appreciating the value of the Australian pound as a means of restoring a stable balance of trade. Fadden and the Country party bitterly fought this proposal because it would strike at the competitive power of Australian primary products in overseas markets. Cabinet, in Fadden's view, was 'on the verge of dissolution'.[60] In the end, Fadden devised a compromise under which the spending power of woolgrowers would be curbed by holding back 20 per cent of the export income from wool as a reserve against future taxation. The crisis was over, but it showed that the Menzies-Fadden coalition was still at least as likely to split under pressure as the opposition. And in July 1951, when the day of economic reckoning could no longer be put off, the remedial measures proposed by the Menzies-Fadden coalition were startling in their pre-Keynesian harshness and their overtones of depression thinking. It was at first planned to dismiss 10,000 federal civil servants, to cut immigration by 25 per cent, to increase taxation, and to prune public works severely. Gentler counsels were eventually to prevail, but the plan showed how little Australian politicians were able to handle and plan for a period of economic growth and prosperity. To a surprising extent their outlook was still dominated by the mentality of the depression.

So as the Australian commonwealth completed its first half-century, there was an odd disparity between the new opportunities for economic growth and national maturity, and the capacity of politicians to recognize and seize these opportunities. The Liberal-Country party coalition was uncertainly cemented and inept in its control of the sophisticated economic controls now at the Australian government's disposal. The A.L.P. was a prisoner of its past, unable to adapt its working-class and socialist origins to the demands of postwar Australia. Yet both groups were building better than they knew during the 1940s. They had drawn Australia out of its British leading-strings by an immigration policy which would permanently enrich and diversify the texture of Australian society, and by foreign policies which brought the nation closer to South-East Asia and the United States, its natural partners in the Pacific world. They had laid the foundations for Australia's future social and economic growth by strengthening the federal government's financial machinery, encouraging the diversification of secondary industry, increasing the range of educational opportunity, widening the scope and provision of social services, and generating a sense of national responsibility and purpose to replace the pessimistic drift of the 1930s. If the Curtin and Chifley

[60] A. W. Fadden, *They Called Me Artie*, Brisbane, 1969, p. 116.

governments deserved praise for initiating many of these developments, the Menzies-Fadden coalition was not slow to preserve and
extend them. Compared to this fundamental similarity of purpose, the
issues which divided Australians – the shrill accusations of Communism and crypto-Fascism, the squabble over power and prestige –
could be discounted as a futile, noisy, and largely irrelevant sideshow,
the hangover of Australia's earlier colonial immaturity.

12

1951-72

W. J. Hudson

*A new watershed—political leadership—the A.L.P. before 1954—
the split of 1954-55—the Petrov affair—Evatt and the Movement
—the Hobart Conference and its aftermath—the D.L.P. and the
Q.L.P.—McEwen, the Country party and the coalition—Menzies
and his elections—Holt and Gorton—the character of the Liberal-
Country party hegemony—expansion of central power and role
of government—dual enterprises and organized marketing—the
immigration programme—the decline of the British connection—
the E.E.C. and the Commonwealth—Australia and the United
States—Americanization—U.S. investment—Australia and Asia—
Vietnam—Australia and China—Japan—Indonesia—Papua and
New Guinea—urbanization—industrialization—wool and wheat
—other primary industries—the mining boom—self-identification
—unions of employees—arbitration and wages—women in
employment—social services and welfare assistance—the Aborigines—education—state-aid to private schools—sectarian relations and religiosity—the quality of cultural life—intellectual
life—leisure—the years of fat.*

To write the history of one's own society's very recent past demands
daring of the writer and tolerance of the reader. When time has not
yet elapsed to allow the shadows of men and events to lengthen or
shorten in the light of subsequent developments, there is a problem of
perspective. When archives are still inaccessible and intimate records
of participants are still unpublished, there is a problem of sources.
When the historian has lived through the period under review, there
is a problem of choice: the significant tends to be what lodged deepest
in his own memory or most encroached on his own experience. And,
probably prone to the academic's occupational hazard of alienation,
the contemporary historian may well be seen to foist his own values
on to a society of which he is not at all typical.

It is not lightly suggested here, therefore, that the two decades to
1970 comprised years of such profound change in Australian experience as to allow a confident prediction that future historians will
see them as a watershed comparable only perhaps with the 1850s.
These were the years during which an overseas British settler society

504

finally left the milieu of the founding nation. At the same time, though not to a degree comparable with the former filial relationship with Britain, Australia transferred the focus of its external interest to the United States. At the same time, again, Australia at last was forced by political change in Asia and the Pacific to abandon its old notion of itself as a dependent outpost and to engage in regional political and economic diplomacy of a formerly unknown kind. Australia was also transformed from an essentially rural export society into a modern western industrial state. Finally, there was a remarkable change in the life styles and expectations of Australians in the period, the ethos of the lean battler giving way to a much fatter society.

Each of these aspects of change in Australian experience will be discussed in turn, but it is appropriate first to note the domestic political context. Certainly, increasingly pervasive bureaucracy, the sophistication of economists, wide acceptance of basic humanitarian canons and the erosion of ideological commitment have tended to narrow the policy gap between major parties in the western democracies, among them Australia – one could almost speak of a flight from policy. Certainly, too, some of the change sprang from developments in the 1940s and earlier, or from developments overseas. Nevertheless, policies advanced by the usually co-operating Liberal and Country parties on the one side, and on the other, by the Labor party, continued to differ at the hustings; in national office Labor probably would have given a significantly different tone to Australian life in the 1950s and 1960s. One must say 'probably' because the striking feature of the period is the unbroken hegemony of the conservative Liberal-Country party coalitions at the national level and their dominance in the states. For a period at the end of the 1960s the only notable power base held by Labor in the whole of Australia was the Brisbane City Council.

Several factors applied here. Until his retirement in 1966, Robert Menzies dominated parliament and a Liberal party almost of his own creation, and in Australia at large he had no close competitor in aura or tactical skill.[1] The Country party was led in the federal parliament until 1958 by Arthur Fadden, by John McEwen until 1971 and then by the much younger Douglas Anthony; all were considerable men, but, with some qualifications in McEwen's case, they were content in the main to work in harness with the Liberals.[2] Labor's revered leader Ben Chifley died in opposition in 1951 and was succeeded by Herbert Evatt, a magnificent foreign minister in the Curtin and Chifley Labor

---

[1] See K. West, *Power in the Liberal Party: A Study in Australian Politics*, Melbourne, 1965. See also the autobiographical reminiscences of R. G. Menzies, *Afternoon Light*, Melbourne, 1967 and *The Measure of the Years*, Melbourne, 1970.

[2] There are as yet no good biographies of Liberal and Country Party leaders. Some have published their reminiscences, for example, A. Fadden. *They Called Me Artie*, Brisbane, 1969: E. Page, *Truant Surgeon*, Sydney, 1963: P. C. Spender, *Politics and a Man*, Sydney, 1972.

governments of 1941–9 but a poor domestic politician utterly lacking capacity for effective leadership of a singularly faction-prone party.[3] Sadly reduced by Menzies' superior flair and his own incapacities, he gave way in 1960 to Arthur Calwell. This veteran of the palmy 1940s almost toppled the coalition in 1961, but age and a sundered party were heavy weights to carry. Menzies' departure in 1966 and Calwell's in 1967 and the succession respectively of Harold Holt and Gough Whitlam closed the charisma gap. With Holt's untimely death by drowning late in 1967 and the Liberals' hesitant choice of the ungroomed John Gorton, the leadership battle, increasingly important at a time of television and consumer packaging of politics, swung Labor's way. The swing became even more pronounced when the Liberals in early 1971 replaced Gorton with William McMahon who, after two decades of success with a wide variety of portfolios, proved unimpressive as a leader. Still, for three-quarters of the period, Menzies' personal qualities comprised a major factor in the coalition's uninterrupted electoral success. A great orator, he exploited the Communist issue in the oppressive Cold War years of the 1950s; early in the 1960s he markedly weakened the once inviolable Labor-Catholic nexus and the protestant tradition of his own party, and he knew how to reap the last grain of electoral harvest from piecemeal social welfare legislation and from Labor's fratricidal tendencies. Australia had not seen his like since Henry Parkes in the previous century, and Parkes was a primitive in comparison.

It is probably the case, too, that, despite abrupt doses of deflation in the early 1950s and again in the early 1960s, the electorate generally was lulled by twenty years of relative economic stability, virtually full-employment, an impression of continuing development, some opportunity for social mobility from the old working class, and probably the conservatism of the new immigrant working class. However, Labor did not become an anachronism. In 1954, 1961 and 1969, Labor's national vote numerically exceeded the coalition's.[4] Further, both sides now wooed Catholic voters with educational aid. With international politics less favourable to coalition campaigns, and with the emergence of younger middle class leaders perhaps with greater impact on a younger and more affluent electorate, Labor's fortunes showed signs of revival late in the 1960s; witness the electoral success of South Australian Labor with Donald Dunstan in 1965 and under him in 1970, and the deep inroads made by federal Labor under Whitlam in 1969 on the huge federal house majority won by Holt over Calwell in 1966. And it is not to follow the customary academic tendency to

---

[3] See L. F. Crisp, *Ben Chifley*, London, 1961: K. Tennant, *Evatt: Politics and Justice*, Sydney, 1970.

[4] For electoral statistics up to 1964 see C. A. Hughes and B. D. Graham, *A Handbook of Australian Government and Politics 1890–1964*, Canberra, 1968. All federal and state elections since 1955 are discussed in successive articles in the Political Chronicle Section of *A.J.P.H.*

focus disproportionately on Labor to suggest that the principal reason for the coalition's twenty-three year tenure of office was the Labor split of 1954–5. A product of left-right factionalism, personal careerism and ineptitude, and also honed sharper by sectarianism (all usual enough in kind but not this time in degree), the split left the Labor remnant for a time sour and alienated and saw the creation of breakaway parties by the expelled and the exasperated. These latter coalesced as the Democratic Labor party which, though it survived to become a party in its own right, remained heavily, and perhaps predominantly, comprised of older men who had been Labor and younger men who would otherwise have been Labor had Labor retained its former colouring. Democratic Labor not only split the Labor effort, it also split the Labor vote by directing preferences to coalition parliamentary candidates. Australian electoral practice prevents appropriate parliamentary representation for smaller, dispersed parties except in the state-wide federal senate electorates (and in 1970 there were five Democratic Labor senators), but a preferential system of voting and Democratic Labor's usual allocation of second preferences to the coalition prevented almost certain coalition defeats. But for the Democratic Labor party, it seems certain that Labor would have achieved office in 1961 and probably in 1969, and might possibly have won in 1958 and 1963.

That the Liberal-Country coalition's survival in Canberra was anything but assured is evident from the politics of the years to 1954. When the coalition won office in December 1949, Labor still controlled the Senate, and Labor governments ruled in Queensland, New South Wales and Tasmania. Frustrated by the Senate, Menzies engineered justification for a double dissolution, but in the subsequent elections in 1951, while the coalition achieved its Senate majority, it lost five house seats to Labor. Later in the year the coalition's bid to alter the federal constitution so as to permit the outlawing of the Communist party was narrowly rejected in a national referendum.[5] At the same time, the coalition skirted dismemberment when Country party ministers had to carry almost to the point of resignation their hostility to some leading Liberals' liking for currency appreciation as a corrective to racing inflation: the retail price index rose almost as much in 1950–51 as over the following thirteen years.[6] In 1952, when the coalition in Canberra brought down a harsh deflationary budget, Labor achieved office in Victoria; in 1953, Labor took over in Western Australia and increased its house majority in New South Wales from two to twenty. Labor now ruled in all the states except South Australia where a rurally-weighted jerrymander kept Thomas Playford's Liberal Country League government secure, although even here Labor picked up seats in 1953. The slide in the federal coalition's fortunes

[5] See L. C. Webb, *Communism and Democracy in Australia: A Survey of the 1951 Referendum*, Melbourne, 1954.

[6] A. Fadden, *They Called Me Artie*, Brisbane, 1969, p. 114.

continued in 1954 when, despite the melodrama of a Soviet Union agent's defection in an atmosphere hurtful to Labor, and despite public dispute in Labor ranks over Evatt's grand social welfare promises at the hustings, Labor still picked up five seats and more than half the national vote. Then, apparently on the brink of sweeping the country, Labor fell apart in a few months later in 1954. National power retreated from its grasp; Labor lost government in Victoria in 1955, in Queensland in 1957, in Western Australia in 1959, and in New South Wales a house majority of twenty slipped to six in 1956 and to four in 1959. In the 1960s, even New South Wales and Tasmania were lost and, except for successes in South Australia later in the decade, Labor was in eclipse and conservative coalitions held majorities in all Australia's seven parliaments.

In the great Labor split of 1954–5, normally competing factions merged to bring down men in power; power was the prize, doctrines and traditions were the ammunition. In the early and mid-1940s, Communists came close to dominating the trade union bureaucracy and, in 1945, the Labor party in New South Wales formed what were called industrial groups to combat Communists in the unions which then, as since, controlled about two-thirds of the party's power bases. The groupers, as they were called, spread quickly to Victoria, South Australia and Queensland. About two-thirds of the groupers were at least nominally Catholics and, of these, about half seem to have been associated with 'the Movement'. The groupers' Catholic ingredient was not too disproportionate; the still largely working class Catholic community was a natural Labor component, more than half the federal Labor M.P.s were Catholics and, in the early 1950s, ten of Queensland's eleven Labor cabinet ministers were Catholics. Led by a volatile young Melbourne lawyer, B. A. Santamaria, 'the Movement' was an episcopally-backed organization dedicated primarily to the destruction of Communist power in the unions but also to the advancement of ameliorative alternatives to capitalism and socialism, notably in the form of industrial co-operatives and intensive land settlement schemes.[7] Between 1948 and 1954, in appallingly bitter and often physically violent strife, the Labor party groupers and their Movement allies were largely successful in wresting trade union control from Communist officials.

In the very process of their Herculean effort, the often younger and better educated groupers posed a threat to other Labor factions, especially to the older generation. Often Catholics of the tribal and unintellectual kind, these latter varied from exuberant mob orators of the left like Sydney's E. J. Ward, to more dogged reformers like Chifley and gentle moderates of the right like Tasmania's Robert Cosgrove. Some, like Victoria's P. J. Kennelly, almost the archetype of the older 'fixer', saw the groups as a threat to their faction-juggling

[7] See B. A. Santamaria, *The Price of Freedom*, Melbourne, 1964: P. Ormonde, *The Movement*, Melbourne, 1972.

power from the beginning. Indeed, in 1950 when groupers won control of the Victorian party executive, Kennelly resigned as secretary after several clashes; he remained federal secretary, but he depended personally on his Victorian Legislative Council seat, and in 1952 groupers deprived him of preselection. In New South Wales, where Tom Dougherty, national secretary of the giant and traditionally anti-Communist Australian Workers' Union, had joined them, the groupers won control of the state party in 1952, displacing the machine of J. A. Ferguson, a Sydney equivalent of Kennelly. In Queensland, too, the A.W.U., for many years controller of parliamentarians and hostile to the left-wing Brisbane Trades Hall officials, supported the groupers.

When Evatt succeeded to the federal Labor parliamentary leadership on Chifley's death in 1951, he seemed to ally himself with the rising grouper faction, less from a sense of common ground than from a need to find a personal power base. However, while the groupers controlled the party in the big eastern states by 1953, they did not quite carry the heights, and this for several reasons. First, they alienated some traditionalists by welcoming and using coalition government legislation to allow easier recourse to supervised union ballots and by clearly welcoming the coalition's attempts to outlaw the Communist party. Second, in a federally structured party the smaller states mattered; with these, and especially with the Western Australian state secretary, F. E. Chamberlain, Kennelly politicked brilliantly to hold the federal executive. Third, the groupers' success in the unions almost inevitably took them into the party's political apparatus and there they became almost *ex officio* opponents of old guard industrialists, especially in Melbourne, who formerly had worked closely with groups and Movement to survive Communist competition. Fourth, although Kennelly and many of the groupers' power competitors were Catholics, and although the Movement was meeting ecclesiastical opposition (especially after the elevation to the episcopacy in 1954 of Labor traditionalist James Carroll as an auxiliary to Sydney's Cardinal Gilroy), there was a protestant-masonic strand among the industrialists to give sectarian bite to their animosity. Fifth, Dougherty withdrew A.W.U. support. Not all the lesser A.W.U. barons had followed Dougherty; E. E. Reece of Tasmania was a friend of Kennelly, and Clyde Cameron in South Australia had helped to deprive the groups of party authorization there in 1951. But A.W.U. support had been vital in Queensland and New South Wales and, to a less extent, in Victoria. All this left Evatt's leadership in jeopardy. He had courted the groupers but they had bitterly deplored his appearance as legal counsel for the Communist interest in a High Court case which ruled unconstitutional the coalition's attempt to outlaw the Communist party by legislation. Many did not approve of his leadership of a successful 'no' campaign in the subsequent 1951 referendum on a constitutional amendment to give the coalition the power to ban the Communist party. When grouper interest in him disappeared utterly as a result of the Petrov affair in 1954, he had either to repair his fences with them, or else he could jump over to the anti-grouper alliance in such a way that they would accept him rather than their favourite, Arthur Calwell. The first alternative was a difficult and perhaps pointless task; given the development of an anti-grouper alliance of the surviving left, alienated industrialists, Kennelly and the old machine men, and the A.W.U., Evatt chose to jump.

Early in February 1954, Menzies learned from the Australian Security Intelligence Organization that a security operative in the Soviet embassy in Canberra was likely to defect. On 3 April, the defector, Vladimir Petrov, was granted political asylum, bringing with him embassy documents. On 4 April Menzies saw these documents. On the evening of 13 April, Menzies informed the House of Representatives of the defection and cabinet's decision to establish a royal commission of inquiry, a decision which was supported on the following day by Evatt.[8] In the campaign leading up to national elections late in May, the press and the Country party capitalized on the Petrov affair, but the Liberals in general, and Menzies in particular, stood on their record and very effective scorning of Evatt's platform of generous social welfare pledges, including abolition of the means test for pension qualification.

During the campaign the royal commission held only a formal session, but after the election, on 13 July, Evatt's press secretary was questioned by the commission about a document he had allegedly written before joining Evatt's staff and had passed on to a Soviet source in Canberra. Two days later others of Evatt's staff were mentioned in connection with another document provided by Petrov and allegedly written by a Sydney Communist journalist. On 13 August, Evatt appeared before the commission as counsel for his staff, making the bitter and often to be repeated claim that the whole Petrov affair represented a plot to embarrass him electorally. That Menzies stage-managed Petrov's defection has passed into Australian lore, but it might be noted that Menzies left it to a royal commission well after the slated elections to bring out aspects really damaging to Evatt, even though he must have been aware of them seven weeks before the elections and doubtless could have found some way of exploiting them. On 1 September, Evatt told the commission that the second document was a forgery and that the inclusion in it of the names of two of his staff was part of a conspiracy against him. On 7 September, the commission withdrew Evatt's right to appear, saying that he was confusing his legal with his political roles. Evatt's activities before the commission further alienated grouper elements in the party (in part, on grounds of feared electoral impact). His long absences from parliament coincided with a quickly widening gulf between left and right in caucus on cold war foreign policy issues and

8 This chronology is Menzies' own. See R. G. Menzies, *The Measure of the Years*, Melbourne, 1970, pp. 154–97.

with good parliamentary performances by Calwell, now casting a heavy shadow over Evatt's leadership.

Evatt made his jump on 5 October, 1954. He released a press statement which, without naming Santamaria or the Movement, claimed that especially in Victoria a small section of Labor membership was subverting Labor at the instigation of an outside organization.[9] That the wording was vague, and that some of the evidence cited was absurd, was beside the point; his evidence included the public attack during the recent elections on his means test abolition proposal by a Victorian M.P., W. M. Bourke, a Catholic but strongly anti-Movement grouper. The sectarian tiger was loosed, the daily press plate was overflowing and the 'outs' in the Labor power game had their banner for an onslaught against the 'ins' in an hysterical atmosphere of conspiracy and Italian plots. The bitterness generated in those weeks after Evatt's statement can scarcely be described; the pressure on non- or even anti-Movement Catholics to rally to what friend and foe alike said was a church standard was immense, as was the pressure on non-Catholic groupers to escape smear by association. Lifetime comradeships disappeared in days. At once rebel unions in Victoria and then New South Wales called for federal executive investigation of their grouper-dominated state party executives.[10]

The federal executive moved into Victoria and called a special conference which elected a new, anti-grouper state executive. Even though it might well have dominated that conference, the old grouper executive boycotted it in the belief that its repudiation could be effected at a federal party conference to be held in Hobart early in 1955. But the whole point of the intervention was to change the colour of the Victorian delegation at the Hobart conference and so at Hobart the grouper delegation was locked out and the new delegation admitted. Even so, numbers at Hobart were almost even and a continued fight by groupers from other states might have saved them but they, too, opted for a boycott. This left the field to their opponents who were now quite free to endorse the new Victorian executive, direct state parties to withdraw recognition from the industrial groups and adopt foreign policy motions in favour of recognizing the Communist government of China and against the use of Australian forces in Malaya.

With the centre-left factions triumphant in Hobart, the knives came out with such savagery that the emergence of a dissident party was made inevitable. The new Victorian executive quickly suspended from A.L.P. membership four state Labor ministers, thirteen state M.P.s

9 The text is reproduced in F. K. Crowley, *Modern Australia in Documents, 2, 1939–1970*, Melbourne, 1973, pp. 286–8.

10 It is impossible here fully to describe the subsequent Labor crises. For an extraordinarily able treatment, see R. Murray, *The Split: Australian Labor in the Fifties*, Melbourne, 1970. See also F. G. Clarke, 'Towards a Reassessment of Dr Evatt's Role in the 1954–5 A.L.P. Split', in *L.H., 19*, November 1970.

and seven federal M.P.s who had attended a meeting called by the old grouper executive. When the suspended ministers were excluded from his ministry by the Labor premier, John Cain, they and twelve backbenchers formed a rebel party in the Victorian parliament. The purge then continued with the expulsion of more than a hundred former executive members, federal M.P.s and city and suburban councillors. At state elections in 1955, only one supporter of the old grouper executive retained his seat, the Labor government was defeated and the Liberal and Country party's Henry Bolte was returned to begin a string of electoral wins still unbroken when he retired in 1972. The left quickly capitalized on the groupers' obloquy; in 1955 and 1956 Communists and A.L.P. leftists co-operated to win back large unions and subsequently preserved leftist control of the state party until 1970, when the federal executive again intervened, this time to make the Victorian party structure more representative of its centre and right membership.

Had the same process followed in New South Wales, the A.L.P. might have disintegrated. A purge on Victorian lines in Sydney, where there was close harmony between J. J. Cahill's Labor government, the party's state executive and the Trades Hall, would have seen the emergence of a rebel party much larger and wealthier than in Victoria. The Kennelly forces, despite frequent and silly statements by a crusading Evatt, therefore sought a more moderate solution; New South Wales Labor men remembered the federal-Lang split of the 1930s. Sydney's Cardinal Gilroy did not encourage Catholic dissidents as Archbishop Mannix did in Melbourne, and most groupers opted for concessions to stay in the party. In tortuous negotiations the old grouper leadership surrendered hegemony, dumped some of their more militant colleagues and accepted the Hobart conference.

The federal effect was catastrophic. The Victorian expulsions saw the creation of a seven-man corner party in the house, later joined in the Senate by Tasmania's George Cole. Two, W. M. Bourke and S. M. Keon, socially mobile intellectuals of a new generation, were a sad loss to the A.L.P. When the Petrov commission's innocuous report was tabled in September 1955, it appeared that the Russians had been trying to do rather ineffectively what Cold War powers were doing everywhere. Evatt then announced in his parliamentary comment that he had written to the Soviet foreign minister, Molotov, to ask if the documents produced by Petrov had been genuine! The A.L.P.s embarrassment was complete, and Menzies at once called for elections to capitalize on the gift of a chaotic Labor under a disturbingly frantic leader. In December 1955 the coalition was returned with twelve additional seats. The Victorian dissidents all lost their seats, but one senator was returned: Frank McManus, assistant secretary to the old Victorian grouper executive.

The anti-grouper forces consolidated in the smaller states with some moderation, but the last act in the split was played out in Queensland and there, even more than in the south, it was a matter of power competition. For years Labor had governed in Queensland on the basis of an alliance between parliamentarians and A.W.U. bureaucrats. Groupers fitted into this situation as an extra component on the A.W.U.-parliamentary side against the generally more militantly left Trades Hall union bureaucracy. R. J. J. Bukowski, A.W.U. boss in southern Queensland, was for a time secretary of the industrial groups. Discord began when Dougherty took the A.W.U. away from the groups in New South Wales in 1954 and Bukowski, due partly to a politically difficult internal A.W.U. situation in Queensland and due also perhaps to an already emerging personal conflict with a less than docile premier, Vincent Gair, followed the Sydney lead. When Gair, a Catholic and pro-grouper, refused with other Queensland delegates to switch at the Hobart conference, the A.W.U. joined with the left to form a slight majority on the party's state executive to bring the politicians into line. One useful issue was that of three weeks' annual leave for workers, formerly a desired target but now laid down as to be implemented immediately despite the Labor government's plea that it was held back by current inflation and straitened state finances. There were others. The government invoked emergency powers to market wool despite a strike by A.W.U. shearers, and a government minister was found guilty of corrupt land dealings in proceedings stimulated by allegations in the A.W.U. press. The government did not first discuss with the party executive two pieces of controversial legislation: to allow University of Queensland staff to appeal on appointments to a committee chaired by a government nominee, and to institute a government-sponsored petrol supply organization following a threat by oil companies to curtail local supplies after they had been refused a petrol price rise. Despite the appearance of sectarianism, this was basically a continuation of the age-old tension between Labor's industrial and political arms rather than simply an extension of the southern split, and even Evatt urged moderation. However, the industrialists had the numbers, the politicians remained adamant and, in April 1957 Gair was expelled from the A.L.P. Apart from J. E. Duggan, a Catholic who stayed to become A.L.P. parliamentary leader, Gair's ministers went with him and these, with supporting backbenchers, styled themselves the Queensland Labor party. With the A.L.P. voting with the opposition the Q.L.P. government was brought down. In subsequent elections, the coalition won and, initially under the Country party's Frank Nicklin, began a period of office still unbroken in 1972.

For a time it seemed that the split might be healed. Many of the expelled and rebellious considered themselves Labor men who would return to the fold when kinder factional balances emerged. In 1957, Rome ruled that the Movement could not continue in direct relationship with the episcopacy and, ultimately renamed the National Civic Council, it became a lay organization with shrinking support from local bishops. Reconciliation, however, did not occur. Chamberlain achieved unusual national Labor cohesion of a violently anti-grouper bent, and too many union and party officials stood personally to suffer if the often more able groupers returned. The other solution, namely the electoral extinction of the grouper remnants who had coalesced in 1957 as the Democratic Labor party, joined formally by the Q.L.P. in 1962, also eluded the A.L.P. Nationally, the D.L.P. vote fell from a peak of 9 per cent in 1958 to 6 per cent in 1969, but in Victoria it held at from 12 to 17 per cent despite Archbishop Mannix's death in 1963 and his successors' neutrality and this, with the personal charisma of Gair in Queensland, ensured the return of D.L.P. senators. On the other hand, with Chamberlain losing his grip and with younger men rising around Whitlam in the late 1960s, it was the turn of the leftist Victorian executive to suffer federal intervention in 1970, partly in the hope that a more broadly based reconstructed party could improve on Victorian Labor's dismal electoral performances. It was notable in the 1970s, too, that, whereas the other parties had thrown up new, younger and better polished leaders, the D.L.P. still personified older, more raucous traditions and still depended on the prowess of its heroes of the 1950s; it had not yet been shown that there would be a second generation of D.L.P. leaders as able, resilient and shrewd as the first.

A usually friendly press, the mores of the key social groups behind the Liberals, a simpler apparatus and almost continual electoral success contributed to much greater cohesion on the coalition side. But the coalition link itself provided some tensions. Menzies and Fadden largely dominated their parties. Both were veterans of the 1939–41 debacle, both were determined to preserve the coalition, and Fadden seemed happy to leave the initiative with the Liberals provided that the Country party was allowed its role as guardian of the rural interest. Fadden was aware that his party's electoral base was shrinking as technology reduced farm labour and expanding secondary and tertiary industry supported an increasingly urban population. But while he supported efforts to wrest country seats from Liberal or Labor control, he reacted coolly to the idea of the Country party expanding its support base by appealing also to urban interests, arguing that a hybrid could not satisfy the party's primary reason for being. Fadden's deputy, McEwen, was not so sanguine about the future, or so content to accept a secondary role in the coalition.

On the coalition's return in 1949, McEwen was given the Commerce and Agriculture portfolio but, foreseeing the party's loss of the treasury on Fadden's retirement, he had the government agree in 1956 to the transformation of his department into the Department of Trade, with a subsidiary department and portfolio of Primary Industry. A significant aspect of the 1956 re-organization was the securing of the link between Trade and Primary Industry and the linking of trade with secondary industry – a link reflected in the new title of Trade and Industry in 1963. McEwen quickly built up trade as a policy rival to the Treasury. When Holt took over as treasurer in 1958 on Fadden's retirement, and when McEwen took over as Country party leader and deputy prime minister, McEwen's different view of coalition politics became apparent. Holt faced a testing novitiate. With a substantial drop in wool income in 1958–9, with drought, with inflation, and with rising unemployment, Holt late in 1960 belatedly and toughly imposed a heavy increase in sales tax on automobiles, raised loan interest rates and tightened credit. In 1961, with unemployment still rising, Holt was forced to ease these restrictions but, even so, the coalition barely survived that year's elections. One aid to the coalition was private dealing by McEwen with Chamberlain for Labor preferences to go to two Country party candidates in Western Australia. And McEwen tended to dissociate himself from the failures of Holt and the treasury in coping with the economic crisis. Although the Country party lost two seats in 1961, the Liberals lost thirteen and in 1962 McEwen spoke as though he saw himself as a future prime minister.[11]

The election result shocked Menzies. He quickly dealt with the buoyant Labor opposition by adopting its policies, including resort to a large budget deficit as an unemployment cure despite previous expressions of horror at the hustings. He dealt with McEwen by himself going to Britain where McEwen had been dominating headlines in his deep mourning of the effect on the Australian economy if Britain should succeed with its first attempt to enter the European Economic Community. Admittedly, Menzies allowed the virtual dismissal of his Minister for Air, Leslie Bury, who disagreed publicly with McEwen's pessimism,[12] but this, together with the premature resignation of the tariff board chairman, Leslie Melville, because of conflict with McEwen, sufficiently alienated Liberal sentiment to end McEwen's immediate prime ministerial ambitions. It was as though he himself accepted this when, late in 1962, he led intransigent Country party opposition to an electoral redistribution scheme favoured by Menzies but now dropped. It would seem that about this time, too, he determined on a new course of salvation for the Country party even though it violated a basic tradition of the party and rocked the coalition boat.

Briefly, it would appear, McEwen concluded that he could expand his party's base by adopting the cause of tariff protection and thus maximizing the value of contacts built up with city manufacturing interests through the trade department's operations. He justified this break with the party's largely free trade tradition by arguing that city workers were the rural industries' best customers, and that only protection would allow continued expansion of the work force through immigration. He countered Liberal and treasury reservations by

[11] It will be obvious that here and in what follows there is heavy reliance on the persuasive and so far uncontradicted A. Reid, *The Power Struggle*, Sydney, 1969.

[12] The episode is partly documented in F. K. Crowley, *Modern Australia in Documents*, 2, 1939–1970, Melbourne, 1973, pp. 430–31.

appealing to the protectionist legend in Labor minds, although its prominent Labor spokesman on trade, Dr J. F. Cairns, at times tended to support the view of informed Liberal backbencher C. R. Kelly, that few workers were employed in some heavily protected industries and these could well be employed elsewhere.

A major hurdle for McEwen came with the Vernon committee's report in 1965. Early in 1963, still tenderly aware of how close economic problems had taken him to electoral disaster, Menzies appointed a committee of economic inquiry led by noted industrialist James Vernon, and including John Crawford, then at the Australian National University but until 1960 permanent head of the Department of Trade and one of McEwen's closest advisers. It happened that later in 1963 Menzies, sensing that current conflict in Labor ranks on the issue of United States military installations in Australia and publicity of rude handling of Labor parliamentarians by the party's federal executive would be useful, brought on a premature election. By skilfully exploiting these issues, Labor became anti-American and the federal conference became the '36 faceless men' dictating to the people's representatives. He also threw in a revolutionary pledge of some state aid for private schools, including Catholic schools, and lifted the coalition majority to a comfortable twenty-one. Consequently, when the Vernon committee's report was submitted in 1965, Menzies felt secure enough to brush aside its main recommendations, including the creation of a federal economic council. But McEwen was damaged by the report's complaint that the wool industry, in particular, was suffering because of excessively protected manufacturing industry. He was fortunate in that, before the report's impact was felt fully at lower Country party levels, Menzies retired early in 1966 and Liberal and government leadership passed to the less awesome Holt.

Difficulties, however, remained. Early in 1966, the Country party had lost a Queensland seat at a by-election to Dr Rex Patterson, a Labor candidate and formerly a highly placed civil servant concerned with northern development. And in cabinet McEwen now faced in William McMahon a firm spokesman for the treasury line against excessive protection. McEwen had power enough in his own party to write a protectionist plank into its platform for elections in 1966, but those elections saw such a massive landslide to the coalition and especially to the Liberals, now holding sixty-one seats to the Country party's twenty-one, that his coalition position was weakened. Moreover, during the election campaign a small but wealthy rural faction calling itself the Basic Industries Group arose to dispute McEwen's tariff policies, echoed early in 1967 by the president of the Australian Woolgrowers and Graziers' Council, part of the Country party's very backbone. McEwen's response was a tactic reminiscent of Evatt's in 1954: to close ranks behind him and distract his critics he dramatically claimed the existence of an outside conspiracy, in this case from the Basic Industries Group which to all appearances had folded up after an ineffectual election campaign. This subdued the Country party, but he was in conflict with the Liberals again in December 1967, when he repudiated cabinet's decision not to devalue the Australian currency in response to Britain's devaluation of sterling and Holt in turn repudiated him.[13]

Holt's death by drowning just before Christmas, 1967, perhaps saved McEwen for another round. McEwen, acting prime minister while the Liberals chose a new leader, declared that the Country party would not support a coalition led by McMahon, Holt's deputy but apparently less than suitably respectful to the Country party veteran. With the coalition's survival at stake, and with the governor-general, Lord Casey, throwing extra-constitutional weight against him, McMahon was passed over. The retired Menzies reportedly lobbied for the very capable but reserved Paul Hasluck, but the parliamentary Liberals elected the little-known Minister for Education and Science, Senator John Gorton. This was the first time since federation that a party represented in the house turned to the Senate for a leader, though Gorton was quickly found a seat in the house, the one previously held by Holt.

Gorton's prime ministerial career was stormy. His casually assertive personality alienated some colleagues and civil servants. His nomination of Hasluck to the governor-generalship early in 1969 and the appointment to external affairs of a junior West Australian, Gordon Freeth, weakened the government. Early in 1969, he suffered some ridicule (and won some sympathy) when a Labor member ventilated, and one of his own Liberal backbenchers pursued, claims that aspects of his personal life militated against effective fulfilment of his public functions.[14] At the same time, the McMahon-McEwen feud showed signs of passing, and Whitlam in the house and Lionel Murphy in the Senate were leading the most vigorous opposition seen for more than a decade. Gorton was humiliated at elections late in 1969. The coalition's majority from 1966 of forty was slashed to seven, with its share of the vote four per cent less than Labor's. With Freeth defeated at the polls and veteran Allen Fairhall now retired, Gorton besides learned early in the new year that the Minister for National Development, David Fairbairn, would no longer serve under him. Now apparently free from McEwen's veto, McMahon contested the leadership and it would seem scored disconcertingly well and was moved to external affairs (renamed during his term foreign affairs), with Bury becoming treasurer. Early in 1971, after public conflict with his defence minister, Malcolm Fraser, Gorton's stocks fell further. When a motion of confidence in his leadership produced a deadlocked vote in the

[13] In 1966, Australia changed to a decimal currency with dollars and cents as units but remained in the Sterling area.

[14] The Liberal took to print: see E. St John, *A Time to Speak*, Melbourne, 1969. He lost his seat at the 1969 elections.

parliamentary party room, Gorton gave his casting vote against himself. Under McMahon, his successor, Gorton survived for a short time as deputy leader and defence minister before his resignation was requested and he retired to a busy life on the backbenches. Despite many years as a very capable minister, McMahon in 1971 and 1972 showed lack of adequate stature as prime minister and failed utterly to meet an unusually brilliant Labor campaign for elections late in 1972. Under Gough Whitlam, Labor was returned with a house majority of nine, though not in control of the Senate. The Liberals faced the mid-1970s, now under Billie Snedden, with more problems than at any time since the early 1940s. A dissident group round Sydney businessman Gordon Barton in the mid-1960s had formed a Liberal reform group which, with inter-state organization and now as the Australia party, by 1972 approached in electoral significance the D.L.P.

The dominance of conservative coalitions imposed a certain air of flatness in government. Dedicated to stability but also to electoral survival, these were not governments of intransigent obscurantists; neither, though, were they governments of visionaries or reformers. There was a marked absence of appeals to the national imagination, of even an occasional grand manifesto of government intent. This is not to say that the quality of government was poor, that constant crusades would not have palled or that low key administration was without at least short-term economic benefit to the country. While immense change was allowed or even encouraged by the coalitions, it came usually with little fanfare, always piecemeal, never integrated into a national design beyond convenience or simple commercial values.

The 'forty-niners' took power in what was partly a campaign against centralist bureaucratization and Labor's alleged disposition towards excessive government. In minor ways, this negative campaign was carried through in office. Federal mining, whaling, oil refining, engineering and shipping interests were cast off; there was some initial amalgamation of government departments; and in 1952, parliament's Public Accounts Committee was revived under the chairmanship of F. A. Bland to expose administrative waste and inefficiency. Between 1951 and 1954 the number of federal employees was cut by more than 5 per cent despite civil service recruitment problems in a period of high employment; the operating privileges of the government airline, T.A.A., were reduced; and the Commonwealth Bank was again placed under a board rather than a single governor responsible to the treasurer. However, while the coalitions continued to pose as the champions of private enterprise in opposition to Labor's statism, and as devout constitutionalists in opposition to Labor's supposed unificationist ambitions (the Country party wing professing even still to want new states),[15] the coalitions in the 1950s and 1960s, in fact if not in

[15] A plebiscite for a new state was actually held in April 1967 in northern New South Wales. It was heavily defeated, largely because the area came as far south as Newcastle and there, and in Cessnock, there were very large hostile majorities.

firm intention, further expanded their central power at the expense of the states and further expanded the role of government as such in Australian life.

The coalitions inherited from the inter-war period federal leadership in the vital field of loan raising; they inherited from the 1939–45 war years federal predominance in the large field of income taxation.[16] There was nothing to stop the states also imposing their own direct taxation but, as the Victorian government found in a High Court case against the federal government in 1957, there was nothing to stop 'Canberra' making states' acceptance of its direct taxation monopoly a condition of reimbursements to them. Nor was there anything to prevent the federal government from supplementing publicly-raised loan funds from its own revenue and specifying how the states should spend the funds allocated to them. In the decade to mid-1968 federal allocations to the states for specific purposes more than tripled; the states were receiving more than half their revenue from the federal treasury and a third of this had strings attached. At the same time, the federal civil service expanded rapidly after a freeze in the early 1950s, and late in the period, when the federal government employed a third of Australia's one million civil servants, the federal sector was expanding much more quickly than the state sector or the population at large.[17] This sprang partly from expansion into fields not specifically envisaged in the constitution, but complementary to the growing practice of allotting finance to the states for particular purposes; for example, in housing and education implementation remained largely with the states, but policy increasingly was determined at the centre where appropriate new portfolios and departments were created. This financial mastery reduced the states to a barren annual exercise of trumpeted advance demands, acceptance of financial rations at federal-dominated loan council and premiers' meetings, and subsequent boasting for political effect of bargains achieved or lamenting of perfidy suffered. Inevitably, this produced strains within the governing parties at the different levels, between, for example, Menzies and South Australia's Playford and between the more candidly centralist Gorton and Victoria's Bolte and New South Wales' Robin Askin.

At a time of world tension, of increasing Australian loneliness in world politics, of survival problems in some rural industries, of domestic demand for government involvement in a host of 'quality of life' areas, there were few Australians disposed to look other than primarily to Canberra for government. In meeting these needs and responding to particular pressures, the coalitions developed considerable pragmatism in pre-empting Labor and retaining office. They

16 See P. E. Joske, *Australian Federal Government*, Sydney, 1967: R. G. Menzies, *Central Power in the Australian Commonwealth*, London, 1967: G. Sawer, *Australian Federalism in the Courts*, Melbourne, 1967.

17 See G. E. Caiden, *The Commonwealth Bureaucracy*, Melbourne, 1967.

accepted for example, the undesirability of allowing unemployment to exceed about 1 per cent of the work force. Avoidance of excessive inflation or deflation also had a high priority. For these reasons among others, the coalition allowed civil service policy departments like the treasury and trade to flourish, used their superiority to control states' spending and transformed the banking system into almost as obedient a creature as even Chifley might have wished. In complex legislation brought down piecemeal in the 1950s, Commonwealth Bank rule solely by a governor responsible to the treasurer was replaced by board rule but with the commonwealth's governor as chairman; the power of the central bank to call up private banks' liquid assets was restricted but remained considerable; the central banking function of credit control was vested in a separate Reserve Bank of Australia; and other functions of the old bank were vested in a Commonwealth Banking Corporation, which controlled trading, savings and development banks.

Some coalition policies were transformed. After a 1949 election campaign along almost classical laissez-faire lines, coalitions in office then evolved a 'two airlines' policy whereby there would be two major domestic carriers and no more – the government-owned Trans Australia Airlines (established in 1946) and the private enterprise Australian National Airways Pty Ltd, (established 1936, taken over by Ansett Airways in 1957). Another policy to be implemented concerned margarine, which could be made more cheaply than butter and almost completely from local products, but coalition governments put quotas on sales to serve the dairying interest. Hostile to Labor attempts to control some aspects of primary production, the coalitions nevertheless erected comprehensive production and marketing systems such that, for example, by the end of the period each wheat grower and sugar cane farmer received a very precise production quota, and even the proud wool industry succumbed to government support. Socialism now was McEwen's orderly marketing. Socialized medicine remained anathema and welfare statism tended at least still to be regretted, but an unwieldy medical insurance system could be instituted and a host of social welfare measures adopted and extended at growing cost to the national purse. Constitutional barriers excused federal inactivity in education, except in the high status area of university education, and until electoral pressures and sheer need induced activity at the secondary level and thought of activity at lower levels still. Not, of course, that there was anything reprehensible in change as such. Democracy presumably anticipates government sensibility to electoral and group wants, and twenty years is long enough that even a dominant party will respond to ministerial mobility and rapid material and attitude changes in its community.[18]

---

[18] For interesting examples of Gorton's attempts to bridge the attitudes of the 'forty-niners' and his own in the 1960s, see J. Gorton, 'Liberal Party: Attitudes and Policies', in H. Mayer, Ed., *Australian Politics: A Second Reader*, Melbourne, 1969, pp. 317–22.

An area of immense change was that of the British connection. In 1950, only perhaps older Irish-Australians saw Australia as anything but British – in allegiance, sentiment, political and professional traditions, education, ethnic composition and even still in foreign policy. By the 1970s, however, Australia had become a white European state rather than essentially a British state. Part of this change was seen in the very substance of the country, in its ethnic composition. Given their leaders' tendencies towards a heavily sentimental anglomania, it would not have been surprising if the post-1949 coalitions had honoured the Labor government's undertaking to receive a relatively large share of Europe's refugees and had then reverted to a traditional emphasis on almost exclusively British immigration. With the refugees apparently accommodated by the community, with trade union tenderness dulled by full employment, with the old security motive reinforced by the fear of a now Communist China, and with a continuing wish to accelerate industrialization, European immigration did not end when the refugee programme petered out in 1950–51 but continued as a matter of high policy priority. Australia subsequently concluded migration agreements with most European states. Migration statistics are more than ordinarily difficult to marshal but, in gross and approximate terms, some 2½ million migrants arrived between 1950 and 1970 in one of the heavier migrations in New World history (a population of 7½ million in 1947 had jumped to 12½ million in 1969). And, of these migrants, over half were non-British. In twenty years, and quite apart from 170,000 mainly eastern European refugees admitted after the war, a self-consciously British community accommodated, for example, 337,000 Italians, 192,000 Greeks, 145,000 Dutch, 120,000 Yugoslavs, 115,000 Germans, and 50,000 Poles. There remained a preference for British and northern European migrants on grounds of sentiment and alleged capacity to assimilate easily, so that whereas 84 per cent of British migrants received assisted passages less than a quarter of the Mediterranean migrants were assisted. However, it was only in the 1960s when European prosperity severely cut continental migration that the British ratio rose markedly.[19]

Declining northern and southern European migration, and the continuing disinclination of the Communist states in the east to encourage migration (apart from Yugoslavia which was keen to dispose of surplus rural labour), took the Australian search as far afield as Turkey, and one could wonder just where the colour bar ultimately would rest. In the period, logic was not exaggerated and, despite the activities of a small immigration reform group, the old racially

[19] A good deal of work of a very high standard has been published on immigration. See especially R. T. Appleyard, *British Emigration to Australia*, Canberra, 1964: C. A. Price, *Southern Europeans in Australia*, Melbourne, 1963: C. A. Price, *Jewish Settlers in Australia*, Canberra, 1964: J. I. Martin, *Refugee Settlers*, Canberra, 1965: A. C. Palfreeman, *The Administration of the White Australia Policy*, Melbourne, 1967. For a very useful guide to further reading see C. A. Price, Ed., *Australian Immigration: A Bibliography and Digest*, Canberra, 1966–1971.

restrictive policy largely was retained notwithstanding boasted changes in its operation from the mid-1960s so as to allow in a trickle of non-whites justified by need for their occupational talents. From March 1966, to September 1970, some 6342 'well-qualified' non-Europeans were admitted for settlement; in about the same period, 4192 relatives of Australian residents were admitted as permanent residents, 5471 previously allowed temporary residence were granted permanency and 18,487 people of racially mixed descent were admitted.

Direct political effects of the Europeanization process were scarcely apparent in the early 1970s. It was coincidental, though, with the disappearance of the old political link involved in Australian security dependence on Britain. This sprang in part from Australia's own increased defence capacity and even more from Australian reliance now on an alliance with the United States, but also because of Britain's own inability any longer to deploy useful force in the antipodes' proximity and her increasing inclination to withdraw to the Atlantic and the Mediterranean and ultimately to the North Sea and Europe. Even in 1950 the lessons of the Pacific war of 1941–5 had been learned and Australia was already embarked on independent diplomacy, but for a time the British connexion remained a chief plank of government policy.[20] Australian forces fought alongside British troops under the United Nations banner in Korea in the early 1950s, as well as against mainly Communist dissidents in British Malaya later in the decade, and against Indonesian campaigners in British Borneo in the early 1960s. A joint Anglo-Australian weapons development project continued in South Australia; and Australia where possible gave Britain diplomatic assistance, as, for example, when Britain's Anthony Eden foolishly conspired with France and Israel to invade Egypt after President Nasser's nationalization of the Suez Canal company in 1956 (Menzies even led a vain western delegation to Cairo to negotiate with Nasser). At the same time, it became clearer year by year that British interest in the Pacific was waning. The Middle East was no longer a potential military theatre for Australian forces and the closure of the Suez Canal after further Egypt-Israel conflict in 1967 little affected Australia. Britain's announcement in 1968 of accelerated and virtually total withdrawal of forces from the whole area east of Suez merely capped the long process.

The effect of all this on Australian attitudes was compounded by British attempts to join the European Economic Community.[21]

---

20 For foreign policy generally see the volumes edited by G. Greenwood and N. D. Harper, *Australia in World Affairs, 1950–55, 1956–60, 1961–65, 1966–1970*. For a brief introduction see W. J. Hudson, *Australian Diplomacy*, Melbourne, 1970. For a further treatment see A. Watt, *The Evolution of Australian Foreign Policy 1938–1965*, Cambridge, 1967. For a more thematic discussion see T. B. Millar, *Australia's Foreign Policy*, Sydney, 1968, and M. Teichmann, Ed., *New Directions in Australian Foreign Policy*, Melbourne, 1969.

21 See H. G. Gelber, *Australia, Britain and the E E C, 1961 to 1963*, Melbourne, 1966.

Britain's submersion in an integrated Europe would severely qualify her headship, however nominal, of a separate, world-wide association of formerly settler states and would substantially reduce surviving Australian economic dependence on Britain. It needs stressing that Australia's experience of the empire and commonwealth had been almost exclusively London-centred, a focus increased rather than lessened by the post-1945 entry into the commonwealth of many Asian and African states, some of them republican. In the 1960s the commonwealth was no longer intimate, no longer white, no longer comprised of members respectful of each others' autonomy, and no longer even particularly British. The black-balling of South Africa from the commonwealth club in 1961, the collective imposition of pressure on Britain to put down white rebellion in Rhodesia and to forgo the sale of arms to *apartheid*-stained South Africa later in the decade accentuated for Australia the discomfort rather than the security of commonwealth membership, the more so when her own interest in Africa was minimal and her own restrictive immigration policies and treatment of her indigenous coloured population exposed her, too, to censure. A commonwealth led by a less than fully independent Britain would mean little to Australia, then, and this was what British entry into Europe promised.

The commercial cord, if not yet cut by British entry into Europe, certainly became much more thinly stretched. Mutual tariff privileges remained considerable, despite inroads as a result of the 'Kennedy Round' of international negotiations under the General Agreement on Tariffs and Trade, but Anglo-Australia trade as such declined in relative significance.[22] In the twenty years from the late 1940s, the British share of Australian wheat, cheese and dried fruits exports halved; that of mutton and lamb fell from 90 to 12 per cent; that of wool shrank from 40 to 10 per cent. Similarly, whereas in the late 1940s about 40 per cent of Australia's imports were from Britain, in the late 1960s the figure was little more than 20 per cent. The British investment contribution, while still growing, also fell behind in comparative terms. In the 1950s public loans raised in the United States comprised less than a fifth of those raised in Britain but by the late 1960s the British share was less than half the American. In the private investment sector, British investment was surpassed on a year-by-year basis by the United States in the early 1960s.

Much of this political and commercial change was not actively sought by Australia and, indeed, was mourned, but it also reflected a new degree of maturity and the erosion of the old colonial ethos. In 1967, the federal government announced that it would restrict appeals to the Privy Council to the extent allowed by constitutional limits. In the period generally, Anglicans showed nationalist tendencies in

---

22 On the history of trade there is a mammoth source book – J. G. Crawford, *Australian Trade Policy 1942–1966*, Canberra, 1968.

organization and episcopal appointments; the universities were becoming more nationally self-reliant in filling their chairs; even the Liberals abandoned precedent with the appointments of Australians (Casey and Hasluck) to the governor-generalship in 1965 and 1969; and in the states the vice-regal sets declined in social significance. It was unlikely that a royal visit would ever again see the public fervour aroused by the tour of the young Queen Elizabeth II in 1954; visits by the United States' President Lyndon Johnson in 1966, Italy's President Giuseppe Saragat and Foreign Minister Amintore Fanfani in 1967 and Pope Paul VI in 1970 better illustrated the new Australia. That Australia in the early 1970s still used the old British national anthem, still recognized the British head of state as its own, still incorporated the union jack in its flag and still accepted British titles and decorations for its citizens illustrated at trivial levels the many Anglo-Australian links that remained, but they also tended to obscure the extent of the change experienced.

A swing away from Britain was matched by a swing towards the United States.[23] Concrete involvement of the United States in Pacific security arrangements was a feature of Australian policy even in the years of submergence in an imperial diplomatic unit. With the virtual eclipse of British power in the Pacific in the early 1940s, ensnarement of the United States became for Evatt a matter of high priority. He failed, not due to faulty diplomacy but because of Washington's estimate of the international situation at the time. Washington's thinking was changed by Communist success in China in 1949, the outbreak of war in Korea in 1950, and a desire both to build up Japan as an anti-Communist buffer and to remove the burden of Japan's post-war sustenance from the American tax-payer. In these circumstances, Evatt's successor, Spender, was able with some finesse in 1951 to achieve not merely United States participation in a Pacific-wide security arrangement but adherence to a tripartite mutual assistance pact involving additionally only New Zealand.

Throughout the period, the ANZUS pact provoked extraordinary debate in Australia. The governing coalitions over-valued it, in part for electoral purposes, and for a time adopted the fatuous practice of asking successive Washington administrations for expressions of continued adherence to it. On the other side of the political fence, there were some inclined to under-value it, arguing that it comprised merely a note which the United States would honour only when her own national interests were involved. With ANZUS as with any treaty, it was, of course, the case that changes in government and international circumstances over time would affect implementation, but the treaty made mutual assistance at least marginally more likely and there were, anyway, interim subsidiary benefits: the treaty provided for

23 See H. G. Gelber, *The Australian American Alliance*, Melbourne, 1968: T. R. Reese, *Australia, New Zealand and the United States*, London, 1969.

periodic meetings of the parties' foreign ministers, and it was undeniably useful for small powers like Australia to have formally guaranteed high-level access to the executive of one of the superpowers; the treaty also provided for continuing military staff liaison, and this comprised a useful additional point of contact.[24]

It seemed that a good deal of the inclination to fault ANZUS came less from a naïve approach to international politics, or even from excessive loneliness with Britain's departure, than from resentment against the concurrent phenomenon of Americanization, a reaction evident in the same period in, for example, Canada and France. This had a military aspect. Australian coalition governments and their supporters closely identified with the United States in the general cold war conflict and were prepared actively to support the United States in Vietnam, to deny recognition to the Communist government of China, to co-operate in the establishment of an American communications centre in the north of Western Australia and of rather more mysterious facilities in Central Australia. In varying degrees, others in the Australian community, especially on the left but not only there, felt that Australia identified too closely with the United States interest and made its client status too obvious; it ran an unnecessary risk of involvement in nuclear war. Holt and Gorton did not help matters by addressing American audiences in terms of grossly sentimental affection perhaps digestible by a courted superior but little liked by nationalists at home. Menzies did not help either when, in 1963 and suspiciously close to national elections fought in part on the alliance issue, he had his Minister for Defence, Athol Townley, contract to buy two squadrons of American fighter-bombers, later known as the F-111 but then still on the drawing board. When Australia eventually took delivery of the planes in 1973 the price had doubled and the plane had been plagued by technical faults.

There was a cultural aspect. Late in the nineteenth and early in the twentieth centuries, Australian society already was one of the most urbanized in the world. The urbanization rate declined between the wars but picked up again after 1945 and, with a much larger population involved, was now much more immediately apparent. As Australia grew into a suburbanized industrial society in the 1950s, Australian entrepreneurs and the mass media turned increasingly to the United States for models, materials and ideas. The Australian press came to give extensive daily attention to American news. Commercial radio stations adopted American formats and accents. Australians proved themselves devoted watchers of television after its introduction in 1956 and television stations found economy and high ratings in heavy buying of American material, much of it old, much of it of poor quality. The local advertising industry flourished along Madison

24 The best general analysis of the treaty is J. G. Starke, *The ANZUS Treaty Alliance*, Melbourne, 1965. For Spender's own account of the negotiations see P. C. Spender, *Exercises in Diplomacy*, Sydney, 1969, pp. 13–190.

Avenue lines and merchandising followed American patterns. In the late 1960s, intellectual youth was turning more to American radical sources than their Euro-centric fathers had done. Overall, Australian culture, and especially popular culture, became very Americanized in a short time. This caused some distress among at least part of the educated minority and among older groups remembering the more distinctively Australian flavour of life in the pre-war years. Distress was deeper in that much of the change sprang from commercial intent so that what was imported tended to reflect the more tawdry aspects of American culture.

Stability and conservative government made Australia an attractive target for United States' private investment and in the 1950s and early 1960s American investment in Australia, while still small in absolute American terms, increased at more than twice the rate of American overseas investment in general. In part, this represented investment for profit of the usual kind; in part, it represented the use of local subsidiary companies better able to market goods competitively behind the Australian tariff wall and close to a growing market.[25] By the mid-1960s, American interests wholly owned more than seventy of the top 300 manufacturing companies in Australia and held a majority interest in a further twenty. This investment was located mainly in metals (investment of $41 million in 1962 in mining and smelting had risen to $144 million in 1966), petroleum and chemicals, agricultural equipment, food processing and motor vehicle production (nearly three-quarters of the motor industry was in the hands of the American big three: General Motors, Chrysler and Ford). Three of the country's four major advertising agencies operated on substantial American capital; the accounting and auditing fields were heavily infiltrated; American techniques became models for reference; and when Australia's largest company, the Broken Hill Proprietary, restructured its organization in 1966–67, it turned to American advisers. Names like Ford, Kellogg, Heinz and General Motors, and phenomena like supermarkets, regional shopping complexes and lubritoriums, became as much part of the Australian scene as the American.

In the face of this profound development, the conservative coalitions opted for day-to-day pragmatism rather than firm, detailed policy. Towards the end of the period, particular forms of investment raised coalition hackles. The purchase of Northern Territory and Queensland pastoral properties and the mainly foreign exploitation of new mineral discoveries led to complaints that the very substance of the country was being lost, and the somewhat more overtly nationalist Gorton warned that his government did not look kindly on the take-over of efficient Australian companies. In general, though, the

25 See especially D. T. Brash, *American Investment in Australian Industry*, Canberra, 1966: D. T. Brash, 'American Investment and Australian Sovereignty', in R. Preston, Ed., *Contemporary Australia*, Durham, N. C., 1969: E. L. Wheelwright and J. Miskelly, *Anatomy of Australian Manufacturing Industry*, Sydney, 1967: B. Fitzpatrick and E. L. Wheelwright, *The Highest Bidder*, Melbourne, 1965.

coalition's assumption was that foreign investment was necessary to economic growth which, in turn, was anxiously to be sought. Perhaps of greater immediate concern to the coalitions was the problem of an unbalanced trading relationship. With a primary sector of her own to safeguard, the United States limited imports of what Australia was best equipped to sell; yet, with the world's leading secondary industry, the United States had much that Australians wanted to buy. It should not be supposed that anti-Americanism was rampant. On the contrary, merchants found American brand names a marketing advantage and governments appealed at the hustings to pro-American feeling. There was, though, a growing awareness of the need to cope with the western pace-setter without loss of identity, to cope with appreciated capital without alienation of the national substance, and to cope with a vastly superior ally without sycophancy. Australians rarely quite managed this in the days of British leadership; it remained to be seen whether they would do better in a sibling than a filial relationship.

One of the oddities of Australia's pre-1940 experience was that her principal point of external contact was with a mothering state as far away as the shape of the world allowed. Nearby south and southeast Asia were submerged in colonial subjection beyond much Australian awareness. In east Asia, China was ignored except to the extent that she comprised an immense deposit of possibly mobile yellow hordes: Australians suffered deeply from mapping conventions whereby some kind of gravity alone seemed to make southward population spills inevitable. In all Asia, the only state to receive intermittent attention, and fear, was Japan. Nationalist revolution in Asia in the 1940s and 1950s suddenly presented Australia with neighbours very different in race, religion, colour, language and institutions, and virtually forced an Australian reaction. In the late 1940s, and despite the handicap of a racially-based restrictive immigration policy, Australia established good relations with parts of the new Asia. Australia's subsequent experience was less happy but it remains that in the 1950s and 1960s she became much more anchored than formerly in her locality.

Australia was largely responsible in 1950 for the Colombo Plan aid programme seen primarily as a destroyer of opportunities for Communist agitation in the Asian area. In the same year, Australia was the first state apart from the United States to commit all three armed services to the Korean conflict against local Communist forces and their Communist Chinese allies. Under the ANZAM agreement with Britain and New Zealand, Australia sent troops and planes to help put down a largely Communist rebellion in Malaya; and although preferring a wider pact involving more Asian states, and especially India, Australia energetically welcomed United States' preparedness in 1954 to underwrite the Southeast Asia Treaty Organization, an exclusively anti-Communist mutual assistance pact which, in the event, did not overcome the problems of limited Asian membership and the growing indifference of European imperial members. In the process, Australia alienated herself to some degree not only from a China under Communist control since 1949 but also from non-aligned and militantly anti-colonial states: notably India, Ceylon, Burma and Indonesia. Thus, where Australia had been an honoured participant at the 1949 New Delhi conference of Asian states discussing mainly the Indonesian independence issue, she was not invited to the 1954 Afro-Asians' Bandung conference dealing mainly with wider colonial issues. One complication was the cold war in which the conservative coalitions opted firmly for the embattled western cause. Nevertheless cold war commitment did not affect Australian status with Asian states themselves committed or at least fearful of Communist incursion: Malaysia, Singapore, the Philippines, South Korea, Thailand, and even Japan. And Sino-Indian hostilities in 1962, a military coup in Indonesia in 1966 (and the decimation of the huge Indonesian Communist party and other leftists in one of the least remarked bloodbaths in recent history), and rising anti-Chinese feeling in Malaysia and Indonesia, all tended to lessen the obloquy that Australia might otherwise have suffered in following the United States into the Vietnamese civil war.

During the Indo-Chinese war of independence against France, Communist and various non-Communist nationalist factions competed for legitimacy and, when the great powers intervened in 1954 to arrange a settlement, this internal struggle was still unresolved. The departure of the French allowed the emergence of two governments claiming Vietnamese jurisdiction: a harshly consolidated Communist government under Ho Chi Minh based on Hanoi in the north and a harshly consolidated anti-Communist government under Ngo Dinh Diem based on Saigon in the south. Early in 1962, Diem appealed for aid against infiltration from the north and almost at once Australia invoked SEATO and sent military advisers to join American advisers already serving in the south. As the position in the south deteriorated, President Johnson increased United States' participation to a level of more than 500,000 troops. Australia expanded its commitment to about 8000 men. Australian governments clearly acted to keep fresh the American alliance as well as to contribute to the containment of Communism, but there was a domestic price.[26] The introduction of military conscription in 1964 to provide troops for Vietnam, and the fact that conscription was not universal,[27] helped to produce a groundswell reaction. So too did the complicated moral issues involved in an undeclared war in David and Goliath circumstances (the Soviet Union and China did not match for Hanoi the scale of American support for Saigon), the inability of the United States quickly to wrap up a conflict the horrors of which television brought into Australian

[26] See H. S. Albinski, *Politics and Foreign Policy in Australia – The Impact of Vietnam and Conscription*, Durham, N. C., 1970.

[27] Birthdates were chosen by ballot, and young men born on the chosen dates were then liable to call-up, depending on their health and their current educational status; deferments were allowed.

drawing roms, and the refusal of traditional allies to participate, notably, Britain. In 1970, this reaction boiled over into the biggest mass demonstrations seen in Australian cities in peacetime. In 1970, however, it also became clear that under President Nixon the United States was withdrawing from the conflict, and Gorton foreshadowed a similar gradual Australian withdrawal. This left Australian defence planning in hiatus. With Britain leaving the area, with the United States withdrawing from the Asian mainland, and with a more self-confident nationalism in southeast Asia, old Australian notions of 'forward defence' were less viable and with a Soviet naval presence growing in the Indian Ocean, Australia faced the 1970s conscious of a greater need to act independently and flexibly than ever before in her history.

The Asian state most feared in a military sense was China, a fear made worse by Australian ignorance and old phobias, as well as by Peking's militant postures.[28] Partly to oblige the United States, Australia did not recognize the Peking government and opposed its entry into the United Nations. There was besides the difficulty of finding a diplomatic formula that would satisfy Peking's comprehensive territorial claims without too harshly dumping the old Chinese republican remnant still governing the island of Taiwan, a problem not made easier by Australia's curious decision in 1966 to establish an embassy on Taiwan. This did not prevent a trading relationship with China of great value to Australia. By the late 1960s, China was taking a quarter of the annual Australian wheat harvest, a good deal of wool and some machinery, while Australia was buying very little from China. In 1971, Whitlam led an A.L.P. delegation on a visit to China, a foretaste of the mutual recognition that was to follow his electoral success in 1972.

The most powerful state in the period was Japan and in this case the relationship posed economic rather than military problems for Australia.[29] With her security guaranteed by the United States and her government for a time markedly pacifist after her nuclear experiences of 1945, and with her population growth rate brought under control, Japan in the period achieved prodigious rates of economic development. Australia signed a commercial agreement with Japan in 1957 and trade between them bloomed to the point when in 1966–7 Australia's exports to Japan surpassed those to Britain and, in 1968–9, Japan took almost a quarter of all Australian exports compared with Britain's 13 per cent. These exports to Japan were mainly in wool, coal, ores, wheat and sugar. In return, Australia imported Japanese textiles and motor vehicles and parts, but the trade was heavily in Australia's favour and it was certain that Japan would press for easier access to the Australian market. It remained, too, that, despite

[28] See H. S. Albinski, *Australian Policies and Attitudes Towards China*, Princeton, 1965.

[29] See W. Macmahon Ball, *Austalia and Japan*, Melbourne, 1969.

Japanese and Australian membership of the Asian and Pacific Council from 1966, Australia by the early 1970s had not established anything approaching intimate political relations with Japan. There was, of course, some surviving antipathy on the Australian side from the early 1940s and some contemporary fears of client status in a lop-sided economic relationship in the case of Japan, but one could wonder whether Australians had committed themselves to *rapport* with Asia to the extent suggested by trade figures. That Australia faced cultural inhibitions in its dealings with Asia in general was suggested by her relations with Indonesia in particular.

Australia was one of the external midwives of Indonesian independence achieved in 1950 but this benign relationship did not last long. First, the Netherlands did not hand over the western half of the island of New Guinea with the rest of the old East Indies to the new Jakarta government and in the subsequent conflict, which dragged on until 1962, Australia sided energetically with the Netherlands. West New Guinea passed to United Nations and then Indonesian administration pending an exercise of self-determination which, predictably, resulted in 1969 in the incorporation of the territory in Indonesia. Australia accepted diplomatic defeat gracefully. Second, Australian governments were disturbed by the size of the powerful Indonesian Communist party, by evident lack of cohesion in the dispersed archipelago republic, by administrative chaos and by the unpredictably volatile President Sukarno. No sooner was the New Guinea issue settled under United States' pressure and threat of Indonesia military action, than Indonesia mounted a vigorous campaign against Anglo-Malayan plans to establish a state of Malaysia comprising Malaya, Singapore and the more distant Sarawak and Sabah, the last two contiguous with Indonesia. Again, Australia came out firmly against Indonesia. The military coup of 1965 saw the displacement of Sukarno, the destruction of the local Communist party, an end to confrontation with Malaysia and assertive diplomacy generally and solid attempts at economic reconstruction. Australia and Indonesia now resumed fully amicable relations, but still of a limited and formal kind. Some aid was offered and some Indonesian students came to Australian institutions. But official contacts were limited and unofficial contacts scarcely extended beyond the interest of a handful of academics, and this even though Indonesian economic problems remained daunting and even though Indonesia now shared a border with Australia in New Guinea which contained the seeds of future problems and perhaps conflict.

After half a century of negligible colonial effort, Australia in the 1950s and 1960s responded to international pressures, as well as to more conscientious domestic interest and greater economic resources by instituting much more energetic administration in Papua and New Guinea. With Paul Hasluck as an unusually effective Minister for Territories from 1951 till 1963, the territorial administration was at once extended and placed more firmly under Canberra's control; educational facilities were multiplied, public expenditure was rapidly increased, indigenous participation in limited local government was extended rapidly, and considerable efforts were made to draw the indigenes away from their subsistence agriculture systems into a cash economy. Hasluck sought deliberately to achieve a slow, comprehensive indigenous advance, less from personal conservatism than from genuine concern for the fate of the territory if it were handed over ultimately to a small, potentially tyrannical and divisive *élite*. In the 1960s, this gradualist policy was displaced and marked advances were allowed on several fronts. This stemmed in part from heavy international pressure by the triumphant anti-colonial camp in the United Nations, which now concerned itself as much with the Australian colony of Papua as with the administratively integrated trust territory of New Guinea, and in part perhaps from revised thinking in Canberra on the strategic importance of Australian control. There was also a conciousness of the diplomatic price of control, and probably some tender awareness of the cost of control (in 1968–9, about $110 million, equivalent to some two-thirds of the territorial revenue). At all events, emphasis in the 1960s was placed on the imminence of self-government or indepen-dence. By 1972, two-thirds of the territory's public servants were indigenes, though few yet held the top positions, and nearly two million of the territory's two-and-a-half million people were represen-ted on local government councils; after the elections of 1968 there were 65 indigenous members and only 29 expatriates in a territorial legislative assembly which now controlled policy and expenditure in some domestic areas of government. A university was opened near Port Moresby in 1966 and soon produced its first Arts and Science graduates, and a comprehensive economic development plan had been in process of implementation since 1968 – unfortunately, in some respects discriminatory against the indigenous interest.

This is not to say that Papua and New Guinea were completing the last dependence lap without profound problems. Racial tension seemed to be growing, centred not only on Australian expatriates' assumptions of superiority, but especially on the tangibles of indigenes' much lower incomes and poorer housing standards in the urban centres. This kind of resentment was a factor in the birth in 1967 of PANGU, a political party based on a dissatisfied, Europeanized, nationalist élite. It was reflected in frequent violence on New Britain where a section of the Tolai people formed the Mataungan Association dedicated to the exclusion of expatriates from local government and the achievement of a bigger share of the local economy. Less than a fifth of the population had progressed well beyond subsistence agriculture; only about half the children reaching school age were in fact attending school. Social fragmentation, once extraordinarily evident, was giving way to wider loyalties, but separatism still threatened territorial cohesion; the populous and conservative highlanders were distrustful of more radical and experienced coastal men, Papuans were inclined to assert superiority over New Guineans, and islanders were suspicious of mainlanders (and with large copper deposits on Bougainville just coming under exploitation by mainly external interests, inclined to consider secession). On the other hand, such was now the scale of Australian public investment in the territory, and such was the likely scale of post-independence aid, that there was danger of conflict with embarrassed Indonesian authorities in western New Guinea, where some disaffection was apparent and where material advancement on the eastern New Guinea level would be beyond Jakarta's capacity in the foreseeable future.[30]

Just as Australia was forced into a mature diplomacy of the kind practised by fully independent states without an insulation of distance, so in the period Australia itself was transformed from a still somewhat primitive economy dependent on a few staple rural exports into a mature industrial state. Urbanization, always pronounced in Australia, accelerated as manufacturing industry boomed, rural industries declined in relative significance and employment opportunities and a mining bonanza erupted; the last was rurally located in terms of ore deposits but directed from metropolitan, and perhaps unfortunately, cosmopolitan bases.

In 1950, about half the Australian population lived in the various capital cities; in 1970, the proportion had passed 60 per cent, and exceeded two-thirds if Newcastle, Wollongong (near Sydney) and Geelong (near Melbourne) were included. The federal seat, Canberra, blossomed from about 24,000 inhabitants in 1950 to 128,000 in 1969 as government departments transferred staff from Melbourne and Sydney. Put another way, almost six million of Australia's population of 12.5 million in 1969 lived and worked in two tight concentrations in the south-east corner of the continent. In economic terms, the position of Sydney and Melbourne surpassed even their demographic superiority to attain a kind of domestic imperialism: in the late 1960s, executives in these two cities controlled more than 90 per cent of the country's leading companies.

Given that the national population in 1950 was only 8.3 million, many changes necessarily accompanied this population pressure on the cities.[31] Especially in Sydney and Melbourne, parts of the inner ring of industrial slums were transformed by European migrants searching for cheap housing, by younger middle class families prepared to renovate as a price for proximity to work and entertainment, and by public authority redevelopment, though too often in the form of aesthetically repulsive and socially harmful high-rise projects. Inner urban development was also marked by proliferation of blocks of

---

[30] For developments in the period, and for discussion of contemporary and anticipated problems see E. K. Fisk, Ed., *New Guinea on the Threshold*, Canberra, 1966: P. Hastings, *New Guinea: Problems and Prospects*, Melbourne, 1969, reprinted 1973: L. P. Mair, *Australia in New Guinea*, Melbourne, 1948, 2nd ed., 1970; W. J. Hudson, Ed., *Australia and Papua New Guinea*, Sydney, 1971, pp. 151–78: H. Nelson, *Papua New Guinea: Black Unity or Black Chaos?*, Melbourne, 1972.

[31] See P. N. Troy, Ed., *Urban Redevelopment in Australia*, Canberra, 1967.

flats and home units, the latter being apartments owned under a system of strata titles and not simply rented. But the great mass of Australians held out for the traditional block of land and bungalow. This involved an immense suburban overflow for which retailers catered with large shopping complexes in middle and outer suburban areas. Employment, however, did not follow the dormitories and shops. Consequently, and at a time when the tertiary sector of the economy mushroomed, more and more workers crowded each day into ever higher city office blocks, straining transport facilities and road capacity beyond their limits and reducing city streets to car-packed nightmares, and then each evening travelled ten and twenty miles back to their homes, leaving the cities husks dotted with restaurants, a decreasing number of theatres and very few actual inhabitants. Governments were not much involved in the economic changes that produced this heightened urbanization, and to the extent that they sought actually to guide development continued for too long to siphon off effort into the rural areas, so that public authorities lagged in the provision of services like sewerage and roadworks. And governments did not significantly decentralize their swelling bureaucracies. Not only were state and municipal services overextended, but the rising demand greatly increased the cost of land and encouraged cheap and unattractive housing developments. Parts of the outer suburban rashes comprised appallingly sterile brick veneer wastelands beset by the delinquency of bored youth, the mental ill-health of lonely wives and social alienation of travel-tired workers.

The industrialization of Australia, begun in the 1920s and greatly stimulated by the demands of a total war economy in the early 1940s, achieved maturity in the 1950s and 1960s.[32] Heavy immigration provided a necessary labour force and expanded the domestic market for goods. Import restrictions in the 1950s protected local manufacturers but the Korean War wool boom early in the decade lifted foreign exchange levels such as to allow the import of capital goods and the tooling up of industries. Tariff protection, too, was high and the Vernon committee found in 1964 that more than half of Australian manufacturing industry was dependent to some extent on tariff assistance. New industries stimulated yet more: for example, large automobile plants provided a market for steel, rubber and a host of other components as well as for the oil industry, and much the same applied to the electrical appliance and chemical industries. British and especially American capital was available for investment, and in the 1960s, when overseas investment was running at about $500 million a year, about a half was going to secondary industry and less than a fifth to primary industry. A building boom was sustained by pressure for urban housing and facilities for a rapidly expanding tertiary sector.

[32] See F. G. Davidson, *The Industrialization of Australia,* 3rd ed., Melbourne, 1962: A. Hunter, Ed., *The Economics of Australian Industry: Studies in Environment and Structure,* Melbourne, 1963: A. H. Boxer, Ed., *Aspects of the Australian Economy,* Melbourne, 1965.

There was a fillip to industry in the 1960s with increased federal spending on defence (the defence expenditure component of gross national product almost doubled in the six years to 1968–9). Finally, acceptance both of full employment and economic growth as basic governmental orthodoxy produced a climate favouring maximum economic activity.

The outcome was that by the beginning of the 1970s Australia enjoyed a fairly well balanced industrial economy. Expanded and diversified productivity was reflected in changing trade patterns: in 1948–9, manufactures earned Australia only some $58 million in export revenue but, in 1967–8, the figure was $536 million; in the same period, manufactures' share of total exports rose from 5 to 19 per cent. There were still problems – overseas proprietorships, dependence on overseas research, and inadequate technical training for young workers and retraining of older workers in new techniques all gave grounds for concern. But the Australian economy had never been as well balanced, and this precisely at a time when the old rural industries on which Australia for so long had depended met immense difficulties.[33]

The primary industries' difficulties stemmed principally from limitations imposed by over-supplied world markets, with, in the case of wool, the additional problem of competition from synthetic products. At last, and reluctantly, Australia in the 1960s came off the sheep's back. Advances in soil chemistry, pasture development and pest control (the ubiquitous rabbit was at last reduced by the man-made virus myxomatosis) allowed an increase in sheep numbers from around 100 million in 1950 to about 170 million in 1970, and wool production rose in proportion. But the great part of the wool clip was for export and, apart from temporarily outlandish prices due to American demand during the Korean War of the early 1950s, and another boom in the early 1960s, export value did not rise generally with production. In 1958–9, between the booms, for example, the clip was worth about $800 million but a decade later it was worth only $700 million and was falling heavily year by year. By 1970, wool growers were receiving government assistance and a government-backed commission was buying wool to sustain the market. British demand fell markedly and Japan now was the vital customer, taking a third of the wool export. It is true that at the end of the period wool still accounted for about a third of the country's export earnings, but pastoralists increasingly were diversifying and some had been forced to leave properties under huge debt. Only in 1972 did higher Japanese demand push prices up to a viable level for growers.

Wheat, Australia's major crop, remained buoyant but met the problem of static or chancy markets. As with wool, advances in agricultural science increased yield and acreage – from 14 million acres in the late

[33] See the essays by W. A. Sinclair and N. G. Butlin in C. Forster, Ed., *Australian Economic Development in the Twentieth Century*, London, 1970.

1940s to 26 million in the late 1960s. Production, stable in the 1950s at around 200 million bushels, then soared, reaching 530 million bushels in 1968–9. With an annual domestic demand for less than 100 million bushels, export surplus was great and the export market did not grow at the same rate. Only the entry of China into buyers' ranks in the 1960s (taking 660 million bushels in 1960–69) allowed boom harvests to be sold. Under a national stabilization scheme, growers were well protected, receiving a guaranteed price for locally sold wheat and part of the export crop, and sharing the export remainder according to Wheat Board success in selling it. But individual production quotas were introduced in 1969 and, especially if China should cut her buying, wheat represented another industry where efficiency and technology allowed much greater production potential than the international market could absorb.

Similar problems faced most other rural industries. Sugar, vital to the prosperity of a long strip of coastal Queensland, remained a very useful revenue earner, but production capacity far outstripped demand and there were here, too, the increasingly normal phenomena of 'orderly marketing': production quota restriction on individual growers, guaranteed local prices and for part of the export produce, a highly organized marketing system. Fruit products and dairying barely held their own and stood to suffer heavily in the event of British entry into the European Economic Community; already, sections of the dairying industry were depressed to the point of poor subsistence levels, but this seemed to comprise too politically thorny a nettle for it to be grasped firmly, least of all perhaps by governments with Country party membership. Other crops, such as tobacco, rice and cotton, were developed but not to the point of rivalling the older rural industries. Only perhaps in the case of beef, so important to much of northern Australia, was there a thriving industry fairly confident of future expansion; at the end of the period, about half of Australia's record 15 million cattle were in Queensland and the Northern Territory. An agreement negotiated with Britain in 1950 assured returns and, when this ran out in the mid-1960s, the United States entered the market precisely for the leaner meat inevitably produced under northern conditions of indifferent pastures, heat and distance from processing plants. This, and a probably growing demand in countries like Japan, seemed to make feasible heavier investment in breeding, pasture improvement and roads.

Luckily for Australia, a vast mining boom roughly coincided with the emergence of the rural industries' profound marketing problems. In 1950 Australia was known to be moderately well endowed with the raw materials for an industrial structure, but no more than that. Large areas of the continent, notably in Queensland and Western Australia, were written off as wasteland of at best marginal pastoral value. There were no known oil deposits of commercial interest, next to no natural gas, no bauxite ore for increasingly demanded aluminium, no nickel, and iron ore only sufficient for domestic iron and steel needs. Yet, less than twenty years later, international consortiums and some local groups were exploiting, or tooling up to exploit, mammoth new iron ore fields in Western Australia and Tasmania. By the end of the period, Australian production accounted for 5 per cent of the world total. Bauxite fields were being developed in northern Queensland, the Northern Territory and Western Australia (comprising no less than a third of the world's known deposits); nickel deposits in Western Australia of still disputed significance; oil fields in Queensland, Western Australia and, richest of all, off the Gippsland coast of south-east Victoria sufficient to meet some 60 per cent of Australia's petroleum needs for a quarter of a century; and immense deposits of natural gas in Queensland, South Australia and off the Gippsland coast suitable for piping to metropolitan and industrial centres hundreds of miles away. Some of this remarkable development sprang from prospecting chance of the old kind, but much came as a result of systematic and technically sophisticated searching and, especially as regards oil and gas, with heavy governmental support. In the decade to 1967, for example, private interests invested about $350 million in the search for oil, but governments contributed $90 million in outright subsidies quite apart from other financial incentives and technical co-operation.

By 1970, these El Dorados were only just getting under way, but their impact was already deep. By no means of least significance was a boost to national confidence for, despite occasionally scandalous or hysterical stock market operations, and the resentment of profits accruing to overseas corporations or fears that the newly-found national heritage was being sold a little too eagerly and cheaply, it remained that Australia enjoyed a new sense of buoyancy. This psychological factor was the more important in view of the national pessimism that might otherwise have been felt with the crash of the wool industry in the late 1960s. More tangibly, there developed an almost embarrassingly favourable balance of payments, new mining towns sprang up, roads and rail lines were laid to link ore fields with new or refurbished ports like Gladstone in Queensland and Western Australia's Port Hedland. Gladstone, north of Brisbane, Kwinana, near Perth, and Westernport, south-east of Melbourne, loomed as future industrial complexes on the scale of Newcastle and Wollongong. The impact on trade was immediate. As late as the mid-1960s, mine and quarry products accounted for about ten per cent of Australian exports, but by the end of the decade the proportion was twenty per cent and rising: their value almost doubled between 1967 and 1970 to nearly $1000 million. In 1960, the export leaders were gold, lead, zinc and copper; during the decade, their production did not falter but by 1970 they had been surpassed by iron, black coal and bauxite-alumina. Much of the new-found iron and more extensively mined coal was going to Japan, thereby deepening an economic relationship which was already causing some unease but with which the Australian community had barely begun to come to terms.

It should be stressed that Australia did not in the 1950s and 1960s cease to be one of the world's major sheep runs or wheat fields, or that she became in addition merely one of the world's major quarries, but rather that she became much more besides. By the early 1970s, Australia was an industrial state, with her people employed very largely in secondary and tertiary industry located in a few large cities, and there was little prospect of this trend halting, let alone reversing. While the national population soared in this period, the rural segment remained almost static at about two million. There was nothing peculiarly Australian in this process: Australian cities, after all, were absorbing not only Australian rural youth but the displaced country dwellers of countries like Yugoslavia. Yet something that was Australian, a set of social characteristics and heroic associations grown into myth since the New World frontier days of the nineteenth century, seemed rapidly to be disappearing. In 1950, the archetypal trade unionist was the itinerant shearer or the then barbarously-employed waterside worker, but in 1970 the more appropriate model was the building worker or the assembly line man in an automobile plant. In 1950 the *Bulletin* was still the country's only major political weekly and was still predominantly a purveyor of rural values and news, but by 1970 it had competitors and, like them, was now, under new owners, a typically glossy middle class urban journal. In 1950 Catholic Action groups could urge closer land settlement in the cause of defence and natural virtue, but in 1970 only perhaps the odd commune of young eccentrics would have found the notion tenable. In 1950, the suburbanite could identify with cattle drovers and fossickers, but in 1970 he was probably less infatuated with the images of the driver of cattle trucks and of oil drillers; and in 1950, poets, novelists and especially short story writers still leant heavily on rural experience for themes but by 1970 they were mainly urban in their preoccupations. This was at least symbolically illustrated in the work of the country's leading novelist, Patrick White, who was awarded a Nobel Prize for Literature in 1973.[34] In the 1950s, his settings were essentially rural, but he moved on to suburbia and finally to city settings. It remained to be seen whether a new pattern of self-identification would emerge in the city complexes despite the pressures towards cosmopolitanism exerted by higher education, the mass media, international corporations, inter-governmental co-operation, personal mobility and the uniformity goals of modern statism.

The beginnings of such a new pattern might have been built around a sustained attempt to achieve a society characterized not only by the formal trappings of approximate parliamentary democracy but by a positive sense of élan in pursuing economic equality consistent with reasonable ambition, the highest possible levels of education (as opposed to selective and merely occupational training), and a good

[34] Principal novels – *The Tree of Man*, 1956; *Voss*, 1957; *Riders in the Chariot*, 1961; *The Solid Mandala*, 1966; *The Vivisector*, 1970; *Eye of the Storm*, 1973.

life for the physically and mentally under-endowed. In the twenty years after 1950, Australia shared the blessings of buoyant world trade and, with the appropriate human and natural resources, also shared in the affluence experienced generally by western Europe, northern America and Japan. Much of this affluence seeped through the Australian community to improve standards of living significantly, but there was no real will to achieve saturation and, certainly, there was little evidence of a proud sense in the country of united pursuit of a nobler mode of existence. On the contrary, governments enacted often impulsive and usually piecemeal reforms, and much was left to the impulses of private organizations.

Among private organizations, clearly the largest and most important in this context were the unions of employees. Trade union membership declined by about 10 per cent to about 50 per cent of the work force, but this remained high in international terms and, although unionism was handicapped by multiplicity (there remained more than 300 unions, some small and poor and many competing for members to the point of demarcation disputes), there was compensation in the growing stature and cohesive power of the Australian Council of Trade Unions.[35] Under the presidency of Labor traditionalist Albert Monk through most of the period, the A.C.T.U. developed a capacity for integrating union strategy and was increasingly accepted even by coalition governments as a body to be consulted on matters of high economic and industrial policy. The strength of the A.C.T.U. was enhanced by the affiliation of the West Australian trade union movement in 1962 and of the country's largest union, the 150,000-strong A.W.U., in 1967. Its potential was made publicly apparent on the succession to the presidency in 1969 of Robert Hawke, a much younger, highly educated and militant man, who had shown his mettle as an industrial tribunal advocate and who envisaged union operations in new fields like housing, retailing and banking.

After the affiliation of the A.W.U., the A.C.T.U. comprised 98 unions and some 1,360,000 workers. However, these by and large were 'blue collar' unions of manual workers, and one of the major developments of the period was the appearance of a more traditional trade union spirit in the more gentlemanly 'white collar' unions and their co-operation with the A.C.T.U. This was the more significant in that employment in increasingly sophisticated industry was not expanding, whereas employment in the tertiary sector, the white collar sector, was expanding. White collar union militancy became evident in the mid-1950s when the loss of quarterly adjustments hurt clerical and professional workers aware that their formerly superior status and income position was being eroded by margins obtained for skilled

[35] See J. E. Isaac and G. W. Ford, Eds., *Australian Labour Relations: Readings*, Melbourne, 1971: P. W. D. Matthews and G. W. Ford, Eds., *Australian Trade Unions*, Melbourne, 1968: K. F. Walker, *Australian Industrial Relations Systems*, Cambridge, (Mass.), 1970.

workers by energetic unions; they were also affected by the beginnings of automation in office work and by wage drift in a period of high employment, that is, by labour shortage inducing industry to pay some manual workers over-award rates and to encourage additional, overtime earnings. The outcome was the founding in 1958 of a federation of almost forty white collar unions with some 300,000 members in the Australian Council of Salaried and Professional Associations which, in 1962, joined with the 78,000-strong Council of Commonwealth Public Service Organizations to form a joint committee with the A.C.T.U. Some new patterns were forged at this time. Ultra cautious groups like school teachers, who had sought professional status as their avenue to improved incomes and conditions, were now in some states, and especially in New South Wales and Victoria, becoming publicly vociferous in their disputes with governments and tactically militant to the point of strikes. Very highly paid airline pilots were now striking. Others like journalists, who had early seen the benefits of combination and use of the arbitration system, were now successfully asserting their professional status and obtaining commensurate awards, but continued the old tendency towards occasional industrial militancy.

This militancy should not be exaggerated; generally, it was noteworthy for its new comprehensiveness as much as for its depth. The ultimate weapon, the strike, indeed, often was more carefully used for several apparent reasons. First, employers in the 1960s increasingly resorted to court insertion of a strike ban clause in awards with penalties to the level of $1000 a day; in the twelve years to 1961, unions were fined only $27,600 in this way, but in 1964 alone the figure was $51,800 and for the decade from 1957 to 1968 it was $280,200, with court costs awarded against the unions amounting to almost as much again. There was also a growing incidence of extra-court agreements between unions and companies incorporating orderly grievance procedures, whilst in some long conflict-prone areas like the waterfront, generally satisfactory working conditions were at last established. Furthermore, Communist leadership in the unions was greatly diminished by the Labor party's industrial groups in the early 1950s and did not recapture all the lost ground even after the Labor split of the mid-1950s; not, it should be stressed, that Communist, militant and striker were at all exchangeable terms. As well, it was probably the case that unionists in an increasingly consumer-oriented society, and with themselves increasingly dependent on regular credit repayments to maintain living standards now taken for granted, were perhaps less inclined than formerly to forgo wages, let alone forgo the overtime payments on which so many were dependent; some of the more restive were those like postal workers whose pay rates were relatively so low as significantly to lessen the pressure to conform. Late in the 1960s the pendulum swung back towards more stoppages and strikes, due partly perhaps to inflationary pressures on workers' incomes and to the new, largely Communist, revolutionary tactic of involving unions in shared agitational experience with other elements in the community on non-industrial issues, but partly, too, to workers' assertiveness at the local plant level making more difficult the task of the unions' central officials, a development ascribed by some to the influence of British migrants used to a tradition of shop steward initiative.

The industrial machinery within which the unions operated – often with ludicrously under-paid, over-worked and self-taught officials – was complex and to a degree liable to change. In 1956 male employees were about evenly divided between federal and state jurisdictions and the federal government sought to rationalize its part of the system with the creation of a two-tier structure: there was to be a Commonwealth Conciliation and Arbitration Commission to concentrate on award determination and a Commonwealth Industrial Court with exclusively judicial functions in matters like appeals and penalties. Criteria used in award determinations continued to include the old ethical factor of a minimum family living standard and, perhaps increasingly, the capacity of industry to pay. Not quite resolved was the extent to which tribunals should take into account the state of the economy, a matter of great importance to unions given employers' and governments' proneness to advance it as a reason for avoiding a rise in industry's wages costs or a further boost to an inflationary wages-prices spiral. In 1952, the chief judge of the then Commonwealth Court of Arbitration and Conciliation, Sir Raymond Kelly, urged employers and employees to accept cuts in profits and wages for the good of the country. This represented extraordinary personal eccentricity; still, in 1953, Kelly and his learned brothers broke the nexus between wages and cost of living indices and early in 1954 froze margins explicitly on anti-inflation grounds. In the mid-1960s, employers sought the replacement of the traditional formula of basic wage plus margins for skill with a total wage for various employment categories and based on productivity criteria. In 1965, the commission refused to tamper with the formula, while a majority accepted price stability as a factor in fixing a new basic wage. In 1966, it swung away from considering as paramount the inflation issue, but in 1967 it finally switched to the concept of a total wage. By the 1970s one could only say that the federal and state industrial tribunals were considering living standards, industrial peace and economic effects in their decision-making.

The success enjoyed by unions in using industrial machinery to obtain higher remuneration and better working conditions for their members, whether in periodic national wage hearings, individual applications or in a host of bi-partite dealings with employers sanctioned by tribunals, is difficult to estimate, especially because this was a system with a built-in wage-price spiral. If one compares the working conditions, the security, and apparent buying capacity of most workers in 1970 with the situation in 1950, then clearly unionists had been well served, but also noting, for example, extensions of annual leave with pay to three and four weeks and the introduction of long service leave with pay. But against this must be set rising expectations which were central to the economic philosophies of governments, entrepreneurs and their friends in the mass media. Experience of affluence alone was such that cars and refrigerators – middle class luxuries in 1950 – were, with television sets, very nearly universally accepted as essentials in 1970. As well, much of the economic expansion of the time was built on the assumption of the ordinary man's acquisitiveness, and, where this was lacking, a booming advertising industry bridged the gap with at best subtle persuasion and at worst trickery. By the end of the 1960s the ratio of people to cars was below three to one. The cost was fantastic: in the period 1950 to 1970 inclusive, traffic accident deaths comprised 54,179 which was almost as many as were killed in action during the 1914–18 war, and getting on for twice the number killed in the 1939–45 war.

Rising expectations and difficulties in meeting them seemed to be involved in two phenomena of the period. The first of these was evident under the surface of the wage drift in the mid-1960s. Most of the workers' above-award income came not from over-award payments by labour-hungry employers but from over-time payments, which accounted for more than 15 per cent of the average weekly earnings of adult males in manufacturing industry. At about the same time, it was found that no less than 144,000 Australians held second jobs. The second was a very rapid rise in the female work force. At the 1954 census it was found that about 13 per cent of married women were employed; by the 1966 census, this figure had more than doubled and a survey late in 1970 showed a figure of 35 per cent. To some extent this sprang from a mild form of sexual revolution encouraged by wartime pressures in the early 1940s, but to a considerable extent it sprang from the need for additional income, whether in migrant families working desperately to establish an economic foothold or in others feeling the pinch of rising costs. This occurred despite remaining problems for working women. In 1966, the federal parliament legislated to allow married women to be appointed, or to remain, permanent officials and to take confinement leave without loss of status, but only South Australia among the states followed suit. Although industrial tribunals in the late 1960s took first steps towards acceptance of equal pay for women in their awards, full implementation of the principle still was a long way off; crèche and kindergarten facilities in most parts of the country met only a tiny fraction of the demand.[36]

Vigilant unions of employees, then, acted to maintain or improve the material living conditions of many Australians. The self-employed and company executives took their chances, and in a period of affluence their chances were good – whether they were plumbers, surgeons or accountants. Another sizeable section of the community,

[36] See N. MacKenzie, *Women in Australia*, Melbourne, 1962: J. Rigg, Ed., *In Her Own Right*, Melbourne, 1969.

however, could scarcely survive by their own efforts, let alone share in the general prosperity, and they depended partly on private agencies and mainly on the state. These were the old, the sick, the handicapped, and the widowed, and there were a lot of them: in 1970, there were 779,000 aged pensioners and 87,000 widow pensioners (20,000 of them deserted wives).

More than their political opponents allowed, the conservative coalitions in Canberra were sensitive and active in this policy area, partly as a matter of electoral survival in conflict with Labor for whom social amelioration was always a prime plank, partly from genuine convictions of the old Deakinite Liberal kind. Thus, in 1950 child endowment was extended to first-born and, from 1963, was paid in respect of dependent children past the former age limit of sixteen years to twenty-one. In 1956 widows' pensions were loaded with rising additions for each dependent child after the first and, in 1963, widows with children were accorded a special domestic allowance. From 1958 supplementary assistance was made available for aged and invalid pensioners and widows paying rent and utterly dependent on pension incomes, and in 1954 the federal government began subsidizing the capital costs of aged people's homes and this subsidy practice was subsequently extended (with variations as to capital and/or maintenance contributions) to home nursing agencies, mental hospitals (through the states), marriage guidance services, accommodation for disabled workers in sheltered workshops and then for the actual workshops. In 1950 a pharmaceutical benefits scheme was introduced to allow free dispensing of life-saving drugs, and in 1951 pensioners were accorded free medical and pharmaceutical services. Besides these more or less radical steps, the coalitions periodically improved the lot of those claiming unemployment or sickness benefits, raised civil pensions, liberalized means tests for pension qualifications, and raised war pensions; a federal repatriation department and an alert R.S.L. so looked to the position of veterans and their dependants as to pose the query whether this welfare sector was excessively favoured. In all these matters Canberra was now the key, with federal predominance in social services launched by Labor in the 1940s made almost absolute by their successors.[37]

Having admitted the coalitions' welfare record, however, it does remain that if the ethical criterion of a minimum acceptable family living standard still was part of the basis for industrial tribunals' wage decisions, a comparable criterion was not the basis for governments' social welfare decisions, and to that extent Australia was no more a welfare state in the early 1970s than it had been in the early 1950s. In the first place, pension increases and other welfare extensions were not tied directly to cost of living indices, but were offered as a rule to trump Labor, or on humanitarian grounds, or in response to agita-

---

[37] See T. H. Kewley, *Social Security in Australia*, Sydney, 1965: T. H. Kewley, *Australia's Welfare State*, Melbourne, 1969.

tion; some pensioner groups in the 1960s became vocal. Humanitarianism was always bounded by broader budgetary policy. In the second place, the extension or institution of welfare measures came piecemeal rather than by integrated design: for example, on the origins of the highly significant decision in 1954 to subsidize accommodation for the aged, Menzies has recalled that 'In 1954, over the dinner table at the prime minister's lodge, my wife made a remark which took root in my mind'.[38] Inevitably, this style produced anomalies and a system of increasing complexity. In the third place, after initially toying with a national insurance scheme so that future welfare recipients would have contributed over a long period to an appropriate fund, the coalitions chose to meet welfare needs from consolidated revenue and, to some degree at least, to retire to a dated aversion to too great a state role lest personal thrift be discouraged and voluntary good works become redundant. The result was that private welfare bodies remained important props for a section of the Australian community. The same ideological flavour permeated the 1953 health scheme whereby people insured themselves with private societies whose payments of members' claims for medical and hospital costs were subsidized by the federal government; by the end of the period more than three-quarters of the population was covered. The extent of the cover varied according to the premium level which the insurer could afford; but that premiums and expenses not covered by them were tax deductions only increased the relative value of the scheme to the more affluent. In general, then, the range of welfare assistance became wider than ever before but not to the point of guaranteeing an ethically acceptable level of comfort and security throughout the population. With the family structure weakening and with inflation fairly constant, this meant in turn the survival of pockets of distress, not now so much in terms of areas inhabited by poorly paid or sporadically employed workers and their families but less evidently in struggling, depressed and scattered old people, deserted wives, widows, the sick and the maladjusted on the fringes of the economic system.[39]

Also hidden from most Australians and yet more thoroughly ignored was the appalling plight of the country's Aboriginal population.[40] By the 1950s federal and state policies were becoming better co-ordinated, favouring assimilation or integration of Aborigines into Australian life. But informal segregation remained, backed up by a degree of officially-induced segregation, notably in Queensland and the Northern Territory, and the gap between black and white seemed to be opening rather than closing. By 1969, there were approximately 50,000 fully

[38] R. G. Menzies, *The Measure of the Years*, Melbourne, 1970, p. 124.

[39] See R. F. Henderson, A. Harcourt and R. J. A. Harper, *People in Poverty*, Melbourne, 1970.

[40] See C. D. Rowley, *Aboriginal Policy and Practice: Vol. I: The Destruction of Aboriginal Society*, Canberra, 1970: F. S. Stevens, Ed., *Racism: The Australian Experience*, Sydney, 3 vols., 1971–2.

Aboriginal Australians, most in the Northern Territory and Queensland, and 90,000 Australians partly of Aboriginal stock, most in Queensland, Western Australia and New South Wales. They were now increasing more rapidly than the population in general and it was expected that by the early 1980s there would be 70,000 in the former category and 184,000 in the latter.

There was some change in the period. All governments stepped up the provision of social services, social work, educational facilities, and abolished some forms of discrimination in matters like the franchise and access to liquor. The tradition of university concern laid by A. P. Elkin and others at the University of Sydney in the 1930s developed further, not only among academics pursuing much needed anthropological, sociological and historical research, but also among students who endowed scholarships for Aborigines and campaigned occasionally against social discrimination in particular and the lot of the Aboriginal Australian in general. And there emerged at last signs of Aboriginal leadership in vigorous, properly angry upholders of Aboriginal rights and values – for example, Kath Walker, a Queensland poet, and Charles Perkins, an Alice Springs Aborigine who graduated from the University of Sydney in 1966. In 1959, there was founded the Federal Council for the Advancement of Aborigines and Torres Strait Islanders which showed increasing signs of giving bite to the periodic agitation of liberal whites. Again, in 1965, the Commonwealth Conciliation and Arbitration Commission at last laid down normal award rates for Northern Territory Aboriginal stockmen; in 1967, a national referendum massively approved a change in the federal constitution to allow aborigines to be treated as Australians in matters like census-taking and to allow the federal government predominance in Aboriginal policy. In the following year, W. C. Wentworth added Aboriginal affairs to his Social Services portfolio, and there was created a high level council to help with advice and a Commonwealth Office of Aboriginal Affairs which showed a welcome tendency to seek Aboriginal staff. Of perhaps accidentally symbolic value was the nomination in 1971 of Queensland Aboriginal Neville Bonner to fill the casual Senate vacancy caused by the retirement of the Liberals' Dame Annabelle Rankin.

Despite these changes for the better, in 1972 almost as much as in 1950, Aborigines and most people obviously of Aboriginal stock were largely depressed city slum dwellers, shanty dwellers on the peripheral wastes of small and usually discriminatory country towns or heavily restricted wards (to use a very kind term) on church or state reserves or settlements. Given that only a handful of the country's Aborigines still lived anything like their traditional life undisturbed, a few statistics adequately illustrate the degree to which Australians were not yet aware of a debt to a dispossessed and decimated people. In the mid-1960s, the infant mortality rate among Northern Territory Aborigines was six times the general Australian rate, and the mortality rate for children under the age of five was even higher. In Western

Australia, Aborigines comprised perhaps 3 per cent of the population but 30 per cent of the state's jail inhabitants; and in 1966–7, there were roughly 20,000 Aboriginal children receiving some kind of primary education, but only 2600 were at secondary schools and just nine were at tertiary level institutions.[41]

If Australians and their governments restrained any inclinations they might have had towards rational and fair-minded welfare policies, and seemed scarcely tempted at all to act on a scale that might have transformed the situation of the Aboriginal minority, they were much more generous in the vital matter of education for their youth. A post-war baby boom and heavy immigration would have demanded considerable expansion of educational facilities merely to have maintained the 1950 position; not only were these demands largely met, but access to higher education was markedly widened.[42] The percentage of gross national product devoted to education more than doubled in the period to more than 4 per cent, and a quarter of the states' expenditures now went on education; the percentage of those in the 17 to 22-year age group engaged in full-time education doubled to 5 per cent. To the end of the 1940s, access to secondary education had been a privilege rather than routine, but by the end of the 1960s half the student population was completing at least four years of secondary schooling and, whereas as late as 1958–9 the states were spending 23 per cent of their educational budgets on their secondary systems, by 1967 the proportion had passed 30 per cent. Even more remarkable was university expansion: where in 1950 there were six straitened state universities and the new Australian National University designed as an institution for advanced research, in 1972 the latter had absorbed the old Canberra University College (a branch of the University of Melbourne) to become as well an undergraduate teaching institution, and the states now had fourteen full universities and several more being planned; the university undergraduate population, less than 30,000 in the early 1950s, had passed 100,000 with another 60,000 in advanced and more or less tertiary level technical institutes.

Such, however, was the sudden demand for education characteristic of many societies at this time, less a matter alone of intellectual frustration than parental interest in social mobility and governmental concern to staff a growing economy, that governments were more criticized for insufficient response than praised for what they achieved. And this although there was more to the prodigious educational expansion than quantity. If anything, pupil-teacher ratios dropped slightly; the academic qualifications demanded of teachers rose and academic standards in schools and universities increased. Dissatisfaction

---

[41] See the chapters by L. P. Hiatt and F. Stevens in A. F. Davies and S. Encel, Eds., *Australian Society*, Melbourne, 1965, 1970.

[42] See E. L. Wheelwright, Ed., *Higher Education in Australia*, Melbourne, 1965.

focused mainly on two issues: the role of the federal government and the role of private education.

As in almost every area of governmental activity, and despite minimal constitutional warranty, the Australian government expanded its role in education relative to that of the state governments to the point where, in 1966, a Department of Education and Science was established in Canberra and the federal share of Australian educational expenditure was 17 per cent, 6 per cent more than a mere five years before. Beyond the increasing dependence of the states for reimbursements, grants and loan allocations from Canberra for educational as much as for other forms of expenditure, the federal government took specific initiatives mainly in the realm of higher education. The conservative coalitions implemented Labor government plans for undergraduate scholarships and from 1951 made matching grants to the states to help universities meet recurrent expenses. In 1957, Menzies invited Britain's Keith Murray to report on the university situation and it was Menzies' basic acceptance of the Murray committee's expansionist recommendations that saw new universities quickly built and others transformed by financing beyond former dreams. The Australian Universities Commission was established in 1959 to advise the government under a system of triennium budgeting involving not merely contributions towards recurrent expenses but matching grants for buildings, student accommodation and teaching hospitals. In 1965, the federal government began contributions to colleges of advanced education (technically and/or vocationally oriented tertiary-level institutions) and in 1967 began outright grants for teachers' colleges. Great as was the expansion in the tertiary sector allowed by this infusion of federal interest and finance, it did not meet fully the demand for scholarships or prevent the imposition by university faculties of restrictive enrolment quotas. At a time of intense demand for educational opportunity, this demand-supply gap produced a sense of grievance aimed now at Canberra rather than the state administrations. One ingredient here was a suspicion of élitism in Canberra's attitudes, in the case of secondary education associated with an element of sectarianism.

The federal government also entered the field of secondary education. Although in 1951 fees to a certain amount had been allowed as income deductions and in 1954 gifts for school building were excluded from taxation, in 1963-4 it began specific grants to the states for expenditure on science blocks and apparatus in secondary schools. both government ('state') and private. More than a quarter of this aid went to private schools and subsequently the federal contribution was raised to allow a further increase in aid to private schools without lowering the amount going to government schools. That this was of immense help to many struggling Catholic schools upset some; that it gave public funds to some socially élite private schools upset others. In 1965, there was a similar reaction when the government introduced scholarships covering the winners' final two years at secondary school, whether government or private. Had the government associated a means test with these measures, the Catholic interest would have been almost as well served and hostility probably would have been much less. Had it shown some particular interest in the primary or junior secondary levels, some hostility would have been avoided. In the event, dissatisfaction mainly among secularists was sufficient to see the emergence in the 1960s of the Committee for the Defence of Government Schools whose electoral candidates' preferences in some seats became significant. After much soul-searching, especially in left-dominated Victoria, Labor moved in the wake of the conservatives, with Democratic Labor keenest of all for state aid.

Some of the dissatisfaction reflected radicals' disenchantment with long years of conservative government. Not only was finance not found to allow unlimited access to education at all levels, but research was showing that those in the system were affected in their performance by, among other things, the cultivation and sense of confidence in their family and school backgrounds. This seemed especially true at the university level where, despite high quota selectivity, failure rates in some faculties were high by international standards. Concern was expressed, too, at wastage in the secondary sector: in 1970, for example, final year enrolments in government schools amounted to only 25 per cent of first year enrolments, whereas the figure for Catholic schools was 32 per cent and for the generally exclusive non-Catholic private schools it was 82 per cent. And this was at a time when three-quarters of the country's secondary students were at government schools. This, of course, reflected the attitudes and experiences as well as incomes of parents. Only the most massive effort, not only in education but in virtually upturning a still stratified and economically unequal society, would have allowed rapid and substantial change. Conservative governments were interested in improving the universities, in ameliorating the plight of Catholic parents (apart from electoral considerations, they did the job more cheaply) and even in lowering the walls of privilege. This last should be remembered, for many tens of thousands of Australians in this period were the first in their families' histories to enter universities and, thereby, the more remunerative and interesting occupations. However, it was not the conservative governments' intention to level society, and this was as evident in their educational policies as in others.

Aid for, among others, Catholic schools after so long a Catholic campaign for it, seemed in 1963 a bold electoral step to win away from Labor some of a large reservoir of traditional support remaining even after the split of the mid-1950s.[43] It may also have reflected awareness in some realist conservative circles of change both in the pattern of religious affiliation and in sectarian relations. With a higher fertility rate and with the proportion of Catholic immigrants greater

[43] See P. J. O'Farrell, *The Catholic Church in Australia: A Short History: 1788–1967*, Melbourne, 1968.

than the national average, census by census the Catholic proportion of the population rose by about 2 per cent until by 1966 it had reached 27 per cent compared with the Anglicans' 34 per cent (down 5 per cent since 1947), the Methodists' 10 per cent (down 2 per cent) and the Presbyterians' 9 per cent (down 1 per cent). Immigration effected other changes, so that the Lutherans and the Orthodox now surpassed the always small Baptist and Congregationalist groups, but Catholic growth was one of the two religious features of the period. By 1966, there were already more Catholic children under the age of four than Anglican, and it was generally anticipated that Catholics would displace Anglicans as the largest denomination by the late 1980s.

The second major change was in sectarian relations. Much greater apparent non-Catholic tolerance of Catholics seemed to spring in large part from changes on the Catholic side. The former Irishness of the church had almost disappeared and with it the old taint of near treason. A new, heavily immigrant working class underneath was also heavily Catholic but of a Mediterranean kind almost as alien to the old Catholic community as to the non-Catholic. Social mobility was taking young Catholics past civil service respectability and security to the more prestigious professions and remunerative ranks of commerce. Unflagging Catholic support for defence preparedness and anti-Communist foreign policies gave community of interest with the Anglican and Presbyterian establishment. As well, the ecumenical spirit of Pope John XXIII was reflected in, for example, the ecclesiastical diplomacy of Hobart's Archbishop Young and 'protestantising' the mass into a vernacular and simpler ritual – aesthetically poorer but no longer affrontingly foreign; custody of the old liturgical glories seemed to pass by default to high Anglican hands. This mutual tolerance was more noticeable among clergy than laity but the grass roots trend was in the same direction except perhaps among Baptists and to some degree Sydney's fervently evangelical Anglicans, for whom reformation battle lines remained fresh and whose Archbishop Loane found himself unable to join with other Anglicans and protestants in prayer with the visiting Pope Paul in 1970.

Religiosity in terms of public observance did not change in the period, but there were problems for all the churches arising from affluence, a much better educated laity, a more hedonistically self-confident youth, pervasive anti-authoritarianism, divisive new theologies, falling clerical recruitment, and weakening family cohesiveness; the federal parliament's imposition on the cluttered states' fields of a new, more rational and permissive divorce code was followed by a climbing divorce rate.[44] For Catholics, there were two particular problems besides: an apparent tendency in lay ranks to ignore episcopal repudiation of contraception (spreading rapidly in the 1960s

[44] For example, the number of divorce petitions rose from 11,132 in 1966 to 15,379 in 1970, with decrees granted in the same period rising from 9859 to 12,198.

with the development of oral contraceptives for women) and, above all, a failing attempt to maintain a comprehensive education system. Catholic school enrolments almost doubled in the period to nearly half a million, but the financial burden in terms of plant and staff, with religious orders becoming increasingly dependent on lay teachers, was great. Estimates varied widely, but it seemed that the proportion of Catholic children in government schools may have jumped by as much as 10 per cent between 1965 and 1970 to something approaching 40 per cent. The potential effects were profound: a survey late in the period suggested that, while 80 per cent of Catholics educated at Catholic schools maintained religious practice in adult life, the same was true of less than half of Catholics educated at government schools.[45]

Wider education, the European migrant infusion, affluence and, it could be suspected, the psychological impact both of a new sense of Australian involvement in the mainstream of world affairs and of a diminishing sense of isolation in the face of revolutionary change in transport and communications, all contributed to immense improvement in that most intangible of phenomena, the quality of Australian cultural life. It was not that Australia suddenly became one of western society's more vibrant cultures, but rather that in a short time a previously somewhat spare, self-conscious and arid intellectual and artistic life gave way to a less frontier and more ordinary western culture. This was most immediately obvious in painting, with proliferating private galleries and steeply rising prices for the work of men like Sidney Nolan, Russell Drysdale, William Dobell and Ian Fairweather. These, and a host of others, often exhibited and drew inspiration from overseas but there was now a domestic milieu financially and to some extent emotionally supportive. In novel writing, former tendencies towards the rough-edged and radically nationalist gave way to greater professionalism and in a few cases greater art, the former most notably in the case of Morris West,[46] commercially very successful on the international market, the latter most notably in the case of Patrick White. In verse, younger men emerged with a variety of approaches, and older poets – A. D. Hope, James McAuley and Judith Wright and others – published work of maturity and authority. Less perhaps was achieved in music, although expatriates like Malcolm Williamson and locally-based composers like Peter Sculthorpe were making their mark.

In the performing arts, individuals still were pulled to the larger audiences and more varied facilities of North America and Europe, such as an operatic singer like Joan Sutherland, a conductor like Charles Mackerras or a number of film and stage actors. Still, what

45 See H. Mol, *Religion in Australia*, Melbourne, 1971.

46 Principal publications *Children of the Sun*, 1957; *The Devil's Advocate*, 1959; *Daughter of Silence*, 1961; *The Shoes of the Fishermen*, 1963; *The Ambassador*, 1965; *The Tower of Babel*, 1968.

formerly had appeared fitfully became constant ingredients of the local scene in the period. Concert series in the capital cities were provided largely by the Australian Broadcasting Commission and directed by eminent local and overseas conductors. Regular ballet and opera seasons by local companies were at times augmented by overseas artists, and overseas tours in the sixties by the Sydney and Victorian symphony orchestras and by a ballet company showed the harvest being reaped from the creative energy of pioneers like Bernard Heinze and Edouard Borovansky. A perhaps declining commercial 'middle brow' theatre was more than off-set by busy and increasingly professional repertory and 'little theatre' companies. Governmental support, for example in the founding of the Australian Elizabethan Theatre Trust in 1953 to subsidize the performing arts, was an essential aid, but there were now audiences and young artists in sufficient numbers to sustain theatrical enterprises. A monument to this flowering promised to be the misnamed Sydney Opera House initiated by the New South Wales government in the mid-1950s and built largely to the design of competition-winning Danish architect Joern Utzon. At the end of the period, and with expenditure of $100 million in sight, work still proceeded at Bennelong Point on Utzon's white dhow-sailed fantasy in concrete. Melbourne, in the meantime, proceeded quietly with the building of a new state gallery-auditorium complex designed by local architect Roy Grounds.

In intellectual life, too, development was on a broad front rather than in the emergence of individual giants, except perhaps in science where Nobel Prizes went in 1960 to Melbourne immunologist Frank Macfarlane Burnet and in 1963 to Canberra neurologist John Eccles. Among historians, for example, and despite an immense quantity of research now being pursued in university departments, only a handful like Manning Clark aspired to an overview of the Australian experience, and at that with muted impact. Indeed, given the way in which university departments tended to monopolize historical, philosophical and even literary talent, it was noteworthy to what degree Australia's intellectual life was stimulated rather by a new breed of highly educated journalist-writers: Donald Horne[47] and migrant John Pringle[48] in Sydney, Bruce Grant in Melbourne and Geoffrey Dutton in Adelaide, to name only a few. Indeed, the higher intellectual level and technical sophistication of sections of the press added a quite new dimension to life in the period, whether in older papers like the *Sydney Morning Herald*, the Melbourne *Age* and the *Canberra Times*, or in the country's first national daily, the *Australian*, launched by Rupert Murdoch in 1964.

Most Australians, of course, still preferred less cerebral use of leisure in clubs, pubs and sport. Sport remained one field in which ambition was respectable, although the old aversion to excessive effort was

[47] His most widely quoted book was *The Lucky Country*, Melbourne, 1964.

[48] He attracted much attention with his book *Australian Accent*, London, 1958.

anyway becoming another casualty of Americanization. Australian tennis players dominated world courts throughout the period, her cricketers were on top for much of the period and her swimmers consistently pushed Australia higher on Olympic Games medal lists than her population made readily comprehensible (including the 1956 Games held in Melbourne). However, while 122,000 people saw Carlton defeat Collingwood for the 1970 Victorian Football League premiership at the Melbourne Cricket Ground, there were signs of a swing away from spectator sport towards participation in golf, fishing, boating, surfing and skiing. The ubiquitous automobile and the urge to escape urban congestion in scarcely less congested coastal ribbons of holiday homes seemed, too, to be changing leisure use patterns.

In summary, these were kind decades for Australia. The mass of her people enjoyed peace, security and stability on a previously unknown scale. Unemployment was minimal; changing attitudes and technology considerably emancipated women; more children were educated to a high level; immigration added immensely to social variety; religious bigotry declined; class divisions were much less bitter despite still very marked income inequality; the pull of the British and Irish traditions weakened and there was a more self-assured Australianness in the press, the universities, the churches and the civil services. Sophisticated Australian journalists, and not brave tourists, now wrote books about the Australian identity.

In the process, there were casualties that could perhaps be mourned. The preceding leaner years produced the brave and bawdy humour of Roy Rene and George Wallace, the stringily valiant boxing of Vic Patrick, the depression-bred toughness of Collingwood and Balmain footballers, the relentless perseverance of Donald Bradman and the larrikin aggressiveness of Sid Barnes, the grinding competence of Ben Chifley and the harsh flamboyance of Eddie Ward, the ceaseless striving of the scholarship boys, Robert Menzies and Herbert Evatt. On the other hand, of course, if the spirit and flair of a Roy Rene were missed, the putrefying slums of his sketches were not. Well-fed sentimentality apart, it was better that the stews of Redfern and Carlton tended now to wear the brighter colours of Mediterranean migrants, that the blood houses of Paddington survived now as the modish haunts of an encroaching bourgeoisie. It is true that Australia in the early 1970s was no utopia. It does remain, though, that there were momentous changes in the 1950s and 1960s such as to produce a society that was much more of a self-confident western industrial state than in 1950, that allowed the allocation among its people of a much larger and tastier social and economic cake, even if not yet in notably equal slices.

Bibliography of Publications

(See Table of Abbreviations)

I

———————

1788-1810

Reasons for the settlement

Blainey, G., *The Tyranny of Distance: How Distance shaped Australia's History*, Melbourne, 1966.

Blainey, G., 'Botany Bay or Gotham City?', in *A.E.H.R.*, *VIII*, 2, September 1968.

Bolton, G. C., 'The Hollow Conqueror: Flax and the Foundation of Australia', in *A.E.H.R.*, *VIII*, 1, March 1968.

Bolton, G. C., 'Broken Reeds and Smoking Flax', in *A.E.H.R.*, *IX*, 1, March 1969.

Clark, C. M. H., 'The Choice of Botany Bay', in *H.S.*, *35*, November 1960.

Dallas, K. M., 'The First Settlements in Australia: Considered in relation to Sea-Power in World Politics', in *T.H.R.A.P.*, *III*, 1952.

Dallas, K. M., 'Commercial Influences on the First Settlements in Australia', in *T.H.R.A.P.*, *XVI*, 2, September 1968.

Dallas, K. M., *Trading Posts or Penal Colonies: The Commercial Significance of Cook's New Holland Route to the Pacific*, Hobart 1969.

Fry, H. T. 'Cathay and the way thither: the background to Botany Bay', in *H.S.*, *56*, April 1971.

Reese, T. R., 'The Origins of Colonial America and New South Wales: An Essay on British Imperial Policy in the Eighteenth Century', in *A.J.P.H.*, *VII*, 2, November 1961.

Roe, M., 'Australia's Place in "The Swing to the East", 1788–1810', in *H.S.*, *30*, May 1958. (see also addendum by B. Atkins in *31*.)

Shaw, A. G. L., 'The Hollow Conqueror and the Tyranny of Distance', in *H.S.*, *50*, April 1968. (see also reply by G. Blainey in the same issue.)

Swan, R. A., *To Botany Bay*, Canberra, 1973.

The early years

Cobley, J., *Sydney Cove, 1788*, London, 1962.

Cobley, J., *Sydney Cove, 1789–90*, Sydney, 1963.

Cobley, J., *Sydney Cove, 1791–1792*, Sydney, 1965.

Collins, D., *An Account of the English Colony in New South Wales*, 2 vols, London, 1798, 1202, reprinted Adelaide, 1971.

Dalkin, R. N., 'Norfolk Island – The First Settlement, 1788–1814', in *R.A.H.S.J.*, 7, 3, September 1971.

Davey, L., Macpherson, M., and Clements, F. W., 'The Hungry Years: 1788–1792', in *H.S.*, *11*, November 1947.

Mackaness, G., *Admiral Arthur Phillip, Founder of New South Wales, 1738–1814*, Sydney, 1937.

Select Committee on Finance, *28th Report*, in British Parliamentary Papers, 1810, No. 348, *IV*, 375; reprinted in *Great Britain: Parliamentary Papers*, reprints by Irish University Press, *Crime and Punishment, I.*

Tench, W., *A Narrative of the Expedition to Botany Bay*, London, 1789. Reprinted Sydney, 1961, under title *Sydney's First Four Years*, edited by L. F. Fitzhardinge.

Tench, W., *A Complete Account of the Settlement at Port Jackson*, London, 1793. Reprinted Sydney, 1961, under title *Sydney's First Four Years*, edited by L. F. Fitzhardinge.

The years 1800–1810, including the Rum Rebellion

Allars, K. G., 'George Crossley – An Unusual Attorney', in *R.A.H.S.J.*, *44*, 5, January 1959.

Bennett, J. M., 'Richard Atkins – An Amateur Judge Jeffreys', in *R.A.H.S.J.*, *52*, 4, December 1966.

Byrnes, J. V., 'Andrew Thompson, 1773–1810', in *R.A.H.S.J.*, *48*, 2 and 3, June and July 1962.

Caley, G., *Reflections on the Colony of New South Wales*, reprinted Melbourne, 1966, edited by J. E. B. Currey.

Evatt, H. V., *Rum Rebellion: a Study of the Overthrow of Governor Bligh by John Macarthur and the New South Wales Corps*, Sydney, 1938, reprinted London, 1968.

Fletcher, B. H., 'The Hawkesbury Settlers and the Rum Rebellion', in *R.A.H.S.J.*, *54*, 3, September 1968.

McMinn, W. G., 'Explaining a Rebellion: An historiographical enquiry', in *Teaching History*, *4*, 1, May 1970.

Mann, D. D., *The Present Picture of New South Wales 1811* . . . , London, 2 vols, 1811.

Mackaness, G., *The Life of Vice-Admiral William Bligh*, Sydney, 2 vols, 1931, revised edition, 1 vol., 1951.

Proceedings of a General Court Martial . . . for the Trial of Lieut-Colonel George Johnston on a charge of Mutiny . . . , London, 1811, edited by D. D. Mann.

Select Committee on Transportation, 1812, *Report*, in British Parliamentary Papers, 1812, *II*, No. 341, reprinted in *Great Britain: Parliamentary Papers*, reprints by Irish University Press, *Crime and Punishment, I.*

Shaw, A. G. L., 'The Rum Corps and the Rum Rebellion', in *Melbourne Historical Journal*, X, 1971.

Sydney Gazette, 1803–10, reprinted Sydney, 1963–70. (8 vols, in 5.)

The legal system

Allars, K. G., 'Richard Dore Re-examined', in *R.A.H.S.J., 50*, 2, July 1964.

Campbell, E., 'Prerogative Rule in New South Wales, 1788–1823', in *R.A.H.S.J., 50*, 3, August 1964.

Currey, C. H., *The Brothers Bent: Judge-Advocate Ellis Bent and Judge Jeffrey Hart Bent*, Sydney, 1968, ch. I.

Windeyer, W. J. V., ' "A Birthright and Inheritance": The establishment of the Rule of Law in Australia', in *Tasmanian University Law Review, I*, November 1962.

The penal system

Bateson, C., *The Convict Ships: 1787–1868*, Glasgow, 1959, 2nd edition 1969.

Cobley, J., *The Convicts 1788–1792: A Study of a One-in-Twenty Sample*, Sydney, 1964, reprinted Sydney, 1965.

Cobley, J., *The Crimes of the First Fleet Convicts*, Sydney, 1970.

Connell, R. W., 'The Convict Rebellion of 1804', in *Melbourne Historical Journal, 5*, 1965.

O'Brien, E., *The Foundation of Australia, 1786–1800: A Study in English Criminal Practice and Penal Colonisation in the Eighteenth Century*, London, 1937, 2nd edition Sydney, 1950.

Robson, L. L., *The Convict Settlers of Australia: An Enquiry into the Origins and Character of the Convicts transported to New South Wales and Van Diemen's Land 1787–1852*, Melbourne, 1965, reprinted 1970.

Shaw, A. G. L., *Convicts and the Colonies: A Study of Penal Transportation from Great Britain and Ireland to Australia and Other Parts of the British Empire*, London, 1966.

Vaux, Hardy, J., *The Memoirs of James Hardy Vaux*, first published London, 1814, reprinted London, 1964, edited by N. D. McLachlan.

The economy

Abbott, G. J., and Nairn, N. B., Eds., *Economic Growth of Australia 1788–1821*, Melbourne, 1969.

Bell, R., 'Samuel Marsden – Pioneer Pastoralist' in *R.A.H.S.J., 56*, 1, March 1970.

Butlin, S. J., *Foundations of the Australian Monetary System, 1788–1851*, Melbourne, 1953, chs 1–3, reprinted Sydney, 1968.

Carter, H. B., *His Majesty's Spanish Flock: Sir Joseph Banks and the Merinos of George III of England*, Sydney, 1964.

Fletcher, B. H., 'The Development of Small Scale Farming in New South Wales under Governor Hunter', in *R.A.H.S.J.*, *50*, 1, June 1964.

Fletcher, B. H., 'Government Farming and Grazing in New South Wales, 1788–1810', in *R.A.H.S.J.*, *59*, 3, September 1973.

Hainsworth, D. R., *Builders and Adventurers: The Traders and the Emergence of the Colony 1788–1821*, Melbourne, 1968.

Hainsworth, D. R., *The Sydney Traders, Simeon Lord and his Contemporaries 1788–1821*, Sydney, 1972.

McCarty, J. W., 'The Staple Approach in Australian Economic History', in *Business Archives and History, IV*, 1, February 1964.

Maude, H. E., *Islands and Men: Studies in Pacific History*, Melbourne, 1968, (ch. 5 'The Tahitian Pork Trade').

Steven, M., *Merchant Campbell, 1769–1846: A Study of Colonial Trade*, Melbourne, 1965.

The New South Wales Corps

Austin, M., 'Paint My Picture Truly', in *R.A.H.S.J.*, *51*, 4, December 1965.

Foster, W., 'Francis Grose and the Officers', in *R.A.H.S.J.*, *51*, 3, September 1965.

Glover, R., *Peninsula Preparation: The Reform of the British Army 1795–1809*, London, 1963.

Parsons, T. G., 'The N.S.W. Corps – A rejoinder', in *R.A.H.S.J.*, *52*, 3, September 1966.

Parsons, T. G., 'The Social Composition of the Men of the New South Wales Corps', in *R.A.H.S.J.*, *50*, 4, October 1964.

Shaw, A. G. L., 'The New South Wales Corps', in *R.A.H.S.J.*, *47*, 2, June 1961.

Exploration

Austin, K. A., *The Voyage of the Investigator: Commander Matthew Flinders, R.N., 1801–1803*, Adelaide, 1964.

Bowden, K. M., *George Bass 1771–1803: His Discoveries, Romantic Life and Tragic Disappearance*, Melbourne, 1952.

Flinders, M., *A Voyage to Terra Australis . . .* , London, 2 vols, 1814, reprinted Adelaide, 1966.

General

Auchmuty, J. J., 'The Background to the Early Australian Governors', in *H.S.*, *23*, November 1954.

Australian Dictionary of Biography, *1–2*, 1788–1850, Melbourne, 1966, 1967.

Clark, C. M. H., *Select Documents in Australian History: 1788–1850*, Sydney, 1950, reprinted 1965.

Clark, C. M. H., *Sources of Australian History*, London, 1957, reprinted 1960.

Clark, C. M. H., *A History of Australia, I*, Melbourne, 1962.

Ellis, M. H., *John Macarthur*, Sydney, 1955.

Fitzpatrick, B., *British Imperialism and Australia 1783–1833: An Economic History of Australasia*, London, 1939, reprinted Sydney, 1971.

Greenwood, G., Ed., *Australia: A Social and Political History*, Sydney, 1955, ch. I.

MacCallum, D., 'Empty Historical Boxes of the Early Days: Laying Clio's Ghosts on the Shores of New Holland', in *Arts* (Journal of the Sydney University Arts Association), *6*, 1969.

Moorehead, A., *The Fatal Impact: An Account of the Invasion of the South Pacific 1767–1840*, London, 1966, Pt. 2, 'Australia'.

Onslow Macarthur, S., *Some Early Records of the Macarthurs of Camden*, Sydney, 1914, 2nd edition Sydney, 1973.

Rienits, R., and T., *Early Artists of Australia*, Sydney, 1963.

Roe, M., 'Colonial Society in Embryo', in *H.S.*, *26*, May 1956.

Smith, B., *European Vision and the South Pacific, 1768–1850: A Study in the History of Arts and Ideas*, Oxford, 1960.

Young, J. M. R., 'Australia's Pacific Frontier', in *H.S.*, *47*, October 1966.

Bibliographical

Fletcher, B. H., 'New South Wales: 1788–1821: An Appraisal of recent historical writings', in *Teaching History*, Sydney, 7, 2, July 1973.

Ferguson, J. A., *Bibliography of Australia, I, 1784–1830*, Sydney, 1941.

2

1810-30

Documents

Clark, C. M. H., *Select Documents in Australian History: 1788–1850*, Sydney, 1950, reprinted 1965.

Clark, C. M. H., *Sources of Australian History*, London, 1957, reprinted 1960.

Hewison, A., Ed., *The Macquarie Decade: Documents Illustrating the History of New South Wales, 1810–1821*, Melbourne, 1972.

O'Farrell, P. J., *Documents in Australian Catholic History: Vol. I, 1788–1884*, London, 1969.

Onslow Macarthur, S., *Some Early Records of the Macarthurs of Camden*, Sydney, 1914, 2nd edition Sydney, 1973.

Ritchie, J., *The Evidence to the Bigge Reports: New South Wales under Governor Macquarie*, Melbourne, 2 vols, 1971.

Ward, R., and Robertson, J., *Such Was Life: Select Documents in Australian Social History 1788–1850*, Sydney, 1969.

Biographies

Australian Dictionary of Biography, 1–2, 1788–1850, Melbourne, 1966, 1967.

Currey, C. H., *The Brothers Bent: Judge-Advocate Ellis Bent and Judge Jeffery Hart Bent*, Sydney, 1968.

Currey, C. H., *Sir Francis Forbes: The First Chief Justice of the Supreme Court of New South Wales*, Sydney, 1968.

Ellis, M. H., *Lachlan Macquarie: His Life, Adventures and Times*, Sydney, 1947, 4th edition (revised) 1965, reprinted 1970.

Ellis, M. H., *Francis Greenway: His Life and Times*, Sydney, 1949, 2nd edition, revised, 1953.

Ellis, M. H., *John Macarthur*, Sydney, 1955, 2nd edition 1967.

Hainsworth, D. R., *The Sydney Traders, Simeon Lord and His Contemporaries, 1788–1821*, Melbourne, 1972.

O'Brien, E., *The Foundation of Catholicism in Australia: Life and Letters of Archpriest John Joseph Therry*, Sydney, 2 vols, 1922.

Steven, M., *Merchant Campbell, 1769–1846: A Study of Colonial Trade*, Melbourne, 1965.

General

Abbott, G. J., and Nairn, N. B., Eds., *Economic Growth of Australia 1788–1821*, Melbourne, 1969.

Bostock, J., *The Dawn of Australian Psychiatry* . . . , Sydney, 1968.

Butlin, S. J., *Foundations of the Australian Monetary System, 1788–1851*, Melbourne, 1953, reprinted Sydney 1968.

Clark, C. M. H., *A History of Australia, I*, Melbourne, 1962, *II*, Melbourne, 1968.

The Cambridge History of the British Empire, VII, i, chs. 4–6, Cambridge, 1933.

Eddy, J. J., *Britain and the Australian Colonies 1818–1831: The Technique of Government*, Oxford, 1969.

Hartwell, R. M., *The Economic Development of Van Diemen's Land 1820–1850*, Melbourne, 1954.

Herman, M., *The Early Australian Architects and Their Works*, Sydney, 1954.

Macmillan, D. S., *Scotland and Australia 1788–1850. Emigration, Commerce and Investment*, Oxford, 1967.

Mann, D. D., *The Present Picture of New South Wales 1811* . . . , London, 1811.

Melbourne, A. C. V., *Early Constitutional Development in Australia: New South Wales 1788–1856; Queensland 1859–1922*, Oxford, 1934, 2nd edition, Brisbane, 1963, edited by R. B. Joyce.

Nadel, G., *Australia's Colonial Culture: Ideas, Men and Institutions in Mid-Nineteenth Century Eastern Australia*, Sydney, 1957.

Newman, C. E. T., *The Spirit of Wharf House: Campbell Enterprise from Calcutta to Canberra, 1788–1830*, Sydney, 1961.

O'Farrell, P. J., *The Catholic Church in Australia: A Short History: 1788–1967*, Melbourne, 1968.

Perry, T. M., *Australia's First Frontier: The Spread of Settlement in New South Wales 1788–1829*, Melbourne, 1963.

Ritchie, J., *Punishment and Profit: The Reports of Commissioner John Bigge on the Colonies of New South Wales and Van Diemen's Land 1822–1823*, Melbourne, 1970.

Robson, L. L., *The Convict Settlers of Australia: An Enquiry into the Origin and Character of the Convicts transported to New South Wales and Van Diemen's Land 1787–1852*, Melbourne, 1965, reprinted 1970.

Rowley, C. D., *Aboriginal Policy and Practice: Vol. I, The Destruction of Aboriginal Society*, Canberra, 1970.

Shaw, A. G. L., *Convicts and the Colonies: A Study of Penal Transportation from Great Britain and Ireland to Australia and Other Parts of the British Empire*, London, 1966.

Steven, M. J. E., 'The Changing Pattern of Commerce in New South Wales, 1810–1821', in *Business Archives and History, III*, 2, August 1963.

Suttor, T. L., *Hierarchy and Democracy in Australia 1788–1870: The Formation of Australian Catholicism*, Melbourne, 1965.

Ward, R., and Macnab, K., 'The Nature and Nurture of the First Generation of Native-born Australians', in *H.S., 39*, November 1962.

Wentworth, W. C., *A Statistical, Historical and Political Description of the Colony of New South Wales and its Dependent Settlements in Van Diemen's Land*, London, 1819.

Bibliographical

Ferguson, J. A., *Bibliography of Australia, I*, 1784–1830, Sydney, 1941.

Fletcher, B. H., 'New South Wales: 1788–1821: An Appraisal of Recent Historical Writings', in *Teaching History*, Sydney, 7, 2, July 1973.

3

1830-50

Biographies and Autobiographies

Australian Dictionary of Biography, 1–2, 1788–1850, Melbourne, 1966, 1967.

Austin, A. G., *George William Rusden and National Education in Australia, 1849–1862*, Melbourne, 1958.

Barry, J. V., *Alexander Maconochie of Norfolk Island: A Study of a Pioneer in Penal Reform*, Melbourne, 1958.

Barry, J. V., *The Life and Death of John Price: A Study of the Exercise of Naked Power*, Melbourne, 1964.

Bassett, M., *The Hentys: an Australian Colonial Tapestry*, London, 1954.

Birt, H. M., *Benedictine Pioneers in Australia*, London, 2 vols, 1911.

Bloomfield, P., *Edward Gibbon Wakefield: Builder of the British Commonwealth*, London, 1961.

Crossland, R., *Wainewright in Tasmania*, Melbourne, 1954.

Dutton, G., *Founder of a City: The Life of Colonel William Light ... 1786–1839*, Melbourne, 1960.

Fenton, J., *Bush Life in Tasmania Fifty Years Ago*, London, 1891, reprinted Devonport, 1964.

Fitzpatrick, K. E., *Sir John Franklin in Tasmania, 1837–1843*, Melbourne, 1949.

Grose, K., 'Sir George Gipps: Prince of all Skinflints?', in *R.A.H.S.J.*, 50, 6, December 1964, pp. 453–65.

Harris, A., *Settlers and Convicts: Or, Recollections of Sixteen Years' Labour in the Australian Backwoods, by An Emigrant Mechanic*, London, 1847, reprinted Melbourne, 1953, 1964.

Herman, M., Ed., *Annabella Boswell's Journal*, Sydney, 1965.

Howell, P. A., *Thomas Arnold, the younger, in Van Diemen's Land*, Hobart, 1964.

Jeffrey, M., *A Burglar's Life: or The Stirring Adventures of the Great English Burglar, Mark Jeffrey ...*, Launceston, 1893, reprinted Sydney, 1968.

Kiddle, M., *Caroline Chisholm*, Melbourne, 1950, 2nd edition 1957.

King, H., *Richard Bourke*, Melbourne, 1971.

Knight, R., *Illiberal Liberal: Robert Lowe in New South Wales: 1842–1850*, Melbourne, 1966.

Levy, M. C. I., *Governor George Arthur: A Colonial Benevolent Despot*, Melbourne, 1953.

McCulloch, S. C., *George Gipps*, Melbourne, 1966.

Miller, E. M., *Pressmen and Governors: Australian Editors and Writers in Early Tasmania*, Sydney, 1952.

Mortlock, J. F., *Experiences of a Convict*, London, 1864, reprinted Sydney, 1965.

Mudie, J., *The Felonry of New South Wales*, London, 1837, reprinted Melbourne, 1964.

Normington-Rawling, J., *Charles Harpur, an Australian*, Sydney, 1962.

Philipp, J., *A Great View of Things: Edward Gibbon Wakefield*, Melbourne, 1971.

Pidgeon, N., *The Life, Experience and Journal of Nathaniel Pidgeon, City Missionary*, Sydney, 1857, 2nd edition 1864.

Porter, H., *The Tilted Cross*, London, 1961. (A novel based on the life of T. G. Wainewright.)

Tucker, J., *Ralph Rashleigh*, Sydney, 1952, edited by C. Roderick.

White, P., *Voss*, London, 1957. (A novel based on the life of L. Leichhardt.)

Wright, J., *Charles Harpur*, Melbourne, 1963.

General

Abbott, G. J., *The Pastoral Age: A Re-examination*, Melbourne, 1971.

Austin, A. G., *Australian Education: 1788–1900: Church, State and Public Education in Colonial Australia*, Melbourne, 1961.

Barnard, A., *The Australian Wool Market 1840–1900*, Melbourne, 1958.

Barrett, J., *That Better Country: The Religious Aspect of Life in Eastern Australia, 1835–1850*, Melbourne, 1966.

Bourke, P. F., 'Some Recent Essays in Australian Intellectual History', in *H.S.*, *49*, October 1967.

Brown, P. L., Ed., *The Clyde Company Papers*, 7 vols, London, 1941–1971.

Buckley, K., 'Gipps and the Graziers of New South Wales, 1841–6', in *H.S.*, *24*, May 1955, and *26*, May 1956.

Burroughs, P., *Britain and Australia 1831–1855: A Study in Imperial Relations and Crown Lands Administration*, Oxford, 1967.

Butlin, S. J., *Foundations of the Australian Monetary System, 1788–1851*, Melbourne, 1953, reprinted Sydney, 1968.

The Cambridge History of the British Empire, *VII*, i, chs 5–8, Cambridge, 1933.

Clark, C. M. H., *Select Documents in Australian History: 1788–1850*, Sydney, 1950.

Clark, C. M. H., *A History of Australia, II, III*, Melbourne, 1968, 1973.

Coghlan, T. A., *Labour and Industry in Australia ...*, London, 4 vols., 1918, reprinted Melbourne, 1969.

Corris, P., *Aborigines and Europeans in Western Victoria*, Canberra, 1968.

Dunsdorfs, E., *The Australian Wheat-Growing Industry 1788–1948*, Melbourne, 1956.

Dyster, B., 'Support for the Squatters, 1844', in *R.A.H.S.J.*, *51*, 1, March 1965.

Dyster, B., 'Prosperity, Prostration, Prudence: Business and Investment in Sydney 1836–1851', in A. Birch and D. Macmillan, Eds., *Wealth and Progress: Studies in Australian Business History*, Sydney, 1967.

Dyster, B., 'The Fate of Colonial Conservatism on the Eve of Gold-Rush', in *R.A.H.S.J.*, *54*, 4, December 1968.

Forrest, J., 'Political Divisions in the N.S.W. Legislative Council, 1847–1853', in *R.A.H.S.J.*, *50*, 6, December 1964.

Forsyth, W. D., *Governor Arthur's Convict System, Van Diemen's Land 1824–1836*, London, 1935, reprinted Sydney, 1970.

Greenwood, G., Ed., *Australia: A Social and Political History*, Sydney, 1955, ch. 2.

Hartwell, R. M., *The Economic Development of Van Diemen's Land 1820–1850*, Melbourne, 1954.

Healy, J. J., 'The Convict and the Aborigine: the Quest for Freedom in Ralph Rashleigh', in *Australian Literary Studies*, *3*, 4, October 1968.

Hobsbawm, E. J., and Rudé, G., *Captain Swing*, London, 1969. (A study of the agricultural rioters.)

Irvin, E., 'Australia's "First" Dramatists', in *Australian Literary Studies*, *4*, 1, May 1969.

Jeans, D. N., 'Crown Land Sales and the Accommodation of the Small Settlers in N.S.W., 1825–1842', in *H.S.*, *46*, April 1966.

Kiddle, M., *Men of Yesterday: A Social History of the Western District of Victoria, 1834–1890*, Melbourne, 1961, reprinted 1963.

Macarthur, J., *New South Wales; Its Present State and Future Prospects Being a Statement, with Documentary Evidence, submitted in Support of Petitions to His Majesty and Parliament*, London, 1837.

Macmillan, D. S., *Scotland and Australia 1788–1850: Emigration, Commerce and Investment*, Oxford, 1967.

Madgwick, R. B., *Immigration into Eastern Australia 1788–1851*, London, 1937, reprinted Sydney, 1969.

McQueen, H., 'Convicts and Rebels', in *L.H.*, *15*, November 1968.

Melbourne, A. C. V., *Early Constitutional Development in Australia: New South Wales 1788–1856; Queensland 1859–1922*, Oxford, 1934, 2nd edition, Brisbane, 1963, edited by R. B. Joyce.

Mills, R. C., *The Colonisation of Australia 1829–42: The Wakefield Experiment in Empire Building*, London, 1915, reprinted London, 1968.

Molony, J. N., *The Roman Mould of the Australian Catholic Church*, Melbourne, 1969.

Morrell, W. P., *British Colonial Policy in the age of Peel and Russell*, Oxford, 1930, reprinted 1966.

Nadel, G., *Australia's Colonial Culture: Ideas, Men and Institutions in Mid-Nineteenth Century Eastern Australia*, Sydney, 1957.

Pike, D. H., *Paradise of Dissent: South Australia 1829–1857*, Melbourne, 1957, 2nd edition 1967.

Roberts, S. H., *The Squatting Age in Australia, 1835–1847*, Melbourne, 1935, reprinted Melbourne, 1964.

Roe, M., *Quest for Authority in Eastern Australia, 1835–1851*, Melbourne, 1965.

Russell, H. S., *The Genesis of Queensland*, Sydney, 1888.

Select Committee on Transportation, 1837–8, *Report*, in British Parliamentary Papers, 1837, *XIX*, 518 and 1837–8, *XXII*, 669, reprinted in *Great Britain: Parliamentary Papers*, reprints by Irish University Press, *Crime and Punishment, II*.

Shaw, A. G. L., *Convicts and the Colonies: A Study of Penal Transportation from Great Britain and Ireland to Australia and Other Parts of the British Empire*, London, 1966.

Shineberg, D., *They Came for Sandalwood: A Study of the Sandalwood Trade in the South-West Pacific 1830–1865*, Melbourne, 1967.

Staples, A. C. 'Maritime Trade in the Indian Ocean 1830–1845', in *University Studies in History*, 1966.

Stevens, F. S., Ed., *Racism: The Australian Experience*, *1*, Sydney, 1971.

Suttor, T. L., *Hierarchy and Democracy in Australia, 1788–1870: The Formation of Australian Catholicism*, Melbourne, 1965.

Townsley, W. A., *The Struggle for Self Government in Tasmania 1842–1856*, Hobart, 1951.

Ward, J. M., *Earl Grey and the Australian Colonies, 1846–1857: A Study of Self-Government and Self-Interest*, Melbourne, 1958.

Ward, R., *The Australian Legend*, Melbourne, 1958, 2nd edition, 1965.

Ward, R., and Robertson, J., *Such Was Life: Select Documents in Australian Social History 1788–1850*, Sydney, 1969.

West, J., *The History of Tasmania*, Launceston, 2 vols., 1852, new edition, Sydney, 1 vol., 1971.

4

1850-70

The Coming of Self-Government

Blackton, C. S., 'The Dawn of Australian National Feeling, 1850–1856', in *Pacific Historical Review, XXIV*, 2, May 1955.

Cell, J. W., *British Colonial Administration in the Mid-Nineteenth Century: The Policy-Making Process*, New Haven, 1970.

Gollan, R., 'Nationalism and Politics in Australia before 1855', in *A.J.P.H., I*, 1, November 1955.

Irving, T. H., 'Some Aspects of the Study of Radical Politics in New South Wales before 1856', in *L.H.*, 5, November 1963.

Irving, T. H., 'The Idea of Responsible Government in New South Wales before 1856', in *H.S.*, 42, April 1964.

Kent, B., 'Agitations on the Victorian Gold Fields 1851–4: An Interpretation', in *H.S.*, 23, November 1954.

Loveday, P., ' "Democracy" in New South Wales. The Constitution Committee of 1853', in *R.A.H.S.J.*, 42, 4, October 1956.

Lumb, R. D., *The Constitutions of the Australian States*, Brisbane, 1963, *I*, 2nd edition, 1965.

Main, J. M., 'Making Constitutions in New South Wales and Victoria, 1853–1854', in *H.S.*, 28, May 1957.

Pike, D. H., *Paradise of Dissent: South Australia: 1829–1857*, Melbourne, 1957, 2nd edition, 1967.

Silvester, E. K., Ed., *The Speeches in the Legislative Council of New South Wales on the Second Reading of the Bill for framing a New Constitution for the Colony*, Sydney, 1853.

Ward, J. M., *Earl Grey and the Australian Colonies, 1846–1857: A Study of Self-Government and Self-Interest*, Melbourne, 1958.

Origins of a Political System

Dickey, B., *Politics in New South Wales 1856–1900*, Melbourne, 1969.

Finnis, B. T., *The Constitutional History of South Australia ... 1836–1857*, Adelaide, 1886.

Lamb, P. N., 'Crown Land Policy and Government Finance in New South Wales, 1856–1900', in *A.E.H.R.*, *VII*, 1, March 1967.

La Nauze, J. A., 'The Gold Rushes and Australian Politics', in *A.J.P.H.*, *XIII*, 1, April 1967.

Loveday, P., 'The Legislative Council in New South Wales 1856–1870', in *H.S.*, *44*, April 1965.

Loveday, P., 'The Member and His Constitutents in New South Wales in the Mid-Nineteenth Century', in *A.J.P.H.*, *V*, 2, November 1959.

Loveday, P., and Martin, A. W., *Parliament, Factions and Parties: The First Thirty Years of Responsible Government in New South Wales, 1856–1889*, Melbourne, 1966.

Loveday, P., and Martin, A. W., 'The Politics of New South Wales, 1856–1889: A Reply', in *H.S.*, *50*, April 1968.

Martin, A. W., 'The Legislative Assembly of New South Wales, 1856–1900', in *A.J.P.H.*, *II*, 1, November 1956.

Martin, A. W., and Wardle, P., *Members of the Legislative Assembly of New South Wales 1856–1901: Biographical Notes*, Canberra, 1959.

Mills, J. E., 'The Composition of the Victorian Parliament, 1856–1881', in *H.S.*, *5*, April 1942.

Quaife, G. R., 'Make Us Roads No Matter How: A Note on Colonial Politics', in *A.J.P.H.*, *XV*, 1, April 1969.

Ryan, J. A., 'Faction Politics: A Problem in Historical Interpretation', in *A.E.H.R.*, *VIII*, 1, March 1968.

Serle, G., 'The Victorian Legislative Council, 1856–1950', in *H.S.*, *22*, May 1954.

Serle, G., 'New Light on the Colonial Office, Sir George Bowen and the Victorian Constitutional Crises', in *H.S.*, *52*, April 1969.

Thomson, K., and Serle, G., *A Biographical Register of the Victorian Parliament 1859–1900*, Canberra, 1972.

Walker, R. B., 'Catherine Helen Spence and South Australian Politics', in *A.J.P.H.*, *XV*, 1, April 1969.

Politics and Social Change

Dyster, B., 'The Fate of Colonial Conservatism on the Eve of Gold-Rush', in *R.A.H.S.J.*, *54*, 4, December 1968.

Elford, K., 'A Prophet without Honour: The Political Ideals of John Dunmore Lang', in *R.A.H.S.J.*, *54*, 2, June 1968.

Gollan, R., *Radical and Working Class Politics: A Study of Eastern Australia, 1850–1910*, Melbourne, 1960, reprinted 1966.

Hawker, G. N., *The Parliament of New South Wales: 1856–1965*, Sydney, 1971.

Hughes, H., 'The Eight Hour Day and the Development of the Labour Movement in Victoria in the Eighteen-Fifties', in *H.S.*, *36*, May 1961.

Kiddle, M., *Men of Yesterday: A Social History of the Western District of Victoria, 1834–1890*, Melbourne, 1961, reprinted 1963.

La Nauze, J. A., 'Merchants in Action: The Australian Tariffs of 1852', in *Economic Record, XXXI*, 60, May 1955.

Martin, A. W., 'Henry Parkes: Man and Politician', in *Melbourne Studies in Education, 1960–1961*, Melbourne, 1962.

Neale, R. S., 'H. S. Chapman and the "Victorian" Ballot', in *H.S.*, *48*, April 1967.

Niland, J., 'The Birth of the Movement for an Eight Hour Working Day in New South Wales', in *A.J.P.H., XIV*, 1, April 1968.

Quaife, G. R., 'The Diggers: Democratic Sentiment and Political Apathy', in *A.J.P.H., XIII*, 2, August 1967.

Raffaello, Carboni, *The Eureka Stockade*, Melbourne, 1855, reprinted Melbourne, 1942, 1963, 1969: facsimile edition Adelaide, 1962.

Reece, R. H. W., 'Henry Parkes as "Parliamentary Martyr for the Working Classes" in 1859', in *L.H., 13*, November 1967.

Reynolds, H., ' "Men of Substance and Deservedly Good Repute": The Tasmanian Gentry 1856–1875', in *A.J.P.H., XV*, 3, December 1969.

Reynolds, H., ' "That Hated Stain": The Aftermath of Transportation in Tasmania', in *H.S., 53*, October 1969.

Walker, R. B., 'David Buchanan: Chartist, Radical, Republican', in *R.A.H.S.J., 53*, 2, June 1967.

Walker, R. B., 'Another look at the Lambing Flat Riots, 1860–1861', in *R.A.H.S.J., 56*, 3, September 1970.

Ward, R., *The Australian Legend*, Melbourne, 1958, 2nd edition, 1965.

Wilson, G., *Murray of Yarralumla*, Melbourne, 1968.

Land

Baker, D. W. A., 'The Origins of Robertson's Land Acts', in *H.S., 30*, May 1958.

Buxton, G. L., *The Riverina 1861–1891: An Australian Regional Study*, Melbourne, 1967.

Meinig, D. W., *On the Margins of the Good Earth: The South Australian Wheat Frontier 1869–1884*, Chicago, 1962.

Powell, J. M., *The Public Lands of Australia Felix: Settlement and Land Appraisal in Victoria 1834–91 with special reference to the Western Plains*, Melbourne, 1970.

Roberts, S. H., *History of Australian Land Settlement: 1788–1920*, Melbourne, 1924, reprinted 1968.

Waterson, D. B., *Squatter, Selector and Storekeeper: A History of the Darling Downs 1859–93*, Sydney, 1968.

General

Australian Dictionary of Biography, 3–4, 1851–1890, Melbourne, 1969 and 1972.

Barnard, A., *The Australian Wool Market: 1840–1900*, Melbourne, 1958.

Barnard, A., Ed., *The Simple Fleece: Studies in the Australian Wool Industry*, Melbourne, 1962, chs 21, 23, 26, 28.

Blainey, G., 'The Gold Rushes: the Year of Decision', in *H.S.*, *38*, May 1962.

Blainey, G., *The Rush that Never Ended: A History of Australian Mining*, Melbourne, 1963, 2nd edition 1969.

Braggett, E. J., 'The Public Schools Act of 1866 and its Aftermath', in *R.A.H.S.J.*, *52*, 3, September 1966.

Butlin, N. G., 'The Shape of the Australian Economy, 1861–1900', in *Economic Record*, *67*, April 1958.

Butlin, N. G., *Investment in Australian Economic Development 1861–1900*, Cambridge, 1964.

Butlin, N. G., *Australian Domestic Product, Investment and Foreign Borrowing 1861–1938/9*, Cambridge, 1962.

The Cambridge History of the British Empire, VII, i, chs 9–11, Cambridge, 1933.

Cannon, M., *'Who's Master? Who's Man? Australia in the Victorian Age*, Melbourne, 1971.

Clark, C. M. H., *Select Documents in Australian History: 1851–1900*, Sydney, 1955.

Currey, C. H., *The Irish at Eureka*, Sydney, 1954.

Eureka Centenary Supplement, of *Historical Studies*, Melbourne, December 1954, revised and enlarged, 1965.

Fitzpatrick, B., *The British Empire in Australia: An Economic History: 1834–1939*, Melbourne, 1941, 2nd edition 1949.

Fogarty, R., *Catholic Education in Australia 1806–1950*, Melbourne, 2 vols, 1959.

Goodwin, C. D. W., *Economic Enquiry in Australia*, Durham, N. C., 1966, chs. 1–3.

Greenwood, G., Ed., *Australia: A Social and Political History*, Sydney, 1955, ch. 3.

Griffin, J., Ed., *Essays in Economic History of Australia*, Brisbane, 1967, chs. 4 and 5.

La Nauze, J. A., *Political Economy in Australia: Historical Studies*, Melbourne, 1949.

Macmillan, D. S., 'Thomas Barker and his Successors: Manufacturing and Marketing Problems, 1859–1875', in *A.J.P.H.*, *XIII*, 3, December 1967.

Molony, J. N., *An Architect of Freedom: John Hubert Plunkett in New South Wales 1832–1869*, Canberra, 1973.

Nadel, G., *Australia's Colonial Culture: Ideas, Men and Institutions in Mid-Nineteenth Century Eastern Australia*, Melbourne, 1957.

Reynolds, H., Ed., *Aborigines and Settlers: The Australian Experience 1788–1939*, Melbourne, 1972.

Rowley, C. D., *Aboriginal Policy and Practice, I: The Destruction of Aboriginal Society*, Canberra, 1970.

Serle, G., *The Golden Age: A History of the Colony of Victoria, 1851–1861*, Melbourne, 1963.

Shann, E., *An Economic History of Australia*, Cambridge, 1930, reprinted Melbourne, 1948, 1963.

Turner, N., *Sinews of Sectarian Warfare?: State Aid in New South Wales 1836–1862*, Canberra, 1972.

Walker, R. B., 'The Abolition of State Aid to Religion in New South Wales', in *H.S.*, *38*, May 1962.

Ward, J. M., *Empire in the Antipodes: The British in Australasia: 1840–1860*, London, 1966.

5

1870-90

Area Studies

Bate, W., *A History of Brighton*, Melbourne, 1962.

Birch, A., and Macmillan, D. S., *The Sydney Scene 1788–1960*, Melbourne, 1962.

Bolton, G. C., *A Thousand Miles Away: A History of North Queensland to 1920*, Brisbane, 1963, reprinted Canberra, 1970.

Buxton, G. L., *The Riverina 1861–1891: An Australian Regional Study*, Melbourne, 1967.

Cannon, M., *The Land Boomers*, Melbourne, 1966.

Crook, D. P., 'Occupations of the People of Brisbane: An Aspect of Urban Society in the 1880s', in *H.S.*, *37*, November 1961.

Crowley, F. K., *Australia's Western Third: A History of Western Australia from the First Settlements to Modern Times*, London, 1960, reprinted Melbourne, 1970.

Cusack, F., *Bendigo: A History*, Melbourne, 1973.

Daley, L. T., *Men and a River: A History of the Richmond River District 1828–1895*, Melbourne, 1966, reprinted 1968.

Grant, J., and Serle, G., *The Melbourne Scene 1803–1956*, Melbourne, 1957.

Greenwood, G., and Laverty, J., *Brisbane 1859–1959: A History of Local Government*, Brisbane, 1959.

Heathcote, R. L., *Back of Bourke: A Study of Land Appraisal and Settlement in semi-arid Australia*, Melbourne, 1965.

Hill, Ernestine, *Water into Gold*, Melbourne, 1937.

Hirst, J. B., *Adelaide and the Country: 1870–1917: Their Social and Political Relationship*, Melbourne, 1973.

Hodder, E., *The History of South Australia: From its Foundation to the Year of its Jubilee*, London, 2 vols, 1893.

Kiddle, M., *Men of Yesterday: A Social History of the Western District of Victoria, 1834–1890*, Melbourne, 1961, reprinted 1963.

Meinig, D. W., *On the Margins of the Good Earth: The South Australian Wheat Frontier 1869–1884*, Chicago, 1962.

Powell, J. M., *The Public Lands of Australia Felix: Settlement and Land Appraisal in Victoria 1834–91 with special reference to the Western Plains*, Melbourne, 1970.

Priestley, S., *Echuca: A Centenary History*, Brisbane, 1965.

Pryor, O., *Australia's Little Cornwall*, Adelaide, 1962.

Richards, T., *An Epitome of the Official History of New South Wales ...*, Sydney, 1883.

Serle, G., *The Rush To Be Rich: A History of the Colony of Victoria, 1883–1889*, Melbourne, 1971.

Turner, H. G., *A History of the Colony of Victoria: From its Discovery to its absorption into the Commonwealth of Australia*, London, 2 vols, 1904.

Walker, R. B., *Old New England: A History of the Northern Tablelands of New South Wales 1818–1900*, Sydney, 1966.

Waterson, D. B., *Squatter, Selector and Storekeeper: The Darling Downs 1859–1893*, Sydney, 1968.

Economic Development

Bailey, J. D., *Growth and Depression: Contrasts in the Australian and British Economies 1870–1880*, Canberra, 1956.

Barnard, A., *The Australian Wool Market 1840–1900*, Melbourne, 1958.

Barnard, A., Ed., *The Simple Fleece: Studies in the Australian Wool Industry*, Melbourne, 1962.

Blainey, G., *The Peaks of Lyell*, Melbourne, 1954, 2nd edition 1959.

Blainey, G., *Mines in the Spinifex: The Story of Mt Isa Mines*, Sydney, 1960, revised edition 1965, 1970.

Blainey, G., *The Rush That Never Ended: A History of Australian Mining*, Melbourne, 1963, 2nd edition, Melbourne, 1969.

Blainey, G., *The Rise of Broken Hill*, Melbourne, 1968.

Butlin, N. G., 'The Shape of the Australian Economy, 1861–1900', in *Economic Record, XXXIV*, 67, April 1958.

Butlin, N. G., *Investment in Australian Economic Development, 1861–1900*, Cambridge, 1964.

Butlin, N. G., *Australian Domestic Product, Investment and Foreign Borrowing, 1861–1938/9*, Cambridge, 1962.

Coghlan, T. A., *Labour and Industry in Australia: From the First Settlement in 1788 to the Establishment of the Commonwealth in 1901*, London, 4 vols, 1918, reprinted Melbourne, 1969.

Fitzpatrick, B., *The British Empire in Australia: An Economic History 1834–1939*, Melbourne, 1941, 1949.

Glynn, S., *Urbanisation in Australian History 1788–1900*, Melbourne, 1970.

Hall, A. R., *The Stock Exchange of Melbourne and the Victorian Economy 1852–1900*, Canberra, 1968.

McLean, I. W., 'The adoption of harvest machinery in Victoria in the late nineteenth century', in *A.E.H.R., XIII*, 1, March 1973.

Roberts, S. H., *History of Australian Land Settlement (1788–1920)*, Melbourne, 1924, reprinted 1968.

Shann, E., *An Economic History of Australia*, Cambridge, 1930, republished Melbourne, 1948, reprinted 1963.

Urbanization in Australia, a special issue of *Australian Economic History Review, X*, 2, September 1970.

Politics

Bartlett, G., 'The Political Orders of Victoria and New South Wales, 1856–1890', in *A.E.H.R.*, *VIII*, 1, March 1968.

Butlin, N. G., 'Colonial Socialism in Australia, 1860–1900', in H. G. Aitken, Ed., *The State and Economic Growth*, New York, 1959.

Deakin, A., *The Crisis in Victorian Politics, 1879–1881: A Personal Retrospect*, Melbourne, 1957.

Dickey, B., *Politics in New South Wales 1856–1900*, Melbourne, 1969.

Gollan, R., *Radical and Working Class Politics: A Study of Eastern Australia, 1850–1910*, Melbourne, 1960, reprinted 1966.

Hawker, G. N., *The Parliament of New South Wales: 1856–1965*, Sydney, 1971.

Loveday, P., and Martin, A. W., *Parliament, Factions and Parties: The First Thirty Years of Responsible Government in New South Wales, 1856–1889*, Melbourne, 1966.

Martin, A. W., 'Henry Parkes and Electoral Manipulation, 1872–82', in *H.S.*, *31*, November 1958.

Martin, A. W., 'Henry Parkes: Man and Politician', in *Melbourne Studies in Education, 1960–1961*, Melbourne, 1962.

Nairn, N. B., 'The Political Mastery of Sir Henry Parkes: New South Wales Politics 1871–1891', in *R.A.H.S.J.*, *53*, 1, March 1967.

Parkes, H., *Fifty Years in the Making of Australian History*, London, 2 vols, 1892.

Taylor, G. P., 'Political Attitudes and Land Policy in Queensland, 1868–1894', in *Pacific Historical Review*, *XXXVII*, 3, August 1968.

Tregenza, J., *Professor of Democracy: The Life of Charles Henry Pearson, 1830–1894: Oxford Don and Australian Radical*, Melbourne, 1968.

Walker, R. B., 'Squatter and Selector in New England, 1862–95', *H.S.*, *29*, November 1957.

Education

Austin, A. G., *Australian Education: 1788–1900 Church, State and Public Education in Colonial Australia*, Melbourne, 1961, 3rd edition, 1972.

Austin, A. G., *Select Documents in Australian Education, 1788–1900*, Melbourne, 1963.

Barcan, A., *A Short History of Education in New South Wales*, Sydney, 1965.

Dow, G. M., *George Higinbotham: Church and State*, Melbourne, 1964.

Fogarty, R., *Catholic Education in Australia 1806–1950*, Melbourne, 2 vols, 1959.

Griffiths, D. C., Ed., *Documents on the Establishment of Education in New South Wales, 1789–1880*, Melbourne, 1957.

Martin, A. W., 'Faction Politics and the Education Question in New South Wales', in *Melbourne Studies in Education, 1960–1961*, Melbourne, 1962.

O'Farrell, P. J., *The Catholic Church in Australia: A Short History: 1788–1967*, Melbourne, 1968, ch. 3.

General

Australian Dictionary of Biography, *3–4*, 1851–1890, Melbourne, 1969, 1972.

The Cambridge History of the British Empire, *VII*, chs 11–13, Cambridge, 1933.

Cannon, M., *Life in the Country: Australia in the Victorian Age: 2*, Melbourne, 1973.

Clark, C. M. H., *Select Documents in Australian History: 1851–1900*, Sydney, 1955.

Dunstan, K., *Wowsers*, Melbourne, 1968.

Grattan, C. H., *The Southwest Pacific to 1900: A Modern History*, Ann Arbor, 1963, ch. 16.

Greenwood, G., Ed., *Australia: A Social and Political History*, Sydney, 1955, ch. 3.

McKinlay, B., *The First Royal Tour, 1867–1868*, Adelaide, 1970.

Nadel, G., *Australia's Colonial Culture: Ideas, Men and Institutions in Mid-Nineteenth Century Eastern Australia*, Sydney, 1957.

Roe, J., 'Challenge and Response: Religious Life in Melbourne, 1876–86', in *The Journal of Religious History*, *5*, 2, December 1968.

Suttor, T., 'The Criticism of Religious Certitude in Australia, 1875–1900', in *The Journal of Religious History*, *I*, 1, June 1960.

Twopeny, R. E. N., *Town Life in Australia*, London, 1883, reprinted Melbourne, 1973.

Walker, R. B., 'Aspects of the Country Press in New South Wales from 1850–1900', in *R.A.H.S.J.*, *50*, 3, August 1964.

Ward, R., *The Australian Legend*, Melbourne, 1958, 2nd edition 1965.

Willard, M., *History of the White Australia Policy to 1920*, Melbourne, 1923, reprinted London, 1967.

Yarwood, A. T., *Attitudes to Non-European Immigration*, Melbourne, 1968.

6

1890-1900

Economic History

Blainey, G., *Gold and Paper: A History of the National Bank of Australasia Limited*, Melbourne, 1958.

Blainey, G., *The Rush That Never Ended: A History of Australian Mining*, Melbourne, 1963, 2nd edition 1969.

Blainey, G., *The Rise of Broken Hill*, Melbourne, 1968.

Boehm, E. A., *Prosperity and Depression in Australia 1887–1897*, Oxford, 1971.

Butlin, N. G., 'The Shape of the Australian Economy, 1861–1900', in *Economic Record*, *XXXIV*, 67, April 1958.

Butlin, N. G., *Investment in Australian Economic Development 1861–1900*, Cambridge, 1964.

Butlin, S. J., *Australia and New Zealand Bank: The Bank of Australasia and the Union Bank of Australia Limited 1828–1951*, London, 1961.

Cain, N., 'Financial Reconstruction in Australia, 1893–1900', in *Business Archives and History, VI*, 2, August 1966.

Cannon, M., *The Land Boomers*, Melbourne, 1966.

Coghlan, T. A., *Labour and Industry in Australia*, London, 4 vols, 1918, reprinted Melbourne, 1969.

Dunsdorfs, E., *The Australian Wheat-Growing Industry 1788–1948*, Melbourne, 1956.

Glynn, S., *Urbanisation in Australian History, 1788–1900*, Melbourne, 1970.

Gollan, R., *The Commonwealth Bank of Australia: Origins and Early History*, Canberra, 1968.

Hall, A. R., *The Stock Exchange of Melbourne and the Victorian Economy 1852–1900*, Canberra, 1968.

Sinclair, W. A., *Economic Recovery in Victoria 1894–1899*, Canberra, 1956.

Labour and Industrial Relations

Fitzpatrick, B., *A Short History of the Australian Labor Movement*, Melbourne, 1940, reprinted 1968.

Gollan, R., *Radical and Working Class Politics: A Study of Eastern Australia, 1850–1910*, Melbourne, 1960, reprinted 1966.

Gollan, R., *The Coalminers of New South Wales: A History of the Union, 1860–1960*, Melbourne, 1963.

Harris, J., *The Bitter Fight: A Pictorial History of the Australian Labor Movement*, Brisbane, 1970.

Henning, G. R., 'Steamships and the 1890 Maritime Strike', in *H.S.*, *60*, April 1973.

Macarthy, P. G., 'Labor and the Living Wage 1890–1910', in *A.J.P.H.*, *XIII*, 1, April 1967.

Macarthy, P. G., 'Victorian Wages Boards: Their Origins and the Doctrine of the Living Wage', in *The Journal of Industrial Relations, 10*, 2, July 1968.

Macarthy, P. G., 'Wage Determination in New South Wales – 1890–1921', in *The Journal of Industrial Relations, 10*, 3, November 1968.

Macarthy, P. G., 'Wages in Australia, 1891–1914', in *A.E.H.R.*, *X*, 1, March 1970.

Macarthy, P. G., 'Employers, the Tariff, and Legal Wage Determination in Australia – 1890–1910', in *The Journal of Industrial Relations, 12*, 2, July 1970.

Merritt, J. A., 'W. G. Spence and the 1890 Maritime Strike', in *H.S.*, *60*, April 1973.

Nairn, N. B., 'The 1890 Maritime Strike in New South Wales', in
H.S., *37*, November 1961.
Piggin, F. S., 'New South Wales Pastoralists and the Strikes of 1890
and 1891', in *H.S.*, *56*, April 1971.
Reeves, W. P., *State Experiments in Australia and New Zealand*, 2
vols, London, 1902, reprinted 1923, 1969.
Spence, W. G., *Australia's Awakening: Thirty Years in the Life of an
Australian Agitator*, Sydney, 1909.
Sutcliffe, J. T., *A History of Trade Unionism in Australia*, Melbourne,
1921, reprinted Melbourne, 1967.
Walker, R., 'The Maritime Strikes in South Australia 1887 and 1890',
in *L.H.*, *14*, May 1968.

Federation

Bastin, J., 'Federation and Western Australia: A Contribution to the
Parker-Blainey Discussion', in *H.S.*, *17*, November 1951.
Bastin, J., 'Sir John Forrest and Australian Federation', in *A.Q.*,
XXIV, 4, December 1952.
Blainey, G., 'The Role of Economic Interests in Australian Federa-
tion: A Reply to Professor R. S. Parker', in *H.S.*, *15*, November
1950.
Deakin, A., *The Federal Story: The Inner History of the Federal
Cause*, Melbourne, 1944, 2nd edition, 1963.
Fredman, L. E., 'The Tenterfield Oration: Legend and Reality', in
A.Q., *XXXV*, 3, September 1963.
Fredman, L. E., 'Yes-No Reid: A Case for the Prosecution', in
R.A.H.S.J., *50*, 2, July 1964.
La Nauze, J. A., *Alfred Deakin: A Biography*, I, Melbourne, 1965.
La Nauze, J. A., 'Who are the Fathers?', in *H.S.*, *51*, October 1968.
La Nauze, J. A., *The Making of the Australian Constitution*, Mel-
bourne, 1972.
Martin, A. W., 'Economic Influences in the "New Federation Move-
ment"', in *H.S.*, *21*, November 1953.
Martin, A. W., Ed., *Essays in Australian Federation*, Melbourne, 1969.
McMinn, W. G., 'George Reid and Federation: the Origin of the "Yes-
No Policy"', in *H.S.*, *38*, May 1962.
McMinn, W. G., 'G. H. Reid and Federation: The Case for the
Defence', in *R.A.H.S.J.*, *49*, 4, December 1963.
McMinn, W. G., 'Sir Henry Parkes as a Federalist', in *H.S.*, *47*, October
1966.
McMinn, W. G., 'The Federal Policy of G. H. Reid: A Rejoinder', in
R.A.H.S.J., *51*, 1, March 1965.
McMinn, W. G., 'Some Observations on the Personal Element in the
Federation Movement: 1890–1894', in *University Studies in
History*, 1965.
McQueen, H., *A New Britannia: An Argument Concerning the Social
Origins of Australian Radicalism and Nationalism*, Melbourne,
1970.

Parker, R. S., 'Australian Federation: The Influence of Economic Interests and Political Pressures', in *H.S.*, *13*, November 1949.

Quick, J., and Garran, R. R., *The Annotated Constitution of the Australian Commonwealth*, Sydney, 1901.

Nationalism, Patriotism

Adams, F., *The Australians: A Social Sketch*, London, 1893.

Blackton, C. S., 'Australian Nationality and Nationalism, 1850–1900', in *H.S.*, *36*, May 1961.

Blackton, C. S., 'Australian Nationality and Nationalism: The Imperial Federationist Interlude, 1885–1901', in *H.S.*, *25*, November 1955.

Blackton, C. S., 'Australian Nationality and Nativism: The Australian Natives' Association 1885–1901', in *The Journal of Modern History*, *XXX*, 1, March 1958.

Cole, D., 'The Crimson Thread of Kinship: Ethnic Ideas in Australia, 1870–1914', in *H.S.*, *56*, April 1971.

Crabbe, C. W., Ed., *The Australian Nationalists: Modern Critical Essays*, Melbourne, 1971.

Haydon, A. P., 'South Australia's First War', in *H.S.*, *42*, April 1964.

Penny, B. R., 'Australia's Reactions to the Boer War – A Study in Colonial Imperialism', in *The Journal of British Studies*, *VII*, 1, November 1967.

Penny, B. R., 'The Australian Debate on the Boer War', in *H.S.*, *56*, April 1971.

Roe, M., 'An Historical Survey of Australian Nationalism', in *The Victorian Historical Magazine*, *42*, 4, November 1971.

Reynolds, H., 'Australian Nationalism: Tasmanian Patriotism', in *The New Zealand Journal of History*, *5*, 1, April 1971.

Shortus, S. P., ' "Colonial Nationalism": New South Welsh Identity in the mid-1880s', in *R.A.H.S.J.*, *59*, 1, March 1973.

Ward, R., 'Two Kinds of Australian Patriotism', in *The Victorian Historical Magazine*, *41*, 1, February 1970.

Political History

Bennett, S., Ed., *The Making of the Commonwealth*, Melbourne, 1971.

Butlin, N. G., 'Colonial Socialism in Australia 1860–1900', in H. G. Aitken, Ed., *The State and Economic Growth*, New York, 1959.

de Garis, B. K., and Stannage, C. T., 'From Responsible Government to Party Politics in Western Australia', in *A.E.H.R.*, *VIII*, 1, March 1968.

Ebbels, R. N., *The Australian Labor Movement 1850–1907*, Sydney, 1960, reprinted Melbourne, 1965.

Encel, S., 'The Concept of the State in Australian Politics', in *A.J.P.H.*, *VI*, 1, May 1960.

Ford, P., *Cardinal Moran and the A.L.P.*, Melbourne, 1966.

Gollan, R., *Radical and Working Class Politics: A Study of Eastern Australia, 1850–1910*, Melbourne, 1960, reprinted 1966.

Gollan, R., 'The Trade Unions and Labour Parties, 1890–94', in *H.S.*, *25*, November 1955.

Graham, B. D., *The Formation of the Australian Country Parties*, Canberra, 1966.

Hawker, G. N., *The Parliament of New South Wales: 1856–1965*, Sydney, 1971.

Hirst, J. B., *Adelaide and the Country, 1870–1917: Their Social and Political Relationship*, Melbourne, 1973.

Ingham, S. M., 'Political Parties in the Victorian Legislative Assembly, 1880–1900', in *H.S.*, *15*, November 1950.

Loveday, P., 'A Note on Nineteenth Century Party Organization in New South Wales', in *H.S.*, *36*, May 1961.

Martin, A. W., 'Free Trade and Protectionist Parties in New South Wales', in *H.S.*, *23*, November 1954.

McRae, M. D., 'Some Aspects of the Origins of the Tasmanian Labour Party', in *T.H.R.A.P.*, *III*, 2, April 1954.

Morrison, A. A., 'Liberal Party Organizations Before 1900', in *Historical Society of Queensland Journal*, *V*, 1, 1953.

Murphy, D. J., *et al*, Eds., *Prelude to Power: The Rise of the Labour Party in Queensland 1885–1915*, Brisbane, 1970.

Nairn, N. B., 'The Role of the Trades and Labor Council in N.S.W., 1871–1891', in *H.S.*, *28*, May 1957.

Nairn, N. B., 'J. C. Watson in New South Wales Politics, 1890–1894', in *R.A.H.S.J.*, *48*, 2, June 1962.

Nairn, N. B., *Civilising Capitalism: The Labor Movement in New South Wales 1870–1900*, Canberra, 1973.

O'Connor, J. E., '1890 – A Turning Point in Labour History: A Reply to Mrs Philipp', in *H.S.*, *16*, May 1951.

O'Farrell, P. J., 'The Australian Socialist League and the Labour Movement, 1887–1891', in *H.S.*, *30*, May 1958.

O'Farrell, P. J., 'The History of the New South Wales Labour Movement, 1880–1910: A Religious Interpretation', in *The Journal of Religious History*, 2, 2, December 1962.

Philipp, J., '1890 – The Turning Point in Labour History?', in *H.S.*, *14*, May 1950.

Picard, F., 'Henry George and the Labour Split of 1891', in *H.S.*, *21*, November 1953.

Rawson, D. W., *Labor in Vain?: A Survey of the Australian Labor Party*, Melbourne, 1966.

Rawson, D. W., 'Labour, Socialism and the Working Class', in *A.J.P.H.*, *VII*, 1, May 1961.

General

Australian Dictionary of Biography, *3–4*, 1851–1890, Melbourne, 1969, 1972.

Blainey, G., *The Tyranny of Distance: How Distance Shaped Australia's History*, Melbourne, 1966, reprinted 1968.

The Cambridge History of the British Empire, *VII*, i, chs. 13–15, Cambridge, 1933.

Clark, C. M. H., *Select Documents in Australian History: 1851–1900*, Sydney, 1955.

Crowley, F. K., *Australia's Western Third: A History of Western Australia from the First Settlements to Modern Times*, London, 1960, reprinted Melbourne, 1970.

Greenwood, G., Ed., *Australia: A Social and Political History*, Sydney, 1955, ch. 4.

Griffin, J., Ed., *Essays in Economic History of Australia*, Brisbane, 1967, 2nd edition, 1970, ch. 6.

Lawson, R., *Brisbane in the 1890s: A Study of an Australian Urban Society*, Brisbane, 1973.

Moore, T. I., *Social Patterns in Australian Literature*, Sydney, 1971.

Dutton, G., Ed., *The Literature of Australia*, Melbourne, 1964, esp. pp. 13–54, 273–87.

Palmer, Vance, *The Legend of the Nineties*, Melbourne, 1954, reprinted 1963, 1966.

Phillips, A. A., *The Australian Tradition: Studies in a Colonial Culture*, Melbourne, 1958.

Ward, R., *The Australian Legend*, Melbourne, 1958, 2nd edition 1965.

Ward, R., and Roe, M., 'The Australian Legend: An Exchange', in *Meanjin*, *XXI*, 3, 1962.

7

1901-1914

Nationalism and Defence

Campbell, P. C., 'Australian Nationalism', in *R.A.H.S.J.*, *14*, 6, 1928.

Cole, D., 'The Problem of "Nationalism" and "Imperialism" in British Settlement Colonies', in *The Journal of British Studies*, X, 2, May 1971.

Gill, G. H., 'The Australian Navy: Origins, Growth and Development', in *R.A.H.S.J.*, *45*, 3, November 1959.

Grimshaw, C., 'Australian Nationalism and the Imperial Connection 1900–1914', in *A.J.P.H.*, *III*, 2, May 1958.

Hancock, I. R., 'The 1911 Imperial Conference', in *H.S.*, *47*, October 1966.

Haydon, A. P., 'South Australia's First War', in *H.S.*, *42*, April 1964.

Jebb, R., *Studies in Colonial Nationalism*, London, 1905.

Kendle, J. E., *The Colonial and Imperial Conferences 1887–1911: A Study in Imperial Organization*, London, 1967.

Lowe, P., 'The British Empire and the Anglo-Japanese Alliance, 1911–1915', in *History*, *LIV*, 181, June 1969.

Macandie, G. L., *The Genesis of the Royal Australian Navy*, Sydney, 1949.

McQueen, H., *A New Britannia: An Argument concerning the Social Origins of Australian Radicalism and Nationalism*, Melbourne, 1970.

Meaney, N. K., 'A Proposition of the Highest Importance: Alfred Deakin's Pacific Agreement Proposal', in *Journal of Commonwealth Political Studies*, *V*, 3, November 1967.

Megaw, R., 'Australia and the Great White Fleet 1908', in *R.A.H.S.J.*, *56*, 2, June 1970.

Nish, I. H., 'Australia and the Anglo-Japanese Alliance, 1901–1911', in *A.J.P.H.*, *IX*, 2, November 1963.

Penny, B. R., 'Australia's Reactions to the Boer War – a Study in Colonial Imperialism', in *The Journal of British Studies*, *VII*, 1, November 1967.

Penny, B. R., 'The Australian Debate on the Boer War,, in *H.S.*, *56*, April 1971.

Perry, W., 'Military Reforms of General Sir Edward Hutton in the Commonwealth of Australia: 1902–04', in *The Victorian Historical Magazine*, *29*, 1, February 1959.

Roe, M., 'An Historical Survey of Australian Nationalism', in *The Victorian Historical Magazine*, *42*, 4, November 1971.

Sawer, G., 'Nationalism in the Working of the Federal Constitution', in *Teaching History*, *3*, 2, September 1969.

Thompson, R. C., 'The Labor Party and Australian Imperialism in the Pacific, 1901–1919', in *L.H.*, *23*, November 1972.

Ward, R., 'Two Kinds of Australian Patriotism', in *The Victorian Historical Magazine*, *41*, 1, February 1970.

Politics

Beazley, K. E., 'The Labor Party and the Origin of the Commonwealth Bank', in *A.J.P.H.*, *IX*, 1, May 1963.

Brigden, J. B., 'State Enterprises in Australia', in *International Labour Review*, *XVI*, 1, July 1927.

Broadhead, H. S., 'J. C. Watson and the Caucus Crisis of 1905', in *A.J.P.H.*, *VIII*, 1, May 1962.

Cahill, A. E., 'Catholicism and Socialism – The 1905 Controversy in Australia', in *The Journal of Religious History*, *I*, 2, December 1960.

Catts, D., *King O'Malley: Man and Statesman*, Sydney, 1957.

Childe, V. G., *How Labour Governs: A Study of Workers' Representation in Australia*, London, 1923, reprinted Melbourne, 1964.

Clark, V. S., *The Labour Movement in Australasia: A Study in Social Democracy*, Westminster, N.Y., 1906, reprinted London 1907, reprinted New York 1970.

Cowen, Z., *Isaac Isaacs*, Melbourne, 1967.

Cowper, N., 'The First Financial Agreement: Its Effect upon Relations between the Commonwealth and the States', in *E.R.*, *VIII*, 15, December 1932.

Crisp, L. F., *The Australian Federal Labour Party 1901–1951*, London, 1955.

Deakin, A., *Federated Australia: Selections from Letters to the Morning Post 1900–1910*, Ed., J. A. La Nauze, Melbourne, 1968.

Eggleston, F. W., *State Socialism in Victoria*, London, 1932.

Encel, S., 'The Concept of the State in Australian Politics', in *A.J.P.H.*, VI, 1, May 1960.

Evatt, H. V., *Liberalism in Australia: An Historical Sketch of Australian Politics down to the year 1915*, Sydney, 1918.

Evatt, H. V., *Australian Labour Leader: The Story of W. A. Holman and the Labour Movement*, Sydney, 1940, reprinted 1942, 1945, abridged edition 1954.

Fitzhardinge, L. F., *William Morris Hughes: A Political Biography*, I, Sydney, 1964.

Gollan, R., *Radical and Working Class Politics: A Study of Eastern Australia, 1850–1910*, Melbourne, 1960, reprinted 1966.

Graham, B. D., 'The Choice of Voting Methods in Federal Politics, 1902–1918', in *A.J.P.H.*, VIII, 2, November 1962.

Groom, Jessie, Ed., *Nation Building in Australia: The Life and Work of Sir Littleton Ernest Groom*, Sydney, 1941.

Heydon, P., *Quiet Decision: A Study of George Foster Pearce*, Melbourne, 1965.

Hirst, J. B., *Adelaide and the Country 1870–1917: Their Social and Political Relationship*, Melbourne, 1973.

Hughes, C. A., and Graham, B. D., *A Handbook of Australian Government and Politics 1890–1964*, Canberra, 1968.

Hughes, W. M., *The Case for Labor*, Sydney, 1910, facsimile edition Sydney 1970.

Jauncey, L. C., *The Story of Conscription in Australia*, London, 1935, reprinted Melbourne, 1968.

Joyner, C., 'Attempts to Extend Commonwealth Powers, 1908–1919', in *H.S.*, *35*, November 1960.

Joyner, C., *The Commonwealth and Monopolies*, Melbourne, 1963.

La Nauze, J. A., *Alfred Deakin: A Biography*, Melbourne, 2 vols, 1965.

Loveday, P., 'Support in Return for Concessions', in *H.S.*, *55*, October 1970.

MacKenzie, N., 'Vida Goldstein: the Australian Suffragette', in *A.J.P.H.*, VI, 2, November 1960.

Main, J. M., Ed., *Conscription: The Australian Debate, 1901–1970*, Melbourne, 1970.

Mansfield, B. E., 'The State as Employer: An Early Twentieth Century Discussion', in *A.J.P.H.*, III, 2, May 1958.

Mayer, H., 'Some conceptions of the Australian Party System 1910–1950', in *H.S.*, *27*, November 1956.

Métin, A., *Le Socialisme sans Doctrines*, Paris, 1901, reprinted 1910.

Murphy, D. J., 'The Establishment of State Enterprises in Queensland, 1915–1918', in *L.H.*, *14*, May 1968.

O'Collins, G., *Patrick McMahon Glynn: A Founder of Australian Federation*, Melbourne, 1965.

Palmer, N., *Henry Bournes Higgins: A Memoir*, London, 1931.

Parker, R. S., 'Public Enterprise in New South Wales', in *A.J.P.H.*, *IV*, 2, November 1958.

Reeves, W. P., *State Experiments in Australia and New Zealand*, London, 2 vols, 1902.

Rawson, D. W., 'Another Look at Initiative and Resistance', in *Politics*, *III*, 1, May 1968 (and replies in *IV*, 1 and 2).

Reid, G. H., *My Reminiscences*, London, 1917.

Reynolds, J., *Edmund Barton*, Sydney, 1948.

Robertson, J. R., 'The Foundations of State Socialism in Western Australia: 1911–16', in *H.S.*, *39*, November 1962.

Robertson, J. R., 'The International Politics of State Labor in Western Australia, 1911–1916', in *L.H.*, *2*, May 1962.

Rydon, J., and Spann, R. N., *New South Wales Politics 1901–1910*, Melbourne, 1962.

Sawer, G., *Australian Federal Politics and Law, 1901–1929*, Melbourne, 1956.

Sherington, G. E., 'The Selection of Canberra as Australia's National Capital', in *R.A.H.S.J.*, *56*, 2, June 1970.

Spence, W. G., *Australia's Awakening: Thirty Years in the Life of an Australian Agitator*, Sydney, 1909.

St Ledger, A., *Australian Socialism: An Historical Sketch of its Origin and Developments*, London, 1909.

Turner, H. G., *The First Decade of the Australian Commonwealth: A Chronicle of Contemporary Politics 1901–1910*, Melbourne, 1911.

Turner, I., *Industrial Labour and Politics: The Dynamics of the Labour Movement in Eastern Australia, 1900–1921*, Canberra, 1965.

Turner, I., 'Socialist Political Tactics 1900–1920', in *L.H.*, *2*, May 1962.

Watson, J. C., 'The Labour Movement', in *British Association for the Advancement of Science: Handbook For New South Wales*, Sydney, 1914.

Westerway, P. B., 'Clichés on Australian Politics, 1900–1950', in *Melbourne Historical Journal*, *3*, 1963/64.

Wright, D. I., 'The Politics of Federal Finance: The First Decade', in *H.S.*, *52*, April 1969.

Wright, D. I., *Shadow of Dispute: Aspects of Commonwealth-State Relations, 1901–1910*, Canberra, 1970.

Labour and Industrial Relations

Atkinson, M., Ed., *Trade Unionism in Australia*, Sydney, 1915.

Birch, A., 'The Implementation of the White Australia Policy in the Queensland Sugar Industry 1901–12', in *A.J.P.H.*, *XI*, 2, August 1965.

Coghlan, T. A., *Labour and Industry in Australia*, London, 4 vols, 1918, reprinted Melbourne, 1969.

Ebbels, R. N., Ed., *The Australian Labor Movement 1850–1907*, Sydney, 1960, reprinted Melbourne, 1965.

Fitzpatrick, B., *A Short History of the Australian Labor Movement*, Melbourne, 1940, 1944, 1968.

Forster, C., 'Australian Unemployment, 1900–1940', in *E.R.*, *41*, 95, September 1965.

Gollan, R., *The Coalminers of New South Wales: A History of the Union, 1880–1960*, Melbourne, 1963.

Higgins, H. B., *A New Province for Law and Order: Being a Review, by its late President for Fourteen Years, of the Australian Court of Conciliation and Arbitration*, London and Sydney, 1922. Also published by the Government Printer, Melbourne, as monographic reprints of original articles in the *Harvard Law Review*, 1915–1920, reprinted London, 1968.

Hill, M. R., 'The Basic Wage, 1907–1953', in *A.Q.*, *XXV*, 4, December 1953.

Iremonger, J., *et al*, Eds., *Strikes: Studies in Twentieth Century Australian Social History*, Sydney, 1973.

Keating, M., 'Australian Work Force and Employment, 1910–1911 to 1960–1961', in *A.E.H.R.*, *VII*, 2, September 1967.

Macarthy, P. G., 'Labor and the Living Wage, 1890–1910', in *A.J.P.H.*, *XIII*, 1, April 1967.

Macarthy, P. G., 'Justice Higgins and the Harvester Judgement', in *A.E.H.R.*, *IX*, i, March 1969.

Macarthy, P. G., 'Employers, the Tariff, and Legal Wage Determination in Australia, 1890–1910', in *The Journal of Industrial Relations*, *12*, 2, July 1970.

Macarthy, P. G., 'Wages for unskilled work, and margins for skill, Australia, 1901–21', in *A.E.H.R.*, *XII*, 2, September 1972.

Morrison, A. A., 'The Brisbane General Strike of 1912', in *H.S.*, *14*, May 1950.

The Economy

Dunsdorfs, E., *The Australian Wheat-Growing Industry 1788–1948*, Melbourne, 1956.

Easterby, H. T., *The Queensland Sugar Industry: An Historical Review*, Brisbane, 1933.

Forster, C., Ed., *Australian Economic Development in the Twentieth Century*, London, 1970.

Glynn, S., 'The Transport Factor in Developmental Policy: Pioneer Agricultural Railways in the Western Australian Wheat Belt, 1900–1930', in *A.J.P.H.*, *XV*, 2, August 1969.

Gollan, R., *The Commonwealth Bank of Australia: Origins and Early History*, Canberra, 1968.

Hall, A. R., *The London Capital Market and Australia, 1870–1914*, Canberra, 1963.

Reitsma, A. J., *Trade Protection in Australia*, Leiden and Brisbane, 1960.

Segal, V. M., 'The Development of Tariff Protection in Australia', in *A.Q., IX*, 2, June 1937.

Wheelhouse, F., *Digging Stick to Rotary Hoe: Men and Machines in Rural Australia*, Melbourne, 1966, reprinted Adelaide, 1972.

Wood, G., *Borrowing and Business in Australia* . . . London, 1930.

General

Atkinson, M., Ed., *Australia: Economic and Political Studies*, Melbourne, 1920.

Bryce, J., *Modern Democracies*, London, 2 vols, 1921.

The Cambridge History of the British Empire, VII, 1, Cambridge, 1933, chs. 16–19: *III*, Cambridge, 1959, chs. 11, 12, 15.

Cole, D., 'The Crimson Thread of Kinship: Ethnic Ideas in Australia, 1870–1914', in *H.S.*, *56*, April 1971.

Crowley, F. K., 'The British Contribution to the Australian Population: 1860–1919', in *University Studies in History and Economics*, 1954.

Crowley, F. K., *Australia's Western Third*, London, 1960, reprinted Melbourne, 1970.

Crowley, F. K., *Modern Australia in Documents, I, 1901–1939*, Melbourne, 1973.

Dingle, A. E. and Merrett, D. T., 'Home owners and tenants in Melbourne 1891–1911', in *A.E.H.R., XII*, 1, March 1972.

Dutton, G., *From Federation to War 1901–1914* in the series *Australia Since the Camera*, Melbourne, 1971.

Fraser, J. F., *Australia: The Making of a Nation*, London, 1910.

Greenwood, G., Ed., *Australia: A Social and Political History*, Sydney, 1955, ch. 5.

Kewley, T. H., *Australia's Welfare State: The Development of Social Security Benefits*, Melbourne, 1969.

Kewley, T. H., 'Social Services in Australia (1900–10) with special reference to Old Age and Invalid Pensions in New South Wales', in *R.A.H.S.J., 33*, 4, 1947.

Northcott, C. H., *Australian Social Development*, New York, 1918.

Serle, G., *From Deserts the Prophets Come: The Creative Spirit in Australia 1788–1972*, Melbourne, 1973.

Yarwood, A. T., *Asian Migration to Australia: The Background to Exclusion 1896–1923*, Melbourne, 1964, 1967.

8

1914-19

The First A.I.F.

Bean, C. E. W., *The Official History of Australia in the War of 1914–1918*, Sydney, 12 vols., 1921–42, (individual titles and authors on the volumes).

Bean, C. E. W., *Anzac to Amiens: A Shorter History of the Australian Fighting Services in the First World War*, Canberra, 1946.
Bean, C. E. W., *Letters from France*, London, 1917.
Cutlack, F. M., Ed., *War Letters of General Monash*, Sydney, 1934, reprinted Sydney, 1935.
Inglis, K. S., 'The Australians at Gallipoli', in *H.S.*, *54* and *55*, April 1970 and October 1970.
Inglis, K. S., 'The Anzac Tradition', in *Meanjin Quarterly, XXIV*, 1, 1965.
Monash, J., *The Australian Victories in France in 1918*, London, 1920.
McLachlan, N., 'Nationalism and the Divisive Digger: Three Comments', in *Meanjin Quarterly, XXVII*, 3, 1968.
Moorehead, A., *Gallipoli*, London, 1956.
Roe. M.. 'Comments on the Digger Tradition', in *Meanjin Quarterly, XXIV*, 3, 1965.
Robson, L. L., *The First A.I.F.: A Study of Its Recruitment 1914–1918*, Melbourne, 1970.
Robson, L. L., 'The origin and character of the first A.I.F., 1914–1918: Some statistical evidence', in *H.S.*, *61*, October 1973.
Serle, G., 'The Digger Tradition and Australian Nationalism', in *Meanjin Quarterly, XXIV*, 2, 1965.

Military Biographies

Bean, C. E. W., *Two Men I Knew: William Bridges and Brudenell White: Founders of the A.I.F.*, Sydney, 1957.
Birdwood, W. R., *Khaki and Gown: An Autobiography*, London, 1941.
Hetherington, J., *John Monash*, Melbourne, 1962.
Hill, A. J., 'Chauvel and Monash' in *R.A.H.S.J.*, *53*, 4, December 1967.
Inglis, K. S., *C. E. W. Bean, Australian Historian*, Brisbane, 1970.
Smithers, A. J., *Sir John Monash*, London, 1973.

Rank-and-File Views of the War

The Anzac Book: Written and Illustrated in Gallipoli by the Men of Anzac, London, 1916.
Butler, A. G., *The Digger: A Study in Democracy*, Sydney, 1945.
Fair R., Ed., *A Treasury of Anzac Humour*, Brisbane, 1965.
Gammage, B., *The Broken Years: Australian Soldiers in the Great War*, Canberra, 1974.
Harris, P. L., Ed., *Aussie: A Reprint of all the Numbers of the Diggers' Own Paper of the Battlefield, Wholly Written, Illustrated and Printed in the Field by Members of the A.I.F.*, Sydney, 1920.

Pictorial Publications

Bean, C. E. W., and Gullett, H. S., *Photographic Record of the War*, being vol. XII of *The Official History of Australia in the War of 1914–1918*, Sydney, 1923.

Dyson, Will, *Australia at War: A Winter Record made by Will Dyson on the Somme and at Ypres During the Campaigns of 1916 and 1917*, London, 1918.

Low, David, *The Billy Book: Hughes Abroad*, Sydney, 1918, concentrates on W. M. Hughes.

Marquet, Claude, *Cartoons: A Commemorative Volume, with Appreciations by Leading Representatives of Literature and Politics*, Sydney, 1920. (Cartoons from the *Australian Worker*, Sydney.)

Turner, L. C. F., *The Great War 1914–1918*, in the series *Australia Since the Camera*, Melbourne, 1971.

Fictional Accounts

Davison, Frank Dalby, *The Wells of Beersheba: An Epic of the Australian Light Horse 1914–1918*, Sydney, 1933, revised edition 1947.

'De Loghe, Sydney', (F. S. Loch), *The Straits Impregnable*, Melbourne, 1916.

Lawrence, D. H., *Kangaroo*, London, 1923, reprinted Harmondsworth, 1950; reprinted 1954.

Mann, Leonard, *Flesh in Armour: A Novel*, Melbourne, 1932, 1944; reprinted Sydney, 1973.

'Parker, Leslie' (Angela Thirkell), *Trooper to the Southern Cross*, London, 1934, Melbourne, 1966. (Also published in London in 1936 under the title *What Happened on the Boat*.)

Poetry

Dennis, C. J., *The Moods of Ginger Mick*, Sydney, 1916.

Dennis, C. J., *Digger Smith*, Sydney, 1918.

Dyson, Edward, *'Hello Soldier!': Khaki Verse*, Melbourne, 1919.

Gellert, Leon, *Songs of a Campaign*, Adelaide and Sydney, 1917.

'Maurice, Furnley', (Frank Wilmot), *Eyes of Vigilance: Divine and Moral Songs*, Melbourne, 1920; and *Poems*, Melbourne, 1944.

Palmer, Vance, *The Camp*, Melbourne, 1920.

The Conscription Controversy

Bastian, P., 'The 1916 Conscription Referendum in New South Wales', in *Teaching History*, 5, 1, June 1971.

Childe, V. G., *How Labour Governs: A Study of Workers' Representation in Australia*, London, 1923, Melbourne, 1964.

Forward, R., and Reece, B., Eds., *Conscription in Australia*, Brisbane, 1968.

Gibson, P. M., 'The Conscription Issue in South Australia, 1916–1917', in *University Studies in History*, 1963–4.

Gilbert, A. D., 'The Conscription Referenda, 1916–17: The Impact of the Irish Crisis', in *H.S.*, 53, October, 1969.

Gilbert, A. D., 'Protestants, Catholics and Loyalty: An Aspect of the Conscription Controversies, 1916–17, in *Politics*, VI, 1, May 1971.

Inglis, K. S., 'Conscription in Peace and War, 1911–1945', in *Teaching History*, I, 2, October 1967.

Jauncey, L. C., *The Story of Conscription in Australia*, London, 1935, reprinted Melbourne, 1968.

McQueen, H., 'Who were the conscriptionists? Notes on Federal Labor Members', in *L.H., 16*, May 1969.

Main, J. M., Ed., *Conscription: The Australian Debate 1901–1970*, Melbourne, 1970.

Robertson, J. R., 'The Conscription Issue and The National Movement, Western Australia June 1916 – December 1917', in *University Studies in Western Australian History*, 1959.

Robson, L. L., *Australia and the Great War 1914–18*, Melbourne, 1969.

Smith, F. B., *The Conscription Plebiscites in Australia 1916–1917*, Melbourne, 1965, 1966, 1969.

Turner, I., *Industrial Labour and Politics: The Dynamics of the Labour Movement in Eastern Australia, 1900–1921*, Canberra, 1965, chs 4 and 7.

General

Bean, C. E. W., 'Sidelights of the War on Australian Character', in *R.A.H.S.J., 13*, 4, 1927.

Brennan, N., *Dr Mannix*, Adelaide, 1964.

Buckley, K. D., *The Amalgamated Engineers in Australia, 1852–1920*, Canberra, 1970.

The Cambridge History of the British Empire, *VII*, 1, ch. 19, Cambridge, 1933.

Crowley, F. K., *Modern Australia in Documents*, *I*, 1901–1939, Melbourne, 1973.

Denholm, B., 'Some aspects of the Transition Period from War to Peace, 1918–21', in *A.Q., 16*, 1, March 1944.

Evatt, H. V., *Australian Labour Leader: The Story of W. A. Holman and the Labour Movement*, Sydney, 1940, reprinted 1942, 1945; abridged edition 1954.

Fitzhardinge, L. F., 'Australia, Japan and Great Britain, 1914–18: A Study in Triangular Diplomacy', in *H.S., 54*, April 1970.

Fitzhardinge, L. F., 'W. M. Hughes and the Treaty of Versailles, 1919', in *Journal of Commonwealth Political Studies*, *5*, 2, July 1967.

Forster, C., 'Australian Manufacturing and the War of 1914–18', in *E.R., 29*, November 1953.

Hughes, W. M., *The Splendid Adventure: A Review of Empire Relations Within and Without the Commonwealth of Britannic Nations*, London, 1929.

Hughes, W. M., *Policies and Potentates*, Sydney, 1950.

Laird, J. T., 'A Checklist of Australian Literature of World War I', in *Australian Literary Studies*, *4*, 2, 1969.

Laird, J. T., Ed., *Other Banners: An Anthology of Australian Literature of the First World War*, Canberra, 1971.

Pearce, G. F., *Carpenter to Cabinet: Thirty-Seven Years of Parliament*, London, 1951.

Sawer, G., *Australian Federal Politics and Law: 1901–1929*, Melbourne, 1956.

Scott, E., *Australia During the War*, Sydney, 1936, (Vol. XI of *The Official History of Australia in the War of 1914–1918*).

Turner, I., *Sydney's Burning*, Melbourne, 1967; Sydney, 1969.

Whyte, W. F., *William Morris Hughes: His Life and Times*, Sydney, 1957.

9

1920-29

Economic Development

Blainey, G., *The Rush That Never Ended: A History of Australian Mining*, Melbourne, 1963, 1964; 2nd edition 1969.

Boxer, A. H., Ed., *Aspects of the Australian Economy*, Melbourne, 1965.

Brigden, J. B., *et al.*, *The Australian Tariff: An Economic Enquiry*, Melbourne, 1929.

Davidson, B. R., *Australia: Wet or Dry? The Physical and Economic Limits to the Expansion of Irrigation*, Melbourne, 1969.

Dunsdorfs, E., *The Australian Wheat-Growing Industry 1788–1948*, Melbourne, 1956.

Eggleston, F. W., *State Socialism in Victoria*, London, 1932.

Eggleston, F. W., *et al.*, Eds., *The Peopling of Australia*, (Further Studies), Melbourne, 1933, London, 1968.

Fitzpatrick, B., *The British Empire in Australia: An Economic History: 1834–1939*, Melbourne, 1941, 1949.

Forster, C., *Industrial Development in Australia 1920–1930*, Canberra, 1964.

Giblin, L. F., *The Growth of a Central Bank: The Development of the Commonwealth Bank of Australia, 1924–1945*, Melbourne, 1951.

Glynn, S., 'Government Policy and Agricultural Development: Western Australia, 1900–1930', in *A.E.H.R.*, VII, 2, September 1967.

Glynn, S., 'The Transport Factor in Developmental Policy: Pioneer Agricultural Railways in the Western Australian Wheat Belt, 1900–1930', in *A.J.P.H.*, XV, 2, August 1969.

Hughes, H., *The Australian Iron and Steel Industry 1848–1962*, Melbourne, 1964.

Hunt, I. L., 'Group Settlement in Western Australia: A Criticism' in *University Studies in Western Australian History*, 1958.

Phillips, P. D., and Wood, G. L., Eds., *The Peopling of Australia*, Melbourne, 1928, London, 1968.

Reitsma, A. J., *Trade Protection in Australia*, Leiden and Brisbane, 1960.

Schedvin, C. B., *Australia and the Great Depression: A Study of Economic Development and Policy in the 1920s and 1930s*, Sydney, 1970.

Shaw, A. G. L., and Bruns, G. R., *The Australian Coal Industry*, Melbourne, 1947.

Spaull, A. D., 'The Rise of the Victorian Briquette Industry, 1895–1935', in *A.E.H.R.*, *IX*, 1, March 1969.

Wadham, S. M., *Australian Farming 1788–1965*, Melbourne, 1967.

Labour and Industrial Relations

Anderson, G., 'The Commonwealth Conciliation and Arbitration Act 1928', in *E.R.*, *4*, 7, November 1928.

Anderson, G., *Fixation of Wages in Australia*, Melbourne, 1929.

Bedford, I., 'The One Big Union 1918–1923', in I. Bedford and R. Curnow, *Initiative and Organization*, Melbourne, 1963.

Brown, W. J., 'The Strike of the Australian Waterside Worker: a Review', in *E.R.*, *5*, 8, May 1929.

de Vyver, F. T., 'The 1920 Civil Service and Teachers' Strikes in Western Australia', in *Journal of Industrial Relations*, 7, 3, November 1965.

Dixson, M., 'The Timber Strike of 1929', in *H.S.*, *40*, May 1963.

Fitzpatrick, B., *A Short History of the Australian Labor Movement*, Melbourne, 1940, 1944, 1968, ch. 13.

Foenander, O. de R., *Towards Industrial Peace in Australia: A Series of Essays in the History of the Commonwealth Court of Conciliation and Arbitration*, Melbourne, 1937.

Forster, C., 'Australian Unemployment, 1900–1940', in *E.R.*, *41*, 95, September 1965.

Foster, H. W., *A Brief History of Australia's Basic Wage*, Melbourne, 1965.

Gollan, R., *The Coalminers of New South Wales: A History of the Union, 1860–1960*, Melbourne, 1963.

Higgins, H. B., *A New Province for Law and Order: Being a Review, by its late President for Fourteen Years, of the Australian Court of Conciliation and Arbitration*, London and Sydney, 1922, reprinted London 1968.

Hutson, J., *Penal Colony to Penal Powers*, Sydney, 1966.

Hutson, J., 'The Amalgamated Engineering Union and Arbitration in the 1920s' in *L.H.*, *14*, May 1968.

Iremonger, J., *et al.*, Eds., *Strikes: Studies in Twentieth Century Australian Social History*, Sydney, 1973.

Mauldon, F. R. E., 'The Australasian Council of Trade Unions', in *E.R.*, *4*, 6, May 1928.

Matthews, P. D., and Ford, G. W., Eds., *Australian Trade Unions: Their Development, Structure and Horizons*, Melbourne, 1968.

Portus, J. H., *Australian Compulsory Arbitration 1900–1970*, Sydney, 1971.

Walker, K. F., *Industrial Relations in Australia*, Cambridge, Mass., 1956.

External Affairs

Dignan, D. K., 'Australia and British Relations with Japan, 1914–1921', in *Australian Outlook*, *21*, 2, August 1967.

Fitzhardinge, L. F., 'W. M. Hughes and the Treaty of Versailles, 1919', in *Journal of Commonwealth Political Studies*, *5*, 2, July 1967.

Hasluck, P., *The Government and the People: 1939–1941*, Canberra, 1952, ch. 2.

Hudson, W. J., *Australian Diplomacy*, Melbourne, 1970.

McCarthy, J. M., 'Australia and Imperial Defence: Co-operation and Conflict 1918–1939', in *A.J.P.H.*, *XVII*, 1, April 1971.

McCarthy, J. M., 'Singapore and Australian Defence, 1921–1942', in *Australian Outlook*, *25*, 2, August 1971.

Megaw, M. R., 'Undiplomatic Channels: Australian Representation in the United States, 1918–39', in *H.S.*, *60*, April 1973.

Poynter, J. R., 'The Yo-Yo Variations: Initiative and Dependence in Australia's External Relations, 1918–1923', in *H.S.*, *54*, April 1970.

Sales, P. M., 'W. M. Hughes and the Chanak Crisis of 1922', in *A.J.P.H.*, *XVII*, 3, December 1971.

Vinson, J. C., 'The Problem of Australian Representation at the Washington Conference for the Limitation of Naval Armament', in *A.J.P.H.*, *IV*, 2, November 1958.

State Politics

Aitkin, D., *The Colonel: A Political Biography of Sir Michael Bruxner*, Canberra, 1969.

Aitkin, D., *The Country Party in New South Wales: A Study of Organisation and Survival*, Canberra, 1972.

Bernays, C. A., *Queensland – Our Seventh Political Decade, 1920–1930*, Sydney, 1931.

Black, D., 'The Collier Government 1924–1930', in *University Studies in Western Australian History*, 1959.

Brigden, J. B., 'State Enterprises in Australia', in *International Labour Review*, *XVI*, 1, July 1927.

Crowley, F. K., *Australia's Western Third*, London, 1960, reprinted Melbourne, 1970.

Davis, S. R., Ed., *The Government of the Australian States*, Melbourne, 1960.

Dixson, M., 'Reformists and Revolutionaries in New South Wales, 1920–1922', in *Politics*, *I*, 2, November 1966.

Dixson, M., 'Ideology, the Trades Hall Reds and J. T. Lang', in *Politics*, *VI*, 1, May 1971.

Eggleston, F. W., *State Socialism in Victoria*, London, 1932.

Ellis, U., *The Country Party: A Political and Social History of the Party in New South Wales*, Melbourne, 1958.

Hart, P. R., 'J. A. Lyons, Tasmanian Labour Leader', in *L.H.*, *9*, November 1965.
Hawker, G. N., *The Parliament of New South Wales: 1856–1965*, Sydney, 1971.
Higgins, E. M., 'Queensland Labor: Trade Unionists Versus Premiers', in *H.S.*, *34*, May 1960.
Hopgood, D., 'The View from the Head Office: the South Australian Labor Political Machine, 1917–1930', in *Politics*, *VI*, 1, May 1971.
Hyams, B. K., 'The Country Party in Western Australia 1914–1944', in *University Studies in History*, 1965.
Lang, J. T., *I Remember*, Sydney, 1956.
Lang, J. T., *The Turbulent Years*, Sydney, 1970.
Maiden, H. E., *The History of Local Government in New South Wales*, Sydney, 1966.
Morrison, A. A., 'Militant Labour in Queensland, 1912–1927', in *R.A.H.S.J.*, *38*, 5, November 1952.
Rydon, J., 'Victoria 1910–1966: Political Pecularities', in *H.S.*, *50*, April 1968.
Schedvin, B., 'E. G. Theodore and the London Pastoral Lobby', in *Politics*, *VI*, 1, May 1971.
Turner, K., *House of Review?: The New South Wales Legislative Council 1934–68*, Sydney, 1969.
Young, I. E., 'A. C. Willis, Welsh Non-conformist, and the Labour Party in New South Wales, 1911–33', in *The Journal of Religious History*, 2, 4, December 1963.

Politics, General

Crisp, L. F., *The Australian Federal Labour Party: 1901–1951*, London, 1955.
Crisp, L. F., and Bennett, S. P., *Australian Labor Party: Federal Personnel 1901–1954*, Canberra, 1954.
Crisp, L. F., 'New Light on the Trials and Tribulations of W. M. Hughes, 1920–1922', in *H.S.*, *37*, November 1961.
Davidson, A., *The Communist Party of Australia: A Short History*, Stanford, 1969.
Davies, A. J., 'Australian Federalism and National Development', in *A.J.P.H.*, *XIV*, 1, April 1968.
Davis, S. R., 'A Unique Federal Institution', in *Annual Law Review*, *II*, 2, December 1952.
Edwards, C., *Bruce of Melbourne: Man of Two Worlds*, London, 1965.
Ellis, U., *A History of the Australian Country Party*, Melbourne, 1963.
Gow, N., 'The Introduction of Compulsory Voting in the Australian Commonwealth', in *Politics*, *VI*, 2, November 1971.
Graham, B. D., 'Graziers in Politics, 1917–1929', in *H.S.*, *32*, May 1959.
Graham, B.D., *The formation of the Australian Country Parties*, Canberra, 1966.
Graham, B. D., 'The Country Party and the Formation of the Bruce-Page Ministry', in *H.S.*, *37*, November 1961.

Heydon, P., *Quiet Decision: A Study of George Foster Pearce*, Melbourne, 1965.

Hughes, C. A. and Graham, B. D., *A Handbook of Australian Government and Politics 1890–1964*, Canberra, 1968.

Kristianson, G. L., *The Politics of Patriotism: The Pressure Group Activities of the Returned Servicemen's League*, Canberra, 1966.

Maxwell, J. A., *Commonwealth-State Financial Relations in Australia*, Melbourne, 1967.

May, R. J., *Financing the Small States in Australian Federalism*, Melbourne, 1971.

O'Farrell, P. J., 'The Russian Revolution and the Labour Movements of Australia and New Zealand, 1917–1922', in *International Review of Social History, VIII*, 1963.

Page, E., *Truant Surgeon: The Inside Story of Forty Years of Australian Political Life*, Sydney, 1963.

Sawer, G., *Australian Federal Politics and Law, 1901–1929*, Melbourne, 1956.

Sherrard, K., 'The Political History of Women in Australia', in *A.Q.*, *XV*, 4, December 1943.

Wildavsky, A., and Carboch, D., *Studies in Australian Politics: The 1926 Referendum: The Fall of the Bruce-Page Government*, Melbourne, 1958.

Young, I., *Theodore: His Life and Times*, Sydney, 1971.

General

Barcan, A., *A Short History of Education in New South Wales*, Sydney, 1965.

Bedford, I., and Curnow, R., *Initiative and Organization*, Melbourne, 1963.

Birch, A., and Macmillan, D. S., *The Sydney Scene 1788–1960*, Melbourne, 1962.

The Cambridge History of the British Empire, VII, 1, ch. 20, Cambridge, 1933.

Cleverley, J. F., and Lawry, J., Eds., *Australian Education in the Twentieth Century: Studies in the Development of State Education*, Melbourne, 1972.

Crawford, R. M., *An Australian Perspective*, Madison and Melbourne, 1960.

Crowley, F. K., *Modern Australia in Documents, I*, 1901–1939, Melbourne, 1973.

Fitzpatrick, B., *The British Empire in Australia: An Economic History 1834–1939*, Melbourne, 1941, 1949.

Fitzpatrick, B., *The Australian Commonwealth: A Picture of the Community 1901–1955*, Melbourne, 1956.

Grant, J., and Serle, G., *The Melbourne Scene 1803–1956*, Melbourne, 1957.

Green, H. M., *A History of Australian Literature*, Sydney, 2 vols., 1961.

Greenwood, G., Ed., *Australia: A Social and Political History*, Sydney, 1955, ch. 7.

Hancock, W. K., *Australia*, London, 1930, Sydney, 1945, Brisbane, 1961, 1964, 1966.

Jones, M. A., *Housing and Poverty in Australia*, Melbourne, 1972.

Kewley, T. H., *Social Security in Australia*, Sydney, 1965, 1973.

McLeod, A. L., Ed., *The Pattern of Australian Culture*, Melbourne, 1963.

Mayer, H., *The Press in Australia*, Melbourne, 1964, 1968.

Rowley, C. D., *Aboriginal Policy and Practice, Vol. I: The Destruction of Aboriginal Society*, Canberra, 1970.

Smith, B. W., *Australian Painting 1788–1960*, Melbourne, 1962, 1965, second edition 1971, 1972.

Younger, R. M., *Australia and the Australians: A New Concise History*, Adelaide, 1970, ch. 19.

10

1930-39

Economic History

Alford, F. S., *The Greater Illusion: A Critical Review of Australia's Fiscal Policy*, Sydney, 1934.

Blainey, G., *The Rush That Never Ended: A History of Australian Mining*, Melbourne, 1963, 1964, second edition 1969.

Boehm, E. A., *Twentieth Century Economic Development in Australia*, Melbourne, 1971.

Boxer, A. H., Ed., *Aspects of the Australian Economy*, Melbourne, 1965.

Burton, H., 'The "Trade Diversion" Episode of the 'Thirties', in *Australian Outlook*, 22, 1, April 1968.

Brogden, S., *The History of Australian Aviation*, Melbourne, 1960.

Butlin, N. G., *Australian Domestic Product, Investment and Foreign Borrowing 1861–1938/39*, Cambridge, 1962.

Campbell, K. O., 'Australian Agricultural Production in the Depression: Explanations of its Behaviour', in *E.R.*, XX, 38, June 1944.

Cheney, S. A., *From Horse to Horsepower*, Adelaide, 1965.

Cooksey, R., Ed., *The Great Depression in Australia*, Canberra, 1970, being No. 17 of *Labour History*.

Copland, D. B., *Australia in the World Crisis 1929–33*, Cambridge, 1934.

Cramp, K. R., 'The Story of Australia's Handling of the Financial Crisis in and after 1929', in *R.A.H.S.J.*, 23, 2, 1937.

Davidson, F. G., *The Industrialization of Australia*, Melbourne, 1957, 1960, 1962, 1969.

Duncan, W. G. K., and Janes, C. V., Eds., *The Future of Immigration into Australia and New Zealand*, Sydney, 1937.

Dunsdorfs, E., *The Australian Wheat-Growing Industry 1788–1948*, Melbourne, 1956.

Eggleston, F. W., *et al.*, Eds., *The Peopling of Australia*, (Further Studies), Melbourne, 1933, London, 1968.

Forster, C., 'Australian Unemployment, 1900–1940', in *E.R.*, *XLI*, 95, September, 1965.

Fysh, H., *Qantas Rising: The Autobiography of the Flying Fysh*, Sydney, 1965.

Giblin, L. F., 'Farm Production and the Depression', in *E.R.*, *XI*, (Supplement), March 1935.

Giblin, L. F., *The Growth of a Central Bank: The Development of the Commonwealth Bank of Australia 1924–1945*, Melbourne, 1951.

Griffin, J., Ed., *Essays in Economic History of Australia*, Brisbane, 1967, 1970.

Hartnett, L. J., *Big Wheels and Little Wheels*, Melbourne, 1964.

Hocking, D. M., and Haddon-Cave, C. P., *Air Transport in Australia*, Sydney, 1951.

Hughes, H., *The Australian Iron and Steel Industry, 1848–1962*, Melbourne, 1964.

Iremonger, J., *et al.*, Eds., *Strikes: Studies in Twentieth Century Australian Social History*, Sydney, 1973.

Louis, L. J., and Turner, I., Eds., *The Depression of the 1930s*, Melbourne, 1968.

Louis, L. J., *Trade Unions and the Depression: A Study of Victoria, 1930–1932*, Canberra, 1968.

Maclaurin, W. R., *Economic Planning in Australia 1929–1936*, London, 1937.

Mauldon, F. R. E., and Polglaze, J., 'Australian Manufacturing in the Depression', in *E.R.*, *XI*, (Supplement) March 1935.

Mitchell, T. J., 'J. W. Wainwright: The Industrialisation of South Australia, 1935–40', in *A.J.P.H.*, *VIII*, 1, May 1962.

Polden, K., 'The Collapse of the Government Savings Bank of New South Wales, 1931', in *A.E.H.R.*, *XII*, 1, March 1972.

Portus, G. V., Ed., *What the Census Reveals*, Adelaide, 1936.

Richardson, L., 'Dole Queue Patriots: The Port Kembla Pig-Iron Strike of 1938', in J. Iremonger, *et al.*, Eds., *Strikes: Studies in Twentieth Century Australian Social History*, Sydney, 1973.

Schedvin, C. B., *Australia and the Great Depression: A Study of Economic Development and Policy in the 1920s and 1930s*, Sydney, 1970.

Shann, E. O. G., and Copland, D. B., Eds., *The Battle of the Plans: Documents Relating to the Premiers' Conference, May 25th to June 11th, 1931*, Sydney, 1931.

Shann, E. O. G., and Copland, D. B., Eds., *The Crisis in Australian Finance 1929 to 1931: Documents on Budgetary and Economic Policy*, Sydney, 1931.

Shann, E. O. G., and Copland, D. B., Eds., *The Australian Price Structure, 1932*, Sydney, 1933.
Smith, R. F. I., 'The Scullin Government and Wheatgrowers', in *L.H.*, *26*, May 1974.
Wadham, S. M., *Australian Farming 1788–1965*, Melbourne, 1967.
Walker, E. R., *Australia in the World Depression*, London, 1933.

External Affairs and Defence

Andrews, E. M., *Isolationism and Appeasement in Australia: Reactions to the European Crises, 1935–1939*, Canberra, 1970.
Andrews, E., 'Australian Labour and Foreign Policy 1935–1939: The Retreat from Isolationism', in *L.H.*, *9*, November 1965.
Ball, W. Macmahon, *Possible Peace*, Melbourne, 1936.
Ball, W. Macmahon, Ed., *Press, Radio and World Affairs: Australia's Outlook*, Melbourne, 1938.
Cumpston, I. M., 'The Australian-Japanese Dispute of the Nineteen Thirties', in *A.Q.*, *XXIX*, 2, June 1957.
Esthus, R. A., *From Enmity to Alliance: U.S.-Australian Relations, 1931–41*, Seattle, 1964, Melbourne, 1965.
Fairbanks, G., 'Isolationism v. Imperialism: The 1937 Election', in *Politics*, *II*, 2, November 1967.
Hasluck, P., *The Government and the People, 1939–41*, Canberra, 1952.
Hudson, W. J., Ed., *Towards a Foreign Policy: 1914–1941*, Melbourne, 1967.
Hudson, W. J., *Australian Diplomacy*, Melbourne, 1970.
Levi, W., *Australia's Outlook on Asia*, Sydney, 1958.
Long, G., *To Benghazi*, Canberra, 1952.
McCarthy, J. M., 'Australia and Imperial Defence: Co-operation and Conflict 1918–1939', in *A.J.P.H.*, *XVII*, 1, April 1971
McCarthy, J. M., 'Air Power and Australian Defence, 1923–1939', in *The Victorian Historical Magazine*, *42*, 3, August 1971.
Megaw, R., 'The Australian Goodwill Mission to the Far East in 1934 and the Evolution of Australian Foreign Policy', in *R.A.H.S.J.*, *59*, 4, December 1973.
Odgers, G., *The Royal Australian Air Force: An Illustrated History*, Sydney, 1965.
Shepherd, J., *Australia's Interests and Policies in the Far East*, New York, 1939.
Watt, A., 'Australia and the Munich Agreement: Underlying Assumptions and Operative Methods of Australia's Foreign Policy (1938)', in *Australian Outlook*, *17*, 1, April 1963.
Watt, A., *The Evolution of Australian Foreign Policy, 1938–1965*, Cambridge, 1967, London, 1968.

Politics

Aitkin, D., *The Colonel: A Political Biography of Sir Michael Bruxner*, Canberra, 1969.

Birch, A. H., *Federalism, Finance and Social Legislation in Canada, Australia and the United States*, Oxford, 1955, 1957.

Campbell, E., *The Rallying Point: My Story of the New Guard*, Melbourne, 1965.

Cooksey, R., Ed., *The Great Depression in Australia*, Canberra, 1970, being No. 17 of *Labour History*.

Cooksey, R., *Lang and Socialism: A study in the Great Depression*, Canberra, 1971.

Crisp, L. F., *Ben Chifley: A Biography*, London, 1961, 1963.

Crisp, L. F., *The Australian Federal Labour Party 1901–1951*, London, 1955.

Davidson, A., *The Communist Party of Australia: A Short History*, Stanford, 1969.

Denning, W., *Caucus Crisis: The Rise and Fall of the Scullin Government*, Parramatta, 1937.

Drummond, D. H., *Australia's Changing Constitution: No States or New States*, Sydney, 1943, 2nd edition 1946.

Edwards, C., *Bruce of Melbourne: Man of Two Worlds*, London, 1965.

Ellis, U., *The Country Party: A Political and Social History of the Party in New South Wales*, Melbourne, 1958.

Ellis, U., *A History of the Australian Country Party*, Melbourne, 1963.

Foott, B., *Dismissal of a Premier: The Philip Game Papers*, Sydney, 1968.

Gibson, R., *My Years in the Communist Party*, Melbourne, 1966, ch. 3.

Howard, F., *Kent Hughes: A Biography of Colonel the Hon. Sir Wilfred Kent Hughes*, Melbourne, 1972.

Hughes, C. A., and Graham, B. D., *A Handbook of Australian Government and Politics 1890–1964*, Canberra, 1968.

Jupp, J., *Australian Party Politics*, Melbourne, 1964, 1966, 1968.

Kisch, E. E., *Australian Landfall*, Melbourne, 1937, 1969.

Kristianson, G. L., *The Politics of Patriotism: The Pressure Group Activities of the Returned Servicemen's League*, Canberra, 1966, ch. 3.

Lang, J. T., *Why I Fight!*, Sydney, 1934.

Lang, J. T., *The Great Bust: The Depression of the Thirties*, Sydney, 1962.

Lang, J. T., *The Turbulent Years*, Sydney, 1970.

Lyons, Enid, *So We Take Comfort*, London, 1965.

McCarthy, J. M., ' "All for Australia": Some Right Wing Responses to the Depression in New South Wales, 1929–1932' in *R.A.H.S.J.*, 57, 2, June 1971.

Maxwell, J. A., *Commonwealth-State Financial Relations in Australia*, Melbourne, 1967.

May, R. J., *Financing the Small States in Australian Federalism*, Melbourne, 1971.

Mitchell, P., 'Australian Patriots: A Study of the New Guard', in *A.E.H.R.*, IX, 2, September 1969.

Page, E., *Truant Surgeon: The Inside Story of Forty Years of Australian Political Life*, Sydney, 1963.

Robertson, J. R., 'Scullin as Prime Minister: Seven Critical Decisions', in R. Cooksey, Ed., *The Great Depression in Australia*, Canberra, 1970, being No. 17 of *Labour History*.

Sawer, G., *Australian Federal Politics and Law: 1929–1949*, Melbourne, 1963, 1967.

Shann, E. O. G., and Copland, D. B., Eds., *The Battle of the Plans: Documents Relating to the Premiers' Conference May 25th to June 11th 1931*, Sydney, 1931.

Watt, E. D., 'Secession in Western Australia', in *University Studies in Western Australian History*, 1958.

Williams, J. R., *John Latham and the Conservative Recovery from Defeat 1929–1931*, Sydney, 1969.

Young, I., 'J. T. Lang and the Depression', in *L.H.*, 5, November 1963.

Young, I., *Theodore: His Life and Times*, Sydney, 1971.

General

Baxter, J., *The Australian Cinema*, Sydney, 1970.

Blake, J., 'The Early Thirties', in *Arena*, 25, 1971.

Bolton, G. C., *A Fine Country to Starve In*, Perth, 1972.

Caddie, pseud. *Caddie: A Sydney Barmaid: an Autobiography written by herself*, Introduction by Dymphna Cusack, London, 1953, Melbourne, 1966.

Coleman, P., *Obscenity, Blasphemy, Sedition: Censorship in Australia*, Brisbane, 1962.

Crowley, F. K., *Modern Australia in Documents, I, 1901–1939*, Melbourne, 1973.

Crowley, F. K., *Australia's Western Third*, London, 1960, reprinted Melbourne, 1970.

Grattan, C. H., *The Southwest Pacific Since 1900: A Modern History*, Ann Arbor, 1963.

Greenwood, G., Ed., *Australia: A Social and Political History*, Sydney, 1955, ch. 8.

Ingamells, R. C., *Conditional Culture*, Adelaide, 1938, reprinted in J. Barnes, Ed., *The Writer in Australia: A Collection of Literary Documents 1856 to 1964*, Melbourne, 1969.

Louis, L. J., and Turner, I., Eds., *The Depression of the 1930s*, Melbourne, 1968.

Moore, T. Inglis, *Social Patterns in Australian Literature*, Sydney, 1971.

Power, F. R., *The Depression Hiatus*, Melbourne, 1973.

Serle, G., *From Deserts the Prophets Come: The Creative Spirit in Australia: 1788–1972*, Melbourne, 1973.

Stephensen, P. R., *The Foundations of Culture in Australia: An Essay Towards National Self Respect*, Sydney, 1936.

Waten, Judah, *The Depression Years: 1929–1939*, in the series *Australia Since the Camera*, Melbourne, 1971.
Younger, R. M., *Australia and the Australians: A New Concise History*, Adelaide, 1970, chs. 20–22.

I I
1939-51

The War

Bateson, C., *The War with Japan: A Concise History*, Sydney, 1968.
Hetherington, J., *Blamey: The Biography of Field Marshall Sir Thomas Blamey*, Melbourne, 1954.
Long, G., Ed., *Australia in the War of 1939–1945*, Canberra, Australian War Memorial, 22 vols., individual authors and titles on the volumes.
The volumes concerning the home front (Series 4, Civil) are:— are:—

> Hasluck, P., *The Government and the People, 1939–1941*, Canberra, 1952, 1956, 1965, and *The Government and the People, 1942–1945*, Canberra, 1970.
> Butlin, S. J., *War Economy, 1939–1942*, Canberra, 1955, 1961; *War Economy, 1942–1945*, (not yet published).
> Mellor, D. P., *The Role of Science and Industry*, Canberra, 1958.

Long, G., *The Six Years War: A Concise History of Australia in the 1939–45 War*, Canberra, 1973.

Economic History

Bambrick, S., 'Federal Government Intervention in the Price Mechanism 1939-49', in *A.E.H.R.*, *XIV*, 1, March 1974.
Blainey, G., *The Steel Master: A Life of Essington Lewis*, Melbourne, 1971.
Brash, D. T., *American Investment in Australian Industry*, Canberra, 1966.
Butlin, S. J., *War Economy, 1939–1942*, Canberra, 1955, 1961.
Copland, D. B., and Barback, R. G., Eds., *The Conflict of Expansion and Stability*, Melbourne, 1957.
Crawford, J. G., *Australian Trade Policy 1942–1966: A Documentary History*, Canberra, 1968.
Forster, C., Ed., *Australian Economic Development in the Twentieth Century*, London, 1970.
Kemp, C. D., *Big Businessmen: Four Biographical Essays*, Melbourne, 1964. (H. Gepp, W. Massy-Greene, L. McConnan, G. Grimwade.)
McColl, G. D., *The Australian Balance of Payments: A Study of Post-War Developments*, Melbourne, 1965.
Nicholson, D. F., *Australia's Trade Relations: An Outline History of Australia's Overseas Trading Arrangements*, Melbourne, 1955.

Walker, E. R., *The Australian Economy in War and Reconstruction*, New York, 1947.

Waters, W. J., 'Australian Labor's Full Employment Objective, 1942–45', in *A.J.P.H.*, *XVI*, 1, April 1970.

Foreign Policy

Albinski, H. S., 'Australia and the China Problem Under the Labor Government', in *A.J.P.H.*, *X*, 2, August 1964.

Ball, W. Macmahon, *Japan: Enemy or Ally?*, Melbourne, 1948.

Dedman, J. J., 'Defence Policy Decisions Before Pearl Harbour', in *A.J.P.H.*, *XIII*, 3, December 1967.

Eggleston, F. W., *Reflections on Australian Foreign Policy*, Melbourne, 1957.

Esthus, R. A., *From Enmity to Alliance: U.S.-Australian Relations, 1931–41*, Seattle, 1964, Melbourne, 1965.

Evatt, H. V., *Foreign Policy of Australia: Speeches*, Sydney, 1945.

Evatt, H. V., *Australia in World Affairs*, Sydney, 1946.

Grattan, C. H., *The United States and the Southwest Pacific*, Melbourne and Cambridge (Mass.), 1961.

Hasluck, P., 'Australia and the Formation of the United Nations: Some Personal Reminiscences', in *R.A.H.S.J.*, *40*, 3, December 1954, and *41*, 5, January 1956.

Hudson, W. J., Ed., *Towards a Foreign Policy: 1914–1941*, Melbourne, 1967.

Hudson, W. J., *Australian Diplomacy*, Melbourne, 1970.

Kay, R., Ed., *The Australian-New Zealand Agreement 1944*, Wellington, 1972.

McCarthy, J. M., 'Singapore and Australian Defence, 1921–1942', in *Australian Outlook*, 25, 2, August 1971.

McIntyre, W. D., and Gardner, W. J., Eds., *Speeches and Documents on New Zealand History*, Oxford, 1971, Pt. 7.

Moore, J. H., Ed., *The American Alliance: Australia, New Zealand and the United States: 1940–1970*, Melbourne, 1970.

Reese, T. R., *Australia, New Zealand, and the United States: A Survey of International Relations*, London, 1969.

Rosecrance, R. N., *Australian Diplomacy and Japan, 1945–1951*, Melbourne, 1962.

Spender, P. C., *Exercises in Diplomacy: The ANZUS Treaty and the Colombo Plan*, Sydney, 1969.

Spender, P. C., *Politics and a Man*, Sydney, 1972.

Starke, J. G., *The ANZUS Treaty Alliance*, Melbourne, 1965.

Watt, A., *The Evolution of Australian Foreign Policy 1938–1965*, Cambridge, 1967, London, 1968.

Politics

Calwell, A. A., *Be Just and Fear Not*, Melbourne, 1972.

Casey, R. G., *Personal Experience 1939–1946*, London, 1962.

Chester, A., *John Curtin*, Sydney, 1943.

Clarke, F. G., 'Labour and the Catholic Social Studies Movement', in *L.H.*, *20*, May 1971.

Crisp, L. F., *Ben Chifley: A Biography*, London, 1961, 1963.

Crisp, L. F., *The Australian Federal Labour Party 1901–1951*, London, 1955.

Dalziel, A., *Evatt the Enigma*, Melbourne, 1967.

Davidson, A., *The Communist Party of Australia: A Short History*, Stanford, 1969.

Dedman, J. J., 'The Labor Government in the Second World War: A Memoir', in *L.H.*, *21*, November 1971; *22*, May 1972; *23*, November 1972.

Dowsing, I., *Curtin of Australia*, Melbourne, 1968.

Fadden, A. W., *They Called Me Artie: The Memoirs of Sir Arthur Fadden*, Brisbane, 1969.

Forward, R., and Reece, B., Eds., *Conscription in Australia*, Brisbane, 1968.

Gollan, D., 'The Balmain Ironworkers' Strike of 1945', in *L.H.*, *22*, May 1972, and *23*, November 1972.

Hasluck, P., *The Government and the People 1939–1941*, Canberra, 1952, 1956, 1965.

Hasluck, P., *The Government and the People 1942–1945*, Canberra, 1970.

Haylen, L., *Twenty Years' Hard Labor*, Melbourne, 1969.

Howard, F., *Kent Hughes: A Biography of Colonel The Hon. Sir Wilfred Kent Hughes*, Melbourne, 1972.

Hughes, C. A., and Graham, B. D., *A Handbook of Australian Government and Politics 1890–1964*, Canberra, 1968.

Kelly, V., *A Man of the People: From Boilermaker to Governor-General: The Career of the Rt. Hon. Sir William McKell*, Sydney, 1971.

Main, J. M., Ed., *Conscription: The Australian Debate 1901–1970*, Melbourne, 1970.

May, A. L., *The Battle for the Banks*, Sydney, 1968.

Menzies, R. G., *Afternoon Light: Some Memories of Men and Events*, Melbourne, 1967.

Menzies, R. G., *The Measure of the Years*, Melbourne, 1970.

Muirden, B., *The Puzzled Patriots: The Story of the Australia First Movement*, Melbourne, 1968.

Ormonde, P., *The Movement*, Melbourne, 1972.

Perkins, K., *Menzies; Last of the Queen's Men*, Adelaide, 1968.

Rawson, D., *Labor in Vain?: A Survey of the Australian Labor Party*, Melbourne, 1966.

Ross, L., 'Jack Curtin – Socialist ... John Curtin – Prime Minister', in *A.Q.*, *XVII*, *3*, September 1945.

Santamaria, B. A., *The Price of Freedom: The Movement – After Ten Years*, Melbourne, 1964.

Sawer, G., *Australian Federal Politics and Law: 1929–1949*, Melbourne, 1963, 1967.

Spender, P. C., *Politics and a Man*, Sydney, 1972.

Spratt, E., *Eddie Ward: Firebrand of East Sydney*, Adelaide, 1965.

Tennant, K., *Evatt: Politics and Justice*, Sydney, 1970.

Waters, W. J., 'Labor, Socialism and World War II', in *L.H.*, *16*, May 1969.

Webb, L. C., *Communism and Democracy in Australia: A Survey of the 1951 Referendum*, Melbourne, 1954.

Weiner, H. E., 'The Reduction of Communist Power in the Australian Trade Unions: A Case Study', in *Political Science Quarterly*, *LXIX*, *3*, September 1954.

West, K., *Power in the Liberal Party: A Study in Australian Politics*, Melbourne, 1965.

General

Alexander, F., *Australia Since Federation: A Narrative and Critical Analysis*, Melbourne, 1967, ch. 5.

Alexander, F., *From Curtin to Menzies And After*, Melbourne, 1973.

Appleyard, R. T., *British Emigration to Australia*, Canberra, 1964.

Aughterson, W. V., Ed., *Taking Stock: Aspects of Mid-Century Life in Australia*, Melbourne, 1953, 1954.

Bolton, G. C., *Dick Boyer: An Australian Humanist*, Canberra, 1967.

Caiger, G., Ed., *The Australian Way of Life*, Melbourne, 1953.

Crowley, F. K., *Modern Australia in Documents*, 2, 1939–1970, Melbourne, 1973.

Green, H. M., *A History of Australian Literature*, 2, 1923–1950, Sydney, 1961.

Greenwood, G., Ed., *Australia: A Social and Political History*, Sydney, 1955, ch. 8.

Jupp, J., *Arrivals and Departures*, Melbourne, 1966.

Kewley, T. H., *Social Security in Australia: The Development of Social Security and Health Benefits from 1900 to the Present*, Sydney, 1965, 1973.

Mansergh, N., *et al*, *Commonwealth Perspectives*, Durham, N.C. and London, 1958.

Oeser, O. A., and Hammond, S. B., *Social Structure and Personality in a City*, London, 1954.

Price, C. A., *Southern Europeans in Australia*, Melbourne, 1963.

Pringle, J. D., *Australian Accent*, London, 1958, 1959, 1965.

Reese, T. R., *Australia in the Twentieth Century: A Political History*, chs. 8–10, Melbourne, 1964.

Rowley, C. D., *Aboriginal Policy and Practice, Vol. 1, The Destruction of Aboriginal Society*, Canberra, 1970.

Serle, G., *From Deserts the Prophets Come: The Creative Spirit in Australia: 1788–1972*, Melbourne, 1973.

12
───────────
1951-72

Foreign Affairs

Albinski, H. S., *Australian Policies and Attitudes Towards China*, Princeton, N.J., 1965.

Albinski, H. S., *Politics and Foreign Policy in Australia: The Impact of Vietnam and Conscription*, Durham, N.C., 1970.

Ball, W. Macmahon, *Australia and Japan*, Melbourne, 1969.

Fisk, E. K., Ed., *New Guinea on the Threshold: Aspects of Social, Political and Economic Development*, Canberra, 1966.

Gelber, H. G., *Australia, Britain and the EEC, 1961 to 1963*, Melbourne, 1966.

Gelber, H. G., *The Australian-American Alliance: Costs and Benefits*, Melbourne, 1968.

Gelber, H. G., Ed., *Problems of Australian Defence*, Melbourne, 1970.

Greenwood, G., and Harper, N. D., Eds., *Australia in World Affairs, 1950–1955*, Melbourne, 1957; *1956–1960*, Melbourne, 1963; *1961–1965*, Melbourne, 1968; *1966–1970*, Melbourne, 1974.

Harper, N. D., and Sissons, D., *Australia and the United Nations*, New York, 1959.

Hastings, P., *New Guinea: Problems and Prospects*, Melbourne, 1969, reprinted Melbourne, 1973.

Hudson, W. J., *Australian Diplomacy*, Melbourne, 1970.

Hudson, W. J., *Australia and the Colonial Question at the United Nations*, Sydney, 1970.

Hudson, W. J., Ed., *Australia and Papua New Guinea*, Sydney, 1971.

Kay, R., Ed., *The Australia-New Zealand Agreement 1944*, Wellington, 1972.

Mair, L. P., *Australia in New Guinea*, Melbourne, 1948, 2nd edition, 1970.

Millar, T. B., *Australia's Defence*, Melbourne, 1965, 2nd edition 1969.

Millar, T. B., *Australia's Foreign Policy*, Sydney, 1968.

Millar, T. B., Ed., *Australian Foreign Minister: The Diaries of R. G. Casey 1951–60*, London, 1972.

Nelson, H., *Papua New Guinea: Black Unity or Black Chaos?*, Melbourne, 1972.

Reese, T. R., *Australia, New Zealand and the United States: A Survey of International Relations 1941–1968*, London, 1969.

Spender, P. C., *Exercises in Diplomacy: The ANZUS Treaty and the Colombo Plan*, Sydney, 1969.

Starke, J. G., *The ANZUS Treaty Alliance*, Melbourne, 1965.

Teichmann, M., Ed., *New Directions in Australian Foreign Policy: Ally, Satellite or Neutral?*, Melbourne, 1969.

Watt, A., *The Evolution of Australian Foreign Policy, 1938–1965*, Cambridge, 1967, London, 1968.

Watt, A., *Australian Diplomat: Memoirs of Sir Alan Watt*, Sydney, 1972.

Politics

Brennan, N., *Dr Mannix*, Adelaide, 1964.

Caiden, G. E., *Career Service: An Introduction to the History of Personnel Administration in the Commonwealth Public Service of Australia 1901–1961*, Melbourne, 1965.

Caiden, G. E., *The Commonwealth Bureaucracy*, Melbourne, 1967.

Campbell, E., and Whitmore, H., *Freedom in Australia*, Sydney, 1966, 1967, 2nd edition 1973.

Davies, A. F., *Private Politics: A Study of Five Political Outlooks*, Melbourne, 1962, 1966.

Davies, A. F., *Images of Class: An Australian Study*, Sydney, 1967, 1969.

Davis, S. R., Ed., *The Government of the Australian States*, Melbourne, 1960.

Encel, S., *Cabinet Government in Australia*, Melbourne, 1962.

Encel, S., *Equality and Authority: A Study of Class, Status and Power in Australia*, Melbourne, 1970.

Fadden, A., *They Called Me Artie: The Memoirs of Sir Arthur Fadden*, Brisbane, 1969.

Gordon, R., Ed., *The Australian New Left: Critical Essays and Strategy*, Melbourne, 1970.

Hughes, C. A., and Graham, B. D., *A Handbook of Australian Government and Politics 1890–1964*, Canberra, 1968.

Joske, P. E., *Australian Federal Government*, Sydney, 1967, 2nd edition 1971.

Jupp, J., *Australian Party Politics*, Melbourne, 1964, 1966, 2nd edition 1968.

Kristianson, C. L., *The Politics of Patriotism: The Pressure Group Activities of the Returned Servicemen's League*, Canberra, 1966.

May, R. J., *Financing the Small States in Australian Federalism*, Melbourne, 1971.

Mayer, H., Ed., *Australian Politics: A Reader*, Melbourne, 1966: also *A Second Reader*, Melbourne, 1969; and (with H. Nelson) *A Third Reader*, Melbourne, 1973.

Menzies, R. G., *Central Power in the Australian Commonwealth: An Examination of the Growth of Commonwealth Power in the Australian Federation*, London, 1967.

Menzies, R. G., *Afternoon Light: Some Memories of Men and Events*, Melbourne and London, 1967.

Menzies, R. G., *The Measure of the Years*, Melbourne, 1970, London, 1972.

Miller, J. D. B., *Australian Government and Politics: An Introductory Survey*, London, 1954, 2nd edition 1959, 1961, 1963, 3rd edition 1964, 4th edition 1971.

Murray, R., *The Split: Australian Labor in the Fifties*, Melbourne, 1970.

O'Farrell, P. J., *The Catholic Church in Australia: A Short History: 1788–1967*, Melbourne, 1968.

Ormonde, P., *The Movement*, Melbourne, 1972.

Overacker, L., *Australian Parties in a Changing Society 1945–67*, Melbourne, 1968.

Page, E., *Truant Surgeon: The Inside Story of Forty Years of Australian Political Life*, Sydney, 1963.

Rawson, D. W., *Labor in Vain?: A Survey of the Australian Labor Party*, Melbourne, 1966.

Reid, A., *The Power Struggle*, Sydney, 1969.

Santamaria, B. A., *The Price of Freedom: The Movement – After Ten Years*, Melbourne, 1964.

Sawer, G., *Australian Federalism in the Courts*, Melbourne, 1967.

Tennant, K., *Evatt: Politics and Justice*, Sydney, 1970.

Truman, T., *Catholic Action and Politics*, Melbourne, 1959, 1960.

Webb, L. C., *Communism and Democracy in Australia: A Survey of the 1951 Referendum*, Melbourne, 1954.

West, K., *Power in the Liberal Party: A Study in Australian Politics*, Melbourne, 1965.

The Economy

Boxer, A. H., Ed., *Aspects of the Australian Economy*, Melbourne, 1965.

Brash, D. T., *American Investment in Australian Industry*, Canberra, 1966.

Crawford, J. G., *Australian Trade Policy 1942–1966: A Documentary History*, Canberra, 1968.

Davidson, F. G., *The Industrialization of Australia*, Melbourne, 1957, 2nd edition 1960, 3rd edition 1962, 4th edition 1969.

Drohan, N. T., and Day, J. H., Eds., *Readings in Australian Economics: Studies in Economic Growth*, Melbourne, 1965, 2nd edition 1968, 1969.

Fitzpatrick, B., and Wheelwright, E. L., *The Highest Bidder: A Citizen's Guide to Problems of Foreign Investment in Australia*, Melbourne, 1965.

Forster, C., Ed., *Australian Economic Development in the Twentieth Century*, London, 1970.

Griffin, J., Ed., *Essays in Economic History of Australia*, Brisbane, 1967, 2nd edition 1970.

Glynn, S., *Urbanisation in Australian History 1788–1900*, Melbourne, 1970.

Hunter, A., Ed., *The Economics of Australian Industry: Studies in Environment and Structure*, Melbourne, 1963.

Isaac, J. E., and Ford, G. W., Eds., *Australian Labour Relations: Readings*, Melbourne, 1966, 1968, 2nd edition 1971.

McFarlane, B., *Economic Policy in Australia: The Case for Reform*, Melbourne, 1968.

Matthews, P. W. D., and Ford, G. W., Eds., *Australian Trade Unions: Their Development, Structure and Horizons*, Melbourne, 1968.

Playford, J., and Kirsner, D., Eds., *Australian Capitalism: Towards a Socialist Critique*, Melbourne, 1972.

Walker, K. F., *Australian Industrial Relations Systems*, Cambridge, (Mass.), 1970, is 2nd edition of *Industrial Relations in Australia*, Cambridge (Mass.), 1956.

Wheelwright, E. L., and Miskelly, J., *Anatomy of Australian Manufacturing Industry: The Ownership and Control of 300 of the Largest Manufacturing Companies in Australia*, Sydney, 1967.

Society

Appleyard, R. T., *British Emigration to Australia*, Canberra, 1964.

Boyd, R., *Australia's Home: Its Origins, Builders and Occupiers*, Melbourne, 1952, 1961, 2nd edition 1968.

Boyd, R., *The Australian Ugliness*, Melbourne, 1960, 1961, 1963, 2nd edition 1963, 1968.

Coleman, P., Ed., *Australian Civilization: A Symposium*, Melbourne, 1962, 1966, 1967.

Davies, A. F., and Encel, S., Eds., *Australian Society: A Sociological Introduction*, Melbourne, 1965, 1966, 1967, 1968, 2nd edition 1970, 1971, 1972.

Elkin, A. P., Ed., *Marriage and the Family in Australia*, Sydney, 1957.

Henderson, R. F., Harcourt, A., and Harper, R. J. A., *People in Poverty: A Melbourne Survey*, Melbourne, 1970.

Horne, D., *The Lucky Country: Australia in the Sixties*, Melbourne, 1964, 2nd edition 1965, 1966, 1967.

Kewley, T. H., *Social Security in Australia: The Development of Social Security and Health Benefits from 1900 to the Present*, Sydney, 1965, 2nd edition 1973.

Kewley, T. H., *Australia's Welfare State: The Development of Social Security Benefits*, Melbourne, 1969.

McGregor, C., *Profile of Australia*, London, 1966, 1967.

MacKenzie, N., *Women in Australia*, Melbourne, 1962, London, 1963.

McLaren, J., *Our Troubled Schools*, Melbourne, 1968.

McLeod, A. L., Ed., *The Pattern of Australian Culture*, Melbourne, 1963.

Martin, J. I., *Refugee Settlers: A Study of Displaced Persons in Australia*, Canberra, 1965.

Mayer, H., Ed., *Catholics and the Free Society: An Australian Symposium*, Melbourne, 1961.

Mol, H., *Religion in Australia: A Sociological Investigation*, Melbourne, 1971.

Palfreeman, A. C., *The Administration of the White Australia Policy*, Melbourne, 1967.

Price, C. A., *Southern Europeans in Australia*, Melbourne, 1963.

Pringle, J. D., *Australian Accent*, London, 1958, 1959, 1965.

Rowley, C. D., *Aboriginal Policy and Practice: Vol. I, The Destruction of Aboriginal Society*, Canberra, 1970.

Stevens, F. S., Ed., *Racism: The Australian Experience*, Sydney, 3 vols., 1971–72.

Stevenson, A. M., Martin, E. M., and O'Neill, J. A., *High Living: A Study of Family Life in Flats*, Melbourne, 1967.

Stretton, H., *Ideas for Australian Cities*, Adelaide, 1970, Melbourne, 1971.

Stubbs, J., *The Hidden People: Poverty in Australia*, Melbourne, 1966.

Troy, P. N., Ed., *Urban Redevelopment in Australia*, Canberra, 1967.

Wheelwright, E. L., Ed., *Higher Education in Australia*, Melbourne, 1965.

General

Alexander, F., *Australia Since Federation: A Narrative and Critical Analysis*, Melbourne, 1967.

Crowley, F. K., *Modern Australia in Documents*, 2, 1939–1970, Melbourne, 1973.

Grattan, C. H., *The Southwest Pacific Since 1900: A Modern History*, Ann Arbor, 1963.

Preston, R., Ed., *Contemporary Australia: Studies in History, Politics and Economics*, Durham, N.C., 1969.

Serle, G., *From Deserts the Prophets Come: The Creative Spirit in Australia: 1788–1972*, Melbourne, 1973.

Younger, R. M., *Australia and the Australians: A New Concise History*. Adelaide, 1970.

Index

Compiled by Elmar Zalums
The Flinders University of South Australia

617

623